Accounting Education: Problems and Prospects

ACCOUNTING EDUCATION: PROBLEMS and PROSPECTS

Editor:
JAMES DON EDWARDS
University of Georgia

Associate Editors:
WAYNE J. ALBERS
Ernst & Ernst
THOMAS R. HOFSTEDT
Stanford University
K. FRED SKOUSEN
Brigham Young University
JAMES SORENSEN
University of Denver
MILTON F. USRY
Oklahoma State University

AMERICAN ACCOUNTING ASSOCIATION
1974

Library of Congress Catalog Card Number: 74-25240
Copyright 1974 by The American Accounting Association. All rights reserved
Printed in the United States of America

Contents

Foreword ix
Preface xi

SECTION I ACCOUNTING EDUCATION: PROBLEMS AND PROSPECTS
   1. Accounting Education: Problems and Prospects, James Don Edwards 1

SECTION II CHALLENGES, VALUES AND CHANGES 7
  PART A Introduction: The Fragile Ecology of Accounting Education, Editors 9
  PART B The Economics of Educational Change, Editors 16
   2. The Dismal Science of Non-Growth, Editors 17
   3. The Coming of Middle Age in Higher Education, Earl F. Cheit 20
  PART C Values as Forces for Change 29
   4. The Over-Intellectualization of Accounting Education, Robert K. Mautz 30
   5. Society, Professions and Accounting Curricula, Harold Q. Langenderfer 38
   6. Toward a Revitalized Accounting I, John P. Fertakis 50
  PART D The Demand for Accounting Graduates and the Design of Curricula 59
   7. Attributes of a New (Public) Accountant, Guy Trump 60
   8. Attributes of a New (Private) Accountant, Arthur P. Bartholomew 64
   9. Relevance, Auditing and Professionalism, Jack C.
      Robertson and Charles H. Smith 67
  PART E The Implementation of Values 78
   10. The Professional School in Accounting Education, Edward L. Summers 79
   11. Rigidity or Systematic Flexibility?, J.C. Kinard and C.H. Stanley 94
   12. Directions in the Academic Study of Accounting, Louis F.
      Biagioni and John W. Kennelly 106
   13. Resource Allocation for Accounting Doctoral Education:
      Quantity or Quality?, Gary L. Sundem and Jerry J. Weygandt 113
   14. Education or Experience?, Charles G. Carpenter and Paul E. Dascher 117
   15. Welfare Economics and Accounting Curricula,
      Levis D. McCullers and Relmond P. Van Daniker 123
  PART F The Master Teacher: Beyond Technique 129
   16. The Master Teacher, Charles J. Woelfel 130

SECTION III A CONCEPTUAL OVERVIEW OF LEARNING FOR ACCOUNTING EDUCATORS 137
   17. A Conceptual Overview of Learning for Accounting
      Educators, James E. Sorensen 139
  PART A Analyzing the Learner 140
   18. Individual Differences: Ability, Personality, and
      Vocational Interest, John Grant Rhode 141
   19. Interpersonal and Social Environment, James E. Sorensen 150
   20. Economic and Cultural Environment: The Special Case of the
      Disadvantaged, Sybil C. Mobley 155
   21. The Special Case of the Culturally Disadvantaged,
      Philip E. Fess and Charles T. Hamilton 163
  PART B The Task of Learning 171
   22. Learning Theories and Accounting, J.J. Willingham,
      I.E. McNeill and E.F. Collins 173
   23. Is Motivation "What Makes Sammy Run?" Michael J. Barrett 181
   24. Arranging the Contingencies of Reinforcement, Joel Macht 187
   25. Inquiry in the Accounting Classroom, James C. Stallman 203
   26. Using Learning Theory to Teach Accounting More Efficiently,
      William F. Bentz 213

Contents

27. Developing Behavioral Objectives for Accounting Education, Doyle Z. Williams and Dan M. Guy 221
28. Objectives of Professional Education and Training, Carl J. Bohne, Jr. 233

SECTION IV INSTRUCTIONAL INNOVATIONS 245
   29. Instructional Innovations: An Overview, Norton M. Bedford 247
  PART A Instructional Innovations: Systems 255
   30. The Modular Concept of Instruction, Donald D. Bourque 256
   31. Self-Paced Instruction, Dempsey Dupree 268
   32. Programmed Instruction, James Don Edwards 278
   33. Computer Usage in Accounting Education, Donald E. Stone 289
   34. The Multi-Media Approach to Classroom Presentation, Clarence G. Avery and Donald F. Istvan 305
   35. Television Related Instruction, Robert W. Koehler 313
   36. The Case Method in Accounting, Robert N. Anthony 329
   37. Team Teaching, Kenneth W. Perry 341
  PART B Instructional Innovations: Techniques 351
   38. A Method for the Integrated Use of Learning Resources in Education, John. F. Rockart 352
   39. A Games Approach to Introducing Accounting, Marvin L. Carlson and J. Warren Higgins 365
   40. The Use of Dynamic, Interacting Business Simulations for Accounting Instruction, Howard D. Leftwich 370
   41. The Use of Role Play Simulation in Accounting Education, Lawrence A. Tomassini 376
   42. Cooperation vs. Competition, R.E. Shirley 383
   43. Financial Statement Content and Use: A Classroom Simulation, James. J. Benjamin and Robert. H. Strawser 385
   44. A Teaching Machine Application in a Basic Tax Course, G. Fred Streuling 388
   45. COMBUD: A Computer Simulation of the Budgetary Process of the Firm, J. Timothy Sale 398
   46. A Computer Simulation Approach for Teaching the Evaluation of Internal Control, David C. Burns 404
   47. Integration of the Computer into Systems and Auditing: A Team Approach, Richard L. Cattanach and Glyn W. Hanbery 412
   48. An Illustration of Four Price Level Approaches to Income Measurement, Harry I. Wolk 415
   49. A Visual Comparison of Direct Costing Versus Absorption Costing Income Effects, H. Milton Jones 424
   50. Teaching Economic Order Quantities in a Price Break System, Edward B. Deakin 427
   51. A Pictorial Discussion of Corporate Tax Reorganizations, D. Larry Crumbley 431

SECTION V EVALUATION OF PERFORMANCE 441
   52. Evaluation of Performance: An Overview 443
   53. Accountability in Accounting Education, Keith G. Lumsden 444
   54. Evaluation of College Teaching, Robert C. Wilson 451
   55. An Improved Instrument for Measuring Teaching Effectiveness, G. Michael Crooch and George W. Krull, Jr. 467
   56. The Student as Godfather? The Impact of Student Ratings on Academia, John A. Centra 475

Contents

57. Some Approaches to Faculty Evaluation, K. Fred Skousen 482
58. A Technique for Summarizing and Presenting Data Relative to Faculty Performance, R.R. Read 505
59. Testing, Grading, and Evaluation of Student Achievement, William J. Turppa 514
60. Grading Systems and the Purposes of Grades, Jonathan R. Warren 531

SECTION VI RESEARCH IN ACCOUNTING EDUCATION 537
61. Research on Teaching Innovations in Accounting, Thomas R. Hofstedt and Thomas R. Dyckman 539
62. A Case Study of Comprehensive Educational Innovation, James D. Newton, Dallas M. Cullen, Ray V. Rasmussen, and Eugene Swimmer 547
63. A Critique of "A Case Study of Comprehensive Educational Innovation" 563
64. Student Attitudes Toward Management Accounting and the Influence of the Management Accounting Course, David M. Buehlmann .. 564
65. A Critique of "Student Attitudes Toward Management Accounting and the Influence of the Management Accounting Course" 572
66. The Effectiveness of Active Student Participation in Meeting the Cognitive and Affective Objectives of an Elementary Accounting Course, Maureen H. Berry 574
67. A Critique of "The Effectiveness of Active Student Participation in Meeting the Cognitive and Affective Objectives of an Elementary Accounting Course" 594
68. A New Introduction to Accounting Combined with a Traditional Textbook: An Empirical Research Study, Allen Sanders 596
69. A Critique of "A New Introduction to Accounting Combined with a Traditional Textbook: An Empirical Research Study" 601

Foreword

The idea for this book came out of a brainstorming session in New Orleans in 1971 by the members of the Advisory Committee to the Director of Education.* At that time there was a strong feeling by the members of this Committee that the American Accounting Association should multiply its efforts in the area of accounting education in order to put an emphasis on education at a level at least parallel with the organization's efforts in the technical aspects of financial and managerial accounting. To help the readers of this book to understand how an initial idea is shaped and molded to the exigencies of the situation, some of the initial thinking behind the early developmental stages should be identified.

Initially, the Advisory Group felt that there was no significant opportunity available for the publication of articles dealing with accounting education matters, including education research, except in the teaching notes section of the *Accounting Review*. There was a general feeling that such articles were not accorded the same status as articles in the regular section of the *Accounting Review* and that this "second class" status for education articles inhibited educators not only from writing about accounting education matters but also inhibited research in accounting education. To overcome these presumed inhibitions and encourage more writing and research of an accounting education nature, the Advisory Committee felt that a fifth issue (regular publication is quarterly) of the *Accounting Review* should be published each year which would be devoted exclusively to reporting on research and other developments in accounting education. The Advisory Committee felt that this would be an initial desirable step which might lead eventually to a separate *Journal of Accounting Education*. This idea was tried out informally by the Director of Education on the members of the Executive Committee, including the editor of the *Accounting Review*. For reasons not entirely clear, the idea of a fifth issue of the *Accounting Review* was not well received, but in the course of the informal discussions it became obvious that a monograph or a book would be an acceptable alternative. With this information available, the Advisory Committee proceeded to make a proposal for a monograph on accounting education to the Executive Committee. The Executive Committee gave the Director of Education the green light to proceed with the qualification that it would be inappropriate to refer to it as a monograph if a number of authors were involved. Thus, it came to be referred to as a book, and in this modified form it appeared to have a chance to "get off the ground."

But in order for the project to "take off," there was the necessity of finding a dynamic editor who not only had a strong interest in accounting education, but who also had the leadership qualities to attract outstanding papers and see the project through to a timely conclusion. James Don Edwards clearly met these qualifications and immediately accepted the assignment when it was offered. Shortly after his acceptance, he met in Atlanta with the Director of Education and with Thomas R. Hofstedt to lay out the parameters of the project and select a number of associate editors to direct the project. In addition, Thomas Hofstedt, Milton F. Usry, K. Fred Skousen, James R. Sorensen and Wayne J. Albers enthusiastically agreed to work with James Don Ed-

---

*The Director of Education at that time was Harold Q. Langenderfer (University of North Carolina). His Advisory Committee was chaired by William Ferrara (Pennsylvania State University) and included the following members: Thomas R. Hofstedt (Cornell University), Carl Palmer (Tulane University), Frank Singer (University of Massachusetts), Vern Odmark (California State University—San Diego), and Thomas Burns (Ohio State University).

wards in editing the book. Shortly thereafter, a full-fledged two day meeting of the editors was held in Atlanta to identify the sections of the book (together with a detailed outline), the title, and the commissioned authors, as well as set out the procedure for a call for papers and the timetable for each stage of the development.

The call for papers elicited over 150 responses which confirmed the thinking that there was a strong interest in accounting education. The editors have worked diligently to screen articles submitted, to edit the articles accepted, and to develop written dialogs to integrate the articles in each section into a cohesive group.

As the Director of Education when this project was launched, this writer would like to take this opportunity to express appreciation to the Executive Committee for its willingness to approve the project, to the Advisory Committee for its creativity in conceiving the project and for the strength of its convictions in promoting it, to the authors for their efforts in providing timely articles of high quality, and finally and especially to James Don Edwards, Thomas R. Hofstedt, K. Fred Skousen, Wayne J. Albers, Milton F. Usry, and James R. Sorensen for their dedication in developing the format and performing the editing task in an energetic and forthright fashion. It is to be hoped that this project will be viewed as a significant milestone in the history of the American Accounting Association in its efforts to promote accounting education.

Harold Q. Langenderfer
Director of Education
1971-1973

Preface

This book, *Accounting Education: Problems and Prospects*, was commissioned by the Director of Education of the American Accounting Association based on a recommendation from the Advisory Committee on Accounting Education. The research of that committee and the experiences of the Editor and Associate Editors of this book clearly demonstrated the need for this book.

We have been fortunate to have more than 80 authors share their experiences in accounting education by contributing to this book. It was not possible to include all of the materials made available to us, but we are grateful for the wide interest in this project.

The Editors have attempted to include a full range of papers on challenges to accounting education: conceptual framework for education, motivation, communication and learning theory, instructional innovation, evaluation of performance for both student and teachers, and the important area of research methodologies applicable in accounting education.

This project would not have been possible without the intellectual contributions of the Associate Editors. They deserve significant recognition from all of us for their contributions to accounting education.

James Don Edwards, Editor
November, 1974

Section I

Accounting Education: Problems and Prospects

Accounting Education: Problems and Prospects

Introduction
James Don Edwards
University of Georgia

Section I

The overriding objective of *Accounting Education: Problems and Prospects* is quite simple: to *improve* accounting education. Startling as it may seem, no comprehensive book has been written on accounting education, prior to this time. This book is intended to fill this void. The intended audience ranges from practitioners and educators to potential professors—(Ph. D. students).

The book has both substantive and purely motivational objectives. Some of these objectives are to review the state of the art in accounting education, provide relevant and specific information to teachers, focus attention on educational problems and present some solutions to these problems, describe what's going on—ranging from theoretical and abstract to "how to do it," motivate and train accounting educators and potential professors, demonstrate the potential for education research in accounting, provide insights for intellectual change, and to serve as a reference work, a Handbook of Accounting Education.

One highly significant attribute of this text is its diversity. The book is composed of papers written by both practitioners and educators, by both critics and participants; and it encompasses a wide range of universities, colleges, and authors. With this diversity of schools and authors comes a wide range of topics and a widespread diversity of viewpoints on these topics. Even with its wide diversity, the book is only a highly selective sample of what's going on in accounting education. It does not systematically cover the accounting curriculum, educational administration, or non-college level accounting. Nevertheless, the content of the book is probably representative of the major issues in accounting education.

Another significant attribute of the book is the continued emphasis on the concept of *accountability* in accounting education. Although there can be no single answer regarding who is responsible to whom for what, the book does stress the importance of effective and efficient uses of resources allocated to accounting education. The importance of adequate techniques for measuring the output of the educational system is emphasized relative to issues of resource allocation.

Yet another significant attribute is the deliberate and continuous reference to concepts of educational psychology. For the professor, the relevant and troublesome question is: What does an accounting educator need to know about learning? The book presents concepts and techniques underlying the teaching and learning process. Learners seem to be influenced by virtually everything; therefore, the accounting educator must appreciate these influences in order to better understand the accounting student. Moreover, the book thoroughly examines the task of learning. Various applications of learning are presented, including motivation and reinforcement of the learner. Educational objectives in the classroom and professional accounting education are also discussed.

Finally, the book is designed for a certain highly important implicit purpose: to elevate the *teaching* of accounting by simply paying formal attention to it and by emphasizing that "teaching" is not a dirty word.

Section II

Section II, "Challenges, Values and Change," attempts to identify and discuss the current set of forces causing major changes in accounting education. "The management of change" has become a trite buzz phrase in business schools and executive suites; nevertheless it does reflect a growing concern about "how to cope." The papers in Section II are intended to heighten the reader's awareness of change and its causes but *not* to provide definitive solutions to specific problems. Their collective function is to establish a sense of perspective, to distinguish between the feasible and the pipe dream, the creative innovator and the crackpot schemer. In short, Section II should serve as an intellectual backdrop for the remainder of the book. Section II as a whole is about those things that serve accounting education, not just about students, the curriculum or any other single aspect of accounting education.

As might be expected from such a description, the papers in Section II should evoke reasonably controversial viewpoints. The intent is to induce a kind of constructive awareness in two sorts of people: those who advocate change for the sake of change and those who oppose change because it is change. The message of Section II is that change is inevitable but malleable.

Specifically, the Section discusses the economic implication of "no-growth reality" for accounting education, the "goals gap"— if there is one—between the professor and the practitioners, the emotional and artistic aspects of teaching and, finally, presents a series of "white papers" which attempt to make the difficult transition from perceived problems to practical solutions. The ultimate impact of Section II will be measured by its immediate and long run effect on educators' attitudes and loyalties, not by any immediate change in behavior.

Section III

"What does an accounting educator need to know about learning?"

Section III is a multi-disciplined response to this question with cogent examples of how the classroom professors can better analyze their learners and better understand and cope with the task of learning.

Learners seem to be influenced by virtually everything, yet the accounting educator rightfully asks such questions as:

How can I capitalize on the ability, personality, and vocational interest of my students in the accounting classroom?

What do I need to know about teacher-centered versus student-centered approaches to learning?

What are the pros and cons of:
• Individual vs. group work?
• Cooperative vs. competitive work and grading schemes?
• Small vs. large class sizes?

Do cultural and economic forces restrict the absorption of various disadvantaged groups into accounting? What are these barriers and how do I deal with them?

Armed with emotional concerns, research finding, and keen personal observations, each question is answered. The suggested answers provide substantive guidance for today's—and tomorrow's—accounting educators who are trying to improve their own teaching ability or to better analyze their accounting students.

But analyzing the student is only part of the issue; what about the task of learning? The accounting educator continues with more questions.

• What are the major learning theories?

How do they relate to teaching accounting?

How do I know when I'm using (or not using) a particular theory?

• What are the current theories of motivation? What are the major differences between need theory, behavorial theory, and expectancy theory?

• How can I apply these varied theories to my classroom?

• How do behavorial objectives fit into the accounting classroom?

• Do educators and practitioners agree on the educational objectives for accounting?

• How are practitioners approaching professional development?

Using perceptive and careful distillation, selections from staggering volumes of materials from multiple sources are used to focus on these crucial questions. After reading this section nearly all accounting educators will come away with new views and skills. Relevant and usable examples are sprinkled throughout the discussions— examples that can be directly imported into today's classroom. The references and bibliographies provide a wealth of hand-selected materials for those who wish to pursue specific learning topics.

If learning about learning is an interesting question, then Section III provides some interesting answers.

Section IV

Instructional Innovation is the focus for Section IV. Innovation is change, so it is only human nature for resistance to occur. Care must be exercised in selecting those methods that are to be amended or cast aside for better ways of achieving improved learning. Staying in the main stream of relevance is not an easy task. Reluctance to give up the obsolete but familiar methods to embark upon the uncertain, unfamiliar course of newer methods is a powerful force. Yet, there may be harm to the learning process from inappropriate abandonment of the old in favor of the new. Obviously, all change is not for the better.

Accounting academicians constantly confront the difficult task of retaining those methods that are effective, discarding or reshaping those that are not, and adding the new. Many instructional innovations are available. The more important task is appropriate implementation. Rote, untempered attempts to mechanically transplant new methods will likely prove unproductive. Accounting educators must carefully select and tailor these working tools appropriate for their purposes.

The section on instructional innovations presents useful methods highlighted by a *maximum emphasis on utility*. Certainly, not every method will be useful to every instructor. But the reader is urged to be open minded. He or she should think about teaching needs, students, subject areas, and courses as the various pragmatic tools are presented in these twenty-three papers on innovative instruction in accounting.

All of the papers are utilitarian and are developed in the context of the needs of accounting instructors. This section, indeed the entire book, is directed to the specific problems and needs of *accounting educators*. It is designed to be used, and its purpose is fulfilled only to the extent of the utility provided its intended audience.

An overview paper in Section IV sets the stage for the instructional innovations section and identifies fundamental notions concerning the section's general theme, previews the included papers, and offers general observations concerning their utility.

Two major subsections follow the overview. The first presents eight fundamental instructional systems. Four papers dealing with the modular concept, self-paced instruction, programmed instruction, and computer usage have a strong individualized instruction orientation. But the wide utility of programmed instruction and the computer in the accounting education environment is also developed. Media usage is highlighted in the discussions of the multi-media approach and television-related instruction. Finally, the essentials of the case method and team teaching are clearly developed.

The second major subsection presents a wide variety of instructional techniques and must be applied in the context of the personality of the individual instructor, the teaching facilities, the quality of students, the teaching objectives, and the subject matter being taught. These fourteen technique papers, as well as many others found in other parts of the book, were selected from responses to the Editor's Fall, 1972 "call for papers" issued in connection with the publication of this book. The response was gratifying both as to quantity as well as quality. Space constraints restricted what could be included. The selection was not an easy task. Those selected seek to demonstrate a wide range of techniques with respect to useful ideas applied to a variety of accounting subject areas.

Included are an integrated method for learning resource usage, simulations, role playing, use of teaching machines, computer applications, and techniques for teaching selected topics in the subject areas of introductory financial and cost-managerial accounting, information systems, auditing, and taxation.

The selections presented are intended as a *sampling* of techniques from many that, given more space, could be included. Instructors are encouraged to study these techniques for useful ideas to apply in their teaching. While conciseness has been a criterion, a primary objective in both the instructional systems and technique papers has been the presentation of sufficient detail to permit adopting and transplanting those ideas useful to individual instructors. The key word is *usefulness*.

Section V

Section V, "Evaluation of Performance," is directly concerned with accountability in accounting education. Accountability poses the question: Who is responsible to whom for what? There is no specific answer. The resources allocated to higher education must be used effectively; however, there has been a lack of attention to the determination of optimum resource allocations for education. There is no controlling group like stockholders to demand more efficient use of educational resources. Greater efficiency by the faculty does not accrue to either the faculty or their respective departments. Hence, stagnation results.

In addition to resource allocation problems, education is faced with measuring the output of the educational system. The system produces multi-dimensional output but does not provide adequate measurement techniques. Neither has there been a proper identification of the underlying production functions.

If there is to be an effective evaluation of college teaching, specific objectives must be established. Effective teaching must be adequately defined and described to assist in identifying instruments and tools to be used in teaching evaluations. In addition, certain measures of teaching effectiveness can be provided by the teacher himself as well as by students, alumni, colleagues, and student achievement. Thus, the components of effective teaching include the students as well as the teachers.

One instrument for measuring teaching effectiveness is the student completed rating scale. Student evaluations provide a formal channel by which students may express their feeling concerning the effectiveness of accounting instruction. However, the effectiveness of the student evaluations is highly dependent upon the students' cooperation and attitudes. The ultimate impact of student evaluations on teaching is dependent upon how the ratings are used. Student evaluations used by instructors as a source of feedback produce desirable results. However, when the student ratings are used in making administrative decisions about the faculty, questionable side effects may be produced. This section presents evidence of the effect of student ratings on individual instructors, the administration, the students, and the colleges as well as on teaching in general. This section also presents some examples of faculty evaluation models currently being utilized. As emphasized by the case illustrations presented, an effective approach to faculty evaluation should be based upon carefully established evaluation criteria.

Once completed, the evaluations of faculty performance must be summarized for presentation. A methodology for summarizing multiple opinions concerning the performance of faculty is demonstrated through the use of an equilateral triangle in which teaching characteristics are classified into three categories: below, center, and above. The evaluations can then be plotted on the triangle before *and* after changing teacher attitudes to test the degrees of improvement. This methodology is especially useful in administrative review of faculty performance.

In addition to faculty evaluations, this section includes a discussion of testing, grading, and evaluation of student achievement. The discussion involves the measurement problems for student achievement including the general principles of testing, grading, and evaluating, as well as the functions of tests and types of test questions. A case study is also provided to illustrate a technique of testing, grading, and evaluating involving test construction, administration, grading, interpretation, evaluation, and final student evaluation.

Grading systems and the purposes of grades are also discussed in this section. Several alternative grading systems exist: the traditional ABCDF system, the ABCX system, the pass-fail system, and the pass-no report system are examples.

In short, Section V discusses the various techniques of evaluating both faculty and students, the problems involved in these evaluations, and the benefits derived from these evaluations.

Section VI

Section VI, "Research on Teaching Innovations," is essentially a workshop. As such, it has two aims. The first is substantive: to present information and data bearing on pedagogical problems. In this respect, the papers in Section VI are intended to advance the art of teaching. The second aim is less direct but nevertheless vital to the overall goals of the book: to motivate empirical education research and to provide "models" for how to conduct (or how *not* to conduct) such research. Obviously, these two objectives are related.

It is ironic that the accounting profession, particularly its academic members, can be simultaneously enmeshed in both research methodology and teaching and yet not make the obvious link between them. To be blunt, education research in accounting has low status, few empiricists and is of generally low quality (when it exists). To the extent that the problems are methodological in character, they are curable; to the extent this problem reflects widely-held values among teachers of accounting, there may be resistance to change. Section VI is concerned with the former rather than the latter problem. To that end, the introductory paper suggests certain evaluative criteria, and each research paper is followed by a methodological critique.

An overview of Section VI is shown in Figure X.

Research will be a key determinant of progress in the classroom. It is vital that such research reflect both methodological rigor and the realities of the classroom. That dual charge is extremely demanding. Section VI is intended to encourage *both* rigor and vigor in educational research in accounting.

A Concluding Comment

The various authors have directed their contributions to those who have a vital interest in accounting education. A wide range of viewpoints and research approaches have been included in this book for critical analysis. It is the editors' hope that every accounting educator will find some material in this book that will not only appeal to him but will be of help in improving his teaching or research effectiveness. The objective of improving accounting education requires both a collective effort and an individual effort. If this book serves as a collective catalyst to stimulate greater individual effort to improve accounting education, its primary objective will have been accomplished.

Figure X

Overview of Section VI

Research on Teaching Innovations

Examples	Research and Design	Independent Variables	Dependent Variables
(1)	Case Study	Multiple Changes in Curriculum and Teaching	Performance and Attitudes
(2)	Pretest/Post Test	Management Accounting Course	Performance and Attitudes
(3)	Non-Equivalent Control Group	Student Participation	Performance and Attitudes
(4)	Solomon 4-Group Design	Price Waterhouse Study Group Course Modules	Performance and Attitudes

Section II

Challenges, Values and Changes

Introduction: The Fragile Ecology of Accounting Education

This section is based on two assumptions. One is indisputable; the other highly questionable. They are the beliefs that in general, the accounting educational system is something less than perfect and that something can be done to improve the situation. If you don't know which of these is indisputable and which questionable, you need not read this section.[1]

That accounting education falls short of being perfect hardly warrants repeating. Critics include the profession,[2] the teachers,[3] the students[4] and almost every other interest group. The litany of complaint includes charges of irrelevance, insensitivity, too much abstraction, too little abstraction and other various sorts of malfeasance. Perhaps most telling of all, any teacher of accounting is acutely aware of his own inability to communicate—sometimes known as the "I taught them that, but they didn't learn it" syndrome. It is both easy and painful to find fault with accounting education.

Is improvement possible? Certainly for every perceived fault, there is a pet remedy. There is no end of activity and tinkering. Committees, commissions, study groups, foundations, deans and others are continually suggesting and even implementing change. But "change" and "improvement" are different commodities, and distinguishing one from the other is a murky business. Many confuse "doing something" with progress (and, of course, equally many view any reform as a step toward anarchy).

The purpose of Section II is to set out some of the major forces for change which are operating on accounting education. There is no attempt to construct an exhaustive list, nor even to rank order the various forces according to their relative importance. Most important, the Section will *not* enable the reader to prescribe any tonic or therapy for accounting education. Hopefully, it will provide a background against which the remainder of the book will stand out. It will identify major schools of thought on certain key issues and, if all goes well, it should leave the reader with an impression of constructive skepticism about either educational reform *or* the status quo. That would seem to represent a healthy state of tension.

A State of Ferment

Symptoms of dissatisfaction are easy to identify. Furthermore, the symptoms are generalized, involving all of the educational system—not just professional education. For example,

> "The institution we call "school" is what it is because we made it that way. If it is *irrelevant*, as Marshall McLuhan says; if it *shields children from reality*, as Norbert Weiner says; if it *educates for obsolescence*, as John Gardner says; if it *does not develop intelligence*, as Jerome Bruner says; if it is *based on fear*, as John Holt says; if it *avoids the promotion of significant learnings*, as Carl Rogers says; if it *induces alienation*, as Paul Goodman says; if it *punishes creativity and independence*, as Edgar Friedenburg says; if in short, it is not doing what needs to be done, it can be changed; it *must* be changed."[5]

In the 1960s, the U.S. spent more dollars on education and training than on defense, in spite of the Vietnam war.[6] In accounting circles, the allocation of the education dollar between institutions (e.g., which schools will receive foundation money for educating minorities or urban management students?), between academic units and firms (e.g., should technical skills be taught by the university or by the CPA firm?), and between academic departments (e.g., do we want a strong MBA or a Ph.D. program?) is a major determinant of change, particularly for any given institution involved in the education of ac-

education of accountants. Postman & Weingartner liken the management of U.S. education to driving a multi-million dollar sports car, shouting "Faster! Faster!", but all the while steering by looking steadfastly into the rear view mirror.[7] To pursue the analogy, it would seem more appropriate to steer the system by looking ahead, by anticipating change.

Therefore, this section seeks to identify those forces which either are currently or soon will be pushing for change.

Multiple & Overlapping Change Agents

Given the many roles that education plays in our society, it is not surprising to find that the educational system mirrors the forces operating in the world around it. Figure 1 provides a crude schematic of some of the major categories of forces which operate on accounting education.

Cultural forces involve those basic shifts in folkways and mores of our society which somehow translate into educational policies (or make existing policies obsolete). Social philosophers and critics have dealt with these shifts at length. In accounting education, they have surfaced in the form of the different values and classroom expectations held by different generations of professional accountants.[8]

Economic forces are probably the most visible change agents operating on accounting education. University financing has changed drastically and many of yesterday's pedagogical necessities have become today's luxuries. The repercussions of steady state psychology are pervasive and often detrimental. A Stanford professor of education noted that

"The earmarks of an institution in financial trouble or declining health ... include faculty and staff job preservation, a frenzied search for new (student) markets, fear of technological change, mutual suspiciousness on the part of faculty and administration, cutbacks of expenditures on research and development, and the insulation of the central administration from the actualities of changing conditions that could lead institutions into even more precarious conditions than they now face."[9]

That such effects are "forces for change" is clear; and it would seem equally clear that the shift in economic fortunes portends some realignment of the ecological structure of the educational system.

Intellectual forces abound, numbered by the disciplines which interface with accounting—most of the behavioral sciences, disciplines with "information" at their center, most of economics, and so on. In each of these, and in accounting proper, something akin to a "knowledge explosion" is taking place. Each increment to knowledge, whether achieved by painstaking research or sudden insight, puts new demands on students and professors. The "turnover" of relevant information increases. Witness the move toward five year programs in accounting, the insistence on more computer skills, more analytical talent, etc.

Professional forces also exist and have (rightfully) tremendous influence on accounting education. Much of this section is concerned with these forces. Pressures emanate from the profession to educators in two ways. First, there are direct attempts at intervention—the visiting lecturer, articles in the literature, participation in education policy decisions, and so forth. Second, there is a significant secondary or indirect force for change which is created by simple supply and demand; i.e., proper education implies graduates get jobs. Closely related to this factor is the simple truth that the profession is a major educator in its own right, via various staff training programs and a rapidly increasing continuing education program.

Finally, there are *pedagogical* forces for change. Occasionally, such forces arise from schools of education. More often, a proven application will be picked up by accounting educators; e.g., the computer (either as an object of instruction or as an instructional aid) and programmed learning materials. Education, particularly teaching, is an art; therefore, continual improvement, recycling of ideas, refinements of technique should be observed. Such a turmoil seems to be a logical accompaniment to any process which seeks to modify the behavior of other persons.

The above catalogue of change agents is hardly exhaustive or even mutually exclusive. Furthermore, the effect of each is

The Ecology of Accounting Education

Figure 1

CAUSE & EFFECT IN ACCOUNTING EDUCATION

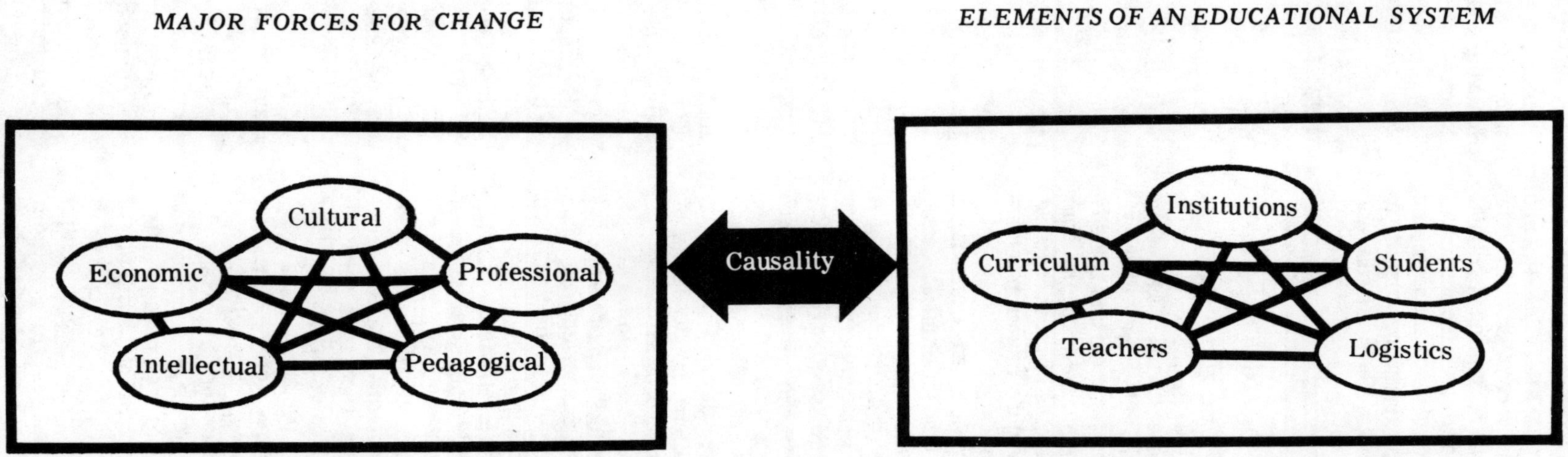

ELEMENTS OF AN EDUCATIONAL SYSTEM

- Students
- Logistics
- Institutions
- Teachers
- Curriculum

Causality

MAJOR FORCES FOR CHANGE

- Professional
- Pedagogical
- Cultural
- Intellectual
- Economic

intermingled with all of the others. Declining enrollment (economic force) is a product of changed attitudes toward education (cultural force) and in turn causes a reappraisal of class size policies (pedagogical) and tenure rules (economic). The effects are multiple and overlapping, so that attributing causality to any one force is extremely difficult and subjective.

Accounting Education Systems: Response Possibilities

Accepting for the moment that the preceding forces are "real" (i.e., they singly or collectively will create change), how can "change" be detected and scaled? Such a question requires a rough identification of the elements of an accounting education system. Figure 1 again provides a partial schematic.

Almost by definition, an educational system must have *teachers* and *students*. They will usually operate within some kind of formal structure or *institution,* using a plan or *curriculum* to signify progress toward some prearranged goal. And, they will typically have *logistical* support systems: books, facilities, etc.

Overt changes in each of these elements are plentiful these days. On the institutional front, there is debate over colleges-without-walls, professional schools and other such innovations. Teachers are changing[10] but probably not as fast as students.[11] Concerning logistics, textbooks and computer facilities both reflect new ideas in accounting education.

However, of the elements listed, *curriculum* is clearly the focal point of most of the controversy and experimentation. Apparently, there is a deep-seated belief that content (what we teach) is far more influential than form (how we teach). It is in the area of curriculum that massive change has occurred.

As with the forces for change, any serious attempt to isolate a single element must ignore obvious and important interactions. The existence of a particular book (a logistical item) may permit for the first time a certain type of instructor (a teacher variable) to teach a new course (a matter of curriculum). One cannot identify shifts in teacher style without simultaneously wondering about concurrent changes in student behavior. One cannot argue for a professional school of accountancy without presenting detailed plans for a curriculum; i.e., institutional forms are defined partially by what they teach.

Planned Change: Some Problems

The interesting issue for educational policy making is not really how to measure change, but rather how to channel it constructively and efficiently. Two aspects of this problem warrant brief discussion.

First, the policy maker must decide which forces he shall attend to. This is essentially a political question, a matter of values, expediency and often temporizing. While this section may clarify some of the positions, it cannot impose an automatic answer on anyone.

Second, the policy maker must predict the outcome of his action on the delicate ecology of accounting education. Such prediction will be fraught with uncertainties, for some of the following reasons.

As Figure 1 illustrates, simple cause-effect relationships are impossible to discover. There is a web of causality. Furthermore, causality runs both ways; i.e., a change in curriculum, for example, may well induce a change in the culture. For example, as "social measurement" enters the accounting curriculum, the attitudes of consumers (a cultural attribute) may well change.

Feedback is delayed and often unattainable at all. A change in teaching method may produce infinitesimal change in the course itself, but may evoke profound change much later. Creating a paraprofessional type of curriculum will cause a myriad of affects, none of which can be assessed until much later, if at all.

The "response options" are much "stickier" than the relatively fluid forces which led to the response. For example, changes in course content, once instituted, acquire a life of their own and will be resistant to termination. Specialized faculty are hired for fixed terms (or indefinitely, in the case of tenured faculty) and cannot be excised simply because their sub-sub-specialty has been made obsolete by cultural or intellectual forces.

Related to this, the very fluidity of the forces for change makes them somewhat suspect. The words "crisis", "new wave", "innovative" and so forth may translate as "fad" or "gimmick" to the experienced educator.

There are, of course, simple strategies for policy makers that abstract from these frustrations; e.g., "muddling through". They may well be appropriate. However, the objective of this section of this book is to make the educator aware of the contending forces. It would be an infringement on the authors and readers alike to attempt more.

Overview of Section II

The first sub-section which follows examines the implications of collegiate cost problems for accounting education. These implications are derived mostly from the deliberations and findings of the Carnegie Commission on Higher Education and its various outputs. Concerning economic forces, it is possible to generalize with some assurance. Conditions are not good, ranging from impending doom in some institutions to prudent optimism in a very few well-heeled areas.

The second sub-section addresses the value issue. By far the most numerous type of challenge to the status quo is phrased as "You—the accounting educator or administrator—are not doing what you ought to be doing." The use of "ought" implies a value system at odds with the educator in question.

Four of the papers dealing with comparative values represent particular points of view about global norms for accounting education. The other two papers deal with specific courses—beginning accounting and auditing. They pose, either explicitly or implicitly, the problems of resource allocation in a different way. Is the accounting faculty, in a collective sense, to strive for excellence in teaching or in research? Should the delicate balance (or imbalance) between professional education and other forms of accounting education be deliberately altered? Is it possible (or even desirable) to construct an "ideal" curriculum within any given institution? What institutional arrangements help and hinder the education of accountants? These and other questions are addressed.

Langenderfer presents a capsule history of accounting education, constructs a framework to encompass different pedagogical goal sets, and lays out alternatives in a neutral tone. The curriculum reformer or disgruntled practitioner is provided with a complete game plan for change according to his lights. The paper provides an excellent background for evaluating the more editorial recommendations of the other two papers (and others in Section II).

Trump and Bartholomew attempt to present a user's perspective on accounting education. Since almost all of the graduates of accounting programs fall within the purview of one of these two organizations, their observations about the skills necessary for success within their field of knowledge are highly relevant to the accounting teacher. It is left to the reader to attempt a reconstruction of the accounting curriculum sufficient for both sets of purposes and needs.

Mautz, writing with the benefit of both professorial and professional perspectives, mounts a very strong and pointed attack on accounting professors, curriculum content and delivery, and esoteric research. His paper commences with a litany of deep-seated problems in present schools and proceeds to a set of recommendations which, if implemented, would radically realign educational priorities and professorial prerogatives. While it is always easy for an editor to label something "must reading", this paper will rally a great deal of support in diverse camps and will demolish any sense of complacency in accounting researchers with any tendency toward reflection.

The third sub-section is like the preceding one except that the papers deal with well-defined objectives and problems and they present a relatively concrete proposal and/or case study of change in the accounting classroom. They are intended to be specific illustrations of how particular value sets have been implemented. As such, they have been selected and edited for their combination of normative and practical. For the most part, these papers are deliberately and necessarily simple-minded (in the best sense of the word); i.e., they have excised a well-defined subset of the educational system for study.

The final sub-section discusses a highly personal, unresolvable challenge: the challenge to be a teacher. There are as many teaching styles as there are teachers.

Some use cases; others see cases as an abomination. Some grade harshly; others leniently. Some have charisma; others impress by sheer force of mind. And so on. But for those who desire teaching (and its counterpart, learning) to be a questing-questioning, meaning-making process for them (and their counterpart, the student), then Professor Woelfel's prescriptions should be useful.

FOOTNOTES

[1] This highly arbitrary treatment of potential readers is paraphrased from the introduction to a book by Neil Postman and Charles Weingartner. *Teaching As a Subversive Activity*. (New York: Delta, 1969). p. 11. The Book is generally relevant to anyone interested in educational reform.

[2] See almost any recent issue of the *Journal of Accountancy*.

[3] Review the "Educational Research" section of any *Accounting Review*.

[4] The reader can probably conjure up his own vivid examples. Otherwise, see Jerry Farber, *The University of Tomorrowland*. (Pocket Books, September, 1972).

[5] Postman & Weingartner, p. 14.

[6] Peter Drucker, *The Age of Discontinuities*. (New York: Harper & Row, 1968). p. 311.

[7] Postman & Weingartner, p. 14.

[8] See for example, James E. Sorensen, John Rhode and Edward E. Lawler, III. "The Generation Gap in Public Accounting". (*The Journal of Accountancy*. Dec., 1973).

[9] *Campus Report* (Stanford University, October 17, 1973).

[10] Paul Aslanian and John Duff. "Why Accounting Teachers are so Academic". (*The Journal of Accountancy*, October, 1973).

[11] Sorensen, Rhode & Lawler.

The Economics of Educational Change

Introduction

This book, welcome as it is, poses a fundamental dilemma. Much of the book is concerned with innovation and change, progress and new programs; yet, it is also apparent that higher education is confronting a euphemism often called "no-growth reality." All sponsors of new programs, experimental classes and educational research projects must reconcile this problem in their own way, but it does seem important to present this elementary fact early in this volume. After all, perspective is a useful thing.

Surely it borders on gratuitousness to tell most accounting educators about scarce funds. The effects of no-growth reality operate on hiring, firing, tenure, class size, research and any other aspect of academic life. However, the new conditions of scarcity do not eliminate the need for change: They sharpen that need and channel it in new directions. In particular, it seems likely (and highly desirable) that attention to pedagogical problems will increase. But, regardless of the ultimate outcomes, a fundamental shift in attitudes will be required.

The Dismal Science of Non-Growth

Editors

Educational innovation is exciting... and expensive. The hard truth of this assertion is that educational values may become secondary to certain economic realities. Consciousness IV in higher education is cost-consciousness.

The implications of this growing realization for a book on accounting education are several. First, the "new realities" often translate into serious constraints on change. Innovations must be budgeted and subjected to feasibility checks. It is no longer true that "No academic experiment ever fails" and such a mentality is rapidly disappearing from the scene. Second, many of the exciting innovations touted in this book are in fact *responses* to the new awareness of scarce financial resources; e.g., teaching evaluation schemes (to use a particularly painful example), computerized introductory courses, and other such efficiency-maximizing devices. Third, it seems useful to recall occasionally that accounting education, like any other economic commodity, is subject to market forces and that the product (the accounting graduate) must bear some passing resemblance to what the employer wants. To be more blunt, the demand for teachers of accounting is a derived demand.

The paper which follows is a description of the present state of financial affairs for higher education, with particular emphasis on the need for attitude adjustments on the part of educators. The author, Earl Cheit, Program Advisor to the Ford Foundation, is the author of "The New Depression in Higher Education", a report sponsored by the Carnegie Commission on Higher Education and issued in 1970. This paper is derived from a follow-up study ("The New Depression in Higher Education—Two Years Later") based on studying 41 institutions.

The report concludes that most of these institutions "have gone from a financial condition of steady erosion to one of fragile stability". Seven key generalizations pertinent to progress in accounting education are:*

1. "The basis for rejoicing over the more stabilized current situation is quite limited." Austerity programs, program cutbacks and even outright bankruptcies are going to continue as part of the new reality.

2. "The responses and the individual institutions' records of expenditures suggest that, on the whole, private institutions are in somewhat better control of their situations than the public institutions." The reasons are not at all clear, nor is the implication for accounting education. If "better control" is achieved via very tight expenditure controls, then it is possible that pedagogical innovations will be viable only in public institutions of higher education. On the other hand, private colleges and universities are thought to have more freedom of action overall. In any case, generalizations about private-public sector well-offness seem hazardous and not as meaningful as the specific condition of the one institution wherein we work.

3. "Although the private institutions are as a group more optimistic, there are greater extremes of financial condition in the private sector than in the public." The range is from the "high-cost, high-quality" liberal arts college to the truly marginal operation.

4. "Within the public sector, the two year colleges are often thought to be a relatively favored type of institution. The

---

*Excerpted from the *Chronicle of Higher Education*, April 16, 1973.

responses from the follow-up study do not tend to support that view." Presently, state colleges are seemingly most secure; research universities see themselves as the most threatened of the public schools. It would seem that the thrust and thinking behind changes in accounting education may come from the "non-research" institutions in the immediate future.

5. "As a group, the research universities seem to be in the greatest state of concern about their future." Whether public or private, such schools express fear about the "qualitative leveling" which may occur. Again, extrapolation of such findings is difficult. It could, for instance, lead to a massive concern with mass production techniques in education. On the other hand, it may divert research attention from more esoteric areas to the very real and pressing problem of how best to educate the student.

6. "Administrators at institutions of all types endorse expanded student-aid programs and believe their institutions would benefit from them; but relatively few believe that expanding student aid alone will solve their institution's financial problems." Some have seen deferred payment plans for various types of student loans as a panacea for universities, but this is not to be. The private university charging almost $4,000 tuition will continue to have to justify that expenditure to students who have the alternative of paying, say, $400 to a state university near home. If students are receptive to such persuasion, it will probably be due to their belief that the educational experience is superior. Once more, logic leads one to conclude that greater devotion to pedagogical matters will be forthcoming, especially at the prestige schools.

7. "...The present condition of stability is very fragile." In short, the above generalizations are risky ones indeed. They depend on highly volatile assumptions about inflation, external sources of financing, entry by new students, and so on. Not the least of these factors is the attitude of the participants—students, faculty, alumni, administrators, etc.

A quantified expression of the future is the Carnegie Commission's statement that institutions of higher education should reduce the rate of expenditure growth to 2.5 percentage points above the rate of inflation. By way of reference, the cost growth in the late 1960s was 8.1 percent, a rate about 3.9 percentage points above the rate of inflation. To some extent, such cold-hearted numerical comparisons will affect accounting education, probably adversely relative to faculty expectations.

It is interesting to speculate about some likely ripple effects of the financial crunch on the teaching of accounting. However, the following are purely speculative and should be viewed as such until corroborated by experience. In any event, most of the articles in this book must be judged at least partially against this background.

First and most obvious, a tension for change will exist and grow. In its most painful form, this may require the reallocation of faculty positions and salaries in the light of changing demand. The dawning awareness of poorer financial circumstances must eventually filter down to operating levels. The obvious remedies to cost growth—fewer faculty, more students, larger classes, etc.—will be tried and will generate resistance of various forms.

Second, change can no longer be accomplished by growth: It must be in the form of substitution or even contraction. Furthermore, such change must be centralized in the sense that a systems perspective must be adopted. Programs can no longer be added willy-nilly, perhaps not at all. Integrating economics into the accounting curriculum may be difficult to sell because it is "redundant". Internships or work-study programs may become casualties due to their "non-academic" character. Resource allocation will be very similar to a zero sum game in the business curriculum.

Change will be evaluated, scaled and measured. Innovations in accounting education will be judged according to whether they "work", which means careful goal specifications and ongoing program evaluations. Ph.D. programs will be rethought and agonized over. The resources given the first accounting course will be reconsidered in the light of increased demand for MBA's relative to undergraduate accounting majors, or vice versa. In its most obvious form, such scaling will consist of teaching evaluation techniques not now used. The fabled autonomy of the individual faculty member is likely to be reduced.

Fourth, class size is likely to increase and, of course, student faculty ratios will rise. Economies of scale will begin to be an important concept in the design of schools, classes and curricula. The highly abstract course which draws relatively few students will be more difficult to justify to a cost-concious dean, and so forth. Obviously, certain courses, faculty, programs and even schools may be forced to justify their existence. Should every school have a Ph.-D. program? Every hospital a heart-lung machine? Every professor a tenured position?

Fifth, the traditional educational paradigm will be challenged and changed. Colleges without walls, continuing education, non-degree programs, summer mini-courses and other experiments will emerge under the pressure of the need for change.

Sixth, educational programs (including experimental new ones) must be shown to be *both effective and efficient*. Such a charge implies a basic and profound reexamination of the objectives of accounting education, leading to questions of professional schools, para-professionalism, continuing education and other perplexing issues. In short, the basic values of education itself are at issue: The mission must be redefined.

Last, although the redefinition process will be traumatic, one of the fortunate by-products should be increased attention to pedagogy and educational research. Hopefully, the heightened awareness and the outcomes from such research will more than offset the losses from cutbacks, retrenchments and similar austerity moves.

As Cheit observes in his paper, the aftermath of the force of growth is bringing to the fore the issue of educational leadership. "But it is not the barren role by which leadership was identified in the past. During the "golden years" leadership was seen as mediating conflicts between ambitious campus departments. During the recent period of campus disturbances, leadership was identified with keeping the peace. Now, in contrast to that recent past, leadership will be identified *in the context of educational policy making.*" (Emphasis added) Such a shift seems both desirable and timely for accounting education.

The Coming of Middle Age in Higher Education*

Earl F. Cheit
Program Advisor to the Ford Foundation

When academic men and women gather to talk about their administrative work these days, they tend to become nostalgic. Not for the immediate past, to be sure. Not for those turbulent times my Berkeley colleagues call "the bad old days." But rather for an earlier time and earlier conditions—for the conditions of a decade ago memorable for their possibilities, which now apparently are lost. How much easier it would be to solve the problems of today if we had the money of yesterday. The talk may concern either new policies—or the traditional concerns—helping a new Ph.D. in history in the job market, or finding money for freshman seminars. Soon, not later, someone will summarize the situation with the lament: "ten years too late."

Anyone who has spent at least the last ten years professing or administering on campus understands immediately that wistful reference to what Hans Jenny calls "the golden years" for higher education, the decade that ended with 1968. The "golden years" had problems, of course. But they were primarily the agreeable problems of growth: staffing, building, new programming. Now the problems of growth are all but gone and are evolving into the problems of adjustment. A glance at the new problems makes obvious why there is nostalgia for the old.

The problem of how to bring new faculty members in is becoming the problem of how to counsel old ones out. Those happy recruitment parties at the scholarly conventions are being replaced by dreary technical meetings on the actuarial foundations of early retirement. Those pioneering building problems—how to build space to house new faculty and new programs—have become the burdensome management problems of how to find budgeted activities to fill those buildings, and how to live with that most deceptive of euphemisms, deferred maintenance. Young faculty members were told their problem was to meet the established teaching, research and service standards and their reward would be advancement to tenure. But now their problem is that we cannot always keep the promise, and our problem is that they are forming unions. Until recently, a persuasive argument for starting a new program was that "someone else is doing it." Today that fact is a respectable argument for *not* starting it.

The problem of what to do with new money has become the problem of how to hang on to the old. Faculty positions that could not be filled at budgeted ranks, or filled at all, produced "budgetary savings," that most valuable of all academic resources, new money. New money was used to fund academic innovation and even support formulas into reverse, the remaining money is being used to fund management innovation and even whole management systems, with prayer.

In the office of student admissions, until recently the problem was how to buy, today the problem is becoming how to sell. A recent advertisement in *The Chronicle of Higher Education* says "Learn How to Recruit More New Students For Your Institution." Admissions procedures that could humble the most confident applicant are today fast on the way to becoming candidates for human relations awards.

---

*Speech before the National Association of State Universities and Land-Grant Colleges. American Association of State Colleges and Universities. Washington, D.C. November 13, 1972

As for research grants, they have always been popular, but as John Gardner recalls from his service as Secretary of HEW during those "golden years", academics were particular about the way they got the money. They insisted on the method he called the "leave it on the stump" approach. Now there is moss on the stump. The new way is the accountable way. At the annual meeting of the Association of Universities and Colleges of Canada this year the Director of Statistics Canada set the tone by warning his colleagues that the "future will be an era of no growth," and the entire meeting was devoted to accountability in research funding.

Put in language the State Department is said to find useful, our plans for the campus were "overtaken by events." With a fair degree of confidence a few years ago we projected student enrollment, assumed financial support, and predicted for higher education a gradual transition to organizational maturity by the end of the decade of the 1970s. It was to have been a slow transition to life in the steady state. But instead events rushed us into the problems of middle age adjustment in the first years of the decade. The transition could hardly be called graceful. Its rites of passage are no more memorable than the last budget fight, which on further reflection, seems indistinguishable from the budget fight that preceded it.

Academics trained to treat organizations for growing pains must now find remedies for the pains of middle age. "Ten years too late" is not a penitent nor a contrite cry, although some say it should be. It's a wistful reminiscence about the future. A full treatise on this academic change of life has not yet been done, but when it is, it could well be called "The Groans of Academe," because one of its conclusions will have to be that although growing pains hurt, they are not nearly as acute as the pains of middle age.

II

When did middle age set in? No single date marks the first signs, but they first began to trouble some institutions late in the 1960s, and have become more general since. The important fact is that they came much earlier than we had expected. Long-range planners in higher education have known that, given the present population which they could count, and enrollment rates which they thought they could predict, enrollment would grow steadily through the decades of the 1970s, level off at the end of the decade, remain fairly stable through the 1980s, and then climb again. Colleges and universities would have to scramble to make ends meet, but as they had done in the past, they could continue to finance this growth and so live at their accustomed life style. People who looked ahead saw adjustment problems occurring as growth ceased. What they did not foresee was the declining rate of income growth, the rising cost pressures, and the changes in attitudes toward higher education, all of which began to occur in the late 1960s. Any one of these factors alone would have caused some adjustment problems; together they produced the circumstances that overtook those long range plans. Today they are forcing upon us an accelerated course in the character building potential of retrenchment.

The growing divergence between cost and income put a heavy premium on tuition. Doubly valuable because it is the only income source that institutions can control directly, and the only "new" (uncommitted) money, tuition was pushed up, and pushed up faster than the rise in per capita disposable income. This increase in tuition (and other charges) together with changed attitudes, a slack job market, and a new draft situation, slowed down the rates of enrollment growth. During the decade of the 1960s enrollment grew at an average annual rate of about twelve percent. An average growth rate of about six percent was predicted for the 1970s. Dr. Garland G. Parker, the authority on enrollment figures, estimates this year's enrollment growth at two percent. Canadian colleges and universities, whose enrollment also grew at the average annual rate of about twelve percent during the 1960s, predicted an enrollment increase of five percent this year. Instead, it has gone up one-half of one percent.

Law schools and medical schools are, of course, growing rapidly, as are a few other special areas on university campuses—forestry and architecture, for example, and most community colleges are still growing at least as rapidly as expected, as are a smaller number of four-year institutions.

But except for a fortunate few, all four-year colleges and universities are affected. It is now reported that the proportion of state budgets going to higher education has stopped growing; and that in two-thirds of the states, the proportion of the budget going to higher education is actually declining. The prospects for substantial new federal funds are poor. For most institutions the transition away from incremental budgeting has begun. Although the degree of adjustment varies from campus to campus, in all of them the work of administrators and the worries of academics have changed enough to render them nostalgic. Plainly put, the college president's job formerly was to give things away; now he must increasingly take things away. The faculty, accustomed to worrying about trading up, now worries about being traded off. That is middle age with a vengeance!

III

No one can say we were totally without warning, early or distant. Articles and speeches were current about academic life in the steady state. One of President Clark Kerr's favorite themes—and he came back to it often in his speeches on the Berkeley campus—was growth and its evolution. Looking ahead through the 1960s and early 1970s, he said the university would be going through a period of "extensive growth." But after that, late in the 1970s, the university would enter a new period of "intensive growth." I remember the speeches clearly; I distinctly remember enjoying and applauding them; I now realize that I did not really understand what they meant. Certainly there was no reason for alarm. Like the "steady state", the concept of "intensive growth" had an agreeable sound. In any case, "intensive growth" was still a long way off. What was hard to understand at the time, but is painfully clear today, is that it meant growth through conscious choice. It meant change, not by addition, but by substitution, or even by contraction.

Perhaps President Kerr meant to tell his faculty that intensive growth is partly the growth of character that comes from making hard choices. If that was his intention he chose a method that was too subtle. It took more than subtlety to raise consciousness of choice in the "golden years." That is not the way we were inducted into the system. My induction on moving west in 1957, along with a couple of hundred thousand or so fellow migrants, came from a colleague at a welcoming luncheon on the Berkeley campus. "There are three things a newcomer to California ought to understand" he explained.

"First, you will now enjoy an entirely new relationship to nature. Until now, she was sometimes your adversary. Now she is your ally. Here nature is always on your side."

"Second," he continued, "we are terribly provincial. When we speak of the government, we don't mean Washington, D.C., we mean Sacramento."

"Finally, and most important, we have repealed the first principle of economics, that dealing with choice. Here is how we handle it. If there are two ways of doing something, we don't agonize about which way to do it. We do both."

Whether or not other new faculty members stumbled into such a heady welcome in the "golden years", the objective conditions on campus could not help but generate optimism. Malcolm Moos, President of the University of Minnesota, describes the "affluent Fifties and Sixties" as a time of "overflowing public coffers from which we virtually shovelled out at will the resources we felt necessary to finance education..." Even allowing for the fact that from the perspective of today, those past years may seem a bit more golden than they in fact were, it was a time not likely to generate serious responses to lectures about intensive growth, nor to articles about the problems of the steady state. The warnings were there, but the conditions that would make them real were not. Now we have the reality.

IV

Facing up to reality is difficult for all organizations. They prefer to change the easiest way—by growing. No one likes to discard activities. It is easier to decide what to do, than it is to decide what not to do, than it is to decide what to do first or than it is to decide what to give up. Our governments, state and federal, tend to be least disciplined about these questions, so they grow. Business is not much different. In his book, *The Age of Discontinuity*, Peter

Drucker reminds us that "Businessmen are just as sentimental about yesterday as bureaucrats. They are just as reluctant to abandon anything. They are just as likely to respond to the failure of a product or program by doubling the efforts invested in it."

For colleges and universities, facing the reality of change without growth is doubly difficult. They are complex organizations of professionals. Peer judgment is an essential ingredient for their most important decisions. Administrators are appointed under a corporate theory, but their academic success depends in large part on their ability to lead by a parliamentary model. By comparison, the organizational problems of business are simple. Many of the achievements we prize most in our academic institutions can be traced to their decentralized structure, their autonomy. But that form of planning and spending is not well suited to the problem of adjusting program to more restricted circumstances. Moreover, educational institutions do not have performance measures that could facilitate judgment of their effectiveness. As of now, there is little agreement about the value judgments which would be implicit in such measures.

Finally, the problems of adjustment are more difficult in colleges and universities than in most other organizations because they have been undermanaged, especially at the departmental level. If no one has offered the colleges and universities as examples of impeccable management, neither has anyone made a convincing case that their problems are primarily ones of bad management. As their alumni and friends discovered during the periods of campus disturbances, the problem is that they have been undermanaged. By any reasonable criterion of administrative support one might apply, colleges and universities compare quite favorably with governmental and even with industrial organizations. That is part of their problem. As recently as eight years ago, one of the nation's leading institutions was operating without a budget. That is an extreme example, to be sure, but it is one that brings knowing and sympathetic nods from academic administrators. Their own institutions, in their own ways, have also been undermanaged. In higher education, facing up depends on catching up.

V

Ask the president of any college or university today what his major concern is, and in one way or another, he will tell you that he is working on the choices forced by the cost-income situation on campus. Listen to the conversations at meetings of the various associations in higher education. Whether it is the Association of University Presses, or the National Collegiate Athletic Association, or the learned societies, or this meeting of Land-Grant Colleges, State Colleges and State Universities. The conversations are never far away from the money problem and the adjustments it forces on the campus. Lyman Glenny, Director of the Berkeley Center for Research and Development in Higher Education, recently warned that the process of adjustment was not moving fast enough; that on same campuses there was still more concern with prestige than with flexibility; that expansionist tendencies are still evident; that some faculty members seem to view the present situation as merely a temporary aberration from the "golden years" pattern.

Scratch a president who sighs "ten years too late" and you may still find a "golden years" builder yearning for a few new Ph.D. programs and a new medical center. But the odds are growing that you will find a new-wave cost-accountant. Or more accurately, a cost-finder, who is busy turning the planning process around. Instead of beginning with aspirations for prestige, leaving eventual costs and educational objectives to take care of themselves, he now begins with the objectives, and the unit costs had better be justified by them or the project will be scrapped. At the University of Minnesota, Malcolm Moos has a program he calls R and R. His R and R does not mean rest and recreation. It means retrenchment and reallocation. Not every campus is doing as much, and it is not always easy for an outsider to know just how much, if anything, is going on because on some campuses the process proceeds under euphemisms. But it is becoming hard to find a campus not involved in reconsideration of its priorities, for all know that sooner or later they will have hard choices to make.

This effort to improve choice by the use of management methods has produced the newest movement on campus—the management movement. The signs are all around us. Look at the titles of popular recent books: *Efficiency in Liberal Education; Efficient College Management; The More Efficient Use of Resources.* The advertisements in educational journals reveal a growing market for consulting services in management.

Consider the important new organizations. From its relatively modest beginnings just a few years ago, the National Center for Higher Education Management Systems (NCHEMS) at the Western Interstate Commission for Higher Education (WICHE) at Boulder, is today a burgeoning force in higher education. The National Center convened its first national assembly just two months ago (September 13-15, 1972), and although registration of a few hundred was expected, about 700 academic administrators from all over the country came. What were the program topics that justified so much travel at this time of tight budgets? "Making Decisions with NCHEMS Tools"; "Faculty Activity Analysis"; "Modern Planning and Management Techniques: Implications for Implementation and Organization"; "Information Exchange Procedures: Significance for Decision Makers"; "Cost Finding Principles." It was one of the first national meetings of the new management movement that is gaining momentum in higher education. The National Center's meeting was clearly a consciousness-raising session, an important early phase in the life of all movements. Every president who reads the incoming mail knows that similar sessions are being held in all parts of the nation. Some parts of this movement—the Commond Fund for example—are devoted to increasing income. Most are concerned with costs.

So sensitive have we become to the forms of this movement that any president who cannot say he is using cost-simulating models described by powerful-sounding acronyms like PROBE or DRIVE or BAMN (no endorsements here) goes unarmed these days to meetings of alumni, Regents, and especially to meetings of presidents, where it could well be assumed he is not up to date, or even worse, that he is not conscious of costs. For it now seems that as a result of the management movement, Consciousness IV is making its appearance on the nation's campuses—it's cost consciousness.

VI

If the colleges and universities were being forced to adjust to a short-term money problem only, I think that even at this early date, the management movement could be proclaimed a partial success. When hard figures do become available, I believe they will show that the management efforts are making progress, both in holding down the rate of growth of expenditures, and in raising more income than would otherwise be the case. Some budget disasters have been avoided, others at least postponed. My overall impression is that the amount of progress is substantial and its consequences significant.

But we are not dealing with a short-term problem. The optimists say the 1970s will be bad; the pessimists say the 1980s—with no enrollment growth to justify income growth—will be worse. Among academic administrators there is general recognition that this is a long-term phenomenon. This explains why one can find nostalgia for the old life style even among those administrators not yet forced to adopt the new one. They know that whatever their differences in size, aspirations, and degree of present difficulty, all institutions will be counting on management methods to help with their money problems for the forseeable future.

When the problems of adjustment are looked at in this longer run perspective, the importance of attitudes toward education becomes apparent. In higher education, issues of money lead eventually to issues of purpose. Although the immediate adjustments of the kind I listed at the beginning of these remarks were for the most part dominated by tactical, fiscal considerations, their longer run solution like the condition of higher education itself, depends upon basic attitudes toward higher education. And as I noted earlier, the colleges and universities are dealing with a money problem and an attitude problem. They are an interrelated product of growth, most of which has been absorbed by the Land-Grant and State institutions.

In higher education, as in other areas of our national life, we are being forced to come to terms with growth and the attitudes about it. In so far as one can tell, the burden of changed attitudes toward education seem to be rather evenly distributed among the nation's institutions of different types. But the ability of individual campuses to meet the educational needs of their potential students, to be of good quality, and in some cases, to exist, will in considerable measure be determined by how the emerging, conflicting views about education are reconciled in the future.

This future situation has special relevance for Land-Grant Colleges and the State Colleges and Universities. They have a major stake in the outcome, of course. But, in addition, these institutions are in a strong position to provide leadership in reconciling the main attitude conflicts due to growth. Let's take a look at growth in this light.

VII

The dominant fact about American higher education is its rapid and successful growth. In the period since World War II, higher education was transformed from an elite to a mass enterprise. In 1940, the enrollment rate—i.e., the ratio of undergraduate degree-credit enrollment to the population aged 18 to 21—was 15 percent. By 1970, that figure was 50 percent of a much larger population. Graduate School enrollments rose in even larger proportion. Graduate degree-credit enrollment was equal to a mere 1.5 percent of the population age 22 to 24 in 1940. By 1970, it had risen to almost 10 percent. It helps to recall the total numbers, the total enrollment in all institutions reporting to the U.S. Office of Education. In 1940, total enrollment was 1.6 million students. Total enrollment in 1970 was 8.5 million students. These numbers emphasize another characteristic of our system of higher education—its egalitarianism. Socioeconomic status does affect access and success, but probably much less than anywhere else in the world.

There is no mystery about how or why this growth occurred. Education was made a mass phenomenon because we were willing to pay for it, first through the G.I. bill, and then through public and private funds made more ample by rising per capita incomes. In short, we were willing to invest in new buildings, in large campuses, in generous support for graduate study, and in support budgets for students and institutions. All this did not happen in a policy vacuum. Higher education, through its teaching, research and service functions, was responding to national purpose: first it was meeting the educational needs of war veterans, and later the nation's need for scientific, technical, and defense skills. NDEA, lest we forget, stands for National Defense Education Act.

One important consequence to the nation of this increased enrollment, as recently shown by a National Bureau of Economic Research study for the Carnegie Commission (NBER Occasional Paper 118), was a significant reduction in the loss of talent, as measured by the fraction of high school graduates who enter college at various ability levels.

And finally, our institutions of higher education achieved this record of growth and egalitarianism while retaining, indeed augmenting, their quality. It is a remarkable record of success, success in responding to national need and purpose.

Ironically, success has generated some new problems and illuminated some old ones:

—justifiable pride in the achievements of our mass system is giving way to complaints about impersonal instruction;

—delight with the rapid expansion of graduate work has become a lament that undergraduates are being neglected;

—enthusiasm for financial support for graduate students has been soured by complaints that it is mainly a method of exploiting labor;

—patriotic feelings that accompanied scientific work for the federal government have been supplanted by feelings of guilt about complicity of a large education establishment with the military-industrial complex;

—the autonomy of our institutions, which made their excellence possible, is now criticized as an unfair, clumsy, and expensive form of governance;

—what academics laud as a reduction in loss of talent is being criticized as a new form of waste. We are now accused of giving a college education to many more people than need it for the labor market;

—the question arises about the large institutions which performed admirably in absorbing so many students, thus producing new forms of irritation, is more better?

VIII

The larger setting, within which the successful growth in higher education and its consequent problems have occurred, served to intensify and to complicate those problems. From a growth-oriented society, giving relatively clear professional, scientific, and enrollment missions to higher education, we are moving toward a society forced to come to terms with growth. We are becoming concerned about the effects of growth on the quality of life. Instead of simple growth, we want desirable growth.

In some obvious ways, we no longer feel as dependent upon higher education as we did just a few years ago; but in other ways we are more dependent on higher education than ever. We look to it to extend opportunity to those still excluded, and for help with the complex problems of growth whose solution will require even more sophisticated technology and training. We are perplexed by the many criticisms of higher education and generally unimpressed by the responses.

Regard for the college was once similar to regard for one of its ancestors, the church. But in the university and the society at large the old reverential attitude toward higher education is disappearing. Although a new attitude has not yet emerged, an unquestioning supportive attitude is all but gone, and as a result the burden of proof about the value of education has shifted. Addressing himself to the similar phenomenon in Canada, Colin Mackay, Executive Director of the Canadian Association of Colleges and Universities, described it this way: "...society, having concluded that higher education became the pampered pet of politicians, is anxious to throw the dog out of doors to seek shelter in the all-but-forgotten dog-house."

If all the recent studies, reports, speeches, books and legislative actions on the problems of higher education are sent out at the same time, there will be no room in the dog-house for the dog. Nor will all this reading matter offer clear directions on how to get higher education back indoors. It contains many criticisms that institutions put too much emphasis on graduate education followed by the actions of legislators in North Carolina, California and probably in states between, creating new universities. Various reports of the task forces and commissions reflect similar conflicts. They deplore the emphasis on credentials, but are at the same time concerned about the cost of dropouts; they advocate diversity which is costly, and economy, which presumably is not; they support autonomy of institutions, but support policies which will shift authority off campus.

IX

It is hard enough to try to keep track of all of these developments, let alone reconcile them. But I believe that in these gropings for a new attitude, we can identify three underlying elements which eventually will shape the others. First, there are the views of those who know what good education is and who are most concerned about its future quality. Put much too simply, their concern, as expressed in some of the objections I noted earlier, is that the great growth in higher education has tended to pollute it. Somewhat disenchanted with what mass higher education has become, they want it restored to human scale, they want it to be better. To the extent that they have a program, it tends to be procedural, and it is put in terms of diversity, attention to individual development, humanized learning, creativity, responsiveness. In policy terms, those who hold these views are seeking high quality and diversity on both the public and the private side.

X

Not everyone is groping for a new attitude toward higher education. Some people have just come to the old one. This is the second underlying element, namely, that those still excluded from it want access to the middle class. For them, the problem of higher education is not impersonal learning, but insufficient growth, for with growth comes access. When only a few people could afford to go to college, there were no outcries of dehumanized learning. Those who still cannot afford to go remind us that disenchantment with growth motivates those who have made it, but it is growth and development that appeal to those who have not. In short, higher education is becoming part of a larger struggle, one which occurs when rising per capita income affords mass access, and brings concerns about quality from those who are enjoying the benefits of growth, and demands for access from those who are still trying to get it. Their program is extending the opportunity for access.

XI

The third underlying element in the developing situation is the growing movement to redistribute the costs of higher education by moving public systems closer to full cost pricing. That idea is not one of those gems privately polished in the inner circles of some Chamber of Commerce. It is being advanced by young economists on your faculties. One of the many ironies in our recent experience is that at the very time the campuses were accused of radicalism and worse, faculty members were making respectable the idea of applying market methods to the most important public service, education.

The growing cost of higher education—from 1.1 percent of GNP in 1960 to 2.5 percent in 1970—made inevitable that it should become the object of scrutiny. The decline in the old reverential attitude toward higher education made it vulnerable to what had heretofore been regarded as a rather weak, shortsighted argument: that the benefits of higher education are essentially private.

Today this argument seems to be in the ascendency. Supported by the arguments that higher education resources are not allocated as equitably, or used as efficiently as they should be, it has little effective opposition. At the same time there is growing recognition of the serious consequences for some private institutions of the tuition gap in our two price system. Actually, it is not necessary to rely on these arguments to increase tuition in state systems. A strong incentive to do so is provided by the basic grant program of the Education Amendments of 1972.

XII

If this analysis is correct, in the coming months and years public policy toward higher education will be shaped by efforts: (1) to move public systems closer to full cost pricing; (2) to have high quality institutions, both public and private; and (3) to extend access. Every campus faces some access, quality and cost conflicts. Indeed, the reconciliation of divergent goals is a continuing activity in higher education. But the formal resolution of these goals is becoming a major new policy issue in many, perhaps most, states.

It seems fairly safe to predict, as most members of a national panel consulted by WICHE recently bid, that as a result of the efforts of state governments, within 10 years "students will pay a greater proportion of the cost of post-secondary education." Would the panel be willing to predict with the same assurance that opportunity for access will be extended, and quality protected? That question was not posed, so we do not know. We do know that all three will be advocated, and we can predict that how they are reconciled will depend in considerable part on whether colleges and universities can unite to exert leadership influence in support of principled, difficult policy choices. We can also predict that a tactic of low profile, or of bickering, given present public attitudes, is almost certain to yield the priority ranking of: full cost pricing, first; high quality, a not-so-close second; extending access, a distant third.

That result will not be what the language of a full cost pricing proposal says, or what its thoughtful advocates intend, but that is the likely eventual result.

Can colleges and universities exert leadership in support of a more principled reconciliation of these partially conflicting goals? It is much too early to tell. There are hopeful but still highly fragile signs in the States of Washington, New York, and undoubtedly others that I do not know about.

Although the basic elements of this emerging policy issue are similar in most states, the local conditions vary enough to make impossible generalizations about the substantive choices that will emerge.

Where colleges and universities seem able to exert leadership influence, however, it is because they can create an atmosphere conducive to trust among all institutions, public and private, and are able to agree that life in the steady state requires cooperation and probably market sharing.

XIII

At this point I should like to be able to assure you that "Life begins at forty" has an organizational counterpart. But if one exists I do not know about it. What I do know is that the force of growth, the aftermath of which is creating adjustment problems on campus and off, is bringing to the fore the issue of educational leadership. But it is not the barren role by which leadership was identified in the past. During the "golden years" leadership was seen as mediating conflicts between ambitious campus departments. During the recent period of campus disturbances, leadership was identified with keeping the peace. Now, in contrast to that recent past, leadership will be identified in the context of educational policy making. On campus and off it will be identified through the choices it makes. On campus and off, those choices will shape the understanding of a conflicted public about higher education and will lead in time to its support.

In other words, desirable growth depends upon principled choice, a conclusion likely to make one nostalgic for those "golden years" lectures on intensive growth. Like the earliest advocates for instruction in the agricultural and mechanical arts, they were ahead of their time, but right.

Values as Forces for Change

Introduction

"Accounting Education" is a complex of people, buildings, courses, curricula and assorted other things. It is hardly a monolithic, unified or steerable entity. It is moved fitfully if at all and trying to assess where it is at any one time is only slightly less difficult than trying to fine-tune it into a new position.

Nevertheless, friends and members of the educational community do adopt certain positions of advocacy in an attempt to influence the direction and force of change. Such positions are often determined by implicit or explicitly stated values. This section is an attempt to portray some of those values. The following section will describe some earnest attempts to implement values in an actual educational setting.

All six of the papers in this section—some more than others—are concerned with the interface between society, the profession and the student, where the accounting curriculum is viewed as a mechanism for imparting both technical and non-technical skills. Each author is arguing for a particular viewpoint, usually with conviction. Since there is no central planning agency for accounting education, each reader must decide for himself which value system is most harmonious with his own and act accordingly.

The point of this sub-section may well be that accounting education cannot be all things to all people, nor should it try. However, it should pay close attention to the complaints of its public.

The Over-Intellectualization of Accounting Education

Robert K. Mautz
Partner, Ernst & Ernst

Introduction

This paper is a general indictment of accounting education. Dr. Mautz contrasts a professor-oriented accounting curriculum with one based on student needs, and perceives a growing intellectualization of accounting education at a time when the need is for professionalization. Issues of theory vs. practice, teaching vs. research, and various offshoots of these issues underly the argumentation in this paper, although the single largest unspoken question is: Who is the better judge of student needs, the professor or the practitioner? Clearly, the question is both subjective and hotly controversial involving as it does the issue of educational values. The answer is likely to be that both professor and practitioner can contribute insights, that neither is (nor should be) dominant. The relationship is symbiotic, not a superior-subordinate situation.

The thesis of this paper is that over the last three decades a changing sense of values has led accounting education to change its priorities in directions that make it less relevant to the needs of students and their prospective employers. During this period there has been a substantial shift in emphasis from teaching to research, from practice to theory, and from experience to publication. Accompanying that shift, and partly as a result of it, accounting education has tended to slip out of the mainstream of educational purpose. Neither its teachings, its publications, nor its research are as relevant to the needs of students as they should be. So a new set of priorities is needed, and this article attempts to make a case for them and to indicate what their nature should be.

Nature of Conditions Influencing Accounting Education

From the end of World War II until the beginning of the current decade, higher education generally, including education for accountancy, has enjoyed a state of near euphoria. A number of reasons account for this. Accounting education has had a plentiful supply of students because there was such a strong demand for accounting graduates. A long period of rapid and continuing expansion of business and industry called for increasing numbers of accountants both in industry and in the public accounting profession. Growth in the size of individual business units intensified the importance of accounting data for control purposes. The rise of professional management became a necessity in order to deal with the problems of both large and diversified companies, and an essential ingredient of professional management continues to be a demand for and reliance on financial data.

The extensive growth of business activity could not have occurred without access to plentiful supplies of funds through the investment market and, as a "people's capitalism" developed in this country, the demand for financial information by analysts, investment counselors, and fund managers also increased. Also recognized was the need for some form of regulation of the flow of financial data which called for still more accountants to participate in and support the regulatory process.

So, with rare exceptions, business schools have had little difficulty in placing their competent accounting graduates. This has assured a steady flow of entering students, almost without regard for the details and content of the curricula offered. As the number of students increased, the need for teachers expanded, which meant burgeoning graduate programs.

This situation provided accounting educators with greatly increased freedom. Their salary conditions were improved, particularly in comparison with other departments whose students were not in such great demand. But more than this, professorial salaries improved in comparison with those of academic administrators. For the first time, outstanding professors with no administrative duties whatsoever found their compensation equalling that of department heads and deans, a fact which gave them both a great deal of satisfaction and a feeling of equality not previously enjoyed.

Because teachers were in short supply, they could demand reduced teaching loads to provide time for research as well as for "moonlighting" in the increasing number of part-time employment opportunities available to them. Also because of the shortage of teachers, those who had created significant personal reputations were free to use their spare time about as they pleased.

During this period, the so-called search for excellence by academic administrators put a high premium upon the services of those teachers who also published. Lacking any better basis for evaluating the quality of their own faculties, administrators tended to view publication as the equivalent of successful research, and research became the order of the day. The competition for professors with outstanding publication records provided no end of opportunities to the successful publisher, a fact which he was not reluctant to bring to the attention of his dean or president.

These circumstances combined to provide those in academic positions with a degree of freedom not previously experienced. There was almost no interference with the individual's choice of what he would teach or how he would spend his research efforts. Changes in curricula, whether brought about by formal or informal means, became almost the sole prerogative of those doing the teaching, and some very young educators with little experience beyond their own undergraduate and graduate courses assumed positions of substantial importance in curriculum development. In some cases, the faculties of expanding universities were staffed almost completely with very young and inexperienced people. In other cases, by sheer weight of numbers, recent additions to the faculty outvoted their more experienced seniors.

During this period, accounting faculty members have enjoyed an enviable position of status and prestige. There has been an almost total absence of criticism of educational content and processes by practitioners, many of whom have been led to believe that the great developments since they left school have rendered their education largely obsolete. Thus, for practitioners to criticize academic programs not only would be interference with academic freedom but might also be an embarrassing display of ignorance. At the same time there has been no absence of criticism of practice by educators who, by and large, have far less acquaintance with the world of the practitioner than that individual has with the world in which the professor reigns supreme.

Because of the high regard in which practitioners have held academics, funds have been made available for research both directly and indirectly. Although specific research grants have not been common, monetary grants with no strings attached have been made to schools which have underwritten research efforts with those funds. In addition, practitioners, both in public accounting and in industry, have cooperated in the supplying of research data to academic researchers.

Funds also have been provided for the support of colloquia, symposia, travel and other efforts of this type so that many academics who otherwise would not attend such activities are able to do so at little or no cost. Typically included is an allowance to publish the proceedings, so the number of opportunities for publication by academics has also grown. Expanding opportunities for consulting assignments, internships, and other arrangements have provided additional ways for professors of accounting to improve their financial condition and exchange views with practitioners. When compared with the funds and opportunities available to academic types in some of the physical sciences, the advantages flowing to accounting educators do not seem at all extravagant. Nevertheless, it represents such a change from previous years that its impact has been significant.

A Professor-Centered System

What has been the net impact of all of these changes? It has led to a professor-centered system of accounting education. Supplied with the opportunity, accounting educators have acted like any entrepreneur under similar conditions. They have tailored their environment and activities to suit their own interests and preferences. To a considerable extent, the interests of the individual professor were put first, whether in scheduling the time of his classes, in establishing the content of his courses, or in proposing research topics and work programs. Because it has had the most to do with his personal advancement, publication has assumed inordinate importance. The emphasis upon publishable research dominated the thoughts of many academicians to such an extent that the entire curriculum became skewed in favor of the professors' interests. To conserve their own time and energies, whether done deliberately or unintentionally, many professors brought to their classes the same issues with which they were working in their efforts to improve their publication records, regardless of the relevance of such issues to their students' educational and career goals. More than one class of elementary accounting students has been overwhelmed by material from a doctoral candidate's thesis when both the students' interests and their needs would have been better served by some less esoteric topic.

The total impact of this tendency is evidenced by a great concern in accounting curricula with topics which are only peripheral to accounting. Those matters that appear new and exciting and which may lead to publication, catch the fancy of the professor. Unless he is subject to either firm self-discipline or is controlled by his department head (an increasingly difficult task these days), there is a great temptation to carry matters of the professor's current interest to class. We have introduced into the curriculum heavy doses of mathematics, statistics, and behavorial science, sometimes without any serious effort to justify those injections in terms of the actual needs of the student.

The rationalization has been that the world is changing, that decision making is a new art, that for today's students to be current and useful during their lifetimes they must have these newer topics. One is hard pressed to defeat such arguments even if one wanted to. Certainly much good comes from introducing more rigorous materials into the curriculum. But the cost has been great. To make room for these subjects, accounting procedures, techniques, and analytical problems have received reduced attention. Some of the educational materials which very successful industrial and public accountants believe contributed significantly to their success no longer receive anything like the attention they once did.

There is a new emphasis on "what should be" rather than on "what now is". And what should be is often based upon nothing more than the views of the individual teaching the course. His views may be unrealistic and may have been reached without any significant acquaintance with practice, yet in today's environment they are viewed as important. Not infrequently, they are highly critical of practice although the basis for criticism may be minimal.

In a sense this is exemplified by the attitude of many academics toward the Accounting Principles Board. Instead of respecting the Accounting Principles Board as a group of volunteered experts engaged in an essentially political process under heavy and conflicting pressures at a time when society's changing standards make their task all the more difficult, we find some educators apparently viewing them with an intolerant and critical eye. Some see the Board as composed of near rascals who have little regard for truth and logic but much concern over their own personal success — which can be furthered, these educators believe, most readily by a blatant catering to those corporate executives who control their appointments as company auditors. To many educators, totally unaware of the difficulties of the Board's mission, the purpose of the Board has been to establish "good accounting theory" as the individual educator would define it and any failure to do this has been viewed with disfavor.

Intellectualization vs. Professionalization

What has happened within the academic sphere is an intellectualization of accounting at a time when it badly needed

contrary. Among the various forces contending for attention in a university, perhaps the least powerful in the last thirty years has been the student who wanted a truly professional education. The attention he receives reflects this fact.

Most universities describe their schools of business administration, in which accounting typically finds its home, as professional schools. Such a description leads people to believe that its emphasis is upon preparation of students for professional careers in subjects in which the school specializes. The implication in this title, "professional school", is that it prepares students for a career at a professional level, in either public or private accounting. Parents send their children to study in such a school because they and their children look forward to a career of some kind in accounting practice. A profession implies practice, service to clients. It implies doing, not merely discussing. It implies helping clients to meet problems. It implies something far more than an intellectual interest in accounting theory. To the extent that professional schools of business administration fail to prepare their graduates to enter into professional practice, they fail to meet the expectations of both those who had entered as students and those who have supported their education.

Determining Student Needs.

Two courses are open to the educator who wishes to determine what his students' needs really are. One is to obtain sufficient first-hand experience through faculty internships, other visits to corporations and firms, conversations with practicing accountants who come to the campus, attendance at professional meetings, and similar efforts so that he discovers the nature of professional practice and the kind of work which the students will be expected to do. A second method is to accept the word of others. The first is much to be preferred. Nevertheless, there are many sincere educators who wish to do right by their students and who are unable, for one reason or another, to obtain the necessary experience directly and promptly. For them, some of the following thoughts might be helpful as they restructure their value systems.

Whether one would prefer it that way or not, the intellectually appealing solution is only one of the important considerations in the formulation of business and accounting decisions. Accounting practice stresses active participation in the prompt solution of mundane as well as empyrean problems. The appropriate solutions to mundane problems often depend as much upon the details of the transaction and the circumstances in which it occurred as they do upon broad theoretical considerations.

To cope with the host of problems of all shapes and sizes that he faces, the career professional puts relatively more weight on technical ability and proficiency than does the educator. The facility with which one accomplishes a given task, the accuracy of one's work, its organization, reliability, and reviewability are all matters of importance. The skilled technician is respected. There is little acceptance of sloppy work. Although the problems faced by the practitioner may appear to be mundane, many of them have the potential for near disaster. Accountants, like others in the business world, live in a contentious and litigious atmosphere. Although there are encouraging signs, contingent fee law suits and huge class actions are still strong possibilities. So there is great emphasis on defensible solutions to the problems facing the practitioner. The cost of mistakes is an ever present consideration. At the least, mistakes may cost the practitioner an unhappy client, customer, shareholder, or other financially interested party. At the worst, one's professional reputation and success are at stake. And when litigation results, as it too often does, the costs are incomprehensible except to one who has had experience with its direct and indirect burdens.

So whether in industry or in public practice, the practitioner is much concerned with quality control. Relying, as he must, on others within large organizations, he unavoidably faces the need for methods of obtaining internal discipline and quality control with a minimum sacrifice of innovative ability and motivation. The means and techniques by which discipline is accomplished are at least as essential to the practitioner as the rules of logic are to the intellectual. They should not be omitted from the students' education. Certainly there is nothing nonintellectual about a professionalization. Intellectualization means an attitude and approach toward the study of accounting that:

1. Advocates the resolution of accounting issues in terms of logic and theory only, without regard to the difficulties and implications of implementation.
2. Exhibits little or no interest in discovering and evaluating the variety of situations and circumstances in which accounting principles must be applied.
3. Includes a disinclination to empathize with the practitioner who finds questions of accounting theory inextricably entangled with matters of equity, precedent, materiality.
4. Exhibits little or no concern for the details which distinguish transactions and situations from one another in spite of apparent similarities.
5. Tends to think of progress, not in terms of pragmatic solutions to relative mundane problems, but as the formulation of grand generalizations that contribute great new insights.
6. Prefers the role of advisor and critic to that of participant and performer.

Another way of viewing intellectualization vs. professionalism is to recognize that there are essentially two ways in which accounting might be presented in a university curriculum. One possibility is to present it as an organized discipline based on certain essential concepts which lead to principles, procedures, techniques, and standards, and which concepts themselves are influenced by unavoidable postulates. By concentrating on a clarification of the current status of these elements of the system and by testing the elements against rules of logic, internal consistency, and observations of the real world, our understanding of these elements can be improved and progress can be made toward better descriptions of what the system should be. This is basically the intellectualization approach.

A second possibility is more operational than theoretical in approach, more professional than intellectual. It emphasizes what accountants do, whatever the nature of their employment. Questions such as the following receive attention: What problems does an accountant face? What tools does he have to work with? How might he best approach different kinds of problems? What should he watch for? To whom is he responsible? When is he in difficulty? What makes some situations differ from others?

Intellectualization reflects emphasis on the construction of theory. Professionalization stresses quality performance of important tasks. Of course, some attention to both is needed. In the early days of accounting education, a how-to-do-it approach prevailed and theory received little, if any, attention. In the last two decades, the balance has swung just about as far as it can the other way. Relatively little time is now spent on how to do it. Considerably more time is spent on how it ought to be done, with all the reasons why the educator thinks so. Education has greatly neglected implementation and application in favor of theorization, including its own diversification movement into peripheral areas. If accounting education has a responsibility to the accounting profession, there is little in its recent history to indicate any recognition of that responsibility. During a period when the nature, obligations, and problems of the profession have been changing substantially, accounting education has shown very little responsiveness to those changes.

This intellectualization of accounting education and accounting research has emerged quite naturally out of the professors' inclination to avail himself of an opportunity to indulge his own interests and advancement. For this reason it is suggested that accounting has become a professor-centered program.

Student Needs as Center of Interest for Accounting Education.

If the professor and his interests are not to be the focus of accounting education, what should be? The student, of course. The student's needs, his ambitions, and his purposes in seeking education are of prime importance. If we go back to original purposes and causes, universities were established to provide students with what they could not obtain as well elsewhere. Professors exist to serve students, not the professional education. Such an education would prepare the prospective practitioner to deal not only with matters of theory but with questions of precedent, equity, and materiality. He must be taught to deal not only with concepts and principles but with their application to real world situations. He must learn to distinguish form from substance and to resist the inevitable pressures that will be a part of his environment.

Emphasis in Professional Education.

What would professional accounting education include? In addition to a sound background in general education and sufficient general business education to permit the accounting graduate to discuss and to understand business operations and activities, it should include the following:

1. A thorough grounding in the current state of the accounting art. This should be a balanced presentation, one that includes adequate attention to both the technical and the conceptual aspects of accounting. It is important that the graduate know what current practice includes. He should also know why it exists in the form that it does, i.e., what the reasons are, historical and otherwise, that accounting has developed as it has to its present state. Beyond this, he should also have a realistic comprehension of accounting's strengths and weaknesses. And this too must be a balanced presentation so that the student has pride in the profession he is joining, yet knows there is much opportunity and need for additional progress.

2. He should have a thorough introduction to professional responsibilities and obligations. Somewhere in his university education he should be introduced to the nature of the obligations accepted by those who aspire to professional status. In the public accounting profession there is a general feeling that the nature of professional obligations accepted by those who aspire to professional status. In the public accounting profession there is a general feeling that the nature of professional obligations are largely neglected in undergraduate and graduate school education. If this is true of the CPA's responsibilities it is far more true of the financial executive generally. Almost no attention is given to the responsibilities of directors, chief executive officers, or chief financial officers. The responsibility of the treasurer or controller in corporate accounting and financial reporting is something that many graduates learn only by hard experience after completing their formal education.

The social, legal, and professional responsibilities imposed by the various aspects of accounting practice should be presented in such a way that the student looks forward to measuring up to them. Rewards tend to follow responsibilities, and it is only as the practitioner measures up to the responsibilities placed upon him by society that he is truly entitled to the rewards that society grants him as a successful professional man.

3. The purpose, nature, and role of regulatory bodies should be a topic of considerable importance and attention. For accountants, this is a confusing pattern indeed with some regulatory bodies existing in the private sector and some in the public sector. But these are the bodies with which the practicing accountant must live and it is well that he know this. Certainly the nature of these organizations, their present rules, and the procedures they follow in promulgating new pronouncements are matters that can be effectively taught within the college atmosphere. The relationship of these regulatory bodies to the professional's responsibilities is direct and should be given the attention it deserves.

4. The student should be given a sufficient historical perspective of the evolving role of the profession so that he can fit current developments into long-term trends. Perhaps no other kind of knowledge will permit him to look forward to future demands and obligations quite as well as a sound understanding of how accounting came to be where it now is.

5. The nature of professional institutions, organizations, and methods of operation are essential knowledge

for the professional who would participate effectively in the advancement of his profession. One of the reasons that so many graduates fail to understand the nature of the profession is that their professors have never had any experience with it. Over the last thirty years, accounting has developed a strong and well organized profession. It differs significantly from the organization of the legal profession, the medical profession, or others, but there is a learnable structure and process. The nature and duties of the several committees, professional organizations, and financial activities within corporations and public accounting firms are all matters of great interest that could be presented quite effectively within the classroom. It only requires that practicing accountants insist upon the organizational overview, and that accounting educators take the necessary steps to draw the material together. For example, the interrelationships among and between the treasurer's department, the financial accounting department, the internal audit department, and the independent accountants, not to mention the influence of regulatory agencies, merit something more than a casual comment during the course of a lecture.

6. Finally, the student should have an awareness of research trends and the potential of research for influencing the development of accounting and accounting practice. The typical practicing accountant has relatively little time for anything more than the kind of research necessary to search his ready references and solve a client's immediate problem as rapidly and efficiently as possible. Yet if he is to take an active part in the advancement of his subject, he must at least know what is going on in it and be able to distinguish recommendations based upon sound research from those which represent little more than someone airing his private and unsupported views. We use the term research so loosely that many practitioners have great suspicion for pronounced research results. Some basis for distinguishing what is reliable from that which is not would be of substantial assistance.

Role of Accounting Research

Perhaps a word should be said here about accounting research for there are many sincere educators who feel that over the years accounting research has been much neglected and that it greatly needs attention. This is a generalization that one can scarcely disagree with. Yet the importance of accounting research must be put in perspective. It is a mistake to equate research in one field with research in another. The *relative* benefits to be produced by accounting research is almost nil. Society supports some kinds of research because society sees that research as beneficial to all its members.

That accounting research is important is not to be questioned. That it is not generally viewed as important enough to receive significant public support is also not to be questioned. The evidence is clear. There are in this country very few, if any, professorships that are endowed for the purpose of conducting accounting research. There are a great number of professorships which are established for the primary purpose of teaching. Some of these have been utilized, with the connivance of educational administrators, to subsidize accounting research at the expense of accounting education. Accounting research is important; it should be supported with a reasonable amount of resources. But accounting education comes first by a wide margin, and teaching is the most important activity in which an accounting educator can be engaged. The educator who neglects his teaching responsibilities in favor of furthering his personal career by attention to publishable research fails in his most important responsibility.

Professional Responsibilities

Much of the support for schools of business, and particularly for accounting education, has come from the accounting profession broadly described. Yet accounting education has largely neglected the needs of the profession as well as the needs of career oriented students. Relatively little effort has been made by many accounting educators to discover what accountants are actually doing in practice, what demands for skills exist in practice, and what students who plan to enter the practice of accounting most need to know so that they can serve effectively and advance with reasonable speed. As matters stand today, the accountant whose name is associated with a set of financial statements accepts a variety of duties and responsibilities to a variety of interests in those financial statements. In some cases, balancing his responsibility to one of the interests against that of another is a complex and difficult task and one for which typical accounting educations do not prepare him. Within our educational system, far more attention should be placed upon the nature of professionalism in accounting, using that term in the broadest context. What should be the accountant's approach to his task? What should be his attitude toward his clients and to those who use his work? Some of the recent cases have suggested that accountants must accept a whole new range of responsibilities for ascertaining compliance with requirements, for disclosure of failures to comply, for revealing conflicts of interest, and for knowing when the confidentiality of information gleaned during an audit must be sacrificed. Professional courtesy and proper relationships with one's colleagues in other firms are also matters to be covered.

Today's accounting graduate enters a world far more complex and risky than did those of twenty years ago. The plea here is that accounting educators dedicate themselves to preparing their graduates for that kind of world. Within the accounting profession there is a great deal of discussion of the accountant's responsibilities. An equal amount of discussion could profitably be devoted within the teaching profession to the educator's responsibilities. If educators will devote themselves to this subject as fully and as fairly as practitioners do to their equivalent topic, some marked improvement in the quality of education made available to students in both public and private universities will result.

Society, Professions and Accounting Curricula

Harold Q. Langenderfer[1]
University of North Carolina

Introduction

Accounting is simultaneously a professional and an academic or scholarly discipline. As such, it is presently being pulled and shaped by contending forces. Accounting education—as the mirror and occasional initiator of these forces—must and will change. Professor Langenderfer reviews the origin, nature and likely outcomes of some of the current trends. His emphasis is on the interplay between the profession, the society and the accounting curriculum. The strongest conclusion emerging from his analysis is the trend toward graduate schools for professional accounting education.

Accounting education is on the threshold of change. The emerging trends are not completely clear, but there appear to be strong forces shaping the future thrust of educations for the profession. To understand more clearly the probable path that accounting education is likely to take in the future, it seems desirable to consider in some depth several questions that have a bearing on the problem. These questions are:

1. How has the educational process evolved in other professions?
2. What is the nature of the changes in society that impinge on the accountant's function?
3. How must the accounting profession change in its knowledge set (common body of knowledge) and in its personnel to cope with society's changing needs?
4. In light of the changing needs of society for accounting services what forces are being brought to bear to make accounting education responsive to these needs?
5. What alternatives are open as to how accounting education should respond to society's evolving needs?
6. What should a university's posture be regarding accounting education?

The Evolution of Education for a Profession[2]

Professions tend to begin by providing, through self-taught practitioners, a service needed by society. Apprenticeship procedures are introduced by which accumulated experience is transmitted to the apprentice. Eventually the body of knowledge becomes large enough to establish professional schools, with the early history of these schools being heavily flavored by experience. The real world is simulated to the extent possible, with teachers using their own experiences as significant input into the educational process.

After a professional school is established, the experience-based knowledge set evolves to an inductively developed knowledge set. Generalizations emerge from examination of actual cases through inductive logic. Eventually research yields laws, principles, postulates, and theories applicable to the professional sphere.

This progression of experience, induction and deduction continuously expands the total body of knowledge of the profession, which in turn leads to a more rigorous academic curriculm, a demand for higher quality students, and eventually an insistence on graduate training as a requirement for admission to the profession, Medicine, theology, and law, for example, already require post-baccalaureate training and there are some indications that engineering also will soon have a graduate requirement.

As evolutionary processes, these are slow and often painful. Subjects based solely on experience are the first to be removed from the curriculum, but not without anguished debate. Roy and MacNeill describe the problem this way:

> Actions taken to diminish the experience component of professional training always raise a hue and cry. Teachers of experience usually are senior faculty, who quite naturally resist discounts from the value of their instruction and the threat of intellectual obsolescence as well. By the same token, each profession, epitomized by its leaders, elder statesmen, practitioners, and professional societies, is more likely to esteem experience than new knowledge not possessed, not understood, and not foreseen by the elders to be applicable, And, more subtly, to change the program they had seems to derogate its quality?[3]

These types of restraints impede, but do not halt, the evolution of a learned profession. Medical training depends less on the clinic than it once did and engineering as an art has, to a large degree, given way to engineering as a science. There are many who think that accounting is on the threshold of changes of this type.[4]

Societal Changes and Accounting

Societal changes are creating and shaping a major new dimension in accounting and in accounting education. No simple statement can adequately describe the changes, but consideration of some significant events and trends will indicate the nature of the changes and their impact on accounting education. These trends, according to one author, may be classified as external or internal.[5] External forces are those changes occurring in society that impinge upon the service function of accounting. Internal forces are those changes occurring within the accounting profession in response to society's needs. Each is considered in turn.

Accounting is useful because the discipline has developed measurement concepts and techniques for use in articulating goals and in measuring progess toward such goals. Conventional structures of double-entry bookkeeping and generally accepted accounting principles have played a major role in this connection during a period of rapid and protracted business development and expansion. These conventions and priniciples have served reasonably well during this period when private enterprise and the profit objective have been the basic contributors to economic expansion.

As we progress through the 1970s, there is growing recognition that the public is demanding that more attention be paid to urgent social problems, which include pollution control, urban deterioration, racial inequality, equitable distribution of wealth and more efficient utilization of resources. Concurrently, there is growing recognition within the accounting profession that accountants do possess, or should possess, the know-how which is critical to the solution of many social problems, or at least certain aspects of these social problems, particularly the issue of accountability and trust. Furthermore, it is doubtful whether present institutional constraints will permit the profession to respond adequately. Such increasing concern has placed strong, new pressures and unusual challenges before the accounting profession. There is a significant need for useful short term evaluation of programs which have long range impacts, and at the same time there is an accelerating demand for planning and control techniques related to social programs and the fulfillment of corporate social objectives.

Traditional measurements of economic phenomena are important, but they are inadequate in the face of future and present needs. Innovative measurement systems must be developed to take account of differences between profit and non-profit oriented organizations. These new concepts and procedures will emerge from significant research and will be disseminated through the accounting educational framework.

Even within the more traditional areas of accounting, changes are taking place. The growth and increased complexity of business organizations, the broader equity markets and the generally heightened sensitivity to current issues all have placed added responsibilities on the accounting discipline as the basic source of public financial information. In addition, strong competitive pressures within the domestic and (more recently) the international economy have caused internal management information to be an even more critical factor in decision making.

These challenges within and without the traditional confines of accounting provide great potential for contributions by accountants. To meet these challenges, the field of accounting must broaden its horizons. It must reorient its measurement and communication activities to a greatly changed hierarchy of multiple goals and desires of individuals and social interest groups. If accounting is to prosper in a changed social and economic environment, accountants and their institutions must anticipate the needs of organizations and society, and then proceed to develop concepts, tools and educational mechanisms to serve these needs.

Thus, the accounting profession has a clear and significant role to play in this changing society. The external forces presently operating suggest that the profession's service functions, ideally, should strengthen the link between private and public welfare by bringing measurement and communications skills to bear on problems in both the private and public domains. However, if logistical and educational efforts ignore this objective, the profession soon will be forced to choose between two paths in its service function role in society. One path would lead to a broader public service role that would move the profession into social auditing and accountability *in addition to* its traditional profit-oriented role. The other path would lead to even greater intensification of financial auditing and of advisory services to profit-oriented institutions. It is to be hoped that the pluralistic trends developing within the profession will lead to the ideal service objective of fulfilling both private and public needs in the future. Such trends have important ramifications for the kinds of people and for the type of education necessary for effective performance in this broadened perspective.

How the Accounting Profession Must Change

The perceived needs of society and the evident desire of the accounting profession to respond to such needs suggest that two significant changes are likely to occur within the profession. One will be an expansion of the professional knowledge set. Another change will be a shift in the type of talent needed to command and utilize the expanded knowledge set. The expanded knowledge set and increased talent are especially needed by the large CPA firms involved in activities ranging over the entire socio-economic spectrum. In this broadened context, they are acting not only as verifiers of information but also as systems designers and problem solvers. Such expertise extends beyond traditional accounting knowledge to include engineering, mathematics, computing methods, and behavioral science. To be sure, all of the skills may not be provided by CPAs as such, but they are likely to be provided within the framework of the accounting profession. Montagna suggests that

> "The accounting profession....- because of its unique position as auditors and advisers in financial and related areas to American and world institutions, is destined to play an increasing important role in social policy and planning. As a knowledge oriented work community, public accounting promises to become a major force in the social construction and elaboration of reality."[6]

Yet, not all accountants will be a major factor in solving societal problems. The need for more capable personnel dealing with an increased knowledge set generally has not affected accounting practice at the local level. A division of labor exists between large and small firms: the attest function and the modern analytical work that characterizes a major CPA practice is generally absent at the local level. Generally, it is the large firms that reflect change and what is new in accounting. The large firms reflect the emergence of accounting within a pluralistic structure, a structure that should be the focus for identifying the changing needs of accounting education, especially for major universities.

John Buckley has identified a knowledge set and a class of people needed to solve society's emerging measurement problems in terms of the quality of the accountant, the requisite knowledge, and the public image of the profession.[7]

Buckley's thesis is that the public image of the accounting profession is primarily determined by the public's contact with accountants. Since the primary contact of the public is with CPAs in small firms doing what might be described as a significant amount of non-professional work (for which certification is not needed), the public image of the accounting profession may be substantially misleading. The crux of the problem is that, both in practice and education, the knowledge set required in accounting has become increasingly sophisticated, but the *majority* of "accountants" have not. Thus, because of their limited and biased exposure to the profession, the public defines the profession in terms of its more visible members (generally the small practitioners), when, in fact, the profession ought to be defined in terms of its normative knowledge set. While this narrow view of the profession has important ramifications for accounting education, the immediate question is whether such misperception has any significant impact on the profession's ability to recruit talented people. If the profession is to respond to developed new solutions to measurement and communications problems, it must employ a larger number of more talented accountants who possess a truly professional knowledge set. If the accounting profession is to do more than just follow the path of least resistance, which at first glance implies an intensification of financial auditing and advisory services, it must build a reservoir of personnel capable of applying new tools and techniques. It will be the job of the educational system to provide this higher quality professional manpower.

Buckley also describes a mutually acceptable objective for the accounting profession and accounting education in terms of the *existing* status of the profession and a *desired* status. The change in status might be diagrammed in terms of the relationship between the quality of the accountant and the type of knowledge he needs to possess:

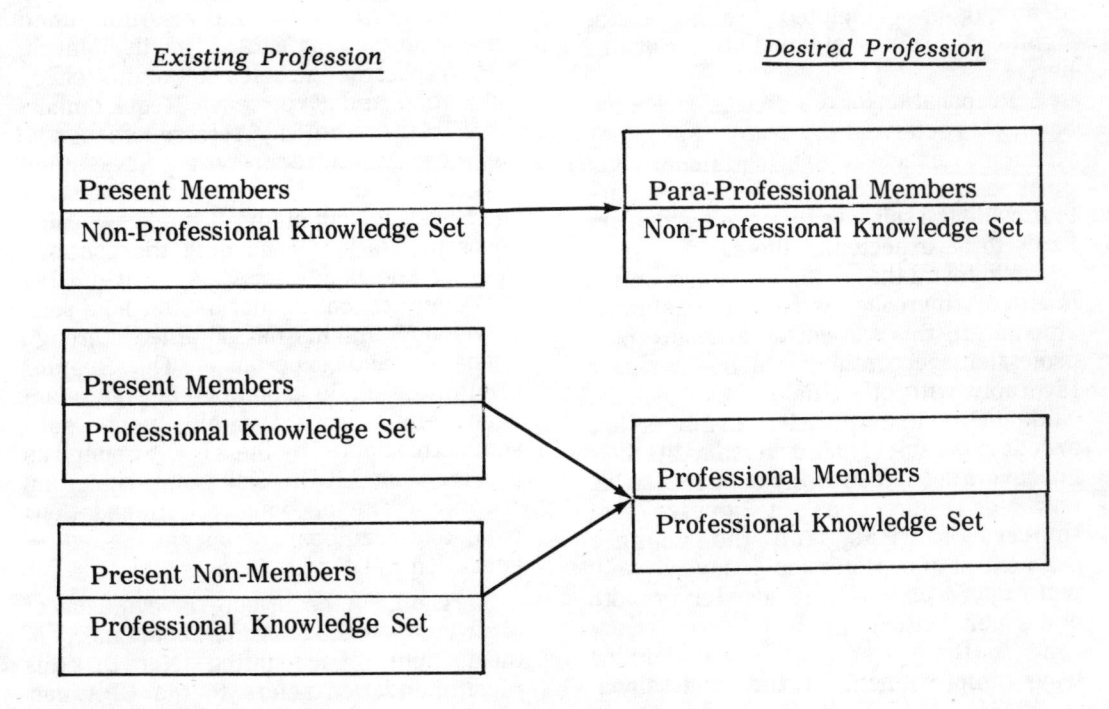

Existing Profession   *Desired Profession*

| Present Members | → | Para-Professional Members |
| Non-Professional Knowledge Set | | Non-Professional Knowledge Set |

| Present Members |
| Professional Knowledge Set | ↘ |

| | Professional Members |
| | Professional Knowledge Set |

| Present Non-Members | ↗ |
| Professional Knowledge Set | |

A shift of the type depicted above is not going to occur immediately, but it might serve as an ideal posture for the accounting profession of the future relative to accounting education. In any case, it is reasonable to assume that the external forces operating in society will demand more from the accounting profession; moreover, the profession's need to develop more accountants with a professional knowledge set will demand a higher quality entry level education. What ramifications do these views have for accounting education? The answer to this question requires a brief look at recent developments and trends in accounting education.

Accounting Education's Response to Emerging Needs

In 1963 the Carnegie Commission and the American Institute of CPAs sponsored a study to determine the common body of knowledge for beginning CPAs. In order to insure a broad approach to the study, the study group or Commission was composed of an attorney, a banker, a stock exchange official, two college deans, two professors of accounting, and five practicing CPAs. The final report *Horizons for a Profession*, written by Roy and MacNeill, was completed in 1966. It set in motion a number of forces that have affected accounting education in ways which are yet to be identified or completed. Some of the significant findings[8] of the study are quoted here:

1. Preparation for practice as a CPA has been characterized by rigor for many years; nevertheless, this traditional rigor must be increased still further if CPAs are to provide the services to society which are likely to be expected of them.

2. We found that research in accounting must . . . increase, and by a substantial amount. In this subjective attribute of a profession, accounting does not compare favorably with other fields. Analogously, while CPAs in impressive numbers are ardent in pursuit of self-development, their endeavors seem essentially to be focused in how-to-do-it directions. It appears that tomorrow's CPAs, and the younger segment of the profession today as well, will require programs of greater breadth and sophistication.

3. In these admittedly hard-to-define ways, improvement in the professional status of CPAs in needed. But, as we can repeat with conviction, the challenges, needs, and opportunities of the field are worthy of the best minds. Evaluation of the success or failure of this report may well depend upon the extent to which we can make clear this attraction to individuals of high quality.

4. We conclude . . . that tomorrow's beginning CPA must have mathematical facility beyond that possessed by his professional forebears; he must also be given fundamental knowledge and skill to understand and use computers and to keep pace with their further development in years to come. We further believe that these requirements, when added to the qualitative factors previously postulated, indicate that preparation for public accounting should come to include graduate study. These conclusions are fundamental to this report.

These broad observations have been followed by four identifiable developments that may affect the evolution of accounting education. These developments include an AICPA committee report, another Carnegie Commission report, the creation of a new professional examination, and a renewed interest in professional schools of accounting.

The first of the developments following the publication of the recommended knowledge set for CPAs was the March, 1969 report of the AICPA committee on Education and Experience Requirements for CPAs (commonly referred to as the Beamer Committee report). This study was a follow-up to the recommendations of the Roy-MacNeill study. It made sweeping recommendations regarding the common body of knowledge for CPAs, but did not make any recommendations on how such knowledge might be obtained through education and experience. The Beamer Committee made a number of significant recommendations which were subsequently adopted by the AICPA Council as representing AICPA policy on accounting education. The following recommendations have a direct bearing on the extent of education needed by CPAs:[9]

1. The CPA certificate is evidence of basic competence of professional quality in the discipline of accounting. (Note that this recommendation refers to the CPA cer-

tificate as a mark of competence in accounting, not just in public accounting!)

2. *Horizons for a Profession* (i.e., the Roy and MacNeill study) is authoritative for the purpose of delineating the common body of knowledge to be possessed by those about to begin their professional careers as CPAs.

3. At least five years of college study are needed to obtain the common knowledge for CPAs and should be the education requirement. For those who meet this standard, no qualifying experience should be required.

4. The states should adopt this five-year requirement by 1975. Until it becomes effective, a transitional alternative is four years of college study and one year of qualifying experience.

5. The college study should be in programs comparable to those described in "Academic Preparation for Professional Accounting Careers" (which set out a model curriculum).

6. (Dealt with when candidates should take the CPA exam).

7. Student internships are desirable and are encouraged as part of the educational program.

8. . . . the accreditation of academic programs is the responsibility of the academic community.

9. Educational programs must be flexible and adaptive and this is best achieved by entrusting their specific content to the academic community. However, the knowledge to be acquired and abilities to be developed through formal education for professional accounting are proper and continuing concerns of the American Institute of Certified Public Accountants.

As an appendix to the report, the Committee made recommendations to provide more specific guidance to planners of accounting curriculums. The committee prefaced its model accounting program with these comments:

The committee notes the expanding role of the accountant in society and believes that the recommendations specified in Horizons (Common Body of Knowledge) need to be adopted if accountants are to be equipped to play this role. We therefore endorse the recommendations of the report. We note, too, the trend toward placing greater reliance on formal education and less on-the-job training as a means of professional preparation. We agree that this development is desirable and believe that the body of knowledge necessary for entrance into the profession will and should be acquired as a part of the collegiate education. But our analysis of the recommendations leads us to conclude that the mastery of the body of knowledge which is commensurate with our public responsibility will require not less than five years of collegiate study. Thus the committee recommends that the Institute recognize the need for education *beyond the baccalaureate degree* (italics added for emphasis) for those who stand prepared to enter the profession. It further recommends that the Institute neither specify in terms of courses or course hours how this education should be attained nor encourage such criteria to be made a matter of law or regulation.

Business education must not only pace but anticipate the changes that take place in business and in the accounting profession. To do this, educational programs must be flexible and adaptive, and this is best achieved by entrusting their specific content to the academic community. Notwithstanding, the committee believes that the scope, purpose and general content of the formal education for professional accounting are proper concerns of the Institute.[10]

A second significant development since the publication of the common body of knowledge study was the establishment of a qualifying examination for management accountants, sponsored by the National Association of Accountants (NAA). This examination will give greater stature to management accountants and will accelerate the trend toward the professionalization of accounting, especially if the examination is a rigorous one. Although the AICPA looks upon the CPA certificate as a mark of basic competence in the broad discipline of accounting, it remains to be seen whether the CMA (Certified Management Accountant) designation for management accountants will emerge as competitive with the CPA certificate or as an indication of specialized knowledge in addition to the basic competence represented by the CPA designation. In either case, the knowledge required to pass these examinations is expanding and is becoming more conceptual and more rigorous, so that education beyond the baccalaurate degree may well be essential if candidates are to acquire the knowledge set necessary to pass these exams.

The third recent development is the recommendation of the Carnegie Commission regarding the college degree. This report, entitled *Less Time, More Options or Education Beyond the High School* made the following recommendations that have relevance to accounting education:[11]

1. The average length of time to a B.A. degree should be shortened initially to 3½ years, on the average, then to 3 years.

2. A degree (or other form of credit) should be made available to students at least every two years in their careers (and in some cases every year).

3. That certain new degrees be widely accepted: "Generally we favor more such degrees calling for two years of study after the B.A., as does the MBA. The two year advanced master's degree would serve occupations which require more formal training than the one year M.A. now provides.

If these recommendations are followed, it would appear that an accounting degree might well be a five year process, with a B.A. at the end of three years and a graduate degree at the end of five years.

A fourth development since *Horizons* is the serious consideration being given by the accounting faculties of some schools to the creation of professional schools of accounting. At the present time, at least three universities (Texas, Houston, and Missouri) are in the preliminary planning stages for such schools. Northeastern University and Rutgers University have had Professional Schools of Accounting for some time.

Professional schools have been discussed at length for a number of years without any definitive position having evolved. At the present time, there seems to be renewed interest in the possibility of professional schools, in part because accounting faculties feel the pressure for more elbow room in the curriculum. Such flexibility is needed to create the expanded knowledge set suggested by the Horizons study and dictated by the emerging needs of society. This thrust is occurring concurrently with the pressure to transform business schools into schools of administrative science with curricula incompatible with professional accounting needs, given the impractability of limiting the accounting curriculum to four years. If business schools tend to reject all accounting education except that which is supportive of education for general management, then accounting faculties with a primary interest in professional accounting problems are likely to look to professional schools as an attractive mechanism for maintaining a professional accounting curriculum. This approach receives support from the public accounting profession because of the profession's concern that business educators are not sympathetic to the academic needs of the professional accountant; i.e., educators often seem to want to keep the accounting curriculum within the same curricular mold as disciplines in the business school, even though those other disciplines are not built on a recognized base of professional examinations and legal recognition.

Many thoughtful accountants recognize inherent weaknesses in a professional school approach and are hopeful that a thriving accounting curriculum can be retained within the framework of schools of business. Whether the forces for change in accounting and in the business school will permit continued compatibility remains to be seen.

Alternatives Open to Accounting Education

John Buckley has addressed the question of what alternatives exist to provide education for the accounting profession. He sees three possible courses of action: 1. Retrench; 2. Upward mobility; 3. Bilateral mobility. A brief discussion of each of these concepts will indicate their relationship to accounting education.[12]

Retrenchment

If the accounting profession rejects the demands of society for solutions to urgent social problems through the development of better measurement techniques and new approaches to problem solving, then the need for an expanded knowledge set will be unnecessary. The old knowledge set will establish the intellectual boundaries of the profession. In turn, the traditional curriculum would be retained. There would be some growth in the knowledge set, through the use of new tools and new applications, but research would be limited and growth would be slow. Accounting education would be more vocational than professional and could be accomplished within the confines of the four-year undergraduate curriculum. Graduate education would be designed primarily to prepare accounting teachers. Since accounting educators do not expect this approach to prevail, it can be set aside without further comment.

Upward Mobility

This posture is likely to occur if accountants accept society's challenge to develop a more sophisticated knowledge set and apply their new tools to the solution of social problems that range far beyond the traditional profit-oriented measurements. As the knowledge set expands, new members will be attracted to the profession by the rigor of the knowledge required and by the challenge of graduate education which necessarily would accompany the increased knowledge set. Many view this upward mobility as the current trend in accounting and as the key force propelling accounting education toward graduate education. A commitment to upward mobility seems to be the basis for the current policy actions by the American Institute of CPAs; e.g., their push for a master's degree in accounting, their growth in management services, their acceptance of non-CPA specialists within the professional orbit, and the strong support of professional schools of accounting.

If upward mobility becomes the standard model, accounting education would tend to become exclusively graduate education, although para-professionals may be able to perform with only an undergraduate degree. Accounting education at the graduate level would become more theoretical and would emphasize problem solving using increasingly sophisticated measurement tools. The public accounting profession would expand rapidly into new areas, such as social measurement and administrative planning and control, where their new knowledge set would provide them with a unique capability for solving problems beyond the traditional sphere of the accountant's function. The term "accounting" would no longer be applicable to accounting's expanded role, unless the public was educated to the broadened concept of its function.

Bilateral Mobility

Buckley suggests that a middle ground between retrenchment and upward mobility is what he terms "bilateral mobility".[13] Under this approach the accounting profession would become pluralistic and specialized, comprising a number of sub-cultures. Each sub-culture would have its own membership and service objective, but some members would belong to more than one group. There would be a basic level of knowledge expected of all members, but beyond that, each group would develop specialists in solving certain types of society's problems. Some argue for a national CPA certificate as the mark of basic competence required to enter the discipline of accounting, with added specialist designations acquired beyond the CPA, such as certified management accountant, certified tax accountant, certified public accountant, etc. All of these specialists would be represented in the large public accounting firms while there would be independent small practitioners providing services in certain sub-fields, such as taxes, small business consulting, and estate planning.

In any case, there would be a wide range of skills in the overall knowledge set which would require a broadened definition of the term "accounting" or the creation of a new term to describe the broadened service functions. This approach would have significant implications for accounting education, including different educational programs for the various sub-elements of the profession. Some sub-elements would require only an undergraduate degree while others would require substantial graduate education. In this framework, it would seem unlikely that all schools would choose to serve the same clientele. Undergraduate schools and community colleges could prepare students for para-professional skills and basic professional skills. Graduate programs would prepare students to be full-fledged professional accountants with one or more specialties, depending upon the student's interests and aptitude. The graduate schools would be educating students primarily for working in large organizations, such as public accounting firms, large industrial organizations, or significant governmental units.

Thus bilateral mobility encompasses both retrenchment and upward mobility. Some schools will want to retain their undergraduate status while others will want to gear their faculty to a higher plateau in the knowledge set they choose to communicate. The accounting program a particular school should develop will depend upon the caliber of their faculty and the market they choose to serve, both of which are critical determinants of the type of student that would be attracted. In short, whether a school operates an undergraduate curriculum, a graduate curriculum within a business school, or a graduate curriculum outside of a business school is a product of how it sees its role in relation to:

1. Its view of society's problems.

2. The knowledge set needed to solve society's problems.

3. Its educational objectives: The similarity of the accounting faculty's aspirations in relation to the school's objectives.

4. The quality of the faculty, existing and planned.

A school's curriculum and degree requirements in accounting ought to be build on the foundation of an understanding of these variables and the faculty's best assessment as to how these variables affect their situation.

Attention can now be turned to where a given school's accounting program should fit within the alternative frameworks just described.

A School's Posture Regarding Accounting Education

The direction that the accounting curriculum takes at a school should be related to its assessment of the following factors:

1. The future scope of the accounting function in society.

2. The knowledge set needed to provide the accounting services of the future.

3. The quality, reputation, and objectives of the school.

4. The capabilities of the accounting faculty.

5. The student market to be served.

Much of the preceding discussion has been devoted to the expected role for accounting in our future society. It seems inevitable to this writer that this role will be expanded far beyond the traditional role of performing the measurement function for profit-oriented enterprises. As was indicated earlier, society's needs for social measurements for problem solving as well as the expanded demand for extended measurements in the profit sphere will necessitate accountants to broaden their knowledge set if they are to be able to operate effectively in this future environment.

Given this evolving environment, what should a school's role be in accounting education? If Buckley is right about the likelihood of a pluralistic profession in the future (and this writer thinks he is), then each school must decide which portion of accounting education it wants to offer. The choices seem to be these:

1. Education of the para-professional.

2. Education for the basic knowledge set required of all professional accountants.

3. Education for the expanded knowledge set to supply accountants for large CPA firms, large industrial organizations, and major governmental agencies.

Buckley has identified these roles in diagrammatic form in terms of the quality of the faculty and the nature of the subject matter, as follows:[14]

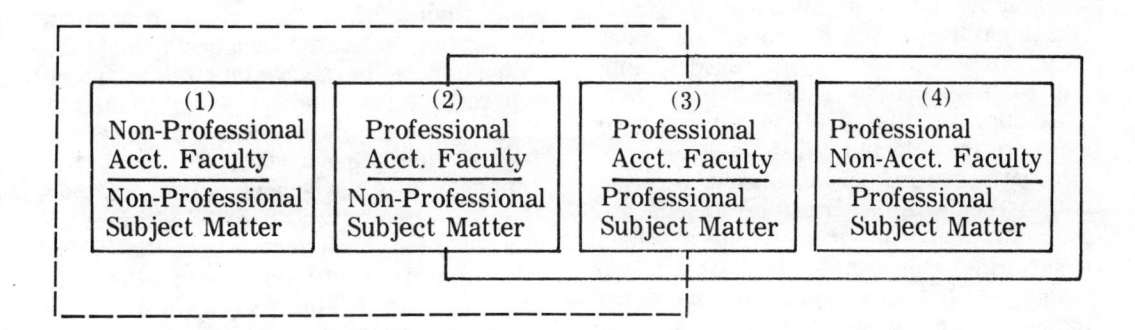

(1) Non-Professional Acct. Faculty / Non-Professional Subject Matter	(2) Professional Acct. Faculty / Non-Professional Subject Matter	(3) Professional Acct. Faculty / Professional Subject Matter	(4) Professional Non-Acct. Faculty / Professional Subject Matter

The dotted boundary is what Buckley describes as the conventional accounting education boundary. The solid boundary is what he describes as the normative accounting education boundary. If a school has been in a leadership position in accounting education, and would like to continue that leadership, it would seem that it ought to provide accounting education within the normative education boundary with particular emphasis on professional subject matter taught by a professional faculty. If this is a valid expectation, the key question becomes what type of education will constitute the normative education boundary of the future?

Taking into consideration the needs of society and the expanded knowledge set that accountants must have to respond to society's needs, and relating these factors to the recommendations of the Horizons study, the Beamer Committee report, and the Carnegie Commission report, there seems to be a clear indication that academic institutions wishing to provide education for the expanded knowledge set and to supply manpower for large organizations intending to solve complex private and public problems must offer graduate education in accounting.

A school with the faculty capability and faculty desire ought to seriously consider moving in this direction. There are more than enough schools to educate students for para-professional roles and for basic accounting education to meet the needs of a pluralistic profession. A school's accounting curriculum must be on a broader scale if it wants and expects to be a leader in accounting education in the future.

If this is the role a school wants to assume, then it is essential that it think seriously about modifying its curriculum and degree requirements to move strongly in this direction. Schools offering basic accounting courses could supply their top students to the "leader" schools which are capable of equipping them with the new measurement tools and new knowledge set necessary to perform effectively in the future environment.

This objective cannot be accomplished within the framework of a four-year program. The typical four-year program is not sufficiently differentiated in content, degree expectations, or length for the outstanding undergraduate accounting majors. There ought to be one school in each state or at least one in each region to offer a differentiated, top quality program that will provide the type of accounting education needed by the accounting leaders of tomorrow. It would seem that this objective requires a graduate program in accounting.

There seem to be three possible alternatives:

1. Accounting concentration within the MBA program.
2. Graduate degree in accounting within the School of Business Administration, but separate from the MBA program.
3. Graduate degree in accounting in a separate professional school of accounting.

It is beyond the scope of this paper to discuss the professional school concept in length. The environment at a new school might make it possible for them to adopt this approach and they should be encouraged to do so. For a large number of schools, however, it appears that the professional school approach is not feasible, not only because of the local environment but also because the institutional framework for education in our society is not presently organized to support such a school in an effective manner.

Assuming the professional school concept is rejected, this reduces the alternatives to an accounting concentration within the MBA program or a separate graduate degree program within a school of business. These might be the only two viable possibilities at many schools. Since many MBA programs operate as general business programs without strong emphasis on specialties, and there is every reason to believe that business school faculties will want them to remain as such, it seems as though a separate graduate degree program in accounting is the most logical choice. A separate program would highlight the *professional* orientation of accounting and would be more likely to attract outstanding students from four-year schools who otherwise would not go to graduate school.

A critical problem in adopting a graduate program is the issue of what to do about the undergraduate accounting program. Should a program offering basic accounting work for undergraduates be continued with the best students channeled into the graduate program or should the undergraduate program be dropped in favor of attracting all students for the graduate program from other schools. State universities may have a continuing obligation to supply basic accounting work at the undergraduate level, but this should be complementary to the main function and consideration should be given to phasing it out once the graduate program is well established.

CONCLUSION

A review of the forces for change in accounting education suggests that the education of the accountant of the future will require a graduate program. In view of these forces, schools ought to carefully review their present curriculum and long range goals. A few schools might conclude that they can accomplish the ultimate in the professionalization of accounting education by creating professional schools of accounting. It appears, however, that a much larger number of schools that want to be leaders in accounting education should develop graduate programs in accounting within the current structure of the school of business. A graduate program in accounting would not be an alternative to an undergraduate accounting major, but would be necessary additional education for the person who wants to be a professional accountant. Undergraduate accounting education then would have as its objectives the education of para-professionals as well as providing basic accounting understanding prior to entering a graduate program in accounting.

Although MBA programs may be appropriate for educating some professional accountants, they are likely to be used primarily by non-business undergraduates who are seeking careers in business and in the process discover that they want to become professional accountants.

Whatever the organization structure used to accomplish the task, it seems clear that a careful reading of the forces impinging on accounting education leads to the conclusion that a graduate program in accounting will be essential for the professional accountant of the future.

FOOTNOTES

[1] I would like to acknowledge the contributions to this paper by the Accounting Faculty at the University of North Carolina, especially R. Lee Brummet, Isaac Reynolds, Junius Terrell, Elba Baskin and Eugene Brooks.

[2] Most of the ideas for this section were drawn from *Horizons for a Profession*, written by Robert H. Roy and James H. MacNeill and published by the American Institute of CPAs.

[3] *Ibid*, p.4

[4] *Loc. cit.*

[5] John W. Buckley, "Identity Issues in Accounting," Accounting and Information Systems Working Paper number 72-14, Study Center in Accounting and Information Systems, Graduate School of Management, University of California, Los Angeles, Calif., 1972

[6] Paul D. Montanga, "The Public Accounting Profession," *American Behavioral Scientist* (march-April, 1971), p. 475-491

[7] Buckley, *op. cit.*

[8] *Horizons for a Profession, op. cit.,* pp. 1-21.

[9] Report of the Committee on Education and Experience Requirements for CPAs, American Institute of CPAs, March, 1969.

[10] *Ibid,* p. 41-42.

[11] *Less Time, More Options* (Education Beyond the High School), The Carnegie Commission on Higher Education, January, 1971.

[12] Buckley, *op. cit.*

[13] *Loc. cit.*

[14] *Loc. cit.*

Toward a Revitalized Accounting I

John P. Fertakis
Washington State University

Introduction

Challenges create change and, in accounting education, the extent of that change is probably best measured by the controversy surrounding the beginning accounting course, for it is there that accounting education involves the most faculty and students. The course content reflects transient fads as well as durable traditions, gimmicks as well as genuine innovations, capricious whimsies as well as planned change. For the student and administrator, the problem is to distinguish one from another. For the educator, the problem is to manage change in such a way that the course shapes and complements student needs and later courses. As the touchstone for the entire curriculum, it must confront change with a systems perspective. Professor Fertakis presents both history and policy recommendations on Accounting I.

Among some people in the world, self-flagellation is used to express one's devotion to and belief in a religious or cultural image. Through punishment of the body, it is believed, true devotion can be expressed. In some ways it seems that beginning education for accountancy is following this practice.

Since the late 1950s, university programs in accounting have been responding to the call for assessment, innovation, and change. A variety of approaches to accounting education have evolved during the 1960s and thus far in the 1970s. Perhaps the greatest impact of the forces for change has taken place in the introductory course, which will be called Accounting I.

The purpose of this paper is to identify some approaches that have evolved in teaching Accounting I, to assess these changes in view of the role of introductory courses in general, and to suggest a more consonant or congruous set of objectives and approaches.

The Traditional Philosophy and Approach

Any attempt to generalize about a "traditional" pedagogy for Accounting I involves the risk of implying a greater unanimity than may have existed. However, some probable attributes of early approaches to accounting instruction can be ventured. First, accounting texts and other materials tended to be predominantly "procedural" in content, with an emphasis on the recording and reporting function in the practice of public accounting.[1] Second, whatever concepts, principles or theories were discussed were supportive of the procedural requirements. Third, substantial emphasis was placed on preparation for further accounting courses. Finally, success in class tended to be measured by procedural and analytical problem solving ability, both in assigned homework and "practice sets" and in examinations. Critical assessments of existing procedures were not generally encouraged. Memorization of details of transactions and accounts was often the accepted mode of learning, and it often seemed that beginning accounting was oriented to a high-stool, green-eyeshade, quill-pen career as a mild mannered and inoffensive Bob Cratchit.

Dissatisfaction and Diminishing Prestige

With the publication of a series of critical examinations of schools of business administration and related disciplines, a strong impetus for change developed. Such publications as the Gordon and Howell,[2] and Pearson[3] reports created an environment which encouraged experimentation, diversity of approach, and multiple objectives for instruction in business and accounting. Newer materials of great variety have appeared and yet further changes are in process.

As other areas of business education expanded and became more conceptual, accountancy did not escape the image of the profession so well described elsewhere[4] . . . the green-eyeshade, bookkeeping-oriented, status-quo stereotype. Its prestige in academic circles declined alarmingly in spite of the prospective evolution in course content in more modern directions.[5]

Newer Philosophies and Approaches

Change came to elementary accounting education courses at the college level in the form of an increase in conceptual and theoretical content and more enlightened textbook materials. Progressive texts at first began to support the procedures that were discussed with references to authoritative recommendations of the Committee on Accounting Principles and its successor, the Accounting Principles Board. Differing points of view were compared and areas of controversy were aired. The dominant technique continued to be, however, a thorough presentation of generally accepted accounting procedures relating to financial statement items and underlying transactions. But further shifts were developing along with the rising expectations of the public and the law with regard to the accountant's work.

Gradually, the procedures began to give way to both the controversial issues and to what might be called motivational and relevance factors. Procedures became regarded by some of the academic community and to some of the practicing profession itself as lacking in excitement, depth and rigor, relevance to the affairs of the nation, and in importance to the social and business systems. The exciting frontiers of space technology, the prestige and accomplishments of engineering and other professions, the relevance of the behavioral and social sciences, and the importance of the growing information technologies to business and society were all contributing factors to the decline of importance of procedural content in Accounting I.

At first, the broader perspective of accountancy was confined largely to the early chapters of texts, with the consequence that texts became either longer or sacrificed some procedural content to make room for newer material. Again at the risk of oversimplification and error, it is desirable to attempt to classify some varieties of approaches that developed.

One approach toward developing interest and motivation in the beginning student was to strike out boldly toward an "adventures in accounting" introduction. The larger economic and social environment in which accountants operate was stressed, along with the diversity and challenge to be found in the work of the accountant. An effort was made to change the stereotyped image of accountants and show them as central figures in our national life.

Presumably, with such a background the student will be motivated to achieve a new view of accountancy and therefore be motivated to endure the necessary learning of procedure, having a more exciting perspective of what lies ahead.[6] An attempt is made to relate procedures to an overall structure, and the student works with problem material that requires intellectual challenge to match transactions with the procedure and with appropriate concepts.

Another approach might be termed that of "relevancy." Accounting is treated in the first course as a logical process pertinent to social, economic and moral issues of the day. It thus contributes to high level of decision making concerning the allocation of resources. The learner is motivated, therefore, to achieve an understanding of accounting concepts as a rational approach to the needs of society. Only those general procedures that contribute to the understanding of concepts are seen as relevant to the learner.

Closely related to the relevance approach is the "managerial approach," which emphasizes the utility of accountancy for decision making and resource allocation within entities.

While some decrease in procedural content was often required to accommodate discussion and contextual material, the above approaches maintained a considerable orientation toward the presentation of problem-solving material as opposed to attitude development. The effect of these changes was by and large salutary. Student interest and motivation were heightened to some degree, and many burdensome details were reduced or eliminated from the curriculum.

Published materials for Accounting I assumed a more generalized orientation during the late 1960s,[7] and seemed to be moving in the direction of an even broader education for economic competency. The presentations of problem-solving procedures and currently accepted accounting principles and practices were even further reduced. Even for the accounting oriented student, some authors came to:

> value conceptual understanding over procedural skill. It would be easy to require the beginning CPA to know how to calculate a standard deviation, but it is much more important for him to understand the meaning of the concept. It would be easy to require the beginning CPA to be competent in the techniques of accounting for depreciation, but it is much more important to specify that he *understand* this complex subject. Ability to apply techniques is easy to specify and as easy to test; conceptual understanding is much more elusive, both to impart and to ascertain.[8]

Another illustration of the recommended emphasis is the following:

> The importance of accounting as a whole to a private enterprise society suggests that the first course in accounting should not be influenced by the educational needs of prospective accounting majors. Instead, it should seek to convey to a general audience of college students the conceptual content of accounting, the overall scope of the accounting function, and the interpretation of accounting reports. Furthermore, it should, in analytical terms, have a primary educational objective of informed citizenship . . . .

The proposal thus envisioned a complete shift in the approach to introductory accounting away from the traditional "preparer of accounting information" premise to a "function and social role of the accounting discipline" premise. Furthermore, it was thought that a social-function-citizenship orientation would minimize attention to procedural detail.[9]

Another source describes a course in which the

> outline does entail a reduction of emphasis on procedures and techniques, which is counterbalanced by an increase in emphasis on such matters as (1) normative as well as positive views of the accounting function, (2) the role of accounting in economic and social processes, (3) an historical perspective, and (4) an exposure to the variety of activities and dimensions which are encompassed by the accounting discipline, including not only financial and managerial accounting, but also auditing, information systems, taxation, quantitative methods, behavioral accounting and accounting theory.[10]

A final example of a broader educational objective and philosophy regarding initial instruction in accounting is summarized in the Preface of a text in introductory accounting:

> . . . Because machines can now perform most of the operations necessary for compiling and summarizing business data, the accountant is free to assume a more active role in management and to concentrate on those parts of accounting which demand creative thought and judgment. Despite these changes, most textbooks in accounting have retained the emphasis which was appropriate before the days of computers; they present accounting as it relates to the manual bookkeeping process. This book makes a significant break with that heritage . . . . it is designed to provide perspective on the difficulties of economic measurement and the strengths and limitations of economic information.[11]

Numerous texts are now available for Accounting I which contain little reference to "accounting" procedures.[12] The uses of accounting data in planning, evaluating, analyzing, controlling and decision making have supplanted even the basic accounting cycle and the systematic treatment of transaction events in some newer texts.

A Schism in the Fabric of Higher Education for Accountancy

A deep division in the ranks of teachers of accounting has occurred over the procedural *vs.* the general education objectives and content of the entire Accounting curriculum. This division is described by Buckley as follows:

> In part, the decline of professional accounting education results from a schism within accounting academe itself. A state of cold war exists between avant garde and traditional faculty. Failure to influence professional accounting and-or accountants leads the avant garde to direct their attentions elsewhere, primarily toward management accounting, information systems and other "exotic" areas. Failure to understand the motives, objectives or methodologies of the avant garde leads the traditionals to man their shrinking bastions in a last-ditch defense of the old empire. The inflexible posture of the traditionalists at some schools has led to the total abandonment of professional accounting education; at other schools the avant garde have left the accounting group to form coalitions with other disciplines or to form such independent areas as computing methods, information systems, planning and control, and so forth.[13]

Professional meeting of educators often become forums for advocates of the differing approaches. The focus for the main philosophical viewpoints is likely to be Accounting I. An emphatic denial of the importance of techniques, procedures, mechanics and "plumbing" approaches in beginning accounting courses has become the vogue. Derisive references to procedures-oriented texts and curriculums seem mandatory among educators who seek to command the respect of their peers and the attention of convention program coordinators.

There increasingly appears to be a de facto two-level education process that has developed around this schism. On the one hand are schools, notably community colleges and smaller four-year institutions, which steadfastly hold to the procedural approach in the beginning course. The primary basis for such a statement is the continuing success of "traditional" texts with a high technical and procedural content in those schools. Adoptions of programed accounting texts and multimedia materials dealing with basic procedures have occurred principally at community colleges and smaller schools without graduate degree programs.

On the other hand, the general education point of view often prevails at the prestige institutions and those with graduate programs in accounting and business administration. Experimental approaches and more general-education-related philosophies seem to emerge from such schools in the form of articles appearing in leading accounting journals and through the willingness of some of these institutions to adopt the non-procedural materials currently available or to develop in-house materials. There seems to be a tendency among schools to implement the procedural vs. general education, managerial, or other approaches to the entire spectrum of courses in the accounting curriculum. And the profession has more or less taken sides.[14] Thus the schism in institutions of higher learning tends to deepen.

In an effort to prevent a more pronounced dispersion of curricula, there seems to be some merit in attempting to seek a discussion which will ameliorate or reconcile the divisions that have occurred. Progress and change are necessary to growth, but disparate positions within academia at the beginning level serve only to confuse the student, distort the education process, and lessen the attractiveness of the profession as a career. The increasing number of states requiring a college degree in accounting as a prerequisite to certification as a CPA, increases the necessity of reconciling different objectives and points of view if a professional orientation is to be preserved. The imposition of curricula defined by state statutes would constitute an unfortunate turn of events.

The Role of the First Course

The introductory course in an academic area is often a survey of that field of study.

It is usually intended to serve the purpose of giving the student an appreciation of the history, methods, attitudes, and techniques which underly the subject. The course in many disciplines is so generalized that it is not recommended for those wishing to prepare for a career in that field. The faculty often establishes an alternative sequence of study which more adequately conveys the basic skills and abilities that will underly further inquiry in subsequent courses.

The first course in accounting has not yet become fragmented and differentiated for the benefit of those seeking general as opposed to preparatory objectives. There is divergent opinion on the advisability of a separation of the introductory course to meet diverse objectives. Even those who enroll in beginning accounting as a general subject seem to desire some degree of ability to handle accounting procedures and financial data as a *sine qua non* to their understanding of the field of accountancy. It is much as the student in a biology course who expects to obtain some ability to discern some major species and identify distinguishing characteristics. Another representative group found in beginning accounting are those students majoring in a business field. They too can be presumed to expect some ability to handle data in a systematic manner, such as they will find in the world of business. Curriculum designers in other fields can be presumed to recommend or require accounting on the assumption that an ability to handle figures and to think in abstract business terms will be gained.

The role of the first course in accounting can now be described as attempting to meet several objectives. First, the student should be exposed to what accountants do. He does many things, but certainly foremost is the operation or supervision of the bookkeeping system. This requires a knowledge of methods and techniques and a viewpoint or attitude with respect to the systematic treatment of data. Second, and closely related to the first objective is the development of some basic skills in observing certain kinds of events, recording significant aspects or attributes of those events, and reporting them in a meaningful way to others. This requires a knowledge of the accounting model and the way in which data is entered into and processed through the system.

A third objective in beginning accounting courses is to capture the imagination and interest of the student so that he can critically evaluate accounting as a career opportunity or to encourage him to understand the relevance of accounting viewpoints and data systems in his intended field of study. A fourth objective is to serve as a preparation for subsequent courses in accounting or related fields such as finance. Finally, accounting courses serve a general education role in the sense that regardless of his major area of study an educated person should obtain some understanding of the society and culture in which he lives. Western culture has an economic and business tradition that accounting, even in its most procedural context, can help the student to understand. But most curricula have other courses which better meet this objective, if it is a primary one, and therefore general education should not be considered a major objective in accounting instruction.

Some obvious omissions from the above objectives are the decision-making planning, controlling, and evaluating objectives mentioned earlier and which are dominant in newer course materials. While important, the meeting of such objectives should be based on a fundamental group of the disciplined approach to the use of data which underlies accountancy. These are complex objectives that are ill-served by omitting fundamentals. The whole meal cannot be in the first bite. This is not to say that Accounting I should not include materials related to the above objectives, but rather that they should serve to illustrate the importance and difficulty of working with the single-dimension structured measurement system they are learning. Educators cannot pretend that systematic data for these other functions exist.

The multiple objectives described for the introductory course represent a wide range of expectations which appear to offer no conflict with the thoughtful presentation of the essentials of bookkeeping systems in the first course. By centering the first course on procedures, some basic needs of the student are also met. Only the first two objectives should be considered primary in the first accounting course.[15] The remaining objectives can be accomplished to some extent in the process of meeting the first two.

Student Needs

The concept of the "educated person" implies the rewards of study for the sake of knowledge. A well-rounded individual has appreciation for his environment and is conversant with many issues of importance outside the realm of his particular economic and social role. Essential to the concept, however, is a basic ability to contribute to society and support himself. A well-rounded person who cannot contribute to society or his own livelihood is often unwelcome in Western culture.

During the 1960s, students noticeably became attracted to the idea of relevance. They questioned the importance of learning areas which failed to relate to the world around them. In a sense, they were on a quest for useable knowledge.

A prime motivational technique in educational processes has been to relate the subject matter to the knowledge, ability, and environment of the student. This serves not only to motivate study but, if the knowledge is shown to be valid and if it can then be employed by the student in a useful way, an important need of the student has been met. The study of accountancy is one area in which the utility of the skills and knowledge learned can carry the student to better motivation and performance in other studies. In secondary schools, the development of such skills as cooking, typing, furniture building, and athletics often serve as springboards to better motivation and performance in other studies as well as providing the intrinsic satisfaction of accomplishment. The mastery of a technical subject requiring a disciplined approach, even at an elementary level, is a rewarding accomplishment in terms of the needs of students.[16]

Coupled with useable and relevant knowledge and the mastery of difficult processes, is the further need to know why. In this aspect of education, the procedures approach in the beginning course carried with it the risk of the student's failure to comprehend evolutionary and theoretical considerations which must be understood before real accounting knowledge is attained. Educators should not overlook underlying principles and concepts which lend shape and substance to the accounting art as they attempt to educate students for mastery and relevance. Meeting the student's need to know why is basic to any true process of education. Rote memorization accomplishes only a limited objective, and it fails to ignite the drive that the learner can bring to bear when truly challenged.

Accounting in Academia

Unlike most other academic disciplines, accountancy and other "professional" programs are inextricably bound to a pragmatic social role. The musings of researchers and theoreticians are necessarily secondary to the process of education for professional competency. It is certainly inappropriate to encourage the undergraduate student to approach accountancy without an understanding that laws and regulations as well as currently accepted practices constitute the bulk of what he must learn if he is to enter practice or understand the data produced by accounting. The essentially "practical" or applied nature of the practice of accountancy places the discipline in a role which is sometimes regarded as inferior in the spectrum of high education. Consequently, education for the professions sometimes lacks academic prestige on the university campus.

There is, however, a recognized place for professional education in the University. Schools of medicine, law, engineering, pharmacy, and education, along with business administration, are a necessary part of publicly supported education in America. This country has achieved stature for both its theoretical and its practical achievements in its technology and its professions. In the case of accountancy, there is general recognition that the ability to conceive and establish a reliable data system which meets established criteria and to become expert in its operation has an intrinsic value to society.

Both academic prestige and respectability are necessary ingredients of higher education. Prestige largely arises from the complexity of the body of knowledge to be studied and other people's opinions of that body of knowledge—generally among peers. Respectability stems from linking the objective of the area of study to proven success in accomplishing its objective. A proper concern in accounting education should center on the respectability of the discipline. A continued development of theoretical and conceptual knowledge at higher curriculum levels may eventually lead to academic prestige. But prestige does not seem a proper focus for the beginning course in accountancy.

CONCLUSION

Traditional approaches to the teaching of Accounting I have been modified and improved by introducing materials relating to the relevance, adventure, and managerial importance of the subject. These areas benefit the motivation of the student in the accounting course and constitute acceptable pedagogical technique. There is, however, little justification in the current trend which tends to reduce the emphasis on underlying procedural content in beginning courses. The needs of the student, the requirement for academic respectability, and the professional orientation of the curriculum seem to require that a study of the accounting model and an understanding of the operation of accounting systems and procedures continue to be course objectives.

Extensive debate and research should be encouraged among accounting educators and practitioners for the purpose of developing a more united approach to accounting education—with particular reference to the first course. The schism which has developed among educators and between educators and practitioners over the procedural *vs.* the conceptual approach must be analyzed and resolved if possible.

The very nature of accounting seems to call for at least some attention to the system which represents what accountants do. The process is in many cases the message. The process in equally many cases is also the problem. Many of the most difficult theoretical, conceptual, and practical problems encountered by accountants originate in the basic model, A equals L + P, and the necessity of making data and events conform to that formula. Little in the way of understanding accountancy, its role, and its problems can be meaningfully grasped by a student unless he has achieved a problem-solving and analytical frame of reference based on the essentials of that model. Concepts and principles in accounting ultimately must face the test of procedure and relate to the systematic processing of data.

The gradual at first and now accelerating movement away from procedural content in accounting texts is to some extent parallel to changes in beginning courses in other professional fields. While such courses are often more exciting and challenging for the teacher, there remains the necessity to adhere to a "systems" viewpoint, a specific subject matter mastery, and a disciplined approach to economic measurement if a student is to feel a sense of accomplishment. As the volume of knowledge in professional disciplines expands and course hours diminish, the luxury of "education for citizenship" philosophies in introductory professional courses must be reconsidered.

There are practical considerations, too, in seeking to place limits on the "generalization" of Accounting I curricula. Accounting *is* an important and fascinating field of study with evidence of its pervasive nature in every newspaper and periodical. More exposure in the public media has created a greater awareness of accounting as an important function with flaws and weaknesses. As the first course becomes more and more related to current events it becomes easy to find interesting topics, problems, questions, and events on which to base class discussion. An attempt to return to the mastery of procedures results in an inevitable clash between the normative and the pragmatic aspects of accountancy. Having learned the importance of current values in managerial decision making—to cite one example—the student finds it difficult to attempt to master the procedures related to historical cost data. Hence, it may be wise to defer some theoretical and practical considerations until the student first understands the procedures which created or relate to them.

Perhaps educators have grown impatient with the mastery aspect of Accounting I, and have come to expect to accomplish too many objectives in the course. In the author's experience, students have expressed feelings of uneasiness in the generalized course. They are impatient to get to the point where they can "solve" problems, make entries, and otherwise "come to grips" with the accounting process they have heard about from others and at which they expect accountants to excell.

Finally, the subsequent courses taken by accounting students have remained largely procedures-oriented. The assumption is that the student either has had some basic record-keeping system or can go off by himself and get it somewhere else. After an exposure to the initial generalized course it is unreasonable to expect the student to be motivated to study and master a basic structure that he has been convinced is irrelevant to today's information realities.

Accounting educators must rethink and attempt to achieve a consensus with respect to the objectives of the first course, the motivations and needs of the student, and the place of accounting procedures in the curriculum of the university. The first course should not dwell at length on accounting failures, shortcomings and inadequacies. Self-flagellation is too primitive a practice and, far from showing devotion to beliefs, may lessen the attractiveness of what a career in accounting has to offer the student.

FOOTNOTES

[1] Robert H. Roy and James H. MacNeill, *Horizons for a Profession*, (New York: American Institute of CPAs and The Carnegie Corporation, 1967), p. 38.

[2] Robert A. Gordon and James E. Howell, *Higher Education for Business*, (New York: Columbia University Press, 1959).

[3] Franklin Pearson and others, *The Education of American Businessmen*, (New York, McGraw-Hill Book Co., 1959).

[4] Don. T. DeCoster and John Grant Rhode, "The Accountant's Stereotype: Real or Imagined, Deserved or Unwarranted," *The Journal Accounting Review*, (October, 1971), pp. 651-664; Don T. DeCoster "'Mirror, Mirror on the Wall . . .' The CPA in the World of Psychology" *The Journal of Accountancy*, (August, 1971), pp. 40-45; L. William Seidman, "The End of the Great Green Eyeshade," *The Journal of Accountancy*, (January, 1972), pp. 51-55.

[5] The state of affairs as recently as 1970 is described in John W. Buckley, "A Perspective on Professional Accounting Education," *The Journal of Accountancy*, (August, 1970), pp. 41-47. The quality of students choosing an accounting career was found lacking in John Ashworth, "People Who Become Accountants," *The Journal of Accountancy* (November, 1968), pp. 43-49, but regarded as high by Roy and MacNeill, op. cit., p. 46.

[6] Some texts utilizing this approach include Arthur L. Thomas, *Financial Accounting: The Main Ideas*, (Belmont, Calif.: Wadsworth Publishing Company, Inc., 1972); Thomas J. Burns and Harvey S. Hendrickson, *The Accounting Primer: An Introduction to Financial Accounting*, (New York: McGraw-Hill Book Company, 1972).

[7] c. f. Ronald J. Patten, "The Trend in Accounting Education," *Managerial Planning*, (November-December, 1972), pp. 34-37; Billy E. Goetz, "A First-Year Accounting Course," *The Accounting Review*, (October, 1969), pp. 823-832; Barry E. Cushing and Charles H. Smith, "A New Emphasis for Introductory Accounting Instruction," *The Accounting Review*, (July, 1972), p. 599.

[8] Roy and MacNeill, op. cit., p. 2.

[9] *A New Introduction to Accounting*, Gerhard G. Mueller, ed., (The Price Waterhouse Foundation, July 1971), p. 2.

[10] Barry E. Cushing and Charles H. Smith, "A New Emphasis for Introductory Accounting Instruction," *The Accounting Review*, (July, 1972), p. 599.

[11] William J. Bruns, Jr., *Introduction to Accounting: Economic Measurement for Decisions*, (Reading, PA., Addison-Wesley Publishing Company, 1971), p. 5.

[12] Paul E. Fertig, Donald F. Istvan, Homer J. Mottice, *Using Accounting Information-An Introduction*, (New York: Harcourt, Brace Jovanovich, Inc., 1965 and 1971); William J. Bruns, Jr., op. cit.; Paul H. Walgenbach, Norman E. Dittrich, *Accounting: An Introduction*, (New York: Harcourt Brace Jovanovich, Inc., 1973); Jack Gray and Kenneth S. Johnston, *Accounting and Management Action*, (New York: McGraw-Hill Book Company, 1973); also a forthcoming text described in *A New Introduction to Accounting*, Gerhard G. Mueller, Ed., (The Price Waterhouse Foundation, July, 1971).

[13] John W. Buckley, "A Perspective on Professional Accounting Education," *The Journal of Accountancy*, (August, 1970), p. 43.

[14] The author's observations indicate that firms employing accountants prefer the procedural curriculum and will shift recruiting efforts to those schools offering more traditional curricula.

[15] Milton F. Usry notes, for example, that "It is vital that early courses build a solid base for further study in accounting for the accounting major and also provide the necessary working tools and a favorable opinion of accounting for the nonaccounting major." *The Journal of Accountancy,* July, 1972) p. 87.

[16] This need is discussed, albeit with criticism, in William H. Whyte, Jr., *The Organization Man,* (Garden City, NY: Doubleday Anchor Books, 1957), pp. 72-75, 88-89.

The Demand for Accounting Graduates and the Design of Curricula

Introduction

The set of three papers which follows reflects the force of consumerism in professional accounting education.

The first two papers are written from the perspective of two of the largest groups of users of the products of accounting education. Guy W. Trump is Vice President—Education and Regulation of the AICPA. Bart Bartholomew is National President of the NAA for 1974-75. Both papers reflect their views and not those of their respective organizations.

As we might expect, these two user groups have different views about the knowledge content of an "ideal" accounting curriculum and the depth to which the accounting student should pursue these various knowledge areas. On the other hand, there is a strong pattern of consistency in the views of both public and private accountants in several very important areas.

Both of these papers offer strong support for a broad educational background as a requirement for success in the practice of accounting. The breadth runs beyond accounting and business subjects, as Mr. Bartholomew puts it, "sufficient courses in the liberal arts to broaden the graduate into a well-rounded person", and, according to Mr. Trump, to provide "the minimum intellectual base considered necessary for a professional man".

Both papers also agree on what some might consider to be the other end of the spectrum. In addition to a broad business and liberal education, accounting majors are expected by both private and public practitioners to have sufficient knowledge of procedures and applications to be productively employable immediately upon entry into their careers. Mr. Bartholomew states the accounting major should have "thorough knowledge in accounting concepts and theory, standards, techniques, systems design, and procedures in their conventional form as they apply to regular accounting activities." Mr. Trump says "the entering accountant is expected to be able to function in client contacts with some orientation assistance by demonstrating knowledge of accounting and auditing standards and procedures in practice."

The breadth of knowledge sought by both public and private accounting practitioners is very much in accord with current philosophies of accounting education. However, their demands for skill in applying accounting knowledge immediately upon entry into the field are being ignored by more and more accounting educators and programs of accounting education. This trend has resulted from the pressures emanating from various sources within the academic environment. Perhaps the time is again approaching for accounting educators to be at least as sensitive to the advice of their fellow accountants as they are to their fellow educators.

The final paper traces the evolution of auditing education through three phases—the traditional, the neo-traditional and the modern. The authors address the "image problem" so prevalent for auditors and present a set of coherent goals for auditing courses. Using survey research techniques, they compare practitioners' ideal auditing course with the "average" auditing course as presently taught and conclude that the present division of educational labor between classroom and practice should be realigned for a more efficient educational blend.

Attributes of a New (Public) Accountant

Guy Trump
Vice President
American Institute of Certified Public Accountants—New York

What basic skills are required for success in public accounting practice? This question must be considered in any realistic program for accounting education. While in individual cases, we would have to define rather precisely a CPA firm's characteristics and operating philosophy as well as current supply and demand for accountants to give a more precise profile, the following will indicate in broad terms characteristics agreed upon by a series of AICPA-sponsored commissions and committees. These represent a long-range goal for qualified entrants to the public accounting profession.

Qualifications to Enter the Profession

The AICPA's present position was established in 1969 by the Committee on Education and Experience Requirements for CPAs (the Beamer Committee). Its principal recommendations included:
1. The CPA certificate is evidence of basic competence of professional quality in the discipline of accounting. This basic competence is demonstrated by acquiring the body of knowledge common to the profession and passing the CPA examination.
2. *Horizons for a Profession* is authoritative for the purpose of delineating the common body of knowledge to be possessed by those about to begin their professional careers as CPAs.
3. At least five years of college study are needed to obtain the common body of knowledge for CPAs and should be the education requirement. For those who meet this standard, no qualifying experience should be required.

The latter recommendation was clarified in 1971 by The Standing Committee on Accounting Education in light of developing circumstances in higher education. These representatives of AAA, AICPA, AACSB and NASBA agreed that the Beamer Committee's recommendation was for the mastery of the body of knowledge rather than for spending any specified period of time in which it was to be acquired; and this group endorsed this recommendation.

These recommendations were made considering the social and economic forces at work during the 1960s, which were seen to be compelling CPAs to broaden their practices beyond the traditional attest function to other areas of attestation and accounting-related services. The brief years since this report seem to have confirmed this demand for broader services.

Modifications Dictated by Short-run Operating Factors

However, long-range plans have a way of being sidetracked by the requirements of short-term operating results, even in a professional firm. In the decade of the 1960s when there was a constantly growing demand for graduates in an accounting education, many firms were unable to find the number of graduates desired with the characteristics sought. Thus firms were willing to undertake the heavy cost of special education and training programs for graduates of liberal arts schools who had outstanding academic records and evidence of leadership in extra-curricular activities. Interest in these programs has declined in the last two to three years as the available supply of trained accountants has increased, though some programs of this type continue on a limited scale.

Furthermore, when demand is high, firms tend to put pressure on a baccalaureate degree holder with a good combination of personal qualities and a basic professional accounting education to come with them immediately rather than wait until he has another year of education or a graduate degree.

Attributes of a New (Public) Accountant

Current Picture Shows Cost as a More Important Factor in Hiring

With the supply of graduates now more plentiful, undergraduate degree holders are, in most cases, becoming economically more attractive than the higher cost master's degree holders to employer firms. Nevertheless, for the master's degree holder with the optimum combination of personal qualities and accounting education, the firms are willing to pay the required premium.

Attributes Sought in New Staff Members

Obviously the varieties of firm size, type of practice, personnel policies and operating policies have a significant effect on the characteristics sought in the staff members engaged. These variables combine in different ratios at different times in moving a given firm to seek a specified combination of the three elements desired in a staff member—intellect, personality and accounting education.

The most important attribute is intelligence. The entire process of higher education is designed to develop this trait. It is needed to enter and to continue in any university as well as to achieve any honors or distinction upon graduation. Higher education screens students so that the survivors are those with the curiosity, the concern and the energy needed to seek out problems and to resolve them. This is the attitude that the certified public accountant must have, essential for the work to be done. Intelligence or intellectual curiosity, the desire to understand conflicts and their solution, is the basic ingredient to which skill in interpersonal relations and technical performance must be added.

The second attribute needed is personality. Since the accountant must constantly work effectively with clients, associates and staff to reach a desired goal in a business situation, he must possess personality traits that include the ability to get along with people, and express his ideas clearly, effectively and persuasively. The educational process helps in the development of one of these traits with its stress on the various means of communication. It also introduces the concept of the variety of personal needs and means of perception in those with whom one communicates. However, many feel that higher education has failed to stress sufficiently the importance of this attribute of personality and ability to communicate as a means to get a job done. While innate personal traits are important, one can also learn to move a task through application of peoples' effort from the idea or concept stage to the appropriate action stage to a final stage of competion with a desired end product. There can be so much emphasis on academic "proof" of how valid the "process" is that one loses sight of the fact that it must be done in this setting, at this time, by these people, and with this deadline. The successful accountant must be a "doer", a mover of people who can conclude an engagement satisfactorily, and on time.

Thus the personality sought should combine energy and drive, the desire to probe a situation to find a problem, to organize and disclose findings and work toward a solution. In this process one must be presentable, reasonable, logical and able to communicate what the situation now is and what the goals are. One must also be persuasive enough to sell the plan of action. Without these interpersonal skills, the powers of great intellect, insight, analysis and planning ability are lost in that they are limited to the strength and benefit of one person.

Technical Skills Required to be Effective in Practice

The technical skills sought come last only because they can be acquired through study and on the job if the other attributes are present. Yet the technical skills are essential in any educational program. They require the mastery of concepts, procedures and techniques which get the job done according to professional standards.

Structure of the Professional Accountant's Educations

Horizons for a Profession is an authoritative description of the common body of knowledge for beginning CPAs. This was agreed to by the Beamer Committee during thorough and widespread discussions with accounting educators, professional accountants in practice, in business and in government as well as many leaders in education, business and government who were not accountants. Here, specific guidelines for a strong accounting education curriculum were described, and these became an adjunct to the committee report as Appendix D, Academic Preparation for Professional Accounting Careers. This remains a useful guide to any school wishing to provide a strong program in professional accounting.

Thus the 30 to 36 semester hours of accounting subjects in the five-year program recommended by the Beamer Committee and *Horizons* provide a blend of theoretical and philosophical concepts and practical and operating knowledge.

The 54 semester hours of general business subjects recommended by the Beamer Committee contain supportive subject matter to the professional accountants' knowledge of accounting and the ability to apply it within a democratic social system. They include knowledge of the social constraints within which business and the professional accountant must operate. They include understanding of constraints generated for accountants by client, consumer and associated service disciplines within the business community. They provide insight into the significance of the accountants' work to the business community and the need for reliable and informative communication of the type that justifies the statutory designation of those qualified to practice as professional accountants.

The 60 semester hours of general education outlined in the Beamer Committee Report indicate the minimum intellectual base considered necessary for a professional man. This is where intellectual vigor and the ability to communicate effectively are to be developed.

Skill and Interest Both are Required

All these attributes and skills are required in the entering professional accountant if he is to fulfill the role demanded for him by society and his profession.

In the rapidly moving current business setting, the entering accountant is expected to be able to function in client contacts with some orientation assistance by demonstrating knowledge of accounting and auditing standards and procedures in practice. With starting salaries at present levels, the client is entitled to expect such performance, the employing firm must have such capabilities, and the student should expect to be able to function in such an entering professional role. Thus accounting education must include a knowledge of what the work is like and what is expected of a staff member in terms of speed and effectiveness in a professional accounting situation. Such work exposure enables a student to know if this is a setting in which he or she can be comfortable as well as challenged. We know from experience that the work of the professional accountant is not to everyone's liking, but for those who enjoy the opportunities it offers, the rewards and satisfactions are substantial. Public accounting firms have found that those without previous accounting training lack the personal assurance and effectiveness that come from better knowledge of the work of the profession.

Professional Schools of Accounting

Unfortunately, many of the business schools have concluded that their objectives are limited to the preparations of "business managers," rather than including the objective of preparing entrants for professional accounting. Accounting programs in such schools have tended to shift emphasis from the preparation of professional accountants to providing tool preparation in accounting for "decision makers."

Professional accountants, as represented in the ranks of practicing members of the American Institute of Certified Public Accountants, have expressed increasing dissatisfaction for this state of affairs. An official position of the Board of Directors of the Institute was adopted in July, 1973, when a policy statement was adopted which included the following:

> The Institute recognizes that during the last several years the professional dimension of accounting as an academic discipline has suffered a decline in many schools—a decline which is of great concern to accountants. The Institute views this as contrary to public interest which requires that strong professional programs be generally available at universities throughout the United States.
> The Institute strongly endorses any action which provides such strong professional programs. As one way,

and perhaps the preferable way, of achieving an increased emphasis on the professional dimension of the discipline, the Institute endorses and encourages the establishment of schools of professional accounting at qualified and receptive colleges and universities.

Skills Needed for Growth

Beyond the entry level, the professional accountant will find a continuing need to use all the basic skills previously mentioned. The technical knowledge of concepts and procedures will move to applications at a higher, more complex level of client operations and will include more concern with financial statement disclosure. The human relations and communications skills will grow to the level of communicating with and obtaining the cooperation of a larger number of persons both within the firm, the client organization and in taxing and regulating bodies involved. There is also a greater need for administrative skills and the ability to plan and to program and to develop staff. As experience and judgment grow, one continues to build on the basic skills outlined and the opportunities expand for the use of administrative and managerial skills.

After demonstrated proficiency in the technical and communications skills, the need to refresh or expand one's knowledge in the managerial areas will become apparent during the conduct of larger segments of an engagement or of larger engagements, and in managing more than one engagement. The entering professional needs an educational exposure to these administrative and managerial areas of knowledge and procedure which he will need later. When he does need them, a continuing education program in the current theory and practice of management will prove useful to the experienced and professional accountant.

Continuing Education

While some of this education needed for growth will be acquired from the experience gained on the job, more will be acquired through formal programs of continuing professional education. In fact, several of the states have adopted, with Institute encouragement, legislation or regulation which requires that CPAs demonstrate that they are continuing their professional education in order to qualify for renewal of their permits to practice. While educational institutions may have some part in this education, it seems clear that the major roles will be those of the larger firms and the state and national professional organizations. The adhesive that holds them together and moves them forward is the ability to use advantageously the strengths of each person and to learn from each other that one person, or one group of very similar persons, seldom provide the only solution to all of the challenges encountered by the group.

CONCLUSION

It is difficult and perhaps unrealistic to try to describe an ideal graduate, the man most likely to succeed in a professional accounting practice. The attributes and skills described here have proved to be significant in the past and should remain so for the foreseeable future. Any professional organization will continue to consist of a variety of individuals with many common characteristics yet with remarkable diversity in intellect, personality and education.

Attributes of a New (Private) Accountant

Arthur P. Bartholomew
National President
National Association of Accountants

What would we expect an "ideal" accounting major to know upon completion of an undergraduate program? In broad terms, the ideal undergraduate accounting major should have acquired the knowledge to enable him to assume an accounting position requiring technical accounting background and to continue his studies either in a graduate program or as formal and informal continuing education effort.

The first objective calls for the type of technical background required in practice. The second objective implies a sound theoretical knowledge at the intermediate level of accounting theory.

Levels of Competence Required

It is relatively easy to identify the major areas of study to be covered in an undergraduate accounting program. A more difficult task is to determine the level of competence to be attained in each of the respective areas.

One may establish three levels of competence: (1) thorough knowledge, (2) familiarization, and (3) general understanding. In the areas in which thorough knowledge is required, the undergraduate major should become expert. In the areas where familiarization is required, he should be able to participate in effective teamwork with the experts in these areas, or call for their assistance as needed in his work. In the areas requiring general understanding, the undergraduate accounting major should know how matters in these areas will relate to and affect his work.

Thorough Knowledge

Areas requiring thorough knowledge are:

a. Accounting concepts and accounting theory, standards, methods, techniques, systems design and procedures in their conventional form (office systems and procedures and those conventional systems which are accounting oriented) as they apply to regular accounting activities (regular meaning routine, periodic, repetitive, and continuous operations). Though a thorough knowledge of the routine systems design procedures is necessary only in their conventional form for undergraduate study, there is a need for further study of the conceptual and technological framework of systems design probably fitting better into the framework of the graduate curriculum.

b. Accounting measurements, including commonly applied statistical and mathematical methods.

c. Accounting information: principal sets of accounting data underlying the accounting information in its various forms and intended uses; documentation, verification and analysis involved in preparing reports; accounting statements and reports (external and internal).

Familiarization

Areas requiring familiarization are:
a. Auditing
b. Computer theory and applications.
c. Organization theory and business applications of behavioral sciences. To be effective in any organization one must have an awareness of problems in the behavioral science area. Therefore, the graduate should have been exposed to the concepts of organizational behavior

dealing with interpersonal communication and leadership.

d. Marketing concepts, including the distribution functions performed by the various marketing agencies, interpretation of marketing policies and distribution costs as well as marketing strategy.

e. Problems in the production area, including quality control methods and the planning and scheduling of material and labor flow with the attendant problems of inventory management.

General Understanding

Areas of general understanding are:
a. Theory of the firm
b. Decision theory
c. Taxation
d. Finance and investments
e. Macroeconomics, socio-economics and an understanding of the business environment

Other Requirements

It is crucial that a graduate be particularly adept at communicating, and, therefore, he should be skilled in the use of the English language. This is important in report writing and other forms of written intercourse, but is even more important in the area of oral communication. Communication clearly falls into the "thorough knowledge" level of our competence scale. The undergraduate program also should provide sufficient courses in the liberal arts to broaden the graduate into a well-rounded person.

Finally, the undergraduate accounting major should have developed good work habits, enthusiasm for his chosen field, and the intellectual curiosity to enable him to function effectively.

Graduate Programs

At the graduate level, the emphasis should shift from the conventional and regular features of accounting to exploration of the issues of particular interest to the prospective manager who can delegate the responsibility for routine applications. In terms of the previously used categories, an outline of the graduate program would be as follows:
1. Thorough knowledge:
   a. Accounting policies and the related theory, including conceptual and technological framework of systems design
   b. Financial statements
   c. Management accounting methods and techniques
   d. Auditing
   e. Organization theory and business applications of behavioral sciences
2. Familiarization:
   a. EDP
   b. Statistical and mathematical methods
   c. Taxation
   d. Ethical problems. Accounting majors in graduate programs should be aware of the ethical problems facing accountants, both public and private. Determining what constitutes ethical behavior is, in many instances, a subjective decision. There are many grey areas and differences of opinion as to what constitutes "ethical" business practice, but recently our courts have been defining ethical practices and graduate students in accounting should be thoroughly versed in the implications of these court decisions.
3. General Understanding
Since the graduate level program would include either a thorough study or familiarization of necessary areas of business management, no specific items are listed here.

The successful completion of a master's program will enhance the graduate's knowledge of accounting as it applies to the day by day management of an organization. He will have thorough knowledge of the concepts of management accounting including responsibility accounting and the recognition of cost behavior patterns, as well as the techniques of flexible budgeting, direct costing and contribution margin reporting.

The planning and control of capital, including long-range capital budgeting techniques for deciding among alternative investment opportunities, and the management of cash are topics with which he will be familiar. Tax planning will provide him with some insight of the methods available within the tax law to minimize the organization's tax liability.

Changes in Emphasis Needed

Some private accountants have indicated their feeling that there is too much emphasis on public accounting in some universities. Since a large number of accounting students will not choose public accounting, more emphasis should be given to those courses leading to competence in management accounting. Such a change in emphasis could concurrently improve the preparation for a public accounting career, as accounting firms move more strongly into the consulting and management services field.

There is also a feeling that the current emphasis on the theory of quantitative analysis needs to be examined carefully. Very few accounting graduates encountered understand when the techniques should be used, when they are not appropriate, and the assumptions and problems inherent in their use. The critics are not certain about "de-emphasis" in this area, but feel that a better method or a more practical method of instruction needs to be found.

Schools cannot continue to feel that one course can adequately cover the concepts and uses of standard costs, flexible budgeting, direct costing information, and all the other managerial accounting areas. This slighting of such a broad range of subjects occurs too frequently and is really a disservice to the profession. Many professors need a greater understanding of current managerial accounting practices to avoid the use of outdated or irrelevant examples and techniques which may prove to be worthless to students when they begin their business careers.

Changes in Methods Needed

Less emphasis is needed on structured problems and more emphasis on unstructured problems. Students are at a loss to sift out relevant data in real world situations because the structured problem approach to instruction does not train the mind to examine and evaluate data properly.

One approach would be more emphasis on a "seminar" method of teaching, at least in courses above the introductory level. All too often, feedback to the instructor is minimal in lecture type courses, and it is difficult to determine, from written testing, the progress being made by students, and the depth of their understanding. If there were more interchange of ideas, the students would probably gain a superior understanding of the subject, and the instructor would be in a better position to evaluate ability.

It seems likely that increased emphasis on this recommended approach would necessitate a longer period of schooling, which might mean a five year undergraduate program.

The practice followed by some schools of scheduling "internship" programs with co-operating organizations for several months during an interim period of the student's training has positive value for the students and should be adopted as a more general practice.

There is a need for development of more meaningful teaching objectives for each course. These objectives must be specific, measureable, and outlined far in advance of the course. What is expected of the student? What concepts and techniques should he or she have mastered? How can we measure what has been learned? These are the types of questions that should be asked, and answered with formal follow-up. Each course should have specific objectives and ways of determining whether those objectives have been accomplished.

Accounting educators need to recognize that they now have many technological developments to help them do their job better. A study of teaching methods in accounting classes would probably find almost exclusive use of the traditional "lecture" approach—the most inefficient method possible. Some universities are doing marvelous things in the areas of teaching method studies but very few are doing them in the accounting departments.

Relevance, Auditing and Professionalism

Jack C. Robertson
The University of Texas at Austin
Charles H. Smith
Arizona State University [1]

Six years ago Professor Ray Sommerfeld wrote that educational efforts in the field of taxation were sorely in need of change and reform to meet changing needs and new complexities.[2] The thesis of the present report is that auditing and professionalism (in general) also suffer the "educational orphans" status in most college curricula today, and the present situation is a close kin to the circumstances that existed earlier in the taxation field.

Even though many accounting graduates find first employment in auditing, and even though the field of auditing itself has expanded (in the scope of its practice, its tools, and its literature), formal auditing education is still in most curricula limited to a one-course, three- or four-semester hour educational experience.[3] It is not surprising therefore to find public accounting firms and State Societies devoting an increasing amount of time to auditing subject matter in professional development programs. If the one-course constraint at the college level is to be accepted as a fact of life, auditing educators in educational institutions and in professional practice need to launch a cooperative effort to decide how to slice the education-training pie.

The approach of this paper is fourfold: (1) To review the importance of an *auditing* education (as opposed to an *accounting* education); (2) To outline the trends in auditing education at the college and university level; (3) To place the image problems of auditors in an educational perspective; and (4) To report the results of a research survey reflecting the views that practicing auditors have about formal and professional auditing education.

Education For Auditors

The educational process for accountants and auditors has been studied and restudied many times over. In practice, auditing instruction consists of two parts: (1) an introduction to the profession of accounting—its rules of ethics, mode of practice, job opportunities, legal responsibilities, and other aspects of professional life, and (2) the theory and practice of auditing in a professional setting—the auditing standards, techniques, procedures, tools, internal control, and forms of reporting (finally reaching the direct connection with "accounting"). Nowhere else in the accounting curriculum does the student receive such a heavy dosage of exposure to what the profession of accounting is all about; nowhere else is the *public* in Certified *Public* Accountant so apparent and meaningful as in the introductory auditing course.

Changing Nature Of Auditing Education

Not too many years ago instruction in auditing was exclusively procedural and technical—designed to enable the neophyte to enter his first public accounting job with some comfort in his technical competence. An important side benefit of the procedural-technical approach was that the student was fairly well prepared to take and pass the Uniform CPA examination. As much as 60-70 percent of the total time available in such courses was devoted to how to audit balance sheet and income statement accounts. In the last few years, however, there has been a discernible movement toward a more conceptual treatment of auditing subject matter and a slight suppression of the procedural-technical aspects.[4] The suppression of the latter subject matter has resulted from educators' efforts to cover new material (Statements on Auditing Procedure, statistical sampling, auditing and EDP) combined with an overall time limitation to the single course.

This emergence of the conceptual material, the studies of accounting and auditing education, and the prognostications of eminent educators and practitioners enable one to type auditing education in three schools of thought. For convenience these three will be termed the *traditionalist*, the *neo-traditionalist*, and the *modern*.

The traditionalist school of auditing education may be characterized by the emphasis on procedural-technical aspects of auditing methodology (probably including the use of an audit practice case) consuming about 60-70 percent of the time in a first course (single course). The remaining time is spent on generally accepted auditing standards, ethics, internal control, the forms of opinions, and two or three important settled legal cases.

The neo-traditionalist educator is really a traditionalist in disguise. He might be called a half-modern or a wolf in a lamb's clothing, depending on one's viewpoint. Characteristic of the neo-traditionalist is his conduct of a course that has an extensive conceptual basis, for example, adding some theory from the *Philosophy of Auditing*[5] to the generally accepted auditing standards, some morals to the study of ethics. The neo-traditionalist may introduce behavioral aspects of internal control, and he will certainly devote considerable time to statistical sampling and the use of the computer and to an exhaustive coverage of recent controversial legal cases (both those settled and perhaps some still in progress in the courts). As a result of his shift in emphasis, procedural-technical material will be treated in a general way in short class time and there will be no practice case.

The modern school of auditing education is probably a rare bird in today's college curricula. A "modern" approach would involve a change in emphasis from the audit of financial statements to the audit of information systems, with an opinion on financial statements being only *one* of the important outputs.[6] Such instruction would undoubtedly include all the elements of professionalism embodied in the standards, ethics, and legal relationships, but the whole frame of reference would depart from the framework of financial auditing and enter the realm of "management auditing." At the same time the modern approach would retain the emphasis of the "public" in its reporting mode, and the course would not be a variation on the traditional management advisory services theme.

Image And The Demand For Change

Auditors still suffer from the "green eye-shade" image. Who among us has not had his work characterized as "poking around in other people's books!" This extreme of the image, of course, does not exist in such obvious form in the eyes of accounting students. At the same time, however, students generally perceive a "halo effect" respecting management advisory services practice and tax practice, particularly since the latter has begun to lean more in the direction of tax planning and consultation services. Auditing suffers in comparison.

Why is it that students are so enamored of the tax and management advisory services consulting areas? Why is it that auditing is perceived as only an entry point, and a rather uninteresting one at that? Perhaps students perceive an aura of excitement about MAS and taxation with their complicated quantitative models and complex laws and regulations which lend themselves to high-level consulting activities. Perhaps students, like many practitioners and educators, want to be known as "consultant" or "adviser" rather than as "auditor." Perhaps auditing is just a dull academic subject for which there is no hope of salvation—a premise that is hard to believe for anyone who has practiced as an auditor. If indeed the academic study of auditing is dull, then perhaps the fault lies with the educators and the courses rather than with the subject itself.

The question most relevant for auditing education is: Where do the students who eventually become the audit practitioners, who carry on the attest function with such apparent fervor, obtain an interest in auditing? In the authors' opinion, real and lasting interest is generated on the job where the new professionals can truly see for themselves the service that is inherent in auditing. Whereas, in the classroom the service potential of MAS and tax consulting is very apparent, the perception of service potential in the audit task somehow surfaces only with practice: Thus, as far as formal education is concerned, educators have allowed MAS and tax practice to take the "halo" that could rightfully be shared by the auditor.

The image-changing task has to begin in the college classroom, and it is the educators' responsibility to accept the goal of preparing students with a new "mental set"—a framework—for their personal and professional future development. In large part, the acceptance of such a responsibility would mean giving up the warm comforts of the traditionalist school of auditing and professional education thought wherein one is able to teach the nuts and bolts—the stereotype—of auditing. The traditionalist school represents a *danger* to the progress of auditing and professional education because of the perpetuation of the stereotype that has created our problems. In addition, the college classroom is a poor place to train auditors in procedures and techniques: The students cannot generate a real interest, and the instructors cannot create realism in the classroom. The training phase is better left to AICPA and individual CPA firm initial staff training programs where real-life auditors can supervise a practice set, and where the need to learn procedures is uppermost in the students' minds. (Practicing auditors have probably long known that they can do this job better than the educators anyway.)

The goal for the college classroom should be to present the attest function in a broader perspective than the traditional financial audit. The classroom time referent should be that of preparing the student for his fourth or fifth year of practice rather than for his first-year job. The role of an education should be to teach students to think for themselves and to contribute to their development of an ability to adapt to a rapidly changing environment of professional practice.

To the extent that the neo-traditionalist school of educational thought can contribute to these goals, then there is *hope* that the image can be improved, and that the result will be a better-educated auditor. Adoption of the modern school of thought holds promise for not only hope but also for *salvation* from the doldrums of the present stereotype.

AUDITING CURRICULUM RESEARCH

In an attempt to identify possible solutions to the numerous problems outlined above, an opinion-attitude survey was undertaken of practitioners (all in Texas). A questionnaire was sent in batches to participating coordinators in nineteen offices representing sixteen different CPA firms. These coordinators distributed the instrument randomly to their respective audit staff personnel. The distribution of, and responses to the instrument are shown in Table 1.

With the research instrument, each respondent was given opportunity to express his opinions on the importance (on a five-point scale) and time allocation requirement of formal auditing education efforts relating to a list of fifty-three potential topics. The two major responses—importance and time allocation—were considered to be independent;[7] that is, the most important topic may not also reflect the heaviest time allocation. The two responses yielded important information to educators for study of auditing educational efforts: The *importance* response enables one to judge his own opinions of importance with reference to the opinions of practitioners; and the *time allocation* gives a starting point for design of the desired audit course.

Demand For Undergraduate Course Content

Powerful forces of supply and demand should operate between accounting employers and auditing educators. Practitioners have to face client demands for service and they have to fill those demands with educated personnel. Educators should seek out knowledge of the demand that is derived from the needs of practitioners, and they should seek to supply accounting graduates who are "properly educated." At the same time, educators must be true to their own conception of proper education

TABLE 1

RESEARCH INSTRUMENT DISTRIBUTION AND RESPONSE

	Distributed	Responded	Per Cent
National CPA Firms (8)			
Firm A	20	7	35 %
Firm B	15	4	27
Firm C	40	30	75
Firm D	40	28	70
Firm E	5	5	100
Firm F	15	14	93
Firm G	18	9	50
Firm H	35	25	71
	188	122	65 %
Regional-Local CPA Firms (8)			
Firm I	5	4	80 %
Firm J	8	3	38
Firm K	15	14	93
Firm L	10	0	0
Firm M	2	0	0
Firm N	12	0	0
Firm O	3	0	0
Firm P	6	0	0
	61	21	34 %
Total distribution and response	249	143	57 %

which generally involves long-run educational goals, not just short-term training goals suitable to satisfy immediate personnel needs of the practitioners. In short, educators must know of the needs of the profession, but they must also prepare students for a lifetime of learning—even if at the expense of producing a graduate who cannot "go out and perform with only minimal indoctrination."[8]

Respondents to the questionnaire were asked to scale (on a five-point scale) each of 53 topics (classified in 13 subject areas) according to the *importance* that an undergraduate student be exposed to the subject matter of the topics. The importance scale response ranged from an indication of "extremely important" to "extremely unimportant." These importance measures for each topic were aggregated to calculate an importance score for the subject area in which the topics were classified. Table 2 contains the scores of subject areas derived from the 143 respondents.

TABLE 2

IMPORTANCE RANKING OF SUBJECT AREAS

Subject Area Content	Average Importance Score*
1. Theory of Auditing Ethics, generally accepted auditing standards, basic concepts, processes of judgment formation based on evidence	3.35
2. Audit Reports Types of audit opinions, long-form reports	2.65
3. Workpapers and Procedures Traditional techniques and procedures for auditing accounts, use of industry data and ratio analysis, audit practice set	2.63
4. Legal Relationships General liability, liability under Securities Acts, recent litigation, historical litigation	2.60
5. Internal Control General principles, narrative descriptions of systems, flow-chart techniques, relation to extent of testing, behavioral dimensions	2.36
6. Auditing Relationships Relationships to accounting and to internal auditing, professional organizations, organization of CPA firms, social significance of attest function	2.20
7. Electronic Data Processing Control characteristics, information processing, auditing "around" and "through" the computer	2.05
8. Sampling in Auditing Judgment sampling, random sampling with classical evaluation, with Bayesian evaluation	2.03
9. SEC Practice and Procedure General filing requirements	1.70
10. Human Relations in Auditing Client relations, leadership, motivation, partner-staff relations	1.25**
11. Extensions of the Attest Function Audits of budgets and forecasts, backlog, capital expenditure appropriations, relationship of financial auditing to management auditing	0.97
12. International Dimensions Comparative accounting and auditing standards, questions of uniformity	0.65
13. Mathematical Models in Auditing Applications of linear and dynamic programming to planning and scheduling, development of computer programs	0.47**

*Average importance scores are the mean of all topic scores in the subject area (except those indicated by 40 percent or more of respondents as being appropriate for professional development coverage, see Table 5.) on the scale of Extremely Important equals 4, Somewhat Important equals 3, Neutral—importance not determinable equals 2, Somewhat Unimportant equals 1, and Extremely Unimportant equals 0.

**All topics under the subject areas of Human Relations and Mathematical Models were indicated as subjects for in-firm training by 40 percent or more of respondents. Scores based on all topics are presented for comparison only.

With reference to Table 2, the Theory subject area ranks a clear first place in terms of importance for undergraduate exposure. The next subject areas of Audit Reports, Workpapers and Procedures, and Legal Relationships are in a virtual tie for second rank; and these are followed closely by Internal Control and Auditing Relationships. Somewhat further behind in seventh, eighth, and ninth rank are the more specialized subject matter areas of Electronic Data Processing, Sampling in Auditing, and SEC Practice and Procedure (general filing requirements only). Not until reaching the tenth subject area does the ranking decline to approximate the "somewhat unimportant" and "extremely unimportant" response scalings.

Allocation Of Classroom Time

The second part of the research instrument required the practitioners to give an estimate of how many class meetings should be devoted to coverage of each topic.[9] A class meeting was defined as a single hour in class augmented by two hours of pre-class preparation. The respondents were requested not to restrict their total meetings to what they thought amounted to a semester of work. Since many auditing courses of both traditional and neo-traditional varieties are available for comparison on the basis of class meeting time, Table 3 contains a presentation of the research responses and comparisons with existing courses.

TABLE 3

ALLOCATION of TIME to SUBJECT AREAS:
COMPARISON WITH EXISTING AUDITING COURSES

Time Allocation:
Number and Percent of Class Meetings

Subject Areas in Order of Average Importance Score	Survey responses (a) Number	%	Traditional courses (b) Number	%	Neo-Traditional courses (b) Number	%
1. Theory of Auditing	9	18.0	5	12.5	6	15.0
2. Audit Reports	4	8.0	3	7.5	5	12.5
3. Workpapers and Procedures	10	20.0	21	52.5	9	22.5
4. Legal Relationships	4	8.0	1	2.5	4	10.0
5. Internal Control	7	14.0	3	7.5	4	10.0
6. Auditing Relationships	4	8.0	2	5.0	4	10.0
7. Electronic Data Processing	6	12.0	2	5.0	2	5.0
8. Sampling in Auditing	3	6.0	3	7.5	6	15.0
9. SEC Practice and Procedure	1	2.0	*		*	
10. Human Relations in Auditing**	1	2.0	0		0	
11. Extensions of the Attest Function	1	2.0	0		*	
12. International Dimensions	0		0		0	
13. Mathematical Models in Auditing**	0		0		0	
	50	100.0%	40	100.0%	40	100.0%

(a) Median number of class meetings per respondents.
(b) Derived from available course outlines: Including the outlines contained in the series by Thomas J. Burns (ed.) *Accounting Trends*. (New York: McGraw-Hill Book Co.)

* Less than one class meeting, but not completely omitted.
**Presented for comparison only. Over 40 percent of respondents indicated that all topics in these subject areas should be handled by in-firm training programs.

The time allocations for existing courses presented in Table 3 must be interpreted with some caution, because it is difficult to derive from a written course outline the exact nature of the material an instructor covers under a given caption. In particular, a traditionalist may weave into his course a great deal of theory when dealing with procedural and technical problems; likewise a neo-traditionalist may cover a good many procedures and techniques under the topic headings of EDP and Sampling. Perhaps the most distinguishing characteristic found in a traditional outline, however, is the large number of meetings devoted to auditing the balance sheet captions. Such coverage is highly condensed and generalized in the neo-traditional course, and the time is otherwise spread out among other subject matter areas. If any generalizations are warranted by this data, perhaps the most obvious is that the neo-traditionalist time allocation corresponds more closely with practitioner demands than does the traditionalist allocation of classroom time.

Earlier in this report, it was noticed that the dimensions of professionalism are generally first encountered by the student in the first auditing course. With respect to the outline of the "core course" found in Table 4, one can observe that all of the topics are *auditing* topics in the traditional sense; and one can observe several that do double duty as topics in the *professional* aspects of accounting and auditing practice. With respect to professionalism, the subject areas of *Theory of Auditing* (generally accepted auditing standards, auditing concepts, rules of ethics, and judgment based on evidence), *Audit Reports* (the types of communications to report users), *Legal Relationships* (historical, current, common law, and statutory duties), and *Auditing Relationships* (relationship of accounting of auditing, social significance of the attest function) contain the types of material that auditors and accountants generally think of as embodying the dimensions of professionalism discussed earlier. All together these topics were assigned twenty class meetings by practitioners—amounting to 40 percent of the total allocated—and in terms of a normal semester of forty meetings, amounting to 50 percent of the typical college course.

When the accounting student takes nine or ten courses to gain the bachelor's degree with a major field in accounting, these professional topics constitute about 5 percent of his accounting educations. This proportion appears small enough to earn the appellation of "orphan" in the accounting curriculm.

Slicing The Education-Training Pie

All education and learning certainly does not occur on the college campus, and in auditing and professionalism the surface of knowledge is only slightly scratched. Buckley phrased the matter in terms of his first pertinent question of a strategic nature—how to divide the educational pie between school and profession in a manner that optimizes the training and performance of the accountant.[10] Respondents to the survey reported herein also had opportunity to indicate whether a topic was appropriate for in-firm training and professional development program coverage in lieu of formal college classroom coverage. The responses presented in Table 5 display the opinions of the 143 practitioners.[11]

The 20 topics considered by respondents as appropriate for PD course coverage have the common characteristics of being either: (1) very detailed and specialized, (2) quite "advanced", and/or (3) amenable to unique firm-oriented philosophy. The message here is quite clear: Topics with these characteristics are best handled in a practice setting. Nevertheless, practitioners also appear to demand that formal education efforts provide a thorough familiarity with generalized procedures and techniques. Depending on the degree of detail attributed to "thorough familiarity with procedures and techniques," there exists a distinct possibility for a useful trade-off between formal education courses and professional development courses.

Professor William B. Shenkir expressed the trade-off in some reflections following his experience teaching in the AICPA Level I staff training program. His comments, which follow, place the conceptual and the procedural aspects of auditing education in a proper perspective.

> These courses (AICPA Level I and in-house staff training are essentially technical and procedure-oriented. It

TABLE 4

AN AUDITING CORE COURSE CONTAINING "IMPORTANT" TOPICS

Auditing Topics — Subject Areas: Number of Class Meetings

Rank*	Theory	Reports	Procedures	Legal	Internal Control	Relations	EDP	Sampling
1. Generally accepted auditing standards	3							
2. Principles of internal control					3			
3. Financial auditing concepts	2							
3. Rules of ethics	2							
3. Types of audit opinions		3						
6. Detail audit procedures			6					
7. Judgment formation based on evidence	2							
8. General legal liability				1				
9. Internal control and extent of testing					2			
10. Relationships of auditing and accounting						2		
11. Recent litigation				1				
12. Internal control in EDP							2	
13. Audit practice set			3					
14. Sampling—classical								2
15. EDP—lecture on auditing "through" computer							1	
15. Historical litigation				1				
17. Liability—Securities Acts				1				
17. Sampling—judgmental								1
19. Use of industry data, ratio analysis			1					
19. Internal control flowcharts					1			
19. Auditing "around" the computer							1	
22. EDP information processing							1	
22. Internal control narratives					1			
24. Social significance of attest function						1		
25. Long-form reports		1						
Total Meetings (=45)**	9	4	10	4	7	3	5	3

*Topics with identical importance ranks were in a tie.
**The other five class meetings were found in topics that were ranked as "Neutral—neither important nor unimportant." One class meeting was assigned to each of the following topics: (1) 26th rank, Auditing Relations subject area—Professional and firm organization, (2) 27th rank—General SEC filing requirements, (3) 27th rank, EDP subject area—EDP-problems on auditing "through" computer, (4) 27th rank—Client relations and (5) 32nd rank—Current practice and management auditing.

TABLE 5

TOPICS APPROPRIATE FOR PROFESSIONAL DEVELOPMENT TRAINING

Twenty topics for which 25 per cent or more of respondents indicated professional development and in-firm training.

Subject Area	Topic	% of Respondents
Audit Reports	Letters to underwriters	45 %
Workpapers and Procedures	Audit problems of:	
	Banks	72 %
	Securities brokers	76 %
	Savings and Loan Assoc.	74 %
	Insurance companies	74 %
	Public utilities	74 %
	Non-profit organizations	69 %
	Local government units	59 %
	Federal programs	71 %
Electronic Data Processing	Auditing "through" the computer; problems on the computer	25 %
	Use of generalized "audit tape" programs and applications	39 %
SEC Practice and Procedure	General filing requirements	33 %
	Details of Regulation S-X	49 %
	Details of SEC report forms	45 %
	Registration under Texas Securities Act	52 %
Human Relations in Auditing	Personal relations with clients' staffs	52 %
	Partner-staff relations, leadership, motivation	65 %
Mathematical Models in Auditing	Linear programming applications	40 %
	Dynamic programming applications	45 %
	Development of computer programs to create audit programs	45 %

goes without saying that parallel programs are a tremendous waste of time and it might be added, a procedure-oriented course in a university environment competes at a disadvantage.[12]

On a time allocation basis (see Table 3) the views of both practitioners and educators argue in favor of a more neo-traditionalist course at the college level. The introduction to auditing and professionalism in a conceptual framework, later augmented with professional development study and on-the-job training, appears to offer the best combination of efforts in the preparation of accountants and auditors.

SUMMARY AND CONCLUSIONS

Educational efforts in auditing and professionalism are presently in need of significant improvement. These two aspects of education for professional accountants are now virtual orphans in the formal curriculum, especially since developments in the field of accounting practice have rapidly changed many dimensions of professional life. The image of auditors and accountants is in need of a face-lifting, and the place to begin is at the grass roots in the college classroom, and the place to continue is in the professional development effort sponsored by the AICPA, state societies, and individual firms.

The *traditional* procedures-oriented first course in auditing can continue to meet neither the changing nature of the profession nor the present demands of practitioner-employers. A *neo-traditional* frame of reference that devotes greater time to teaching students how to think and that gives them a solid background for post-college personal development is presently the most viable framework for formal auditing education.

Educators and practitioners must recognize and accept the fact that each group can contribute more usefully in certain areas than the other group. College educators can provide a classroom experience that develops a mental set—a professional attitude—that has significant breadth and sufficient depth to prepare a student for further development on the job and in professional development courses. Practitioner instructors (whether a senior accountant on the job or an instructor in an organized program) can make the college experience truly meaningful by their efforts to impart a true *working* knowledge of complicated auditing and accounting matters in a real-world setting. With a useful slicing of the education-training pie, neophyte accountants may obtain a rich, coordinated formal and practical education for the profession.

FOOTNOTES

[1] The authors are indebted to Professor James R. Boatsman, Oklahoma State University, for his valuable assistance in designing and executing an analysis of variance of the survey data.

[2] Ray M. Sommerfeld, "Taxation: Education's Orphan." *Journal of Accountancy,* (December, 1966), pp. 38-44.

[3] John H. Ziegler, "Current Trends in the Teaching of Auditing," *Accounting Review,* (January, 1972), 170.

[4] Evidence of this movement may be found in: D.R. Carmichael and John J. Willingham, "New Directions in Auditing Education," *Accounting Review* (July, 1969), pp. 611-615. John H. Ziegler, "Current Trends in the Teaching of Auditing," *Accounting Review* (January, 1972), pp. 167-170.

[5] R.K. Mautz and Hussien A. Sharaf, *The Philosophy of Auditing,* (American Accounting Association, 1961).

[6] W. Thomas Porter and John C. Burton, *Auditing: A Conceptual Approach* (Belmont, California: Wadsworth Publishing Co., Inc., 1971), p. 154.

[7] Analysis of the responses showed that the 53 topics fell into two categories—29 having reasonably high importance and 24 which were considered minor in importance. The Spearman rank correlation coefficient comparing the 29-high importance topics ranked as to (1) importance, and (2) time allocation was 0.69—a positive, but not strong relationship. The rank correlation coefficient for the other 24 minor topics was 0.91, which showed that these were uniformly minor both as to importance and as to amount of time considered necessary for instruction.

[8] Ziegler, *op. cit.,* p. 168.

[9] During the process of preparing a course outline and materials for the Fall, 1972 semester, the authors have derived much benefit from these opinions on time allocation requirements.

[10] John W. Buckley, "A Perspective on Professional Accounting Education." *Journal of Accountancy* (August, 1970), p. 41.

[11] It is clear that a judgment has been made to the effect that an item is appropriate if 25 percent or more of respondents indicated support for it. The authors felt that less than 25 percent represented an insignificant minority.

[12] William G. Shenkir,"The Auditing Course in the Accounting Curriculum: A Professor's View." Paper presented at the Twenty-third annual meeting of the Southeast Regional Group of the American Accounting Association, April 30-May 1, 1971.

The Implementation of Values

Introduction

One may favor a "liberal education", "professional schools", "socially conscious accounting graduates", "diverse educational experiences" or any number of other equally grand-sounding things, but until something concrete emerges from that wish, it is both premature and hazardous to debate the merits of that particular favored position. Or, to use more elegant phrasing . . . .

"When I use a word," Humpty Dumpty said, in a rather scornful tone, "it means just what I choose it to mean—neither more nor less".
"The question is," said Alice, "whether you can make words mean so many different things."
"The question is," said Humpty Dumpty, "which is to be master—that's all."
   Lewis Carrol, Through the Looking Glass

The six papers in this section have in common an emphasis on implementation, on finding ways to imbed values in ongoing educational structures. They deal with diverse topics in equally diverse fashions, but they do provide models, concrete illustrations and/or data which will serve as prototypes for imitators. Section IV on "Instructional Innovations" is in the same vein; however, the innovations in this section provide a more direct link between the motivating value system and the instructional system which results.

The Professional School in Accounting Education

Edward L. Summers
University of Texas at Austin

Is a professional school of accounting both desirable and possible? If so, what form is it likely to take and what problems and benefits may be foreseen? The purpose of this paper is to address these issues by presenting a paper prototype of such a school.

Most accounting education now takes place in professional multi-disciplinary schools of business administration. Within such schools, no accounting department controls all aspects of its own curriculum, selects its own students, raises funds independently for its own uses, controls its own budget, or entirely determines its own faculty identity or aggregate activities and programs. As a result, the perquisites most commonly associated with professional schools are, to a greater or lesser degree, substantially denied to accounting educators. Furthermore, the impact of the traditional organizational form has been observed and objected to by professional accountants with increasing vehemence.

The literature to date has tended—with cause—to concentrate on the need for change, rather than on the bureaucratic details of organizing such an entity. This paper will favor the latter approach.

The immediate effects of *not* having professional schools of accounting education are evident. Specializations such as professional accounting are discouraged, for example, and accounting is expected to be taught as a "tool" for managerial decision making.[1] The business faculty prefers that coverage of accounting reveal the use of accounting but not its structure; much, perhaps, as typing courses concentrate on the use of a typewriter rather than on its construction. As a result, only a fraction of the total educational function in the accounting profession is performed at institutions of higher education. The writer has been told that one of the "Big Eight" accounting firms annually spends a greater sum on in-house education than the sixty biggest departments of accounting in the United States combined! No other major profession relies so little on institutions of higher education in terms of relative resource commitments.

Character and Programs of the School of Accounting

Schools of accounting would produce many changes in the education of an accountant. Figure 1 summarizes just a few of these changes.

Accounting schools would probably function as two or three-year schools following two years of general preparation. Students would be full time students. The thrust of instruction would be to familiarize students with the interaction of accounting theory and business practice in the context of the accountant's professional relationships with others. In the school of accounting, relatively more resources would be devoted to pursuing research ideas than in the typical present department of accounting.

The professional school's faculty would be committed to performing the important function of *transfer of knowledge* from research and applications in accounting and other disciplines to accounting practitioners. The knowledge transfer function is one of the most important professional school functions. It is substantially not performed by present departments of accounting, and exists only in splintered form in the educational program of large CPA firms and professional accounting organizations. These programs are often supplementary and do not provide uniform, coordinated coverage of all important potential accounting applications. The school of accounting would bring this

Figure 1

Education of An Accountant

The character of accounting education fully conforming to recognized professional standards would differ from existing accounting education. This figure relates some of these differences at important stages in education for the accounting profession.

Where Stage Occurs...

Stages in education for accounting	Conforming to traditional concept of education for a profession	Existing accounting education
1. Broad and general education background	Outside School of Accounting	In and Out of School of Business
2. Basic theory and principles of accounting (i.e., first 30-40 credit hours of accounting)	Within School of Accounting	Available only to extent accounting is a "tool" of business; courses shared with non-accounting students.
3. Basic theory and principles of selected accounting-related disciplines such as computer science, psychology, economics, finance and management.	Outside School of Accounting from faculty of those disciplines.	Fundamental principles and use of "tool" concepts such as management and finance in business; taught in school of business.
4. Application and intergration of contributing disciplines into accounting Body of Knowledge	Within School of Accounting	Limited additional accounting specialization available; usually shared with non-accounting students.
5. Practical experience	Accounting Professional Practice	
6. Continuing education	Available from school and profession in coordinated programs	Available only from profession.

function's full benefits to accounting practitioners for the first time.

The school of accounting would serve as a comprehensive education-research-communication center for accountants, just as law schools do for the legal profession and medical schools for physicians.

The following section outlines some approximate solutions to the purely organizational problem involved in (1) "spinning off" a subunit of a business school and (2) establishing the new unit within the university decision making system. Two points should be noted. First, the suggestions are just that—one set of many possible solutions to such problems. Second, such problems are merely transitional, i.e., experimentation and experience will yield optimal organizational schemes.

The Professional School: Organizational Issues and Tentative Solutions

Fitting a major new professional school into a university administration structure would be a delicate operation. Governance of universities and their subunits is complicated because there is no ready agreement on measurable parameters of performance, production functions, or assurance of educational success or excellence.

As a starting point, a typical organization structure for a typical university is something like Figure 2.

Figure 2

University Organization Structure

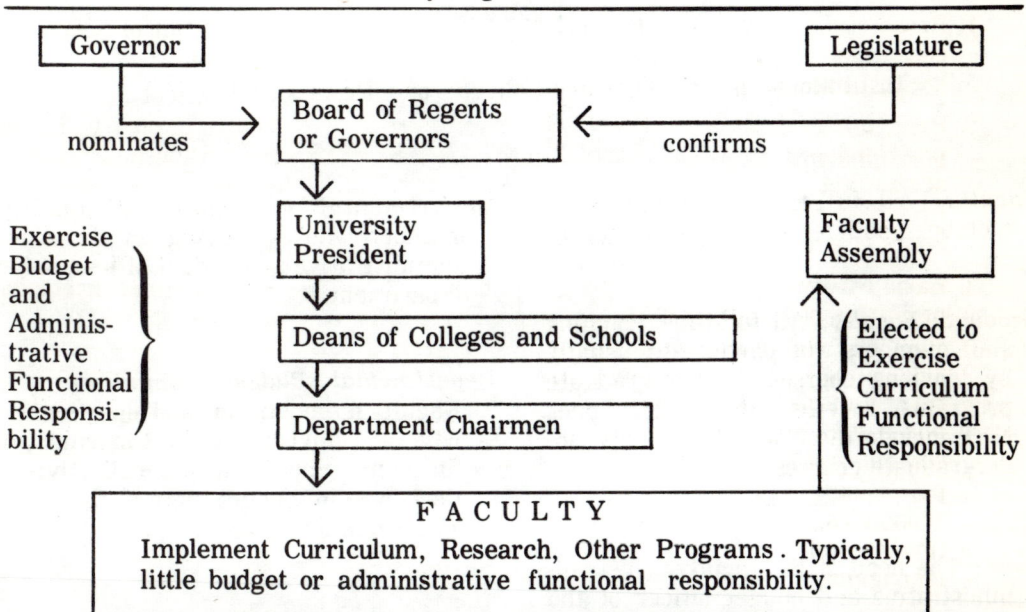

```
     Governor                                          Legislature
        |                                                  |
        v                                                  v
                 Board of Regents    <---
  nominates -->  or Governors             confirms
                        |
                        v
Exercise          University                          Faculty
Budget            President                           Assembly
and                     |                                 ^
Adminis-                v                                 |
trative     Deans of Colleges and Schools          Elected to
Functional              |                          Exercise
Responsi-               v                          Curriculum
bility          Department Chairmen                Functional
                        |                          Responsibility
                        v
            ┌─────────────────────────────────────────────┐
            │                F A C U L T Y                │
            │ Implement Curriculum, Research, Other Programs. │
            │ Typically, little budget or administrative      │
            │ functional responsibility.                      │
            └─────────────────────────────────────────────┘
```

The regents approve all major operational changes, including those necessary to implement a school of accounting.

Well down the administrative structure are deans and departmental chairmen. A dean will be responsible for formulating and administering procedures for the faculty's teaching and research in all major educational programs in the school.

Departments are usually the smallest, least formal responsibility centers. They are formed along natural lines of specialization within curriculum areas. Since situations arise which departments cannot handle, deans must also do some mediating and coordinating. The dean is constrained in these activities primarily having scarce educational resources which must be used to obtain balanced programs rather than to pursue any single program (such as professional accounting) to the extent its advocates propose.

There are three major types of functional responsibility necessary to implement any educational program: budget, curriculum, and administration. Definitions of these responsibilities follow:

Budget:
Funding of all teaching, research, publications, continuing education, and other programs. Set faculty and staff levels, hire new faculty, approve requests for research grants and/or time off, approve faculty and staff promotions, approve equipment purchases, reimburse faculty travel or other expenses, establish faculty and staff salaries

Curriculum:
What graduate and undergraduate courses will be offered, the content of courses, combinations of courses that will be considered a degree program; admissions, probation, and continuance standards; attendance, examinations, grading transfer credit, awards and scholarships; interdisciplinary cooperation with other departments or colleges

Administration:
Carrying out budget or curriculum policies; originating and carrying out administrative policies. Administrative authority must schedule courses, assign office space, calculate travel expense reimbursements, and manage staff resources. Administrators engage in fund raising and meet and talk with other administrators, casual visitors, alumni, and state officials.

These responsibilities are carried out through entities created especially for that purpose. These entities are summarized in Figure 3.

Figure 3

Institutions in a Typical College or Professional School

Faculty: All full-time teaching staff members, both tenured and nontenured.

Graduate Faculty: All full-time teaching staff members who participate, usually by teaching courses, in the graduate programs, In effect this faculty does NOT include those who teach only undergraduate courses.

Dean: The head of the faculty, chief administrative and budget officer of the faculty.

Departments: Associations of faculty, usually on the basis of common teaching interest.

Departmental Chairman: A faculty member who is serving as the chief administrative and budget officer of his department.

Departmental Budget Committee: Faculty members in a Department who are advisory to the Chairman, or (in many schools) whose collective decisions in budget matters the Chairman executes.

College Foundation, Institute, or Center: An administrative entity responsible for all activities other than straight teaching and college-related administration. It is controlled by the Dean or Faculty Senate.

Figure 4 is a matrix depicting in summary the present distribution of responsibilities among a college's ruling institutions.

Figure 4

Present Distribution of Functional Responsibility Among College Institutions

Types of Institutions	Budget	Curriculum	Administrative
Faculty	None	Undergraduate Program Policies, Teaching	None
Graduate Faculty	None	Graduate Program Policies, Teaching	None
Dean	Prepares college budget; may change departmental budgets	Carries out faculty's policies	Carries out budget policies; proposes and carries out college administrative policies
Department Chairmen	Prepare departmental budget	Schedule courses	Carries out budget policies; proposes and carries out departmental administrative policies
Department Budget Committees	Approve departmental budget	None	Approve departmental administrative policies
College Foundation, Institute, or Center	Manages research, periodicals, alumni and outside relations, continuing education fund raising	None	Resources for special projects, publications, seminars colloquia, etc.

Advocates and opponents of professional schools are well aware that any restructuring results in power shifts. In order for a school of accounting to exist, the above responsibilities will have to be redistributed. One possible redistribution of responsibilities between accounting and business is shown in Figure 5, grouped in combinations that exemplify three unique concepts of self-control for professional accounting education. Each concept is discussed in some detail.

Figure 5
Allocation of Functional Responsibilities to
Accounting and Business Education

Status of Accounting Educations	Curriculum	Administrative	Budget
ACCOUNTING PROGRAM, NO SCHOOL OF ACCOUNTING	All to school of business: Entire business faculty controls graduate and undergraduate programs	Dean and departments (including an accounting department) share administrative responsibility, with dean retaining authority over departments.	Dean retains all authority, but delegates authority for initiating certain budget recommendations to departments. The department heads (or chairmen and budget committees) make budget recommendations for their departments and formulate and administer budget policies within their departments.
INDEPENDENT SCHOOL OF ACCOUNTING	Accounting faculty controls graduate programs only in accounting; entire business faculty controls all other programs.		Two or more autonomous units exist in the college, but they both have the same Dean. The Dean must meet separately with each unit, and each unit makes and administers its own budgetary policies.
SCHOOL OF ACCOUNTING WITHIN COLLEGE OF BUSINESS	Accounting faculty controls graduate and undergraduate programs only in accounting; business faculty (excluding accounting) controls all other programs.	Two administrative units are formed, each completely autonomous from the other, having separate Deans.	There are two or more autonomous budgetary units, each with its own Dean, which submit separate budgets to University officials.

Accounting Program, No School of Accounting

Curriculum: All authority is shared by entire business faculty. Entire business faculty controls graduate and undergraduate programs.

Administrative: Dean and departments (including an accounting department) share administrative responsibility, with dean retaining authority over departments.

Budget: Dean retains all authority, but delegates authority for initiating certain budget recommendations to departments.

Under this arrangement (approximately the status quo), the accounting programs would be administered by a Department of Accounting with autonomy approximating that of the other departments in the college. In particular, the accounting programs would be subject to the department chairman, the college of business administration dean, the entire college of business administration faculty, and to the rules, policies, and resource allocations satisfactory to the entire college of business academic community. In every significant respect, accounting would be part of the overall management programs of the college business.

This is the structure under which accounting education once prospered and which has been exploited to its limits in achieving excellence in the accounting profession.

School of Accounting within College of Business

Curriculum: Accounting faculty controls accounting programs; business faculty (including accounting faculty) control all other programs.

Administrative: Two administrative units are formed from the original one, each completely autonomous from the other, having the same dean.

Budget: Two or more autonomous units (one of them, the school of accounting) exist in the college, but both have the same dean and submit a single budget to University officals

Under this arrangement, the professional accounting programs would be concentrated in the hands of a "School of Accounting" which would be an administrative part of the college of business. Although at first glance this appears to be merely a name change imposed upon the previous arrangement, it does have important differences.

1. The School of Accounting would be headed by a Director responsible to the dean of the college of business, rather than by a chairman as a department would be. The School of Accounting also would offer non-professional accounting programs, including accounting courses intended for non-accounting majors and the first accounting course sequence.

2. There would be no possibility of college of business faculty determining the character of professional accounting courses and programs (although their *advice* should be sought).

3. Admission to the professional accounting programs would be through the School of Accounting. Thus, admission to the college of business would not guarantee admission to the School of Accounting.

4. The Master's degree in accounting would be controlled through the School of Accounting faculty, without participation by the college of business faculty.

Features of existing systems which would be retained would be:

a. The budgetary responsibility, including the decisions bearing on faculty and staff levels, promotions, and compensation, would continue to reside in the Dean's office.

b. Most administrative matters would continue to be handled through the Dean's office.

In the area of outside relations, autonomy should be granted the School of Accounting within a business school. It would be natural for the name, "School of Accounting" itself to be visible and attractive to accountants, and their tendency would be to deal with this welcome new institution directly rather than through the dean of the college of business. The college and School should capitalize on this tendency by establishing separate outside responsibilities for the School of Accounting. For example, the typical college of business has a "College of Business Foundation" which collects money from outsiders and uses it to supplement the entire college's regular budget. It would not affect the appeal of such a foundation to create a "Research Center for Professional Accounting" appealing directly and exclusively to the accounting profession for support of School of Accounting programs. The overall financial support of the college would be increased, and that of the accounting programs would be greatly increased. But a truly professional program needs a higher level of financial support than that received by accounting programs today, and the greater inflows of financial support could only further enhance the likelihood of success for the new school.

Figure 6 shows the distribution of functional responsibility in a college of business which includes a school of accounting. A comparison with Figure 4 will show the changes necessary to implement this accounting education concept.

Independent School of Accounting

Curriculum: Accounting faculty controls graduate and undergraduate accounting programs; business faculty controls all other programs.

Administration: Two administrative units (one of them, the school of accounting) are formed from the old one, each completely autonomous from the other, having separate deans.

Budget: The college is split into two autonomous budgetary units (one of them, the school of accounting), each with its own dean, which submit separate budgets to University officials.

The independent school of accounting would have no special relationship with the school of business or with any other college or school in the university. Its Director or Dean would have status equivalent to that of any other dean on the campus in budget and administrative affairs. No college, department, or other school could modify its programs, change its budget, or designate its administrators. Only the normal university-wide authority of the president and the board of regents or governors would apply to the school of accounting. The visibility of the independent school of accounting to the public would enhance the prestige, morale, and ethical force of the accounting professions.

The matrix representation of the fully independent school of accounting is depicted in Figure 7. Figure 8 shows the corresponding university organization chart. Although the setup is much simpler than that for the semi-independent school of accounting, we choose to illustrate as explicitly as possible the total separation of curriculum, budget, and administrative authority between the two educational entities.

Figure 6
School of Accounting within College of Business— Distribution of Functional Responsibility

Type of Institution	Budget	Curriculum	Administrative
Faculty A. Accounting B. Business	None	A. Professional accounting programs, courses. B. All other undergraduate program policies, teaching.	None
Graduate Faculty A. Accounting B. Business	None	A. Accounting PhD. Program. B. Graduate non-accounting programs, policies, teaching	None
Dean, School of Business and School of Accounting	Prepares Business and Accounting budgets; may change Accounting and departmental budgets	None	Carries out all budget policies; proposes and carries out Business School administrative policies. Head of college Center
A. Director, Accounting School B. Department Chairmen.	A. Prepare Accounting budget for Dean B. Prepare departmental budgets for Dean	A & B. Schedule Courses. Accounting Department staffs nonprofessional accounting courses.	A. Carries out Accounting budget; proposes and carries out Accounting administrative policies; head of Accounting Center. B. Same for Departments except no Department Centers.
A. Accounting School Budget Committee. B. Business Dept. Budget Committees	A. Approve Accounting School Budget B. Approve Departmental Budgets.	None	A. Approve Accounting School Administrative Policies. B. Approve Departmental Administrative Policies.
Accounting Center Business Center	Accounting research, periodicals, alumni & outside relations, continuing education, fund raising. Same, but for Business School	Finance release time from teaching.	Resources for special projects, publications, seminars, colloquia, etc. for Accounting School.

Figure 7

Independent School of Accounting—
Distribution of Functional Responsibility

Type of Institution	Budget	Curriculum	Administrative
Faculty		Approve professional accounting programs, policies, teaching.	
Graduate Faculty		Approve Accounting Ph.D program, policies, teaching.	
Dean, School of Accounting	Prepare Budget		Carry out budget policies, carry out administrative policies. Head of Accounting Center.
Curriculum Committee		Propose professional accounting programs and policies.	
Budget Committee	Advise Dean with respect to Budget, approve budgetary policies.		
Advisory and Policy Committee			Advise Dean with respect to administration; approve administrative policies.
Center for Professional Accounting	Accounting research, periodicals, alumni and outside relations, continuing education, fund raising, knowledge transfer.		Administrative resources for special projects, publications, seminars, colloquia, etc.

Type of Functional Responsibility

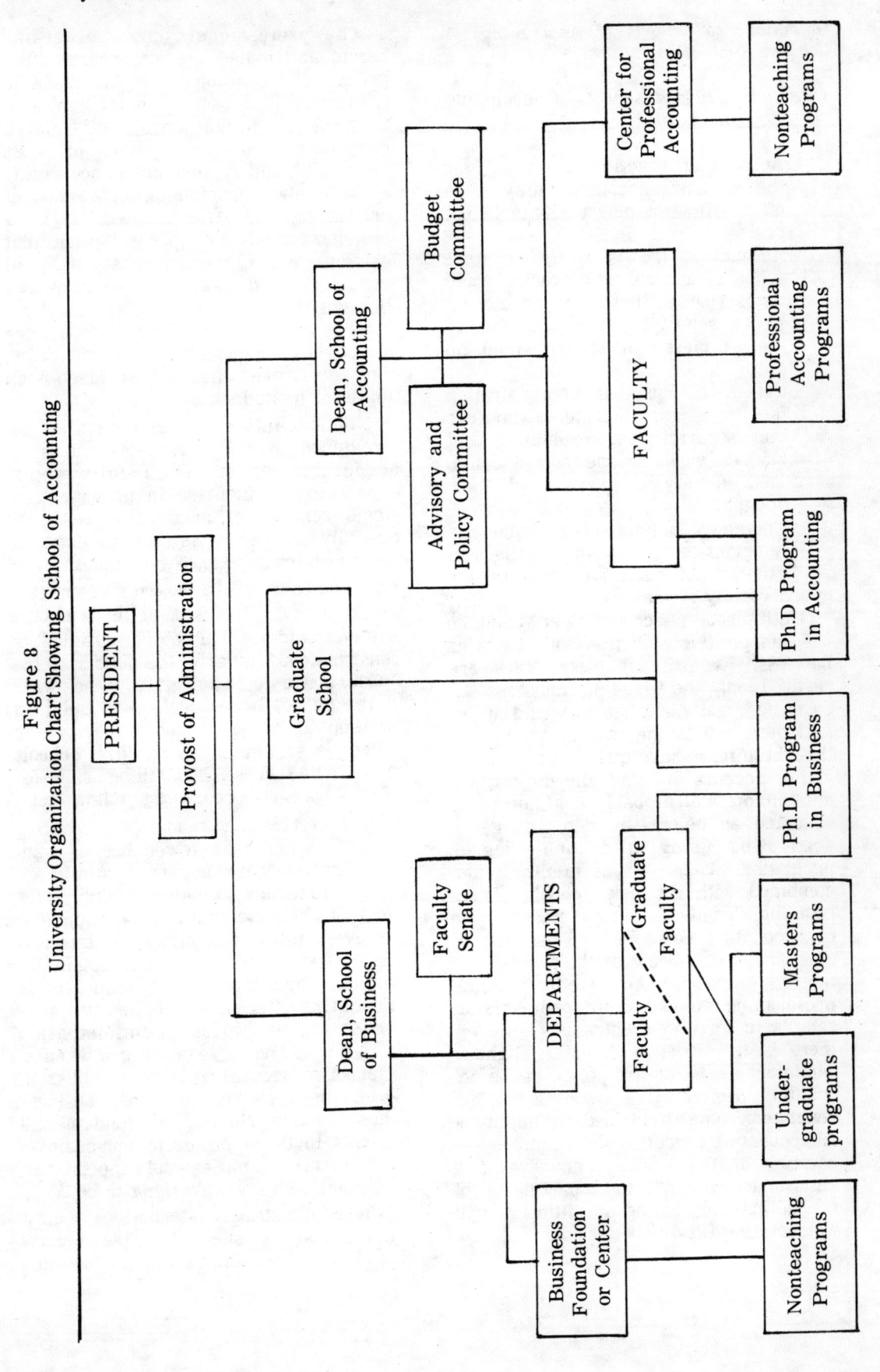

Figure 8
University Organization Chart Showing School of Accounting

Objections to Schools of Accounting: A Critical Evaluation

Those who object to schools of accounting fall into four classes:

> Accounting practitioners who fear that schools of accounting may choke off the flow of new entrants to the profession.
>
> Accounting faculty who fear that school of accounting curricula would be narrow, or that if they could not join a school of accounting faculty their professional status would be diminished.
>
> College of Business Administration faculty or administrators who fear that separation of accounting and business would reduce their students, their faculty numbers, and their budgets.
>
> University administrators who are reluctant to approve any changes in existing administrative structures for a variety of reasons.

Until schools of accounting are tried, no one can positively dismiss such fears as baseless. Even if all these fears are realized, only the first few schools of accounting initially in existence would suffer. And there are strong reasons to suppose that these fears have little basis.

For decades to come, the majority of accountants will probably continue to be educated as before—by departments of accounting using traditional degree programs. These departments, when combined with the new schools of accounting, should not alter the present scale of accounting educations. Expansion of programs should occur as the profession's needs require. Admittedly, some professions do use their professional schools to limit new entrants; however, there is no evidence that the slightest sentiment exists for this policy in the accounting profession. As schools of accounting become established, the quality of an accounting education should improve—certainly in the schools themselves and almost as certainly in departments of accounting. Accounting practitioners will welcome the flow of better-educated new CPAs.

The professional school programs herein anticipated are not narrow. The pattern of education would be to obtain fundamental accounting in the school of accounting, fundamentals of related disciplines from the faculties of those disciplines, and applications in accounting of these related disciplines in the school of accounting. This would appear to be a broader educational approach than that currently found, in which substantially all career-related material is acquired through the school of business faculty—most of whom are not primarily computer scientists, sociologists, mathematicians, and so on, even though they teach such material to students.

No accounting faculty member is threatened by the advent of schools of accounting. Accounting faculty would experience an increase in prestige if a single school of accounting was successfully established. As a broad analogy, a person who owns a $20,000 house is happy to have someone build a $40,000 house next to his; it increases the value of his own house and he would not think of discouraging its construction. Similarly, the builder of the $40,000 house would be pleased if the owner of the $20,000 house decided to build an addition to it; again, the value of both houses is enhanced. As the first schools prove to be successful, it will be easier for more schools of accounting to follow them.

It is certain that school of accounting students would take fewer business administration courses; they would go directly to faculties in other disciplines for most knowledge outside accounting. However, other disciplines in business administration may also be trending in this direction, and the specific reduction in accounting students enrolled in non-accounting business administration courses would occur regardless of whether a school of accounting were established. Given the crowding in most business schools, some shifting of fundamental students to the appropriate non-business administration faculties would appear to be a prudent and desirable thing to do.

The administrative alternatives in most universities are such that the faculty available for accounting and information systems could be retained in the college of business administration for academic reasons and still, for budgetary purposes, be attached to a school of accounting. The use of joint appointments, cross-listed courses, and interdisciplinary programs appears to have sufficient flexibility to preserve faculty ties between accounting and business administration. While the school of accounting accommodates intensive attention to accounting students, there should be no lack of willingness on the part of accounting faculty to offer accounting courses to college of business administration and other non-accounting students and to hold open for non-accounting students a number of seats in courses intended for school of accounting students.

Another likelihood is that colleges of business administration will develop non-accounting courses in the area of information management to offer as electives to their own students. Information management is a discipline relating to

> ...a widely felt need for individuals who can bring to bear the relevant computer technology on the information requirements of particular organizations....A body of knowledge exists for both organizational functions and information technology, but this knowledge is currently offered in diverse areas....[2]

Colleges of business, schools of accounting, and computer science departments may join to create truly interdisciplinary programs in information management as a major contribution to business knowledge and practice.

University budgets are affected by factors other than organizational structure. In general, if one administrative unit is split into two or more units, the sum of the budgets of these units is more than the budget of the original unit. A school of accounting and a college of business could expect to split more money than the original college budget. University administrators know this and tend to resist administrative-unit proliferation unless it is consistent with the public interest. Thus, the prospect of schools of accounting is actually a prospect for more funds for non-accounting programs in schools of business, not less; particularly since a separate identity will enhance fund-raising abilities.

Accounting curricula may *increase* in academic content as they come under control of schools of accounting. There will be more lines of communication for faculty and students to primary disciplines and there will be more applied research in problem areas of accounting. A diminishing of academic content has not occurred in the programs of any of the major professions;they are too closely related to both practice and the primary disciplines for such a diminishing to be long unnoticed or uncorrected.The fear of diminished academic content in accounting programs appears to be one of the least likely to be realized.

As for competition to win prestige and other intangible attributes of success, the school of accounting will address itself to a constituency fundamentally different from that of the college of business. Business managers and professional accountants are different groups. In the areas of overlap (such as information systems) competition should be desirable so long as it avoids duplication of degree programs and course offerings. Neither accounting nor business adminstration need fear competition. There is already beneficial competition among colleges of business administration and departments of economics, mathematics, engineering, and computer science.

The inflexibility of college administrators derives from their reluctance to bend the university structure to every passing fad and style in higher education. Most administrators are found to be reasonable and cooperative if they are approached with a well-conceived proposal with demonstrated support by substantial elements of the community. The school of accounting concept can be made into such a proposal and the proposal can generate public support at any number of major universities.

The ultimate response to objections to

schools of accounting will be the performance of these schools when they finally exist. In anticipating this performance and the contribution it will make to accounting and the public interest, it is well to remember that no one is at present suggesting that law schools be reorganized as "law departments" in schools of political science, or that medical schools be made into "departments of medicine" within colleges of applied life science. The professional schools are part of their profession, and their independence is one of the most jealously guarded sources of renewal and continuity of a profession. If schools of accounting already existed, surely no one would seek to reform them into departments!

SUMMARY AND CONCLUSIONS

Accounting has developed to the point at which, as a profession, it needs what all other mature professions have: schools of accounting, controlled by their faculties and responsive to the needs of the accounting profession. Although departments of accounting have served the profession in the past and will surely continue to do so, they cannot serve as the comprehensive and diversified education centers accounting needs.

Creation of schools of accounting may be complex and difficult, but should not be impossible since no person or institution will be worse off as a result of their emergence. Professional programs could be offered effectively through schools of accounting which were either fully independent or within schools of business. An independent school could expect to be placed in a division headed by a "Provost of Administration" and including also schools of public administration, business administration, and perhaps economics. The greater the degree of autonomy for the school of accounting, the more flexible and responsive it could be in serving as an education center for the accounting profession.

Ultimately, the justification for schools of accounting must be the services rendered by the accounting profession itself in the public interest, for those services may not continue or expand without schools of accounting.

How might a particular faculty go about establishing a school of accounting? No one procedure will be successful at all schools, but a few generalizations are possible. An accounting faculty at most universities cannot "step out" of the university administrative structure and directly petition the board of governors for a school of accounting. Yet, this group will have to approve any major change, and such proposals are slow to work their way up through their prescribed channels. Indeed, a board of governors or regents will be reluctant to act unless they perceive broad accounting profession and public support for schools of accounting. A first step would seem to be to establish that such support exists and is visible.

Assume that this has been done. Perhaps a group of practitioners may approach the board of governors with a request that the institution they govern establish a school of accounting. The board will seek the advice of the president, who will in turn go to the dean of the college of business and the accounting faculty.

Since the advice of non-accounting faculty will be sought by the president and the board of governors, it is important that the accounting faculty take the time and have the patience to explain the school of accounting to the non-accounting faculty.

Thus, no school of accounting proposal that is conceived as simply "putting one over" on hostile business faculty associates or escaping the authority of an unfriendly dean is likely to be successful. The school of accounting proposal must from the first be approached as something that will be beneficial to all affected parties, and when presented must attract their support.

The board of governors should, after being presented a proposal by influential professional accountants and having the proposal recommended favorably by its administrative officers, approve the proposal and establish the school of accounting.

The accounting profession needs schools of accounting now. It is possible to establish them. The responsibilities of practitioners and faculties should be clear: prepare proposals and secure support (in and out of the University) for them and the schools they will create.

FOOTNOTES

[1] See, for example,

Robert A. Gordon and James E. Howell, *Higher Education for Business*, (New York: Columbia University Press, 1959) pp. 194-197

John J. Clark and Blaise J. Opulente (eds.) *Professional Education for Business*, (Jamaica, New York: St. John's University Press, 1964) pp. 105-107.

The Pierson Report takes an equivalent tone.

[2] ACM Curriculum Committee on Computer Education for Management, "Curriculum Recommendations for Graduate Professional Programs in Information Systems," *Communications of the ACM*, May, 1972, pp. 364-398.

REFERENCES

Buckley, John W., "A Perspective on Professional Accounting Education," *The Journal of Accountancy*, August, 1970, pp. 41-47.

Burton, John C., "An Educator Views the Public Accounting Profession," *The Journal of Accountancy*, September, 1971, pp. 47-53.

Carey, John L., "Teachers and Practitioners," *Accounting Review*, January, 1969, pp. 79-87.

Cheek, Billy K., "The Development of a Professional," in Education & Professional Training section, *The Journal of Accountancy*, February, 1971, pp. 85-87.

Davidson, Sidney, "The CPA and the Educator," in Education & Professional Training section, *The Journal of Accountancy*, February, 1971, pp. 85-87.

Lockley, Lawrence C., "Some Comments Regarding University Education," in the Education & Professional Training section, *The Journal of Accountancy*, May, 1969, pp. 94-97.

Lynn, Edward S., "Professional Schools of Accountancy," *The Journal of Accountancy*, May, 1965, pp. 87-89.

Miller, Herbert E., "The Environment of Accounting Profession," *The Journal of Accountancy*, January, 1966, pp. 80-83.

Paton, William A., "Accounting's Educational Eclipse," in Editor's Notebook, *The Journal of Accountancy*, December, 1971, pp. 35-37.

Paton, William A., "Earmarks of a Profession—and the APB," *The Journal of Accountancy*, January, 1971, pp. 37-45.

Phillips, Lawrence C., "A Professional School of Accountancy: An Alternative to a School of Management," *The Texas CPA*, July, 1972, pp. 30-34.

Savoie, Leonard M., "The Professional School of Accountancy," in Editor's Notebook, *The Journal of Accountancy*, November, 1971, pp. 33-35.

Smith, C. Aubrey, "Accountancy: Circa 2000 AD," *The Accounting Review*, January, 1954, pp. 64-71.

Stone, Williard E., "The Challenge of the Beamer Committee Report," in Education & Professional Training section, *The Journal of Accountancy*, March, 1971, pp. 86-88.

Welsch, Glen A., "Is Accountancy An Academic Discipline?" in the Education & Professional Training section, *The Journal of Accountancy*, May, 1966, pp. 81-82.

Williams, Thomas H., "MAS and the Expanded Meaning of an Accounting Education" working paper 72-11, distributed by Bureau of Business Research, The University of Texas at Austin, 1971, p. 19.

Rigidity or Systematic Flexibility?

J. C. Kinard
C. H. Stanley
Ohio State University

Introduction

The college accounting classroom is rapidly changing its character. One of the many causes and symptoms of change is the increasing participation on the part of the student. Professors Kinard and Stanley provide a cogent historical review, a strong philosophical statement in favor of constructive participation and—perhaps most useful—a documented set of materials as the nucleus for any attempt at implementing one's belief in "different courses for different students." Their paper is an interesting translation of liberal educational philosophy into an eminently practical introductory accounting course.

The course of the history of innovations in educational theory and practice may be charted along any of a number of dimensions. A dimension which we find particularly revealing is one which views the movement of education away from rigidity and toward flexibility. The philosophical viewpoints which underlay the medieval scholastic conception of education as the servant of theology metamorphosed into a conception that education in the liberal arts could also serve such proximate goals as preparation for life, including practice of the learned professions of law and medicine.

This enlargement of the goals of education occurred gradually, almost imperceptibly, over a long period of time. Having happened, however, goal expansion inevitably required the introduction of subjects into the curriculum which were specific to the particular program or course of study elected by the students. Multiple goals suggested the need for multiple paths to achieve those goals. Multiple paths suggested the need for a basic unit of academic bookkeeping—the course or credit hour—which could be used to describe and record the student's progress toward his degree goals. This scorekeeping scheme granted the student an impressive measure of freedom to change his degree goal, his program of major study, even his academic institution.

The use of an input measure—the credit hour—to define a unit of output—learning—is not without its problems, both philosophical and practical. Still, it is entirely appropriate to view the dramatic expansion of the alternatives open to the student as evidence of a rejection of a rigid formula for a single educational path for all students in favor of a system more responsive to the individual goals of the students. Indeed, the virtual hegemony of the credit-hour system is a milestone in educational philosophy and practice marking the demise of scholasticism and the birth of the system in existence today.

But the progression toward academic flexibility is far from complete. The rigidity which once characterized the entire macro-educational system finds its modern counterparts not only in the specification of formulas for degree requirements, such as 180 quarter hours of credit earned in a specified distribution, but also in the syllabus of requirements set for a specific course.

The attack on the first type of rigidity is well advanced through such studies as *Less Time, More Options*, published by The Carnegie Commission on Higher Education, and such activities as The

College Level Examination Program operated by The Educational Testing Service. In this paper, we are primarily interested in addressing the second problem—the problem of rigidity within an individual course.

Inflexibility Within a Course:

An almost universal description which one may give of the educational process in conventional college courses of instruction is "inflexibility." Typically, students may receive information through *scheduled* lectures and *required* textbooks; feedback on learning is gleaned through a number of *scheduled* examinations and *required* exercises; each student is treated *exactly like* any other student in terms of the course syllabus of topics, the pace of coverage of the topics, as well as other elements of the course.

The instructor in any course is typically faced with a student group composed of individuals with widely different backgrounds, both in terms of their previous exposure to the topics covered in the course and in their aptitude for and interest in various instructional approaches which the instructor might use. These same students may also have widely different reasons for taking the course and quite varied expectations concerning the nature and utility of what is to be learned in the course. At the same time, the instructor has both personal educational and institutional goals in offering the course, together with knowledge of the available or potentially available resources and technology for achieving both his and the students' goals.

In this section of the paper, we shall discuss some of the dimensions of flexibility which are available in any course of study, whatever the level or subject. In the following section, we shall describe an approach for implementing substantial flexibility in an introductory accounting course, the accounting course in which there is the largest potential for impact.

A student may be differentiated from his fellow students along any or all of the following dimensions, among others, in connection with a particular course of study:

1. prior knowledge of the content included in the course;
2. speed of learning and need for repetition;
3. learning media preference;
4. feedback timing preference;
5. purpose for taking the course in terms of type and depth of knowledge sought.

The scheme described below is one approach to treating each student in a course as an individual in terms of each of the dimensions described. First the instructor must carefully analyze the course topic content. We have chosen the term "module" to represent the smallest unit of knowledge into which the topic material will be divided, and "topic" to mean the logical grouping of these modules. Topics are the conventional subdivisions of a course syllabus. Furthermore, the instructor must analyze the material in terms of his conception of the best definition and sequencing of modules within topics. The result of this analysis will be a set of topics which defines the course content. In specifying the order of topics, the instructor is specifying both his educational goals relative to the subject matter and his pedagogical strategy for promoting the students' learning of the material.

Some instructors make such a detailed analysis of their course content, but many do not. As will become apparent in the following discussion, this analysis is essential for the other components of the design.

The second step is to construct a diagnostic plan to evaluate each student's entering knowledge level about each topic in the course. To implement this diagnostic phase, two steps are necessary. The first step is to recognize that the basic unit of diagnosis may be markedly different from the basic pedagogical elements previously described. A single diagnostic element, for instance, might provide for inferences about one, two, or perhaps more modules. Alternatively, several modules might be included in a single pedagogical element. The second step in the diagnostic phase is the practical one of developing the diagnostic instruments to be used.

Based on the results of the diagnosis, the instructor can supply a prescription of pedagogical elements which will allow the student to move from his entering knowledge level of each topic to a level of competence in the topics of the course determined by the place and purpose of the course in the curriculum.

The third, and a very important stage in the design, involves the learning environment in which the prescription may be "filled" by the student during the time frame of the course. Given the instructor's goals as evidenced in the content matrix, and given that the student can express his expectations and goals in equivalent terms, to the extent that these two sets are not equivalent, there is a fundamental political question of whose goals will be built into the course. The "answer" to this question found today in most courses in most schools gives complete weight to the goals of the instructor and invites the student to accept these goals on an all or nothing basis by registering for the entire course. Students have expressed some dissatisfaction with this system, not only by their comments, but also by their pressure to adjust the conditions in which courses may be taken to include "auditor" as well as "pass-no credit" registration status. Such differential registrations permit the student to exercise at least some of his goal preferences while at the same time exempting the instructor from the necessity of adjusting the standard specifications of his course.

But the achievement of diversity within the constraints imposed by uniformity is not the only possible answer to the political question. It might also be possible to permit students to have at least some voice in the specification of the content and goals of the courses they will be studying. One possibility is for the instructor to design the course after a series of votes by the students on dimensions of variability in the course, constraining the dimensions to those which are believed to be within the competence of the students. In this system, the educational desires of the majority are substituted for those of the instructor, but the results may indeed be no more nearly optimum than would be the case if the instructor simply designed the course based on his own experience.

A second possibility is to permit each student to design his own course within whatever constraints may be specified by the instructor and by the institution. In this system, there is a fair chance that at least a Paretian optimum, compared to the conventional approach, would be reached since each student would be following an individualized course of study which he helped to design and no student's choices would constrain those of any other student. Such individualized programs have indeed existed for some time in a variety of tutorial and honors programs, but they are very expensive relative to other modes of instruction, and this has limited their use.

Honors and tutorial programs have also in general failed to provide an answer to the question, "How shall the course allow for students' different aptitudes for and interest in the various available instructional techniques?" In response to this question, we believe that a flexible learning system should be provided so that, for each module within a subject, a variety of alternative learning media can be available for use by students. Any one learning medium is flexible in some ways (e.g., a live lecture is "interactive" while video-taped lectures are not) and inflexible in others (e.g., live lectures are at a fixed time and non-repeatable while video-taped lectures are flexibly timed and repeatable).

The Merits of Flexibility

There are several advantages for a flexible learning media system. First, it permits each student to play to his own strengths and preferences by choosing the learning media which he believes are the most efficient and enjoyable. Second, its use allows the student to escape from the tedium and the tyranny of a system which forces him to read his textbook chapter by chapter and attend a series of lectures whose relentlessness within a term is relieved only occasionally by an Act of Congress establishing Monday holidays. The student cannot only build a degree of variety of learning media into his course of study, but can also exercise a significant degree of control over the pace at which he will undertake his studies. Third, the student may use more than one learning medium for a particular module if he believes it would be beneficial for whatever reason.

The achievement of these advantages for students does not come without cost, and much of the cost must, of course, be borne by the instructor. Some resistance to the introduction of such a system must be anticipated from those who believe the substitution of student preferences for those of the instructor will result in a lowering of standards. We do not believe this argument to have much merit, but those who would attempt to implement the ideas we describe here would be wise to be prepared to justify them to some of their colleagues. The major cost is in the nature of an investment of the instructor's time and effort in collecting and developing the learning materials which manifest the learning media to be made available to the student for each module. Most of the materials currently available were designed to fit into another system, and their use in our system requires that transitional material be prepared which will articulate the various parts of the course. This is an enormous, unending task. Fortunately, once established this system turns out to be flexible from the standpoint of the instructor as well as the student, for the instructor can withdraw any learning medium for a particular module for revision without affecting the rest of his course.

The end result of the prescription phase of an introductory course such as we envision is a syllabus of study for each student which specifies modules which the student needs to study and lists the media of instruction which are available to the student for each module. Armed with this information, the student can formulate a plan of study which satisfies his learning media preferences, his learning rate preferences, and repetition preferences. The dimensions of flexibility which are considered here are to offer a variety of learning media for each pedagogical module, to offer at least one repeatable type of learning medium and at least one non-scheduled type so that a student may vary the speed of coverage from the conventional "lock step" progression, and so that repeated coverage of a module is possible.

Finally, step four would be to provide feedback on the student's knowledge of any topic at any (or, at least, many) points during the time frame of the course.

An Individualized Introductory Accounting Course:

The implementation of the approach described in the preceding section in the context of a comprehensive introductory accounting "course" (which might represent a two-semester or three-quarter introductory course sequence at the undergraduate level or a one-semester or two-quarter introductory course sequence at the MBA level), is described in the following paragraphs.

The following topic-module list and sequence network are illustrative of the first step described above. Each topic is described in terms of modules for both diagnostic and pedagogy purposes. Following the topic list is a diagram illustrating the sequence-of-topic-coverage assumptions which underlie the topic-module list.

COMPREHENSIVE INTRODUCTORY ACCOUNTING COURSE
PROFIT-ORIENTED ENTITY FINANCIAL ACCOUNTING MODEL SECTION

Topic	Module	Diagnosis	Pedagogy
1. BALANCE SHEET:	Entity Concept	1	1
	Definition of Asset, Liability, Residual Ownership	1	1
	Balance Sheet Algebra: A-L equals RO	1	1
	Stock (Point-in-time) Concept	1	1
	Chart of Accounts for Balance Sheet	2	2
	Categories and "Term" Classification Conventions	2	2
	Uses of the Balance Sheet	3	3

Topic	Module	Diagnosis	Pedagogy
2. TRANSACTION ANALYSIS:	Transaction as a Flow (Change in Account Balances)	1	1
	Transaction Measurement: Cost Basis Valuation	2	2
	A Processing Model for B/S Account Changes	2	3
3. INCOME STATEMENT:	Flow (Thru-time) Concept	1	1
	Flow Algebra: A = L+RO+R-E	1	1
	Chart of Accounts for R & E	1	2
	Income Statement Internal Structure	2	3
	Adjusting and Closing Entries	2	3
	Uses of the Income Statement	2	3
4. ALTERNATIVE ACCOUNTING INFORMATION PROCESSING MODELS:	Double Entry: Original Entry General Journal "T" Account	1	1
	Matrix Model	2	2
	Single Entry: Special Journal	3	3
	Double Posting: Subsidiary Ledger	4	4
5. TIMING OF MEASUREMENT OF FLOWS:	Timing or Recognition Issue	1	1
	Cash and Accrual Basis	1	1
	Adjusting Entries	1	2
	Closing Entries	1	2
6. VALUATION:	Valuation Concepts: Exchange and Use Value	1	1
	Historical and Current Exchange	1	1
	Opportunity Cost	1	1
	Entry and Exit Exchange	1	1
	Economic Behavior Based on Valuation	2	2
	Decision Rules Based on Valuation	2	2

Topic	Module	Diagnosis	Pedagogy
7. TIME VALUE OF MONEY:	Time Preference (Opportunity Cost)	1	1
	Resource Flow (Cash) Patterns	1	2
	Present Value and Future Value	2	3
	Computational	2	3
	Rate of Return	3	4
8. EQUITIES:	Capital Funding	1	1
	Capital Structure	1	1
	Borrowing Decision	1	1
Liabilities:	Classification of Short Term Items	2	2
	Long Term Liabilities and Time Value	3	3
	Interest Rates	3	3
	Discount-Premiums	3	3
Residual Equities:	Contributed Capital	4	4
	Convertible Debt	4	4
	Retained Earnings	5	5
	Dividends: Asset & Stock	5	5
9. ASSETS:	Assets: Concepts	1	1
	Monetary vs. Non-Monetary	1	1
Monetary:	Short-Term: Cash Receivables (Valuation)	2	2
	Long-Term: Marketable Securities	3	2
	Notes-Bonds-Treasury Bills	3	2
	Notes Receivable	3	2
	Bonds Receivable	3	2
Non-Monetary:	Short-Term: Inventory (Decisions)	4	3
	Acquisition Cost	4	3
	Cost Flow Concepts	5	3
	Market Valuation (LCOM)	5	3
	Marketable Securities (Stocks-Market Valuation)	6	3

Topic	Module	Diagnosis	Pedagogy
	Long-Term: Acquisition Cost	7	4
	Expected Salvage: Physical Life / Economic Life / Productivity	7	4
	Straight-Line Amortization Model	8	5
	Production Amortization Model	9	5
	Sum of the Years' Digits	9	5
	Declining Balance at X Times SL Rate	9	5
	Alterations	10	6
	Retirement	10	6
10. FUNDS:	Flow Definitions: Funds Flow / Cash Flow / Income Flow	1	1
	Representation of Funds Flow in Processing Models	2	2
	Operations vs. Investment-Capital Structure	3	3
	Uses and Interpretations of the Funds Statement	3	4
11. BUSINESS COMBINATIONS:	Methods of Acquisition & Control	1	1
	New Entity Valuation on Combination or Acquisition	2	2
	Separate Entity Consolidation / Investment Accounting / Inter-Company Transactions	3	3
12. PRICE LEVELS:	Price Changes: General / Specific	1	1
	Accounting for Price Level Changes	1	2
	Used to Modify a Valuation Method	2	2
	Gain or Loss from Price Changes / Monetary / Non-Monetary	3	3
13. INCOME TAXATION:	Taxable Income vs. Financial Income	1	1
	Tax Liability Accounting	2	1
	Tax Rate Structures	3	2
	Decision Impact of Taxation	3	2

Rigidity or Systematic Flexibility?

Topic	Module	Diagnosis	Pedagogy
14. THE AUDITOR'S REPORT:	CPA Opinions & Attestation	1	1
	Statement Footnotes	1	1
15. FINANCIAL STATEMENT INTERPRETATION:	Ratios	1	1

MANAGERIAL ACCOUNTING MODEL SECTION

Topic	Module	Diagnosis	Pedagogy
M1. PRODUCT COSTING:	Costing Concepts: Cost Flow (Attachment) with Physical Transformation	1	1
	Cost Allocation Where Joint	1	1
	Costing Models: Job	1	2
	Process	2	2
M2. STANDARD COSTING & VARIANCE ANALYSIS:	Variable Cost Inputs	1	
	Capacity Concepts and Fixed Cost Inputs	2	1
	Incurred Cost vs. Standard Cost and Rationale for Variances	3	2
	Variance Algebra	4	3
M3. COST & REVENUE BEHAVIOR:	Cost Behavior Measurement	1	1
	Revenue Behavior Measurement	1	1
	Breakeven Concept	1	2
	Measurement Techniques	2	3
M4. MARGINAL ANALYSIS FOR DECISIONS:	Incremental Flows	1	1
	Comparison of Alternatives	1	1
	Selection Criteria	2	2
	Direct Comparison	3	2
	Present Value	3	2
	Rate of Return	3	2
	Risk	4	3

Topic	Module	Diagnosis	Pedagogy
M5. BUDGETING:	Forecasting	1	1
	Pro-Forma Statements	1	1
	Planning	1	2
	Control	2	3
	Budget Variances	2	3
M6. DECENTRALIZED OPERATIONS :	Entity Reconsidered	1	1
	Responsibility Accounting	1	2
	Cost and Profit Centers	1	2
	Goal Congruency	1	2
	Economic Model & Artificial Prices	2	3

NOT-FOR-PROFIT-ORIENTED ENTITY
FINANCIAL-CONTROL ACCOUNTING MODEL SECTION

Topic	Module	Diagnosis	Pedagogy
F1. "FUND" ACCOUNTING SYSTEMS :	Entity	1	1
	Chart of Accounts: Budgetary Accounts Appropriations Encumbrances	2	2
F2. PLANNING & CONTROL SYSTEMS :	Cost-Benefit Analysis	1	1
	Budget Methods: Object of Expenditure Program	2	2

Rigidity or Systematic Flexibility? 103

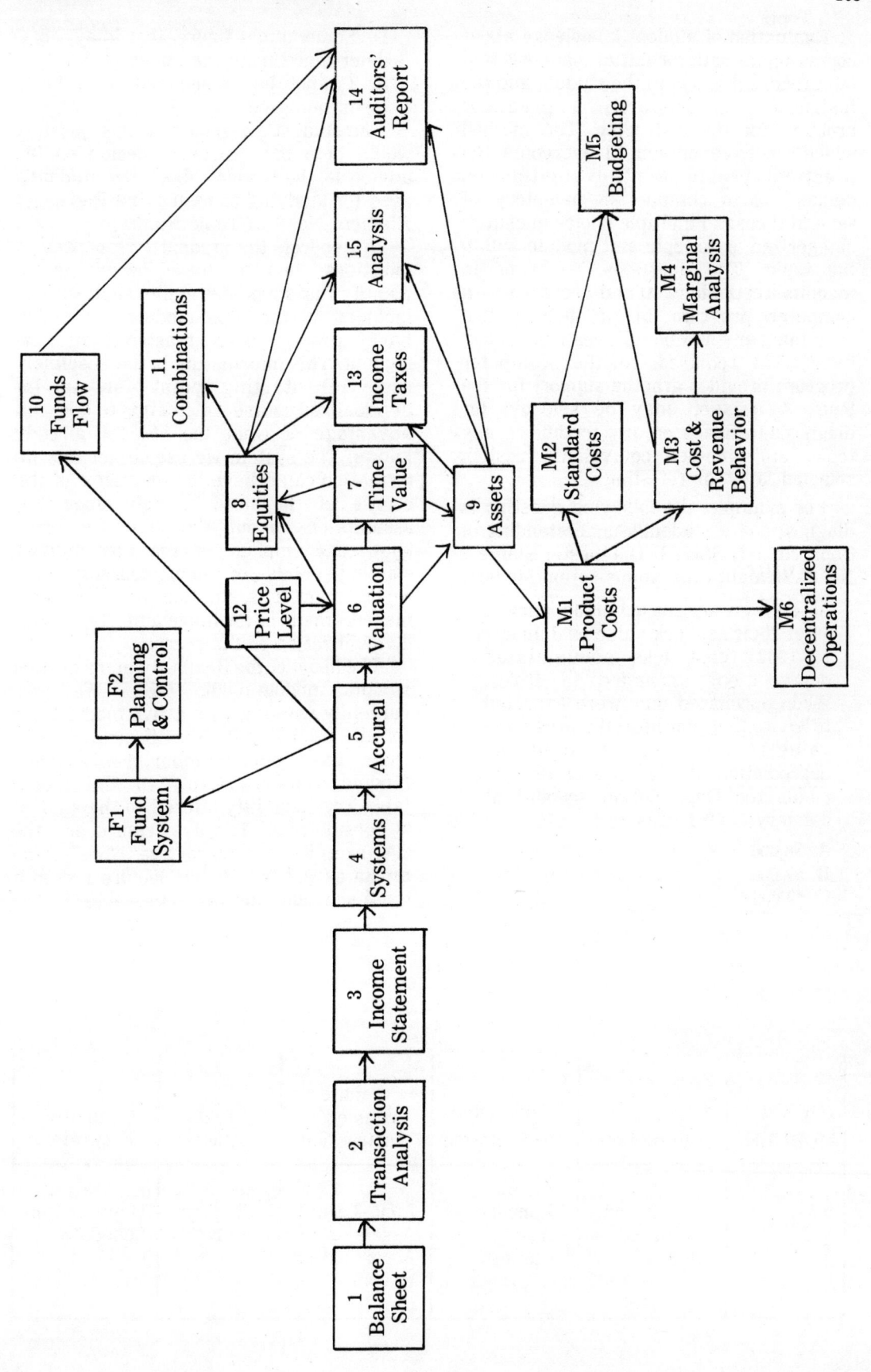

1 Balance Sheet
2 Transaction Analysis
3 Income Statement
4 Systems
5 Accrual
6 Valuation
7 Time Value
8 Equities
9 Assets
10 Funds Flow
11 Combinations
12 Price Level
13 Income Taxes
14 Auditors' Report
15 Analysis

F1 Fund System
F2 Planning & Control

M1 Product Costs
M2 Standard Costs
M3 Cost & Revenue Behavior
M4 Marginal Analysis
M5 Budgeting
M6 Decentralized Operations

Evaluation of student knowledge about course topics both for initial diagnosis and later feedback (to both the student and the instructor) is primarily a practical problem for the instructor. The method which we have chosen to overcome the practical problems of evaluation on demand is to compile an inventory of several thousand multiple choice questions categorized as to topic and module within the topic. The questions are kept in machine readable form and accessed by a computer program to produce a test containing any number of questions on any topic(s) as required. Another computer program provides grading support for the tests. A question may be selected for diagnosis-feedback on any module in any topic, and another equivalent question selected later for retesting.

For example, the following question is diagnostic of a student's understanding of Topic No. 9 (ASSETS) Diagnostic Element No. 8 (Straight-Line Amortization Model):

Assets were purchased on January 1, 1960. Their net book value on January 1, 1962 (cost less accumulated depreciation) amounted to $6,000. When purchased they were expected to have a five year life with no salvage value. Assuming straight-line depreciation, the balance of the Accumulated Depreciation account at January 1, 1961, was:

A. $8,000
B. $7,500
C. $2,000
D. Some other figure that may be determined from the above
E. Cannot be determined from information given

The student's response to this question would help the instructor decide on his advice to the student about the student's need for studying or restudying Pedagogy Element No. 5 in Topic No. 9.

In general, the student's responses to questions such as these permit us to identify those modules within each subject included in the topic-module list which have already been mastered by the student. This information is the absolutely essential starting point for an individualized course which aims to take full advantage of what the student already knows. The system we use to get this information can relieve the instructor of the course of the need to rely upon the assumptions about the student's prior knowledge implicit in the conventional starting points of such courses. This replacement of assumption with diagnostic measurement is an important step to individualization of the course.

The heart of the flexibility in the system is the module-media table. We are currently working with a five-media table for the module list. For illustration consider the Topic number 9—Pedagogy Module number 5 row in the media table. The flexibility offered to the student is considerable. The live lecture and the CAI exercise are interactive. None of the media except for the live lecture are on a fixed schedule and are repeatable.

<u>MEDIA</u>

TOPIC-MODULE	Live Interaction	Video-Tape Presentation	Computer Assisted Instruction	Text-Book	Computer Program
9-5	Lecture on 13 March 1973	Long-Term Assets Cassette	Long-Term Assets Amortization Exercise	Chapter 7	Depreciation Schedule Generator

The Advantages of a Flexible Course:

"Treating each student as an individual" is the purpose of the course flexibility which we have described.

In the context of a regular university course, we envision several advantages for such flexibility. First, a student can be given, based on the diagnostic phase, a course syllabus customized to reflect the knowledge which he as a unique individual needs to gain to satisfy the course requirements. Also, it permits each student to choose the learning media which he prefers. In addition, a student can monitor his progress by reentering the diagnostic phase at any time, for with several thousand questions available we can automatically generate any number of different exams which are equivalent in terms of topic coverage and difficulty. Finally, a student may use more than one learning medium for a particular module if he feels it would be beneficial for whatever reason.

Although we have limited our attention here to the development of the introductory course, the same conception can be extended, by the addition of topics and modules, to cover the more advanced subjects usually found in the accounting major courses. Similarly, as technological innovations in learning media are developed, they can be appended to our system at a relatively small cost. Such sensitive problems as the transferability of credits from junior to senior colleges and the use of experience to satisfy at least some degree requirements can be fairly handled in our system.

An unexplored, but perhaps more novel, use of such a scheme is outside a fixed course environment. A person interested solely in acquiring knowledge of a subject (perhaps a highly customized subset of the broad topic set) rather than in course credit should find such a system extremely efficient and responsive. Also, in the continuing education area where work and lecture schedules often conflict or in a "refresher" mode of study, a flexible system offers interesting possible advantages.

Directions in the Academic Study of Accounting

John W. Kennelly
University of Oklahoma
Louis F. Biagioni
University of Iowa

Introduction

Institutional diversity is a highly prized norm for Professors Kennelly and Biagioni. Their paper develops the links between teaching and research, between concept and procedure and between costs and benefits in education. In arguing for the desirability of diversity, the authors challenge the notion of a global norm as advocated by the Price Waterhouse Study Group on the introductory course.

Questions about the direction of accounting education are important and current. For any of us to think that these issues can be resolved on "a once and for all" basis is, in our judgment, inappropriate. No answer can be expected to persist over time, given the continuing evolution of the underlying discipline. Further, we submit that no single view at any point in time is necessarily appropriate for all educational institutions. As the title of this paper indicates, we are most concerned with "academic" study; however, to ignore other vehicles for generating and transmitting the subject matter to interested parties would lead to a clear danger of sub-optimization. Put another way, we wish to consider "academic" study in the context of study generally, including self-study, on-the-job training, and other mechanisms.

In this paper, we set forth some strong views on the study of accounting and the education of accountants, where the latter is treated as a sub-set of the former. In the course of our argument we express some disagreement with the Price Waterhouse Foundation Study Group, despite our sympathy with some of the ideas advanced by the Study Group[1] Our major contention is that a *single answer* cannot be expected to answer a set of significantly *different questions*. We would supplant the Price Waterhouse *question:* "(implicitly) How should (all) students be introduced to the subject of accounting?" with a set of questions relating the same question to *subsets* of the student population but recognizing important *differences* between as well as similarities amoung sub-sets of the student population. We depart in several ways from the line of reasoning set forth by Porter in his summary of the 1970-71 symposia on the AICPA Committee on Educations and Experience Requirements (CEER)[2] Porter, of course, was attempting to reflect the symposia conclusions, and the symposia were directed toward the "academic preparation for professional accounting careers."[3] We submit that this function is only a part of the goal structure of academic institutions, in the large, although some institutions may properly specialize in such a manner.

Our approach to explicating the issues, and to developing our comments on them, may be summarized as follows: First, we consider the study of accounting generally, not limiting the discussion to academic study. Second, we use this perspective to consider the aspects of the study of accounting which appear (at least) to be most appropriately conducted in an academic setting. Third, we attempt to set forth those elements of academic study most integral to the educational preparation of accountants. Finally, we consider the institutional structure of academic study in an effort to identify the attributes of curriculum, staffing and resource employment which must concern us in planning future directions for academic institutions.

The central theme of our remarks, as implied above, is one of diversity—in students, in institutions, and in educational goals. We should recognize that we should not, even if we could, seek homogeneity across institutions or over time. The fundamental bases for this contention are : (1) differing resource limitations within and among educational institutions, and (2) uncertainty about the future directions of the discipline and (3) the costs of adjustment. These premises are explored more fully below.

The Study of Accounting

We hesitate to characterize "accounting" in a very strict fashion because, at the boundaries, the field is continually evolving. We can perhaps agree that the production of periodic financial reports for investors is an accounting function. However, some other topics, for example, "non-financial" performance reports, have been subject to debate as to whether or not they are "accounting" topics.[4] On the other hand, some have attempted to bound accounting by drawing distinctions between "accounting" and "bookkeeping." We wish to avoid such semantic arguments. Hence, we characterize accounting in a way which is admittedly arbitrary.

Accounting is characterized as the set of report generating systems charged with supplying decision-makers with summaries of the financial effects of economic events. In turn, the study of accounting is the study of how these systems perform and the comparison of such performance with that of proposed alternative systems. The way(s) study of the "performance of accounting" is conducted is obviously a function of the purpose of the inquiry.

We submit that it is convenient to look at accounting in several dimensions. First, we can treat the *levels of accounting choice:* between models, methods, or techniques. Second, we can establish *perspectives of analysis:* "private" or "social" perspectives. Finally, we can establish the *scope of analysis:* accounting systems or information systems (of which accounting systems are a part). The relation between level of choice and scope of analysis is illustrated in Table 1. In this table we have for simplicity suppressed the dimension "perspectives of analysis".

As to the second dimension, perspective of analysis, we can look at either the individual(private) choice problem, or the social (public) choice problem.[5] Within the first kind of analytical perspective one seeks to understand the forces shaping supply and demand for information. The second perspective of analysis deals with the ways in which social welfare is affected by the resources devoted to informations sytems.

The above characterization of dimensions of accounting aggregates to quite a bit of material for potential study. We suggest that no aspect of it should be ignored. On the other hand, an attempt to equally weight all aspects within the curricular constraints of two and four year undergraduate programs would result in a relatively shallow treatment of all. We suggest that we need to specialize the study of accounting in academic programs relative to other educational mechanisms. The question which then arises is : Where to concentrate our efforts?

The answers to this question are to be found partly in value judgments as to the relative importance of aspects of the discipline and partly in looking at the structure of the educational (or study) process itself. As academicians we wish to design curricula to transmit knowledge of those aspects of accounting which we think are : (1) most valuable to the students we serve, and (2) most efficiently transmitted in academic programs. We suspect that our answers to the first question will differ widely, and properly so.

In this sense, we find the Price Waterhouse Study Group report unsatisfying. Perhaps the Group was able to achieve consensus (though probably through compromise), but its answers to what should be taught, in Chapter 2, must be viewed as one of a set of possible orientations with no *a priori* reason to suppose that this orientation is superior to alternatives[6] We suspect instead that the best we can hope is that this report will be useful for *some* schools.

In the next section, we consider the second question just advanced: what knowledge is most efficiently transmitted in academic programs.

Academic Study of Accounting

We wish to avoid the commonly alleged distinction between teaching and research, especially as it pertains to academic programs. In our opinion, a student of the field of accounting has a choice of instruments (1) personal reading, (2) on-the-job study, (3) attendance at professional pro-

Table 1

The Study of Accounting
Illustrated in Two Dimensions*

	Scope of Analysis	
Level of Choice	Accounting	Information
Models	Accrual accounting vs. Current Cash Equivalent Replacement Cost	Accounting systems vs. other reporting systems as a basis for decisions—Economics of information
Methods (Assuming accrual model)	LIFO vs. FIFO Income Tax Deferrals	Decision-models as a basis for specifying accounting data requirements
Techniques (Assuming accrual methods)	Periodic v. Perpetual procedure in inventories	Forecasting properties of accounting data series

*Perspectives of analysis is suppressed in this table

grams and seminars, (4) attendance at degree-granting academic programs, to name a few broad categories. Note that if we define academic programs from the viewpoint of the student, the distinction between research and teaching disappears. The student uses an educational institution as an access mechanism to the subject field. Properly, then, the teacher serves as both an acquirer of the base (through research) and transmitter of acquired knowledge (through teaching). The student is substituting the teacher's research capability for his (her) own. The educational institution and the teacher are economically justified only to the extent that they represent less costly access mechanisms than alternatives, for example, self-study. Whether this is the case depends upon the teacher, the student, and the attributes of the field which are the subject of study. In any event, our function as academicians is to draw from the field (conduct research) and to transmit this to students directly (through "teaching") or indirectly (through publication of our findings).

What follows is an initial approach to cost-benefit analysis which the student of accounting might conduct in choosing the optimal combination of study instruments. Academic programs have distinct advantages and disadvantages relative to alternatives.

Academic programs emphasize transmittal to groups rather than to individuals. This confers certain economies in areas of common interest and concern in exchange for suppressing the unique interests of specific individuals. To the extent that a "common body of knowledge" exists, academic institutions may be the most efficient way of transmitting it to students. On the other hand, to the extent that individual students have unique requests for knowledge (based upon unique capabilities and unique interests) the advantage of academic, hence collective, programs diminishes relative to on-the-job, or self-study programs. If on the other hand students can be aggregated into sub-groups of varying capabilities, diverse academic programs can be developed which attempt to serve these various knowledge requests.

In this way, we need not reduce the field (in academic programs) to a single, therefore most general subject matter. Different programs can emphasize different aspects of the field, thus reducing the size of groups of concern and moving toward individual interests to the extent that they are diverse.

The amount of specialization will depend in part upon the diversity of student interests, and the relative importance of diverse versus common interests. It will depend in part upon the relative costs of serving these interests.

A major problem which arises here is the provision of sufficient knowledge of the available choices to students, many of whom are relatively unsophisticated at the entry level. It is incumbent upon us to provide this knowledge to students making the study choice. We suspect, for example, that study of accounting at different schools (even within one state) is quite different between schools. We suspect also that we each are guilty, to some extent, of granting to our own programs the unqualified evaluation of "better" or even "best". In fact, we merely are "different." We would each attempt to combine our faculty and students in ways which are optimal given that the products of us all can be "better" than the products of each of us. The important point to be made is that *there is no single "best" accounting program within the resource constraints which we all face and the nature of the field and the diversity among its students.*

Of course, the extent to which we specialize leads to two kinds of consequences. On the one hand, we become more valuable to students who share our interests and orientation. On the other hand, the number of students for whom this occurs can be expected to decrease. At some point which we are not prepared to suggest here, specialization (or generalization) becomes self-defeating because of these conflicting forces. For example, consider the teaching of managerial accounting and the case of "inventory accounting". More than 1,400 different inventory decision-models are now employed in industry. The differences are reflections of differences in situations. If we attempted to "teach" all of these models we would get hopelessly bogged down in detail. On the other hand, we do not think any of us would seriously suggest that the topic be entirely ignored. What most of us do is to choose one or more prototype models to illustrate common elements of inventory models—stock-out costs, etc.—

then leave specialization in particular techniques to firm programs, on-the-job training, and self-study.

To attempt to focus on particular details is too costly for (generalized) academic programs relative to (specialized) firm programs.

We submit that this observation holds for a wide range of accounting topics. We must learn to *emphasize the illustrative role of procedures* in academic programs. Too often this is forgotten, and we make the dangerous comparison between one member of the set of acceptable procedures and one member of the set of unacceptable procedures, giving the student the incorrect perception that there exists a "right" and a "wrong" procedure. This error is not prevented by most text materials available for our use.

Further, the foregoing observation leads to the illusory conflict between "conceptual" and "procedural" or between "theoretical" and "practical."[7] None of us, we hope, would go to either extreme. If "theory" does not have "practical" implications it is doubtful usefulness, at best. On the other hand, procedures cannot be understood without some organizing concepts to explain them and their interrelationships.

In terms of our earlier explication of the subject matter of accounting, we may choose to emphasize model, method, or procedure *choice*. Each becomes more specialized, and none can really ignore the others, though those not emphasized may only be treated implicitly. The point to be made is that whatever the level of choice, it is the *choice* which is of concern to the accountant, not procedures, methods, or models *per se*.

In order to make choices, we must find relevant ways of characterizing the alternatives, of characterizing the scope of analysis, and of characterizing the criterion employed. Hence, we require that our students study cognate fields relevant to these aspects of accounting choice. This is also the reason that students other than students of accounting *per se* are commonly required to study accounting as a subject cognate to their areas of primary interest.

This observation leads naturally to the distinction we draw in the next section between the study of accounting and the educational preparation

Educational Preparation of Accountants.

We have already suggested that educational institutions may specialize to fulfill certain aims of students in their programs. Within institutions we can observe the same specialization, reflected in part by "majors" in programs. To the extent that "majors" differ in areas of substantive study we can expect courses to offer these specialized studies. To the extent that subject matter is common across interest groups, we can see the courses generalizing instead of specializing. One of the major questions facing academic program decision-makers generally and accounting curriculum decisions in particular is the degree of specialization within collegiate level academic programs. Once again, we suggest that a diversity of responses is more appropriate than any attempt to reach consensus about a single "best" program. The more specific a student's goal in study becomes, the more specific a program of study can become, at least potentially. At the poles of this sort of continuum, are specific on-the-job training or self-study which are highly specific, and at least some undergraduate liberal arts programs which are highly general. Academic programs in accounting can hardly be expected to supplant either of these extremes. However, this still leaves an incredibly wide range of options open. We are convinced that the preferred circumstances would be those in which schools would offer *different* options rather than attempting to converge to some "golden mean".

In this sense, we are not sympathetic to alarmists who would see a "submergence" of accounting as a specialization or chauvinists who would see an expansion of accounting to subsume all information systems under an accounting mantle.

We see neither generalized education nor "professional" schools of accounting as global answers because we do not see a global question. Rather, we see these as extreme solutions along a continuum. In our judgment, common attributes of conceptual, analytical approaches serve to identify the domain of academic study, but within this general framework a range of answers regarding specific content and structure of academic programs is appropriate.

An important sub-set of the population of students is the set of individuals with little education beyond public school level who have tentatively selected to pursue an accounting career. Another set is the group of individuals with various non-accounting baccalaureate degrees who wish to become accountants with the aid of graduate academic study. Individuals already engaged in the profession but wishing to pursue further academic study of their chosen field constitute a third important group. In this section we focus upon such groups, for the moment suppressing the wishes of others desiring academic study of accounting (for example, managers who must deal with accounting and accountants on a regular basis).

The question we seek to answer is: to what extent are the academic subjects and the approach to these subjects distinct for accountants relative to others?

We characterize the central function of the accountant as one of choosing between alternative accounting system and of implementing the choice. (that is, we see the production of accounting reports as a process analogous to the production of any other economic good, and we assign the role of manager in the general case to the accountant in the special case).

Users of the accounting product (reports) wish to know product characteristics, and they wish to know enough of the production process (accounting system) and quality control process (auditing) to assess the degree of reliance which may be placed upon the product.

On the other hand, the accountant wishes to know what users of the product desire and how much they wish to pay for it so that he can design and produce the product at a supply cost justified by the demand price. The production and control decisions are left largely to the accountant.

Given the foregoing, we can conclude that the accountant can be differentiated from other students of the subject in the following ways:

1. The accountant's concern for the use of accounting reports is limited to understanding how this affects demand for his product; and
2. The accountant's concern for available technologies to produce accounting reports is greater than that of users, as is his concern for the alternative costs of these available technologies; and,
3. The accountant should be concerned about research and development of "improved" products and technologies.

All of this leads to the not surprising conclusion that accountants should study more accounting than other students of the field, sacrificing the study of correlate disciplines relative to other students. This leads to the conclusion that at minimum, we would expect most accountants to "major" in accounting at the undergraduate and graduate levels.

More importantly, and perhaps less obviously, the academic preparation of accountants should carry a strong research flavor. As the field evolves, substantive answers to substantive questions become obsolete. Thus the accountant must devote a share of time consistent with the scope and pace of change to identifying and understanding the products of research and development of accounting and auditing and of changes in decision-making paradigms which alter the demand for accounting reports.

Thus, a central function of an academic program, we submit, is the development of the research skills of the student *qua* accountant. We feel that emphasis should be upon the methods of finding answers to accounting questions rather than on the answers to particular (illustrative) questions.

Again, we hasten to add that the relative emphasis upon any dimension of the knowledge set can and should be adapted to the audience which a particular (academic) institution hopes to attract and serve. However, we also note that the more a program restricts itself to current answers to current questions the more it attempts to compete with non-academic study alternatives.

Directions for Academic Institutions

We have suggested that the teaching-research dichotomy is illusory, if it exists. We also have suggested that research orientation, coupled with conceptual-analytic approaches are the hallmarks of academic programs. Straying from these elements of special advantage leads to several kinds of problems. First, it dilutes comparative advantage, lessening the case for academic programs and the demand for such programs relative to alternatives. Second, it changes the character of the students which are attracted by the programs, tending to discourage the analytic, research-oriented individual which we think is needed in larger measure in the profession. Finally, it fails to attract professional academicians of the sort who can exploit the special advantages of academic studies. However, we must again qualify our rather strong opinions about these issues to admit diversity in programs. As we stated earlier, we are not prepared to assess the "proper" or "optimal" balance of conflicting forces nor do we feel that others have supplied *an* acceptable answer to date. We therefore argue for continuing diversity, in a sense "experimentation." We suspect that no single best solution exists for all students nor for all institutions.

As a result, our major thesis is that the question of optimal academic program does not, and perhaps will not ever exist. Thus we should be less concerned about how each of us differs from another than with developing a firm rationale for whatever options we choose to take, individually and collectively.

FOOTNOTES

[1] Gerhardt G. Mueller, ed. *A New Introduction to Accounting,* A Report of the Study Group Sponsored by the Price Waterhouse Foundation, 1971.

[2] W. Thomas Porter, Jr. *Higher Education and the Accounting Profession,* A Summary Report on the Haskins and Sells 75th Anniversary Symposiums, 1971.

[3] Porter, p. 5.

[4] Report of the Committee on Non-Financial Measures of Effectiveness, *Accounting Review, Supplement* (1971), pp. 165-211.

[5] See Jacob Marschak, "Economics of Inquiring, Communicating, Deciding," *American Economic Review,* (May, 1968), pp. 1-18.

[6] Mueller, Chapter 2. Even if Chapter 2 is accepted, in whole or in part, by educators, Chapter 3 is certainly not purported to be the optimal way. We find ourselves more sympathetic to the recommended approach than to the experimental implementation, a disagreement beyond the scope of the present paper.

[7] The choice of "theoretical-practical" or "conceptual-procedural" as a way of characterizing the debate seems to be bases upon which "side" is taken by the speaker. We think that this, like the "teaching research" dichotomy is over-drawn. No such either-or choice should exist.

Resource Allocation for Accounting Doctoral Education: Quantity or Quality?

Gary L. Sundem
University of Washington
Jerry J. Weygandt
University of Wisconsin

Introduction

One of the more observable effects of the growth in accounting education has been the proliferation of Ph.D programs in accounting. Since the rate of growth has slackened, an evaluation of the present portfolio is due. Professors Sundem and Weygandt editorialize about the problems of too many similar Ph.D programs pursuing the same goals. Essentially, misallocation of resources results from the difficulty of quantifying outputs and the intense competition for too few dollars. Also, the large number of programs poses a serious information-acquisition problem for the prospective and naive Ph.D student. A variety of institutional and logistical suggestions are offered as potential remedies.

Resource allocation for doctoral level education is a complex and inexact science. Many of the costs involved in doctoral level education are joint costs that are impossible to separate from overall costs of operating other elements of the university. Many of the outputs are difficult to measure since there is wide disagreement about what constitutes a "well-educated" scholar. Because of difficulties attendant to input and output valuation, the price system traditionally is not used for such resource allocation.[1] Within broad guidelines, presidents and their administrative staff and faculty are expected to apply professional judgment to the management of the university so that benefits are commensurate with the resources used. The complexity of this decision process is indicated by Powel and Lamson: "Most authors question—even in theory—the possibility of determining a single level and mix of resource allocation which can be considered to maximize the effectiveness of resource use in higher education."[2] Yet, despite these difficulties, educators must face questions of resource allocation. Especially in the current environment when support of higher education is being severely questioned, the use of scarce resources for doctoral programs must be justified. The purpose of this paper is to point out possible considerations for resource allocation in accounting doctoral programs and to generate discussion that may lead to a more efficient allocation framework than presently exists.

Cost Versus Benefits

To be socially desirable an accounting doctoral education must produce benefits to the population of greater value than its cost. However, a Ph.D is by no means a homogeneous product, and the costs of producing an accounting doctorate vary greatly. Thus, it is extremely difficult for the consumer, both students who receive a direct benefit and society in general, which receives indirect benefits, to know what or how much they are buying.

On the cost side, estimates of the direct cost of supporting one business administration doctoral student for a nine-month school year range from $532.00 to $7,669.00, depending on the school, with a median of $3,529.00. Full costs have been estimated at 136 percent to 230 percent of direct costs.[3] If one assumes that cost is directly related to quality this may not suggest any misallocation of resources.

However, data from doctoral programs in other fields leads us to believe that such a relationship is not likely.[4]

The benefits of a doctoral education in accounting are even more difficult to specify. As a broad goal, doctoral programs attempt to produce graduates who are able to teach accounting and perform scholarly research. However, the relative weights put on each of these goals and the success in achieving each varies greatly among schools. It is widely acknowledged that students graduating from a given doctoral program have characteristics peculiar to that particular program. Benefits of a doctoral education are therefore very much dependent on the school from which one receives his degree. Yet, despite the wide differentiation in the product, there seems to be a distinct lack of recognition of this difference on the part of consumers of this product, namely the students and the general public.

The Two-Party System—Students and the General Public

Potential doctoral students are one major recipient of the benefits of any given doctoral education. When students enter a doctoral program, their direct costs are identifiable as tuition and fees and the opportunity costs associated with the income foregone while in the doctoral program. Despite the importance of the student's decision in the selection of an accounting program, it is often made with little knowledge about the wide differentiation in doctoral degrees. While bachelor and masters degree graduates often invest much time in searching for the proper job, these same individuals frequently base their selection of a doctoral program on little, if any, substantive information. A lack of foresight on the part of the student is partly to blame for this phenomenon, but biased information on doctoral programs coupled with subsequent frustration in a personal information search are often to blame. It follows that the benefits to and the disadvantages of various accounting doctoral programs are often not explained adequately to the potential Ph.D candidate.

Another recipient of the benefits of an accounting doctoral education is the general public, which enters into the resource allocation decision through its support of state institutions of higher education. Originally most state institutions had little to do with doctoral programs, as most doctorates were granted by private universities and only a select few state universities. But since World War II "the teachers college or mining institute has become the state college, then the state university, and ultimately a Ph.D granting institution."[5] The growth in accounting doctorates granted has been primarily in the state universities.[6] One reason for this is the federal government policy of "deliberately distributing research and fellowship funds to a longer and longer roster of institutions, reinforcing the efforts of state governments to upgrade the status of their institutions of higher education by the addition of graduate programs."[7] This growth of doctoral education in the state universities is due at least in part "to the wish of state governments—and even more the wish of the institutions themselves—to build graduate programs for purposes of prestige."[8] This growth then has come about not because of the excellence of the doctoral programs, but due to the availability of resources. The result may be an application of Gresham's Law to doctoral programs: the proliferation of relatively low quality programs is making it hard for the high quality programs to survive.[9] The actions of generous public support in the late 1960s may well result in a deterioration of doctoral education in accounting as well as other fields.

Solution to Existing Problems

The solution to the resource allocation problem for doctoral programs is complex. However, there are several areas where we believe that improvements could be made in the allocation process. First, explicit recognition of the heterogeneity in doctoral programs should be emphasized and documented. Not every institution should attempt to provide every type of doctoral education a student may want.

The scarcest resource for doctoral education is qualified faculty. With fifty-six accounting doctoral programs in the United States, it is impossible to staff all of these programs with across-the-board faculty competence;[10] specialization in accounting doctoral education is needed. At least three specialities exist: research, teaching and non-academic.[11] To successfully allow specialization several criteria must be met. The rigor of the programs must not differ by speciality, thus helping avoid specialization based on prestige. Resources must be made available to all three specializations as demand for the output warrants.

Flexibility must be maintained in all programs. Research, teaching and non-academic careers have much in common, and the commonality as well as the differences must enter into planning doctoral programs in each area. Finally, the specializations must be communicated to the consumers. Because the title "Ph.D" evokes a quite narrow, research-oriented response set, it may be necessary to actually create at least three different degrees. The D.B.A. and Ph.D. have traditionally implied different degrees, but the distinction is becoming less pronounced. If the difference in the degrees were well defined, this could provide a starting point. A Doctor of Arts (D.A.) degree for a teaching emphasis has been used elsewhere, and may provide another alternative.[12] Both specialization and communication of that specialization are necessary.

The second area where improvement is necessary is in providing information about alternative doctoral programs to prospective students. Accountants are concerned with providing unbiased information to financial investors, but academic accountants provide little information to those about to invest in an accounting doctoral education. Perhaps because the reputation of a doctoral program is based largely on its graduates, educators sometimes covet their outstanding undergraduate students. Rather than provide all of the information available and let the investors make the decision, these students are often directed along a path chosen by a faculty who want to insure that these "good students do not get away". Perpetuation of a system set up like this can only lead to a misallocation of resources, totally unresponsive to user needs. If prospective students had complete unbiased information about the alternative programs, specialization would likely come about on its own. Each school wishing to attract doctoral students would have to evaluate itself carefully and critically and plan a program based upon its unique features. Thus, a weak, across-the-board doctoral program might not attract students, but the same school with the same resources may well be able to specialize and attract students interested in that speciality.

The American Accounting Association (AAA) should also play a large part in this information presenting process. Acting as an unbiased intermediary, the AAA should certify the unbiasedness of program descriptions. It could also update the information, and make it available to prospective students. The information should include some independent assessment of programs as well as presentation of content. A bold step in this direction by the AAA would greatly enhance the resource allocation process for accounting doctoral students. Therefore accountability of the highest magnitude is necessary to assess the quality of existing doctoral programs. Like it or not, scarce resources must be allocated and schools must make a realistic assessment of their priorities within these constraints.

CONCLUSION

We are concerned by the proliferation of accounting doctoral programs in the late 1960s and the resulting resource allocation problems it presents. Too many faculties have invested a vital resource in an area where only a few should be involved. Methods of making the transformation back to more effective and meaningful level of doctoral programs involves two concepts—information and specialization. Information must be supplied by faculties in a unbiased manner, completely devoid of any institutional jealousies. Secondly, within a given set of doctoral programs, specialization may be quite appropriate and helpful to the allocation process. We are cognizant of the many problems that our proposed solutions suggest, but we believe that new and innovative approaches to the allocation problem must be found, or else accounting education at the doctoral level may find itself in a period of very little quality, but plenty of quantity.

FOOTNOTES

[1] For a more extensive discussion of this see John H. Powel, Jr. and Robert D. Lamson, *Elements Related to the Determination of Costs and Benefits of Graduate Education.* (The Council of Graduate Schools, Washington, D.C., March, 1971), pp. 5-6.

[2] *Ibid.,* p. 6.

[3] There are many shortcomings and limitations to these data. For a detailed analysis see Powel and Lamson, pp. 237-255.

[4] See Powel and Lamson, pp. 257-262. Regressions run with cost as the dependent variable and Roose-Andersen rating of graduate faculty among the independent variables showed that there is a positive relationship between quality and cost but that it lacks statistical significance in most instances.

[5] "Newman Unit's Report of Graduate Education," *The Chronicle of Higher Education* (March 12, 1973), p. 17. While the character of these schools has changed along with the name, the result has been a proliferation of Ph.D. granting institutions.

[6] Between 1965 and 1970 the number of accounting doctorates granted increased by 92 percent (from 75 to 144) compared to a 62 percent increase in total doctorates granted in all fields. In the period from 1968 to 1970 alone, eleven schools began offering an accounting doctorate, a 25 percent increase. The statistics for accounting doctorates are from William F. Crum, "The Second Survey of Doctoral Programs in Accounting," *The Journal of Accountancy* (June, 1971), pp. 86-88, and those on total doctorates from "Newman Unit's Report...", p. 19.

[7] "Newman Unit's Report...", p. 19.

[8] *Ibid.,* p. 19.

[9] More details about this possibility are given in "Newman Unit's Report....", p. 19.

[10] Across-the-board competence can be defined in either a vertical or horizontal framework. Virtually all departments cannot expect to be competent in all three areas of educational training—undergraduate, masters and Ph.D. work. Horizontally, the difficulty of providing competence in the many areas necessary for training of a successful Ph.D. candidate should be apparent.

[11] According to the Newman Report, doctoral programs should have a "greater emphasis on graduate curricula which will give students career options outside academic settings," especially those aimed at "solving the social problems of the 1970s and 1980s." Thus, non-academic goals are included with the traditional teaching and research as possible specializations. See "Newman Unit' Report...", p. 20.

[12] In the fall of 1971 there were sixteen humanities and seventeen natural and social science departments in thirteen universities offering D.A. degrees. See Robert Ear Wright, *A Study of Doctoral Level Programs for the Training of Teachers for Undergraduate Colleges: The Doctor of Arts (D.A.) Degree,* unpublished Ph.D Dissertation, University of Washington, 1972, p. 42. The D.A. degree may substitute a project in pedagogy for the dissertation.

Quality assessments could be derived from surveys, statistics on placement of graduates, statements by respected individuals in all phases of accounting, etc.

Education or Experience?

Charles G. Carpenter
Pennsylvania State University
Paul E. Dascher
Drexel University

Introduction

A chronic dilemma confronting accounting educators and students is to find a optimal tradeoff point between experience and education. In its most extreme form, this requires the choice between advising a student to seek a job after a baccalaureate degree or to proceed to graduate school, thereby foregoing current income for future income. Historically, the accounting internship has been a common compromise. It is conjectured that a primary by-product of the internship is changed attitudes, certainly more so than improved skills although that may also develop. Carpenter and Dascher bring some tentative empiricism to bear on this issue. The findings are limited by the methodology, but are suggestive for both proponents and opponents of internship programs.

Professional experience as a requirement for admittance into a given profession has generally existed for some time. In the early years of the public accounting profession, the skills necessary for participation as a professional were acquired substantially through practical experience. Subsequently, as the discipline underwent maturation and evolution, there came increasing recognition of education as a necessary component for the adequate development of the professional. The most recent decades have seen a trend toward reducing further the requirement of experience as the prerequisite for the right to sit for the CPA examination. A recommendation by the Beamer committee for the elimination of the experience requirement with a corresponding recommendation to adopt a five year educational requirement in place of the frequently encountered four-year educational requirement and either a year or two of professional experience, seems to complete the trend. The greater objectivity of measuring the compliance with educational requirements over practical experience may have contributed in part to the designation of the CPA as evidence of an individual's qualification as an "entrant" into the profession.

However, coincident with this trend has been the recognition by many practicing CPAs and educators of the value of practical experience in the development of the professional.[1] At least two distinct possibilities for introducing professional work experience into educational programs appear to exist: the co-operative work-study arrangement whereby the student attends class and works for an accounting employer, either concurrently or on an alternating basis; alternatively, the educational institution may adopt some plan whereby during all or part of a term, the student is released from on-campus responsibilities and participates in an internship with an accounting employer.[2]

Of these alternatives, the internship appears to be the more frequently utilized, having received strong endorsement from several committees of the American Accounting Association and the American Institute of Certified Public Accountants as an excellent supplement to the formal classroom learning experience.[3]

The report of the Commission on Standards of Education and Experience for Certified Public Accountants,[4,5] and the more recent Beamer Committee[6] reccommendations to the AICPA membership have very strongly supported internships as a bona fide part of the academic curriculum.

In 1956, the Commission stated that:

> .... (it) recognizes the value of practical experience in the training of the public accountant, but it believes that from the longrun standpoint most of such experience should come after the individual has met the prerequisites for the profession through the formal educational process and satisfactory completion of the CPA examination. At the same time the Commission considers some exposure to actual accounting operations and procedures to be a highly desirable part of the formal education of an individual interested in public accountancy. For this reason the Commission is recommending the inclusion of an internship program as part of the education requirement (4, pp. 134-35)

In 1969, the AICPA Beamer Committee recommended that:

> We believe that student internships are desirable and should be encouraged as part of the educational program because, carefully planned, they bring more meaning to subsequent college study. The standards under which internships should be established are those set forth in "Statement of Standards and Responsibilities Under Public Accounting Intership Programs" (6, pp. 14-15)

The standards referred to by the Beamer Committee are those suggested by an AAA committee for the participating university or college, student, and CPA firm.[7]

In a study undertaken in 1964, Lowe found 102 colleges and universities offering accounting internship programs among 386 institutions responding to a questionnaire mailed to 448 colleges and universities which offered majors in either accounting or business administration.[8] The length of the internship programs varied between 10, 11, 12 weeks for 38.4 percent of the responding schools, 4, 5, 6 weeks for 24.6 percent of the schools, and 7,8, 9 weeks for 13.7 percent of the schools, with the remaining schools offering a wide variety of time lengths for the internship. Lowe also found that one limiting factor in the growth of the internship programs was the semester system, a factor which contributed to the abandonment of 11 of the 16 internship programs among the schools surveyed. This factor also contributed to the failure on the part of some of the respondents to organize an internship program.

Even though internship programs appear to have achieved some degree of acceptance in accounting, little information is available concerning the intern's reactions to the internship experience, the exceptions being a plethora of descriptive and/or laudatory articles authored by former interns. The current study was undertaken to assess the impact of the internship experience on job preferences (for example: industry, government, local CPA firm, national CPA firm) of accounting students and the job characteristics they consider to be most important. Student reactions to these matters were gathered prior to the internship experience and again upon the students' return from the internship by means of a questionnaire. Although many influences on student perceptions were possible, the internship experience remained as a common intervening variable among the participants. Identical questionnaires were distributed to the student participants both before and after a ten week internship. The results reported in this study reflect student attitudes and perceptions of job characteristics associated with various aspects of professional accounting.

Results

Fifty-two senior accounting majors at The Pennsylvania State University participated in the internship programs and were included in the sample for the current study. The interns were asked to express their personal career plans upon graduation. The results of this question, including responses given both before and after the professional experience, are presented in Table 1.

By individual item, no significant shift in student plans was evident. The number of students anticipating full time postgraduate study in business, law, or other disciplines did decrease; eleven students (21.2 percent) anticipated engaging in such advanced study before the internship while eight students (15.4 percent) planned on post-graduate study after internship ex-

Table 1
Career Plans

	Percentage* Before	After
Graduate study *in* business prior to permanent employment	15.4	11.6
Graduate study *outside* business prior to permanent employment	0.0	1.9
Law school prior to permanent employment	5.8	1.9
Graduate or law study while employed full-time	21.2	28.8
No plans for advanced study	57.6	55.8
	100.0	100.0

*Percentages are calculated on the basis of 52 respondents.

perience. The overwhelming majority of the participants (44 or 84.6 percent) planned a primary commitment to their professional careers. Some, however, indicated a desire to pursue graduate or law studies while employed full-time. Clearly, the majority of the interns participating in this study were primarily oriented toward their future professional careers. Given these expectations and their proximity to graduation, it is reasonable to expect that they, as individuals, should be interested in exploring all aspects of a professional career. They should be receptive to new information about accounting careers and, to the extent that experience is a teacher, information gained during their internship program should be evident in subsequent perceptions.

The interns were asked to rank four alternative types of employers as to three different job characteristics: compensation, advancement, and overall desirability. There were no changes in the rankings before and after the internship. National CPA firms were ranked highest and government lowest on all three categories. Industry was ranked second on compensation but third in advancement and overall desirability and local CPA firms third in compensation but second in advancement and overall desirability both before and after the internship.

The interns were asked to indicate the job characteristics which they considered to be most important in evaluating alternative employment opportunities. The rankings of eleven possible characteristics are presented in Table 2. Nature of work and opportunity for advancement were ranked highest and fringe benefits, company reputations, prestige of industry and opportunity for graduate study were ranked lowest, both before and after the internship experience. Job security decreased from third to fifth in the ranking of importance while training programs dropped from sixth to seventh place. Working conditions, starting salary and location all advanced one place in the rankings reported after the internship.

The interns were asked to indicate their impressions of each category of employer, (national CPA firms, local CPA firms, industry and government) with respect to ten selected characteristics on a seven point semantic differential scale. The rankings reported by the students before and after the internship are reported on Table 3. Table 4 extends the presentation by focusing on the changes in perceptions which took place.

Table 2

Rankings of Job Characteristic Preferences

Before Rank	Before Mean Ranking*	Characteristics	After Rank	After Mean Ranking*
1	8.81	Nature of Work	1	9.75
2	8.35	Opportunity for Advancement	2	8.14
3	7.44	Job Security	3	7.33
4	6.96	Working Conditions	4	7.35
5	6.77	Starting Salary	5	7.34
6	6.06	Training Program	6	4.90
7	5.56	Location	7	5.94
8	5.37	Fringe Benefits	8	4.89
9	5.00	Company Reputation	9	4.80
10	3.67	Prestige of Industry	10	3.18
11	2.81	Opportunity for Graduate Study	11	2.35

*Average of the rankings given by students. The particular characteristic ranked highest was given a score of 11; the second highest a 10, etc.

For national CPA firms, the ratings of eight of the ten characteristics decreased during the internship experience. The greatest decrease was relative to job security with growth potential, fringe benefits, and prestige of the firm following in that order. It is interesting to note, however, that both individually and in total the interns' perceptions of the management of national CPA firms as being progressive increased.

The perceptions reported for local CPA firms after the internship also decreased for seven of the ten times. The greatest decreases were reported in the areas of compensation and prestige while students were more favorable in their perceptions of the availability of training opportunities in these firms. Perceptions as to the client orientation and management philosophy of local CPA firms also increased after the internship.

With regard to industry, perceptions decreased in nine of ten characteristics (all except progressive management), with the greatest decreases taking place in growth potential, training programs, compensation, advancement and prestige.

Although generally displaying the lowest overall scores, the changes reported for government were more favorable (seven of the ten characteristics showed increases). The greatest decreases were noted for opportunities for advancement and growth within the organization.

CONCLUSIONS

Student internships are generally considered to be both educationally and practically advantageous. Educational benefits stem from the diversity of actual experience generally afforded to the student. In a practical vein, many employers feel that internship programs present an opportunity to attract high quality entrants into the profession. This study focused, to some extent, on the latter view.

Obviously, this study was constrained by many factors, including sample size and environment. Variables other than employer characteristics could prove to be valid measures of changes induced by the internship program. These tend to inhibit generalization of the results. However, the intent of this study was exploratory in nature. The results, therefore, might prove useful for inducing further research in the area and possible correlations or extensions of the reported findings.

Table 3

Perceptions* of Alternative Employer Characteristics
Relative to a Professional Position

	National CPA		Local CPA		Industry		Government	
	Before	After	Before	After	Before	After	Before	After
Advancement	5.48	5.42	4.62	4.46	4.58	4.04	3.94	3.62
Job Security	4.92	3.98	4.81	4.75	4.89	4.79	5.71	5.60
Training Programs	5.75	5.60	3.67	3.94	4.48	3.77	4.10	4.33
Compensation	6.25	6.27	4.77	4.21	5.10	4.48	3.65	3.94
Fringe Benefits	5.27	4.87	4.04	3.92	5.13	5.12	5.20	5.40
Profitability	5.56	5.44	4.88	4.75	5.23	4.90	2.96	3.37
Growth Potential	5.96	5.44	4.92	4.73	4.90	3.35	3.94	3.69
Prestige	6.27	5.94	4.98	4.71	4.56	4.06	3.61	3.73
Client Oriented	5.52	5.44	5.44	5.62	3.63	3.19	2.88	2.81
Progressive Management	3.75	4.21	3.67	3.85	3.88	4.06	2.86	3.00

*As reported on a scale of 1 (lowest) to 7 (highest).

Table 4

Changes in Before and After Perceptions
of Alternative Employer Characteristics*

	National CPA	Local CPA	Industry	Government
Advancement	(.06)	(.16)	(.54)	(.32)
Job Security	(.94)	(.06)	(.06)	(.11)
Training Programs	(.15)	.27	(.71)	.23
Compensation	.02	(.56)	(.62)	.29
Fringe Benefits	(.40)	(.12)	(.01)	.20
Profitability	(.12)	(.13)	(.33)	.41
Growth Potential	(.52)	(.19)	(1.55)	(.25)
Prestige	(.33)	(.27)	(.50)	.12
Client Oriented	(.08)	.18	(.44)	.07
Progressive Management	.46	.18	.18	.14

*Shown as the change between the before and after response with a decrease indicated by brackets.

FOOTNOTES

[1] Philip Wolitzer and Arthur Hirschfield, "Effective Staff Recruitment Through Internships," *The New York Certified Public Accountant*, (July 1967), p. 523.

[2] Elmer G. Beamer, "The Co-operative System and Education for Public Accountancy," *The Journal of Accountancy*, (May, 1960), pp. 72-76.

[3] "Report of the Committee of Internship Programs," *The Accounting Review*, (July 1952), pp. 316-323.

[4] *Report of the Commission on Standards of Education and Experience for Certified Public Accountants*, (Ann Arbor, Michigan: The Bureau of Business Research, University of Michigan, 1956.)

[5] Lawrence L. Vance, "Education for Public Accounting With Special Reference to the Report of the Commission on Standards of Education and Experience for Certified Public Accountants," *The Accounting Review*, (October 1965), pp. 573-580.

[6] *Report of the Committee on Education and Experience Requirements for CPAs*, (New York: American Institute of Certified Public Accountants), 1969.

[7] "Report of the Committee on Accounting Personnel of the American Institute of Accountants. and of the Committee on Faculty Residency and Internship Programs of the American Accounting Association," *The Accounting Review*, (April 1955), pp. 206-210.

[8] Ross E. Lowe, "Public Accounting Internships," *The Accounting Review*, (October 1965), p. 839.

Welfare Economics and Accounting Curricula

Levis D. McCullers
Relmond P. Van Daniker
University of Kentucky

Introduction

As the need for socio-economic measurements has become increasingly obvious in recent years, accountants have been called upon to measure social performance in such areas as pollution control, anti-poverty programs, and human resource accounting. The purpose of this paper is to argue that: (a) Accounting graduates are not likely to have the background necessary to be measurers of social performance, (b) Such background could be facilitated by the study of welfare and institutional economics.

The need for socio-economic measurements has become increasingly obvious in recent years. For example, *The Wall Street Journal*, in December 1971, presented a series of articles on the need for new methods of measuring the success of business firms. The concern of businessmen was summarized in the following comments:

As the social role of business expands, the timehonored standards of corporate performance have come into growing disrepute. Businessmen and their critics alike increasingly agree that the concepts of growth and profit as measured by traditional balance sheets and profit-and-loss statements are too narrow to reflect what many modern corporations are trying to do.

Some of those things which accountants are being called on to measure include: corporate efforts in pollution abatement, cost-benefit analysis of anti-poverty programs, and the value of the firm's human resources.

The purpose of this paper is to demonstrate that accounting graduates are not likely to have the economic orientation necessary to be measurers of social performance, and that such orientation could be facilitated by the study of wefare and institutional economics.

Support for the first hypothesis will be drawn from a recent study conducted by the authors which revealed that the economics background of accounting graduates of American Association of Collegiate Schools of Business (AACSB) schools is typically limited to micro and macro economic theory. These courses are not designed to deal with the increased concern for the social consequences of business activity. Such courses typically place primary emphasis on profit maximization. Courses in welfare and institutional economics, because of their normative orientation, would facilitate a change in attitudes on the part of accounting majors from profit maximizers to reporters of social performance.

The second hypothesis will be supported by reference to welfare and institutional economic models. Illustrative welfare economic models, which will provide accountants with techniques for evaluating whether a policy of business or government has a net positive effect on society, will be discussed. Institutional economics will be described in terms of the role of the myriad institutions of society and the effect that these institutions have on the economy.

Changing Economic Environment

Any observer of our society is aware that changes are taking place. The following items are indicative of the change in the economic environment from a profit maximizing philosophy to a more socially oriented philosophy.

1. The 1st National Bank of Minneapolis in its 1971 annual report outlined how it hoped to measure 10 components that taken together should give an indication of the quality of life in the Twin Cities. Among the categories to be measured were job opportunities, environment, housing, health and income.

2. Some popular textbooks in introductory economics have now included material on measures of economic welfare as an alternative to GNP. These measures adjust GNP for pollution and ecological costs as well as the benefits of increased leisure.

3. The United Church of Christ has published a booklet entitled "Investing Church Funds for Maximum Social Impact". As investment criteria it offers such areas of social importance about a company as its products, influence on public policy, internal practices, and philanthropic giving.[3]

4. The Dreyfus Third Century Fund, Inc., says that "while seeking investments suitable for long-range capital appreciation," it will nonetheless limit itself to firms that have done work to "improve the quality of life in the United States."[4]

These comments are indicative of a growing concern for the failure of our present economic measurement system. Some critics charge that the American preoccupation with quantity has led to a neglect of quality. The critics would evidently like to see developed social indicators that would measure national well-being.

From the accounting point of view a firm's goal accomplishments are measured in terms of profits. Any goal that does not fit into the profit maximizing model is ignored. For example, a company's effort in pollution-abatement is reflected as an expense in traditional financial statements. Consequently, companies may not be motivated to make socially and environmentally desirable changes unless the method of measuring their success is changed because they will strive to maximize their performance on the measurement scale actually used.[5] Thus, accounting may be an unwitting accomplice in the reduced social commitment on the part of firms. A proposed solution to this dilemma, in which profits and purposeful activities are conflicting goals, is:

> not in the negation of profit motivation or of social concern, nor is it in a diluted middle-of-the-road position in which a dirtied economic hand is rubbed clean by the hand of social charity. The solution ... is twofold: first, business needs an objective method of measuring and evaluating the non-revenue producing aspects of corporate activities; second, business needs to adopt standards and practices that will enable it to incorporate the "value" of these activities into broad financial statements that reflect a company's quantitive and qualitative contribution to society.[6]

Current Economic Orientation of Accounting Majors

In order for accountants to meet the enlarged responsibilities expected of them by society, the colleges and universities must bear the burden of providing the opportunity to obtain the necessary measurement skills. However, evidence reveals that a major weakness exists relative to the economic education of accounting students.

In a recent survey of the AACSB schools,[7] the authors found that most accounting students are likely to be exposed only to micro and macro economic theory. As Table 1 indicates, if a school has only a six-hour economics requirement, the two courses would usually be micro and macro theory. In addition, schools with more than a six-hour requirement tend to specify the courses taken by accounting majors. These additional courses would usually be intermediate micro or macro theory. However, as shown in the Table, other courses may fulfill the requirement.

Table 1

CLASSIFICATION OF REQUIRED HOURS

Subject Area	Credit Hours 3	6	9	Total
	Number of Schools			
Micro Economics	87	24	1	112
Macro Economics	81	29	2	112
Institutional	10	2	0	12
Econometrics	7	1	0	8
Public Finance	4	0	0	4
Labor Economics	3	0	0	3
Welfare	1	0	0	1
Other	17	3	0	20

Table 2 presents the elective courses which are available to accounting majors in meeting the economics requirement. However, only 9 percent of the total hours required by the schools in the sample may be selected by the student.

Table II

CLASSIFICATION OF ELECTIVE COURSES

Course	May Elect Yes	No
Labor	55	58
Public Finance	54	59
Econometrics	51	62
Micro	50	63
Macro	50	63
Institutional	45	68
Welfare	36	77
Other	40	73

While most schools appear to have socially oriented economics courses available, there is little emphasis on requiring those courses or permitting the student to elect those courses as part of the requirement. Thus, it would appear that the average accounting major will not be exposed to the economic courses which may be more appropriate to modern society.

Economics of a Changing Society

There have been various transitions in economic thought during the 200 years since Adam Smith. One of the more significant changes was Keynesian economics which shifted emphasis from a free enterprise economy to a recognition of the need for government participation in the growth of the economy. However, both classical and Keynesian economics place emphasis upon the maximization of profit by the individual firms and the growth of the Gross National Product. In the past 10 to 15 years, many economists have raised questions concerning whether we are measuring the right things. The basic question is whether we should measure the "quantity of output" or the "quality of life."

The concern for measuring the quality of life is not a new phenomenon. Jeremy Bentham was unsuccessful in his attempt to develop a "moral thermometer" in the 18th century. Over the years, other attempts have also proven futile because of the many difficulties inherent in quantifying social progress. However, because of the increased interest in measuring the quality of life, several attempts have recently been made to develop a model of economic welfare. One of the more promising efforts has been that of Professors Nordhaus and Tobin. They have attempted to adjust the GNP to a MEW or Measure of Economic Welfare. In their model, GNP is adjusted to MEW by adding in the value of leisure and household work and deducting such things as defense spending, police protection, cost of pollution, and congestion.

There are some inherent difficulties in this model or, for that matter, any model of economic welfare. For example, how do you value leisure or household work? However, such things must be measured if we are to develop an indicator of economic welfare.

Welfare Economics

The branch of economics which has typically been most concerned with policy matters relative to the maximization of social good is *welfare economics*. Thus, welfare economics is essentially normative in contrast to the more positive nature of micro and macro theory. Those branches serve to develop the analytical tools which can be used in making normative judgments. Since accounting is based on judgments, having the exposure to the normative branch of economics should be beneficial to accountants whether or not they are engaged in the measurement of social performance.

Some topics covered in welfare economics that are not usually covered in other courses include:

1. *Pareto Criterion-*
This maximizing criterion states that any change which harms no one and which make some people better off (in their own estimation) must be considered to be an improvement because the total social welfare is greater. In other words, a change in which the value of gains is greater than the value of the losses is an optimum.

   This criterion might be adapted to evaluate the results of operation of a firm. For example, if a firm has a profit of $1,000,000 measured by current accounting practices, but contributes pollution costing the community $2,000,000, a Pareto optimum has not been attained. The net economic welfare is a negative $1,000,000 and perhaps the results of operation should be reported as $1,000,000 loss rather than a profit.

2. *Edgeworth Box-*
The Edgeworth Box is an exchange model based upon two sets of indifference curves. The model is an attempt to promote greater efficiency in the distribution of goods and increase social welfare by a redistribution of goods through voluntary exchanges. The purpose of the model is to demonstrate how total satisfaction may be increased by exchanges which will leave one person no worse off than before while increasing the satisfaction of another person. Some knowledge of this model

may provide background for accountants in decisions relative to acquisitions of other firms, allocation of resources, and distribution channels. The model is generally described in terms of two individuals but the principles can provide insights into increased social consciousness on the part of corporations and thus, perhaps, contribute to an increase in the quality of life.

3. *Kaldor Criterion-*

This maximizing criterion states that a change is an improvement if those who gain evaluate their gains at a higher figure than the value which the losers set upon their losses. The difference between the Kaldor and Pareto optimums is that Kaldor criterion requires only that the gainers perceive the gain at a greater rate than the losers perceive their losses. Thus, the gainers would have the *potential* to compensate the losers.

A study of the Kaldor model might provide insights into the measurement of such things as: cost-benefit analysis of a welfare program, guaranteed annual incomes, justification for progressive taxation, etc. Additionally, this model may be adaptable to the entire question of fringe benefits; e.g., does the fringe benefit provide greater perceived value to the employees than the cost to the firm. If the benefits are perceived to be greater than the cost, there is a net social gain. There are other models that could have been cited as providing background into the normative branch of economics. The models discussed were not selected because they were necessarily the best, or because they are without problems, rather because they are indicative of the philosophy and orientation of welfare economics. These three models should be adequate to indicate the basic difference between welfare economics and traditional micro and macro theory.

Institutional Economics

The value of Institutional Economics cannot be illustrated with precise models such as those for welfare economics. The role of the myriad institutions of society and the effect that these institutions have on the economy pervades many courses. However, as illustrated in Table 2, 45 AACSB schools offer elective courses in institutional economics.

Since the subject matter of Institutional Economics deals with the institutions of society, a study of these courses will afford the accounting major the opportunity to assess the contributions of the institutions to society. Many years ago a prominent accounting writer, DR Scott, expressed the need for understanding institutions when he said that "a theory of economic value must draw its validity from a particular scheme or ideal of social organization. It must rest on social ends or values."[8] The institutions to which Scott referred includes economic, legal, governmental, political, etc.

Since there are clearly changes occurring in these institutions, if economic values are based upon those institutions, then economic value must also be changing. As a barometer of the effect of the institutions, consider the activity of the stock market. The fluctuations in the stock market, frequently brought about by factors other than profit, indicate that the market is based upon many institutional influences other than profit. Thus, the market does not exist apart from the institutions which created it. The institutions influence the market and, at the same time, the market influences the institutions. In a broad sense, the stock market is part of the machinery of government just as the principles which underlie the theory of market control are part of the prevailing system of law.

CONCLUSIONS

In a brief way, we have tried to convey the view that a change in the economics orientation and background of accounting majors is needed. There is no doubt that the environment, in which business and accounting operates, is changing. If the environment is changing, business and accounting must also change. Society is demanding a greater accountability from business relative to its contribution to the quality of life as well as profits.

There are those who maintain accountants have no special role or skills relative to the measurement of social welfare. We do not contend that accounting majors should be welfare or institutional economists, but neither should they be micro or macro theorists. However, we strongly believe that exposure to the concepts and ideas embodied in welfare and institutional economics will enhance their ability to exercise appropriate judgments in the measurement of a firm's goals and social contribution.

Attempts at measuring social progress will be made in the future. As measurers of business performance, accountants should take the initiative in this area. Problems such as pollution control and the desirability of individual government programs demand an accounting at the present time. If accountants do not measure these things, then others, more willing to make normative judgments but untrained as measurers, may assume this role.

Furthermore, we are convinced that few schools are moving in the direction of encouraging courses in welfare and institutional economics for accounting majors. Thus, if accounting education is to take the direction which we have proposed, then accounting educators must influence and encourage the economics faculties to offer courses in these areas. In addition, the accounting faculty must impress upon the accounting majors the need for exposure to these areas of economics. These two proposals can be accomplished by (1) the substitution of courses in welfare and institutional economics for courses beyond introductory micro and macro theory, (2) advising accounting majors to elect courses in welfare and institutional economics, and (3) including in accounting courses references to the measurement of social goals. Through such activities, future accounting graduates will be in a better position to understand the attitudes of society and thus, be better able to contribute to the measurement of social progress.

FOOTNOTES

[1] *The Wall Street Journal.* December 9, 1971.
[2] *The Wall Street Journal.* May 18, 1972.
[3] *The Wall Street Journal.* December 9, 1971.
[4] *Ibid.*
[5] Robert K. Elliott, "Statements in Quotes," *Journal of Accountancy* (July 1972), p. 72.
[6] William C. von Berg, "Statements in Quotes," *Journal of Accountancy* (November 1972), p. 72.
[7] For a more complete discussion of the study see Levis D. McCullers and Relmond P. Van Daniker, "Socio-Economics and Accounting Educations," *The Accounting Review* (July 1972), pp. 604-06.
[8] DR Scott, *The Cultural Significance of Accounts*, Lucas Brothers Publishers, p. 94.

The Master Teacher: Beyond Technique

Introduction

If teaching is an art, then it must be practiced by artists. Surely, it can be and has been mechanized, computerized and even depersonalized. Just as surely, it can be and is essentially a human, creative and intensely personal sort of interchange. Teaching is a curious blend of mysticism, charisma, style and other equally tangible things. Professor Woelfel presents here his own teaching creed, and introspective statement about the interplay between values and teaching. He sets no rules, suggests no gimmicks, but he does sketch the outline of a Master Teacher. Regardless of the universality of the creed, it seems absolutely imperative to reflect that technique cannot do it alone, that some intrinsic committment to students is a vital ingredient in the process of learning and teaching.

The Master Teacher

Charles J. Woelfel
Southern Illinois University

As "The Lord" said in the play Green Pastures, "Everything nailed down is coming loose." This seems to be the case today in teaching. I would like to try to nail down some of the things which have come loose in education during my lifetime. That is the main purpose of this attempt to refine my thoughts, experiences, and writings on teaching which have evolved during an unaudited span of years.

Teaching has something to do with the education of man. This being an acknowledged part of the human condition, those engaged in this noblest of art forms must occasionally reflect on the nature and scope of their endeavors. This is especially true for those engaged in the teaching of a discipline such as accountancy which is highly structured, complex in its arrangements, extensive in its embrace, and demanding in its exercise. The flaw in those who teach accountancy lies not so much in their academic unpreparedness (since they are usually highly qualified in their field), nor is it the lack of practical experience in the subject they teach (for many of them have known the challenge of public or private practice); rather, the flaw, if flaw exists, may be in their not having sufficiently contemplated the art of teaching and the commitment it requires. If this is so, the defect can be remedied. It is with this in mind that I would like to now consider those essentials which relate to the art of teaching at its highest level.

The Beginning

I want to dialogue with you about the handwriting on the classroom wall which we educators are unable to see because we have our backs up against it. In particular, I want to talk with you about the high art of teaching as practiced by the master teacher. (See Table 1). Wall-to-wall teaching has something to do with getting the job done. It has everything to do with how we teachers perform with excellence and survive with integrity. Wall-to-wall teaching won't make teaching easier, but it should make teaching better. It is not for underachievers.

In Italy during the thirteenth century, the student guilds devised the most effective procedure known to man for getting the most efficient teaching from their instructors. In that enlightened century, the students paid, hired, and fired their professors. (That is almost like turning the asylum over to the lunatics.) Medieval students were empowered to command their teachers to lecture three, four, and even five times faster than normal conversation. Ill-prepared lecturers were hooted off the rostrum and driven from the town. The students were paying for an education, and they wanted full measure, shaken down and overflowing. Let us not dwell on this unappealing alternative.

Assuming that ten thousand accounting teachers read this article, then I can assure you that there are approximately ten thousand different ways for each to become a master teacher. Teaching is so personal that I hesitate to fool with it. Now that I have told you that there is no one way to describe the master teacher, I am going to do just that. That's chauvinistic logic for you.

I would begin by telling you that masterful teaching cannot be taught. It has to be learned. A teacher becomes a teacher by teaching. A teacher becomes a master teacher by teaching masterfully. You don't become a master teacher by reading about it. It's like art—you don't become an artist by collecting art.

Becoming a master teacher is like the blooming of a flower or the aging of good

Table 1
WALL-TO-WALL TEACHING

COMMITMENT TO TRUTH
A. Reality
B. Common Sense.

CONCERN FOR PERSONS
A. Sensitivity
B. Maturity

in an environment of

OPENNESS
A. To ideas; toward persons
B. A high regard for privacy

FREEDOM
A. Intellectual psychological spiritual, etc.
B. A respect for order; personal responsibility

visibly expressed in

COMPETENCE
A. Subject Matter:
  1. Learning Process:
    a. Romance
    b. Precision
    c. Wisdom
  2. The authority of knowledge
B. Teaching Methods
  1. Logic/judgment
  2. Communicative skill
  3. Human Nature:
    a. Motivation
    b. Guidance
    c. Discipline
C. Cultured/Liberal

CREATIVITY
Do it your own way; plow a field with a different plow; taste the forbidden fruit.

RESPONSIBILITY
To yourself, to your neighbor, to your country, to your God.

CONFIDENCE
A. Culmination of competence, creativity, responsibility
B. Ideals indentity
C. Commitment/involvement

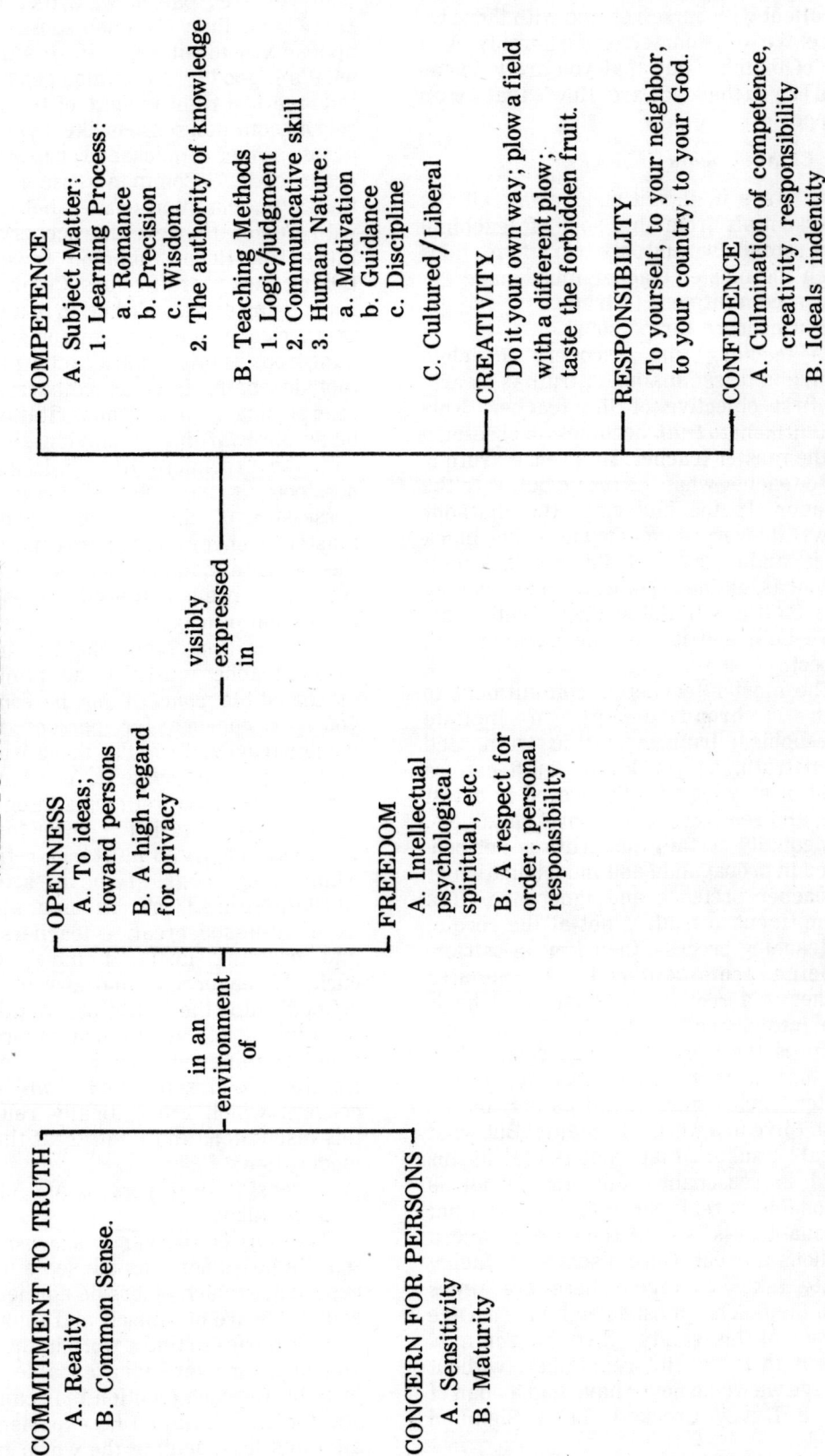

whiskey. It takes time. Nature understands this aging process; we don't. We are too impatient with ourselves and with those we serve. We judge ourselves too harshly. As a rule of thumb, I say that you are twice as good as you think you are. How's that for an opener?

The Commitments

As I see it, if you strip away all the nonessentials from this soul of teaching, there remain two and only two affirmations which the master teacher must make:
1. a commitment to truth
2. a concern for persons.

In teaching, the discovery, development, and dissemination of truth is clearly the first objective of the teacher. This *commitment to truth* becomes an obsession for the master teacher. In a sense, truth is to the teacher what the brave bull is to the matador. In the bull ring, the matador knows at every moment where his black bull is, and he does not turn his back on it without assuming certain sharp and deadly risks. So it is with the teacher. Truth is his brave bull, and it must be handled with respect.

The master teachers's commitment to truth is broad enough to include philosophical truth, scientific truth, and moral truth. As you know, truth can be found in a syllogism, discovered in a test tube, and read off a pair of broken tablets. It is equally certain that truth is not contained in propaganda and indoctrination or in teacher pretense and ignorance. If a commitment to truth is not at the core of the teaching process, then I'm an ostrich.

Being truth-centered, the master teacher is a *realist*. He knows that he is born into a real world. He knows that reality is the world which surrounds him and that he is a part of this world. The master teacher may be a dreamer, but he doesn't live in a world of dreams. But what is real? I submit that what is real in this world is reasonable, and that what is reasonable is real. Now you tell me what reasonableness is, and then we'll have a solutions manual. Once discovered, facing reality takes courage. There are times when the teacher must stretch his courage as well as his sanity when he commits himself to truth. But remember, without courage we would never have had a Joan of Arc, a Davey Crockett, or a Sigmund Freud.

If facing reality is one handle of this truth-centered ball of wax, then *common sense* is another. Common sense is like an appendix, a tonsil, or a tail. It's there, but what's it good for? Common sense is what tells me I'm right in spite of the facts. To rely on common sense is like trying to walk across a river of quicksand or to swim in an ocean of lies. Common sense is a lot of things, but common sense is not riding out with Custer to view the scenery on the Little Big Horn. Common sense is not talking back to traffic cops. Common sense is not using shrinkable cotton in a bikini. In inexperienced hands, common sense is as dangerous as mistaking a cactus plant for a mohair chair; it is as embarrassing as interpreting a wink for an invitation; it can be as unrewarding as playing gin rummy with the Cincinnati Kid; it is as misunderstood as the rules of logic. It is a possession of the master teacher. The master teacher knows approximately when the delicate balance between truth and common sense is achieved and so he is in possession of a pearl of great price.

Along with a commitment to truth, the master teacher must have an immense and inexhaustible *concern for persons*. Once you put concern for persons into the master-teacher formula, there isn't much left to do but to refine it. You have to be very careful about refining a thing because the power to refine is the power to destroy. I have seen spirited mustangs refined into whimpering nags. I have seen good whiskey refined into rubbing alcohol. I have witnessed creative teachers refined into cringing idiots. I have seen the curiosity, eagerness, and awe of students refined into the dullness, apathy, and fearfulness of institutional morons. To avoid refining concern for persons to a frazzle, I will select only two areas of concern which are critically relevant to this discussion, and I will treat these with moderation:
1. sensitivity to persons and ideas
2. maturity

The master teacher is a *sensitive* person. He hears notes on the scale of human experience which others do not hear. He is acutely aware of himself and things about him. He tries to find a word in the English language for every idea capable of being thought, for each emotion that can be felt, and for any sensation he experiences. He attempts to articulate the world tumbling around him so that his students can start where he leaves off.

We cannot leave our discussion of concern for persons without touching on *maturity*. I doubt if maturity can be defined. If it could, I am not sure that it should. Maturity is a condition. It is a state of mind. It is a way of looking at things. The mature person takes into consideration the long-range implications of his actions. He distinguishes the relevant from the irrelevant. The mature person sticks with something that is worthwhile until it is finished. He does not impulsively change jobs, careers, friends, or wives. The mature person deals with frustrations and failures, discomforts and disappointments on a rational level rather than as an emotional outburst. In terms of transactional psychology, maturity takes the position that "I'm O.K. You're O.K."

A concern for persons humanizes the teaching process. It transforms the classroom from a brutalizing and demeaning training session for circus cats into a civilized gathering of free men and women who have come together to share an experience of living.

The Environment

If education has anything to do with the process of man becoming man, then I am convinced that the master teacher must know something of the environment in which man becomes man. Becoming man is essentially a product of two imperatives:

1. the openness with which he encounters people, ideas, and things;
2. the freedom with which he is allowed to exercise that openness.

Openness and freedom are essential to man's growth and development. They alone are capable of dispelling those forces which compel him to assume artificial, superficial, and hypocritical poses. Openness and freedom increase an individual's awareness of himself as a person and as a member of the group to which he belongs. The behavioral scientists know this and are trying to tell us.

The master teacher must be completely open to ideas and persons. In teaching, there is no place for the closed mind or the closed heart. To be truly effective, openness requires elbow room in which to operate. Elbow room is another name for freedom. The master teacher must be free. He must be his own man. He was born free; he must remain free. Unreasonable rules and procedures account in a large part for the lawbreakers in our prisons and the larger number of the uncommitted in our classrooms and faculty lounges. When laws or rules conform to reason, we feel comfortable with them because somehow they reflect us as does a mirror. If laws and rules do not conform to reason, then the reflection is a caricature of ourselves, and we are overcome with feelings of anger, frustration, and injustice.

When it comes to freedom, I'll cast my lot with the rebels. I say let us sweep the slate clean and start all over. Let us do away with all the unnatural educational encumbrances which make education impossible—encumbrances such as credit hours, quarters and semesters, yearbooks, and special fees. Let us abolish all honor rolls, dean's lists, and cum laudes. Get rid of all the status symbols such as assistant professors, executive vice presidents, and academic deans. Burn all diplomas, cancel all baccalaureate programs and commencement exercises. Do away with bells, clocks, schedules, and calendars. This is the folly that waits to be scraped off the blackboard of education before the master teacher can truly perform the single function for which he was born—to instruct the ignorant. Don't tell me that this won't work. I know it won't work, but in your heart you know I'm right.

Openness and freedom are two variables in education which have never been adequately tested. I would like to see an in-depth experiment undertaken to determine the extent to which openness and freedom are a prerequiste of man becoming man. To show my good faith, I volunteer to be the first pigeon in such an experiment. Do I have any takers?

In order that I not be completely misunderstood or judged incurable, nothing I say about openness and freedom should be construed as carte blanche approval for invasion of privacy or for the abandonment of good order and personal responsibility.

The Outcome

As you may have suspected, the teacher's function is to make education competitive with Miami Beach. Teachers, like parents, are in the business of raising children. If I had children of my own, I know what I would want them to be like. I would want my sons to be able to distinguish between God, cadillacs, and girls in cashmere sweaters. I would want my child to grow up and become a person who was—

1. *competent* in his chosen profession,
2. *creative* in his approach to the problems he would be called upon to face,
3. *responsible* to himself, to his neighbor, to his country, and to a Supreme Being,
4. *self-confident* in his ability to deal with life as it comes his way.

While these qualities of competence, creativity, responsibility, and self-confidence are those qualities which I try to cultivate in my students, I believe that they also are the very qualities which the master teacher should possess—and possessing them, put them on exhibition for his students to observe and perhaps emulate.

The master teacher knows that competence in the teaching profession refers to competence in the subject matter he teaches and competence in the application of methods of teaching. Put another way, competence means that what is taught must be taught thoroughly; e.g., it must be taught with *dedication* and *skill*.

The mastery of subject matter is a three-fold process. In education, the learning trip consists of three stages:[1]

1. a romantic involvement
2. the attainment of precision
3. a striving for wisdom

A romantic involvement with learning starts with inquisitiveness, curiosity, and excitement. Romance is what attracts and disposes us to open doors and windows, introduce ourselves, take a book off a shelf, ask a question, sign on the dotted line, and enter into other seemingly harmless adventures. The novel, the exceptional, and the unknown have always been the seed corn of wanting to know more.

After a romantic involvement comes the striving for precision. Teaching requires a degree of expertise. Precision puts order into facts, figures, and life. Precision provides procedures and techniques. During the precision-seeking and acquiring stage, skills are acquired and habits formed. Systems are constucted and adjustments reached.

To remain mired in the precision stage is what happens to the technician; and you shouldn't let it happen to you. To stop with precision is to stop short of fulfillment. The ultimate step in learning, in teaching, and in living is the attainment of wisdom. Wisdom is the fruition of precision. Wisdom arrives at an understanding, appreciation, and acceptance of reality that goes beyond merely knowing how to do something. Wisdom knows why.

As far as teaching methods are concerned, the master teacher knows that he is there to give assistance by signs, symbols, and experience. He provides order, guidance, and motivation. He knows the objectives of the course; he sets the pace; he insists on concentration; he evaluates achievements and deficiencies. As a teacher, it is his responsibility to understand human nature and not to judge it.

Creativity is another special attribute of the master teacher. Creativity has to do with insights, awareness, the subconscious, and black magic. Creativity is a process, conscious or otherwise, of discovery, invention, and insight. It is part inspiration and part perspective—but total originality. Creativity is a product of the most primitive powers and the most highly developed faculties of man. In dreams and in rational processes, creativity is an outlet for the original, the novel, and the exceptional. Surprise, excitement, relief, and awe accompany the act of creation and are its certification.

Creativity is human in that it comes from not knowing when to stop, from not accepting textbook answers, from doing it your own way, from not leaping in the dark, from looking after leaping, from starting over, from giving a damn. Creativity comes to those who risk everything, to those who ignore the obvious, to those who get lost in a cave, to those who sit on an ant hill, to those who split the atom of truth, to those who laugh at taboos, to those who taste the forbidden fruit, to those who censor the censor, to those who pay the piper. In the final summation, creativity is man at this finest hour. Without it, man is just another beast of burden. With it, man touches the finger of God.

Along with competence and creativity as basic to teaching excellence comes responsibility. Responsibility is an attitude—a frame of mind and a determination of will. The responsible man keeps promises he makes and doesn't make promises he doesn't intend to keep. For the responsible man, failures, defeats, and disappointments are lessons, not fiascoes. The responsible man doesn't expect to just "muddle through", "luck out", or "come up smelling like a rose". He doesn't "cave in". He is not a day late and a dollar short. How do you tell if a man is responsible or not? I judge a man by what he does in the dark.

Finally, we come to confidence, the last trait of the master teacher. Self-confidence is the last of the old-fashioned virtues. Self-confidence is part competence, part creativity, and part responsibility. The self-confident man is a person who has adopted a realistic set of ideals. Ideals are values and, as such, they are not entirely worthless. Possessing ideals, the self-confident person knows the extent of his convictions and the limits of his commitments. A failure of ideals precedes a collapse of confidence. Once ideals go down the drain, there's no place left to go but out.

Self-confidence comes with an awareness of who you are, what you are, and why you are. Everybody seems to be going through his identify crisis these days. Some people are known to have pulled out of it without leaving any visible scars. Somehow, self-confidence seems to come with self-acceptance.

CONCLUSION

Man is so concerned with getting somewhere these days that when he does get there, he has forgotten why he came. Now we must try and conclude the journey we started a few pages ago. We've been talking about the master teacher. Well, that bit of status plus a quarter will get you a cup of coffee at any truck stop.

What is needed in teaching today is the leadership of men and women who have moral and professional standards above the ordinary and who are willing to be judged according to these standards. This is also the type of person who should be the end product of our educational process. If we've missed this, what else have we failed to see?

We have all read Alice in Wonderland. You may recall that at the end of this fairy tale the grinning Cheshire cat, which gives Alice advice, slowly vanished until nothing is left but its smile. The master teacher is like the Cheshire cat who, when his job is done, vanishes leaving behind nothing but the shadow of a smile.

FOOTNOTES

[1] Aristotle, Hegel, and Whitehead have written on this three-fold process. They are entitled to a reading whatever you might have heard about their idiosyncrasies.

Section III

A Conceptual Overview of Learning for Accounting Educators

A Conceptual Overview of Learning for Accounting Educators

James E. Sorensen, Associate Editor
University of Denver

Introduction

Human beings learn. Although few would seriously challenge this simple statement, virtually no one can give a complete explanation of the learning process. Although the vast numbers of variables related to learning and the great volumes of material devoted to these variables are staggering, the analysis is still incomplete. Yet accounting educators do need an understanding of certain learning issues. The specific topics presented in this section bear directly on the issues that should be better understood and better managed by accounting educators—topics that focus on the issues of the learner and the learning process. In sum, this section contains an amazing matrix of vital issues and ideas; some are based on empirical research and some on personal observation but all are focused to help the accounting educator do a better job.

Section Overview

In this multi-faceted approach to analyzing the learner and the learning process, no discipline or method prevails. An abbreviated section outline reveals an emphasis on diverse perspectives:

I. Analyzing the Learner
   A. Individual Differences: Ability, Personality, and Vocational Interests
   B. Interpersonal and Social Environment in Learning (including class size)
   C. Cultural and Economic Environment: The Special Case of the Disadvantaged

II. The Task of Learning
   A. Theories of Learning
   B. Theories of Motivation
   C. Objectives in Accounting Education
      1. Professional Education and Training
      2. Behavioral Objectives for the Classroom

Each topic touches key factors affecting the success or failure of accounting educators in the classroom. The authors bring highly abstract and complex issues into specific and understandable focus to facilitate practical classroom application. For a series of general topics the degree of specificity is amazing. Topics such as sensorimotor stages of mental development, development of symbolic abilities, psychogenetics, language, coding, the unconscious, mental health in the classroom, and others have been deleted from this overview because of space limitations and their highly specialized nature. What has been included should be of practical benefit.

Analyzing the Learner

Editor's Introduction

Learners seem to be influenced by virtually everything they are exposed to, and perhaps some error is committed when the influences are split into separate units such as:
A. Ability
B. Personality
C. Vocational interests
D. Interpersonal and social settings
E. Economic and cultural environment

But only by viewing these smaller sections one at a time can the whole be seen more clearly. Accounting educators may wonder which of these influences could be of utility to them in better understanding the accounting student. Without attempting to explain all of the variations of the learner, each of these five key variables is explored because of a known or assumed significance in learning.

Ability, personality, and interests as well as interpersonal and social environment are viewed as they apply generally to accounting students while the examination of the economic and cultural environment is focused specifically on the disadvantaged—especially one of the most significant minorities in accounting, the black.

Individual Differences

At a time when the professions are undergoing the strain of absorbing greater numbers of new members, few topics have greater relevance than the ways in which people differ and the effect of these differences on academic and professional performance. Professor John Grant Rhode reviews the ways in which

Intelligence and special abilities
Personality
Vocational interests

can affect performance. Professor Rhode distills the complex area of individual differences and explains how these differences—with the possible exception of personality—have been useful predictors of certain types of career behavior, especially educational progress and occupational status.

Individual Differences: Ability, Personality, and Vocational Interest

John Grant Rhode
University of Washington

Introduction

People differ greatly...even the most casual observer is impressed with the amazing array of physical differences among people. But people also differ in a myriad of other less easily discerned qualities, such as intelligence, abilities, skills, motivation, and temperament.[1]

Individuals and Some of Their Differences

Although physical differences provide us with a simple means of identifying individuals, the necessary information to facilitate judgments on whom, how and when to best educate are frequently derived from measures of ability, personality and vocational interests. And, because these characteristics are subtle and more complex then physical attributes, they must be studied and their effects carefully monitored. Of these important mental characteristics, perhaps ability, or intelligence, has the largest impact on what an individual can learn—in accounting or any other discipline. This ability to learn, if properly utilized, will have a lot to do with the eventual station one reaches in life and that station may further assist in maintaining a preferential life-position for one's family. This differential preference is in direct contrast to a statement in the Declaration of Independence indicating that, "We hold these truths to be self evident, that all men are created... equal..." The idea that men (women) are created unequal is now self evident and exclusive of health, wealth and family position, intelligence and its learned application is likely to be the major source of inequality.[2]

Some of the most common characteristics contributing to inequality, or differences, are physique, age, sex, race, social class, culture, avocation, motivation, personality and ability. Although these may all indicate important individual differences, attention is focused on those differences related to ability, personality and vocational interest.

Ability Differences: Intelligence

Psychologists have determined that the distribution of individual differences follows a normal curve. Whether looking at the height of English-born men,[3] the lung capacity of male college students,[4] the tendency of women to dominate their associates in face-to-face contacts of everyday life,[5] or, most importantly, the intelligence quotient (IQ) of a representative sample of children,[6] the plotted distribution for large samples reveals a normal curve. Consequently, people are not always characterized with sharp qualitative distinctions, but fall along a continuous scale where differences are more a matter of degree rather than absolute.[7]

Given that IQ differences resulting from organic intelligence are normally distributed, and that accounting educators are usually concerned with students at the top end of an IQ distribution who have survived several years of successive academic evaluations to reach their terminal years in undergraduate and graduate programs, of what concern is a knowledge of intelligence to accounting educators? One initial answer is to know what ability does or does not represent, and to dispel some of the myths attendant to intelligence.

IQ scores: Potential Rather Than Accomplishment.

For example, a high IQ may be a necessary but not sufficient condition for outstanding performance since the potential may never be realized unless accompanied by motivation, creativity and leadership.[8] Persons referred to as unmotivated geniuses come easily to mind—particularly in an academic environment where nonproductive faculty may be insulated by the tenure granted their position.

Mind and Body Stereotypes.

Despite the popular stereotype associating strong minds with weak bodies, the published research indicates that intellectually gifted individuals tend to be physically superior and emotionally well adjusted—both as superior children and later as successful adults. These data are obtained from the longitudinal reports of the Stanford Gifted Child Study directed by Terman.[9] In sum, the research on this largest of test groups analyzed over so lengthy a time period presents a highly favorable view of the educational, social, emotional and physical status of intellectually superior children and their adult lives.[10] Consequently the stereotype of strong minds and weak bodies is subject to data-based criticism and should be considerably tempered if not discarded.

IQ and Careers.

Another interesting comparison is often made between intelligence and economic success. Yet, again, the effect of IQ scores on earnings and occupational status is somewhat inconclusive. From an extensive study on occupational inequality, the data do not support the theory that occupational success depends heavily on the genes that influence IQ.[11] Because of our credential oriented society where employers frequently recruit for positions using educational degree criteria, and since the correlations between educational attainment and IQ test scores is between .60 and .70,[12] intelligence clearly plays a strong role in determining who eventually is hired in desirable occupations.

Effect of Heredity and Environment.

An issue on intelligence and ability which has remained basically unanswered — whether heredity or environmental factors are more responsible for IQ scores — may be approaching a position of definitive answer. As recently reported[13] some psychologists consider intelligence to be due primarily to inherited genes rather than to environment and upbringing.[14] The discussion has previously vacillated between a nature-nurture preference, or balance, without being decided in favor of heredity or environment. The controversy may have a considerable impact on directing educational efforts since those who believe that environment principally affects intelligence have brought into reality such compensatory educational programs as Head Start. Although, if compensatory education is ineffectual, then perhaps higher education will be directed mainly at elitists whose birth right and family genes permit entrance to high quality education and to maintain that privilege primarily for their descendents.

Of all the evidence supporting heredity-based intelligence, perhaps the studies by Jensen on 122 sets of identical twins separated early in life and raised in different environments offer the strongest argumentive defense. The IQ scores for the identical twins raised apart correlated .89, sibling with identical sibling.[15] Since identical twins have identical genes and because unrelated children growing up in the same environment have a correlation of .27 between sibling and non-related sibling, some psychologists have concluded that between 73 and 89 percent of the differences in IQ are due to heredity rather than environment.[16]

To be sure, individuals with a superior IQ who are not intellectually stimulated will not likely demonstrate their full potential. But, at the same time, persons with low IQs seldom do well enough to reach the top of a socio-economic scale including such occupations as lawyers, scientists and academicians.[17] This means there is little, if anything, accounting educators can do to affect the organic intelligence, of their students. Whatever effect heredity or environment has on IQ has been determined well before students face accounting professors at college and universities. What accounting educators can do is ensure a challenging environment for learning so the brightest students will be stimulated to use their intellectual potential. Accounting educators should concentrate on building functional intelligence or, usable knowledge, and on improving the learning environment. The potential to learn, or basic IQ, cannot yet be increased very much by university professors. The data are too strong to ignore—especially from the studies of identical twins reared apart.

One of the benefits of teaching in a college environment rather than at primary or secondary school systems is knowing that the students are generally of superior intelligence. This allows professors to devote more of their time to the subject matter and less to counseling sessions and IQ scores. Given how controversial psychological testing is and how sensitive IQ scores are regarded, it is comfortable to know that administrators and admissions officials take care of almost all pre-classroom evaluative testing. Such freedom is a luxury for college level instructors—especially with the unsolved issues of test validity and cultural bias.

For More Reading

For a more extensive reading into some of the literature on intelligence and psychological testing, see Buros[18] for an evaluation for all tests in print, Anastasi[19] for a summary of problems surrounding psychological testing, Hunt[20] for a review of research on what intelligence represents, Guilford[21] for an in-depth examination of mental measurement theory and technique, and Cronbach[22] for a survey on the entire area of psychological testing. These references contain essential material for anyone interested in either establishing a psychological testing program or obtaining a better knowledge of results from existing programs.

Ability Testing in the Profession

Ability testing is not the sole responsibility of psychologists but is also found within the medical, legal and accounting professions. To date, the most widely used accounting ability and knowledge testing program is that of the American Institute of Certified Public Accountants (AICPA) and its Uniform CPA examination.[23] The AICPA is also involved with tests of accounting knowledge and ability through its level I and II Achievement and Orientation test programs. These tests together with The Accounting Classification Test (TACT),[24] a test of 40 accounting and quantitative analogies, represent the latest attempts to blend the principles of psychological testing with accounting knowledge for predictive purposes when counseling students and employees. Consequently, ability testing for accountants and by accountants is already here, not just in classroom examinations, but in the form of validated tests like TACT and the AICPA testing program.

No less sensitive than ability testing is personality testing and its implications. The theories and research on personality provide the second testable measure of individual differences discussed.

Definitions and Theories of Personality

Apart from ability, personality is one of the most important attributes related to success in vocational, social and emotional relationships. Personal characteristics such as compulsiveness, diligence, self-discipline, allegiance, conformance, submission, flexibility, honesty, perseverance, or erasability, to list but a few, contribute substantially to how individuals are evaluted and rewarded for their work or non-work. It is easy to recall examples of persons whose work was not up to standard, who, nonetheless were either retained or promoted because of a desirable personality. It is also not too difficult to think of individuals whose personality was unacceptable to the extent that promotion and salary increase reward was either delayed or insufficient—in spite of a fine output of work. Wherever work is evaluated, personality characteristics usually are examined along with the measured output. Like it or not, this co-evaluation exists. One only has to think of the last faculty promotion and salary review meeting for close personal examples.

Just What Is Personality?

Psychologists have wrestled with the term from the time they first began to study personality. One of the popular definitions comes from Guilford[25] who considers personality so extensive that it includes all of an individual's traits, physical characteristics, intellectual qualities, aptitudes, talents, temperamental qualities, interests, expressive behavior, and pathological symptoms. So broad a definition is not particularly useful, since meaningful classifications are difficult. But even a general definition works as a departure point because psychologists have early reported [26] that there are some 3,000 to 5,000 words which describe personal qualities. And, since personal qualities are the basis for personality, broad-stroke descriptions emerge to satisfy our need for definitions.

Other definitions consider personality as the dynamic organization within the individual of those psychophysical systems that determine characteristic behavior and thought,[27] a prediction of what a person will do in a given situation,[28] and those habits of social importance that are stable and resistant to change.[29]

One of the most recent definitions purports that personality is a *stable* (emphasis added) set of characteristics that determines commonalities and differences in the psychological behavior of people.[30] This definition is interesting in that it associates stability with personality much like the life-long stability of intelligence discussed earlier.

Perhaps the best conclusion regarding a personality definition is provided by Hall and Lindzey[31] following a thorough review of several theories. They conclude, and are supported in this view by another prominent personality scholar,[32] that no substantive definition of personality can be applied with any generality. In other words, personality as we recognize it, is one of our most individual of individual differences. Other than fitting into extremely broad definitions and classifications, the literature suggests that personality is a set of characteristics singularly unique to each of us.

Important Theories.

Although several theories share positions of importance in the personality literature, none of them dominates to the extent that other theories are overwhelmed—very likely because of the nongeneralizability which permeates each theory. Because one theory may explain the behavior of several, but not all, individuals, and another may explain the acts of a few, but not very many people, it is more worthwhile to briefly list the highlights of several theories than to search for the one dominant theory.[33] No attempt is made to rank-order the several theories in importance, and their place in the summarized listing holds no meaning other than near assocation with other theories.

Freud, perhaps the most familiar name of the personality theorists, formulated a theory which attempts to maximize instinctual gratification and minimize guilt and punishment. Within five psycho-sexual stages—oral, anal, phallic, latency and genital—individuals will attempt to protect themselves psychologically with several defenses. Among them are projection— attributing to others an objectionable trait which you actually possess, denial—not perceiving the existence of a threatening person, object, or event, intellectualization —substitution of a ficticious socially acceptable reason for one's actions, repression— removing from consciousness those actions which are threatening or unpleasant, and sublimation—diverting unattainable, destructive desires into socially acceptable channels. One interpretation of personality theory[34] indicates that in Freud's view the basic outlines of personality are essentially fixed by age five—with remaining life a complex reflection of early patterns.

Similar to Freud's theory is the work of Murray[35] who contributed the additive concept of a needs list which must be satisfied. Murray's list numbers some forty in total and includes such needs as achievement, power, affiliation, and nurturance.

Another prominent personality theorist is Erikson who, unlike Freud's emphasis on sexuality, is concerned with the conflict between children and parents. His theory centers on a lifetime of evolvement through eight stages of tradeoff situations; Trust v. Mistrust, Autonomy v. Shame and Doubt, Initiative and Responsibility v. Guilty Functioning, Industry v. Inferiority, Identity v. Role Diffusion, Intimacy v. Isolation, Generativity v. Stagnation, and Ego Integrity v. Despair.[36]

Sullivan contributed the notion that individuals seek to maximize satisfaction and minimize insecurity. In doing so they may, at different stages in their development, be self-absorbed, incorrigible, negativistic, nonintegrative, a stammerer, ambition-ridden, asocial, inadequate, homosexual, or chronically adolescent. Critical to Sullivan's theory is the thesis that individual behavior is most strongly determined by avoiding the insecurity of disapproval from relevant others.[37]

Specifying only two personality types, the fully functioning person and the maladjusted person, Rogers bases his theory on whether individuals receive unconditional or conditional positive reward.[38] The core of his theory concerns itself with whether someone is able to actualize their inherent potential. This is in contrast to essential conflict germane to the personality theories of Freud, Murray and Erikson.

A theory in strong agreement with Rogers is the hierarchy of needs proposed by Maslow. Stating that individuals move from the satisfaction of need levels starting with physiological and moving through safety, belongingness, and esteem until self-actualization is reached,[39] Maslow, like Rogers, also provides a conflict-free theory.

Very briefly, other theories include Rank's conflict notion that individuals simultaneously minimize fears of life and death,[40] Angyal's proposition that conflict arises from our attempts to maximize expressions of autonomy and surrender,[41] Jung's premise that people have a tendency toward attainment of selfhood,[42] Adler's concept of striving toward superiority or perfection,[43] Allport's thesis that people fuction in a manner individually expressive of one's self,[44] Fromm's theory that individuals must relate or not relate with others, have an identity and frame of reference while expressing one's human nature,[45] and Kelly's suggestion that individuals attempt to predict and control the events they experience.[46] Based on these descriptions, there is a substantial amount of overlap between the various personality theories. The overlap may be corroborative, or simply an unnecessary duplication.

Any individual whose behavior is being catalogued may be consistent with the listed behavior in some setting but not in others. Consider, for example, the consistency some one may exhibit in honesty toward relatives and associates. The same person may not be consistently honest toward associates yet may be totally honest with, say, brothers and sisters. Many years ago Hartshorne and May[47] noted these results when measuring such qualities as honesty, generosity and self-control. Given this finding and the myriad of definitions on personality theory, it is not suprising that Hall and Lindzey[48] conclude that no substantial definition of personality can be generally applied.

Personality and the Accounting Educator.

The critical question following this review is: "Of what benefit are these theories to an accounting educator?" Other than recognizing the individuality of students and maintaining respect for their individual differences, little is to be gained by such knowledge. The theories tell us that people are motivated by anxiety, guilt, frustration, accomplishment, conflict, and fear of disapproval. If the theories are generalizable at all, then students, as people, are also so motivated. *Consequently, accounting professors should try to stimulate whole classrooms of students with varying personalities rather than trying to assess the individual personality attributes of each student in those classrooms.*

Protected Privacy

Today individuals have the right to retain or release information on their intelligence scores, personality profiles and vocational interests. Hopefully that privacy will be maintained. And when considering the individual differences in ability and personality that exist in students, accounting educators will look primarily to data on classroom performance—not to their analysis of individual student personality characteristics. A review of the psychological literature on personality, indicates that a vast academic area exists for counseling that is well beyond the understanding level of accounting educators unless they are also trained counselors. Given the tremendous amount of education time investment essential to becoming a trained counselor, accounting educators are likely best able to affect accounting education by being simply better educators and not by attempting to analyze the personalities of students.

Individual Differences in Vocational Interests

Vocational interests, unlike inherent individual differences of ability and personality, are learned or experienced and take a considerable amount of time to crystallize during the formative years. Moreover, these do not become highly stable individual qualities until the age of about nineteen. Once individuals are exposed to the influential experiences, working persons, courses of academic study, professions, and, of course, media representations that affect perceptions of what is enjoyed or not enjoyed, vocational interest remain remarkably constant for several years. For example, on the average, male college students with high scores on certain occupational scales of the Strong Vocational Interest Blank (SVIB) are approximately four times as likely to be working in that occupation nearly twenty years later than are other male college students who had low scores on the same scales.[49]

Almost all individuals attempt to find a satisfactory matching of their abilities, personality and vocational interests in the occupation of their choice. This is no less true of accountants (and accounting students) than it is of doctors, lawyers, or anyone else. Campbell has eloquently summarized enthusiasm for work as one of the world's most exciting topics.[50]

> Under the guise of employment, men allow themselves to be manhandled physically (professional football players), to be subjected to public ridicule (politicians), to be displayed publicly (cocktail waitresses, Bunnies and strippers) or to be deprived of all material possessions (priest and monks). The excitement of occupation has led men into more risks—undercover espionage, space travel, Antarctic exploration—than could money or fame; the fanatic commitment of some men to their jobs has probably caused more divorces than has marital infidelity; the possibility of better employment has created larger mass migrations than has religious fervor, and the absence of meaningful work has likely created more mental depression than any other single factor. For most people, where they work is where the action is.

For accounting students, particularly those who enter the professional world of public accounting, work is clearly where their action is—if only because of the legendary amount of hours they are at work—especially during the filing season for tax and calendar year financial statements.

Vocational Interests: SVIB

Since accounting educators do commit a large amount of time and their students' time to some accounting related occupation, what are the vocational interests which assist in making this choice and what useful knowledge is there about the vocational interests of accountants? To assist in answering these questions, attention is focused on the SVIB[51] since that test is both empirically derived and the source of the largest amount of vocational interest research.

The empiric foundation of the SVIB means its scales were developed from actual responses of persons in some seventy different occupations -- not from armchair speculation as to how they might respond. Consequently, the CPA scales within the SVIB are derived from responses made by CPAs and not from someone's guess as to how CPAs might answer items such as respond "Like," "Indifferent," or "Dislike" to being an actor, architect, author of novels or airplane pilot. After the responses of a sample group of CPAs are tabulated for some four hundred items, then their collective responses (percentages of like, indifferent or dislike) for each item are contrasted to a representative group of Men-In-General (MIG). When some 75 items emerge which indicate a preference (like) or rejection (dislike) which are unique to the CPAs relative to MIG, then a SVIB scale of these unique items is established for CPAs. And, all subsequent individuals who take the SVIB will see how their responses to the entire test of four hundred items compares to the responses of the CPA norm group and norm groups for some seventy other occupations. Correspondingly, the vocational interests of individuals represent a collection of their four hundred item responses, a scale score on seventy occupations, and a basic interest score on twenty-two scales such as public speaking, office practices, science, nature, social service, music, or writing. All of these contribute to a person's vocational interest profile.

Each of the norm groups, whose item responses contrasted with the MIG sample, are comprised of members who are *both* satisfied and successful in their work. As a result, students should be cautioned against entering an occupation or profession where they have unusually low scale scores and should be encouraged to work at a job where they have a high comparability of vocational interests with their colleagues and co-workers. Again, as with interpretations of ability and personality test scores, counseling on vocational interests should be done only by trained psychologists and counselors.

Data on CPAs

When a recent sample of CPAs were scored on the basic interest scales they distinguished themselves by receiving their highest scores on the law-politics, mathematics, public speaking, business management, religious activities, office practices, merchandising and adventure scales. Their lowest basic interest scale scores were on the agriculture, mechanical, nature, art, technical supervision and science scales. All of the other basic interest scale scores for the CPAs (social service, teaching, writing, recreational leadership, sales, music military activities, and medical service) fell in between the two extreme groupings.

On some of the individual items where CPAs differ in a unique way from the Men-In-General (MIG) group, one gets a brief glimpse at the detailed vocational interest preferences or rejections of CPAs. For the following items, CPAs have a *stronger* preference for the item than does the MIG sample: cashier in bank, factory manager, income tax accountant, judge, corporation lawyer, manufacturer, office manager, statistician, stockbroker, algebra, arithmetic, bookkeeping, calculus, economics, geometry, golf, bridge, going to church, writing reports, living in the city, optimists, people who have made fortunes in business, and work where you move from place to place. For these items the CPAs have a uniquely lesser preference (or stronger rejection) for the item than does the MIG sample: actor, artists, city employee, farmer, inventor, poet, sculptor, agriculture, art, botany, nature study, zoology, art galleries, social problem movies, looking at a collection of antique furniture, democrats, physical activity and inventivenes.

No value judgments should be placed on whether the vocational interests of CPAs are good or bad. What is important is to recognize that these preferences or rejections represent the set of vocational interests which are *uniquely* descriptive of CPAs. Moreover, individuals considering a career in accounting should, at some time before entering the profession, determine if their ability, personality and vocational interests adequately match those of successful and satisfied accountants already in the profession. An awareness of this essential matchup is something accounting educators should be concerned about—if for no other reason than the high professional staff turnover rates observed in public accounting.

SUMMARY

Organic intelligence and genetic personality characteristics change very little beyond the early formative years. Accounting educators should not attempt to affect these attributes in their students since any changes that result are not likely to be lasting or significant. Most importantly, individuals should be recognized for their individuality. Vocational interests, on the other hand, are quite malleable through the undergraduate years for most students. Because these interests may be seriously affected by accounting educators, these educators should portray only the most realistic picture of professional accounting. Moreover counseling experiments involving ability, personality, or vocational interests should be conducted only by accredited psychologists.

Accounting educators should concentrate on the learning setting—make it as stimulating as possible—no matter what individual differences in ability, personality, and vocational interest may exist among the class members. Educators should be more concerned about the personality characteristics of their colleagues than of their students. When ability and knowledge of students are approximately equal, effective learning is probably more stimulated (or not stimulated) by the personality of the classroom professor than by any other personal characteristic.

FOOTNOTES

[1] Marvin D. Dunnette, *Personnel Selection and Placement* (Wadsworth Publishing Company, Inc., 1966), p.1.

[2] For an insightful treatment of this issue, see Roger J. Williams, *Free and Unequal: The Biological Basis of Individual Liberty* (John Wiley & Sons, Inc., 1964).

[3] G.U. Yule and M.G. Kendall, *An Introduction to the Theory of Statistics*, 13th Edition (London: Griffin, 1949), p.95.

[4] J.A. Harris, C.M. Jackson, D.G. Paterson and R.L. Scammon, *The Measurement of Man* (University of Minnesota Press, 1930), p.94.

[5] R. Ruggles and G.W. Allport, "Recent Application of the A-S Reaction Study," *Journal of Abnormal and Social Psychology* (1939, 34), pp. 518-528.

[6] L.M. Terman and Maud A. Merrill, *Measuring Intelligence* (Houghton Mifflin, 1937), p.37.

[7] Anne Anastasi, *Differential Psychology: Individual and Group Differences in Behavior*, Third Edition (The Macmillan Company, 1963), p.23.

[8] Ibid., p.446.

[9] For an analysis of the 1528 individuals originally tested as children and followed for 35 years see: Barbara S. Burks, Dorthea W. Jensen and L.M. Terman, *The Promise of Youth: Follow-Up Studies of a Thousand Gifted Children* (Stanford University Press, 1930), L.M. Terman and Melita H. Oden, *The Gifted Child Grows Up* (Stanford University Press, 1947), and L.M. Terman and Melita H. Oden, *The Gifted Group at Midlife* (Stanford University Press, 1959).

[10] Anastasi, p. 447.

[11] Christopher Jencks, *Inequality: A Reassessment of the Effect of Family and Schooling in America* (Basic Books, Inc., 1972), p.188.

[12] Ibid., p.185.

[13] Jerry E. Bishop, "The Argument Over Heredity and IQ," *The Wall Street Journal* (June 20, 1973), p.14.

[14] For a complete review of the studies see Arthur R. Jensen, *Genetics & Education* (Harper & Row, 1973), R.J. Herrnstein, *I.Q. in the Meritocracy* (Atlantic-Little-Brown, 1973), and Theodosius Dobzhansky, *Genetic Diversity & Human Equality* (Basic Books, 1973).

[15] Bishop, p.14.

[16] Ibid.

[17] Ibid.

[18] O.K. Buros, Jr., editor, *Mental Measurements Yearbook* (Gryphon Press, 1965).

[19] Anne Arastasi, editor, *Testing Problems in Prospective* (American Council on Education, 1966).

[20] J. McV. Hunt, *Intelligence and Experience* (The Ronald Press Company, 1961).

[21] J.P. Guilford, *Intelligence, Creativity and Their Educational Implications* Robert R. Knapp, 1968).

[22] Lee J. Cronbach, *Essentials of Psychological Testing*, 3rd ed. (Harper & Row, Publishers, 1969).

[23] American Institute of Certified Public Accountants, *Uniform CPA Examination, November 1972, Questions and Official Answers* (AICPA, 1973).

[24] John Grant Rhode, Edward E. Lawler III and Edward H. Murphy, *The Accounting Classification Test* (Seattle, Washington: Professional Affiliates, Ltd., 1971).

[25] J.P. Guilford, *Personality* (McGraw-Hill, 1959).

[26] G.W. Allport and H.W. Odbert, "Trait-names, A Psycholexical Study," *Psychological Monographs*, (47(1)).

[27] G.W. Allport, *Pattern and Growth in Personality* (Holt, Rinehart & Winston, 1961), p.28.

[28] R.B. Cattell, *Personality* (McGraw-Hill, 1950), pp. 2-3.

[29] E.R. Gutherie, "Personality in Terms of Associative Learning," in J.Mc.V. Hunt (Ed.), *Personality and the Behavior Disorders*, Vol. 1 (Ronald Press Company, 1944), p.48.

[30] Salvatore R. Maddi, *Personality Theories: A Comparative Analysis* (The Dorsey Press, 1972,) p.9.

[31] Calvin S. Hall and Gardner Lindzey, *Theories of Personality*, 2nd edition (John Wiley & Sons, Inc., 1970), pp. 8-9.

[32] Irwin G. Sarason, *Personality: An Objective Approach*, 2nd edition (John Wiley & Sons, Inc., 1972), p.15.

[33] The essence of these theories is synthesized primarily from Hall and Lindzey, Maddi, Sarason, and Albert Mehrabean, *An Analysis of Personality Theories* (Prentice-Hall, Inc., 1968).

[34] Maddi, p.39.
[35] H.A. Murray, *Explorations in Personality: A Clinical and Experimental Study of Fifty Men of College Age* (Oxford, 1938).
[36] E.H. Erikson, *Childhood and Society* (Norton, 1950).
[37] Harry Stack Sullivan, *Conceptions of Modern Psychiatry* (William Allanson White Psychiatric Foundation, 1947).
[38] Carl R. Rogers, "A Theory of Therapy, Personality, and Interpersonal Relationships as Developed in the Client-Centered Framework," in S. Koch (ed.), *Psychology: A Study of a Science* (McGraw-Hill, 1959), Vol.3.
[39] Abraham H. Maslow, *Motivation and Personality* (Harper & Row, 1954).
[40] Otto Rank, *The Trauma of Birth* (Harcourt, Brace, 1929), and Otto Rank, *Will Therapy and Truth and Reality* (Knopf, 1945).
[41] Andras Angyal, "A Theoretical Model for Personality Studies," in D. Krech and G.S. Klein (editors), *Theoretical Models and Personality Theory* (Duke University Press, 1952), pp. 131-142.
[42] Carl Gustav Jung, *Modern Man in Search of a Soul* (Harcourt, Brace & World, 1933).
[43] Alfred Adler, *The Practice and Theory of Individual Psychology* (Harcourt, Brace & World, 1927), and Alfred Adler, *Individual Psychology* in C. Murchison (editor), *Psychologies of 1930* (Clark University Press, 1930).
[44] Gordon W. Allport, *Becoming: Basic Considerations for a Psychology of Personality*, (New Haven, Conn: Yale University Press, 1955).
[45] Erich Fromm, *Man for Himself*, (New York: Holt, Rinehart & Winston, 1947).
[46] George A. Kelly, *The Psychology of Personal Constructs* (New York: Norton, 1955), Vol. 1.
[47] Marvin D. Dunnette, *Personal Selection and Placement* (Wadsworth Publishing Company, Inc., 1966), p. 63.
[48] Hall and Lindzey, *loc. cit.*
[49] E.K. Strong, Jr., *Vocational Interests of Men and Women* (Stanford, California: Stanford University Press, 1943), and E.K. Strong, Jr., *Vocational Interests 17 Years After College* (Minneapolis, Minnesota: University of Minnesota Press, 1955).
[50] David P. Campbell, *Handbook for the Strong Vocational Interest Blank* (Stanford, California: Stanford University Press, 1971). p. 7.
[51] The context for the section on individual differences in vocational interests is primarily developed from three sources: E.K. Strong, Jr. (Revised by David P. Campbell), *SVIB Strong Vocational Interest Blanks Manual for Men's Forms and Women's Forms* (Stanford, California: Stanford University Press, 1966); David P. Campbell, *SVIB Strong Vocational Interest Blanks Manual 1969 Supplement* (Stanford, California: Stanford University Press, 1969); and David P. Campbell, *Handbook for the Strong Vocational Interest Blank* (Stanford, California: Stanford University Press, 1971).

Interpersonal and Social Environment

James E. Sorensen
University of Denver

Following Professor Rhode's suggestion to focus on groups of individuals leads to a discussion of the accounting classroom. Because the classroom is an organized social environment, person-to-person relationships have both psychological and social character. To understand the psychological events in a learning situation requires an understanding of the social context in which they occur and vice versa. While no single discussion could cover all of the conditions and effects of individual interacting in group learning settings, two major topics have been singled out for their possible special significance to accounting educators:

A. Teacher-centered versus student-centered approaches to learning
B. Student groupings
   a. individual versus group work
   b. cooperation versus competition
   c. small versus large class sizes

Each topic has been researched extensively and only a few highlights of the central concepts and findings are presented. More detailed descriptions are available by consulting the cited references.

Each of these topics departs from a varying foundation of social norms. "Social norms are ideas held by two or more persons about how categories of persons should behave in specified types of situations."[1] While social norms specify many guides for classroom behavior for both the instructor and the student, conformity to and deviation from these norms is variable:

Conformity appears to be a function of such factors as: the person's knowledge of the norm, the strength of the norm, the strength of the person's attraction to the group, the likelihood the conformity or deviation will be observable by others, the strength of the sanctions expected for conforming or deviating, personality predispositions (such as dependency, acceptance of authority, self-confidence). Whether or not a person will conform will depend not only factors but also on the strength of the tendency to deviate which is determined by parallel considerations (e.g., is the tendency to deviate from the norms of one group a tendency to conform to the norms of another group to which the person belongs?).[2]

Leadership Styles

The foundation of varying leadership styles—teacher-centered or learner-centered—is built on social norms that specify different types of behavior for both the instructor and the student. The teacher-centered style is roughly equivalent to an authoritarian, directive, controlling style while the learner-centered style is roughly equivalent to a democratic, permissive, and considerate style. The now-classic Lippitt and White[3] experiment studied the effect of different styles of leadership on children's motivation. Children led by authoritarian leaders (who set policy, dictated activities, and made arbitrary evaluations) were productive only when the leader was present. When the leader left the room, productivity decreased and aggressive behavior increased; work was generally done carelessly and the children showed little initiative toward and pride in the class activities.

In contrast, the children led by democratic leaders (who encouraged and guided group discussions and decisions about policies) revealed less dependence on the leader and little change in behavior when the leader left the room. While the Lippitt and White results have been supported generally by other researchers[4], authoritarian leadership can be more successful under certain conditions. Fiedler[5] found that highly favored or highly unfavored leaders can do well with authoritarian, controlling, directive styles while moderately favored leaders fare better with democratic, permissive, considerate styles. Additionally he finds the authoritarian, controlling directive style more effective if the task is routine rather than nonstandard; nonstandard ("creative") tasks are better performed in democratic, permissive, considerate settings. Personality enters too. Campion[6] found that persons with high need for authoritarianism and low need for independence performed better under nonparticipative (authoritarian) styles while those with low need for authoritarianism and high need for independence performed better under participative (democratic) conditions.

At best, the research on the impact of teacher-centered ("authoritarian") or learner-centered ("democratic") normative structures is mixed. Besides the difficulty of labeling the kinds of teaching methods within each category, the modest research findings available are contradictory. In general the leadership research suffers from inadequate conceptualization and the studies in educational settings are no exception. Anderson concludes "we cannot state with any certainty that either teacher-centered or learner-centered methods are associated with greater learning".[7] No one teaching style appears to be uniformly effective and this finding suggests a diversity of teaching styles can be effective. Yet, as in the case of non-academic research settings, interest and satisfaction seem to be higher in the learner-centered ("democratic, permissive, considerate") settings than the teacher-centered classes. Perhaps there is an implication for accounting educators: would learner-centered approaches attract and retain more majors and graduates in accounting programs?

Individual vs. Groups

But what about the norms and interpersonal relationships among students? Are students more productive when they work alone or together in a group? While all students do not profit equally from a group format, most of the research[8] favors the superiority of groups over solitary learning. Group work is facilitated by:

1. stimulation from the presence of others
2. pooled resources
3. higher probability of able persons included in group
4. correction of blind spots and errors
5. stimulation of ideas by building on each other's ideas
6. learning from the experience of others

Yet groups can be less effective than individual work because of:

1. conflicting goals, interests, and habits of the members
2. communication difficulties, especially as group size increases
3. coordination difficulties
4. distraction and overstimulation
5. excessive dependence upon others or work avoidance

Probably the greatest benefit in groups is that the least able and those with the least resources are likely to be helped most. If accounting educators were encouraged to expand their use of group work (in and out of the classroom), perhaps increased individual learning can be achieved.

Cooperation vs. Competition

Both of these variables can affect the relationships between students and instructor as well as relationships among students. One of the most interesting uses of cooperation and competition is in grading. Many studies of cooperative versus competitive grading suggest substantial effects on communication, perceptions, attitudes toward one another, and type of task orientation. In describing a study by Deutch, Deutch and Hornstein[9] summarize the similarity of these studies.

The sections which were graded cooperatively were characterized by much friendlier discussion; they learned each other's names more rapidly, they were more attentive and more influenced by what other students said and were more nearly satisfied by their discussions, and they felt more secure personally. In the competitive sections students showed more aggressive, obstructive, oppositional, and self-defensive behavior; there was also less sense of being listened to or of being understood; there were more misunderstandings and more frequent need for repetition of what had just been said in these sections.

Of greatest interest to accounting educators is the fact that in general the students in either grading system seemed equally motivated while there were no significant differences in individual learning as a result of the grading procedure. Accounting educators should carefully review traditional testing procedures; perhaps it is possible to achieve comparable individual achievement along with a substantial improvement in social relationships. (For the details of an actual application of cooperative grading in accounting, see Professor Shirley's article "Cooperation Vs. Competition" in Section IV.)

Small versus Large Classes

Concern over classroom size stems from:

1. Desire to optimize learning
2. Impact of class size on educational costs

Up to this point, the research studies of class size simply are not conclusive. Depending on the research cited[10], smaller classes versus larger classes are favored from five to one to no advantage at all. Generally smaller classes are credited with greater variety in instructional methods and more desirable instructional methods[11] such as:

1. Increased opportunities for students to select learning materials and greater variety in learning materials
2. Increased face-to-face relationships between students and the instructor
3. Increased knowledge by instructors of their students' abilities and potential
4. Increased instructor attention to informal student guidance
5. Increased instructor attention to non-overt student behavior denoting emotional stability
6. Increased work with both the able and the less-able
7. Increased attention to grouping and greater flexibility of grouping.

When class size increased, these practices were used with less frequency and consistency.

While the evidence tends to favor the smaller class, Varner[12] summarizes several decades of research and policy statements of various educational bodies by restating the question:

...Rather than looking for the optimum figure, as has been done in the past, the question should read "Best classroom size for what ends and under what circumstances?" New methods of classroom organization and staff utilization which include team-teaching, non-grading, flexible schedule with large-small groups and independent instruction, use of paraprofessional personnel, and vertical and horizontal grouping have been . . . considerations . . . of grade levels from kindergarten through college . . .

Use of *varied* class size for varying objectives as outlined by Besvinick[13] provides special insights for accounting educators:

1. Classes of *unlimited size* would enable efficient "one-way transmission" of knowledge, information, and opinion by instructors and guest speakers. Class discussion or question-answer sessions would not be attempted.
2. The purpose of classes of *moderate size* (40-50 pupils) would be skill development (e.g., mathematics, physical education, typing). The teacher would supervise individuals, but would not attempt to communicate with the class as a whole.
3. Classes of *activity size* (25 pupils)

would be appropriate for science or language laboratories, art classes, or vocational shops.
4. Discussion, clarification, and exploration would take place in *small groups* of 10-20 pupils.
5. Provisions for *independent study* would involve assigning pupils to central "subject-matter stations," where they would work on material of their choice but related to that station's emphasis. As a student showed proficiency in a certain area, he would be released from reporting to the teacher and would then be free to concentrate his attention wherever he wished. The student would gradually be allowed more freedom of action, as he was able to use the latitude given him.

For accounting educators, perhaps two conclusions may be useful:

1. In undergraduate skills building courses such as accounting and related quantitative methods, moderate sized classes (25-50 students) or smaller appear to provide an opportunity for desirable teaching practices to emerge.
2. Accounting educators should experiment with class size using varied educational techniques and adequate research design so varied educational objectives, cost structures, and class sizes can be assessed more clearly.

FOOTNOTES

[1] J. Eugene Haas and Thomas E. Drabek, *Complex Organizations: A Sociological Perspective* (New York: The Macmillan Company, 1973) p. 127.

[2] Morton Deutsch, "Group Behavior", *The Encyclopedia of the Social Sciences*. 1968, pp. 265-276.

[3] R. Lippitt and R. White, "The 'Social Climate' of Children's Groups," in R. Barket, et al., *Child Behavior and Development* (New York: McGraw-Hill, 1943), pp. 485-508.

[4] J. P. Campbell, et. al. "Managerial Style: Research Results and a Social-Psychological View," *Managerial Behavior, Performance, and Effectiveness* (New York: McGraw-Hill Book Company, 1970), pp. 415-422.

[5] F. Fiedler, "Engineer the Job to Fit the Manager," *Harvard Business Review*, Vol. 43, 1965, pp. 115-122.

[6] J. E. Campion, Jr. "Effects of Managerial Style on Subordinates' Attitudes and Performance in a Simulated Organization Setting." Unpublished Doctoral Dissertation, University of Minnesota, 1968.

[7] R. C. Anderson, "Learning in Discussion: A Resume of the Authoritarian-Democratic Studies," *Harvard Educational Review*. Vol. 29, 1959, p. 206. Also see, S.S. Boocock, "Toward a Sociology of Learning: A Selective Review of Existing Research," *Sociology of Education*, Vol. 39, 1966, pp. 1-45.

[8] G. Watson, "An Evaluation of Small Group Work in a Large Class", *Journal of Educational Psychology*, Vol. 44, 1953, pp. 385-408.

[9] M. Deutsch and H. Hornstein, "The Social Psychology of Education," in J. Davitz and S. Ball, *Psychology of the Educational Process* (New York: McGraw-Hill Book Company, 1970), p. 199.

[10] Sherrell E. Varner, *Class Size*, (Washington, D.C., National Education Association, 1968) pp.5-33.

[11] Harold Richman, *Instructional Practices as Affected by Class Size*, Unpublished doctoral dissertation, Teachers College, Columbia University New York, 1955.

[12] Varner, *op. cit.* (in document resume) Educational Resources Information Center (ERIC) Document No. ED 032 614.

[13] Sidney Besvinick, "Scheduling Problems: How Many? How Long?" *Clearing House* 39: 425-27 March 1965 as reported in Varner, *loc. cit.*, p. 34.

Cultural and Economic Environment and the Disadvantaged

Introduction

Cultural and economic background are potent factors that differentiate one student and one professor from another. As accounting educators seek to attract and propel disadvantaged groups into accounting careers, the role of cultural and economic differences create difficulties. What emerges from the next two articles is a realization that there is a vital hidden eco-cultural curriculum which appears to have a major effect on the success or failure of the official accounting educational process. Professor Mobley identifies some of the key forces reducing the absorption of several minorities—in this case, blacks—but the arguments appear to be generalizable to other groups. She concludes with specific suggestions for accounting educators on the key topics of testing and communications. Researchers Fess and Hamilton explore the results of a large midwestern university's specific program to attract and retain minorities in academic programs. While the results are encouraging the pervasive impact of economic and cultural variations are still quite visible.

Economic and Cultural Environment: The Special Case of the Disadvantaged

Sybil C. Mobley
Florida A and M University

Introduction

The failure of teachers to respect the cultural heritage and mental ability of disadvantaged students creates a demoralizing atmosphere which precludes academic accomplishment. A more positive, less patronizing attitude is required for a meaningful study of group differences in test performance and communication.

Accounting has been called one of the least integrated professions in America.[1] To correct this situation, employers have committed themselves to a recruitment program for achieving meaningful integration. However, people cannot be recruited directly into the accounting profession; they must first be recruited into schools. Efforts of employers to integrate their staffs will be futile if sufficient numbers of minorities are not enrolled and graduated from accounting academic programs. Accounting educators have the responsibility to investigate the issues involved in the training of disadvantaged youths for the accounting profession.

Although there are many opportunities for effective action by disadvantaged groups, these opportunities are not the concern of this paper. Also, the problems of counseling, recruiting and teaching disadvantaged groups are too numerous for full discussion here. This paper is limited to some of the issues involved in teaching accounting. The references presented are drawn from a limited study and experimentation with only one group, blacks. However, because these inferences suggest changes for accounting educators the proposed changes hold implications for all disadvantaged groups.

The Economic Environment

The economic environment of disadvantaged students poses two critical problems. First, these students will need funding if they are to be permitted to share in the educational process. Second, education may not reap the same economic benefits for them as for their advantaged counterparts.

The commitment of educational institutions to provide funding for disadvantaged students has not extended to any great degree beyond their willingness to administer federal funds.[2] There is little evidence of these institutions reallocating those funds which have historically been restricted to the advantaged group.

Many educators have not shown adequate concern when the economic benefits of an accounting education are less for disadvantaged groups than for advantaged groups. Typically, disadvantaged groups are viewed as high risk students who "stretched" themselves to get through school and their failure to enjoy the full economic benefits of an accounting education are the result of their personal inadequacies as opposed to possible flaws in the operation of the economic system.

The failure to address the economic problems is largely a function of the cultural environment and, therefore the cultural environment deserves special intensive study.

The Cultural Environment

The cultural environment generates two critical problems:

1. Being a part of a culture which is

labeled "disadvantaged" carries tremendous handicaps; there is an assumption of inferiority which extends beyond the mores and folkways of the group to an assumption of its mental and sometimes moral inferiority.

2. Different cultural patterns tend to develop different competencies and approaches to academic competencies which are often unrecognized and unappreciated.

Efforts of teachers to deal with disadvantaged students are usually one of two types:

1. To identify an exception and promote him as a "lucky find." No substantive changes occur either in the attitudes of the majority community toward minorities or in the overall plight of the minority group. Little concern is shown for the total impact on the selected student. Generally because the student is recognized as "different", the student will become the recipient of great economic rewards and this, in turn, is supposed to make the student forever grateful to his benefactors. The psychological dilemma resulting from half acceptance and half rejection is the price paid for such success.[3]

2. To gather disadvantaged youth as guinea pigs in a funded research project (often assigned a patronizing acronym which belies the perceived superiority of the experimenter). The true cost of the research project is not limited to the funds spent; its greatest cost may be the destruction of the self-confidence of minorities and the appearance of credibility given the charge of racial inferiority. If the project succeeds, the mental superiority of the white is apparent because he succeeded at a difficult task, but if the project fails, the altruistic concern of the white is documented; either way the suspicions of inferiority relayed by society are reinforced and the group's self-image is damaged even further. This approach has little regard for the sensitivity of the minority student. Minorities are assumed to have no pride or to suffer no embarrassment at being labeled "disadvantaged," "the minority problem" and other terms that denote inadequacy.

Psychological Impact.

An understanding of the psychological repercussions which minorities suffer as a result of their presumed inferiority is a prerequisite for the education of the disadvantaged.

Knowlton has referred to this problem in saying: "But the general 'anglo' presumption of cultural superiority tends to destroy his (the disadvantaged) confidence in himself and in his home and ethnic group. It often contributes to an emotional confusion and inhibits his intellectual advancement and affects his personal opportunities."[4]

Rosenthall and Jacabson reported that:

"The reaction of disadvantaged students to teacher expectations has been shown to be of major importance. Indeed, one study suggests that almost all of the variance in learning by children from low-income families is a function of the teacher's belief that these children cannot achieve as well as others".[5]

Others have commented:

"Teachers influence student motivations and expectations by such behavior as fluctuations in their voices or changes of facial expression. Students may respond to these expressions with discouragement. All too often teachers bluntly and even cruelly tell students that their abilities are low. As a result, those students may make little or no effort."[6]

"Children are responsive to the expectations of their environment. They read clearly both the conscious and the unconscious message. The ordinary process of learning vaults him (the black child) into the center of everyone's conflict, namely: Will I be smart, clean, clever, obedient, loved, successful, important, rich (and white), or will I be stupid, dirty, awkward, defiant, despised, and an unimportant, impoverished failure (who is black)?"[7]

Cultural Differences

If innate equality were assumed, efforts should be directed toward changing those forces in society that have created disadvantaged groups. However, efforts have been concentrated, not on the cause, but on the effect.

For integration, as defined by the educational system, is a one-way process. It involves the "uplifting" or "headstarting" of black kids into a white world. It centers on terms like "culturally deprived," which means simply that the identified culture is not acceptable to white, middle-class standards, although it is clear that Negroes have a very distinct and rich culture of their own.[8]

Knowles and Prewitt report that:

As the situation now stands, the "white experts" in the educational system tend to view black students as potential whites with little consideration given to their distinct culture and style of life. Our educators have insisted, consciously or unconsciously, that black children be educated out of their blackness.[9]

There is a strong urge to use the term "culturally different" instead of "culturally disadvantaged." However, the reality of the situation prevails. In a society where punishment for being different is great and rewards for displaying the culture of the dominant group are significant, practicality dictates the disadvantages for minority cultures must be recognized.

Cultural Appreciation

Educators should strive to develop a noncondescending appreciation for the culture of the disadvantaged.

Minority values deserve preservation, and motivation for school success is strengthened by the self-esteem and aspiration for achievement that arise in part from pride in one's inheritance.[10]

This (implied rejection of the disadvantaged student's culture) is a rejection of much that is precious to him personally and may be of great worth to society in general. The damage done to his self-image and ultimately to his attitudes and motives may be irreparable.[11]

The above arguments nave been advanced principally through quotations. In this way evidence is marshalled to show the need for a non-condescending cultural appreciation and to demonstrate its recognition by diverse authorities. But have these notions fallen on deaf ears? Faced with a choice of protecting a group's selfhood, sense of personal worth, capacity to perform, self esteem and confidence, and promoting the dominent group's own culture, the majority community's sense of values may simply favor the dominant culture.

NEW DIRECTIONS IN TESTING AND COMMUNICATIONS

The balance of the discussion advances new approaches and suggests opportunities for study and action of two topics of great concern to educators:

1. test performance
2. communications

Test Performance

Much has been written in the explanation of the low level of test performance of disadvantaged groups. The three most popular theories are

1. the poor educational background of the groups,
2. the cultural bias of the tests,
3. the genetic deficiency of racial groups.[12]

Most educators endorse only the first two. For some disciplines, these two theories are valid in some degree. Acceptance of these theories by accounting educators may suggest tacit endorsement of theory three, however. If accounting teachers prefer students who have not had accounting prior to entering college, if accounting transcends cultural boundaries, and if accounting educators sincerely believe in the innate equality of disadvantaged groups, there must be a concentrated search for more acceptable explanations of poor test performance records.

Impact of Culture

The cultural patterns suggested earlier tend to develop certain competencies and approaches to academic work. These competencies and approaches account for much of the difference in test performance. To make sure the issues identified relate to the cultural and economic environment (i.e., postnatal factors) and not innate ability (i.e., racial factors), the discussion includes factors related to differences in performance within the majority community. These differences cannot be explained in biological terms; they are related to the cultural and economic environment.

Blacks perform at a lower level than whites and southern whites perform at a lower level than northern whites. Documentations of these generalizations have been recorded for decades.[13] Inferiority of schools does not provide an adequate explanation of these results nor does the theory that the content of the tests reflects a cultural bias offers a full explanation. The effect of culture as it relates to cultural competencies needs to be examined.

The economic environments of the North and the South are technologically different. "The technology of an economic system imposes a structure on its society which not only determines its economic activities but also influences its social relationships and well being."[14] The cultural and economic environment are interdependent. The economic differences between the North and the South are reflected as differences in their cultures. The South is viewed as friendly and more conversational than the North. Personal contacts are more frequent, more acceptable and more complete than in the North. These cultural differences are postnatal influences which find expression in the development of different competencies and approaches.

The economic environment for blacks and other disadvantaged groups is technologically different from the majority group. This is generally true notwithstanding the geographical closeness of the groups. These technological differences impose a different structure on the black society which is reflected in the competencies and approaches developed.

Actually the differences in northern whites and southern whites and in whites in general and blacks in general are the same in terms of direction; they vary in magnitude but both differences are quickly decreasing. As a result of industrialization of the South and the advent of new economic opportunities for minorities, the South is becoming more like the North and blacks are becoming more like whites. Television, other media, and travel by individuals influence changes in both the North and the South, both white and black.

The method by which these groups were taught has a great influence on their level of performance on typically administered tests. Southerners and blacks have learned more by listening and less by reading than have northerners and whites.[15] Students are required to search more for their answers in the North; they are instructed more in the South. Assuming that the same course content is transmitted, each group develops different competencies.

One who has learned by listening has developed the ability to interpret facial expressions, voice inflection, emphasis, etc. He does not have to rely totally on words to get an understanding. One who has learned by reading has developed the ability to interpret precisely the written word.

The implications of these observations are great when one considers that accomplishment is typically evaluated only through written tests. This limitation, the form of test more so than its content, constitutes a significant cultural bias in the major national tests. Tests measure not only how much of a given body of knowledge students have learned by the competencies they have developed in the learning process. The cryptic nature of most standardized tests indicates that many tests tend to measure one's ability to decipher more so than the mastery of course content. Little consideration is given to the possibility that other valuable abilities have been developed and should be measured.

Cultural Content vs. Cultural Skills

Explanations of differences in performance have centered on the portion of learning that takes place outside of the classroom in one's cultural setting and that some cultures offer a richer body of knowledge than others. Sutdents who are culturally advantaged therefore have a better opportunity to score high on the standardized tests. Because the comparative results of test performance are tabulated in terms of specific subject matter learned, these explanations have centered on cultural content while overlooking cultural skills.

Different environments develop different abilities. For instance, Earnest A. Haggard, has shown when test items read aloud to the deprived children while they followed in their booklets, the children did much better.[16] Children are "deprived" as a result of their economic and social environment. The same children with the same innate talents would have developed differently in a different environment. Southern and black students may know the answers, but they may not know the questions. Frank Riesmann quotes Irving Taylor, formerly Project Coordinator on the staff of the Institute of Developmental Studies as saying:

> He (Taylor) says that they (disadvantaged children) use words in a different way and are not as dependent on words for their sole form of communication, but nevertheless they are imaginative at the verbal level...Taylor feels that deprived individuals are not as restricted by verbal forms of communication, but tend to permit language to interact more with non-verbal means of communication, such as gestures and pictures. The interaction with other kinds of communication gives them the potential for for 'breaking through the language barrier,' they are not forced to think in terms of the structure of language as are so many people. They are less word bound.[17]

How Riesmann could quote Taylor and still arrive at his patronizing "slow-gifted child" is difficult to explain.[18] Taylor referred to abilities developed as a result of being disadvantaged as economic and cultural influences. "Gifted" identifies group differences as innate; this approach reverses the cause-effect relationship so that the disadvantaged condition is viewed as a result of innate qualities.

Valid Tests?

Before evaluating students by test, the legitimacy of the tests should be established. Conventional tests only document the ability of students to "read writing" but do not test the ability to "read people." Both abilities are important. Assuming that advantaged and disadvantaged groups have the same distribution of innate abilities, their different environments reflect different cultural patterns which in turn tend to develop different strengths. However, a variety of strengths is needed, only one of which is generally emphasized in schools.

This unbalanced emphasis possibly accounts for the disturbingly low correspendence between high academic averages and success in life.[19] The world is not all written. If education is to prepare one for life, the school value system should hold greater correspondence with actual world values.

Changes in Accounting

There are some encouraging signs in accounting education; the behavioral dimension of accounting education has recently emerged and is a move in the people-skills direction. Public accounting is alleged to be one-half public and one-half accounting; traditionally schools have only trained for the accounting half and neglected the other half dealing with the public—or people skills. In the financial departments of industrial firms, more and more financial executives want accounting reports in oral-flip-chart form and in color graphs that authorities suggest are the preferred form for disadvantaged students.[20]

The Real Problem

The real issue is this: students are not searching for the precise word meaning of questions but rather they are attempting to get the "feel" for a question; this process is often accompanied by inappropriate assumptions and when the students' inappropriate assumptions are singled out for analysis, performance will improve.

Communications

While many students have inadequate communication skills, many agree the communication skills of disadvantaged groups, blacks and other minorities, are lower than for other groups. A close look at the circumstances is warranted.

Blacks are unique in that they have a changing, flexible language—changing every month, every year. The circumlocution which was historically necessary for survival has evolved into a refined art which binds blacks together with a sense of identity and group solidarity.[21] Evasion in speech is accomplished in part by permitting facial expression, mood, emphasis, etc. to change connotations from positive to negative (and negative to positive) and to change adjectives to nouns, nouns to verbs, etc. Blacks do not serve words; words serve blacks. Blacks are without challenge in the mastery of an art which has added music, romance, beauty and fascination to a generally dull language.

However, the accomplishment is not without its disadvantages. Knowledge is cumulative and can be transmitted from generation to generation only through words that hold a consistent meaning through time. Regardless of the color and joy that can be added when one is no longer word bound, a precise, fixed language is needed for the communication function. Formal English is a requisite for progress. Even so, all lives could be enriched if our day to day contacts were not so rigidly structured with a word bound language.

Impact of Changing Language

If a native of Italy came to the United States at age three, eighteen years later, at age twenty-one, there would be little evidence that he once spoke the Italian language. If a native of Italy came to the United States at age thirty, eighteen years later, at age forty-eight, it is very likely that there would be substantial evidence that he once spoke the Italian language. The longer a language is spoken, the more it becomes a basic part of one's personality; the more difficult it is to change. At age eighteen, most advantaged people in the United States have spoken the same language for most of their lives. Speech is a fixed, stable part of their personalities. Because Blacks have a shifting, flexible language they remain in a position comparable to the three-year old Italian cited above; they can change completely.

Disadvantaged whites are not masters of formal English. However, they have made the *same* errors for a lifetime; these errors are a basic, very difficult to change part of their personality. Blacks are not masters of formal English and they have made *different* errors throughout their lives, neither of which has become a basic part of their personality.

When blacks are placed in a different environment, they will acquire the speech of that environment *provided they are made to feel a part of that environment and they are permitted to retain their confidence*. In other words, if blacks are made comfortable in their new environment, they will quickly and effectively acquire the language of their new setting. The role of personal comfort in speech is easy to understand, for most people can recall instances of persons considered exceptionally articulate who when required to speak unexpectedly to an unfriendly or a hostile audience, committed serious grammatical blunders. One's inner emotions, insecurities, confidences, happiness, fears, threats, love, hate, arrogance, modesty, compassion, are reflected in speech. When those factors that contribute to a black's comfort are present, his speech will automatically adapt to that of the environment; when those factors that contribute to a black's discomfort are present, the discomfort will be reflected in a deterioration of his speech. These cause-effect relationships are true to some degree for all groups, but the impact is more significant for blacks. Because of the flexibility of the shifting language, the black's speech is vulnerable. He can generally take on new speech patterns at a fast pace and likewise his speech can be impaired more easily than others.

This vulnerable quality places blacks in a unique position. If blacks fail to improve their communication skills, the schools, the teachers and the advantaged students should accept a good measure of responsibility.

SUMMARY

Whatever strengths or weaknesses the individual student brings with him to the university are greatly influenced by cultural and economic background. The attitudes and actions of instructors and peers will have a great deal of impact on the achievements of disadvantaged groups. Three key suggestions are summarized to improve the educational environment and achievement of the disadvantaged student:

1. Develop a sincere respect for the uniqueness of disadvantaged students. Do not destroy their self-confidence by thinking of them as inferior.
2. Recognize the cultural bias of written tests; develop a more balanced testing program using both verbal and written tests—tests which will more accurately indicate success in life and the world of both paper and people.
3. Do not accept differences in patterns of communication as differences in intellect; accept the responsibility of providing an environment conducive to acquiring a mastery of formal English.

FOOTNOTES

[1] See Bert N. Mitchell "The Black Minority in the CPA Profession" *The Journal of Accountancy* (October, 1969), pp. 41-46. Also Committee on Minority Recruitment and Equal Opportunity, Report 1973,(American Institute of Certified Public Accountants, New York), pp. 3 and 8.

[2] See editorial by Gene I. Maeroff, "Minority Enrollments, Some Second Thoughts", *The New York Times,* Sunday, May 20, 1973.

[3] "The learned black man found himself isolated by society generally as one who was "different" an "exception"—which was to say that his accomplishment was set to one side and the prevailing view that all black people were ignorant continued in full force.

"This view fostered his own alienation from his group as well, offering him rewards not for his scholarship, but often on the basis of his being a curiosity, much as one pays to see a seal play a piano. If, then, he is to capitalize on his efforts, he must accept this role and affirm the general view that he is an exception and that in fact no blacks can learn. And this continues to be the dilemma of the black intellectual—fighting to maintain a tie with his people but paid for being so curiously different from the mass of them." William H. Grier and Price M. Cobbs. *Black Rage* (Basic Books, Inc., 1968) p. 117.

"The white community sees him as "different" from his darker brothers and capable of being viewed as one of their own when such meets their convenience. The net effect is an alienation from his roots with no substitute available." *Ibid.* p. 127.

[4] The Research and Policy Committee, *Education for the Urban Disadvantaged,* (Committee for Economic Development, New York, New York, 1971) p. 27.

[5] Robert Rosenthall and Lenore F. Jacabson,"*Teacher Expectations for the Disadvantaged.*" *Scientific American,* Vol. 218, No. 4 (April, 1968) pp. 16, 19-23.

[6] The Research and Policy Committee, *op. cit.,* pp. 49-50.

[7] Grier and Cobbs, *op. cit.,* pp. 110-111.

[8] "Kelyn and Carolyn" by Bill Ayers, *The Harvard Educational Review,*(Winter, 1968).

[9] Louis L. Knowles, Kenneth Prewitt, et. al., *Institutional Racism in America,* (Prentice-Hall, Inc., Englewood Cliffs, N.J.) p. 33.

[10] The Research and Policy Committee, *op. cit.,* p. 31.

[11] *Ibid.,* p. 36.

[12] See Arthur R. Jenson "How Much Can We Boost IQ and Scholastic Achievement," *The Harvard Educational Review* (Winter, 1969), pp. 1-123. Also William Shockley, "Dysgenics, Geneticity, Raceology: A Challenge to the Intellectual Responsibility of Educators, *Phi Delta Kappa* (January, 1972) pp. 297-307.

[13] See Audrey M. Shuey, *The Testing of Negro Intelligence*. (J.P. Bell and Company, Inc., 1958), pp. 179-219; also James S. Coleman, et. al., *Equality of Educational Opportunity* (Washington: U.S. Government Printing Office, 1966), pp. 217-333.

[14] Sybil C. Mobley, "The Challenges of Socio-Economic Accounting," *The Accounting Review* (October, 1970), p. 763.

This should not be difficult to believe if the reader will attempt to recall the difference in the activity which goes on on public transportation in the North and in the South. Passengers generally read while on metropolitan subways; they generally talk while on southern city buses.

[16] Frank Riesmann, *The Culturally Deprived Child* (Harper & Row), (1962) p. 54.

[17] *Ibid.*, pp. 77-78.

[18] *Ibid.*, pp. 63-73. Riesmann describes deprived children as slow, careful, patient, perservering rather than quick, clever, facile, flexible; they are slower readers, slower problem solvers, slower at getting down to work, slower in taking tests. However, Riesmann claims that as slow-gifted children, once they do learn basic concepts, they may use these ideas in a thoughtful, penetrating fashion.

[19] This lack of correspondence is discussed in Christopher Jancks, et. al., *Inequality: A Reassessment of the Effect of Family and Schooling in America* (New York: Basic Books, 1972).

[20] See Kenneth Ells, et. al. *Intelligence and Cultural Differences* (The University of Chicago press, 1951) pp. 209-229.

[21] Grier and Cobbs, *op. cit.*, pp. 103-108.

The Special Case of the Culturally Disadvantaged

Philip E. Fess
University of Illinois (Urbana)

Charles T. Hamilton
University of Illinois (Urbana)

Introduction

In recent years the accounting profession has given increased attention to ways of increasing the number of individuals from minority groups, especially blacks, in the accounting profession. As accounting educators seek to attract and to train more students from disadvantaged groups, the forces affecting these efforts should be identified and probed. This article describes the program the University of Illinois at Urbana-Champaign has established to provide educational opportunities for individuals from minority groups and identifies some of the major difficulties encountered.

Special Education Opportunities Program (SEOP)

In September 1968, 502 culturally deprived students were admitted to the first year of the Special Education Opportunities Program (SEOP) at the Champaign-Urbana campus. Though the program is multi-ethnic, black students made up 85 percent of the enrollment with the others coming from white, Puerto Rican, and Mexican-American families.

Although culturally, economically and educationally disadvantaged when compared to the average university student, these students demonstrated a desire for and a motivation toward achievement in higher education. They offered evidence of ability to complete their college education successfully if supportive services were provided as part of the program. Students admitted to the SEOP program were required to show economic need ($1,200 short of a year's expenses at the Champaign-Urbana campus) and to be residents of the State of Illinois.

The traditional four year undergraduate cycle is now completed for the first SEOP class and a number of questions concerning the performance and retention of students in the SEOP can now be addressed. These include the following:

1. Are there significant differences in retention rates for the specially admitted students compared with regular students?
2. Are there significant differences between specially admitted students and regular students in the speed with which they amass credit hours toward graduation?
3. How do retention rates and ability levels for the specially admitted students compare to those of disadvantaged students who were regularly admitted in past years?

The first two questions can be addressed from experiences of the Department of Accountancy, the College of Commerce and Business Administration, and the University with the SEOP. The third question will be addressed only at the university level because of the relatively small number of disadvantaged students enrolled in accountancy programs in past years. For example, there were only 233 black students among the 22,000 undergraduates at Urbana-Champaign when the SEOP was initiated and an extremely small number of those were in accountancy programs.

Accounting Program

At the Champaign-Urbana campus, the first principles of accounting course was generally presented in each of the first two semesters to all freshman students in the College of Commerce. For most students in

SEOP this requirement was waived until the sophomore year to provide them with additional time to adjust to the college environment and to take restructured courses in such subjects as rhetoric and mathematics before enrolling in an accounting course. The Department of Accountancy had its first classroom contact with these students in September 1969.

At the outset the Department decided that the normal academic standard would be upheld in all SEOP courses. Any special aid would take the form of extra tutorial assistance, adding more class hours to the normal class schedule, providing more individual attention, etc. For this first effort, the department improvised and developed the program on a day-to-day basis. The class schedule was expanded from three to four hours of class meetings per week. The class size was kept to a small size (approximately 15-20 students) so the instructor could provide more individual attention and direction. Students were encouraged to make frequent visits to the instructor in his office and to use the tutorial service of SEOP.

Of the 50 students who registered for the first course in accounting, 14 or 28 percent withdrew and transferred to another college within the university. Only 18 or 50 percent of those remaining (36 percent of those originally enrolled) successfully completed the course. Both the number who withdrew from the course and the number who were unable to successfully complete the course were significantly different from regularly enrolled students. A comparison of the first year SEOP with regular students is presented in Table 1. The high level of statistical significance (x^2 equals 35.05) suggests a real difference between the outcomes of the two groups.

After participation in the specially designed first year accounting course, the SEOP students were integrated into the regular university programs. Subsequent analysis of the progress of the 1968 SEOP class (which was enrolled in the basic accounting course in 1969) indicated that only 7 of the 18 who completed the basic accounting course graduated at the end of the traditional 4 years. Of the remaining 11 students, 6 were still enrolled in the College of Commerce and making normal progress towards a degree at the end of the 4 years (3 were majors in accounting). Of the remainder, 4 withdrew from the university and 1 changed colleges.

The department's experience with this first SEOP class highlighted several significant differences from regular programs:

1. The failure rate in the first course in accounting for SEOP was significantly higher than regular students.
2. A significant number of the SEOP students originally enrolled in the College of Commerce transferred to other colleges.
3. Most SEOP students were unable to graduate within the normal 4 years which is considered the usual measure of academic success.

In an effort to explain the low percentage of those originally enrolled in the College of Commerce remaining in the College and the inability of the SEOP students to graduate within the normal four years, statistics accumulated on the overall University SEOP were examined.

University Performance

After four years of experience with the SEOP the University was able to formulate some preliminary results regarding the inability of the SEOP students to graduate in the traditional four years and the transfer of SEOP students between colleges.

Measure of Academic Success

The experience of the Accountancy Department and the College of Commerce with the SEOP did not indicate success in meeting the normal expectation of graduation within four years. The overall University experience with the SEOP was similar and led the University officials to conclude that this usual measure of success could not be applied to the SEOP students for the following two reasons:

1. Gift aid to SEOP students provided only about 50 percent of the money needed for the education experience. Because the student's families could not provide the remaining funds needed, the students themselves had

TABLE 1

PATTERN OF S.E.O.P. AND REGULAR STUDENTS 1969-1970 FOR THE BASIC ACCOUNTING COURSE

Outcome	Regular Students #	Regular Students %	S.E.O.P. Students #	S.E.O.P. Students %
Withdrew and transferred Colleges	5.5	11	14	28
Completed Course Successfully	36.5	73	18	36
Failed to Complete Course Successfully	8.0	16	18	36
TOTAL	50.0	100	50	100

$x^2 = 35.0585$

$p < .005$

to assume responsibility for the remaining 50 percent. This often required them to work during school terms and carry a reduced academic program.

2. Most of the SEOP students required special courses their first year to help correct environmental and cultural deficiencies, and, therefore, they did not begin a normal college curriculum until their second year.

In an effort to determine whether or not the SEOP was a success, a comparison was made of the academic status of the SEOP students admitted in 1968 with the academic status of regularly admitted students of that year. Table 2 is based on the first six semesters of study at the University.

Large differences exist between the status of the regular and SEOP students. At the end of six semesters, two-thirds of the regular student's original class remained in the University; this compares to only one-third for the SEOP students. However, these results are not so discouraging when the first year performance of the 1968 SEOP group was compared with black students admitted in regular programs in the preceding two years as presented in Table 3.

Table 2
Academic Status of Regular Students and SEOP Students

PART A: Class 1968 REGULARLY ADMITTED

Semester Number	Clear[a] n	%	Probationary[b] n	%	Dropped[c] n	%	Not enrolled[d] n	%
1	4173	84.8	700	14.2	47	1.0		
2	3887	79.0	600	12.2	211	4.3	222	4.5
3	3620	73.6	470	9.6	99	2.0	731	14.8
4	3685	74.9	300	6.1	55	1.1	879	17.9
5	3438	69.9	226	4.6	97	2.0	1157	23.5
6	3287	66.8	171	3.5	66	1.3	1315	28.4[e]

PART B: Class 1968 SEOP ADMITTED

Semester Number	Clear[a] n	%	Probationary[b] n	%	Dropped[c] n	%	Not enrolled[d] n	%
1	321	63.9	163	32.5	18	3.6		
2	242	48.1	177	35.3	37	7.4	46	9.2
3	175	34.8	151	30.1	7	1.4	169	33.7
4	192	38.2	111	22.1	18	3.6	181	36.1
5	171	34.1	102	20.3	21	4.2	208	41.4
6	178	35.5	67	13.3	20	4.0	237	47.2

Note:
a = Clear = maintained a semester grade point average of 3.0 out of a possible 5.0
b = Probationary = in any one semester received a grade point average between 2.0 and 3.0
c = Dropped = in any one semester received a grade point average below 2.0
d = Not enrolled = withdrawn or graduated from the University
e = 1.6 % of regularly admitted students graduated in six semesters

Source: Jane Loeb, "Performance and Retention of Students in the Education Opportunities Program," Research Memorandum No. 72-11, University Office of School and College Relations, University of Illinois, Urbana-Champaign, 1972, page 4.

Table 3

Outcome of Blacks in Regular Programs and SEOP

OUTCOME	Blacks 1966	1967	Average 1966-67	SEOP 1968
% cleared	50%	53%	51.5%	64%
% probationary or dropped	50%	47%	48.5%	36%
	100%	100%	100.0%	100%

x^2 equals 30.167 (Average 1966-67 and SEOP columns)
$P < .005$

Source: Jane Loeb, "Performance and Retention of Students in the Education Opportunities Program", Research Memorandum No. 72-11, University Office of School and College Relations, University of Illinois, Urbana-Champaign, 1972, page 9.

Based on the average performance of the black students enrolled in the University in 1966 and 1967, an estimated expected performance for the first SEOP class was calculated and the x^2 distribution was evaluated. The difference between the 1966-67 average and 1968 is significant at the .005 level. Although SEOP students have not done as well when compared with regularly admitted students, the program has *improved* the assimilation of minorities into the University. With more time and experience, the program should further narrow the gap between SEOP and regular students.

Transfers Between Colleges

Many SEOP students transferred from the College of Commerce to other colleges within the University. Although the movement between colleges is not unusual, a survey was conducted to compare regular and SEOP students' movements between colleges during the 1968 school year. The most significant figures of Table 4 are between the diagonal lines. Groups 1 and 2 show a significantly higher retention rate for regular than SEOP students. Retention rates for groups 3 and 4 are more comparable for the two groups of students. (Group 5, LAS general, is designed for students who do not want to declare a major until later in their studies. The majority of these students subsequently transferred to Groups 3 and 4).

Transfer of Groups

The transfer patterns noted in Group 1 are relevant to this paper. This group consists of professionally oriented coursework in various colleges of the University. One possible explanation for transfer could be related to the subject matter requirements, especially since in most of these fields, quantitative methods (including mathematics) are an important part of the curriculum. Using Scheffe's test for non-orthogonal comparisons and a statistical cut off of .05, the following questions were tested using the School and College Ability Test (SCAT) data from Table 5.

Table 4
Patterns of Major Shifts and Entering Majors
SEOP vs. Regular 1968

Curriculum Groups #	College enrolled in 6th term--percent				
	1	2	3	4	5
1 Regular	73%	6%	11%	7%	2%
SEOP	49%	0%	33%	10%	8%
2 Regular	11%	73%	11%	4%	1%
SEOP	25%	33%	25%	17%	0%
3 Regular	5%	2%	76%	10%	7%
SEOP	7%	0%	67%	26%	0%
4 Regular	3%	1%	8%	83%	5%
SEOP	0%	0%	6%	90%	4%
5 Regular	14%	8%	40%	28%	11%
SEOP	16%	2%	1%	26%	16%

(College enrolled in 1st term-percent)

Groups 1 through 5 are defined as follows:
    Group 1 consists of all of *Commerce;* all Engineering; FAA architecture, landscaping, urban planning; LAS hard science; PE recreation and PEM; Aviation.
    Group 2 consists of all Agriculture except home economics; LAS biological science.
    Group 3 consists of LAS languages, social sciences, and humanities.
    Group 4 consists of FAA arts; Education; LAS speech, English, and home economics; Agriculture home economics; PE health education and PEW.
    Group 5 consists of LAS general.

Source: Jane Loeb, "Changes in Abilities and Interests From Freshmen to Senior Year Among Regularly and Specially Admitted College Students," Research Memorandum No. 72-13, University Office of School and College Relations, University of Illinois, 1972, p. 7.

QUESTION:	ANSWER:
1. Are regular SCAT Verbal scores significantly different from regular SCAT Quantitative Scores?	NO
2. Are SEOP SCAT Quantitative scores significantly different from regular SCAT Quantitative scores?	YES
3. Are SEOP SCAT Verbal scores significantly different from SEOP SCAT Quantitative Scores?	YES
4. Are SEOP SCAT Verbal scores significantly different from regular SCAT Verbal scores?	YES

TABLE 5

SCAT SCORES FOR 1968 CLASS

SCAT SCORE	SEOP $\overline{X}$	SEOP Std. Dev.	REGULAR $\overline{X}$	REGULAR Std. Dev.
Quantitative	13.5	5.4	32.8	8.5
Verbal	17.2	7.1	32.5	8.9

Source: John Bowers, "The Evaluation of a Special Education Opportunities Program for Disadvantaged College Students," Final Report Project No. 9-E-136, University of Illinois, 1972, p. 13.

Since the verbal and quantitative scores of the regular students do not differ (Question No. 1), and since the SEOP students have lower quantitative scores than regular students (Question No. 2), the quantitative emphasis may be one of the major reasons for SEOP students' shift from Group 1 to Group 3, 4, and 5 where there is less quantitative analysis. This conclusion is supported by the significantly different (higher) SEOP verbal scores when compared to SEOP quantitative scores (Question No. 3). If SEOP students are transfering to colleges that are more verbal and less quantitative, they can still expect some difficulty since the SEOP group has a lower verbal score than the regular student (Question No. 4).

Interpretation

SEOP students are different from regular students on both verbal and quantitative SCAT scores. If innate ability is randomly distributed, the cultural dimensions appear to heavily influence these comparisons. Although no statistical survey was conducted, many of the SEOP students appeared to transfer out of the first course in accounting and out of the College of Commerce because of the heavily quantitative oriented curriculum. Another reason appeared to be that business was not related to their culture and background. As Bert N. Mitchell has commented:

> Many of these students have no prior exposure to the world of business; hence they must learn everything about accounting in the classroom. One should appreciate how difficult it is for a person who has spent a life of deprivation in the ghetto to grasp the concepts of accounting for stock rights or for a pooling of interests. Such a person has never heard about stocks or bonds before reading the accounting textbook.[1]

CONCLUSION

Special programs similar to the SEOP are an important part of the overall effort to provide opportunities for the disadvantaged in accounting. Such programs recognize that the disadvantaged tend to have low scores on college entrance examinations which are designed for children of middle-class families. People who have grown up in a different culture are not familiar with these typical middle class symbols and therefore must be given special consideration for entrance into universities and colleges.

Traditional admissions procedures therefore may be modified and/or special means of assisting students may be developed to bridge the academic gap. If the normal graduation standards must be upheld, and as long as the disadvantaged are willing and able to meet these conditions, all colleges and universities have an obligation to give the disadvantaged youth the same chance as the average youth.

In the SEOP developed at the University of Illinois the number of black students among the undergraduates at Urbana-Champaign has increased from 223 to 1,040 in 4 years—a percentage gain from 1.04 to 4.5 percent of total undergraduate student body. At the University level, the percent of blacks who are able to remain in good standing has been increased by the SEOP from approximately 50 percent to 64 percent of original enrollees for a first year of study. Against these positive results is a retention rate of SEOP students that is only about one-half that of the regular students at the University level. And the SEOP has not substantially increased the number of blacks in the College of Commerce and the programs of the Department of Accountancy. The rate of transfer from the College from the SEOP was approximately double that for regular students. The failure rate for SEOP students in the first accounting course was also about double the normal rate. The reason for the high transfer rate from the College and the high failure rate in the first accounting course may be traced to the background brought to the University in the quantitative area by the SEOP students. This condition can be corrected in the long run by better training in mathematics in the grade and high schools. In the short run, by presenting additional courses in mathematics for the culturally disadvantaged and/or giving additional attention to the review of relevant mathematical concepts in the traditional programs, this weakness can be partially corrected.

The representation of blacks and other minority groups among college students is far below their representations in the college age population and all segments of the education process—grade schools, high schools, junior and senior colleges—can and must contribute their fair share if the situation is to be improved. As for the role of the colleges and universities in this process Alexander W. Astin, Director, Office of Research, American Council on Education summarizes an appropriate conclusion:

Presumably, educational institutions exist in order to educate students. Their mission, then, is to produce certain desirable changes in the student or, more simply, to make a difference in the student's life. Given these goals, they should strive in their admissions practices to select those applicants who are most likely to be favorably influenced by the particular educational program offered at the institution. Instead, the typical admissions officer today functions more like a handicapper: he tries merely to pick winners. He looks over the various candidates, evaluates their respective talents, and attempts to select those who are most likely to perform well. Handicappers, it should be stressed, are interested only in predicting the horse's performance— not in improving his performance, in trying to make him run better and faster. The problem here is that an educational institution is supposed to function less like a handicapper and more like a jockey or a trainer; it has a responsibility to improve the performance of the individual, not just to identify those with the greatest potential.

The mission of the college is not simply to maximize its output of distinguished alumni by maximizing its input of talented students. Such a static view puts the college in the role of a kind of funnel, where what comes out is purely a matter of what goes in. Colleges and other educational institutions exist in order to change the student, to contribute to his personal development, to make a difference.[2]

FOOTNOTES

[1] Bert N. Mitchell, "The Black Minority in the CPA Profession," (October 1969), p. 48.

[2] Alexander W. Astin, "Folklore of Selectivity," *Saturday Review,* (December 20, 1969), pp. 69-70.

The Task of Learning

Editor's Introduction

Various learning theory researchers have focused on:

1. Tasks ranging from simple skills to complex reasoning and attitudes.
2. Varying types of learners ranging from earthworms and rats to animals and humans
3. Differing conditions varying from artificial to real-life situations

From this research have emerged vocal partisans for varying major learning theories. While each major school has varying qualities to recommend it, each theory is derived from a wide range of behaviors most would label "learning." To be useful to accounting educators, the theories must be ordered and summarized. Using the broad divisions of

1. Contiguity or stimulus-response psychology
2. Cognitive psychology

Professor Willingham, McNeill, and Collins provide a non-technical distillation of these two major approaches to learning. The analysis concludes with a comprehensive table with accounting related examples. (For those interested in more technical and elaborate analysis, a list of optional readings is suggested.)

Another way of viewing learning is through the motivation of the learner. Professor Barrett presents a non-technical introduction to motivation: three major streams of thinking--need theory, behavioral theory, and expectance theory--are briefly explored in "What Makes Sammy Run?" Professor Barrett may startle some accounting educators when he concludes that behavioral incentives and expectancy outcomes, not motivation, may be more productive viewpoints for accounting educators. Such a conclusion may demand a re-thinking of how accounting educators view and approach students in the classroom.

Drawing cues from the papers on learning theory and motivation, Professor Macht explores and illustrates how reinforcement can be used in an accounting classroom. His article reveals the convergence and overlap of a stimulus-response learning theory and behavioral motivational theory. Starting with M & M chocolate candies, Professor Macht develops an approach which could lead to widespread improvement in accounting education.

The next two papers explore different configurations of learning theory. Using cognitive approaches Professor Stallman explores an innovative classroom technique-- the "inquiry" approach--while Professor Bentz advances research hypotheses for new teaching approaches by suggesting the use of generalized algorithms rather than the traditional problem-solving approach.

This section concludes with objectives. Professors Williams and Guy explore the formulation and measurement of educational objectives; moving from the trite discussions that usually characterize educational objectives, they probe the power of behavioral objectives in the accounting classroom. The final paper is by Mr. Bohne, a partner of a national CPA firm, who reviews the objectives of professional accounting education from his perspective as a national director of education for his firm. Perhaps there is no more fitting conclusion to a discussion of educational objectives than the viewpoint of a seasoned practitioner.

Learning Theories And Accounting

J.J. Willingham
I. E. McNeill
E. F. Collins
University of Houston

Introduction

The purpose of this paper is to survey briefly some of the explanations for learning. No complete explanation of how or why students learn exists, but nevertheless individual educators can often apply individual concepts or bits of theory in the classroom. First, some of the more classical theories of learning and the conditions under which they take place will be explored. Secondly, some suggested inferences of the theories will be presented with reference to accounting classroom instruction.

THEORIES OF LEARNING

Before turning to the theories of learning, the nature of learning or, more precisely, the meaning of the term "learning" should be defined. Most individuals think of learning as acquisition of knowledge or skills. While this may be an inadequate definition, psychologists can add little more in the way of precision to this concept. The psychological literature extends this definition somewhat by specifying that if learning takes place, a change in behavior of an individual will result—while learning itself cannot be observed, individual performance can exhibit the effects of learning. Generally, most psychologists would go one step further and note that if learning has taken place, behavioral change should be relatively permanent. In turn, educators hope that relatively permanent behavioral changes will be manifested in the acquisition of knowledge, success in examinations, and a productive and contented post-university experience.

Contiguity Learning Theories

Although an over-simplification, all contiguity theories of learning can be described by the phrase "we learn by doing". An individual's experience (what he does) is what he learns. The term "contiguity" derives from the view that whatever a person experiences becomes a stimulus for a response that occurs at the same time--the stimulus and response are contiguous. If the same stimulus reoccurs, it should evoke the same response evoked the last time he noticed the signal or stimulus.

Theories that fall into the category of contiguity theories are often "conditioning" theories. In fact, the classical conditioning theory is the well known one identified by Ivan Pavlov. His experiments with dogs are so well known that the details need not be included here. Classical conditioning theory states simply that to learn, an individual must be conditioned to respond to the same stimulus with identical responses each time. The emphasis of this theory is on repetition. If a single stimulus is repeated enough times an individual will learn to respond identically to it each time.

Almost all of the research in the area of classical conditioning has dealt with physical responses and the responses that have been elicited by stimuli are those governed by the automatic nervous system of animals. Some behavioralists, therefore, discount the applicability of classical conditioning to learning situations involving human beings. Research in classical conditioning has revealed that by pairing a conditioned stimulus (e.g., the sight of a white rat) with an unconditioned stimulus (e.g., hearing a loud noise), one can eventually make a conditioned response happen (e.g., startled reaction) with the conditioned stimulus alone (e.g., sight of the white rat leads to a startled reaction). Furthermore, in some studies a response can be elicited from stimuli that are similar but not identical to the original conditioned stimulus (e.g., small white rat leads to a startled response). However, if the conditioned stimulus is conditioned without pairing it with the unconditioned stimulus, the conditioned response will ultimately fade and disappear (e.g., startled reaction no longer occurs at the sight of the white rat). See lines 1a and 1b of Table I.

A second contiguity theory of learning was developed by B. F. Skinner. It is known, when it does not bear his name, as "operant conditioning". The focus of operant conditioning is upon the response which typically occurs without any specific stimulus imposed by an experimenter or teacher. The theory states that if such a response is propery reinforced, both the strength and probability of reoccurence of this response will increase. The purpose of most operant conditioning research is aimed at controlling responses through proper reinforcement. Most behavioralists would agree that the types of behavior exhibited by a human being that are not the result of apparent stimuli are much more numerous than those that are. The term "operant" in fact is derived from the thought that most behavior not elicited by an obvious stimulus has the function of simply allowing an individual to operate in his environment.

Research into the controlling of responses has, like classical conditioning, been carried on to a large extent with laboratory animals. The basic difference between the accomplishments in the area of operant conditioning in comparison with those in the area of classical conditioning is the complexity of the behaviors that can be taught to animals through operant conditioning. Classical conditioning has been successful only in teaching a single response to a single stimulus. Operant conditioning experiments have extended learning ability of laboratory animals to short series of tasks by offering rewards to reinforce response patterns. Animals have taught three or four sets of tasks in a series to reach a final, more complex objective. Generally, classical conditioning forces a response through the stimulus while operant conditioning assumes a response and the conditioning is accomplished through reward or punishment. For the most part, classical conditioning must deal with rather involuntary responses while operant conditioning definitely deals with voluntary responses, thus, making it on the surface at least, far more applicable to the learning of human beings.

Operant conditioning is the most prominent of the reinforcement approaches to learning. All of the reinforcement approaches, including Skinner's, emphasize reinforcement of the learner when a student or subject makes a correct response and at the same time discourages incorrect responses by the learner.

The nature of the reinforcement is an interesting subject in itself. Reinforcement must take the form of reward but psychologists are undecided as to what that reward can be, at least when applied to human beings. Some say the reward is simply being right, while others theorize that the reward is a state of reduced fear or anxiety in the student or learner. This latter view is being questioned rather widely, primarily because it tends to be a negative approach to motivation of students. Skinner and others believe that satisfaction of being right, correct, or of learning, is a more satisfying view of reward in reinforcement theories of learning and satisfying activities tend to be repeated by people.

In a classroom situation, for the most part, the professor provides the reinforcement or reward or punishment. In effect the teacher becomes the motivator of students to learn. While there is some recent research suggesting negative reinforcement may have some unappreciated qualities, many behavioralists tend to believe that a teacher should use a positive approach and recognize correct responses from students but not ridicule incorrect ones. The effective teacher will redirect incorrect responses or ignore them. See lines 1c and 2a & b of Table I.

Cognitive Learning Theories

Perhaps the most satisfying and appropriate theories of learning are the cognitive ones because cognitive theorists strongly emphasize the intellectual processes of human beings and their role in learning. These theories are generally applicable only to human beings. A cognitive theorist would not deny the importance of involuntary motor responses to stimuli or the importance of operant conditioning. Most would not even completely discount the importance of eliciting responses and reinforcing them. However, to cognitive theorists all of these previously discussed approaches to the understanding of learning simply do not explain the way people learn. Cognitive theory recognizes that individuals have goals and objectives and that learning takes place when an individual is helped toward fulfillment of them. They stress the understanding of complex concepts, generalization, synthesization, and problem solving. The cognitive area of psychology is often known as Gestalt psychology or "patterning". When an individual is confronted with a problem, he tends to try to see new patterns of the situation with which he is confronted. Obviously, this field of learning deals with rather broad metaphysical segments of the experience of life and not with simplistic and mechanistic segments with which contiguity theories deal.

The central concept of cognitive theories is motivation, which is seen by adherents of this school of thought as much the same as purpose toward an end, goal or objective which a learner desires. In a sense, then, his goal determines his behavior rather than a series of patterned responses either to stimuli or without stimuli but with reinforcement. These theories of learning are more satisfying because they clearly give the teacher the task of helping the learner to clearly define and limit his goals and to establish worthwhile and realistic goals. Unfortunately, as most professors are aware, sometimes the goals of students are achievement oriented in terms of grades and recognition rather than subject motivated.

Often a learner may have conflicting motives and these, of course, can have a significant effect upon his success. Teachers can, in effect, fail to manage conflicting motives by creating situations where students must choose between two unpleasant approaches. This situation is highly unlikely to produce effective learning. Another situation can be created by a teacher where the same situation is both attractive and at the same time threatening to the student. A student might feel that he needs help but feels that the teacher is not approachable and the student does not want him to know that he needs help. Generally, teachers can motivate and lead students successfully by avoiding the creation of conditions that may lead to conflict. See lines 3, 4, 5 and 6 of Table I.

SUMMARY

In summarizing the contiguity and cognition theories of learning, the theories can be combined; they are not totally inconsistent. A teacher can properly reward students for correct responses and, in effect, practice operant conditioning while at the same time recognizing the intellectual capabilities and motives of students emphasized by the cognitive theorists. The major theories and several accounting examples are shown in Table I.

Memory and Forgetting

Memory and the prevention of forgetting is a natural topic following a discussion of learning. Very little is known about the physical operation of the brain of a human being, but psychologists have widely assumed ideas or information acquired can be recalled because so-called "traces" of past experiences are retained. Cognitive theorists generally recommend that learners attempt to synthesize and gain the main general ideas or concepts and that details can be filled in later from recall of the main ideas. A simpler task for most learners is to recognize later, things that they have already learned. Often essay examinations require recall while multiple choice examinations require only recognition and the former are much more difficult. While interesting experiments have been carried out with the intent to measuring memory, at the present time, however, little is known about the manner in which not forgetting can be assured. In the area of concept learning, individuals tend to generalize from examples, and when asked to classify instances into correct classifications, they have a much higher probability of correct classification when the instance is similar to previous examples than when it is dissimilar. At this point in time, determining what causes undergeneralization, overgeneralization or complete misconception of a concept is difficult to assess.

TABLE I SUMMARY AND SOME IMPLICATIONS OF
MAJOR LEARNING THEORIES *

Learning model	Description	Elements needed	Some Major researchers & theorists
Stimulus response model: (1a) Classical conditioning	Previously neutral conditioned stimulus is associated with conditioned response	An initial unconditioned stimulus followed by unconditioned response, repetition, & contiguity	Pavlov, Watson
(1b) continguity Associates	Stimulus is linked to a response	Contiguity of stimulus and response	Guthrie
(1c) Reinforcement	Stimulus is linked to a response when the response is followed by reinforcement.	Stimulus followed by contiguous response followed by early reinforcement, repetition	Thorndike & Skinner
(2a & b) Generalization and discrimination	Similar stimuli either do (or if appropriate do not) elicit the same response as the original stimulus had elicited	Similar stimuli repetition, differential reinforcement	Kendler & Kendler
Cognitive Theories: (3) Concept learning	Understanding of common characteristics making up a class	Many instances of lower order (learnings (1a, b, c, d) and 2a, b above. Some language skills	Harlow, Wertheimer, Piaget
(4) Principle learning	Seeing the relationships among concepts	Knowledge of concepts, juxtaposition of the concepts	Gagne, Bruner Kersh & Wittrock

Application to education	Examples in an Accounting setting	Desirable teacher behavior	Teacher's & student's relative role
Learning emotional reactions to previously neutral stimuli	Student learns to dislike accounting when embarrassed by severe reprimands after making errors in debiting and crediting accounts	Provides positive emotional experiences in conjunction with accounting related work	↑ ↑
Learning-rote responses to simple questions	Student learns to recognize accounting like asset, liability, etc. Student learns to respond assets = liabilities + owners equity when asked what is the fundamental equation	Presents stimulus and obtains quick, accurate responses by student to it	
Shaping student's behavior by modifying existing patterns more firmly establishing existing behaviors	Student does neater homework after instructor points out a portion of problem done well followed by praise. Student participates even more after teacher congratulates him on comment	Analyzes behavior desired of student. Reinforces student as his behavior approximates desired behavior. Selects appropriate reinforcers and reinforcement schedules.	Increasingly teacher dominated / Decreasingly student dominated
Student correctly responding even though stimulus changes somewhat (tasks involving transfer of training)	Student correctly recognizes that assets are not liabilities Students correctly post all entries to proper journal	Systematically, differentially rewards correct responses. Extinguishes incorrect responses	
Student groups specific learnings thereby improving recall	Student learns to group subordinate category words such as cash, accounts receivable, into superordinate category word such as assets	Structures basic experiences underlying the concept. Encourages verbalization	↑ ↑
Student relates various conceptual learnings. Student can apply knowledge to new situations	Student knows that current ratio is current assets ÷ current liabilities; the student is told profitable companies have current assets > current liabilities. Student can infer that a bankrupt company may have current liabilities > current assets.	Has student examine component concepts. Either by presenting these concepts inductively or the principle deductively, gets student to see relationship	

TABLE I SUMMARY AND SOME IMPLICATIONS OF
MAJOR LEARNING THEORIES * *(Continued)*

Learning model	Description	Elements needed	Some Major researchers & theorists
(5) Problem solving	Using principles to reach goals otherwise blocked	Knowledge of principles flexibility in using them	Dewey, Ausubel, Luchins, Wertheimer
(6) Creative behavior	Socially significant new ways of solving a problem	Relatively low anxiety, supportive environment, basic knowledge, flexibility	Mackinnon, Ausubel

* Adapted from Joel R. Davits and Samuel Ball, *Psychology of the Educational Process* (McGraw-Hill, Inc., 1970), pp. 50-51.

Some Inferences

Are there some inferences from learning theory that are useful to accounting education? The educator's impact is perhaps greatest in his role as a teacher and as a creator of the classroom environment. The educator as a participant in the learning encounter affects the change in basic personal skills of students. By creating a learning environment, by communicating reinforcing feedback, by being cognizant of relevant peer groups (in some cases a positive force, in others a negative one), by inculcating scholastic values in the student's value system, the instructor can have a major impact on the student's approach to and achievement in accounting.

Major factors in facilitating learning are:
1. Specifying, clarifying, and gaining internalization goals.
2. Aiding in development of positive self-image and raised aspiration levels of students.
3. Identifying and organizing learning materials and aiding in structuring learning patterns.
4. Clarifying and relating facts and concepts.
5. Reinforcement during the learning process.

Accounting educators, in their emphasis on relating concepts to problem and case situations and on problem solution, are likely to give almost exclusive attention to the fourth factor. In fact, this may be envisioned by some instructors as the primary factor or, perhaps, the only significant factor in their role as learning facilitator. Coupled with this may be the concept of the teacher as a fact transferrer or communicator. Experiments and experience with contract learning and the use of self-study materials largely contradict this position. There is evidence many students learn better with no fact transfer from the instructor. Great emphasis on fact transfer, if it duplicates presentations in textbooks or other study materials, may be interpreted as loose performance standards. This could be expected to lower the student's study standards and, perhaps his learning aspiration levels.

If accounting educators focus on learning theories and some of their inferences, they can improve the amount and level of learning by accounting students. Students will learn in many ways and educators can teach in many ways. The basic idea is to improve learning.

Application to education	Examples in an Accounting setting	Desirable teacher behavior	Teacher's & student's relative role
Student solves problems either presented by teacher or perceived by himself	Student calculates earnings per share using official pronouncements. Student looks up financial material to see how funds from operations increased	Encourages flexibility in applying principles. Teacher attempts not to be dogmatic himself.	↓ ↓
Student presents original solution to problem	Student writes paper on how to use accounting to account for pollution. Student analyzes complex case and suggests cost control system	Warm, supportive non-directive	↓ ↓

REFERENCES

Ausubel, D. P. "The use of advance organizers in the learning and retention of meaningful verbal material." *Journal of Educational Psychology,* 1960, pp. 267-272.

Ausubel, D. P. *Psychology of Meaningful Verbal Learning.* (New York: Grune & Stratton, 1963).

Ausubel, D. P. "How reversible are the Cognitive and Motivational Effects of Cultural Deprivation?" Implications for teaching the culturally deprived child. *Urban Education,* 1964, pp. 16-38.

Ausubel, D. P. *Educational Psychology: A Cognitive View.* (New York: Holt, 1968).

Bandura, A., Ross, D., & Ross, S. A. "Imitation of Film-Mediated Aggressive Models," *Journal of Abnormal and Social Psychology,* 1963, pp. 3-11.

Bandura, A., Ross, D., & Ross, S. A. "Vicarious Reinforcement and Imitative Learning,: *Journal of Abnormal and Social Psychology,* 1963, pp. 601-607.

Bandura, A., & Walters, R. H. *Social Learning and Personality Development.* (New York: Holt, 1963).

Bigge, M. L. *Learning Theories for Teachers.* (New York: Harper & Row, 1964).

Bruner, J. S. *The Process of Education.* (New York: Vintage Books, 1960).

Bruner, J. S. "The Act of Discovery," *Harvard Educational Review,* 1961 pp. 21-32.

Fester, C.S., & Skinner, B. F. *Schedules of Reinforcement.* (New York: Appelton Century Crofts, 1957).

Gagne, R. M. "The Implications of Instructional Objectives for Learning," in C. M. Lindvall (Ed.) Defining Educational Objectives. (Pittsburgh: University of Pittsburgh Press, 1964, pp. 37-46.)

Gagne, R. M. *Conditions of Learning.* (New York: Holt, 1965).

Gagne, R.M., & Bassler, O. C. "Study of Retention of Some Topics of Elementary Nonmetric Geometry." *Journal of Educational Psychology,* 1963, pp. 123-131.

Gagne, R. M., & Brown, L. T. "Some Factors in the Programming of Conceptual Learning." *Journal of Experimental Psychology,* 1961, pp. 313-321.

Guilford, J. P. "Three Faces of Intellect." *American Psychologist,* 1959, pp. 469-479.

Guthrie, E. R. "Condition: A Theory of Learning in Terms of Stimulus, Response, and Association," in B. H. Nelson (Ed.) The Psychology of Learning, (Forty-first yearbook, Part II, National Society for the Study of Education. Chicago: University of Chicago Press, 1942, pp. 17-60.

Guthrie, E. R. *The Psychology of Learning,* (Rev. ed.) New York: Harper, 1952.

Hilgard, E. R., & Bower, G. H. *Theories of Learning.* (3rd. ed.)(New York: Appelton Century Crofts, 1966).

Holt, J. *How Children Fail.* (New York: Pitman, 1960).

Kendler, H. H. "Stimulus-Response Psychology and Audiovisual Education". *A. V. Communication Review,* 1961, pp. 33-41.

REFERENCES *(Continued)*

Kendler, H.H., & D'Amato, M.F "A Comparison of Reversal Shifts and Non-Reversal Shifts in Human Concept Formation Behavior." *Journal of Experimental Psychology,* 1955, pp. 165-174.

Kendler, H. H., & Kendler, T. S., "Effect of Verbalization on Reversal Shifts in Children." *Science,* 1961, pp. 1619-1620.

Kendler, H. H., Kendler, T. S. "Vertical and Horizontal Processes in Problem Solving." *Psychological Review,* 1962, pp. 1-16.

Kendler, H. H., Kendler, T. S., & Wells, D. "Reversal and Nonreversal Shifts in Nursery School Children." *Journal of Comparative Physiology and Psychology,* 1960, pp. 83-88.

Kersh, B. Y. "The Adequacy of 'Meaning' As an Exploration for the Superiority of Learning by Independent Discovery." *Journal of Educational Psychology,* 1958, pp. 282-292.

Kersh, B. Y., & Wittrock, M. C. "Learning by Discovery: An Interpretation of Recent Research." *Journal of Teachers Education,* 1962, pp. 461-468.

Lumsdaine, A. A. "Educational Technology: Programmed Learning and Instructional Science," in E. R. Hilgard (Ed.), Theories of Learning and Instruction, (Sixty-third yearbook, Part I, National Society of the Study of Education. Chicago: University of Chicago Press, 1964, pp. 371-401).

Mackinnon, D. W. "The Nature and Nuture of Creative Talent."*American Psychologist,* 1962, pp. 484-495.

Maltzman, I., Eisman, E., & Brooks, L. O. "Some Relationships Between Methods of Instruction, Personality Variables, and Problem-Solving Behavior." *Journal of Educational Psychology,* 1956, pp. 71-78.

McKeachie, W. J. "Research on Teaching at the College and University Level," in N. L. Gage (Ed.), *Handbook of Research in Teaching.* Chicago: Rand McNally, 1963. pp. 1118-1172.

Pavlov, I. P. *Conditioned Reflexes.* Trans. by C. V. Anrep. (New York: Dover, 1927).

Piaget, I. "The Stages of the Intellectual development of the Child." *Bulletin of the Menniger Clinic,* 1962, pp. 120-128.

Skinner, B. F. *Walden II.* (New York: Macmillan, 1948).

Skinner, B. F. *Science and Human Behavior.* (New York: Macmillan, 1953).

Skinner, B. F. *The Technology of Teaching.* (New York: Appleton Century Crofts, 1968).

Thorndike, E. L. *Educational Psychology.* (New York: Teachers College, Columbia University 1913.)

Thorndike, E.L. *The Fundamentals of Learning.* (New York: Teachers College, Columbia University, 1932).

Watson, J. B. *Psychology From the Standpoint of a Behaviorist.* (Philadelphia: Lippincott, 1919).

Watson, J. B. *Behaviorism.* (Chicago: University of Chicago Press, 1924).

Watson, J. B., and Rayner, R. "Conditioned Emotional Reactions", *Journal of Experimental Psychology,* 1920, 1-14.

Wertheimer, M. *Gestalt Theory,* in W. D. Ellis (Ed.), *A Sourcebook of Gestalt Psychology* (New York: Harcourt, Brace, 1945).

Wolf, R. The Measurement of Environments, in W. H. MacGinitie, & S. Ball (Ed.), *Readings in the Psychological Foundations of Education.* (New York: McGraw-Hill, 1968).

Is Motivation "What Makes Sammy Run?"[1]

Michael J. Barrett
University of Minnesota

"What Makes Sammy Run?"[2] must be considered from several viewpoints because psychologists disagree about how his behavior is to be explained. Many psychologists, but not all, believe that Sammy is a hedonist and his motivation specifies the vigor, persistence and the direction of his running. The argument begins in earnest when motivational psychologists of different persuasions are asked why Sammy runs. Three major streams of thought (with their own varieties) have emerged:

1. Need theory
2. Behavioral theory—drive and incentive varieties
3. Expectancy theory—achievement and instrumentality varieties.

A need theorist is likely to state that Sammy runs to become competent (White) or to satisfy his self-actualizing desire to become a superstar (Maslow). Behavioralists explain Sammy's motivation differently. Some will say he must run to reduce a temporary but insistent deprivational state such as thirst; while arresting the drive that pushes him, Sammy is likely to learn a useful habit -- the quickest way to reach the water fountain (Hull and Miller). Other behavioralists will insist the various incentive characteristics of rewards and perhaps punishment (including size, quality and the time delay between running and receiving a reward) are more important causes of Sammy's behavior than his thirst (Spence and others). Expectancy or cognitive motivational psychologists, in contrast, will argue that both Sammy's desire for a valued goal and knowledge of how to get it explain his motivation to run. But within this expectancy framework there is a difference of opinion. For some, the strength of Sammy's motive to achieve *and* how difficult he thinks it is to win, jointly determine how fast he is likely to run (Atkinson); other cognitive psychologists believe Sammy's running is co-determined by his expectancy of success and the association he perceives between running a particular speed and the likelihood of acquiring a valued object (Vroom). If none of these alternative motivational explanations appears satisfactory, perhaps some combination of these possibilities may possess greater appeal.

But which account *best* explains Sammy's motivation to run? The answer largely depends on how each explanation and its supporting evidence are evaluated. Many different interpretations are possible because the comparative evaluative process is a function of several important conceptual and methodological considerations. Distinctions in terminology are seldom clearly stated or operationally anchored. Contrasting objects often are studied. And different methodological tools and analytic techniques are frequently employed. Some investigators treat motivation, motive and need as different concepts, while others ignore these distinctions. For example, behavioral psychologists interested in motivation will study Sammy's prior history of reinforcement and his current status to infer the antecedent determinants of his motivation to run. Expectancy theorists will search the future to anchor the causes of his behavior in its expected consequences. And need theorists will root his motivation in his prior experience in various social settings. The behavioralist will marshall a narrow, yet precise explanation that is heavily dependent on rigorous definitions which are operationalized in a highly controlled laboratory setting. The cognitive psychologist will produce an explanation which has greater appeal, but to do so he will relax the precision of his concept definitions as well as the degree of control he establishes for the environmental context within which Sammy's behavior is studied. The need theorist will further relax these constraints and rely upon clinical observation to infer his motivational explanation. Many study the motivation of animals, but usually only one species. Some study humans. Yet only a very few study both animals and humans. These differences and others make it difficult to directly compare the results of competing motivational explanations, even in the unlikely event that they happen to agree!

Incentives & Expectancy: A Convergence?

But comparisons must be made and certain beliefs strengthened at the expense of others if new knowledge is to be created. After considering many comparisons there is an appealing similarity between the explanations of the behaviorally oriented incentive theorist and expectancy accounts of motivation. Although conceptualized and studied differently, psychologists of both persuasions are likely to agree that the judicious use of rewards and punishments will motivate Sammy to run faster or slower. Those interested in an incentive explanation of Sammy's behavior are likely to tell Sammy's coach or teacher to give some attention to varying the size, quality and delay characteristics of various rewards and punishments to alter Sammy's pace. The expectancy theorist would also tell Sammy's teacher to concentrate on the consequences of Sammy's performance. If the coach knows which consequences are perceived by Sammy to be rewarding or punishing, his coach may be able to influence Sammy's pursuit of each consequence. For example, providing Sammy a clear statement of what is expected and what he will receive if he performs at a particular level *may* enhance his chances of winning the next react. In a similar vein, if Sammy's coach places greater reliance on incentives, perhaps the coach will spend more time developing better advertising campaigns and more attractive training conditions. Rather than attempting to help Sammy satisfy his need for achievement or his desire for self-actualization, the coach might try to alter Sammy's demand for various commodities. Providing a greater array of rewards and punishments of different sizes, qualities and temporal delays, besides grades and credit hours, for running at different speeds, may convince Sammy that he should give up smoking and train harder. Perhaps varying the size and quality of a rewarding consequence will not only increase Sammy's chances of winning but also reduce the overall cost of giving him a suitable reward. For example he might run harder if promised a free ticket to the Super Bowl and the opportunity to have lunch at his coach's expense provided Sammy is willing to undertake his training program largely on his own without the presence of his coach. One inference derived from considering incentive and expectancy motivational accounts of behavior seems to be this: Sammy's coach should shift his attention from how Sammy acts on various outcomes to how such outcome payoffs appear to affect Sammy's speed.

If Sammy's coach decided to pay more attention to the observable affects of various incentive consequences on Sammy's running activity rather than search for elusive, inferred internal motivational causes presumed to govern running, motivation might become a concept having little practical usefulness. This is the conclusion of psychologists studying behavioral modification (behavioral psychology or behavioral theory). For example, Bolles states that "...a motivational theory must necessarily involve all of the terms incorporated in a reinforcement theory and must include a few others in addition."[3] He and others believe with further conceptualization, empirical study and refinement, psychologists may be able to develop adequate explanations of behavior *solely* in terms of responses, environmental stimuli and the reinforcers that are operating in the particular social context in which Sammy operates. If Bolles' belief is eventually validated, a reinforcement account of behavior may prove to be a more parsimonious explanation of Sammy's running. If this possibility is realized (recent strides made by those interested in behavioral modification[4] suggest it might), the concept of motivation may fall into disuse by psychologists and coaches trying to get Sammy to run faster.

Problems Still Remain

The theory and technique of behavioral modification, however, has a number of unresolved problems. Perhaps the most significant today concerns the meaning and operation of reinforcement and reinforcers. B. F. Skinner[5] and others interested in operant conditioning have produced an abundance of evidence demonstrating that subjects will work at different rates under different schedules of reinforcement (or delay characteristics of incentives). However, there is disagreement about the nature of reinforcement and only a dim awareness of what are useful "reinforcers." Some behavioral psychologists argue that the satisfaction of an organism's physiological need for water constitutes reinforcement. But others contend the consumption of water (or merely the sight of it) rather than its ingestion and thirst relaxant effects, governs the rate of the organism's behavior. Beyond these debates, knowledge of which particular reinforcer governs an organism's specific response in one setting, does not necessarily mean the same reinforcer can produce the same or other responses with different settings or subjects. One man's reward may be another man's poison. One of the costs of applying behavioral modification techniques may be that Sammy's coach will not be able to adequately train 50 sprinters and a similar number of distance runners each year because he must determine which particular reinforcers (from a rather large domain of possibilities) have the greatest enhancing effect of *each* runner's speed. Sammy's coach may have to hire more coaches or cut the size of his squad or he may simply decide that Sammy runs because the devil makes him do it.

FOOTNOTES

[1] The discussion below represents some reflections derived from a detailed analysis of several significant motivational theories. Michael J. Barrett, "Theories of Motivation: Their Description and Relevance," *Graduate School of Business Administration Working Paper,* No. 15 (University of Minnesota, September, 1973), 51 t.p.

[2] "What Makes Sammy Run" is a novel by Budd Schulberg (Modern Library, 1952) which deals with a "Sammy" running with and against his social context. This enjoyable book provides a vehicle to explore several competing motivational theories.

[3] R.C. Bolles, *Theory of Motivation* (Harper & Row, 1967), pp. 211-212

[4] L. Krasner, "Behavioral Therapy," *Annual Review of Psychology* (1971), pp. 485-505, presents a rich and lucid introduction to this rapidly accumulating body of knowledge.

[5] B.F. Skinner, *Contingencies of Reinforcement: A Theoretical Analysis* (Appleton-Century-Crofts, 1969).

SUGGESTED REFERENCES

General:

    Cofer, C.N., and M.H. Appley, *Motivation: Theory and Research* (Wiley, 1964).

Need Theory:

    Maslow, A.H., "A Theory of Human Motivation," *Psychological Review* (1943), pp. 370-396.
    Maslow, A.H., *Motivation and Personality* (Harper & Row, 1954).
    Murray, H.A. *Explorations in Personality* (Oxford University Press, 1938).
    White, R.W., "Motivation Reconsidered: The Concept of Competence," *Psychological Review* (1959), pp. 297-333.

Behavioral Theory:

Drive Variety:

Hull, C.L., *Principles of Behavior* (Appleton-Century-Crofts, 1943).
Miller, N.E.,"Studies in Fear as An Acquired Drive: I. Fear as Motivation and Fear Reduction as Reinforcement in The Learning of New Responses," *Journal of Experimental Psychology* (1948), pp. 89-101.

Incentive Variety:

Hull, C.L., *A Behavior System* (Yale University Press, 1952).
Logan, F.A., "Decision Making by Rats: Delay versus Amount of Reward," *Journal of Comparative Physiological Psychology* (1965), pp. 1-12.
Sheffield, D., and T. B. Roby, "Reward Value of a Non-Nutritive Sweet Taste," *Journal of Comparative Physiological Psychology* (1950), pp. 471-481.
Spence, K.W., *Behavior Theory and Conditioning* (Yale University Press, 1956).
Young, P.T., Motivation and Emotion (Wiley, 1961).

Expectancy Theory:

Achievement Variety:

Atkinson, J.W., *An Introduction to Motivation* (Van Nostrand-Reinhold, 1964).
Birney, R.C., H. Burdick and R.C. Teewan, *Fear of Failure* (Van Nostrand-Reinhold, 1969).

Instrumentality Variety:

Graen, G.B., "Instrumentality Theory of Work Motivation: Some Empirical Results and Suggested Modifications," *Journal of Applied Psychology: Monograph*, Part 2 (1969), p. 25.
Vroom, V.H., *Work and Motivation* (Wiley, 1964).
Vroom, V.H., and E.L. Deci, *Management and Motivation* (Penguin Books, 1970).

AN EXAMPLE OF REINFORCEMENT THEORY

Good accounting educators are usually concerned about their performance in the classroom. Most want to do a good job and advice on how to improve instructional performance is generally welcomed. While the effect of a professor's style on student performance cannot be proved conclusively through existing research, the impact has been assumed for many years. Professor Macht shows how an accounting instructor can improve his classroom performance using behaviorism. This special field of psychology holds a particular promise for accounting education primarily because accounting educators probably have been using behavioristic concepts for years— perhaps without being aware of it! But wading through complex psychological experiments that range from rats to people to glean a few key ideas—ideas which might be useful to an accounting educator—is an unappealing and unrealistic approach. An alternative approach is used to review the key concepts of this area—an interview with a professor who teaches educational psychology and behavior modification. Professor Macht prefers the interview format because it enables him to express his ideas in his favorite mode—the conversational mode—and this takes out most of the drudgery of learning about how behavioral psychology might be used by accounting educators.

Arranging the Contingencies of Reinforcement

Joel Macht
University of Denver

EDITOR:
I've recently read Dr. Skinner's text, *The Technology of Teaching*, and I am impressed with the observation that most of the ideas presented by Dr. Skinner are not at all new. They, in fact, are ideas which I believe have been considered and used for many years. Do you agree?

J.M.:
You're right. I think it is safe to say that every teacher, at one time or another, has used some, if not all, of what Dr. Skinner talks about in that particular book. What is happening today is that more teachers are using the operant conditioning principles more carefully and consistently and the result is that their classrooms are more productive. And, their classrooms are usually much more enjoyable.

EDITOR:
You have told me that you use these principles in your classes. Do you mean that you literally reinforce your students' performance.

J.M.:
I try.

EDITOR:
Are you saying that you give your students M & M's chocolate candies when they do well on tests? I've heard that behavior modification has been called the M & M psychology.

J.M.:
I have, on occasion, given students M & M's, but, again, not too often. Let me go a little further on this point. I use the principles in my classes for two reasons. First, the principles do work! I have been able to increase many of my students' performances by using positive reinforcement along with some of the other procedures we will discuss. But I also use application of the principles to show them how the whole system works. I do this because I want them to see that what we are talking about has a great deal of practical utility — that they will be able to use it when they begin teaching. Let me give you an example of what I mean.

Circa: Spring quarter, 1971, University of Denver. I was teaching a course entitled Behavior Modification in the Classroom. It was an undergraduate course and the enrollemnt was approximately sixty. I solicited the help of two students to assist me in a previously unannounced project. During the earlier part of the week, the class and I had been discussing the effectiveness of positive reinforcement and I was interested in presenting an *in vivo* demonstration. I selected a target behavior —writing in a notebook. The "reinforcers" to be used were M & M chocolate candies. No one, with the exception of the two student assistants and myself, knew of the project.

The assistants and I walked into the classroom just as class was to begin. Without any conversation or explanation, we began to walk around the room placing one M & M on the desk of each student who was either writing or closely approximating the task. As could be expected, many of the students began to laugh and talk with their neighbors. However, as each minute passed (and more M & M's were passed out) the class became quiet and the number of students who began to write increased markedly. Within fifteen minutes of the class period, almost everyone was writing something. There were no specifications as to what had to be written. Reinforcement was simply contingent upon writing.

There was, however, one group of six students, sitting together in the back of the room, who failed to write or approximate the task. Instead, they looked around the room, talked with each other, and offered comments as to "how dumb this whole thing was." Again, without saying a word, I walked to the back of the classroom. I stood in front of the "mavericks" waiting for some approximation which could be reinforced. I remained there about three minutes. The class and I had recently discussed how difficult it can be to initiate or maintain a behavior when there is little reinforcement for doing so. I decided, therefore, to seize upon this situation with the six students to review that point. Just as I was about to return to the front of the room, one of the six looked at me and said, "This is really silly. I know what you want me to do; it didn't take much time to pick it up. I just think this is kind of dumb. Besides," with an audible chuckle, "I don't like M & M's. However," with a slightly louder chuckle, "if you have some chocolate covered peanuts...."

Fortunately, I had purchased one bag of M & M chocolate peanuts along with the plain ones. With a noticeable smile on my face, I nonchalantly removed the unopened bag of peanuts from my back pocket. By this time, many of the other students had turned toward the back of the room and were watching what was going on. When my "holdout" saw the bag of peanuts, she laughed loudly, picked up her pen, and began to write with gusto. The writing behavior was immediately followed by several reinforcers. I think it is safe to say that we both were pleased. She received her peanuts and I "received" her writing.

EDITOR:
I am now wondering how I would have reacted to one of my mentors had he carried some cashews around with him. I would do almost anything for a handful of those things! Seriously, how did your students react to the demonstration?

J.M.:
Interesting that you mention cashews, because one of the students asked if I was suggesting that all professors carry little bags of peanuts around with them, plopping peanuts on a desk when a student did something which pleased the professor. Before I had time to respond, a retort followed from another student that most professors could "care less" whether a student does or doesn't do his work. A third mentioned something about an increase in cavities. But a fourth student raised some very salient points.

He indicated that in his view, a professor had three choices. "First, he might not care one way or another—if the student writes, he writes. If he doesn't write, that's the way it goes. Second, he *could* carry 'peanuts' around with him. In other words, he could try and provide something for the students, a reason for writing or a reward for writing. Third, he could get the student to write, but not with the use of rewards of positive consequences. He could, as most professors do, indicate what will happen if the student does *not* write. "You are either going to fail this course or get a low grade if you don't write."

Then the student asked his classmates a series of questions: "How many of us do things in order to avoid something unpleasant? Do you read your textbook because it is interesting and enjoyable or because you know there is going to be a test on it? Do you come to class because the lectures are stimulating or, again, because of a test?"

One student responded that in her class, the professor took roll and deducted points when the students were absent.

"That's the point," the fourth student answered. "You go to class to avoid losing points toward your final grade. That's negative reinforcement, not positive. I'd rather work for 'peanuts' than work to avoid something."

"You are placing too much responsibility on the professor and the college," another student added. "You keep talking about having the college provide reasons for learning. I don't think a professor should have to give you something just to get you to study. It's up to the individual student. If he doesn't want to learn, he shouldn't be here. I don't expect anything from my professors. They present the material. It is my responsibility to learn or not to learn, not his. I maintain a high grade point average and it's certainly not because my professor gives me anything."

"I don't think that is true," the fourth student responded. "Don't you work hard to get good grades?"

"Yes."

"Then you are working for something. For you, grades are important. I would guess that grades have been important to you for a long time. Do your parents ever tell you that they are proud of you because of your grades? If so, then they're giving you something. Do you want to go to graduate school? You know, of course, how important and necessary it is to have high grades for graduate admission. Again, you are working for something. The point is that grades, and your parents' recognition, and admission to graduate school are your rewards. You are not working for nothing. Your environment has given you something to work for and when you work, your environment pays you. Let me ask you this, what are you going to do when you finish school?"

"I'm going to be a teacher."

"Are you going to try to provide reasons for your students to work?"

"Of course, but it's different. I'm not going to be teaching college students. My students will be in elementary school. They must be given reasons to work. Most of them will probably go to school because they have to, not because they want to. I'm going to try to make school fun for them so that they will enjoy being there."

"Then you *are* going to give them something to work for. You are going to reward their behavior. Why can't the same attitude be adopted at the college level?"

"I just do not think it can. Little children can be rewarded with candy and extra recess periods. They'll like it when their teacher smiles at them or pats them on the back. Those things are meaningless to college students."

"All you are saying is that the rewards are different. Instead of candy, we work for grades—in place of recess periods, graduate school admission. In place of smiles and pats, we work for good jobs, money, advanced degrees, recognition by our peers, and even congratulations from our professors and our parents. The principles are the same. The main things that vary are the rewards. Doesn't that make sense?"

EDITOR:

I'm not certain how your student responded to that last question, but the previous argument does seem to make sense. I don't think I have thought about it that way—grades in place of candy, graduate school admission instead of recess periods, jobs, money, professional community recognition—they are powerful rewards for most of us, aren't they?

J.M.:

I think they are and I also think that we know that they are for many students. We've all seen the student who apparently requires very little reinforcement to maintain his academic behavior for many years. Perhaps, it is his own thoughts about the prospects of his future reinforcers which help to maintain his present behavior. That I do not know, but I think it would be incorrect of me to suggest that most students' academic performance can be sustained for four years simply on the basis of long range goals. That picture is just too incomplete. Something else is needed—something which will bridge the gap between the time the student enters college and the realization of some of his desired environmental payoffs. A four-year delay between entering behavior and reinforcement is most often too long. This delayed reinforcement can result in too many "towels" being thrown in, too many valuable prospects being lost along the way, too many goals being unattained, too many resources being wasted. As I see it, if colleges rely almost exclusively on long range goals to maintain their students' performance, they will undoubtedly lose more than they will gain.

Look for a moment at your own field of accounting. Suppose one of your students expresses an interest in becoming a certified public accountant. Maybe he sees himself as a member of an established firm. He realizes that an accountant is a highly respected member of a community—perhaps this appeals to him. He also realizes that his position will afford him the opportunity to make a good living which will enable him to have many material things he presently does not have—perhaps that is appealing to him. There are, of course, other possible long range reinforcers but he is going to have to wait a good length of time prior to obtaining them. Who is going to help him maintain his own performance for those many years? How about the student who expresses an interest in accounting but who has little intention of using his acquired information in a public sense. Rather, the information will be for himself—not as a preparer, I believe that is your term. Most of us enjoy having a non-major in some of our classes. How do we maintain his behavior? After all, he is paying good money to take our course, therefore he is entitled to something.

Bridging the Reinforcement Gap

EDITOR:
I'll accept the possibility that this delay factor, which you've just mentioned, can result in the loss of some very high-powered students. What can the college professor do about it? We must keep in mind that for the most part, the college professor sees his students only in academic circles and the time spent in these circles may be quite brief.

J.M.:
While the time spent with our students is relatively brief, I am going to suggest that you and I as teachers are in the best position to help bridge the gap between long-term and short-term rewards for learning. We, the college professors, can mediate the delay between the students' entering behavior and their attainment of their goals. In fact, I am going to suggest that we must assume the responsibility for bridging this gap. If we fail to do so, we, like our colleges, will lose much more than we will gain.

With few exceptions, you and I know relatively little about the reinforcement histories of the students who enroll in our classes. We observe that some come into our rooms highly motivated. They put forth considerable effort without a great deal of help from us. We often seek them out, cherishing them when the opportunity arises. We derive so much reinforcement from them that we, in turn, shower them with recognition, attention, and words of encouragement. Our consequences maintain their efforts which, in turn, effectively maintain ours. The cycle is beautiful, and many professors have been heard to say that it makes everything else worthwhile.

Other students, however, fail to put forth a great deal of effort. They rarely participate in class discussions. They often perform poorly on examinations. Their attendance is spotty. They sometimes come up with the most ingenious explanations for why a quiz was missed or a project not completed. They give us little reinforcement, and we give them about the same. We indicate to them that they have little interest in our subject matter. They indicate to us that we do not care much about them. The cycle is somewhat less than beautiful. The irony of this situation is that the first groups' behavior could be maintained with much less of our attention while the second group requires so much more. Given, however, the assumption that our reinforcing behavior (or lack of it) and our students' reinforcing behavior (or lack of it) is maintained by the same principles, then our reactions to our students become predictable.

Perhaps by looking at some of the principles that influence behavior, we will be able to obtain a better understanding of how our behavior effects our students' behavior and how theirs affects ours. Equally as important, we should be able to come up with some ideas about how to bridge the so-called "reinforcement gap" and help our "unmotivated" students experience success and positive reinforcement while under our tutelage.

EDITOR:
Before you begin, I would like to raise a question or two. Would you agree that certain academic subject areas lend themselves to intrinsic reinforcement? What I mean by that question is that certain subjects, like art and music, are reinforcing in themselves, thus the professor's job is much easier. In line with my point is a concern that accounting may not be one of those easily reinforced subject areas.

J.M.:
I believe that potentially, all subject areas have intrinsic reinforcement qualitites. Art and music classes are intrinsically reinforcing to those students who truly enjoy art and music. But the same can be said for physics, organic chemistry, French, and

accounting. For example, a freshman who has had the opportunity to help his father or friend balance books or even help the same person prepare a tax return may find a course on debits and credits exciting and challenging. For that student, working with figures and solving problems may be enough to maintain his academic enthusiasm despite what his professor does or does not do. On the other hand, a second freshman may react exactly the opposite. He may find a beginning course in art or accounting very dull in which case the chances for intrinsic reinforcement are slim. This is when you and I must step in to show the student that the subject matter can be enjoyable.

EDITOR:

I think you will find many professors who will question even the possibility that certain courses can be made enjoyable -- particularly the mechanical type courses where one lays the foundation for application at a later date.

J.M.:

You are probably right, but what is there to prevent us from combining mechanics and application. It may be true that children have to crawl before thay can walk but I do not believe that the same idea has to hold for our course work. For example, while I lecture on the mechanics of positive reinforcement I pose an example of a problem that a teacher is having with a child. The students are often asked to make an attempt at solving the problem even before the necessary terminology is learned. In many cases, they appear to enjoy floundering—particularly when I openly share the fact that I have floundered on many occasions myself. The combination of the practical and the mechanical spices up what otherwise might be dull, rote memory. There is no reason to assume that an accounting professor can't do the same. Suppose that you are discussing the effects of transactions on a balance sheet. You can talk about net income, expenses, revenue, assets, and I suspect a host of other things. At the same time that these points and terms are bing discussed, the professor can present a relevant example of a company or individual who is experiencing considerable financial difficulty. Maybe the combination and the attempts at solving the problem would enhance the professor's presentation and make the situation more enjoyable for the students.

Please understand that the task of motivating students is by no means easy. The variables affecting our college students are numerous and complex. To make matters more difficult, our technology of teaching is far from complete. Combine these items with our overcrowded classrooms, our many required extracurricular obligations, and the endless little "nitty-gritty" items that must be handled, and it becomes quite obvious that our work is cut out for us. But in my view, if we do not make the effort to motivate our students, I cannot imagine who will. The responsibility, therefore, is on our shoulders.

Behavior is Affected By Its Consequences

One of the most important facts we know about the acquisition and alteration of behavior is that behavior is affected by its consequences. This means that the future probability of a response is largely dependent upon how the environment responds to that behavior. From a practical standpoint, this statement means that you and I can influence the future probability of the occurrence of a particular form of behavior by our reactions to that behavior. If we want our students to use sophisticated analytical techniques to help, for example, Smith & Sons, Inc. to determine whether they will be solvent next year, then when the students demonstrate the analytical behavior we should react to them—or more appropriately to their behavior—in a positive way. By doing so, we indicate to them that we are pleased with their performance and that what they are doing is correct. We, of course, do not have to react positively. We can rely on other variables such as the material itself, the grade that is given, or any number of other things to maintain the students' behavior. My own personal feeling is that the latter approach is an unnecessary gamble since the time that it takes us to show our positive recognition is minimal and from the students' standpoint, our reaction may be very powerful and important to them.

Environmental responses to behavior may take various forms. Let's look at two general types — positive reinforcers and punishing or aversive stimuli.

Positive reinforcers. These events are defined by the observation that behaviors which precede their application are *more* likely to occur in the future.

Applied reinforcers serve the purpose of increasing the future probability of a behavior.

A positive reinforcer is often defined as any stimulus which an individual is willing to put forth effort to obtain.

Two categories of positive reinforcers. Positive reinforcers may be primary or unlearned as in the case of food, water, air, and sexual contact. They may also be called conditioned, acquired, or learned as in the case of social approval, recognition, money, grades, and the like.

Punishing or aversive stimuli. Aversive stimuli are defined by the observation that behaviors which precede their application are *less* likely to occur in the future, given similar circumstances.

Applied aversive stimuli serve the purpose of decreasing the future probability of a behavior.

An aversive stimulus is often defined as any stimulus that an individual is willing to work hard to avoid.

Two categories of aversive stimuli. Aversive stimuli may be primary or unlearned as in the case of extreme heat or cold, loud noises, very bright lights, or physical pain. They may also be called learned or conditioned aversive stimuli as in the examples of social disapproval, "poor" grades, or threatening verbal statements.

EDITOR:
Would I be correct in assuming that a particular stimulus might be positive or negative depending upon the individual's personal background?

J.M.:
Yes. You see, the effects of conditioned stimuli, both positive and aversive, are learned. As such, not only can a specific stimulus be either positive or negative, but at some time during the life of an individual, it can actually be both. For example, the grade of "C" might be a very positive stimulus during one part of a student's career in school, while becoming a conditioned aversive stimulus at a later date.

EDITOR:
How then do we know whether a stimulus is or is not a positive stimulus?

J.M.:
The only way to really know is to observe the student's behavior. If he is working hard to obtain the stimulus then the stimulus is probably positive at that time. On the other hand, if we observe that the student is working hard to avoid that stimulus, then it is a good bet that it is perceived as negative by the student. I am glad that you asked your question because I'll offer a few examples where I will be assuming that a stimulus is positive. If I indicate that a teacher reinforces a student's behavior with the statement "very good," I do not mean to indicate that that verbal statement will definitely be a reinforcer. For our discussion, I will make that assumption, but again, it is the student's performance which is the ultimate barometer.

Quite obviously, you and I as professors are interested in increasing appropriate academic performance from our students. I doubt that any of us would be particularly satisfied if one of our students finished our course knowing only the same amount of information as he did when he first enrolled. I would like, now, to introduce two procedures which are used to initiate, increase, and maintain behavior. Although you may not be familiar with the names I am certain you will recognize their operations. The two procedures are known as positive and negative reinforcement. (Negative reinforcement is often confused with punishment. Their differences should become apparent in a moment.)

Positive reinforcement. The procedure of positive reinforcement is being used when one *applies* a positive reinforcing stimulus contingent upon a response. When a teacher praises a student for a piece of academic work, he is using positive reinforcement. All things being equal, the probability that the student will repeat his performance at some time in the future has increased. (Again, please note that I am assuming that for this student, praise is, indeed, a positive reinforcer.)

Negative reinforcement. As indicated, the procedure of negative reinforcement also increases behavior. The operation of removing an aversive stimulus contingent upon a response is known as negative reinforcement. Note that the stimulus being employed is aversive—one that the individual would work hard to avoid. Note also that the stimulus is not being applied, but withdrawn. When an aversive stimulus is withdrawn, and the behavior preceding the withdrawal increases, the stimulus is called a negative reinforcer.

When a behavior enables an individual to *avoid, postpone,* or *terminate* an aversive stimulus, that behavior has a higher probability of occurrence under similar circumstances in the future. Let us assume that a student desires to pass a course. Said in another way, he would like to avoid failing the course. His experience has taught him (hopefully) that by studying, there is a greater chance of passing a course or avoiding failure. "Studying behavior" is, therefore, maintained by negative reinforcement. The studying enables the student to avoid the aversiveness of failure. When you and I drive our cars at 30 mph in a 30 mph zone, we do so primarily to avoid a ticket or accident. Our 30 mph driving behavior is maintained by negative reinforcement. Again, we have learned *what to do* in order to avoid an aversive stimulus. When a student goes to a college classroom so as to avoid losing points toward his grade, his attendance is being maintained by negative reinforcement. I am certain that you know that our students' attendance could be maintained by positive reinforcement.

Let me mention two other procedures which can be used to decrease certain behaviors. They are called extinction and punishment.

Extinction. The operation of *withholding* or *withdrawing* a positive reinforcer contingent upon a response is known as extinction. When, for example, a teacher consistently withholds attention from a disruptive student (and all other sources of reinforcement are also withheld — primarily peer reinforcement) disruption should ultimately diminish in frequency.

EDITOR:
I can see where extinction would fit in with younger children, but I'm not certain how we would use it in a college classroom.

J.M.:
I suspect that few college professors use extinction with the excessively noisy and talkative college student. However, I would guess that you would be very surprised to know that many college professors do use the procedure, accidentally I should add, to decrease a behavior which they certainly do not wish to decrease. Earlier, I indicated that many students come into our classrooms already well motivated. And, I said that despite what we do, their appropriate academic behavior continues. These are students who are motivated by sources other than the professor. But some students' behavior is truly maintained almost exclusively by his professor and for those students, the professors reinforcement is very important. What do you suppose happens to a student's initiative, effort, and performance when those behaviors are never followed by reinforcement?

EDITOR:
I can guess!

J.M.:
And you'd be right! His efforts and performance will begin to weaken and if there is a prolonged condition of non-reinforcement, the student may quit.

EDITOR:
I can see where that situation would lead to the negative cycle which you talked about. The student, gaining little, if any, reinforcement from his class begins to slack off

in his work. He gets further and further behind; does poorly on his tests; gives his professor little reinforcement; and, in turn, is given an equal amount from his professor. The student blames the professor— the professor probably admits to himself that the student wasn't "much good" in the first place—and they both lose.

J.M.:

Sadly enough, I believe your analysis is correct. I am certain that all of us wish we could avoid such a situation, but I think that the practical world of the college professor dictates that complete avoidance, today at least, is most difficult—if at all possible. Do you mind if I put a plug in for a pet peeve? This is a perfect spot and maybe an administrator or dean is in the audience.

EDITOR:

Be my guest.

J.M.:

For me, the size of the college classroom is a critical variable. It is almost impossible not to lose a few students when we have thirty or more students in one class. Some professors appear to do a very fine job with that size class. I must admit, quite honestly, that I have a very tough time with class sizes more than thirty. I wonder how many of your readers would agree with me? End of editorial; let me move on.

> *Punishment.* The operation of punishment involves the contingent *application* of an aversive stimulus. When a behavior is immediately followed by an aversive stimulus, the behavior weakens. I doubt that any examples are needed for this procedure since most of us are quite familiar with it.

It should be apparent that all of us, at one time or another, have used each of the described procedures. It is likely that we all use them daily. They were not invented by any one man, and they are not the exclusive right of any one "camp" of psychology. (I remember one student saying to me, "You mean that that man from Harvard didn't invent these things?") They have been used to reduce the occurrence of thumbsucking in young children (Baer, 1962); to help the elderly acquire new skills (Lindsley, 1964); to reduce the frequency of enuresis (Wickes, 1958); to increase cooperative responses in children (Hingtgen and Trost, 1964); to train nurses to deal with institutionalized patients (Ayllon and Michael, 1959); to train mothers to deal with their own children (Hawkins, et al., 1966); and to train teachers to deal with their students (Madsen, et al., 1968). They are used every day to teach reading, writing, and arithmetic. They are used to help the alcoholic, the narcotic, and the psychotic. They are used daily in all forms of psychotherapy. They are used by parents and by their children. They are used by professors and by their students.

Behavior is Affected By Its Consequences

The procedures work automatically. This means that one need not be aware of the contingencies in operation in order for the contingencies to work. Rather, it is the temporal relation between behavior and the environmental consequence that is critical. As Jack Michael and Lee Meyerson (1960) have said "any behavior which is followed by reinforcement—in all of the many species studied, and above all in man—is more likely to occur again in the same or a similar situation.... To increase the occurrence of a particular class of behavior, it is necessary only to ensure that reinforcement occurs relatively soon after the behavior." (See references).

The basic principle is quite simple: behavior is affected by its consequences. One can increase and/or decrease the future probability of behavior by altering the ways in which the environment responds to that behavior. All of us are agents of the environment. We all respond to behavior. To deny the use of the procedures is not the same as saying that the procedures are not being used. For we all use them. The ends for which they are used, however, is a whole new question and a most serious one. The potential ramifications of the technology are immense. At times they are overwhelming. They have spawned many emotional discussions. The resulting questions seem to preclude simple answers. Still, questions must be raised and answers must be tested. (If you are interested in these issues may I suggest that you read two very provocative articles — the Rogers and Skinner debate, "Some Issues Concerning the Control of Human Behavior: A Symposium," and Leonard Krasner's article, "Behavior Control and Social Ressonsibility." Both articles can be found in *Control of Human Behavior,* R. Ulrich, et al., listed in the references.)

Shaping Behavior

The effects of the described procedures work automatically. There are times when we are influencing our students' behavior without being aware of it. Capricious relationships between the responses of our students and our following reactions are often sufficient to bring about changes in student behavior. But capriciousness, by definition, involves inconsistency, and educational inconsistency rarely results in the rapid acquisition of behavior.

An alternative to capricious education is a well-planned program, a program that includes not only positive reinforcement but also a planned approach for presenting academic material. In fact, the two go hand in hand, for by presenting our material in a systematic way, we can increase the probability of reinforcing our students' performance. Although the last statement would appear to be an obvious one, many professors fail to incorporate a systematic presentation of materials in their teaching. Numerous outcomes can come about as a result of this failure, but two possibilities stand out. First, the student may not learn as much as the professor intended. Second, the student will likely miss out on considerable positive reinforcement. If one or the other possibilities actually occurs, student performance probably will decrease. When student performance decreases, instructor performance also may decrease. These outcomes, however, can be avoided, and I would like to illustrate how.

All too often, you and I rely upon the procedure of negative reinforcement to increase and maintain our students' behavior. We do this for several reasons, but probably the main one is that it appears to us to be effective. As a result of the explicit or implied threats of failure, the student performs (or at least he hands in his assignments) and he takes his tests. He may not be learning anything, but he does complete the requirements. We also use negative reinforcement because in our view, positive efforts have simply not worked: the student gives us promises and assurances, but no work. There are times, of course, when we might like to use positive reinforcement instead of negative reinforcement, but our students do so little, that finding something to reinforce positively is difficult in itself. Research clearly indicates, however, that excessive use of negative reinforcement can result in undesired side effects. (For a discussion of the side effects of punishment and negative reinforcement as they pertain to education, see B. F. Skinner's *Technology of Teaching,* Appleton-Century-Crofts, 1968, pp. 95-104; 148; 161; 185 ff.) Although negative reinforcement may result in immediate performance by a college student, it is most unlikely that his desired behavior will be maintained for very long.

But what can we do with a student who puts forth little effort in our classroom? How can we apply positive reinforcement when desired academic responses are so few and far between? It goes without saying that it is most difficult to reinforce a behavior which doesn't occur.

There is a technique, known as shaping, which can be used to increase behaviors that are presently occurring at very low frequencies. As with the previously described procedures, shaping is a technique which all of us have used. In fact, it is unlikely that there has ever been an instructor who has not used some form of it, granting, of course, some instructors use it more effectively than others.

Essentially, the technique of shaping can be broken down into four subconcepts: criterion, baserate, successive approximations, and contingent positive reinforcement. The criterion is the professor's goal or objective. It is that which the professor wishes to accomplish. Ideally, the criterion should be carefully defined and described in objective and observable terms. In this way, both the professor and the student know what it is that they are trying to achieve. There may be a daily criterion — for a small section of a subject matter, or there may be a weekly or monthly criterion.

The baserate is an accurate evaluation of how much of the criterion the student already has in his repertoire. In a sense, it is a measure of how much of the criterion he brings with him into our class. The baserate measure is a critical feature of the shaping process. Without this measure it will be very difficult to know where to start the shaping program.

Successive approximations are the small steps that take the student from *his* baserate to *your* criterion. These are the stepwise increases that are found in programmed instruction. They bridge the gap between what the student knows and what you want him to know. Each step successively approximates the goal. They increase in difficulty and complexity. Whereas the first successive approximation will likely resemble the student's baserate, the final approximation will be very similar to your goal.

Finally, contingent positive reinforcement is the motivator that maintains the student's efforts and also tells him when he has made a correct response. The student receives positive reinforcement for each successful completion of an approximation.

EDITOR:
Could you give us an example of how this shaping process might be used in one of our classrooms?
J.M.:
I will try, but you will have to allow me a little room for error—particularly when it comes to accounting's technical language and to my guesses as to what materials are necessarily prerequisite to others.

I have in front of me a text entitled *Accounting: An Introduction.* Let us assume that you are the instructor in an undergraduate course for accounting majors and that your course is roughly titled "Generally Accepted Accounting Principles — Their Justifications and Limitations." Let us look at the first three subconcepts of shaping and see how they relate to your course.

> *Criterion.* One of the first things we need to do is to establish a goal or goals for our course. We want to make certain that our goal is clearly defined and objectified so that we, as professors, will know when our students have reached the predetermined goal. Perhaps we want our students to be able to define and use correctly, in an example, each of the following terms: accounting entity, accounting period, materiality, conservatism, consistency, full disclosure, etc. We might also wish for our students to explain accurately the need for and function of "generally accepted accounting principles." Let us assume that those are the main goals for our course. We decide that we will measure our students' performance regarding these goals by means of a paper pencil test and a short verbal discussion in which each student will serve as class leader.

> *Baserate.* Our next step is the determination of where our students are in reference to our goals. In other words, we need to find out how much of our goals our students already have in their repertoire. To accomplish this, we will give our students a baserate examination. The exam will be made up of several questions which will sample the materials established in our goals. In preparing our test, all we need to keep in mind is that we need an accurate and reliable measure of how much prerequisite material our students bring to our class.

J.M.:
Notice that these two determinations tell us where our students are in reference to where we want them to be.
EDITOR:
Can you briefly tell us why these two determinations are so important?
J.M.:
Our goal, of course, is really a statement of where we would like to go. It gives us, and our students, some direction. Almost every one of us has some idea as to our goals for our classes, although some are more clearly defined than others. As I see it, the critical measure is the baserate. The entering skills of our students certainly vary: some know a great deal about our subject,

others know little. In my experience, the fact that students have had the necessary prerequisite courses to enter my class does not always tell me a lot. I, therefore, must find out what they know. If I happen to start my presentation of material at a point where I think the students should be, I may lose half of them. I may be over the heads of some, while boring the others to tears. Of course, I may be lucky. I may hit their entering behavior right on the button — but that's unlikely. To be safe, I give them a baserate examination. I give them a sample of my goal and see exactly where they are. Let us look at the situation this way. Simply because a student has taken intermediate accounting does not mean that he is necessarily ready for advanced accounting. Even the fact that he received a better than average grade in the previous course does not tell us how much he got out of the course. He could come into our class with a great deal more or less information then we would predict. If we know where they are (as a result of our baserate test) we will be in a better position to not only reinforce their progress but also to assign certain work which we believe would be helpful for them. More importantly, if we wait for them to do what we think they *should* be able to do, we may have to wait a long time and we may initiate or continue that negative cycle. The baserate evaluation is critical and it doesn't take that much time.

Successive approximations. These are really nothing more than small steps which bridge the gap from where the student is to where we want him to be. Most of us already have sequential steps built into our lecture notes and texts. What changes we may have to make will depend upon our students' measured entering skills. For students who are far behind our anticipated level we will need to develop new steps. In a sense, we ask ourselves, what do our students need to know in order to understand or use the necessary concepts or skills already outlined in our goals? We break the skills and concepts down into component parts and these parts are the approximations.

My entire point is that I strongly believe that you and I must maximize the frequency of positive reinforcement for our students. I do not think that we can afford to rely upon long range reinforcers to maintain a few of our students. Shaping and reinforcement give us a chance to get to some of our students who are not under the influence of what will happen to them two, three, or four years from now. Shaping helps us increase the chances that more of our students will receive reinforcement from our classes. We know where they are so we know where we must begin with them. In a sentence, shaping and reinforcement increase the chances that our students will experience success, and that may be the necessary reinforcement to really turn them on.

We know that positive reinforcement is very effective. We also know what happens to behavior when it results in little, if any reinforcement. We further know that if we do not use positive reinforcement, we must rely upon threats of punishment to produce behavior, and the behavior produced may not be what we desired. I believe, therefore, that it is our responsibility to "catch our students doing something 'good.'" By finding out where our students are in reference to where we want them to be, and by programming our material into small sequential steps, I believe we stand a better chance of catching them at the proper moment and reinforcing them.

Applying the Principles

The validity of the principles of behavioral psychology are now well established. The principles, again, were not invented by man. They simply describe how learning has taken place in the past, how learning takes place now, and how learning will take place in the future. The principles function apart from our awareness of them. Our intentions do not interfere with the relationship that exists between behavior and how the environment responds to behavior. In my view, the only significant choice we must make is whether we will or will not consciously employ the principles as we approach our task as professors. We, of course, do not have to employ the principles. We can rely upon chance, upon a capricious relationship of behavior and environmental reactions. But, on the other hand, we can make a concerted effort to employ the knowledge that our technology has afforded us. Granted, we may not always succeed, but we can certainly increase the likelihood of success.

The principles described above have now been used in the development of a wide variety of programmed materials, teaching machines, and various forms of computer-assisted instruction. In teacher education classes today major emphasis is being placed on the formulation of precise behavioral objectives. Teachers are also being trained in the use of the described principles as well as being given the opportunity to practice the procedures prior to receiving their teaching degree. In fact, entire classes and schools have been redesigned according to the principles of behavioral psychology. One of the major explanations for the adoption of these principles is that in most instances, they have been found to be a tremendous aid in the learning process.

PY 112

The perfect ending to this discussion would be twenty separate descriptions of how the above information has been successfully used in twenty separate college classrooms. Unfortunately, I do not have twenty. As a matter of fact, I do not have ten. Nor five. Nor two. But, I do have one!

PY 112 was (and perhaps still is) a psychology course taught at Arizona State University. Rather than describe the course to you, I am simply going to quote excerpts from a handout that was given to all the students who enrolled in that course. I believe the philosophy of the course is particularly relevant to what we have been discussing.

> This course is an attempt to develop a rather different way of teaching psychology. You are about to begin studying what is as yet a young experimental science. The course itself will be an experiment—guided, at least in part, by the very principles of the science about which you will be learning. As you learn more about these principles of behavior, we hope you will be able to criticize constructively our methods and perhaps suggest new applications to improve these teaching procedures.
>
> In general terms, the objective of this new procedure is to offer *individual* instruction and attention within the framework of mass education. The hope is that each person will in fact master the basic material appropriate to a systematic first course in psychology.
>
> Two special characteristics of this method merit immediate and special attention. First, each student should be able to move at his own pace through the entire course. The rapid worker should not be held back by a slower student or forced to waste time listening to several repetitions of information he has already learned. Equally important, the student lagging behind should not be forced to move ahead at the sacrifice of comprehension. Some of you may finish this course before the end of the semester. That is fine. You will merit the free time that this will make available. Others may not finish the course within the time marked off as a normal semester unit. This may create special problems. How fast you go depends on you.
>
> Second, material will be presented only as you are prepared to deal with it. The student who 'missed the point' but is allowed, or forced to proceed, soon compounds his slight misunderstanding into total confusion—the stuff that 'F's' are made of! The subject matter of this course is broken up into a series of units. You will be required to show mastery of each unit before moving on to the next. In this way a small mistake can be corrected before it results in the ultimate disaster. Sophocles wrote, 'One must learn by doing the thing; for though you think you know it, you have no certainty until you try.' You will be asked to try often. To demonstrate your mastery of each unit, you will be required to pass a 'readiness' test before proceeding

further. For those who are willing to put a *little* effort into the job, there can be no such thing as failure in the normal sense. Your *success* may even be *fun*.

The information you will be asked to acquire will come in five kinds of packages — reading, laboratory, discussion, demonstrations and lectures. These, however, will not occur merely because it is Monday, Wednesday, or Friday. Some material is more appropriate for one type of presentation than another. There will be periods of concentrated reading and other periods when you will spend your time in the laboratory. A reading assignment should not be undertaken until you have passed the readiness test associated with the end of the previous unit. Likewise, laboratory experiments can only be done when you demonstrate you are prepared to profit from them (by passing the previous unit).

The lectures and demonstrations in this course will have a different relation to the rest of your course work than is usually the case. They will be provided only when you have demonstrated your readiness to appreciate them; no examination will be based upon them; and you need not attend them if you do not wish. When a certain percentage of the class has reached a certain point in the course, a lecture or demonstration will be available at a stated time, but it will not be complusory.

A great deal has been said about the "readiness" tests. These are not examinations in the usual sense. Your grade will not depend upon them. Their only function is to indicate to you your degree of understanding and indicate to us where you are having trouble and where help is needed. If you fail a readiness test, you will be required to re-do the unit and try again before you proceed — but there is no penalty in terms of a grade for failing these tests, even two or three times.

A final word. This is your personal course, which as noted above aims to give individualized instruction within the framework of mass education. Our method was first tried out at the University of Brasilia, in Brazil, in 1964, and during the past four terms at Arizona State. We believe that it is a better method than those in common use within large universities, but we know that it can still be improved. To help us do this we wish that you would take time out occasionally to think about its effectiveness for you. Then, if you come up with a comment or suggestion that you think might be helpful, please send it along to your instructor. In this way, you may be of help to yourself, to us, and to your classmates, as well as to those students who will follow you in classes to come.

While the technology of teaching has now become a rather well developed science, much remains to be done in applying what we know to the tasks faced daily by the college teacher. We know that human behavior is very complex. We know that the variables operating in college teaching are equally complex. Yet we cannot allow the acknowledgement of complexity to inhibit our efforts. Instead, the acknowledgement must serve as our catalyst. H. G. Wells once said, "Human history becomes more and more a race between education and catastrophe." I know that we all agree that none of us can afford to lose that race.

REFERENCES

Ayllon, T. and Michael, J. "The Psychiatric Nurse as a Behavioral Engineer," *Journal of the Experimental Analysis of Behavior,* 1959, *2,* pp. 323-334.

Baer, D.M. "Laboratory Control of Thumbsucking by Withdrawal and Representation of Reinforcement," *Journal of Experimental Analysis of Behavior,* 1962, *5,* pp. 525-528.

Hawkins, R.P., Peterson, R.F., Schweid, E., and Bilou, S.W. "Behavior Therapy in the Home: Amelioration of Problem Parent-Child Relations with the Parent in a Therapeutic Role," *Journal of Experimental Child Psychology,* 1969, *4,* pp. 107.

Hingtgen, J.N. and Trost, F.C., Jr. "Shaping Cooperative Responses in Early Childhood Schizophrenics: II. Reinforcement of Mutual Physical Contact and Vocal Responses." Presented at the American Psychological Association, Los Angeles, September, 1964.

Krasner, Leonard. "Behavior Control and Social Responsibility," *American Psychologist, 17,* 1964, pp. 199-204.

Lindsley, O.R., "Geriatric Behavioral Prosthetics," in R. Kastenbaum (ed.), *New Thoughts on Old Age,* New York: Springer Publishing Company, Inc., 1964.

Madsen, C.H., Jr., Becker, W.C. and Thomas, D.R., "Rules, Praise, and Ignoring: Elements of Elementary Classroom Control," *Journal of Applied Behavior Analysis,* 1969, *1,* pp. 139-150.

Meyerson, L. and Michael, J.L., "The Measurement of Sensory Thresholds in Exceptional Children: An Experimental Approach to Some Problems of Differential Diagnosis and Education with Special Reference to Hearing." *Monographs in Somato Psychology,* 1960, *4.*

Rogers, Carl and Skinner, B.F., "Some Issues Concerning the Control of Human Behavior: A Symposium," *Science, 124,* 1956, pp. 1057-1066.

Skinner, B.F., *The Technology of Teaching,* New York: Appleton-Century-Crofts, 1968.

Wickes, I.G., "Treatment of Persistent Enuresis with the Electric Buzzer," *Archives of Disease in Childhood,* 1958, *33,* pp. 160-164.

SUGGESTED READING

Sidman, Murray. *Tactics of Scientific Research.* New York: Basic Books, Inc., 1960.

Ulrich, Roger, Stachnik, Thomas, and Mabry, John. *Control of Human Behavior, Volume 1.* Glenview, Illinois: Scott, Foresman and Co., 1966.

Ulrich, Roger, Stachnik, Thomas, and Mabry, John. *Control of Human Behavior, Volume 2.* Glenview, Illinois: Scott, Foresman and Co., 1970.

USING COGNITIVE PSYCHOLOGY

Inquiry is essentially the process of building and testing theories. Prior to the beginning of formal education a child learns almost exclusively through inquiry. In school, however, learning is generally directed and sequenced for the child by the teacher who sets the goals and guides the learning process. The result of many years of such guiding and directing is that students become dependent learners requiring external motivation (often weak and superficial) to continue with the learning process. Perhaps accounting classes contain dependent learners.

The purpose of Professor Stallman's approach is to describe the use of some teaching procedures which have been shown to be effective in enabling students to regain the inquiry mode of learning. He describes the development of teaching materials and techniques which should provide the primary conditions necessary for stimulation and support of inquiry in the managerial accounting classroom. The use of materials and teaching methods like those described are believed to produce skill and understanding of the inquiry process and relatively efficient assimilation of accounting course content.

The inquiry mode of learning can have a number of highly desirable consequences including increased learner motivation, a greater sense of autonomy, and higher self-esteem—all of which can lead to improved forms of productive thinking. Such qualities seem desirable in light of the continued demands for increased competence and creative and adaptive thinking on the part of today's professional accountant.

Inquiry In The Accounting Classroom

James C. Stallman
University of Missouri-Columbia

Whether they serve in the role of auditor, systems analyst, tax specialist, or controller, accountants face demanding professional responsibilities. One of the accountant's most pressing responsibilities is maintaining the competence required for his particular job in the face of accelerating changes in business practices, technology, government regulation, and accounting principles (or standards). This task requires a continuing effort to keep abreast of a diverse set of developments, an ability to sense which among them are likely to affect the accountant's job or the way it must be performed, and the flexibility to adapt to these changes.

The effective performance of this task requires a commitment to continual learning. The accountant cannot rely solely on what he has learned in the past. The changes which produce the necessity for performing this task are by definition outside the domain of knowledge already possessed. The accountant must be able to think independently, to relate what he perceives to what he knows, to modify his notions of how things relate in the light of new information, to draw implications from changing conditions, to creatively seek solutions to new problems, and to evaluate the ideas which he generates. In short, the accountant must be capable of autonomous productive thinking.

In view of this demand on students after graduation, perhaps accounting classes should be examined to assess their influence on the productive thinking required of students for continued professional growth. Technical competence is, of course, a necessity. A quick review of the course content, the text books, and the quality of the teaching staff which is typical in the curriculum offering of most accounting departments suggests ample opportunity for students to absorb a considerable number of facts and to attain proficiency in an assortment of technical skills which constitute the *content* of the accounting discipline as practiced at that time. But what assistance is given to the student in learning the *process* by which he can independently increase the breadth and depth of his understanding of our rapidly changing discipline and the forces underlying its changes?

Implicit in the approach each teacher takes to his classes is a model of the teacher-student roles in the learning process. One model which is apparently Widespread views the student's mind as an empty bucket. The teacher's job is to fill the bucket with knowledge as fast as possible. This task is complicated by the limited amount of time the teacher has to shovel in the knowledge (during class time and through homework assignments) and the growing pile of knowledge demanding to be shoveled. While most would reject this model as a view of teaching, the pressure of daily tasks sometimes forces instructors to act as though it were true.

A contrasting model might view the student's mind as a gasoline engine ready to function independently if it can just be given the fuel, the spark, and a little tuning. In this view the teacher's job is quite different than the frantic shoveling of knowledge in the previous mode. Here the teacher judiciously selects from the available knowledge that which he feels is most relevant, strikes the spark and observes the functioning of the engine, adjusting and tuning for smooth and efficient performance. He depends on the interest and motivation of the student to carry him far beyond the bounds of the classroom in his search for knowledge. While the first model suggests a style of teaching where the student is dependent on the teacher, the second suggests a style which attempts to make the student intellectually independent.[1]

While all the questions regarding the effects of teacher style and design of teaching materials on student achievement and creative thinking abilities have not been answered, a considerable amount of research has been carried out with regard to many of the basic questions. Much of the research has suggested the desirability of teaching styles which promote more active participation of the student in the learning process by allowing him freedom to take the initiative in structuring and sequencing his learning. A number of studies building on this basic research have developed teaching methods and materials which have been shown to be quite useful in promoting independent, productive thinking with regard to a number of subject areas. One such study, The Illinois Studies in Inquiry Training, developed an approach to learning in which the *content* of the subject area is learned while the students are actively engaged in developing facility with the *process* of acquiring knowledge itself.

This paper will provide a very brief description of the "Inquiry Training" approach and illustrate its adaptation to the teaching of accounting.

Inquiry and Inquiry Training

...When a person is confronted by an event that is no more than partially meaningful to him he may be motivated to take some kind of action to increase the level of meaning available to him. A perceived event or object that is at odds with one's knowledge and past experience appears to fly in the face of reality. Such discrepant events put a person in the position of having to find a way to match what he perceives with what he knows. This internal pressure to "find out why" is one motivation for inquiry. When a discrepant event is suddenly rendered meaningful and assimilable with what is already known and understood there is a release of tension and a feeling of closure and satisfaction. This form of reward is directly associated with inquiry....

The expectation of closure is not however a *necessary* condition for motivation of inquiry. The activity of gathering and processing information is in itself exciting and pleasurable[2].

Inquiry is a fundamental mode of learning. Long before the process of formal education begins infants are exploring their environments, gathering data, and constructing rudimentary conceptual schemes to represent the characteristics of the world as they perceive it. The infant grasps a pot, picks it up, feels it, turns it over, puts blocks into it, dumps them out, and so on. He performs an endless series of transactions not only with his physical world but with his social world as well. He begins to store and symbolize the structural and functional characteristics of his environment. Through the use of symbols and other abstractions he extends his power to recognize, understand, interpret, and predict, control, and explain aspects of his world.

Infant inquiries are generally exploratory and unsystematic... Increased familiarity through exploration of the structure and function of objects brings a sense of power and control. There is an increasing awareness of order and predictability, which is a prerequisite for being surprised and curious about discrepant events. As the child develops and matures cognitively his search for order becomes more purposeful and controlled.

The developing child repeatedly refines his strategies of inquiry. During the elementary school years he is more likely to be searching for specific end results, performing orderly manipulations of the environment, to discover systematic relationships between his operations and their respective consequences (concrete operations). He orders and groups these correspondences in an attempt to bring relationships to light.

By adolescence he becomes concerned not only with observed regularity but with the formulation of laws that embody the logical necessity of observed relationships. The child wants to go beyond the data to construct theories by which he can predict or control events. He uses empirical operations to test these theories and determine their tenability.[3]

To activate and utilize the power and motivation of this natural mode of learning in the training of accountants, the classroom must create and support it. The Illinois Studies found three conditions to be necessary although not always sufficient. These were characterized as focus, freedom, and response.[4]

Focus means that inquiry is usually directed toward some phenomenon or problem which is disturbing to the learner because he is unable to understand or assimilate to his own satisfaction what he has perceived. Focusing marks out an area of concern, gives inquiry a direction to move in, and sets the process in motion.

Freedom has two dimensions. One is external freedom afforded by the environment that minimizes constraints on the learner's cognitive movement in the collection of data, the manipulation and reorganization of ideas, and the construction and testing of theory. The second freedom is internal to the inquirer. He must accept the freedom afforded by the environment and utilize it to carry out his own self-directing thinking.

Response refers to the ability of the environment to provide the data required for building and testing theories. The learner must be able to observe, analyze, and manipulate the environment in order to generate the needed data in a reasonable amount of time.

THE CONDUCT OF AN INQUIRY SESSION IN MANAGERIAL ACCOUNTING

The Accounting Mini-Case

The inquiry session begins with the presentation of a single event (related to the subject matter of the class) which will provide focus to the inquiry. The event is deliberately selected and presented to maximize its discrepant nature, that is, the event should be puzzling and difficult for the students to explain at their particular stage of learning. In the Illinois Studies brief motion picture films were used to present discrepant events. In the accounting classroom the focus of events may be presented in the form of "mini-cases" which may be distributed to the students in written form or acted out by two or three students in front of the class.

The mini-case presents just enough information to pose a problem but very little more. Additional data must be obtained by the students by asking questions. The mini-case presents just enough information to pose a problem but very little more. Additional data must be obtained by the students by asking questions. The mini-case is used only to stimulate inquiry, not to sustain it. The latter function is performed by the inquiry session which follows immediately after the presentation of the case. The following product mix case, which might be used in a fundamentals class in managerial accounting after the students have become familiar with break-even analysis and the notion of contribution margin, is presented for purposes of illustration:

At the beginning of the month ...
Mr. Jones:
Here Hal is an order for 500 cabinets of type A. That new salesman Joe hired is really doing a great job.
Hal:
But Mr. Jones, didn't anyone tell him that the Type B cabinets are more profitable. The accountant told me that the contribution margin for the Type B cabinets is $80 but only $50 for the Type A cabinets. We can make the A's, but I'd like to go on record as being against it so it won't be my fault when my department's profit falls off this month. We were at full capacity using all available labor hours to produce type B cabinets last month. We can't do better than that.
Mr. Jones:
Well Hal, I guess I'd better talk to the sales people, but in the meantime you had better go ahead with that order.

At the end of the month ...
Mr. Jones:
I just got the profit report for your department Hal, and your profits are up, not down as you expected. How did that happen?
Hal:
I don't know Mr. Jones, we worked the same number of labor hours as last month. The accountant must have fouled up the report.

QUESTION:
WHY DID HAL'S DEPARTMENT SHOW HIGHER PROFITS WHEN THE LESS PROFITABLE PRODUCT WAS PRODUCED?

The Inquiry Session

After the presentation of the mini-case the students are allowed to inquire by asking questions and verbalizing theories which might account for the observed event. In this way freedom is extended to the students in the form of an open question-asking session and the response environment is created by the teacher who attempts to answer all data-seeking questions posed by the students. All contributed ideas are treated with respect and accepted without critical judgment. The students can work independently or in groups, but the session is deliberately kept as unstructured as possible to give the students room to operate in ways that are best suited to their individual needs by trying out their ideas and methods of attack on the problem at hand.

Two specific rules are followed, however, to encourage the independence of student thinking. First, the students are required to use only "Yes or No" questions as a simple barrier against the "Why" or "How come?" question. If the latter were allowed, the students would elicit explanations from the teacher and by-pass the important task of formulating and testing their own theories and explanations.

Second, a student should be formally recognized before he is allowed to ask a question in order to maintain some degree of order. Once he has the floor, however, he is allowed to ask as many questions in a row as he wishes. The reason for this rule is to promote analysis through a series of questions which encourages planned sequences or strategies, as well as allowing the student to ask follow-up questions based on answers to his previous questions.

Almost any question asked in the course of an inquiry session can be categorized in the matrix presented in Table I. The row categories refer to the inquiry operations from the most specific (verification) to the most general (synthesis). The column categories describe the focus of the student's operations from the most concrete to the most abstract. Sample questions related to the Product Mix case illustrate such categorizing.

The type of question asked is of course related to the job it is supposed to perform. The choice of questions to be used will vary with the level of knowledge of the inquirer as well as his style of thinking, the availability of data, and the level of sophistication of theory construction. For example, analytical students are likely to employ verification questions early in an inquiry session to pinpoint the parameters of the problem-focus event. (Were any new, more efficient machines used in production? Were all available labor hours used in both months? Was the profit measured by subtracting both fixed and variable costs from revenue?) Experimentation questions might then be used in an exploratory manner to uncover important relationships. (Would profit have increased even more if more than 500 units of A had been produced? If the number of direct labor hours required per unit for each type of cabinet had changed would the result have been different?) Verification and experimentation questions can be answered directly by the teacher.

Necessity questions are attempts to establish necessary conditions as a basis for explaining the problem-focus event. The fact that a condition is necessary for a given event can never be positively proven, only the unnecessary conditions can be established. Thus the formulation of necessary conditions is inferential in that each individual must decide for himself what evidence he will require before he considers a condition necessary on the basis of available data. When a student asks whether a condition is necessary he is really asking for an evaluation of his theory. Since the students are encouraged to evaluate their own theories, such questions are not answered directly. Instead, the student is asked to decide for himself on the basis of the data he has already collected or through the gathering of more data.

Synthesis questions deal more directly with casual relationships. They are also not given a direct answer because it is possible for the student to answer his own question through further inquiry by experimenting with the effects of varying events and conditions.

There are times when the teacher must give a qualified or extended answer. These are permissible as long as he does not return to an expository role. The inquiry process is the students' responsibility. Should the teacher provide too much information in the answering of questions, the students may tend to return to their former roles of dependency. The following series of questions and answers should illustrate the use of such answers:

Student:
Would profit have increased more if the order had been for 600 A's? (Verification)
Teacher:
Yes
Student:
700? (Verification)
Teacher:
Yes
Student:
800? (Verification)
Teacher:
Yes, but let me save you time by telling you that producing and selling more units of cabinet A will increase profits unit a level of 2,000 units is reached. (Extended)
Student:
Does it have anything to do with the number of direct labor hours required to produce the two types of cabinets? (Synthesis)
Teacher:
Can you think of a way of answering that question for yourself from the data you already have or by obtaining additional data?
Student:
Was the number of direct labor hours required to produce one cabinet of type A the same as was required for on of type B? (Verification)
Teacher:
No
Student:
Was the requirement for the type B cabinets greater? (Verification)
Teacher:
Yes
Student:
If the number of direct labor hours required to produce the two products was altered, would the result have changed. (Experimentation)
Teacher:
That depends. (Qualified)

Student:
On the direction of the changes? (Verification)
Teacher:
Yes

The inquiry session continues in the manner illustrated with proposals of theories, verification or experimentation, revision of theories, etc. Sometimes silences occur. If they result because students are thinking, it is best to let them break the silence themselves. It may be, however, that the students have run out of ideas. When this happens it is sometimes useful to pose questions which are subproblems of the larger problem.

When a silence indicates that the students have a sense of closure and seem satisfied with their theories, the teacher may adopt a "closure-busting" strategy. This strategy may take the form of

1. Posing specific instances which the theory should account for..."How does your theory account for the fact that if more than 2,000 cabinets of type A are produced profit begins to decrease again?" or
2. If more than one theory has developed, the students may be asked to reconcile them, or
3. A student may be asked to test his theory or predict from it.

The purpose of early inquiry sessions is to create the conditions that will stimulate and sustain inquiry. The students should be given a certain amount of time to become comfortable with their new roles in the learning process before any structuring is introduced. Students usually begin operating intuitively and may theorize before they verify. As soon as a theory is offered it should be identified.

When students offer their own theories or explanations and ask whether such explanations are "right" they are told that they have presented a theory and that they will have to determine *for themselves* whether or not they wish to retain the theory or reject it. As students begin to recognize the difference between synthesis behavior and verification or experimentation, the opportunity may arise for a brief discussion of where theories come from, how they might be tested, and how they should be evaluated.

The students begin to evaluate their theories, first as to their reasonableness, then with regard to their power to predict, to control, and to explain events. Theories become valued in terms of what they can do (as predictors or explainers) rather then whether they represent some kind of "truth". The students begin to test their theories operationally by deduction of hypotheses, which are statements of what must follow if the theory holds. They recognize that through the operations of verification and experimentation they can test empirically a hypothesis which was derived from their theory and that their test is simply a way of increasing their faith in the theory or of rejecting it.

The teacher can help the student become aware of operations by taking the opportunity to point them out as they arise spontaneously during the session. He can identify the operation directly..."You just performed an experiment," and he can help the students understand the function of the operation and their relation to theory..."Now what does that tell you about your theory?" As their strategies for gathering information improve, the students are able to see how they can improve their knowledge.

The two major categories of things the students focus their operations on are properties and conditions. Conditions are the specific states of the objects or systems in the perceived event. Properties are the characteristics or attributes of the objects or systems and how they behave under varying conditions. The students gradually become aware of how their operations effect their knowledge of properties and conditions, how their theories are inferred from knowledge of properties, and how knowledge of conditions helps them explain a specific event.

Inquiry vs Teacher-Engineered Learning

The traditional teacher engineers learning by lecturing, demonstration, and planning a specific sequence of information presentations. The teacher tries to draw on the student's past experiences and focus his attention, through verbal instruction and exposition, on selected aspects of the subject matter of the course. In order to be effective in doing this the teacher must be reasonably well acquainted with the conceptual systems of the students and keep a constant check on the ways in which these systems are changing. To the extent that the teacher is deprived of feedback on these, he has no way of knowing precisely what effect his teaching is having on his students at any given time and consequently cannot make optimal decisions as to when to leave one topic and go on to the next.

Most accounting instructors probably adhere to fairly rigid preplanned schedules so that they are sure to get to the end of the text by the end of the semester or at least cover all topics which are prerequisites for the next class. But there is really no way of judging how much time should be devoted to the various topics without feedback on the level of understanding of the students and their readiness to proceed.

Inquiry cannot replace didactic teaching. There are many situations where didactic instruction is appropriate and highly effective. But the danger is that teaching can become so completely verbal and teacher-controlled that the learner begins to lose his autonomy. If students are given little opportunity to think their way through a problem to their own conclusions, they become dependent consumers of knowledge and lose touch with the ongoing process of inquiry through which knowledge is created and organized. When the inquiry process is used, learning is directed largely by the students. They formulate their own ideas in terms which are meaningful to them at the time. They learn to evaluate their own ideas and those of others and by self-directed data seeking to test and revise the theories which underly their understanding of the subject matter. This process breeds independence and self-confidence in their thinking which leads to further inquiry and other forms of productive thinking.

Some Additional Comments

The Mini-cases are easy to write and an afternoon of thinking can produce a dozen or more which are capable of focusing inquiry on the various aspects of accounting to be covered in a course. Some experimentation may be required to determine what events will be discrepant to students at a particular level of learning, what data should be put into the case and what data is best left for the data gathering process. During the actual inquiry session the teacher bears a great burden acting as the data source, and it is important that he be quite familiar with the problem-focus event and the conditions and properties of the objects or systems involved. This is important so that proper data is readily available when requested, and so that when students reach closure with regard to the original problem, inquiry can be re-stimulated, if desired, by challenging the theories that have emerged to account for specific events in the case or by introducing sub-problems or altered conditions which require a modification of theories and explanations.

The following list provides a brief description of some events which may be discrepant to beginning students in managerial accounting:

1. A series of volume increases result in increased profits until suddenly one increase results in a sharp profit decrease - step costs.

2. Cost estimates used in the construction of overhead budgets based on a straight line assumption result in confusing overhead variances - true relationship is curvilinear or costs are related to some variable not used in the estimating equation.

3. Performance evaluation and bonus based on a particular divisional profit measurement leads to wrong decisions in a transfer-pricing situation.

4. Inventory decrease causes different profits on two identical companies operating at the same production level - different inventory flow assumptions.

5. Variable costs per unit change - results from learning and set-up costs when production lot sizes change or because of the use of less efficient workers and machines or higher spoilage rates when production rates hit peak levels as they fluctuate with demand due to increased efforts to hold inventory levels to a minimum.

These events illustrate the type of situations which might by used to focus inquiry on various aspects of managerial accounting. There is certainly no reason why a similar list couldn't be prepared for a financial accounting, tax, governmental accounting, or systems class. Perhaps an especially valuable application might arise in auditing where discrepancies in reporting might be used to focus inquiry on possible explanations of the discrepancies and audit procedures which might verify such explanations.

The use of inquiry sessions on a fairly regular basis appears to have several highly desirable results:

1. Students seem to be highly motivated by the process of gathering data and proposing and testing theories for the purpose of explaining a puzzling situation related to the course material they are trying to learn. This motivation often carries over beyond specific inquiry sessions and results in the highly desirable outcome of students challenging ideas presented by the teacher or the text.

2. Students gain confidence in their own abilities to think through difficult problems independently and to evaluate their own ideas and those of others.

3. The inquiry sessions give the instructor important clues as to the progress students are making in understanding course materials so that he can spend time with the portions of the course which are difficult for the students and cover rapidly the areas which the students find easy.

The main disadvantages seem to be:

1. The inquiry sessions are somewhat time consuming. It would obviously take less time to explain to students that when some production factor such as direct labor hours is limiting production, the optimal product mix depends not only on the relative contribution margins per unit of the products but also on the rates at which the constraining resource is consumed in the production of the various products than to let the students attempt to discover this for themselves through inquiry.

2. The traditional teacher may find that relinquished control of the learning process during portions of his class is highly uncomfortable to him. He may even feel that his

authority is threatened when he finds students willing to challenge his ideas in class.

These disadvantages certainly deserve consideration. The second is probably the easiest to evaluate. Many teachers who have never heard of inquiry teach with a style which is easily adapted to that required during inquiry. They can rapidly gain skill in handling inquiry sessions and acquire a comfortable feeling about their role during the sessions. Other teachers may be able to accept the role required with somewhat greater difficulty. Some experimentation should provide an opportunity for an instructor to evaluate his effectiveness in using the technique.

The first problem is probably less easy to evaluate. While a given amount of course material can no doubt be covered more quickly using strictly didactic teaching, the quality of the learning may not be the same. It should also be remembered that students are acquiring a deeper understanding of the inquiry process itself, are gaining experience and confidence in using it to build their understanding of accounting, and as a result are developing the ability to think independently through problems that arise in their understanding. Such an ability would be especially desirable in light of the continual demands for increased competence and creative and adaptive thinking by today's professional accountant.

FOOTNOTES

[1] James J. Gallagher, "Teaching Method Changes," *Teaching Gifted Students*, James J. Gallagher, editor (Boston: Allyn & Bacon, Inc., 1965), p. 160.

[2] Richard J. Suchman "Inquiry and Education," *Teaching Gifted Students*, James J. Gallagher, editor (Boston: Allyn & Bacon, Inc., 1965), p. 195.

[3] Suchman, "Inquiry and Education," pp. 193-194.

[4] The description of the inquiry training process in this section of the paper was influenced heavily by descriptions by Suchman, "Inquiry and Education," and those of Sybil Carlson, Carla Lotta, and Sandra J. Stallman, "The Theory of Inquiry," and "Guidelines for Inquiry Sessions," *Teacher's Handbook for Inquiry Training* (Mimeo) (Urbana: The University of Illinois, 1964), pp. 1-34.

Inquiry in the Accounting Classroom

TABLE I

Matrix of Inquiry Operations and Operanda as Exemplified by Question Types

	Events or Objects	Conditions	Properties	Variables
Analytical	Were the cabinets altered in any manner? Did the Accountant make any errors in the report?	Did the efficiency of production change? Were all available labor hours used in both months? Did the # of available labor hours change?	Was the # of DLH required to produce A the same as to produce B?	Was the CM of A really $50 and B $80? Was profit measured by subtracting Var. & Fixed costs from Revenues?
Verification	Were any new, more efficient Machines used in production?	Were all machine hours used too?		Did the prices of either cabinet change? Did the variable costs of producing either cabinet change?
Experimentation	Would profit have increased this month anyway without the order for 500 A's? Would profit have increased more if more units of A were produced?	If the # of DLH were increased would the result have been the same?	If the # of DLH required per unit of the two products were altered, would the result have changed?	Would the profit have increased if it were measured by direct costing?
Inferential				
Necessity	Was it necessary that two consecutive months were used in the profit comparison? Did the products have to be cabinets?	Was it necessary that DLH constrain production levels?	Did the CM per unit have to be greater for B than for A to get this result?	
Synthesis	Did profit increase because fewer defective units were produced?	Did the profit increase because demand for the product increased?	Was it because the # of DLH per unit was different between the two products?	Did the manner in which fixed costs were allocated have anything to do with it?

USING ALGORITHMS TO INCREASE LEARNING

Some complex accounting methods can be formulated as general algorithms which can be learned more efficiently. Professor Bentz provides an explanation of the cognitive learning theory concepts involved in this approach as well as contrasting the approach with more traditional learning methods implied in problem-solving. Improved learning and retention are hypothesizd by focusing on well-defined algorithms rather than solving sequences of problems in accordance with implied algorithms. A lateral transfer of knowledge is hypothesized by applying each general algorithm to a wide variety of contexts. Finally, with general algorithms, students are hypothesized to comprehend better the mathematical structure and limitations of an accounting method.

Using Learning Theory To Teach Accounting More Efficiently*

William F. Bentz
University of Kansas

INTRODUCTION

The purpose of this paper is to present several hypotheses about the potential advantages of learning accounting methods as generalized algorithms, as opposed to learning them by solving a sequence of problems. A synthesis of relevant learning theory principles provides the conceptual foundation for these hypotheses and the supporting analysis. The analysis is limited in scope to a particular type of learning in accounting; nothing is alleged about the many other types of learning that must take place in accounting.

The focus is placed on the formulation of hypotheses for both communication and research reasons. Different methods of learning accounting algorithms can be expected to lead to different learning outcomes. The exact nature of expected outcomes can be specified and then communicated in the form of hypotheses. These same hypotheses form the basis for any expost evaluation of the alternative learning methods, in terms of the desired outcomes.

The appropriateness of this approach can be clarified by contrasting it with the way changes have tended to occur in accounting education. Both teachers and students have been exposed to many changes in accounting pedagogy. Some readily apparent changes include a shift to a more conceptual approach to accounting thought, the development of audio-visual materials, and the development of computer based exercises and games. Although many of these are believed to be changes for the better, there is little evidence in the literature to suggest that very much attention has been given to the learning theory concepts that are relevant to these developments. Further, since the precise benefits of these developments are not always specified, it is difficult to determine if any particular change has resulted in any meaningful improvement in accounting education.[1] Consequently, instructors are being asked to make changes for which the consequences are unclear. The problem then is to adopt an approach to research and development in accounting education that both incorporates the extant body of knowledge about learning and is amenable to empirical testing.

The approach taken in this paper is an outgrowth of two underlying premises. One premise is that different types of learning are best facilitated by different methods of instruction.[2] The implication of this premise is that it may be useful to have a mixture of instructional methods in every accounting course. There is little evidence to suggest that instructors now use a wide variety of teaching methods within each course, so the validity of this premise may not be self-evident.

A second premise is that the scientific method, as it is reflected in the systems approach to problem solving, is a useful way to approach the task of designing, implementing and testing systems for accounting instruction.[3] As envisioned here, the systematic approach requires the development of a conceptual model of the learning process of interest in order to:

1. Set specific instructional objectives that serve to guide the educational process.[4]
2. Formulate hypotheses, based on learning theories developed in related

---

*An earlier version of this paper was presented on June 12, 1972 at the 1972 Conference on Computers in the Undergraduate Curricula in Atlanta, Georgia.

contexts, about the expected contributions of alternative methods of instruction to the specified accounting instructional objectives;

3. Develop performance dimensions and measurement methods that indicate the relative contribution of alternative instructional methods to the set of instructional objectives;

4. Efficiently select a set on instructional materials, based on their hypothesized benefits as indicated by theories of learning, for further development and experimental testing; and even to

5. Investigate successful systems of instruction in order to identify and isolate the important elements of these applications and to determine the precise nature of the success achieved, if any.

This study is concerned with and limited to the formulation of hypotheses about the expected contributions of alternative methods of instruction to the learning of certain algorithms in accounting.

Algorithms and Accounting

The superstructure of accounting has been studied by a number of researchers, including Ijiri,[5] Mattessich,[6] Moonitz[7] and Sterling.[8] Although they differ in many respects, these studies are similar in that they are attempts to describe the structure, or the set of axioms, common to all of accounting. They are attempts to describe accounting in as compact a manner as is possible. At least two practical benefits can be expected from such efforts.[9] First, by capturing the essential structure of accounting in a few axioms or laws, one can better communicate the essential characteristics of accounting to those outside the discipline; and secondly, one can describe accounting more efficiently to students.

While an understanding of the fundamental structure of accounting is important for education purposes, this is not sufficient. A number of accounting models are consistent with any set of general axioms. This means that one cannot deduce a single, unique accounting mode from a given specification of the general structure of accounting. Moreover, Mattessich argues that in future years it may be useful to develop several "monopurpose" accounting systems that serve different needs even though they have a common structure in the abstract.[10] The other researchers cited are user-oriented also, so the need to develop monopurpose accounting systems whenever they are cost-effective seems to be well-accepted.

The issues at hand can now be restated. For educational purposes, those features of accounting that are common to all of accounting, present and future, should be consolidated. However, given the many different purposes served by accounting, a diversity of accounting methods and techniques can be expected to persist. The problem, then is to achieve a level of generality that is useful for education purposes in a discipline that is replete with specific techniques.

The thesis offered here is that the structure of accounting can be studied effectively by focusing on the algorithms that relate to particular topic areas, rather than focusing either on very general axioms, or on individual exercises. "An algorithm is a procedure for solving a problem."[11] In more formal terms, an algorithm is a procedure that can be carried out on an idealized machine, called a Turing machine. Although the properties of Turing machines have been more precisely defined, let it suffice to note that a Turing machine can do anything a stored-program computer can do.[12] For this purpose those procedures that can be performed by a stored-program computer are called algorithms.

Algorithm learning is a way of learning the mathematical structures of accounting that tend to be common to a number of topics. Algorithms tend to be general in the sense that they can be applied to a number of different problem areas. In addition, algorithms are reflective of accounting practice since they are procedural in nature. In this sense, algorithms satisfy some of the student's needs to learn enough procedural information to be able to solve the types of problems that must be solved in accounting practice.

The Importance of Algorithms in Accounting

Many accounting techniques can be characterized as algorithms; the learning of accounting techniques involves the learning of algorithms. Typically, students learn accounting techniques by reading through a demonstration problem and observing the sequence of steps used therein. Then, the student works several problems, mimicking the sequence of operations that are executed in the demonstration problem. The sequence of operations (an algorithm) necessary to solve an exemplar of a class of problems becomes apparent to the student during the process of examining the demonstration problem, or while working the homework problems. If the method is understood, it is understood as a technique which is applicable to problems other than the particular one at hand. The student who understands the method can apply it to a new problem with little difficulty, while the student who rotely learns a sequence of operations to solve problem X may have difficulty solving problem Y, even though X and Y are of the same class of problems. Although other types of learning may take place while one works problems, the learning of accounting algorithms, and the practice involved in applying them to specific situations, are the major functions served by procedural-type homework problems.

There are two additional reasons for focusing on accounting algorithms. In auditing, the professional accountant is faced with the problem of evaluating the system of internal controls that assures the quality of the accounting data on which an opinion must be rendered. Because many accounting records and recording processes are being automated, modeling or flow-charting the processing system is of utmost importance on almost every audit.

Part of what is being modeled or flow-charted is the algorithm that represents the method by which a machine transforms input into output. The auditor must be prepared to deal with algorithms in their general form, not with a particular solution method for test problem X. Precisely because the clerical procedures performed inside the machine cannot be observed, the modeling of these unobservable algorithms is perhaps more important than ever before.

The construction and testing of algorithms is an equally important function of the management consultant. In designing a new system, or in revising an existing system, the management consultant must specify how activities are to be accomplished. At some stage in the design process, a designer must specify the detailed procedures to be executed by the system. This specification is, in essence, an algorithm even though the system being designed may not be an automated system. For management consultants, the specification of accounting algorithms is an integral part of the system design process.

Learning Accounting Algorithms

The accounting methods that are algorithms can be learned in at least three different ways: (1) the traditional problem solving approach, (2) reception learning of generalized algorithms, and (3) discovery learning of generalized algorithms. The relative advantages and disadvantages of these three methods are analyzed next in order to formulate some hypotheses.

The Traditional Method

In freshman through junior level courses, the instruction sequence usually includes the presentation of some concepts, propositions, and background information. This material is followed by the working of accounting problems which serve to clarify and illustrate the concepts presented, and the accounting methods involved. As mentioned in the previous section, the usual approaches to problem solving by the student follow one of two patterns. First, if a demonstration problem is presented, the student may work the assigned problems after having examined the demonstration problem and then put it aside. Or, he may work the assigned problem while using the demonstration problem as a guide. In either case, the student is actively attempting to discover for himself the sequence of arithmetic operations involved in the accounting method. Understanding of the method can be regarded as complete when the student can apply the method to similar problems (application), or even to novel situations which have not been related to the technique before.[13]

Several criticisms of the "problem" method of learning implicit algorithms are in order. First, since the student never sees the algorithm in its general form, he may stumble through several problems before understanding the methodology embodied in the undisclosed algorithm. Second, the slower learner may not receive sufficient feedback from a few homework assignments to fully grasp the method. Third, the

learning of a method by working problems may only result in pre-verbal understanding which cannot be retained as long as a verbally created description. Fourth, even if a student learns a method by working problems and can verbalize that understanding, he may have difficulty remembering the more important features of the method unless he has the opportunity to work with an abstract model which characterizes the method. Further, the more general and clearly defined algorithms should be more easily remembered than a collection of less general methods which are not clearly differentiable.[14]
Fifth, there is a tendency to teach business terminology and business practices by introducing them in assignment problems. While learning about business practice is important, the superimposing of concept learning, proposition learning and problem-solving may only confuse the student and impede the learning of accounting algorithsm.

Reception Learning of Generalized Algorithms

A second way of learning accounting methods is to encounter them in complete form, and then to apply the method, or algorithm to particular problems.[15] The sequence of instruction would include a presentation of concepts, propositions and background information, as before, followed by a presentation of the accounting algorithm in general form. After the algorithm is studied, it is applied to a series of problems which serve to clarify the student's understanding of the algorithm, as well as demonstrating the range of applications associated with the algorithm being studied. Each student's understanding of the algorithm is tested in the same manner as described above.

Algorithms can be presented for reception learning by means of several different devices. Flowcharts, decision tables and computer programs coded in procedure-oriented languages can be used to describe almost any accounting procedure. As computer courses become required, these tools become more and more familiar to all business students, so their classroom use is feasible in many schools.

Note that the two methods of learning described so far are very different. In the first case, the algorithm must be inferred from an example, or from the feedback provided while the student is attempting to solve problems "correctly." In the second method, the student learns the algorithm by reception, rather than by discovery. The algorithm is presented in its final form, so that the student need not construct it for himself.

There are several criticisms of the reception learning method, as there were of the traditional method. First, students may apply the algorithm to specific problems in a rather mechanical manner, which may not require them to think about the method itself. Second, even when students think about the algorithm as a generalized technique, they may attain only a preverbal understanding of the algorithm. Preverbal understanding is only an intermediate phase of the learning process and does not represent a terminal learning objective. Third, the act of applying a specified algorithm to a set of problems may lack the motivational qualities of a problem or puzzle, that must be solved.

Presenting accounting methods as algorithms does have several advantages which alleviate the limitations of the traditional method as described above. First, by focusing on the algorithm itself, the instructor is indicating to the student what is important. In the process of solving individual problems, without knowing that a general solution method exists, a student may not be able to separate the important features of each homework problem from the trivia. Secondly, by working with a defined algorithm, rather than attempting to discover the algorithm, a student may be able to learn more about its structure and essential features because it has been fully specified for him, in a general form.

Another important reason for learning algorithms is probably clear to most readers. Some ideas are simply vague and somewhat ill-defined until expressed in equation form, or as algorithms. For example, the time value of money is a concept which is readily accepted by students on an intuitive level when first explained. After a careful and tedious presentation of present value concepts, many students can handle straightforward interest problems with the use of interest tables, but only the students with some mathematical sophistication seem to grasp the process of discounting a series of payments to determine their present value. The ability to work with symbols and equations seems to be necessary if a student is to understand interest problems.

In summary, presenting accounting methods to students in the form of algorithms has certain advantages over the more traditional problem solving approach. Specifically, understanding is hypothesized to be more nearly complete and retention is greater when students study and apply explicit algorithms rather than discovering accounting methods by solving problems. This hypothesis is based on Ausubel's theory of the learning and retention of meaningful material (see footnote 2).

Discovery Learning

Another method of learning algorithms involves the use of discovery learning as opposed to reception learning. It differs from traditional methods in that the focus is on the construction of an algorithm rather than on solving a sequence of individual problems. In the next section, the learning of algorithms by discovery is contrasted with the learning of algorithms by reception. In addition, the ways in which computer assisted instruction can be used to alleviate the disadvantages of learning algorithms by reception are discussed.

Computer Assisted Discovery Learning of Accounting Algorithms

An alternative to reception learning is the discovery learning of accounting algorithms. As before, the sequence of instruction would include a presentation of concepts, propositions and background information. Based on his study of the text and any sample problems, the student begins to formulate a general algorithm to solve problems of the type being studied. From the start, the goal is to construct an algorithm that can be used to solve a variety of problems, rather than the solving of a sequence of individual problems. With careful planning, information can be presented to students in a manner that facilitates the formulation of a basic algorithm which can be expanded to include more and more refinements.

Text materials, illustrative problems and handouts can be used to specify the accounting method, but the student must generalize the method himself in order to formulate the algorithm. Each student's algorithm may be specified in the form of a flow-chart, a decision table, or an operation computer program coded in a language such as BASIC, FORTRAN, or COBOL.

What are the potential benefits of having students reconstruct accounting algorithms by writing computer programs? First, the potential motivational benefits are considered. In the process of writing a program, the student receives a lot of feedback which tends to support continued work on the problem (a hypothesis). The feedback is in the form of error listings from the computer and the computed answers to a test problem. If a student gets an incorrect answer, he has a clear signal that his algorithm contains some errors. Discussion with the other students who congregate at the computer center and comments by the instructor also serve as valuable feedback. Incidentally, to follow the logic of a student's program is relatively easy when the procedure being programmed is a familiar one and when a list of suggested variable names has been provided as part of the assignment.

Second, people tend to think about incomplete tasks more than they do about completed tasks.[16] Working on one computer program for N days is hypothesized to maintain more concentrated student attention than working and completing several different problems over the same time period. Another motivational aspect is the greater opportunity for satisfying ego-fulfilling needs when the student must construct an algorithm which is not presented to him in complete form. Constructing the algorithm is satisfying itself. Learning computer skills is satisfying to many in itself, and learning computer skills in satisfying to many students because of the career opportunities associated with a knowledge of computers.

One final motivational benefit is the opportunity to complete satisfactorily a task before submitting it for final approval. Some students find it very frustrating to spend hours working complex accounting problems, to achieve only partial success. With programs, if enough lead time is provided, diligent students have the opportunity to write programs that are correct, not just partially correct.

The potential cognitive learning benefits of the process of constructing accounting algorithms are dependent on the claim that the student will thoroughly understand an accounting procedure if he has written a computer program for it. Further, understanding an algorithm is hypothesized to provide a higher level of abstraction than can be achieved by most students in the process of solving particular problems. To the extent that these claims are true, a student's knowledge of the accounting procedure that he programmed should be integrated into his cognitive structure as a generalized method which is clearly differentiable from other accounting methods.

These are several conditions which can be expected to facilitate greater cognitive learning behavior. First, the construction of an algorithm requires more active participation in the learning process than does the learning of an algorithm presented in final form (reception learning). Some students will critically evaluate new ideas to "make sense" out of them while working at the task of incorporating them into a cognitive structure. However, all too many students are passive listeners when propositions or problem solving methods are presented to them in final form. To the extent that more active learning can be induced by requiring students to construct algorithms, greater learning is hypothesized. Experience indicates that most students do need some inducement to become actively involved in the learning process.

Second, the benefits of massed learning, as opposed to distributed learning, are related to the learning of algorithms.[17] In this case, the alternative learning methods being compared are the learning of accounting methods by solving individual problems as opposed to constructing algorithms for subsequent application. In solving a sequence of problems, usually of increasing difficulty and complexity, the student encounters two problems: forgetting between problem-solving sessions, and the warm-up required to recall the methods and settle into the new problem. It seems plausible that forgetting can be a factor since most undergraduate students take five or six different courses each semester, plus working and being involved in other activities. Further, since accounting problems usually represent complex tasks, substantial warmup and reorienting of one's thinking may be required each time a new accounting problem is encountered. Under these conditions, massed learning can be more efficient than learning that is distributed over a number of sessions.

To the extent that there is a sizable threshold of effort required to discover and fully grasp accounting algorithms, the massed learning that is usually associated with the writing of a computer program may be more efficient than the solving of a series of individual problems over time. Because of the difficulties created by forgetting between problem-solving session, and the warm-up required to settle into a new problem it is hypothesized that the benefits of massed learning are applicable to the construction of computer programs, thus improving learning.

Greater lateral transferability of knowledge should also be facilitated by having students write programs. Gagne[18] theorizes that applying one's knowledge in a number of different contexts increases transferability, even though we know little about the precise factors which are involved. A student can use his own program, or a previously written program, to solve a variety of problems, thus emphasizing the generality of the techniques without increasing the busywork that is usually associated with working a large number of problems. A student can be encouraged to generalize his conception of a technique.

Suggested Topics For Algorithm Learning

Process cost accounting, the allocation of service department costs among reciprocally dependent service departments, the allocation of profits among reciprocally owned corporations, corporate budgeting models, and the financial and managerial accounting methods that involve present value calculations are all complex topics that involve some common algorithms. Process-costing tends to have a structure all of its own, even though some costing operations can be carried out using matrix algebra. Service department cost allocation techniques, profit distribution techniques, and corporate budgeting models all involve the use of matrix operations to solve systems of simultaneous linear equations. Their common structure becomes quite apparent to students when they write or use programs to implement the accounting techniques associated with these topics.

Similarly, the common structure of lease contracts, pension plans, bonds, and long-term investments becomes apparent when students use interest-methods to determine accounting information. After constructing an algorithm to find the present value of a series of payments, students seem to understand present value techniques better. Students are hypothesized to better understand the foregoing accounting topics when a common algorithm is used in their solution. More specifically, knowledge about present-value techniques is hypothesized to be more transferable if students clearly see its applicability in a number of different contexts.

SUMMARY

Several writers and committees have explicitly recognized the pedagogic value of model-building and abstraction in accounting.[19] This paper provides an explanation of the learning theory concepts involved in this approach as well as contrasting it with more traditional methods of problem solving. In general, learning is hypothesized to be improved by focusing on well-defined algorithms rather than solving sequences of problems in accordance with the implied algorithm. Students are hypothesized to learn and remember explicit algorithms better than implicit ones. The lateral transfer of knowledge is hypothesized to be improved by applying an algorithm to a wide variety of problems. Students are hypothesized to better understand and analyze an accounting method if they can work with the general algorithm.

FOOTNOTES

[1] Unless there is agreement on objectives, even the most thoughtful of debates will be inconclusive. This problem is illustrated by the debate about the relative roles of computing and mathematics in accounting education. See A. Wayne Corcoran, "Computers Versus Mathematics," *The Accounting Review* (April 1969), pp. 359-74; and James B. Cowie and James M. Fremgren, "Computers Versus Mathematics: Round 2," *The Accounting Review* (January, 1970), pp. 27-37.

[2] For a discussion of the different types of learning, see David P. Ausubel and Floyd G. Robinson, *School Learning* (Holt, Rinehart and Winston, Inc., 1969), pp. 59-74.

[3] The implications of this premise are explored in C. West Churchman, *Challenge to Reason* (McGraw-Hill Book Company, 1968). The systems approach is described in some detail in C. West Churchman, "On the Design of Educational Systems," Working Paper No. 86, Center for Research in Management Science (University of California, Berkely, 1964); and C. West Churchman, *The Systems Approach* (Dell Publishing Company, 1968).

[4] Some of the more readable materials on the use of specific objectives for instruction include James Evans, "Behavioral Objectives are No Damn Good," in Aerospace Education Foundation, *Technology and Innovation in Education* (Frederick A. Praeger, Publishers, 1968); and Robert F. Mager, *Preparing Instructional Objectives* (Fearon Publishers, 1962).

[5] Yuji Ijiri, "Axioms and Structures of Conventional Accounting Measurement," *The Accounting Review* (January, 1965), pp. 36-53.

[6] Richard Mattessich, *Accounting and Analytical Methods* (Richard D. Irwin, Inc., 1964), pp. 16-51.

[7] Maurice Moonitz, "The Basic Postulates of Accounting," *Accounting Research Study No. 1* (American Institute of Certified Public Accountants, 1961).

[8] Robert R. Sterling, "An Explication and Analysis of the Structure of Accounting Part One," *Abacus* (December, 1971), pp. 137-52; and "An Explication and Analysis of the Structure of Accounting Part Two," Working Paper No. 23, The School of Business, The University of Kansas (1969).

[9] Postulates may also be used to analyze and evaluate accounting practice. This use is illustrated in Raymond J. Chambers, "Why Bother With Postulates?" *Journal of Accounting Research* (Spring, 1963), pp. 3-15.

[10] Mattessich, p. 9.

[11] T. E. Hull, *Introduction to Computing* (Prentice-Hall, Inc., 1966), p. 1.

[12] *Ibid.*, p. 170.

[13] This is called problem-solving learning. Ausubel, p. 504.

[14] *Ibid.*, Chapter 5.

[15] In both statistics and operations research, the usual approach is to present the general model first, and then the general model is applied in particular problem contexts. The approach used in accounting has been very different.

[16] Ausubel, p. 498.

[17] For a discussion of massed learning of low-level capabilities, see Stanley Stevens, *Handbook of Experimental Psychology* (John Wiley and Sons, Inc., 1951), pp. 636-40; and Robert S. Woodworth and Harold Scholsberg, *Experimental Psychology* (Holt, Rinehart and Winston, 1965), pp. 786-94.

[18] Robert M. Gagne, *The Conditions of Learning* (Holt, Rinehart and Winston, Inc., 1965), p. 235.

[19] American Accounting Association Committee (1964) on Courses and Curricula—Electronic Data Processing in Accounting Education," *The Accounting Review* (April, 1965), pp. 422-28; Cowie and Fremgen, pp. 30-33; Werner Frank, "A Computer Application in Process Cost Accounting," *The Accounting Review* (October, 1965), pp. 854-62; Mattesich, p. 7; and George I. Prater, "Time-sharing Computers in Accounting Education," *The Accounting Review* (October, 1966), pp. 619-25.

Developing Behavioral Objectives For Accounting Education

Doyle Z. Williams
Dan M. Guy
Texas Tech University

Introduction

At one time or another, every accounting educator has talked about the educational objectives of his class. Most probably feel they have their objectives well in mind and it is neither necessary nor productive to be more specific. Professors Williams and Guy believe this general condition has led accounting educators to a preoccupation with teaching activities rather than with learning outcomes. If the outcomes of accounting education are poorly stated, perhaps this is because few accounting educators know how to proceed. Professors Williams and Guy distill and explore behavioral objectives embellished with specific accounting examples. They believe educational efforts using behavioral objectives offer the accounting educator the potential for improving and measuring the student's educational experience.

Accounting education, like other disciplines, has witnessed in recent years increased attention to curriculum integration and accountability. Accounting educators are increasingly being called upon to relate their courses to a "total program" and to assess in new ways the effectiveness of their efforts. One vehicle widely applied in other disciplines for assessing the effectiveness of instruction has been the development of behavioral objectives.

The purposes of this paper are to: (1) explain what behavioral objectives are and discuss their potential contribution to the educational process, (2) present a model for applying behavioral objectives, with illustrative application to elementary accounting and auditing, and (3) discuss inherent limitation of the model.

The Nature of Behavioral Objectives

Accounting educators (as do others) have a tendency to express instructional objectives in terms of: (1) subject area covered, (2) teaching activities (e.g., what the professor is going to do), and (3) the learning process (rather than as a learning product). Consider for example the following:

The purpose of today's lecture and the related assigned text material is to:

Subject Orientation—Expose you to the statement of changes in financial position.

Teacher Orientation—Instill in you an appreciation of professional ethics.

Process Orientation—Increase your ability to understand earnings per share.

All of these statements are deficient in that they fail to focus on learning outcomes or student behavior. Stating objectives which focus on the subject matter, the teaching process, or on the learning process prevents determining whether or not the intended learning outcomes have been achieved by the student. Until objectives are expressed as observable, overt behavior on the part of the student, one can never know whether or not the desired level of learning has been achieved. Moreover, the objectives of the learning situation are sometimes so vague that the student fails to learn primarily because he does not know what to learn.

Stating instructional objectives behaviorally contributes to the learning process by: (1) providing direction for the instructor, (2) conveying expected learning outcomes to students, (3) establishing guidelines for the selection of teaching methods and materials, and (4) fostering construction of relevant instruments for evaluating student achievement.

Behavioral objectives are usually classified into three domains, often referred to as Bloom's Taxonomy.[1] These domains are: (1) the cognitive, (2) the affective, and (3) the psychomotor. The cognitive domain deals with knowledge, understanding, and thinking skills. The affective domain is concerned with interests, values, and attitudes. The psychomotor domain deals with motor skills such as typing, articulating, and writing. To date, the psychomotor classification system has not been completed, and the affective domain is somewhat advanced for a discipline that has yet to implement behavioral objectives within the cognitive domain; consequently, the following model concentrates on the latter. (Editor's Note: As an interesting aside, much of the existing educational research in accounting is in the affective domain as is illustrated by the contents of Section VI on "Research In Accounting Education".) It should not be implied, however, that the three domains are mutually exclusive. In any learning model the cognitive, affective, and psychomotor domains interact within the thinking process.

The Cognitive Model

Learning activities in a formal educational setting should be designed to form an integrative educational experience. Each accounting instructor should seek to relate the specific courses he teaches to the total accounting program which in turn should be interfaced with the total program in business. This process may be termed the *systemic* approach to the development of behavioral objectives.

Using the systemic approach, the instructor conceptualizes the course and identifies specific learning outcomes based upon these formulations. A systemic model for achieving behavioral objectives in the cognitive domain is presented in Figure 1. The chief steps of this model are: (1) defining the course concept, (2) specifying the course generalizations, (3) developing a course content outline, (4) specifying the desired levels of learnings, (5) identifying behavioral objectives, (6) developing a table of specifications for testing performance, and (7) constructing performance tests.[2]

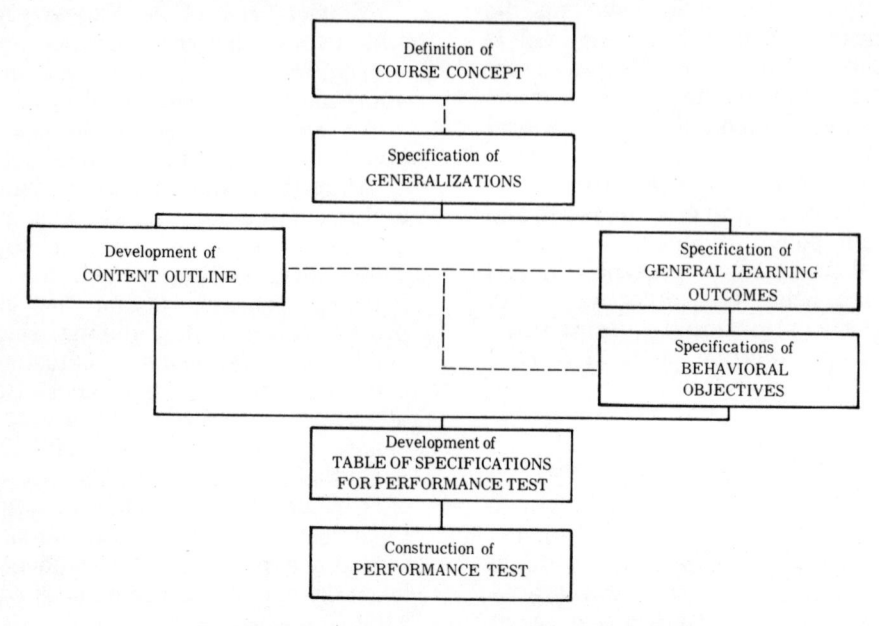

SYSTEMIC MODEL FOR ACHIEVING BEHAVIORAL OBJECTIVES

Figure 1

Defining the Course Concept

A curriculum should be designed like a multi-course meal, appetizers should precede the protein dishes while desserts should be served last. Each course, like each dish, must be related to the whole endeavor and each carefully measured.

Defining courses in terms of *course concepts* serves the purpose of interfacing each course with the total program while at the same time clarifying for both the instructor and the student the dimensions of the course. A carefully developed and clearly stated course concept establishes the boundaries for the course and should be all encompassing. Two examples of course concepts in accounting might appear as follows:

Elementary accounting course concept: Accounting accumulates measures, reports, analyzes, and interprets selected economic events of economic entities for the purpose of planning, controlling and decision-making by capital suppliers and management.

Auditing course concept: Auditing is the examination of information by an independent third party other than the preparer or user, with the intent of establishing its reliability, and the reporting of the results of this examination with the expectation of increasing the usefulness of the information to the user.

An elementary accounting course based on the above concept should give attention to eight major activities: (1) accumulation, (2) measurement, (3) reporting, (4) analyzing, and (5) interpretation of economic events for economic entities. The course also includes how this information might be used for (6) planning, (7) controlling, and (8) decision-making by creditors, owners, and management.

Likewise, given the above auditing course concept, the course should give prime attention to four major aspects of auditing: (1) examination of information, (2) by an independent third party, (3) for establishing reliability, and (4) reporting results of the examination.

Specifying Course Generalizations

After conceptualizing the curriculum through defining specific course concepts, the next task of the instructor is to specify course generalizations based upon the course concept. Specifying course generalizations fleshes out the conceptual framework for the course and serves as a point of departure for developing both the specific content of the course and the levels of learning to be achieved. Course generalizations should be formulated for each major element of the course concept. For example, the first element of the above elementary accounting course concept is *accumulates*. A formulation of course generalizations for this concept might take the following form:

Elementary accounting course generalization: The accounting system accumulates accounting data by (1) selecting the economic events to be captured and (2) anaylzing, classifying, and aggregating these events.

    A. In general, the accounting system recognizes economic events upon the occurrence of a transaction, the expiration of service benefits, and-or the performance of a service.

    B. Economic events recognized by the accounting system are analyzed, classified, and aggregated in a prescribed sequence in terms of their effect upon the basic accounting model, utilizing common processing techniques.

As an additional example, generalizations based on the concept of *independent third parties,* a key element of the auditing course concept presented above, might be expressed as follows:

Auditing Course Generalization: The auditing process adds credibility to information communicated from one party to another by the intervention of an independent third party in the communication flow.

    A. The independent third party is generally a CPA if the information communicated is intended for external (nonmanagerial) consumption.

    B. The independent third party is generally an internal auditor if the information communicated is intended for managerial consumption.

Developing the Content Outline

By first defining the core concept for the course and then developing the generalizations, the instructor's next task of determining the specific topical content becomes much simpler. Specifying course content becomes a matter of listing specific topics for the generalizations. To continue with the example of elementary accounting, a partial course content outline for the concept of *accumulation* might appear as follows:

Elementary Course Outline:

Accumulation

A. Basis for recognition of economic events by the accounting system.
 1. Types of transactions recognized
 2. Timing of transactions recognized
  a. Point of sale
  b. Performance of service
B. Accumulation systems
 1. Accounting processing model
  a. Accounting equation
  b. Transaction analysis
  c. Accounting cycle
 2. Basic elements of accounting system
  a. Chronological record (journal, transactions tape)
  b. Aggregation (account, computer record)
  c. Grouping (ledger, computer file)
 3. Product cost determination procedures
  a. Merchandise operation
  b. Manufacturing operation
  c. Service enterprises

As an additional illustration, if *independent third party* is accepted as a core element of an auditing course, then given the generalization noted above, the auditing course outline might include the following:

Auditing

Independent Third Party

A. Certified Public Accountant
 1. Professional independence
 2. Independence in fact
 3. Independence in appearance
  a. As defined by the AICPA
  b. As defined by the SEC
B. Internal auditor
 1. Organizational status
 2. Systems independence (should not develop and-or install procedures)

Development of the course outline is a requisite to selecting or preparing course materials for student study and for presentation by the instructor. The course outline is also beneficial in subdividing the course into individual class periods, assignment units or modules and helps in establishing the relative emphasis to be given to each subsection of the larger instructional unit. As discussed later, specification of the course content is a prerequisite to testing.

Specifying General Learning Outcomes

Levels of learning.

Concurrently with the development of the course outline, the instructor should also give attention to the *levels of learning* to be achieved by students in the course. Figure 2 relates the levels of learning in the cognitive domain to learning outcomes for elementary accounting and auditing students.

Each level denotes a progressively higher intellectual achievement. Accordingly, the mix of the levels of learning should vary with the type of course. For example, a course in financial accounting might place greater emphasis on knowledge, comprehension, and application whereas an advanced accounting theory course might place more emphasis on analysis, synthesis and evaluation. The relative mix notwithstanding, all levels of cognitive learning should be represented in all accounting courses.

Guidelines for stating general learning outcomes.

Stating general learning outcomes requires practice and often times can be a difficult task. The following five guidelines are useful for preparing general learning outcomes.

First, each general learning outcome should begin with a *verb* describing *terminal behavior* (knows, understands, applies, uses, etc.). For example, consider the following two general learning outcomes:
 1. Understands basic accounting terms
 2. Accounting principles

Obviously, the first of these is stated in terms of a learning outcome whereas the second consists of only a subject-matter topic. There is no indication of what the student is expected to *do* with regard to the principles of accounting.[3]

Figure 2

AN ILLUSTRATION OF THE RELATIONSHIP OF THE LEVELS OF LEARNING IN THE COGNITIVE DOMAIN TO GENERAL LEARNING OUTCOMES FOR ELEMENTARY ACCOUNTING (OR AUDITING) STUDENTS

Major Categories in the Cognitive Domain	General Learning Outcomes
Knowledge	Knows basic accounting (auditing) terms and concepts.
Comprehension	Understands basic accounting (auditing) terms and concepts.
Application	Applies basic accounting (auditing) techniques to new situations.
Analysis	Analyzes accounting (auditing) information into its component parts.
Synthesis	Combines accounting (auditing) information into new patterns or structures.
Evaluation	Interprets and evaluates basic accounting (auditing) information.

Second, each statement should be constructed in terms of *student performance* (rather than teacher performance). For example, consider the following two statements:
1. To increase the student's understanding of financial statements
2. Understands financial statements

The first statement gives the impression that it is the teacher who is going to do the increasing rather than the student, whereas the second statement contains a learning outcome for the student.

Third, each general learning outcome should be stated as a learning *product* (rather than in terms of the learning *process*). Consider these two statements:
1. Gains knowledge of accounting principles
2. Applies knowledge of accounting principles to new situations

The second statement clearly indicates what the student can do at the end of the instruction. The first statement emphasizes the gaining of knowledge (learning *process*) rather than the type of behavior that provides evidence that learning has occurred.

Fourth, each statement should be constructed so that it includes only *one* general learning *outcome* (rather than a combination of several outcomes). For example, examine the following statement:

Knows and applies auditing concepts and techniques

The student may know the auditing concepts and techniques (i.e., be able to describe them) but may not be able to apply them. With separate statements, the instructor can define each outcome in specific behavioral terms and thus determine how well each objective is being achieved.

Fifth, each general learning outcome should be stated at a level of generality that clearly indicates the expected learning outcome and that is readily definable by specific types of student behavior. In developing a list of general learning outcomes for a course, the objective is to obtain a list of goals to work toward not a list of specific types of behavior to be attained by all students. The verbs chosen should be specific enough to provide direction for instruction without overly restricting the teacher or reducing the instruction to the training level. They should also be specific enough to be easily defined by a brief list of the types of behavior the students are to demonstrate when the objectives have been achieved.

As a rule, general learning outcomes should not contain references to specific subject matter. By not including a reference to subject matter in general statements of learning outcomes, the instructor can develop a limited set (say ten to fifteen) of outcomes that are useful with various units of instruction throughout the course.

Stating Specific Behavioral Objectives

After developing a tentative list of general learning outcomes, the next step is to define each outcome in terms of specific student behavior that is to be used as evidence that the objective has been achieved. Stated differently, the task is to develop for each general learning outcome a representative sample of *behavioral objectives*. Through this procedure prior steps become operational for both the student and the instructor.

To illustrate the relationship of behavioral objectives to general learning outcomes, listed below are two general learning outcomes for a course in elementary accounting. Under each are listed three specific behavioral objectives.

Elementary accounting behavioral objectives related to the cognitive domain:

A. Knows basic accounting terms and concepts
  1. Relates terms that have the same meaning.
  2. Selects the term that best fits a particular definition.
  3. Identifies terms and concepts used in reference to particular accounting information.
B. Synthesizes accounting information
  1. Designs an accounting information system to produce reliable information in an efficient manner.
  2. Compiles relevant accounting information to solve a practical problem.
  3. Classifies accounting information into proper summaries for a decision.

An auditing illustration might be as follows:

Auditing behavioral objectives related to the cognitive domain:

A. Understands auditing concepts and techniques
  1. Identifies examples of auditing concepts and techniques.
  2. Describes auditing concepts and techniques in own words.
  3. Points out the interrelationship of auditing concepts and techniques.
B. Interprets and evaluates auditing information
  1. Identifies relevant limitations of audit evidence for testing a particular assertion.
  2. Relates auditing information of specific report decisions.
  3. Judges the adequacy of conclusions drawn from audit evidence.

Stating the general learning outcome first and clarifying it by listing the types of specific behavior that characterizes the outcome makes clear that the desired learning outcome is *knows* (referring to the elementary accounting example above) and not *relating, selecting or identifying*. These latter types of behavior are simply samples of the types of performance that represent *knowing*. They serve the purpose of indicating to the student the types of specific behavior that will be acceptable in demonstrating that he has achieved the general learning outcome. Hence, they serve as the basis for performance testing. Given these purposes for behavioral objectives, their listing need not be all encompassing for instruction above the minimum essentials or training level.

Preparing Specific Behavioral Objectives.

Like stating general learning outcomes, preparing behavioral objectives requires care and practice. First, since each behavioral objective seeks to indicate measurable terminal behavior, the statement should always begin with a verb representing observable student behavior. Hence, the verbs used in preparing specific behavioral objectives must describe specific student reactions representing achievement of the general learning outcome. For example, consider the following two statements:

1. Realizes the limitations of conventional financial statements.
2. Explains the limitations of conventional statements.

Only the second statement indicates behavior that is definite and clearly observable. The first statement does not specify how the student will demonstrate that he realizes the limitations of conventional financial statements. Among the verbs that might be appropriate for preparing specific behavioral objects in accounting are the following:

Appraise	Describe	List
Breakdown	Diagram	Name
Calculate	Distinguish	Prepare
Classify	Estimate	Reconstruct
Compare	Explain	Relate
Compile	Extract	Select
Compute	Graph	Solve
Criticize	Group	State
Defend	Identify	Summarize
Define	Illustrate	Tabulate
Demonstrate	Interpret	Use

Specific behavioral objectives, like general learning outcomes, should also:

1. Be constructed in terms of *student performance* (rather than teacher achievement);
2. Be stated as a learning *product* (rather than in terms of the learning process); and
3. Include only one *terminal behavior* (rather than a combination of behaviors) to facilitate observing and measuring the attainment of specified objects.

After learning how to write specific behavioral objectives, the next step is to determine how many specific behavioral objectives should be prepared for each general learning outcome. There are not hard-and-fast rules for this. Obviously, simple knowledge and skill objectives require fewer behavioral objectives than more complex ones. In this fashion, the level of the course will have a bearing on the number of behavioral objectives which should be prepared. In general, the list of behavioral objectives for courses above the skills or training level should be comprehensive enough to clarify the instructional intent and short enough to be manageable and useful.

In preparing behavioral objectives care should be exercised in matching the specific behavioral objectives with the relevant general learning outcome it is defining. The difficulty is compounded when it is remembered that the levels of learning in the cognitive domain are hierarchial. For example, since knowledge is a prerequisite for comprehension, there may be a tendency to list the specific types of behavior for both goals under any objective concerned with understanding. This practice should generally be avoided, for if carried to an extreme, the highest level of learning outcomes (i.e., evaluation), would have to include all of the specific behavioral objectives listed under all of the other general learning outcomes. Consequently, for operational utility, each general learning outcome should be defined by the specific behavioral objectives that are unique to that particular objective. By defining knowledge of auditing concepts and techniques separately, for example, the instructor is able to identify those students who can demonstrate achievement of knowledge but not of understanding. This ability enhances the diagnostic value of the objectives for both teaching and evaluation.

Selecting Relevant Objectives

After preparing general learning outcomes and specific behavioral objectives, the problem remains of selecting those outcomes and objectives that are most pertinent for a particular course or instructional unit. At this stage there is a clear definition of the course, and its content becomes highly useful. By examining the course content outline, a number of behavioral objectives are likely to become crystalized. The course concept adopted by those responsible for the curriculum will provide learning outcomes considered to be most important. Referring to the course concept, generalizations, and content outline aids the instructor in preventing any serious omissions and provides greater assurance that the final list of objectives is in harmony with the total program.

In selecting behavioral objectives, all logical general learning outcomes should be included. There may be a tendency to include only the lowest levels of learning outcomes to the exclusion of the more complex objectives, when in reality it may be the more complex (i.e., evaluation) that may achieve the greatest endurance.

Finally, behavioral objectives should be in harmony with the basic principles of learning. While the principles of learning are beyond the scope of this discussion, the more complex learning outcomes tend to be retained longer and to have greater transfer value. When they are appropriate to the developmental level of the learner, the more complex outcomes also have the greatest potential for arousing and maintaining student interest.

Preparing Test Specifications

Defining behavioral objectives is not only beneficial in planning classroom instructional content and activities, but they also serve two important purposes in test preparation. First, they indicate the sample of specific learning outcomes that the instructor is willing to accept as evidence that the objectives are being achieved, and second, they specify in precise terms the student behavior that is to be measured by the test items.

Because an achievement test is designed to measure a sample of student behavior, the behavior to be exhibited by the test items should be both relevant and representative. Experience indicates that these conditions are more likely to be met by a carefully detailed description of the intended outcomes of instruction.

An achievement test should not only be representative of the types of behavioral outcomes expected, but should also be representative of the course content. The topical outline developed for planning the course is also valuable for preparing the performance test.

One means of assuring that the performance or achievement test is representative of both the course content and the various levels of behavioral outcomes is to prepare a table of specifications that relates the various levels of learning in the cognitive domain (stated in terms of learning outcomes) to the course content. This two-fold *table of specifications* enables the instructor to classify each test item in terms of both content and objectives. A completed table indicates the number of test items needed to obtain a balanced measure of the behavioral objectives and the course content.

A sample table of specifications, based on the previously illustrated course in elementary accounting, is shown in Table 1. For illustrative purposes, only the general learning outcomes and major areas of content are shown. Although this procedure is acceptable in many instances, more detail may be desirable in some situations.

The number in each cell in the table reflects the number of test items to be constructed in each area. The total number of items in each column indicates the relative emphasis to be given each learning outcome, and the total number of items in each row indicates the relative emphasis to be given to each area of content.

Constructing Test Items

The next task is to construct test items for the general learning outcome and content areas of each cell. For example, to construct a test item for content area B (measurement), and general learning outcome (knows basic accounting terms and concepts), the instructor should (1) select one of the specific behavioral objectives listed under the first general learning outcome, (2) select one of the important accounting terms or concepts, and (3) construct a test item that calls forth the specific behavior indicated by the specific behavioral objective. To illustrate:

General Learning Outcome:
1. Knows basic accounting concepts and terms

Specific Behavioral Objective:
1.2. Selects the term that best fits a particular definition

Test item:
1. Costs that change directly and proportionately with changes in volume are known as:
   a. Sunk costs
   b. Out-of-pocket costs
   c. Variable cost
   d. Fixed costs

Clearly, each test item should be focused on a previously defined behavioral objective and related to the content of the course.

TABLE 1
TABLE OF SPECIFICATIONS OF TEST ITEMS
Elementary Accounting

Content Area	1. Knows Basic Accounting Terms and Concepts	2. Understands Accounting concepts and Techniques	3. Applies Accounting Concepts and Techniques to new Situations	4. Analyzes Accounting Information	5. Synthesizes Accounting Information	6. Interprets and Evaluates Accounting Information	Total Items
A. Accumulation	1	2	1	2	2		8
B. Measurement	1	2	1	2	1	1	8
C. Reporting	3	2	1	1	2	2	11
D. Analysis	1	2	2		1	1	7
E. Interpretation	1	2	2	1		1	7
F. Controlling	1	3	2	2	1	1	10
G. Decision-making	1	2	2	2	1	1	9
Total number of test items	9	15	11	10	8	7	60

General Learning Outcomes (Cognitive Domain)

Limitations of the Cognitive Model

Once behavioral objectives are developed for a given course or learning module, they should be subjected to the following test: Are objectives included from both the cognitive and affective domain? One of the shortcomings of the cognitive model presented herein is the exclusion of affective goals. The major categories of the affective domain are:

Receiving—the student becomes sensitized to the existence of certain phenomena and stimuli.
Responding—the student does something with or about the phenomena.
Valuing—the student displays consistent behavior reflecting a general attitude.
Organizing—the student brings together different values, resolving conflict between them.
Characterizing by a value or value complex-the student's value system becomes a way of life.

Development of conditions conducive to attainment of specified affective learning outcomes is and should be a major part of accounting education. Concentration on cognitive behavior to the exclusion of affective goals will result in preparing a *trained* accountant but not an *educated* one. Many of the inadequacies in the present educational system can be attributed to the lack of attention to the affective domain. Applied to accounting, this means determining which affective goals should be developed to foster a professional attitude in students and how attainment of such goals can be evaluated.

Although the primary purpose of this paper is to give impetus to the construction of behavioral objectives in the cognitive domain, the authors hope also to stimulate efforts directed toward development of affective behavioral objectives. For accounting educators interested in developing behavioral objectives beyond the cognitive domain, four warnings are in order:

1. Cognitive goals are more traditional and more clearly defined than affective goals.
2. Attainment of affective goals is difficult to measure. The affective objective and the overt behavior excepted as attainment are sometimes widely separated, relative to cognitive goals and behavior.
3. Traditional evaluation techniques are not effective in measuring affective goal attainment. A variety of evaluation instruments (rating scales, subjective questions, interviews, class discussions, etc.) must be employed. In addition, affective student behaviors are very slow in development.
4. Since measurement should take place in an unstructured situation, affective domain objectives should not be communicated to the student.

CONCLUSION

Developing behavioral objectives via the cognitive model described herein requires a significant investment of time. Behavioral objectives must be rewritten a number of times until each objective will be clearly understood by students. This is not an easy task. Many objectives will appear to be trivial and not representative of what the instructor is trying to accomplish. Moreover, questions can always be raised about the objective and the sample behavior that will be accepted as evidence of objective accomplishment.

As an alternative to the cognitive model, accounting educators might elect to continue "as is". Consequently, most accounting course objectives will persist in focusing on teaching activity rather than on learning outcomes. For example, accounting educators will continue demonstrating to students how to compute cost of goods sold using Lifo inventory methods. Once the Lifo demonstration is completed (the teaching activity), the objective is achieved, *whether or not the students have learned anything!*

There are many advantages to formulating and stating *explicit* behavioral objectives that are based on observable performance, e.g., "The student is able to prepare a statement of changes in financial position," as opposed to vague generalizations, e.g., "The student appreciates the concept of funds." Behavioral objectives are currently receiving much attention in other disciplines and appear to have significant potential for accounting education.

FOOTNOTES

1 Benjamin S. Bloom, Editor. *Taxonomy of Educational Objectives, Handbook I: Cognitive Domain* (New York: Longmans, Green and Company, 1956). See also: David R. Krathwohl, Benjamin S. Bloom, and Bertram B. Masia *Taxonomy of Educational Objectives, Handbook II: Affective Domain* (New York: David McKay Company, Inc., 1964.)
2 Items 4 through 7 and their subsequent discussion are adapted from Norman E. Gronlund *Stating Behavioral Objectives for Classroom Instruction* (New York: The Macmillan Company, 1970).
3 Following is a list of verbs often appropriate for use in preparing general learning outcomes:

Knows
Comprehends
Applies
Uses
Interprets

Understands
Analyzes
Synthesizes
Appreciates
Evaluates

APPENDIX A

REFERENCES USEFUL IN DEVELOPING BEHAVIORAL OBJECTIVES

Bloom, Benjamin S., et. al. *Taxonomy of Educational Objectives: Cognitive Domain.* New York: David McKay Company, Inc., 1956.
Developing and Writing Behavior Objectives. Tucson: Educational Innovators Press, 1968.
Developing and Writing Performance Objectives. Tucson: Educational Innovators Press, 1971.
Eiss, Albert F. and Harbule, Mary Blatt. *Behavioral Objectives in the Affective Domain.* Washington, D.C.: National Science Supervisors Association: A Section of the National Science Teachers Assocation, 1969.
Gronlund, Norman E. *Constructing Achievement Tests.* Englewood Cliffs, New Jersey: Prentice-Hall, Inc., 1968.
─────. *Stating Behavioral Objectives for Classroom Instruction.* New York: The Macmillan Company, 1970.
Krathwohl, David R., et. al. *Taxonomy of Educational Objectives: Affective Domain.* New York: David McKay Company, Inc., 1964.
Mager, Robert F. *Preparing Instructional Objectives.* San Francisco: Fearon Publishers, 1962.

APPENDIX B

QUESTIONNAIRE FOR EVALUATING COGNITIVE OBJECTIVES*

Adequacy of the List of General Objectives

1. Does each general instructional objective indicate an appropriate outcome for the instructional unit?
2. Does the list of general instructional objectives include all logical outcomes of the unit (knowledge, understanding, skills, attitudes, etc)?
3. Are the general instructional objectives attainable (do they take into account the ability of the students, facilities, time available, etc)?
4. Are the general instructional objectives in harmony with the philosophy of the university?
5. Are the general instructional objectives in harmony with sound principles of learning (e.g., are the outcomes those that are most permanent and transferrable)?

Statement of General Objectives

6. Does each general instructional objective begin with a verb (e.g., knows, understands, appreciates, etc.)?
7. Is each general instructional objective stated in terms of student performance (rather than teacher performance)?
8. Is each general instructional objective stated as a learning product (rather than in terms of the learning process)?
9. Is each general instructional objective stated in terms of the students' terminal behavior (rather than the subject matter to be covered)?
10. Does each general instructional objective include only one general learning outcome?
11. Is each general instructional objective stated at the proper level of generality (i.e., is it clear, concise, and readily definable)?
12. Is each general instructional objective stated so that it is relatively independent (i.e., free from overlap with other objectives)?

Behavioral Definition of General Objectives

13. Is each general instructional objective definded by a list of specific learning outcomes that describes the terminal behavior students are expected to demonstrate?
14. Does each specific learning outcome begin with a verb that specifies definite, observable behavior (e.g., indentifies, describes, lists, etc.)?
15. Is the behavior in each specific learning outcome relevant to the general instructional objective it describes?
16. Is there a sufficient number of specific learning outcomes to adequately describe the behavior of students who have achieved each of the general instructional objectives?

(*) Adapted from Norman E. Gronlund *Stating Behavior Objectives for Classroom Instruction* (New York: The Macmillan Company, 1970), pp. 51-52.

Objectives Of Professional Education And Training

Carl J. Bohne, Jr.
Director of Training
Arthur Andersen & Co.

Introduction

This paper evaluates the objectives of professional education and training from the viewpoint of the practitioner in public accounting. Objectives as stated by academic representatives are compared with the actions by the members of the accounting profession. The training programs of Arthur Andersen & Co. are used as a measure of the accomplishment of the objectives.

Is there a clear distinction between education and training? If there is a distinction, does one fall wholly or in part in the province of either the educators or the practitioners? Is there also a real demarcation in time or in the location where the objectives are achieved?

There is a clear distinction between the term, education, in the broad sense and the term, training, in the narrow sense of instruction and practice in manual skills. Today the chief distinction in the use of the terms is to consider education as the learning that occurs in formal university courses in the development of the general and special abilities of the mind. Training is the descriptive term for the learning which takes place in practical education or practice, usually under supervision, in some art, trade or profession.

If education is thought of as instruction in subjects with rigorous intellectual requirements, or in conceptual as distinguished from procedural matters, or as taught in formal classroom style by masters of the content, or in similar terms, then all of these characteristics apply to a greater or lesser degree in the learning programs in use in public practice. There is much hands-on instruction in such areas as data processing but that approach is also used in many university courses on that subject. The formal instruction in universities, however, is seldom referred to as training although it would not be totally wrong to use that term for preparatory course work required for a particular career. On the other hand some of the instruction given in practice is so narrow or superficial that it cannot be described as education.

Professional development is a continuing process throughout the career of the individual. Professional development starts and may continue with formal instruction in the university and later with personal efforts to increase competence by a combination of study and experience. There is no time or place where development should stop although the form and circumstances will change. Professional development is highly personal; the individual must have the desire to increase his competence. Others may advise or instruct him and he may join forces to promote more efficient and effective self-development, but it must be a personal effort to be effective. The individual cannot be forced to develop professionally although incentives may be employed to make development more attractive, easier, or perhaps difficult to avoid.

In this paper, the profession will be assumed to be practitioners. This assumption is a convenience because the accounting profession is much larger than this in scope if not in numbers. Accountants in industry and government are certainly members of the profession as well as those in education. Practitioners also include a large number of persons from other disciplines. Their knowledge of accounting may be different from that of a CPA, but they are members of the accounting profession in many important respects, not the least of which is the necessity for professional development.

Objectives As Stated By Educators

Accounting is "essentially a *creative* process of generating useful, quantitative, economic information."[1] Educational institutions undertake to prepare a student for positions of responsibility in accounting (whether to become practicing CPAs or to become proficient in other areas of the field). Therefore the primary objective of accounting education, using Ralph Swick's words, is "to better prepare students to evaluate conditions and situations whether they be business, public, or private, in which monetary or economic considerations are paramount, yet with a full awareness, on the part of the evaluator of the moral and ethical considerations involved."[2]

The objective for accounting education basically agrees with Pierson's objective for general business education: "Business careers involve many elements which lie outside the purview of higher education. The principal contributions which business schools can make is to help students apply general knowledge and special abilities to significant business problems . . . Colleges and universities should concentrate on strengthening the student's powers of imaginative thinking".[3]

The Committee on the CPA Examination of the American Accounting Association, reporting in the Supplement to the Accounting Review, XLVII in 1972, received the following response to a questionnaire survey: "The primary purpose of our accounting program is to provide a sound and vigorous conceptual framework on which a student can build for the thirty to forty years following his graduation." This, too, is in agreement with the Swick objective stated earlier.

Summarizing this objective in a somewhat different manner, with more detail, the Committee on Courses in Financial Accounting of the American Accounting Association stated:

. . . financial accounting curriculum, among other things, should:

1. Provide a basic understanding of the conceptual framework underlying the measurement and communication of economic data.
2. Provide the future accountant with the technical competence for effectively measuring, assimilating, and communicating economic data, including the capability to use the *best* tools and techniques available, as well as those which are 'generally accepted'.
3. Provide an understanding of alternative models for measuring and communicating economic data, primarily for external use.
4. Be relevant to current problems and adaptive to changing social and economic conditions.
5. Cultivate a keen, analytical, inquiring mind.
6. Provide the student with the incentive to grow and keep pace with ever-changing issues, conditions, forces, and ideas.[4]

The foregoing citations seem representative of the collective opinion of educators but they ignore several issues of deep concern to many of them:

1. Which and how many non-accounting courses should be in the curriculum?
2. How many accounting courses should be offered and at what level?
3. Should the emphasis be procedural or conceptual?
4. Is accounting a discipline worthy of the name?
5. Should there be special graduate schools for persons destined for public practice?

These issues are not ignored because they are unimportant, but because they are not germane to the approach of this study. Educators are in agreement their task is to prepare students to *become* professional accountants and today's professional accountants are a product of the universities despite, or because of, the obvious diveristy of opinion of the educators.

Objectives As Stated By The Profession

Practitioners and their professional associations have also studied and written on the objectives of professional education and training. Attention to university level objectives was sparked by the Ford and Carnegie reports on business education and the study sponsored by the American Institute of Certified Public Accountants on the common body of knowledge required for entrance to the profession. The opinion of practitioners who are members of large public accounting firms has been well stated by William W. Werntz:

> Formal education in accounting should not, in my opinion, be regarded as an end in itself but rather as a quick and more efficient means of acquiring necessary knowledge than, for example, home reading or an apprenticeship. It is equally true, however, that the qualified professional today cannot be merely a technician. He must also be an educated man in the true sense of the word.
>
> It seems to me far more likely that a four-year graduate with a minimum technical education will be impelled to acquire technical training for his chosen field than that a thoroughly trained technician will thereafter acquire the skills, knowledge, and disciplines of the courses omitted in favor of technical courses.
>
> To attain maximum objectives, the accounting courses should be tightened up with minimum attention to the mechanics of bookkeeping, an increased emphasis in depth on basic accounting, auditing, and data presentation, and a reversal of the trend . . . toward a great proliferation of 'special' courses . . .[5]

The Committee on Education and Experience Requirements for CPAs was composed of a cross section of members of the American Institute of Certified Public Accountants representing all segments of practitioners. The opinion of the Committee in the words of Elmer Beamer, its chairman, follows:

> The Committee notes the expanding role of the accountant in society and believes that the recommendations specified in *Horizons* need to be adoped if accountants are to be equipped to play this role. We, therefore, endorse the recommendations of the report. We note, too, the trend toward placing greater reliance on formal education and less on on-the-job training as a means of professional preparation. We agree that this development is desirable and believe that the body of knowledge necessary for entrance into the profession will and should be acquired as a part of the collegiate education. But our analysis of the recommendations leads us to conclude that the mastery of the body of knowledge which is commensurate with our public responsibility will require not less than five years of collegiate study. Thus the Committee recommends that the Institute recognize the need for education beyond the baccalaureate degree for those who stand prepared to enter the profession. . .
>
> The Committee is aware of the growing practice in the undergraduate business schools of limiting the number of hours that the student is permitted to take in any one area. And to the extent that the trade-off of depth of understanding in one area accomplishes the objective of honest breadth of understanding, we are inclined to be sympathetic with the objective of the practice. Nonetheless, we are concerned with the preparation of young people for careers in professional accounting, in which breadth of education does not justify deficiencies in accounting understanding. If it were necessary to sacrifice accounting competence in order to gain the desirable breadth of education, we would need to oppose that trade-off . . . While we feel that conceptual understanding is to be desired over procedural skill, we do not believe that a trade-off is required here either.[6]

To the extent that the preceding quotations are representative of the attitude of the accounting profession, there is general agreement with the educators that the broad objective of university education is to prepare the student to *become* a professional accountant. A broad base of liberal arts studies should be the foundation for business studies. The value of the conceptual approach is admitted, but the practitioner is not convinced that the procedural approach in accounting education should be abandoned entirely.

There is not unanimity in the profession, nor among educators as to whether there should be a graduate professional accounting school and what courses should be included in programs of varying length. Universities rightly must be concerned to prepare their students to enter the accounting profession in government and industry as well as in public accounting. This broad requirement is the source of some differences of opinion, primarily it seems, over the means to the ends and not over the ends.

Does The Practitioner Agree?

If there is no real conflict between the spokesmen from the universities and the accounting profession at large as to overall objectives, is there also unanimity of opinion among the members of the profession? Disagreement seems obvious when consideration is given to expressions of opinion by invididual practitioners. Much is said and written about the deficiencies observed in university graduates. The primary reason for much of the discussion of deficiencies is that all practitioners do not look for the same qualities and skills in their employees nor can there be one ideal or average employee to match against these diverse needs.

The real problem in understanding the controversy over objectives and the criticisms of university graduates is the virtual impossibility of establishing a generalization about which all parties can speak. There are no average entrants into public practice, engaged largely in similar tasks, and thus providing a standard product to evaluate in terms of the validity of the objectives of professional education at the university level. The relative merits of the conceptual versus procedural approach cannot legitimately be assessed because business conditions have changed so dramatically from the time when most accountants were educated under the procedural approach.

Persons enter public practice upon leaving high school, junior colleges, trade schools, and universities of varying quality. The formal accounting preparation of the entrants ranges from the now rather rare bookkeeping courses (in residence or by extension) to holders of doctoral degrees with a concentration in accounting. Some of the entrants will have had part-time accounting work during their period of schooling or have participated in an internship program in public accounting. Others will have turned to public accounting after some experience in industry or government. To make a fair generalization, a number of entrants with very specific backgrounds would have to be selected, but even this step would not provide a reliable basis for comparison and study.

The employers of these persons will range from the individual practitioner who hires one person every few years to the large international public accounting firms employing many hundreds every year. The business practice of the employer will range from one of predominantly write-up work and preparation of tax returns to the enormously varied and complex practice of the large international firms. If a specific group with similar backgrounds was to be selected for study, there would be the difficulty of defining the average tasks with the average employer.

Another significant factor in the evaluation of objectives of professional education is the presence of large numbers of persons in practice who have no or only minimal accounting training in their academic background. Many persons with formal education in law, mathematics, computer sciences, engineering, finance, and other disciplines are employed directly in the tax and management services divisions of large firms. Others with these same backgrounds work for a time in the auditing division and then transfer to their areas of special interest. The assessment of the special needs of these non-accountants and fair evaluations of their performance are complicated by the presence of experienced accounts who transfered from the auditing division to these other areas of practice.

Objectives Implied By Training Programs

Objectives can be inferred from training programs. There are a number of organizations of professional accountants that have elaborate learning programs. The Professional Development Division of the American Institute of Certified Public Accountants has a wide range of excellent professional development materials. Many of the state societies of CPAs have programs of continuing education or professional development. Some of these societies have an imposing list of subjects and employ a variety of latest teaching techniques.

All persons in public practice worthy of professional status must devote considerable time to self-development programs including research, study and reading. The large public accounting firms have elaborate and costly professional development programs under the fulltime direction of a number of persons and part-time activities of many. Few small firms and individual practitioners have formal training programs, but professional development does occur. On-the-job instruction occurs in varying degrees, and experience is gained on work assignments. In addition, practitioners can participate in the programs offered by various professional organizations.

Certain subjects appear in almost all of these programs, but it is difficult to generalize the needs and attempt to evaluate prior academic education. The depth of treatment of the topic varies from an overview to extensive coverage and cannot be appraised without study of each course. The prerequisites for attendance are usually not stated or are described in terms which do not have a universal meaning. The course offerings may signify no more than an effort to meet the needs of a relatively small or unusual segment of the profession or they may be an attempt to meet a wholesale need. The courses may be attended by persons recently graduated from college or by experienced persons whose academic preparation ended many years ago. Obviously a number of reliable conclusions can be based on studies of a number of training programs, but without a massive study, an evaluation of the overall objective of professional education and training would be meaningless if not misleading. No service would be rendered by inferring approval or disapproval of the quality and skills of university graduates and the degree programs which produce them.

The Training Program Of One Firm

Perhaps one insightful approach would be to examine the objectives and content of the professional development program of a specific public accounting firm. To the extent that the programs are in fact necessary, they imply the needs of the firm's professional personnel. If the needs could or should be met at the university level, it would be fair to evaluate the objectives of university education and to compare them to the practitioners' conceptions of the objectives of professional education and training.

The accounting firm of Arthur Andersen & Co. has approximately 10,000 professional personnel of which 70 percent are in the auditing division, 15 percent in administrative services. All of these persons have an undergraduate degree and a large percentage have advanced degrees. The training programs cover all personnel in all divisions from the newly employed through the most experienced partners. Some courses are taken by all persons at specific career points such as immediately after employment or at the time of promotion to senior. Most of the courses, however, are taken immediately before the opportunity for application is likely to arise, and their frequency is based on the needs of the individuals and their rate of development.

Objectives of the Training Programs

The broad objective of the entire training program is to increase the quality of service to clients. To accomplish this objective requires the professional development to the individual.

Experience, correctly gained, is an effective teacher for those who survive the process of acquiring it over an extended period. However, there are many common skills required on many engagements and these can be taught in advance. Marginal performance can often be improved or avoided if deficiencies are corrected in advance. All engagements differ in the experience to be gained, even from the same client in succeding years; therefore, the learning from experience must be supplemented to increase the rate of development.

Every professional must devote a considerable amount of time to individual study in his area of special interest merely to maintain a minimum level of competence. Some of this study can be accomplished more efficiently on an organized group basis. Acquisition of knowledge of critically important of sweeping developments in technology, regulations, etc., cannot be subject to possible delays and oversights inherent in individual study programs.

As persons become more deeply involved in areas of special interest, keeping abreast of developments in other professional activities becomes increasingly difficult. The day of the broad generalist is gone, but all professionals must have varying degrees of awareness of developments that bear directly or indirectly on the specializations. On an organized basis it is possible for experts to devise programs for each specialization which will teach the desired amount of information on developments in other specialized areas.

There is merit in the informal, day-to-day exchange of information and experiences among individuals, both intra- and inter-disciplinary. Even in a one-office firm, this process in uncertain and ineffective. In a world-wide organization, informal interchange is impossible. The exchange-of-information process must be highly structured both within a specific area of specialization and among allied and interdependent specializations.

An appreciable number of persons become interested in areas of specialization closely allied to or widely different from their main field of academic preparation and/or previous experience. The change may be as small as a tax partner, expert in family planning, who rather quickly has an increasing number of clients with reorganization problems. At the other end of the scale is the history major who decides upon graduation to become an auditor or a data-processing specialist. These needs must be met, and formal instruction provided by the firm, in whole or in part, is necessary.

As a consequence of the factors like the foregoing, the broad objective--increasing the quality of service of clients--can be divided into several instructional objectives as follows:

1. To teach the application or reinforce the understanding of theory and techniques learned in formal university instruction.
2. To teach new skills or bodies of knowledge.
3. To provide supplemental instruction in areas not previously covered in sufficient depth in academic preparation, in background, or in experience.
4. To provide instruction necessary to update the knowledge, skills, and techniques of experienced professional personnel.
5. To provide instruction necessary to supplement and broaden the skills and techniques of experienced personnel.
6. Provide a forum or channel of communication for experienced personnel for the exchange of information, techniques, new developments in professional practice, technological advances, etc.
7. To teach the practices, policies, and organization of the firm.

At this point, there is not obvious conflict between the cited opinions of educators, the profession at large, and Arthur Andersen & Co. over the objectives of professional education and training. The educators believe their task to be to prepare the graduate to become a professional accountant and the authorities cited from the profession agree. The educational objectives of Arthur Anderson & Co. are based on the assumption that the large majority of persons entering the firm do indeed have the broad base of qualifications upon which experience and formal learning programs can build to produce truly professional accountants. Whether there are things that could or should have been done better at the university level remains to be resolved.

Training in the Auditing Division

For the persons entering the auditing division who have made accounting their major field of study at the undergraduate or graduate level, there is no need to teach accounting concepts, principles and practices. In a minority of cases, instruction is required for professional developments and pronouncements that have occured since graduation or perhaps since the last revision of the accounting text books used in their classes. Accounting majors have no difficulty in moving directly from the college classroom to the client's office insofar as their comprehension of financial accounting is concerned. The training programs in accounting matters for auditors throughout their professional careers are devoted to new developments and not to remedial efforts. The extent of such subsequent training in accounting is directly proportional to the complexity of the subject and the experience of the participants.

In recent years the new employee in accounting tends to be somewhat unfamiliar with the mechanics of accounting and the flow of documentation underlying business transactions. The problem is not sufficiently serious to require special training efforts and it quickly disappears with experience. Considerable criticism is directed at this issue in some quarters. If it is a trade-off with conceptual understanding, it is a worthwhile bargain.

Special attention should be given to the frequent criticism that new employees (and some not so new) "do not understand business." Where it is possible to inquire about specific examples, a particular factor is frequently responsible for the criticism. Often the employee seems to have difficulty in analyzing a business problem and identifying the concept or theory involved. This condition may result from classroom instruction which too often signals the topic and requires only the appropriate solution; if the lesson plan calls for instruction on valuation of inventory, for example, it is most likely that case problems and examples will contain this problem. Perhaps a simple lack of business experience is responsible. The rapid exposure to positions of responsibility today reveals inexperience more often than in the days when beginning accountants had too many years of exposure to routine tasks.

There is also the criticism that new employees tend to marshall all of the pros and cons on a theory point or problem and are reluctant to take a positive stand on what is right or preferable. This condition might stem from too much emphasis in the university on every conceivable aspect of a point of view without adequate discrimination. Perhaps this is the result of a human tendency to avoid the consequences of making wrong decisions.

Another criticism somewhat related is that too often the new accountant facing non-accountant client personnel has difficulty in proposing, defending, and debating an accounting point in terms of business facts and conditions. The cause of this problem is so complex that generalizations are difficult. Perhaps this results from the university accounting classroom environment or from a lack of understanding of the economics of business or from a failure to recognize the simple rule of salesmanship in considering the viewpoint of the client.

Usually these matters tend to disappear with maturity and job experience. Training is purposely conducted with case problems and instruction simulating actual business situations. On-the-job training hopefully gives special consideration to these factors. The weakness tend to disappear rather quickly, and it is not possible to say whether training, experience, or some combination are responsible. The interesting point, however, is many blanket indictments of university-level accounting education are based on no more than these specific points.

There are two additional areas that receive immediate and constant attention in all training programs. University graduates know little if anything about government regulation of business, the regulations or the economic and business results. Regulated industries pose special and complex business problems, and the auditor must be well versed in all ramifications of governmental regulations and their effects on business. Little if anything is taught in many universities on the subject; its complexities do seem worthy of considerable attention at the university level.

The second area is closely allied to the first. The complexities and innumerable diversities of modern business--national, international, and multi-national--are well known. A modern-day audit of most companies cannot be performed without a deep understanding of the business facts, circumstances, and economics of the particular company and its industry. There is more to know about many industries than can be learned by years of experience. If responsibilities are to be assumed rapidly, the learning process must by aided and quickened by training programs devoted to the problems of specific industries and taught by experts in these subjects. In the past there was a time for accountants to be exposed to and develop expertise in a number of industries; cross fertilization between industries was possible. Today there must also be a formal approach to the exposure of specialists in on industry to problems of certain other industries in order to broaden the auditor's approach and take advantage of solutions to similar problems developed in other business.

Formal instruction at the university level possibly could do more to educate students in the accounting and business problems of a number of industries. Anything that can be verbalized can be taught but may not for a number of reasons. Course development would require a depth of understanding of all business aspects of an industry plus constant up-dating in current problems. The effort would require an inordinate amount of the time of the instructor. There is also the distinct possibility that the student would not have the necessary experience in general business to benefit from the specialization. Experience indicates that more can be accomplished if the concentrated industry-problem training is delayed until the trainee has had two or three years' experience and until a real interest in a particular industry has been proved. Teaching accounting by industries is to be avoided. An advanced course on business problems common to one or more industries should be challenging and beneficial but the emphasis should be placed on the business facts and not on the accounting.

Little needs to be said about the training programs in the field of auditing. While there are exceptions, new employees have received little or no university instruction for auditing skills and techniques needed in their first two or three years. Most personnel have received excellent instruction in professional ethics, the auditor's opinion, the organization of profession, auditing standards and principles, and similar subjects. This instruction provides valuable insights in their early training and job experience but it is not possessed by sufficient number to be able safely to rely on this prior knowledge. These topics are covered in the firm's training programs, but usually at the career point where they are most important. Where possible, they are not covered as separate topics but in conjunction with practices or events which require their consideration.

Auditing is an intensely practical and common sense skill or art. A first-hand knowledge of business and the cause and effect relationships in business transactions and decisions is essential. Such concepts as materiality and internal control are more easily understood with more field experience. The emergence of rule making in auditing by professional bodies, governmental agencies, and others has added untold complications both to formal training programs of public accounting firms and to the self-development efforts of the individual. Except for the overview of the profession, its standards and ethics, and its professional liabilities, the teaching of auditing seems best left to the profession.

Training in the Tax Division

Professional development in the area of taxation also has complexities. All auditors, at the very minimum, must have a basic knowledge of taxation and its effect on business and business decisions. Far more than this minimum is required by the tax expert even at the beginning level. There are graduate programs in taxation in a number of universities which provide a sound base for direct entry into the tax division of the firm. Graduates of these programs often are able to bypass the elementary instruction required of most graduating from conventional programs.

Teaching the application of tax concepts and the tax code and regulations is a necessary part the first training in the division. A most vital part from the beginning and throughout all advanced training is the necessity to develop an understanding of the economic concepts of taxation and its effect on business and business decisions. The object is to teach the application of taxes in a business situation.

While every tax expert must have a high level of understanding of the entire field of taxation, there is the necessity for, as well as the individual personal desire, to specialize. This specialization creates a particular problem because the specialist must not become obsolete in the general tax issues. The specialization problem is made even more challenging and difficult by the opportunity to concentrate on the tax problems of specific industries. All of these problems place a special burden of the tax expert for self-development and study in addition to the formal education programs of the firm.

There are a number of schools with excellent graduate programs in taxation and more universities should be encouraged to develop similar programs. These programs are typically used by persons who have decided to specialize in taxation. The great majority of those whose major field of interest is financial accounting too often have only an exposure to tax rules and the preparation of simple tax returns (if they were required or chose to take a tax course). This approach barely satisfies the minimum requirement of the beginner in professional accounting and certainly does not meet the need of one who would specialize in the subject. A great improvement in many university courses would be to teach tax concepts, the code and regulations with a focus on applied business problems.

Training in the Administrative Services Division

Meaningful generalizations about the professionals entering the administrative services (systems) division are the most difficult. A majority have advanced degrees, but less than half of the input consists of persons with accounting majors. The others consist of persons with undergraduate or graduate degrees in fields other than accounting, for example, finance, engineering, mathematics and marketing. Some of those with accounting backgrounds have transferred from the auditing division. The universities represented are very diverse, but there is probably a preponderance of graduates from schools emphasizing management aspects of accounting and quantitative measurement.

Few universities, if any, attempt to teach the approach to systems work as it is practiced by Arthur Andersen & Co.--the conceptualization and design of complete business information systems. Many schools, however, teach the concepts of various components as envisioned in management accounting, quantitative measurement, computer science, engineering, etc. Generalizations about objectives, therefore, are most difficult to make.

Although only one element in the consideration of business information systems, computers draw an intense interest, especially the diversity of opinion in universities about how much and what kind of computer knowledge should be taught. The computer is an integral part to today's business information systems and knowledge of computer science is essential. In many universities, computer courses are in various stages of development and maturity. A recent sampling of accounting graduates entering the firm disclosed that 90 percent had taken college courses which, in their opinion, covered computers and or their application. About 75 percent said that they had learned a language (generally, FORTRAN), had done simple flowcharting, and had keypunched cards. The same percentage thought that they understood how a computer works, the function of input and output devices, and the difference between hardware and software. Beyond this point, the responses showed varying and lesser percentages of persons having any depth of knowledge of or hands-on experience with a computer.

All persons entering the administrative

services division immediately are assigned to an extensive course teaching the basic skills of systems work. Such subjects are covered as techniques of fact-finding, flowcharting, problem definition, analysis of priorities, approaches, scope, and design of key procedural and control systems. The first course is followed by basic computer training including instruction in computer fundamentals and basic programming (logic charting, coding, programming in BAL and COBOL, testing and debugging).

After completing these courses, they embark on a three-to four-year program of formal course work interspersed with on-the-job, hands-on experience intended to produce the degree of knowledge of systems skills and computer competence considered necessary for all persons in the division. The program (as with some other CPA firms) includes building competence in:

1. The various systems-skills disciplines practiced by the firm (financial planning and control, production control, operations research, performance standards systems, etc.); and
2. technical skills in computer systems design, installations and project control (documentation of reporting requirements; design of processing flow, file and input requirements; controls; equipment evaluation; estimation of computer time and installation schedules; evaluation of software; preparation of run specifications; supervision and control of projects; etc.).

Persons interested in specific areas of specialization, such as computer technology, operations research, and financial planning and control, pursue their specializations concurrently with the program described above. This is accomplished through highly specialized and advanced technical training courses developed by the firm and through increasing responsibility on client engagements.

The systems field requires and enormous amount of instructional effort to keep pace with technological developments. The mere revision and updating of course material is a very expensive and time-comsuming effort, usually done on an emergency basis. In addition, there is the problem of keeping all specialists adequately informed about developments in other specializations and systems work.

At this time, it is not appropriate to make sweeping generalizations about the adequacy of university objectives insofar as the firm's systems work is concerned. The firm's approach—the conceptualization and design of business information systems—is different from the university's objective to build conceptual knowledge. For a number of the disciplines involved in systems work, (quantitative measurement and accounting, for example), no attempt is made by the firm to teach these subjects. The instructional effort is to teach the application of the discipline using actual cases at the working level.

Many universities are deeply involved in computer science. Computer instruction at the university level is in the developmental stage, and the objectives of the universities are not always clear. Today the majority of the university graduates in accounting and engineering, for example, have much greater knowledge of computer concepts than was true even a few years ago. Certainly in the short term, accounting graduates will have sufficient knowledge of computers to form a solid base for instruction and experience in the use of this tool in accounting and auditing. Whether it is possible, or even desirable, to produce a quantity of combined accountant-computer science graduates or engineering-computer science-accounting graduates sufficiently able to perform computer systems work as practiced in Arthur Andersen & Co. is an open question.

Other Training Programs

Client problems are extremely complex and cut across divisional skills. No one person can be a master of all skills. Individual random efforts merely to keep acquainted with other disciplines are relatively ineffective. Training every person in the application of every skill in every division is impossible; even if the original training effort could be accomplished, the continuing effort to keep up to date as well as train all newly employed persons in inter-disciplinary skills would be beyond the resources of the firm and the ability of the individuals. The response to the problem takes several forms.

There is general agreement on certain intra- and inter-disciplinary skills which must be taught, for example, an agreed level of skill in certain areas of taxation must be developed in all auditors. The partners in charge of various functional divisions and specializations in consultation with others decide the skills, information, etc., from their areas which should be imparted to their personnel in the firm.

The most important response to the problem is the formation of teams, usually by industry, composed of experts from the functional divisions—auditing, taxes, and administrative services. A high level of expertise in all skills is focused on the accounting, tax and systems problems of an industry. The team members decide which and how much of the skills of their areas are to be taught to any or all persons working in that industry. Generally the training objective is to develop a working relationship among the disciplines involved in an industry team but not to attempt to produce experts in all skills.

There is another advantage to this sytem in the cross-fertilization among disciplines and among industries. Often the functional-division experts are assigned to more than one industry. There are frequent mettings of all specialists within a functional division. Through these channels, information on new techniques, new answers to continuing problems, and developments in other functional specializations are disseminated.

CONCLUSION

Educators and the accounting profession at large are in agreement the objective of professional education and training is to prepare the university graduate to *become* a professional accountant. To meet this need, there seems to be a majority opinion in the academic community favoring the conceptual, as opposed to procedural, approach to teaching accounting and other business subjects. The training programs of Arthur Andersen & Co. operate on the basis the university graduate has a solid conceptual understanding of his discipline and a working knowledge of other disciplines taught in accredited business schools. As a generalization, no attempt is made in the firm to teach any of the disciplines of the business schools except where the supply of university-educated persons in a particular discipline does not meet the demand. Personnel who are almost all from schools of business have also proved they have the ability to develop their skills to meet the changing and increasingly complex problems of business; they rapidly assume great responsibilites.

The intent and expectations of the universities are that today's education will meet the needs of their graduates throughout their business careers. Experience shows that these aims have been realized so far and gives no indication that it will be different in the future. At this point what more could be asked of the universities?

FOOTNOTES

[1] "Report of the Committee of Basic Auditing Concepts, 1969-71", *The Accounting Review* (Supplement to Vol. XLVII, 1972), p. 23.

[2] Ralph D. Swick, "Objectives of Accounting Education", *The Accounting Review* (October 1961), pp. 626-30.

[3] Frank C. Pierson, *The Education of American Businessmen* (McGraw-Hill Book Company, 1959), p. 84.

[4] "Report of the Committee on Courses in Financial Accounting," *The Accounting Review* (Supplement to Vol. XLVII, 1972), p. 295.

[5] William W. Werntz, "Accounting Education and the Ford and Carnegie Reports," *The Accounting Review* (April 1961), pp. 186-90.

[6] Committee on Education and Experience Requirements of CPA's, "Academic Preparation for Professional Accounting Careers," *The Journal of Accountancy*, (December 1968), pp. 57-63.

Section IV
Instructional Innovations

Instructional Innovations: An Overview

Norton M. Bedford
University of Illinois

The functions of university education in accounting, as contrasted with other sources of accounting instruction, include (1) the development of new conceptual knowledge on information for decision situations, (2) the transmission of the newly developed and the accumulated knowledge from present to succeeding generations, and (3) the elimination from the accumulated accounting curriculum of obsolete knowledge regarding both content and instructional methods. Of the three functions, the first—under the appealing title of "research"—has attracted by far the greatest interest of academics. The second has received considerable verbal support but has been viewed more as a required or necessary function than as an area of investigation. The third function has been almost completely neglected. No theories or criteria have been developed to deal with the task of removing non-relevant facts and outdated instructional methods from the accounting curriculum. Intuition and feelings have been used on a situation by situation approach. Without standards or theory to support decisions to eliminate obsolete material, accounting curricula tend to suffer from an inability to discard traditional material and conventional instructional systems. While not normally related to instructional innovation, the great research potential for instructional innovation in accounting education may be in the area of developing standards for eliminating or trading-off traditional accounting educational material and instructional techniques not relevant to future society. The big instructional problem may be to induce change rather than to be innovative.

In terms of immediate payoff for university education in accounting, given the state of the art, proposals for gaining acceptance of innovations in the transmission of knowledge function appear to have the greatest chance for effecting improved accounting instruction. One must distinguish between innovation (new ideas) and change (application of new ideas) and recognize the great difficulty of inducing the latter, particularly if it involves discarding familiar and widely used educational material. There is both empirical evidence and intuitive support for the belief that fruitful proposals for instructional innovation in transmitting accounting knowledge must give consideration to the likelihood that the proposed innovation will be accepted and that change will result. With this caveat in mind, an overview of accounting instruction may well start with the realization that the instructional function is directed to (1) the development of a thinking man appropriate for modern society, and (2) the preparation of a professional man for the performance of the accounting function in society.

In an environmental overview sense, a total picture in broad outline, accounting instruction in a time of rapid technological and social change must be recognized as dealing with the transmission of a unique body of knowledge, information development and information processing, and instructional methods influenced by that substance. This means instructional innovations must be evaluated with four considerations in mind:

1. The particular material taught.
2. The resources available for teaching.
3. The person or object doing the teaching.
4. The capacity of the person taught.

This broad view of the scope of applicability of accounting instructional innovations is essential, for in all four areas accounting instruction is becoming broader and more precise than has been typically associated with the accounting instruction function. Breaking from the traditional but now restrictive boundaries imposed by a limited view of the term "accounting instructional function," accounting instructional methods must now relate to the broad task of developing highly educated people capable of providing financial and socio-economic information to multiple decision-makers in society.

EXPANDED EDUCATIONAL CONTENT

In recognition of the need to base the accounting education curriculum at the university on the foundation stone of the concept of information, information development and information processing, accounting educational programs have expanded in scope and have been related back to the basic disciplines. Accounting systems courses have been related back to the somewhat ill-defined field of information systems with particular emphasis on the role of the computer in developing suitable storage and retrieval systems. Class discussions relating to accounting ethics tend to search for a base in concepts of fairness and justice and to an area of philosophy relating to ethics. Courses on accounting analysis require the prior study of basic courses in algebra and calculus as they relate to the field of management science. Similarly the auditing courses involve students in the use of statistical sampling methods and legal rules of evidence. Theory courses on accounting disclosures deal with the psychology of decision making and the behavioral aspects of accounting information in general. Many of these courses tend to find a base in human communication theory which involves both linguistic and psychological factors. The variety of all the material to be taught makes accounting instruction more difficult each year.

Along with the broadening of the accounting curriculum to relate accounting subject matter to basic disciplines, there has been a simultaneous expansion of the scope of the university accounting educational materials as educators have sought to maintain the relevancy of their courses to the expanding activities of accounting practice. Emergence of accounting problems relating to leases, pension funds, investment credits, mergers, sophisticated management techniques, the rise of financial analysts, and the general practical response to the increasing public's right to know as reflected in court decisions, have increased the technical body of applied accounting required of the student.

IMPROVED TEACHING RESOURCES AND METHODS

Out of the expansion in scope of educational material and the related increase in instructional cost to cover it, coupled with the development of a number of technical communication devices, has arisen considerable interest in the improvement and cost-effectiveness of accounting instruction. This interest has resulted in an emphasis on research and innovation in accounting instruction and has created the problem of inducing broad acceptance of successful innovations.

A review of the various types of teaching resources and instructional methods proposed by the various contributors will provide a base for placing this overview in more meaningful perspective. This section of the book contains papers dealing with instructional systems (the first eight papers of this section, pp. 256-350) and instructional techniques (the fourteen papers found on pp. 352-439). Instructional systems encompass the modular concept, selfpaced instruction, programmed instruction, multi-media presentations, television presentation, use of the computer for instructional purposes, the case method approach, and team teaching. The technique papers offer a variety of ideas useful in performing the instructional function in a variety of accounting subject areas.

INSTRUCTIONAL SYSTEMS

Professor Donald D. Bourque's classification of instructional innovation into the four categories: (1) programmed instruction, (2) self-paced instruction, (3) individualized learning, and (4) modular-flexible scheduling reflects modern thinking about instructional innovation. He notes that the idea of a module is common to all categories and proceeds to examine the notion of a module as it is used in modular scheduling and learning models. Using the common idea that a module is a building block, course structuring and scheduling is viewed as a composition of modular units of time, class size, and course structure. The idea is to break educational materials down into basic building blocks of time periods, class size, and course content and then combine them to fit space, time, class size, and content into systematic structures and schedules for instructional purposes. The aim is to attain specific educational objectives efficiently and effectively. Learning modules replace time periods as units of instruction. Each learning module has a specific educational objective and is pursued by each student on an individual basis. While construction of learning modules requires consideration of the learner's interests, readiness, rate of learning, and past learning habits, there is reason to believe the learning modules have been effectively used at a few universities and appear to be a significant instructional innovation.

Professor Dempsey Dupree's examination of self-paced instruction centers on the need to insert flexibility into the instructional process to serve the needs of all types of learners. Self-paced instruction differs from individualized instruction in that it applies to variation in the speed at which a student moves through common instructional material whereas individualized instruction includes content, sequence of presentation, and communication means appropriate for each learner individually. Self-paced instruction really represents a return to much older teaching approaches existing prior to the lockstep, fixed time schedules for classes of students. Under self-paced instruction, the teacher becomes an "educational manager" rather than an "information disseminator." Modular arrangement of single concept study units and explicitly stated course and module objectives are effective parts of self-paced instruction.

The first of Professor Bourque's categories of instructional innovations is programmed instruction. Professor James Don Edwards describes the stimulus-response-reinforcement cycle of programmed instruction as follows:
 1. Give the learner a small amount of information and ask him to answer a question based on the information.
 2. Have the learner answer the question.
 3. Have the program give the correct answer.

Noting that the program is the total of all the sequential frames in the learning module, Professor Edwards emphasizes that programmed instruction is not only beneficial to the student but causes the instructor to engage in creative teaching. Various applications of programmed instruction are included to deal with the problem of inducing the change in accounting instructional methods.

Professor Donald E. Stone covers the ways the computer can aid and extend accounting instruction. In particular he examines changes in the subject matter of accounting because of the impact of computers on accounting practice. He points out that it is important in applying computers to classroom use to have a clear understanding of the distinction between teaching students about computers and using computers to teach. Dealing with the latter, the following educational applications of computer power are discussed: canned programs, computerized cases and practice sets, games and simulated environments, computer-aided instruction, data-based systems, and student-development programs. While these applications merely extend the subject matter of accounting, some of them are specifically designed as individualized teaching aids using diagnostic feedbacks to the student.

Professors Avery and Istvan recognize the multi-media approach is not an instructional innovation while observing it has become more sophisticated as modern technology has developed. In a narrow sense, the term "multi-media" merely refers to the use of a large number of audiovisual materials. In a broad sense, it is a methodology based on the idea that various audiovisual media can be coordinated and reinforces the value of each.

Specifically, the multi-media approach involves identifying the media available for use and determining how they should be used.

Turning to more specific instructional innovation, Professor Koehler reviews television-related instruction. He describes the combined approach, television with live laboratory sessions, in some detail and cites such other television-related instruction as prerecorded tapes, educational networks, and television without labs.

Professor Robert N. Anthony's review of the case method as a teaching device and disclosure of new developments in the use of cases clarifies the use of this instructional tool. He calls attention to several types of cases such as issue cases, appraisal cases, blind cases, iceberg cases, and series cases and then classifies cases by source as armchaired, published source, or field. Innovations in the use of the case method include computer-assisted cases, assumption development cases, grading group discussions, and question development cases.

Professor Kenneth W. Perry's review of team teaching calls attention to the variety of features of this instructional method. He suggests this instructional innovation is most effective in opening up personal relationships between teacher and student, fosters continuous student involvement, and provides respect to the student as an individual.

INSTRUCTIONAL TECHNIQUES

Instructional techniques vary widely and must be applied in the context of the personality of the individual instructor, the teaching facilities being used, the quality of the students, the objectives of the teaching, and the subject matter to be taught. The various authors illustrate a number of effective instructional techniques.

The technique papers were selected from response to the "call for papers" issued in connection with the publication of this book. The response was gratifying. Space constraints restricted those that could be included. Those selected seek to demonstrate a wide range of techniques with respect to useful ideas applied to a variety of accounting subject areas.

Professor Rockart's award winning description of the integration of learning methods and resources illustrates a technique for applying the fruits of technology to an accounting course. Noting that instruction has been a labor-intensive industry, Rockart accounts for the rise of innovative instructional systems in terms of the need to increase productivity of higher quality learning in the educational process by allowing the student to learn, at his own pace, knowledge relevant to his particular needs. He illustrates an objectives-material-methods-resources development process as a technique for applying multiple techniques to an accounting course in a controlled experiment. Specifying seven course objectives, classifying course material into six functional activities, and using eleven learning methods, Professor Rockart suggests that the three instructional resources (professors, students, and technology) can be coordinated to reduce instructional costs and improve learning.

The use of a game for introducing students to accounting is proposed as a teaching technique by Professors Carlson and Higgins. While the game is played during the first two class sessions, Carlson and Higgins found that students became intensely involved in the accounting issues included in the game and the authors observed a high motivational feature of the game.

Two papers focus on the use of simulation techniques:

1. Professor Leftwich's description of the use of the business simulation technique in teaching accounting places the technique in realistic perspective. While business simulation cannot replace the lecture and problem solving, he suggests simulation can be used to call forth knowledge under circumstances that are favorable for retained learning. His conclusions are based on the learning theory principle that reward and reinforcement can be used to "condition" more permanent changes in behavior.

2. Professor Tomassini provides three illustrations of the use of role-playing in accounting education. After providing a justification for the role-playing technique and describing various forms of role-playing, he suggests a ten-stage course of action for implementing the role-play technique. He does caution that users should integrate the technique "within the framework of their own instructional needs and objectives."

Professor Shirley illustrates the use of group assignments as a technique of fostering cooperation and minimizing competition in order to orient students toward learning rather than winning as the study objective.

Professors Benjamin and Strawser

describe the use of financial statements in the classroom in "hands on" learning how to use actual financial reports. They use the technique of modifying annual reports systematically and collecting student estimates of earnings per share from different versions of the financial reports. They report the technique relieved some of the "drudgery" of the problem-lecture approach and stimulated interest in accounting material.

The use of a teaching machine technique as a supplemental alternative to lectures in a basic tax course is discussed by Professor Strueling. While the technique requires the use of teaching machine equipment and substantial effort to develop the programs for the machine, significant success with the technique was reported.

Three papers focus on computer applications and, as such, relate to the papers by Donald E. Stone, "Computer Usage in Accounting Education," pp. 289-304. Professor Sale describes the use of a computer simulation of the budgeting process, labeled "COMBUD", as a technique for teaching illustrates the "real meaning of comprehensive budgeting" to the students. He appears to believe an illustration of a "real life" situation will foster learning and retention.

The second computer application lends support to the technique of inserting "real life" situations into the teaching process through computer simulation. Applying simulation to the teaching of internal control evaluation using both a computer program and written class handout material, Professor Burns proposes a classroom teaching technique that is effective in dealing with the difficult internal control evaluation problem.

In the third paper on computer applications, Professors Cattanach and Hanbery illustrate the use of students and faculty from a variety of courses to reinforce basic concepts of one course by examining these concepts in other courses. They apply their technique to three courses: accounting systems, advanced data processing, and auditing. They call attention to several problems but conclude the technique is superior to the traditional approach where concepts of each discipline are studied in isolation.

Professor Wolk uses the technique of the price level aspects of accounting. By relating the different concepts to each other with illustrations, he implies a better understanding of the problem is conveyed to the student.

Professor Jones illustrates the use of a chart to contrast the income effects of direct and absorption costing. He reports the chart technique helps students understand the income implications of each method.

Professor Deakin presents a technique for determining when to take advantage of quantity discounts by extending the economic order quantity analysis. The technique is particularly significant because it represents a means for including useful quantitative material in accounting courses.

Professor Crumbley's pictorial presentation of tax laws in a logical fashion illustrates a technique he found could improve the communication skills of a tax instructor. He reports that pictorial diagrams, if effectively used as transparency projections or mimeograph handouts, can aid in the teaching of complex concepts.

SOME GENERAL OBSERVATIONS

In recognition of the obvious phenomenon that students, rather than classes, learn, the instructional innovations provide arrangements for individual learning as the basic objective. Class instruction becomes merely one technique for teaching under this conception of the learning objective. While the economies of class rather than individual instruction will necessitate the use of class instruction, the instructional innovations uniformly accept the proposition that effective learning requires active student involvement in both physical and mental participation in the learning process. The participation required is not merely the physical "taking part" in the activity but also the mental perception by the student that what he is doing is relevant to his objectives and that he knows how well he is learning.

One observes the convergence of learning theory with the instructional innovations proposed. Objectives, types of learners, and environmental conditions are used in selecting appropriate learning methods and theories. Several kinds of learning are recognized and the older notion that learning is a unitary phenomenon is replaced so the student may be subjected to awareness learning, intellectual learning, behavioral learning, depending upon his needs.

Noticeable among the contributions is agreement that teacher-student interaction is not always the most effective learning process. Insulation from the teacher is effective for learning certain types of materials and for certain idiosyncratic learning patterns of different students. The broad central theme of the contributions to instructional innovations is that good teaching should both develop a desire on the part of the student for learning and cause students to learn how to learn, but that these broad objectives must be used more as guidelines for the development of specific operational teaching objectives. None of the contributors attempted to deal directly with the two broad objectives, but many of the operational innovations proposed contribute to their attainment.

The most far-reaching inference of the contributors, as a whole, is that effective instruction must be adapted to the needs, abilities, and backgrounds of the learners as individuals. While this is not a particularly new notion, the far-reaching implication is that class-directed instruction is unsatisfactory as an end in itself and must give way to learner-directed instruction as an objective. No general method of instruction, applicable to all situations, exists. The consequence of this learner-directed philosophy is that accounting instruction will become more complex and this complexity extends to require elaborate equipment, specialized facilities, and innovative instructors. In this context of complexity, instructional approaches such as television and automated instruction are useful primarily as methods for improving the quality of accounting instruction, and should not be viewed solely as a means for providing quantity instruction at low cost.

In the contributions to instructional innovations is an implicit outline of the future accounting educational process. The clear trend is that instruction will be increasingly individually designed to meet the needs and abilities of each learner. In this future accounting education process, the teacher emerges as one responsible for program development for each student according to his needs and capabilities and for the selection of appropriate instructional methods from the kit of instructional tools: classroom lectures, discussions, books, programmed learning, computer instruction, and the like. Most important will be the teacher's role in developing educational materials and in the determination of effective teaching systems and techniques. Extensive research in both areas seems to be the great current need.

SUMMARY

The terms "curriculum" and "instruction" are not as distinct as they intuitively appear. While "curriculum" may imply consideration of the subject matter of what should be taught and "instruction" may imply the procedures to be used in the teaching process, the extensive interaction between the two areas precludes independent treatment of them. On the other hand, attempts to treat the two subjects as one merged topic results in a number of ambiguous and imprecise notions.

Dealing with instruction alone, it becomes possible to specify instructional objectives in terms of observable behavior of the learner, either as actions taken or products produced by the learner. To be operational and useful to the instructor, these behavioral objectives must be stated clearly and in such a manner that success can be measured in some way, such as the results of an examination before and after the instructional effort. Instructional innovation also includes new means for attaining these objectives. Both types of instructional developments arose in response to a perceived inadequacy in prevailing methods of mass education. The objective is to be more efficient in transmitting a given quantity of information and effective in the quality of the presentation of subject matter.

Technology is the primary feature of recent accounting instructional innovations, because it offers many opportunities for increased cost efficiency, such as that resulting from machine-graded tests. Technology also offers opportunities for increasing accomplishments or effectiveness but because effectiveness refers to that learned by the learner, it is less easily measured and applications of technology in this area have not progressed rapidly though a number of applications have been reported.

Three topics, covered in the first four papers, related to individualized instruction warrant special consideration as a unit in any summary of accounting instructional innovations. They are individual instruction, programming learning, and computer instruction. To distinguish them, recall that individualized instruction is a flexible system, as demonstrated by the paper "The Modular Concept of Instruction," pp. 256-67, and can be used to attain various educational objectives. It involves the development of an individually directed instructional system based on specified or selected behavioral objectives, learner attitudes, and environmental factors which are correlated with particular instructional techniques, testing results, and curricula materials. The basic objective is behavioral in that it aims to develop the student's self-initiation and his capacity for the self-direction of his own learning. It may also include the more purely educational objective of developing the student's problem-solving ability. An important feature of certain types of individualized instructional systems is that the student moves through the learning process at his own rate. The paper, "Self-Paced Instruction," pp. 268-77, deals with this type of system. This type of learning has been applied with some success but it depends entirely upon the quality, coherence, and completeness of the instructional system. These systems are costly and difficult to develop and require a certain homogeneity of educational development and knowledge in the group which uses them.

The second of the three topics related to individualized instruction is programmed instruction. Once again there is a learning "sequence" determined in advance. The student typically moves at his own rate through a series of small steps, each of which requires an overt response. As Professor Edwards observes, each of the steps should be small enough so that the student is able to give a correct response, which is then "reinforced" by disclosure of the correct answer. While the programming is basically linear, it also contains branches for the student to use if he fails to make the correct response. Normally, the branches attempt to explain the probable cause of the error. As Professor Edwards points out, the *basic* features of programmed learning are that the learner is active in the learning process and receives immediate feedback. Programmed instructional materials have applications beyond individualized instruction and are used effectively in classroom situations.

The third application of the "learning sequence" of individualized instruction involves the use of a computer to store and present the subject matter for discovery by the student. The retrieval speed of the immense data-storage capacity of a computer gives it obvious advantages over written programmed learning materials though, essentially, the principles of operation are the same. Additionally, the computer has instructional utility beyond that of the individualized approach as demonstrated by the wide range of educational applications presented in the paper, "Computer Usage in Accounting Education," pp. 289-304.

The three related innovations share a number of common characteristics. In the first place, all represent an attempt to "tailor" instruction to the abilities of the individual student. Secondly, all require constant student manipulation of the subject matter. Third, student manipulation of the subject matter and interaction with the steps of the learning sequence replace or reduce the amount of student-instructor interaction. All of these characteristics are "built-in" to the learning system involved, and are supposed to have favorable behavioral consequences. The result of all three systems is learning plus development of a positive student attitude toward learning in general.

The cost function for most accounting instructional innovations differ from the lecture method. Sunk set-up costs are high for almost all individualized instructional innovations since they involve large initial outlays in developing, testing, refining, and implementing the learning system involved. In contrast to the high set-up costs, subsequent costs of maintaining and operating the system are on an individual student basis quite low. This means that individualized instructional innovations are economically feasible only on a large scale. The University of Illinois Programmed Logic for Automated Teaching Operations (PLATO) system represents an attempt to develop a basic logic system for application in a variety of systems, which might permit significant cost reductions in individualized instruction. The objective is to develop a universal logic of instruction which could then be applied in a variety of specific situations at low cost.

Other instructional innovations of media transmission form are not related to individualized instruction. Usually, they involve integration of the new instructional media techniques into the traditional "chalk, talk, and book" presentation. Such media aids include the use of television, films, tapes, and various combinations of still pictures and recorded commentary. The papers on the multi-media approach and television related instruction are devoted to these aids. They must be used as supplements to traditional presentation and cannot totally replace student-instructor interaction. Unless media presentation allows for some sort of interaction or manipulation of the subject matter, experience indicates that retention declines. In particular this guideline applies to films, tapes, and similar one-way presentation devices. Television does allow for some interaction, and closed circuit broadcasts can be made to numerous locations simultaneously and if supported by a "conference" telephone link can provide the potential for interaction. But in the main, instructional innovation in the form of media transmission of information are supplemental devices.

The case method affords a highly useful instructional system for a wide variety of situations. Still other instructional innovations which involve variations in teaching technique may be used effectively when several levels of educational material is to be taught. Different teachers may be used for different purposes. In this connection, some schools are experimenting with the use of "aides" or paraprofessionals who work extensively with students, but who do not teach. Essentially, this involves separation of the presentation and interaction functions of teaching. Along with the use of paraprofessionals has come team teaching. Team teaching is best used when diverse subject matter requires the use of different instructors to present and explain the different areas of interest within a course. One of its main limitations is the need to coordinate team activities. Normally it should be used only when course material is interdisciplinary or cuts across areas of specialization within a discipline.

Overall, the techniques to be used depend upon the subject matter to be taught and the capacity of the learners. As is usually the case with the less sophisticated audio-visual aids, new techniques are often mere window dressing. On the other hand many of the innovative techniques can be integrated into traditional classrooms and methods in an effective manner. In the main, however, the innovations designed to supplant traditional methods apparently can only do so under certain limited conditions and only when the subject matter is susceptible to somewhat mechanical presentation.

Because the more elaborate and technologically involved innovations are costly and their effectiveness is not known until large amounts have been invested, they are risky. While this risk was covered in the 1960's by the impetus for innovation because of the shortage of trained teachers and the large inputs of federal money in response to a perceived "crisis" in quality of education, in the future there will be a surplus of teachers and much less money. Logically, instructional innovations would then tend to be evaluated more on the basis of both demonstrated cost-benefit efficiency and on educational effectiveness in order to reduce the risk feature involved in thier use. Exchange of information on the application of new instructional methods among accounting professors seems to be the need of the times.

Instructional Innovations:
Systems

The Modular Concept of Instruction

by
Donald D. Bourque
State University of New York at Albany

Introduction

Instructional technology is a systematic way of designing, carrying out, and evaluating the total process of learning and teaching in terms of specific objectives. It is based on research on human learning and communication and the combination of human and non-human resources to bring about more effective instruction. The module is one of the basic software ideas used in the application of technology to the instructional process. The module is the basic working unit employed in individualized instruction and curriculum (modular) scheduling. This paper discusses the role of the modular concept as a part of the modern instructional system.

The instructional methods employed by accounting professors today are hardly distinguishable from those employed in the 1800s. The typical instructional system uses a textbook, lectures, and problems. The mix and the quality of these components vary substantially. For the most part, the accounting professor, like his colleagues in other disciplines in the university, has almost completely ignored the communication revolution that has swirled around him for the past twenty-five years.[1] Few significant instructional innovations have been introduced as a way to break out of the rigid system that marches accounting students, lockstep, through a series of almost identical classroom situations where the teacher dominates and does most of the talking and the student is in a passive role with little opportunity to either think or respond.[2]

There are signs about us today, however, that changes are in the wind. University educators and administrators see value in the educational technology movement and experimentation and innovation are taking place in the instructional process. Resources are beginning to flow into university centers for instructional development. At the top level of some university organizations are individuals designated as vice president for instructional development.[3] All of this is taking place in a professional environment that provides little reward for improvement in the instructional process. A university professor is usually still better off in the current reward structure (salary or promotion) to write the article or book rather than use his time to innovate in the classroom.

The aim of much of the innovation that is taking place in instruction (organizational, curricular, and technological) is directed at making instruction more precisely meet the individual needs of each student. The result hopefully will be a more scientifically based learning system that recognizes that students learn in different ways at different rates. In this writer's opinion, the present system generally ignores individual learning differences, motivation, and most human behavior traits associated with the instructional process.

Educational innovation has taken and is taking a wide variety of forms. Programmed instruction was clearly one of the first large moves to make the instructional process both more scientific and at the same time more individual. In fact some suggest that the current application of communication technology to education would not have been possible without the advent of programmed instruction and the Skinnerian concept of reinforced learning. The Skinnerian organization form and emphasis on differential reinforcement provided educators with the basis and the opportunity to apply modern communication technology.[4]

Other innovations have taken the form of more *self-paced instruction, individualized learning*, and *modular-flexible scheduling*. Each of these developments offers a unique arrangement of resources, in order to achieve the goal of more effective instruction. Common to all of these innovations is the idea of a module. The module is the basic organizational unit used by these innovative systems, although the specific definition of this term is different in each case.

This paper examines the application of the modular concept in modern instructional systems. The paper specifically explores the notion of the module as it is used in modular scheduling and learning modules and places particular emphasis on the instructional or learning module because in the author's view it is an application that: (a) has immediate use in accounting education with minimal capital and training investment, (b) is an approach that has been successfully tried in accounting at a number of schools, (c) is an approach that emphasizes competency-based education, (d) is an idea with a high degree of flexibility in its application, and (e) has the potential of being used in a conventional classroom situation or in a completely individualized learning system tailored to the needs of the student.

DEFINITION OF THE MODULAR CONCEPT

In general usage a module is any unit that is capable of being joined with another unit to form a larger structure. It is a relatively simple idea that has provided the basis for a near revolution in the fields of electronics, architecture, construction, and education. In education the basic idea behind the module is not new. For years, the entire educational system has been predicated on a building block idea. Schools and colleges have held classes that make up courses that are taken during an academic term. On a smaller scale the building block approach is found in lesson plans which subdivide class sessions into lessons. In modern educational terminology the term "module," however, has taken on a number of different meanings.

In *programmed instruction* the term "module" refers to a collection of frames that make up part of the instructional program. The frame is the basic unit used in programmed instruction and consists of a stimulus-response pattern that ends in a learned skill or concept. The frames provide a step-by-step pattern through the educational material to achieve a stated goal or objective for each frame and for each module.[5]

In *self-paced instruction* the term "module" also refers to a building block but in this case unless programmed instruction is used, frames may not be involved. A module in a self-paced system like *Alex* consists of a unit of instruction on a specific topic.[6] As the student starts the topic he is informed of the objectives and importance of the subject. In the *Alex* system a series of visual and audio lessons transmit the skills and concepts using a film strip. Although the material is not programmed, questions are asked during the module.

The size of a module in programmed instruction is based on the number of frames included. Since a subunit, the frame, is used, programmers have been more concerned about the length of the frame measured in words, sentences, or ideas than the module. In self-paced instruction, the module is the basic unit. Its length will depend on the designer of the instructional system and therefore may vary considerably. For example, in *Alex*, the module is 15 to 20 minutes in length, while in the Merrill system, the modules are 40 to 60 minutes in length.[7]

The module in *modular scheduling* is a segment of a curriculum that is made up of units measured in class size, time, and course structure. In this application the curriculum is viewed as an area or portion of a course to be scheduled. The size of this scheduling module is measured vertically in time (hours or minutes) and horizontally in students in a specific course. A complex scheduling problem develops when these modules are organized into a master schedule.

A *learning or instructional module* is a

unit of instruction that is self-contained and scientifically structured. The instructional module covers a specific topic and has carefully stated learning objectives specified in operational terms. The typical module uses multiple-media forms to communicate facts and ideas and utilizes carefully developed tests to measure achievement of learning objectives.

These different applications of the term "module" in education all have in common the general idea behind the term--that of a building block. Each, however, represents a very different building block. This paper examines the application of the term in modular scheduling and instructional modules. Programmed instruction and self-paced instruction are discussed in other papers in this book.

MODULAR COURSE STRUCTURING AND SCHEDULING

In curriculum planning, the curriculum, conceived of as *an area* to be scheduled, is made up of subparts called "modular units." These units are derived from units of *time*, units of *class size*, and units of *course structure*. When the curriculum is thought of as an area the horizontal dimension is usually defined as students while the vertical dimension is time in the schedule module.[8] Diagram 1 illustrates a schedule module, the basic unit is curriculum planning when flexible modular scheduling is being used.[9]

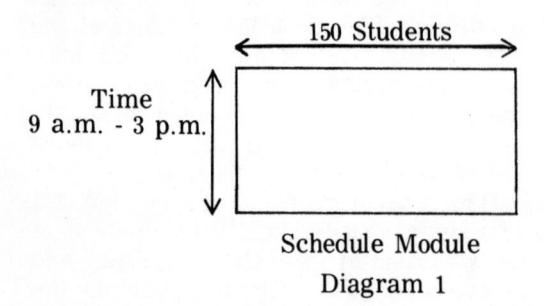

Schedule Module
Diagram 1

In the schedule, module time is chosen by selecting the maximum amount of time multiples which would provide the desired time period lengths for any instructional purpose. For example, if instruction periods of 40, 60, or 120 minutes are desired, then a 20 minute time module would be appropriate. The modular unit of class size would be the minimum size desired for instructional purposes. Although class size need only be estimated, it is important to note that period length is rather finite. In modular scheduling a scheduling module may be any size desired, but to gain maximum flexibility and reduce the complexity of the scheduling function, a larger modular unit is better than a smaller unit. For example, for a module of 15 students meeting for ½ hour, the basic scheduling module would be:

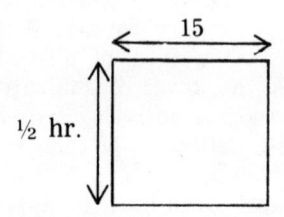

This unit provides a wide variety of *course structures*.[10]

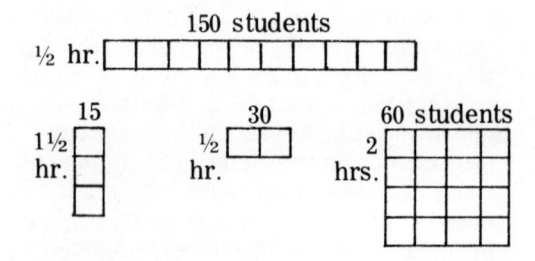

Course Structures

Modular course structure is the application of the scheduling module concept to a course. The course structure consists of phases and sections. A *phase* is a subdivision of the structure for which students, instructors, and the time period length remain constant. Normally capital letters are used to denote a phase when diagramming a course structure. A *section* is a subdivision of a phase. The number of sections in a phase is determined by dividing the total course enrollment by the permissible size of each section in a phase.[11] Sections are denoted by lower case subscripted letters. In Diagram 2, for example, phase A involved all students and is the same as section a. The difference between phase B and D (other than time) is that different groups of students are involved and different instructors may also be involved. As noted early in the scheduling module discussion, the vertical scale is an index of time and the horizontal

The Modular Concept of Instruction

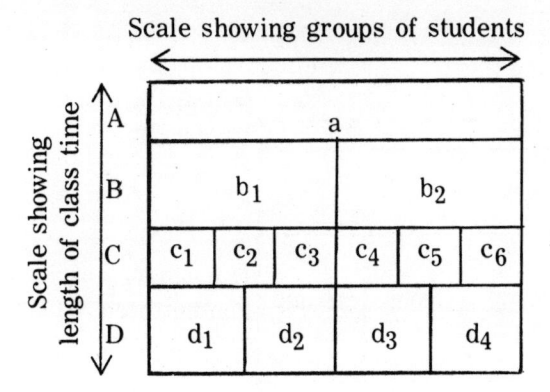

```
                Scale showing groups of students
              ←─────────────────────────────────→
      ┌─A─┬───────────────────────────────────────┐
      │   │                   a                   │
      │ B ├───────────────────┬───────────────────┤
Scale │   │        b₁         │        b₂         │
showing│  ├───┬───┬───┬───┬───┬───┤
length │ C │c₁ │c₂ │c₃ │c₄ │c₅ │c₆ │
of class│  ├───┴───┬───┴───┬───┴───┬───┴───┤
time   │ D │  d₁   │  d₂   │  d₃   │  d₄   │
      ↓└───┴───────┴───────┴───────┴───────┘
```

Structure of a Basic Accounting Course
Diagram 2

scale the number of students. In the example in Diagram 2 it can be observed that the instructor planning this course for the week represented on the vertical scale planned to meet all the students in phase A and then divide the class into two large groups in phase B. Further division of the group takes place in phase C, while in phase D larger groups are utilized. Each of these phases involves some different aspect or dimension of the educational process. Each phase may be tailored to large or small groups or individualized learning situations depending on the subject matter. For example, course structures may appear as they do in Diagram 3. Diagram 4 illustrates an application to a large accounting course.

The variations in course structures shown in Diagram 3 illustrate the value of defining and thinking of the curriculum as an area to be scheduled. Once a basic modular unit is selected for the program or school, each course can be planned with a structure that is particularly suited to the instructional situation. The modular concept does not require any structured change from that of the conventional course unless the instructor desires to do so. It does provide the ability to modify the structure.[12]

If modular scheduling is adopted by a school, two distinct kinds of problems must be resolved: those involving scheduling and those involving curricular requirements. The problem of scheduling must be resolved on a university wide or program wide basis. To utilize a flexible scheduling system, a school, college, or department must have control over faculty time, student time, and physical facilities. If this scheduling system is to work, the school must have the latitude to use large classrooms, laboratories, and small classrooms when needed. The problem of scheduling must be solved by fitting together the various pieces that result from the variety of course structures that might be developed. For example, in the first week of classes all courses may require large group meetings. As the semester progresses, courses will need large and small classrooms, laboratory space, individual learning stations, and students will be taking different phases of courses at different times. The flexible schedule must anticipate in advance all these needs.[13]

	Example 1				Example 2				Example 3			
A	a_1	a_2	a_3	A		a		A	a_1	a_2	a_3	a_4
B	b_1	b_2	b_3	B	b_1	b_2	b_3	B		b		
C	c_1	c_2	c_3	C	c_1	c_2	c_3	C	c_1	c_2	c_3	c_4
D	d_1	d_2	d_3	D	d_1	d_2	d_3	D	d_1	d_2	d_3	d_4
E	e_1	e_2	e_3	E	e_1	e_2	e_3	E	e_1	e_2	e_3	e_4
F	f_1	f_2	f_3					F	f1	f2	f3	f4

Examples of Possible Course Structures
Diagram 3

First Week of Basic Accounting

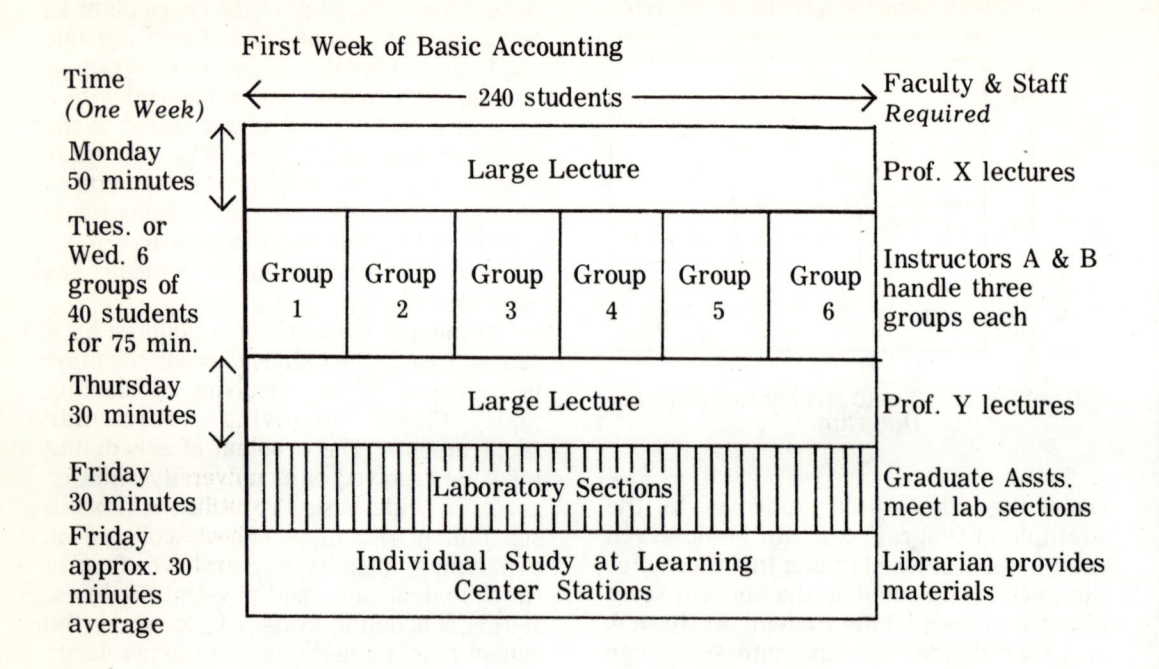

Time (One Week)	240 students → Large Lecture / Groups / Lab / Study	Faculty & Staff Required
Monday 50 minutes	Large Lecture	Prof. X lectures
Tues. or Wed. 6 groups of 40 students for 75 min.	Group 1 | Group 2 | Group 3 | Group 4 | Group 5 | Group 6	Instructors A & B handle three groups each
Thursday 30 minutes	Large Lecture	Prof. Y lectures
Friday 30 minutes	Laboratory Sections	Graduate Assts. meet lab sections
Friday approx. 30 minutes average	Individual Study at Learning Center Stations	Librarian provides materials

Accounting Course Application of Modular Structuring
Diagram 4

Curricular design adds to the complexity of the scheduling task. It must be known, for example, what courses will be taken, by which students, and how much time within the course structure will be allocated to each student grouping. Although the modular idea increases the complexity of the scheduling task, it is easier to alter the total amount of time allocated to any one course. The computer can assist in solving most of these matching problems.

An Overview of the Application of Modular Scheduling

In the discussion on scheduling modules and modular course structuring, the basic ideas underlying flexible scheduling were presented. Diagram 5 brings all the ideas together, providing an overview of the results of an application from the course level, student level, and school level viewpoint.

Modular structuring results in constantly changing course structures from week (or scheduling period) to week. As the semester passes, each course has different instructional situations and classroom needs because of the modular concept.

Students have a new schedule for each scheduling period. No week or schedule period will be exactly the same because of the modular structuring. A new schedule for various groups of students must be prepared for each scheduling period.

The task of preparing an integrated schedule is undertaken at the school level for students, professors, classrooms, and subjects.

Some Advantages and Disadvantages

Flexible modular scheduling encourages a curriculum design and course structure that best meets the instructional requirements of the material and the educational needs of the student. The system allows the use of faculty specialists in specific fields in phases and sections of a course as that expertise is required. Non-

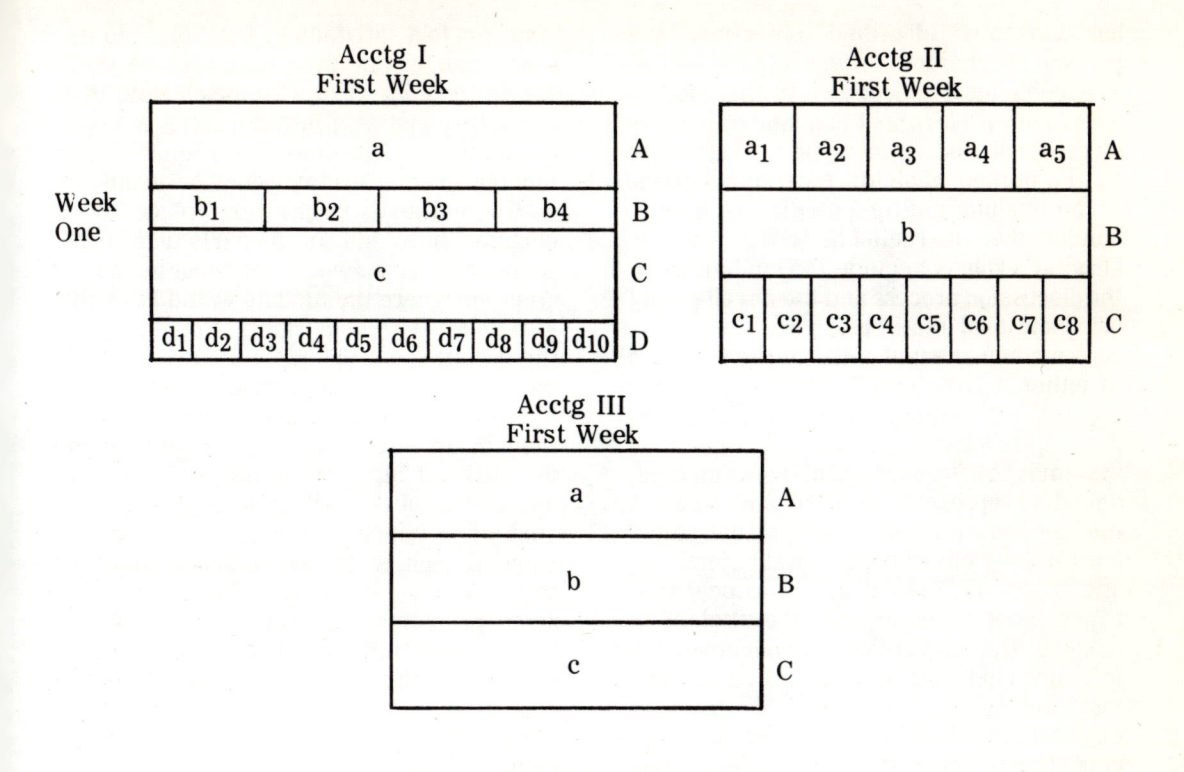

Overview of Modular Scheduling
Diagram 5

faculty technical personnel are easily integrated into this system to help develop educational materials, laboratory sessions, or the control of individual learning materials. This approach to scheduling clearly breaks the lockstep pattern found in most universities under conventional scheduling. The system requires and encourages cooperation and teamwork among the faculty.

The complexity of the scheduling task is not the main reason that most colleges and universities are not using modular scheduling. The main problem is the nature of the university and the university professor as compared to the teacher and a primary or secondary school. Universities are in the business of creating new knowledge as well as disseminating knowledge. Faculty at universities view themselves as independent scholars first and teachers second. They have not been trained as teachers but as researchers. The university reward structure rewards research and publication and merely acknowledges improved instructional methods.[14] A system that restricts the traditional freedom of the university faculty would normally meet with more than normal resistance. Modular scheduling has been tried at the university level in a number of special programs like MBA programs, law schools, and medical schools.[15] In these applications, the program orientation provides the synergistic force necessary to engender cooperation from the faculty, leading to improved student learning. The units involved are autonomous from the university and therefore have the necessary control over faculty, students, and facilities to achieve the flexible scheduling goal.

INSTRUCTIONAL OR LEARNING MODULES

The instructional module is a product of the educational technology movement and is a unit of instruction or knowledge which has carefully identified objectives expressed in behavioral or operational terms. The behavioral objectives of the module interface with terminal learning objectives of the total instructional unit (course) to form a unified whole. In most applications of the module, multiple media are used to handle the instructional task. The instructor's role is to guide the student using the discussion process and the development of educational materials.

A module as a unit of instruction is found in either a time constrained or non-time constrained setting. In a completely *individualized learning system* [16] where the system is both open ended and unregulated, a module represents a unit of *knowledge*. A module consists of specifically stated learning objectives (behavioral objectives) and a set of individualized educational experiences necessary for the student to achieve the objectives. Achievement is measured in terms of a test called a "post-test" because it comes after the learning experiences. In this idealized kind of educational situation the student may pass through or experience the learning materials as many times as he likes before he takes the post-test and achieves a satisfactory level of performance. In this non-time constrained learning situation it is assumed the rate of learning is completely unconstrained. A student, therefore, may move as rapidly or as slowly as desired. If this concept of education is followed to its logical conclusion, a baccalaureate degree would consist of so much *knowledge* (rather than time) with certain minimal performance levels specified. A student would then proceed to acquire this knowledge as rapidly or as slowly as he liked. The present educational system is time constrained. For an undergraduate degree it is typically four years and some universities have rules stating that it cannot take more than six years before a loss of credit for work taken in early years is experienced. It is felt by some educators that the time dimension is an important variable to relate to knowledge acquisition.

When the learning module is viewed in a time constrained environment it almost becomes an entirely different concept than in the unstructured situation. The module is viewed as a unit of *instruction*. The knowledge in the unit must not only be acquired to a satisfactory level prior to the next module, but this must also be done within the context of a time schedule that typically consists of either a class, a week, a month, a semester, or a quarter. A module in this format would be a unit of instruction that might take place at a certain time and in a particular time sequence. This would of course be a situation where the module would have the maximum time constraints. For example, the instructional module may be used as a part of a rather conventional course that meets on particular time schedules rather than in an unconstrained, completely individualized learning situation.[17] In this application of the instructional module the student may be asked to go to a library or learning center to see a short film (15 minutes) on a topic and then work with some problems with illustrated solutions available on film strip. He might then take a post-test. The student would then attend a class prepared to discuss and work on more advanced applications of the concepts.

Design of Instructional Modules

The elements considered to be the basis of all successful educational systems consist of:
  1. Defining objectives or goals to be achieved.
  2. Frequent feedback.
  3. Continuous reinforcement.
  4. Individual pacing.

There is evidence to show that people vary considerably in their ability to learn, mode of learning, study habits, interest, and other facts considered essential to the educational process. In fact, learning appears to be a highly individualized process. In order to meet the challenge of increased individualized learning, the instructional module was developed. It takes all of the key elements of learning into consideration and provides a basis for the application of modern educational technology. An instructional module whether considered a part of a larger learning unit (course, etc.) or an individual unit (modular scheduling) is designed to provide a logical vehicle to allow an individual learner to achieve the objectives established. The sections of the paper that follow provide insights into the design details essential if accounting instructors are to be able to successfully apply this concepted modularized instruction.

Some Essential Preliminaries

Most university professors take for granted a significant number of issues that have concerned primary and secondary teachers for some time. These are *critical variables* in the teaching-learning process and vital to the successful development of useful instructional or learning modules. If these variables are ignored, even though the most advanced instructional technology is applied, success is questionable. Before starting work on the development of an instructional module, the teacher must:

1. *Consider the Learner's Interest.* Is the module required or an elective? How can it be made relevant to a particular student's past experiences? What design or media applications will increase the student's interest? Things like music, color, visual effects, audio effects, and special graphic treatments should be considered. Those working in the field of advertising use all of these effectively to achieve their goal. Educators must learn to do the same.

2. *Consider the Learner's Readiness.* What prior work is being assumed? What skills are necessary to successfully work on the material in this module? What level of prior knowledge of topics or subjects considered prerequisite to this module is necessary?

3. *Consider the Learner's Rate of Learning.* What is the intellectual mix of the group based on past experience or available test scores? How will this influence the level of work (depth of understanding) and the time required to complete the module?

4. *Consider the Learner's Past Learning Habits.* Is the maturity level such that little difficulty can be expected in unguided work or is some degree of guidance necessary? How much effort will be necessary to encourage participation and continuation to avoid drop out?

The Structure of an Instructional Module

The instructional module idea has been applied in three settings. The module is used in individualized instruction where no course *per se* is involved. It is used in what might be thought of as mini courses (one credit hour units) that are completely autonomous from other courses, and the idea has been applied to a regular university course that is held during a semester or fixed time period. In the conventional course application the course is broken down into modules. In any of these applications of the module the structuring steps are essentially the same and therefore no distinction will be made here between applications. The physical format of the module generally consists of: a *title, behavioral objectives, pre-test and post-test,* and *instructional method alternatives* and resources.

Title. Each module should have a title to identify it. The selection of modular subjects and the problems relating to selection (size, etc.) are discussed later in this paper.

Behavioral Objectives. Behavioral objectives are precise statements of what the student will be able to do in behavioral or performance terms upon completing the module. For example, prepare an income statement, distinguish an asset from an expense, or apply the LIFO technique.

The development of objectives in behavioral and measurable terms is a difficult and important task and their importance cannot be overemphasized.[18] With objectives precisely stated, it is possible to evaluate the effectiveness of an instructional system. Using objectives there is a sound basis for selecting and sequencing learning experiences. Objectives mean that the instructor does not confuse the difficulty of content with its importance and students become goal-oriented and motivated.

In formulating a statement of objectives that communicates the intent of the instructor, the following three questions should be kept in mind:[19]

1. What will the student be doing when he demonstrates he has achieved the stated objective? (Since it is impossible to view the mind of another, the state of his intellect must be judged using his actions as a surrogate.)

2. What special conditions will be imposed on the student when he is achieving the objective? (May notes be used? May a calculator or slide rule be used, etc.?)

3. What are the accepted levels of satisfactory performance? These must be spelled out in detail.

In the development of behavioral objectives statements of performance should be made up for the attitudinal objectives as well as for those that are content-related or cognitive skills. For example, when the objective asks the student to *appreciate, develop confidence,* or *evaluate,* these are different in terms of being able to specifically state expected behavior as can be done in the case of *prepare, calculate,* or *determine*. The instructor must decide just what kind of behavior will be accepted as evidence of "confidence" or "appreciate." What does a student do to show he has achieved these goals? This question must be answered as the modular objectives are determined.[20]

Pre-test and Post-test. The pre-test is designed to determine if the student already has the knowledge contained in the module. Since the pre-test is a criterion examination it is based on the same objectives as the post-test and therefore may be the same examination.

In developing the post-test it is absolutely essential that the identified learning objectives are followed. In order to insure this, it is advisable to prepare the post-test before the education media and subject outlines have been prepared.

The post-test is developed by building into the examination items that provide solid evidence of achieving instructional objectives. This means that the instructor must decide in advance what he considers "passing" or "acceptable" performance.[21] Note that performance is not based on a curve or by peer comparison but on absolute performance standards.

Instructional Method Alternatives and Resources. The application of multiple-media forms to the module is the heart of the learning module concept. Alternative media applications distinguish the learning module from all other forms of instruction.

Once the module topic has been selected, the behavioral objectives established, and the criterion examination set, the question that remains is what media to use to perform the instructional task. In most conventional courses, the book, the classroom blackboard, the problem, and the instructor are the media employed. The learning module should draw on the most effective media available for the instructional task. Some media that most instructors will consider immediately are film, cassettes, film strips, video tapes, books, cases, problems, and exercises. Other media that may not come to mind immediately are role playing, simulation, real world practice, and tutorial assistance. In one module it may be necessary and desirable to use several different media forms. For example, when students study the treatment of long term debt on financial statements and the impact of interest rates on the price of the note or bond, the module or modules may use the following media:

1. A movie on capital markets and how they function.
2. A cassette and work book asking questions about the movie.
3. A film strip showing the calculation of bond prices under different interest rates and hence discount and premium situations.
4. A series of exercises applying the concepts discussed in the film strip.
5. A movie on financial statements of corporations and how they treat long term debt.
6. Reading SEC and AICPA statements on treatment of debt.
7. As a part of a simulation, apply for a loan or sale of bonds to actual investment bankers by preparing all necessary financial papers.
8. Do (7), but instead of bankers, let older students play the role of the bankers.
9. Students come to a discussion session and discuss a real world case problem.
10. Several text books used as references.

This example illustrates the kind of imaginative media applications that are possible using learning or instructional modules as the vehicle for the application of educational technology. The main drawback is the resources necessary in both time and money to do this kind of instructional job. Fortunately the results and the rewards usually offset the costs when resource use is carefully planned.

In this type of instructional system the role of the teacher changes dramatically. Instead of being the major fact supplier through lectures and instead of dominating the conversation in the classroom, the instructor becomes a learning manager. As a manager, the instructor must be wise enough to know what Edward Thorndike wrote in 1912 is still true today: "A human being should not be wasted in doing what forty sheets of paper or two phonographs can do. Just because personal teaching is precious and can do what books and apparatus cannot, it should be saved for its peculiar work."[22] Clearly the technology of today is even more superior than in 1912 to man's ability to communicate facts and concepts. The teacher must do what the technology cannot do. The "peculiar work" Thorndike refers to is the discussion and dialogue process that the instructor is able to bring into the classroom.

Steps in Developing Instructional Modules

After considering the basic ideas relating to designing the instructional module and determining the learning objectives, the next step is a concise statement of the procedures involved in applying the modular idea to a course.[23]

1. Select a course, or a part of a course, or a topic for application. This should be an area a person knows exceptionally well from both a technical as well as a conceptual viewpoint.

2. State the overall objectives for this unit in operational terms. These will become (after some reworking) the terminal objectives of this unit. They should reflect the nature of the audience expected in the course.

3. Develop a subject outline for the unit. This outline should reflect the logical flow of topics and the interrelationship between topics.

4. Using the subject outline, identify modular units. When selecting modules, try to select units that are relatively small and relatively autonomous. Work with smaller units rather than larger ones. Precise behavioral objectives are easier to establish with a smaller unit.

5. Write down in specific performance terms the behavioral objectives for each module identified. As indicated in the early discussion on learning objectives, this is a critical area and the more precise the statements, the better the educational results.

6. Write down the evidence or the performance level that is considered adequate for each objective specified in 5 above. Performance levels should be evaluated in terms of the terminal objectives. Not all students desire or need to learn the same amount about every topic. Performance levels should be adjusted to reflect the expectations found in the terminal objectives.

7. Develop a test that measures the statements made in the behavioral and performance objectives. Provide the student with several self-tests.

8. Examine the various media available to communicate ideas and facts. Remember students learn most effectively by doing and that the chances of communicating are highest if more than one sense is used in the communication process. Select, with the help of a technician, the best media for the educational situation.

9. Compare the terminal objectives and the modular objectives. Are they consistent?

10. Select the first module and prepare a detailed outline or flow chart of the topics in the module. Develop the educational materials necessary to communicate each topic and meet the specified learning objectives. Apply the media selected to communicate the materials. Do this for all modules.

11. Prepare a schedule for students and faculty to be used in connection with each module. This schedule lists deadlines, locations of discussion groups, location of resources, etc.

12. Select a test group of students for testing the structural learning situations and acquire feedback for necessary revisions.

Applications of the Instructional Module Idea

A number of universities are working to apply educational technology to courses using the modular approach. Syracuse University, under the direction of Robert Diamond, has applied the idea to at least six courses ranging from basic English to advanced physics. Most courses have substantial enrollments. The results have been extremely rewarding from a student as well as a faculty point of view. Students have assumed their responsibilities as a part of the instructional process, learned more, and performed better than students either in the past or in parallel sections not using the modular system. Dull classes become exciting classes because the students are talking and interacting. Instead of dull lectures that described an event or an instruction, pictures, plays, visits, or experiments replaced the less interesting means of communicating in facts and ideas.

Jay Smith and his associates at Brigham Young University (BYU) have applied the modular notion to intermediate accounting. In this application, the year-long course is divided into ten modules. Each module is further subdivided into two or three quiz modules. The usual instructional module format of terminal objectives for the course, objectives for each module, post-tests, and individualized media applications are evident in this application. In order to individualize the modules in the first semester to accommodate the varied backgrounds of 200 students, three tracks have been developed. All three tracks cover the same material at different rates of exposure. The tracks cover thirteen, fifteen, and nineteen weeks. Students are able to move back and forth between tracks. Teachers also move with the topics to different tracks as their expertise is needed.

The BYU experience with this application of the learning module idea has been positive. They perceive students working harder under this system than under the conventional system even though, as in the Syracuse application, more responsibility is placed on the student for learning. The approach is clearly more organized and more scientific than many university classes in which the objectives of the course may not even be stated. BYU plans continued development.

CONCLUSION

Of the two major applications of the module in education discussed in this paper (modular scheduling and learning modules), the latter has the greatest immediate potential to accounting education. It represents an organized approach to apply the many media available to the educational process. Learning modules enhance students' opportunity for learning by not only increased use of a wide range of technology but by more profitably using the talents of the teacher. Much of the energy and intelligence which teachers now expend in lecturing in the classroom can be shifted in learning modules to working with students in tutorial and small group discussions, and to preparing potental educational materials. The new forms of technology give the teacher added capability and extend the possibilities of education. The "live teacher" cannot and should not "say everything." Students should discover things for themselves and the technology provides this ability. For example, in physical education, slow motion photography, or a recording of a diseased heart beat in medicine, are far better than a teacher's verbal description.

Group-paced and group-prescribed instruction is less individualized and more dehumanizing than the application of machines or technology to education. Students using the learning module approach are able to move to a greater degree at their own pace than they are in group instruction even though both may be time constrained. The use of technology and the module increases the educational alternatives and permits the student his own direction while it encourages work toward established educational objectives.

FOOTNOTES

[1] The Carnegie Commission on Higher Education, *The Fourth Revolution: Instructional Technology in Higher Education* (New York: McGraw-Hill Book Company, June 1972) p. 37.

[2] Commission on Instructional Technology, *To Improve Learning* (Committee on Education and Labor, House of Representatives, March 1970, Doc. No. 40-715-0) p. 29.

[3] U. S. Department of Health, Education and Welfare, *Report on Higher Education* (Doc. No. HE 5.250:50065) Newman Task Force, 1971.

[4] W. Kenneth Richmond, *The Concept of Educational Technology* (Oxford Circle, London, England: Weidenfeld & Nicolson, 1970) p. 17 and *passim*.

[5] See the paper by James Don Edwards, "Programmed Instruction," pp. 278-88 of this book for a more detailed discussion.

[6] D. Dupree, M. Marden, and F. Carter, *Accounting: a Learning Experience* (ALEX) (New York, New York: Prentice-Hall, 1973); also see D. W. Curry and Robert Frame, *Accounting Principles: A Multimedia Program* (Columbus, Ohio: Charles E. Merrill Publishing Co., 1973).

[7] See the paper, "Self-Paced Instruction," pp. 268-77 of this book for a more detailed discussion.

[8] A *schedule module* is that period of time in curriculum scheduling during which the master schedule does not repeat itself. In conventional scheduling this may be one day.

[9] Robert Bush and Dwight Allen, *A New Design for High School Education* (New York, New York: McGraw-Hill Book Co., 1964) p. 21.

[10] *Ibid.*, p. 25.

[11] *Ibid.*, p. 26.

[12] *Ibid.*, p. 29.

[13] Gaynor Petrequin, *Individualized Learning Through Modular-Flexible Programming* (New York, New York: McGraw-Hill Book Company, 1968).

[14] James Koerner, "Educational Technology: Does It Have a Future in the Classroom?" (New York, New York: Saturday Review, May 1973) p. 44.

[15] "Business Schools - A Decade of Ferment," *MBA* (April, 1973).

[16] An individualized learning system is one where the method of instruction has been tailored to individual needs. Note this is different from a self-paced system which has a fixed media application but is usually flexible in the amount of time each student spends on each module within the semester.

[17] A conventional course is defined to be a situation in accounting where the instructional systems consists of a classroom, learning materials, students, and an instructor.

[18] Robert F. Mager, *Preparing Instructional Objectives* (Belmont, California: Fearon Publishing Company, 1962) p. 3.

[19] *Ibid.*, p. 13.

[20] For a discussion of how to prepare behavioral objectives, see D. Z. Williams and D. M. Guy, "Developing Behavioral Objectives for Accounting Education," pp. 231-32 of this book.

[21] *Ibid.*, p. 33.

[22] Edward Thorndike, *Education* (New York, New York: McMillan Co., 1912) p. 167.

[23] See James Lewis, *Administering the Individualized Instruction Program* (West Nyack, New York: Parker Publishing Company, Inc., 1971) for a detailed statement on development and testing.

REFERENCES

Banathy, B., *Instruction Systems* (Belmont, California: Fearon Publishers, 1968).

Bjerstedt, A., *Educational Technology* (New York, New York: John Wiley & Sons, Inc., 1972).

Bush, R., and D. Allen, *A New Design for High School Education* (New York, New York: McGraw-Hill Book Company, 1964).

Carnegie Commission on Higher Education, *The Fourth Revolution* (New York, New York: McGraw-Hill Book Company, 1972).

Commission on Instructional Technology, *To Improve Learning* (Committee on Education and Labor Report, House of Representatives, 1970).

Lewis, James, *Administering the Individualized Instructional Program* (West Nyack, New York: Parker Publishing Company, 1971).

Mager, Robert F., *Preparing Instructional Objectives* (Belmont, California: Fearon Publishers, 1969).

Petrequin, Gaynor, *Individualized Learning Through Modular-Flexible Programming* (New York, New York: McGraw-Hill Book Company, 1968).

Piper, Peter, *Practical Programming* (New York, New York: Holt, Rinehart & Winston, Inc., 1966).

Report on Higher Education (U.S. Department of Health, Education and Welfare, 1971).

Richmond, W. Kenneth, *The Concept of Educational Technology* (Oxford Circle, London, England: Weiderfield and Nicolson, 1970).

Weisgerber, Robert, *Perspectives in Individualized Learning* (Itaska, Illinois: Peacock Publishers, Inc., 1971).

Self-Paced Instruction

Dempsey Dupree
Clarion State College

Introduction

In its earliest stages education was self-paced and individualized. After a number of so-called educational revolutions, self-paced learning is coming back in vogue—this time aided by modern developments in technology. Accounting can be learned very well through self-paced instruction, which promises significant benefits for students, instructors, and school administrators. For best results, self-paced accounting instruction must be carefully controlled by a competent accounting instructor who believes in the learning system being used.

The results of several studies have contributed to a general loss of faith in the contemporary educational process. A 1966 study concluded that the socio-economic level of a student's home was the most significant factor influencing his achievement.[1] Follow-up studies led to the conclusion that "additional school expenditures are unlikely to increase achievement, and redistributing resources will not reduce test score inequality."[2]

Accounting instructors have not been excepted from the pressures for change. As a result, accounting educators are becoming more interested in methodology. Until recently, articles and seminars on techniques for teaching accounting were hard to find. Now some accounting doctoral programs require one or more courses that concentrate on teaching methodology.

New educational buzz words have been coined for novel teaching approaches-- more often than not these are just variations of older teaching methods. One of these approaches, self-paced instruction, is the subject of this paper.

Self-paced instruction is what the name implies–instruction which gives each student a considerable degree of control over his rate of progress. The term is often equated with *individualized instruction,* though individualization suggests that somewhat more than the pace of a course is being tailored to each student's needs. For example, the content of a course, the order (sequence) of progress, and the means of communication (written word, spoken word, visual pictures, etc.) might all be adjusted to the particular needs of each student.[3] Self-pacing applies more specifically to variation of the speed at which a student moves through instructional material.

The degree of control that the student has over his progress may vary considerably with the circumstances. At one extreme, there may be no limit to the time allowed; on the other hand, a student may be permitted to vary his progress only within short time spans, or segments, of a total time allowed to complete the subject.

INITIATING SELF-PACED INSTRUCTION

Professors, like other people, sometimes feel threatened by change. Only those who are unable or unwilling to adapt to a changing world, however, have any reasons for concern. Self-paced instruction may change the teacher's role, but it can never replace him.

Actually, the professor's mission can be upgraded through advances in educational technology. He can become an "educational manager" instead of an "information disseminator." Learning programs and teaching assistants can take over the more drudgerous aspects of the educational process. The professor will then have more time for planning and coordinating his courses, and for motivating students through personal contact that has previously been impractical.

Modular Arrangement

Self-pacing is facilitated by breaking a course down into manageable sub-units, often referred to as "modules." Textbook chapters are, in a sense, modules; and so are class periods, for that matter.

For self-paced instruction, modules should be as autonomous as possible. Each module then constitutes a self contained "mini-course." Modules dealing with only one clearly identifiable topic are sometimes referred to as "single-concept" study units. Conceivably, a student could be given credit for completing a fraction of a total course, even if he never finishes all of the modules.

Modular arrangement aids in tailoring a course to individual student needs. A particular student may be allowed to bypass modules dealing with subject matter that he has covered somewhere else. Instructors or students also have more flexibility in rearranging the order of the modules to suit their own needs.

Behavioral Objectives

Any course of study can be improved by explicitly stating the course objectives. With self-paced instruction, performance objectives should be stated for each module (sub-unit) of instruction. Students should be told in as precise terms as possible just what is expected of them. Before objectives can be communicated to students, instructors must know what these objectives are themselves. In the past, relatively few college instructors have bothered to state learning objectives in behavioral terms; accounting instructors are no exception.

A *behavioral objective* is simply a statement of the kind of performance that will be accepted as proof that the student has learned something.[4] It tells the student what he must be able to do. Thus, most behavioral objectives start with the words "be able to," followed by a description of some observable behavior. For example, at some stage in their study of accounting, students should "be able to prepare a general journal entry in proper form."

The use of vague words that can be misinterpreted should be avoided. The idea is to communicate to the student as specifically as possible just what he is supposed to learn. Of particular importance is the clarity of the verbs used. Explicit action verbs are preferred over fuzzy terms indicating mental states. For instance, it is difficult to determine whether a student appreciates something, or if he knows, understands, or likes a thing. On the other hand, it is easier to observe students stating, writing, listing, differentiating, or building things.

The objectives for the more conceptual aspects of a course are somewhat more difficult to state in unambiguous terms. We may want a student to "be able to defend his views" on some controversial accounting matter. But just how is he expected to defend his views—with his fists? Remember, objectives should deal with observable actions. Perhaps the practical way to judge a student's ability to take a stand is to have him state why he believes as he does, either orally or in writing. A student might be expected to "be able to state in his own words arguments for and against the cost basis concept of accounting." Furthermore, he might be asked to "state his opinion as to whether or not the cost basis concept should be abandoned" as a result of his analysis of the pros and cons of the matter.

Any number of other conceptual-type objectives might stem from those already stated as examples. A student might be expected to "be able to state the effects on other accounting assumptions of substituting a current value concept for the cost basis concept." The fact that the more conceptual objectives are difficult to pin down should not prevent us from stating them as well as we can.

Sequencing Instructional Material

Instructional materials should be arranged in a sequence which is easy to follow. Teachers and writers are more apt to employ a reasonable sequence of steps when they have behavioral objectives clearly in mind. Instructional materials should move, step by step, toward accomplishment of the objectives of a study unit.

Sequencing means about the same as programming—data are arranged in an orderly series of steps that are easy to follow. Programs may be either tightly or loosely structured; they may be in linear or branching form, or a combination of both.[5]

The means, or channels, by which communication takes place are known as "media." The media employed by most instructors have been books and lectures. Written materials involve only one of the student's senses—that of sight. Additionally, word symbols must be converted by a reader into mental images to be meaningful.

Lectures involve both sight and sound senses, but students still have to convert words into mental images. Through use of visual aids, a lecturer may get his message across more effectively. Books, too, may contain visuals that help to convey messages to the reader.

Some individuals comprehend better from one medium than from another. For example, some people gain more from listening than by reading; others absorb more readily from the written word. Generally speaking, however, the rate of learning increases as more senses are employed in the learning process. You certainly have a better idea of what a lamb is when you see it, hear it, touch it, and smell it, (and even taste it) than if someone were to describe one to you in words. The same observation holds for spinach, sex, swimming and, yes, also accounting. The more completely involved people are in the learning process, the faster they learn and the longer they retain what they learn.

A considerable range of equipment (hardware) is now available for use by educators. In fact, hardware capacity far exceeds the software (educational programs) available for use on it. The present position of learning technology might be compared to that of information processing the 1950s. Although computer equipment of that time was much less sophisticated than today, its capacity far exceeded the computer programs available.

Early computer programs unsurprisingly attempted to have the computers duplicate what had previously been done by hand. As time passed the newly developed programs were uniquely suited to computer capabilities. This is not too different from the tendency of most educators to use a media like television to simply broadcast lectures. And then they ponder why they get the same performance results with television that they did with live lectures.

Much of the media currently available is capable of conveying simultaneous audio and video signals. Slides and filmstrips have been around a long time, but inexpensive equipment that will advance visuals automatically in sequence with an audio track only recently became available. Visual motion display with sound has been available a long time also, in the form of movies. Television, though somewhat younger, has been on the scene for many years.

Self-paced instructional programs should use media best suited to the message to be conveyed. Of necessity, equipment used for self-paced instruction must be efficient and economical enough for individualized use.

Testing

Testing becomes more important than ever with self-paced instruction. In fact, a student might not be allowed to go beyond a module until he has proven that the objectives for that module have been attained to a reasonable proficiency level.

Clearly stated objectives in behavioral terms leave no doubt in either students' or instructors' minds as to what will be tested. Ideally, the objectives for each module should be tested as the module is completed. If the objectives are clear enough, they can serve as criteria, or standards, by which a student's success is measured.

Some instructors prefer to keep secret the criteria by which students are to be judged. Under these circumstances a course is more of a game than a joint educational endeavor between the instructor and the student. The student's success, as measured by the grade he receives, depends on his ability to guess what the instructor intends to test.

Testing can also help to determine the route that each student takes through educational materials. Students may be given tests before they commence study to identify what they already know about the subject matter. Carefully administered pre-tests can determine what objectives the student can already attain, thus allowing him to by-pass some of the instructional material. Tests administered for the purpose of determining what a student does and does not know are sometimes called "diagnostic" tests.

Grading

In the words of the American Association of State Colleges and Universities, one of the challenges to be met by contemporary education is that "traditional grading practices should be replaced with competence-based evaluations that attest to what a person knows rather than how many credits he has earned as a result of attending fifty-minute classes three times per week for four years."[6] Tests are nothing more than evaluation devices. Any type of grading system presumes an evaluation system by which a student's performance can be compared to something. Testing and grading go hand in hand.

Traditional grading practices are not particularly useful for instruction which is truly self-paced. Ideally, every student should be able to achieve at a satisfactory level, provided a sufficient amount of time is spent with the instructional materials. Students with exceptional ability and background simply progress at a faster rate than those who are less fortunate. Those who fail to achieve at a satisfactory level, regardless of the time taken, would seem to lack either interest in, or aptitude for, the subject. They should then be counseled to shift their efforts to other areas for which they are more suited.

Some teachers have long been disenchanted with the practice of grading by quality levels, as though students were products of a production process. A person's self-esteem is surely damaged when he is labeled as a failure, or even as a substandard performer. One is hardly "at fault" for having been born with low intellect, or into an environment that has inhibited his intellectual development.

Yet people seem to need some indication of how well they "measure up"—or at least they want to know when they are ready to move on to more difficult material. Potential employers, graduate schools, and others also need to differentiate between applicants, so as to select those most likely to succeed in jobs or educational programs.

Criterion testing can help to assure that students have achieved at the required level before they move on. One who is absolutely incapable of achieving would presumably never reach the end of a course of study that is too difficult for him. In fact, the time required to complete a course might be substituted for letter grades as a measure of achievement. As with letter grades, there would be no obvious disclosure of the reasons why a student performed as he did. He may have been ill, disinterested, disorganized, or mentally deficient. If he completes a course, however, no matter how long it takes, this will indicate, at least, the student has tenacity.

Employers, graduate schools, etc., can use specially prepared tests to differentiate between individual applicants. The results of such tests, along with the time intervals taken to complete self-paced courses, would provide measures of a student's relative suitability for advanced academic work, for employment, and for other endeavors.

Instructional Programs Available

Two different instructional programs suitable for self-paced accounting instruction are currently available from publishing companies. Both programs are for the introductory accounting course, and were introduced in 1973. Other programs will likely become available in the future. A number of schools have experimented with their own locally-produced materials.

Accounting: A Learning Experience (ALEX), by Dupree, Marder, and Carter is available from Prentice-Hall. It is a flexible system suitable for individualized, small-group, or large-group use. ALEX consists of fifty modules, each containing a coordinated filmstrip and audio tape, a *Student Outline*, and separate *Student Resource Materials* in written form. The *Student Resource Materials* also contain extensive questions and problems. The audio-visual unit is the core of each module, and may be used independently of the written materials. The study-testing sequence for using this package on a self-paced basis is illustrated in Figure 1.

Accounting Principles: A Multi-media Program, by Curry and Frame is available from Charles E. Merrill Publishing Company. This program consists of a

STUDY-TESTING PROCEDURE FOR SELF-PACED STUDENTS

Figure 1

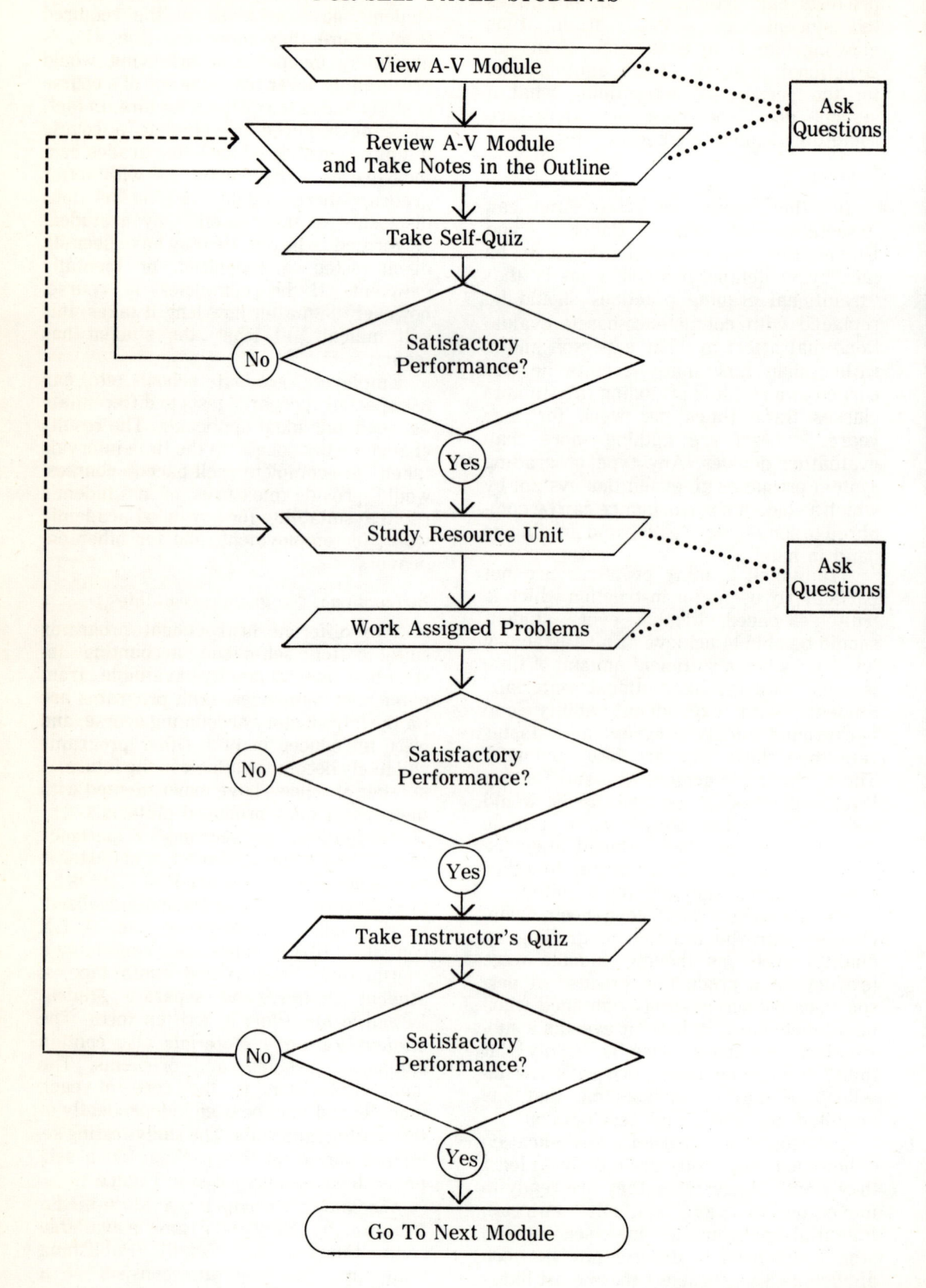

written textbook with integrated filmstrips and coordinated audio tapes. There are thirty modules somewhat comparable to textbook chapters, which are further subdivided into sections. Some of the sections are in written form, while others are in an audio-visual format.

ADVANTAGES OF SELF-PACING

A number of benefits may stem from self-paced instruction, as compared to more traditional lockstep approaches to education. Students, instructors, and administrators may prefer self-pacing because of the advantages of this approach to learning.

Student Advantages

Self-paced instruction is oriented more towards learning than teaching. Students' needs are considered to be more important than those of instructors and administrators.

There can be no doubt that students' interests and abilities differ. To require that all students in a course move along together is rather unreasonable. In the past this problem has been minimized by the selection processes operating in the academic marketplace. Students' abilities have been equalized to some extent through admissions requirements, and by their preferences for certain schools over others.

College admission policies, as well as the preferences of students for certain colleges, have tended to group students with similar abilities and interests together. High achievers have generally sought admission to the most prestigious colleges--provided, of course, they could afford the cost. Conversely, the more prestigious colleges have generally attempted to limit admissions to those who were high achievers. The next most "deserving" layer of students in terms of ability, interest, and wealth chose to attend colleges that seemed to fit them, and so on down the line.

In recent times, admission policies have been turned topsy-turvy. For one thing, over-expansion in higher education has resulted in stiff competition for college students. For another, the traditional measures of "ability" are being seriously questioned. Finally, traditional admission policies are being questioned on moral grounds. Many thoughtful people contend that college admission standards have helped to perpetuate social class divisions by denying opportunities to the underprivileged.

Student abilities, backgrounds, and interests are apt to vary over a wide range. Learning approaches should make allowances for these individual variations. Self-paced (and individualized) instruction makes sense under these circumstances.

Self-pacing makes it possible for students to progress through instructional materials at their own speed. One student with unusual ability and a high level of interest may finish a course in a few weeks; another student may want to take several academic terms to complete the same course. Because of his own unique background, ability, or interest, a particular student may take more (or less) than average time with particular topics within a course.

Students may choose the hours during which they study when instruction is self-paced. Some people are better able to comprehend things in the morning, others in the afternoon, and some are at their mental peaks late at night. Additionally, job or family responsibilities oftentimes conflict with scheduled class hours. Finally, the length of time that people can continue to study productively varies. Self-paced instruction allows students to establish study patterns that meet their individual needs.

Instructional materials that have been adapted for self-paced use also offer other student advantages. By their nature, they are readily available for review at later points in time. Even students in advanced courses may need to go back to elementary modules to overcome deficiencies, or just to refresh their memories.

Self-paced instruction personally involves students in the learning process. A student who fails to progress at a satisfactory rate is forced to assume at least some of the responsibility for his plight.

Instructor Advantages

Although oriented more towards learning than teaching, self-paced instruction can also assist instructors. Learning materials that have been organized into a carefully sequenced, modular format may be used over and over again. Once initial planning has been done, an instructor's preparation time can be reduced considerably. The time saved can be used for personally relating to students, testing, evaluating, and for supervising teaching assistants. Teaching aides, graduate assistants, and even students in advanced courses can assume routine duties of administering the program.

Instructors may vary to suit themselves the order in which learning modules are used. For example, some accounting instructors like to introduce manufacturing accounting to students relatively early; others prefer to postpone this topic until students have had more exposure to the subject. Instructional modules covering manufacturing accounting can be shifted by the instructor to meet his own preferences.

Administrative Advantages

Self-paced instruction also offers some overall administrative advantages. For one thing, it can help to standardize the content and quality of instruction in a particular course. Most schools schedule multiple sections of introductory accounting, taught at various times by a number of accounting instructors. The instructors' qualifications vary in terms of ability, experience, dedication, etc. Clearly stated behavioral objectives, a standard core of instructional materials, and criterion-based testing can help to assure that students will be able to perform at a standard quality level.

Self-paced instructional materials can be easily adapted to a variety of circumstances. Courses may be taken at extension centers or by correspondence without losing as much quality as was necessary in the past. Students who have acquired knowledge in limited areas through work experience can be routed around the modules they do not need. A well-designed, self-paced program is equally suitable for continuing education, external degree curricula, or for preparation of students for obtaining credit by examination.

Transferability of credit for what one already knows is much more feasible when well-defined objectives, content, and testing are available. Gaps in a student's background are easy enough to remedy once they are identified. Previous college work in a self-paced program should be relatively easy to evaluate. Once again, individuals should be able to review at any point in time learning materials with which they are already familiar. This is the quickest way to bring one's knowledge level back up to where it was at the time a course was completed.

Self-paced instructional modules can be kept more current than more traditional books and other materials. Modules can be selectively improved and up-dated, always keeping the best materials and discarding those that are inferior or out-dated.

As mentioned earlier, pressures are mounting to either abandon or improve traditional grading policies. For one thing, a particular letter grade means different things at different schools, and even to different instructors within the same school. Some instructors have no clearly defined grading standards and their students, in particular, are frustrated in attempting to perform at some unidentifiable quality level.

Failure rates should be minimized. Conceivably, outright student failure could be eliminated with self-paced instruction. Students might be allowed as much time as necessary to meet the required performance standards. Where students' aptitudes or interests are inadequate for accounting (or any other subject) they may be counseled to shift to other areas more suited to their particular needs.

Some progress measure may be desired by students, instructors, and others. Time can be substituted for letter grades as pointed out earlier in this paper. A student who completes a course (or a college curriculum) in record time must be superior in some respects unless, of course, other valid demands on the time of other students slowed their pace. Also, time is considerably less subjective than letter grades as a performance measure. Students are less likely to complain about the time *they* have taken to complete a course than about letter grades that an *instructor* assigns to them.

Self-paced instruction is not likely to be a budget panacea. It would appear, however, to offer economies under the proper circumstances. Highly paid professors can handle more students effectively when teacher aides are available to take over routine paperwork and tutoring chores. They should have more time for solving unusual problems, relating to students, course development, and for research and writing when they do not have to prepare continually for daily lecture "performances."

The need for lecture halls should also diminish. In fact, instructional materials may be used in laboratories, libraries, dormitories, cafeterias, or almost any place else. Learning laboratories may be kept open as many hours as necessary to meet the students' needs. Instructors do not care to lecture late at night, but many students prefer to study at these hours.

PROBLEMS WITH SELF-PACING

Self-paced instruction is not all sunshine and roses. Some problems with self-pacing are inherent; others develop when planning or administration has been defective.

Student Problems

Probably the greatest student problem with self-paced instruction is the tendency of many to put off study. Most of today's college students have been brought up on lockstep instruction. They are accustomed to being pushed through courses on an inflexible schedule. Many, if not most, students have difficulty adjusting to a program in which they must assume responsibility for their own progress. They tend to procrastinate, especially when they are enrolled at the same time in other courses that are conducted on a lockstep basis. They may do assignments for other subjects to meet class deadlines, leaving self-paced work for a mythical future time when demands on their time are expected to be lighter.

Students who have been pushed and "spoon fed" for so long may have to learn how to organize their time, and how to rely on their own self-motivation. As an interim step, instructors can set periodic deadlines when segments of self-paced work are supposed to be done. They may have to cajole, plead with, and even threaten individual students to get them to maintain a pace that is reasonable for them. Students must also learn to seek help from instructors, tutors, and classmates when it is needed. This problem can be overcome to some degree by providing tutors or lab assistants in areas where students normally study.

Instructor Problems

The instructor's role in self-paced instruction is an extremely important one. Self-paced instruction must be carefully organized and administered--otherwise, the result will be utter confusion and disorganization.

Keeping track of students' progress is no easy matter when each student is at a different point in the course at any one time. The paperwork burden is inherently greater than with a traditional lockstep approach. Use of frequent, criterion-based tests further compounds paperwork problems. Experimenters at Clarion found that a host of manila folders and a honeycomb set of in--and--out baskets helped considerably in keeping track of paperwork of all kinds.

Maintaining control over quizzes and tests is another problem that instructors encounter. This problem is not as serious, however, as one might expect--provided frequent, criterion-based testing is employed. Once detailed performance objectives are pinned down, the instructor may be relatively unconcerned about just how the student becomes able to achieve. In the ALEX accounting program, for example, students are provided with self-quizzes and recommended solutions that closely parallel the instructor's quizzes on the learning objectives.

Cumulative, problem-type accounting tests are also fairly safe from cheating attempts. Tests may be easily differentiated by changing a few key figures, without detracting to any degree from their comparability. Consider, for example, a test problem on the accounting cycle for a small, service-type business. Students who can perform successfully on one problem should also be able to do others, regardless of how they learned to perform. Additionally, use of a considerable number of quizzes and tests makes it unlikely that any one student will have managed to gain access to very many in advance—especially when a number of differentiated versions are in use. At Clarion, for example, students in the first-semester accounting course are subjected to approximately thirteen hours of testing—and this does not include the assigned "homework" problems that must be done.

Administrative Problems

Some problems encountered with self-paced instruction are of particular concern to administrators. Not the least of these is the initial investment required for both equipment (hardware) and instructional programs (software). Equipment suitable for audio-visual programs is expensive, though it can usually be utilized over a number of years. Programs suitable for self-paced use must either be purchased or produced locally; either way, a substantial investment is required. Once acquired, however, software can usually be used for a number of terms, depending upon the speed with which materials become obsolete.

Another administrative problem is encountered when both self-paced and lockstep instructional programs are used simultaneously. A variety of scheduling problems can result when students are completing a subject at times other than the end of a term. One compromise approach is to permit students to go at their own speed within a school term, but to require them to complete each subject by the end of one term. Students who complete a course early should have something productive to do during the time remaining in the term. If another self-paced course is not available, they might be encouraged to undertake an "independent study" project for extra college credit.

CONCLUSION

Progressive accounting instructors should be able to adapt to current trends in higher education with little difficulty. "Traditional" accounting courses have long incorporated some of the learning approaches that are just now being embraced by other subject areas. For instance, accounting education has always been performance-oriented as evidenced by the type of tests that have been given. The step to behavioral objectives and criterion-based testing should be easy for accounting teachers.

The step to self-paced instruction is a more difficult one. A significant investment in both hardware and software is required. At this point in time, equipment capacity far exceeds the software programs available. Instructional programs for introductory accounting are now available from publishing companies in an audio-visual format suitable for self-paced use.

Self-paced instruction can hold benefits for students, instructors, and administrators. There are, of course, some problems that must be overcome—particularly when students and institutions have had experience only with lockstep approaches to education.

FOOTNOTES

[1] James S. Coleman et al., *Equality of Educational Opportunity* (Washington, D.C.: U.S. Government Printing Office, 1966).

[2] Christopher Jencks et al., *Inequality: A Reassessment of the Effect of Family and Schooling in America* (New York: Basic Books, Inc., 1972) p. 109.

[3] For a discussion of the broader concept of individualized instruction, see the paper by J.C. Kinard and C.H. Stanley, "Rigidity of Systematic Flexibility? An Individualized Introductory Accounting Course," p of this book.

[4] For a description of how to prepare behavioral objectives, see D.Z. Williams and D.M. Guy, "Developing Behavioral Objectives for Accounting Education," pp. of this book.

[5] For a brief, uncomplicated coverage of programmed instruction techniques see *Developing Programmed Instructional Materials* by Espich and Williams (Belmont, California: Fearon Publishers, 1967).

[6] American Association of State Colleges and Universities, "Academic Change and Improvement."

REFERENCES

American Association of State Colleges and Universities, "Academic Change and Improvement," undated pamphlet, Washington.

Ashby, Eric, "Machines, Understanding, and Learning: Reflections on Technology in Education," *The Graduate Journal*, Vol. 7, No. 2, Austin, Texas 1967.

Carnegie Commission on Higher Education, *The Fourth Revolution: Instructional Technology in Higher Education* (New York, New York: McGraw-Hill Book Company, 1972).

Coleman, James et al., *Equality of Educational Opportunity*, U.S. Government Printing Office, Washington, 1966.

Espich, James E. and Williams, Bill, *Developing Programmed Instruction* (Belmont, California: Fearon Publishers, 1967).

Feinsot, Aaron and Sigel, Efren, *Breaking the Institutional Mold* (White Plains, New York: Knowledge Industry Publications, 1971).

Fink, Ronn, "Committee Recommends State's First Open University," *Pennsylvania Education*, Vol. 4, No. 7, Harrisburg, Pa., March 1973.

Jencks, Christopher et al., *Inequality: A Reassessment of the Effect of Family and Schooling in America* (New York: Basic Books, Inc. 1972).

Mager, Robert F., *Preparing Instructional Objectives* (Belmont, California: Fearon Publishers, 1962).

Young, Roger et al., (Editors) *A Guide to Independent Study Through Correspondence Instruction* (National University Extension Association, Washington, 1970-72).

Programmed Instruction

James Don Edwards
The University of Georgia

Introduction

Accounting educators are constantly exploring new innovations in educational technology to provide students with a greater opportunity to learn. In recent years, the development of programmed instruction methods such as the linear and intrinsic techniques have brought about a revolution in education generally, and the adaptation of such programming methods to accounting education is proceeding swiftly. In order to fully appreciate the implications of programmed instruction in future years, and understanding of its basic concepts, applications, and limitations is needed by all accounting educators today.

Programmed instruction, while viewed by many as a recent development in education, can be traced to 1809 when H. Chard was granted a patent for "a device designed to teach reading."[1] However, B. Fred Skinner, a present authority in the field of programmed instruction, attributed Halcyon Skinner with the invention of the first true "teaching machine"— another piece of equipment for teaching reading, patented in 1866.[2]

Later, the efforts of psychologist S.L. Pressey in the 1920's to create a machine which could be used for multiple-choice testing as well as for teaching, was a significant development in the study of the possible application of programs to "produce changes in the effectiveness of instruction."[3] His machines were the first to utilize the concept of "feedback" — a fundamental characteristic of all modern programmed instruction.

However, the modern foundations of programmed instruction date from the 1954 paper entitled "The Science of Learning and the Art of Teaching" by Professor B. Fred Skinner of Harvard.[4] He contended that educational material "could be regarded as an accumulative repertoire of behavior which could be analyzed logically into a number of small 'steps' representing increments of successive approximation to final mastery."[5]

Before describing in detail the theory and design underlying a typical program of today, an examination of the basic principles of learning is needed. An educational system should be designed to conform to these principles to insure effective instruction and maximum learning. Although several principles have been advanced by numerous authors, W.A. Johnson listed seven fundamental ones:

1. *The Principle of Reinforcement.* The learner should be reinforced in the learning situation. Reinforcement should be positive in nature whenever possible, and should be as continuous in nature as possible.

2. *The Principle of Active Participation.* The learner should be actively involved in the learning situation and not just a passive observer. This activity does not necessarily have to be physical.

3. *The Principle of Discovery.* The learner should discover relationships and principles himself rather than having these relationships and principles demonstrated to him.

4. *The Principle of Motivation.* The learner must be motivated to learn. This should be intrinsic, positive motivation whenever possible.

5. *The Principle of Meaningfulness*. The material should be as meaningful as possible in nature and be readily internalized into the cognitive structure of the learner.

6. *The Principle of Sequence*. The material should be organized in such a way as to move logically to the end goal, and that goal should be clearly in sight.

7. *The Principle of Transfer*. The material should be taught in such a way as to facilitate proper transfer to other situations.[6]

What are the essential characteristics of programmed instruction and how do they relate to these learning principles? Although several different variations of programmed instruction are now widely used, all of them conform to the following generally recognized characteristics, compiled here by J.L. Hughes:[7]

Every student is able to pace himself throughout the program, thereby allowing "more latitude for individual differences in learning ability."[8]

The student is given a "relatively small" bit of information (called a frame) and then asked to answer a question or to complete a statement based on the information presented to him. "This is known technically as the *stimulus*."[9] The student then answers the question or completes the statement, or in "technical terms, he is said to be making a *response* to the stimulus presented."[10]

Next, the program gives the correct response to the student. If he was incorrect, the program explains why the response was incorrect. "By this kind of *feedback*, he is rewarded (reinforced)"[11] if he gives the correct answer. This same cycle of "stimulus—response—reinforcement of the correct answer is repeated" for each frame until all of the desired material is presented.[12] The *program* is the total of these numerous sequential frames. The objective of such programs is to reduce the error rate of the student.

A logical question at this point would be: How does programmed instruction contrast with more traditional forms of teaching? The student is more active in the learning process with the use of programmed instruction materials because he is required to respond at more frequent intervals than in more conventional forms of instruction. Greater reinforcement is also claimed with the use of programmed instruction because of the immediate feedback the student receives in each frame.

By structuring material into smaller segments, programmed instruction also requires less time and preparation by the student before a test of his comprehension is made. In conventional forms of instruction, such as lectures and traditional textbooks, "there may be gaps in the presentation which the student is left to fill in for himself. It is therefore possible for a student to miss something during the early stages of a presentation and never fully understand the subsequent material."[13] Because typical programs are the result of much testing and the results of actual performances by selected samples of students, they are generally more logical in material presentation, are more flexible to change, and are more sensitive to student demands on the effectiveness of the presentation. A more exhaustive examination of the advantages and disadvantages of programmed instruction, along with empirical research findings, will be presented at the conclusion of this paper.

Several noteworthy comments can be made regarding programmed instruction. First, programmed instruction is often erroneously compared to other recent innovations in multi-media instruction, such as educational films and television. The latter type material is designed primarily for group presentations, i.e., the pace of all the students is the same, as is the case with more conventional methods. However, programmed instruction enables the student to proceed with the material at his own pace.[14]

Another common misconception is that programmed instruction replaces the teacher. In this regard, Wilbur Schramm has said, "The argument that programmed instruction will replace the teacher is a kind of sensational and uninformed journalism which is unworthy of attention."[15]

Although learning materials are programmed primarily to benefit the student, there are benefits accruing to the instructor. The primary one is that they allow the instructor to engage in *creative teaching*. Because of the degree of comprehension attained by the student, the instructor is relieved of the rather boring task of repeating over and over again the material from the text. He is able to devote his time to guiding and planning the student's learning experiences for him and with him in order to further stimulate and motivate the student. The teacher is also able to devote more class time to relate his own experiences in order to make the subject matter he presents in the classroom more realistic, relevant, and interesting.

In short, the instructor using programmed instructional materials has the opportunity to be more creative, rather than repetitious, in the classroom. Greater assurance is provided that the student interacts with the material. Streuling and Holstrum have stated, "programmed material requires continued active responses on the part of *each* student in the class; whereas under the conventional teaching methods, the instructor is often limited to a response from one student at a time."[16]

Programmed instruction more clearly delineates the role of the teacher and the student in the learning process. Although the teacher is able to engage in more creative teaching, he cannot and should not try to "learn" for the student. The use of programmed instructional materials places the responsibility for learning squarely on the student himself. *The instructor teaches; the student learns.*

APPLICATION OF PROGRAMMED INSTRUCTION TO ACCOUNTING

To this point, the main objective of this paper has been to briefly describe the history, theory, and essential characteristics of programmed instruction. Perhaps the most important question that we as accounting educators can ask is whether or not programmed instruction can be applied to the subject matter of our discipline. To answer this question, consider this definition of programmed instruction by Wilbur Schramm:

Programmed instruction consists of a reproducible series of learning acts arranged in sequence to lead a learner efficiently from some behavior he has mastered to some new behavior which is the goal of the instruction.[17]

As is evident from this definition, programmed instruction is most effective when the subject matter itself can be subdivided into small increments. Obviously, such subjects as creative writing, art or music appreciation, etc. are not very adaptable to programmed instruction, but the field of accounting, particularly at the elementary level, is.

At least two possible applications of programmed instruction in accounting courses are readily apparent, (1) the text itself is programmed and the course is structured around the text, and (2) programmed instructional materials could be used as a supplement in more traditionally oriented course designs for certain aspects of a part of the course (the accounting cycle, for example).

In his article, "Programmed and Non-Programmed Instruction: Integration Criteria in Curriculum Design," John W. Buckley classified accounting subject matter into these four principal types:

1. *Concepts* (terms and definitions)
2. *Techniques* (formulae and procedures
3. *Structured Problems* (problem-solving)
4. *Unstructured Problems* (problem-discovery).[18]

According to Buckley, "These information types are basic—they exist within each unit of study and within the overall course... It is important to recognize and classify subject matter types because each type (and sub-type) may be learned most efficiently by using a particular instructional method."[19] In order to have an effective curriculum design, he asserts that an "understanding of the nature of the body of knowledge on the one hand and of available learning conduits on the other" is essential.[20] The decision whether or not to utilize programmed instruction would thus be unique for each course; it would consider the various instructional media available—lectures, printed materials, audio visuals, etc., as well as the learning environment.[21]

Buckley also stated that "Student adaptation to a coordinated system of non-programmed and programmed learning will occur readily if curriculum design is sound. They (students) are likely to be more confused with programmed learning where it is used as a distinct and non-roordinative adjunct to conventional learning."[22] To be most effective, therefore, the use of programmed instructional materials as a supplement in conventional accounting courses should be well planned and integrated into the design and presentation of the course.

If used correctly, Billy E. Askins concluded from one study that "adjunct programs, designed to familiarize students with the use of accounting manuals as well as to teach technical skills, can be effectively developed by using a combination of programming techniques."[23]

TYPES OF PROGRAMMED INSTRUCTION

Skinnerian Programs

As was noted earlier, modern programmed instruction was pioneered largely by the efforts of Harvard professor B. Fred Skinner in the 1940's and 1950's. He attempted to apply the results of operant conditioning on animals to the art of teaching humans. "Operant conditioning is a process whereby animal or human subjects are stimulated to behave toward predetermined goals through a series of small actions and consequent reinforcements. These small steps of action form a chain of *successive* approximations of behavior until the desired end behavior is displayed by the subject."[24] Skinner found such a process to be quite effective when written as an adjunct program to one of his psychology courses at Harvard.[25]

At the heart of "Skinnerian" programs lies the assumption that the process of learning takes place most efficiently if questions are structured in such a way as to induce a correct response from the student. The learning concept of reinforcement is thus achieved, and immediate feedback is available to the student. As applied to humans, reinforcement "may be simply knowledge of the results of their responses, most people being pleased to learn that they have acted correctly."[26] For a program to be most effective, it should be designed in such a way as to minimize the possibility of student errors. An error rate of 5-10 percent is generally deemed acceptable.

The main characteristics of the Skinnerian program have been analyzed by Wilbur Schramm to be:

1. an ordered sequence of stimulus items
2. to each of which a student responds in some specified way
3. his responses being reinforced by immediate knowledge of results
4. so that he moves by small steps
5. therefore making few errors and practicing mostly correct responses
6. from what he knows, by a process of successively closer approximation, toward what he is supposed to learn from the program.[27]

Compare these characteristics with the essential principles of learning listed on pages 278-79. It is no wonder that the Skinnerian program has been claimed as a truly revolutionary advance in educational technology. Incidentally, Skinnerian programs are often referred to as *linear* because all students, regardless of their individual pace, proceed through the same steps (or *frames*) in the same order.

As is true with other types of programming, linear programs utilize the concept of *fading* or *vanishing* cues or prompts. "In the beginning of the program, the learner is prompted, given some broad hints or *cues* that, in context, provide relatively easy signs to successive response."[28] As the program progresses, the number and extent of such cues is diminished. The goal of such action is "to make the learner finally independent of the program";[29] his responses should come more from his own understanding of the material.[30]

While the basic requirements of all linear programs is that frames be presented in sequential order, several techniques are now in use to accomplish this objective. In one variation the information and question of the first frame is presented at the top of the page and the student turns to the top of the next page to check his answer. Thereafter the student turns the next page to read the next frame, also at the top of the page. He then turns to the following page for the correct response. In this way, the student proceeds through the program text until he has read all of the frames and answers at the tops of the pages. He then starts over at the first page, reading the second row of frames and answers until he reaches the last page of the text. He then begins on the first page reading the frames and answers on the third row from the top of the page. This process is repeated until all of the frames of the program have been completed in sequential order.

Often, the student will be required to write his responses on a separate sheet of paper, thus permitting several students to use the same programmed text.[31] In order to reduce the number of pages, often the correct response to a frame is located on the back of the page, or to the left or right of the next frame. All of these variations are termed "horizontal" presentations, for obvious reasons.

"Vertical" presentations, on the other hand, present the frames in much the same way as does a conventional textbook.[32]

The correct response is printed immediately before or to the left or right of the next frame. Usually some material is needed to cover the answer to prevent the student from "peeking" at the correct response before he has attempted to answer the question.[33]

Most of the variations discussed above were designed primarily to improve the presentation format as well as to reduce the size and cost of programmed materials.[34]

According to Wilbur Schramm, "about 19 out of 20 programs being made today are Skinnerian programs."[35] Several linear programs have been written to assist in accounting instruction. One such effort is *The Accounting Process: A Program for Self-Instruction* by Gerald O. Wentworth, A. Thompson Montgomery, James A. Gowen, and Thomas W. Harrell. As its title implies, the text is primarily designed as a supplement to the typical elementary accounting course. Note the linear format of the following frames from this text, dealing with a review of the steps in the preparation of a balance sheet:

8-1 Remember that one major responsibility of the accounting system involves preparation of the Balance Sheet and the Income Statement. This responsibility is that of _____ _____reporting.	financial
8-2 The financial reporting responsibility involves the periodic preparation of two outputs, the_____ _____and the _____ _____ _____.	Balance Sheet Income Statement
8-3 The first step in preparing the Balance Sheet is to make sure that all entries reflecting the period's transactions have been journalized and posted to the proper accounts in the __ _____ _____.	Ledger
8-4 Next, all the ledger account balances are summarized to verify that the "books are in balance," or in other words, that total debit balances equal total _____ _____. This step is called taking a trial balance.	credit balances

Programmed Instruction

8-5 After making sure that all entries have been journalized and _____to the Ledger, the accountant takes a _____.

posted

trial balance

8-6 The trial balance involves summarizing all Ledger account balances to see if total _____balances equal total _____balances.

debit

credit

8-7 Next, the accountant makes special adjusting entries, which will be described later. After this, the accountant makes his closing entries, which eventually consolidate such temporary holding accounts as the revenue and expense accounts into the permanent account_____.

Retained Earnings

8-8 After making special adjusting entries, the accountant consolidates temporary holding accounts into the permanent, or real, accounts by making appropriate_____.

closing entries

8-9 The final step in preparing the Balance Sheet is to list all the _____account balances on the conventional Balance Sheet form.

permanent (real)

8-10 To review, the first step in preparing the Balance Sheet is to _____. (Answer in your own words.)

Make sure that all entries have been journalized and posted to the Ledger

8-11 The second step is to take the _____.

trial balance

8-12 The third step is to make special adjusting entries. The fourth is to make the _____entries, which consolidate all temporary holding accounts into the _____ accounts.

closing

permanent (real)

8-13 The final step is to list all the _____ account balances on the conventional _____ form.

permanent

Balance Sheet

Also note the use of cues and the review frames. Much the same format is used in *The Accounting Process: A Programmed Adaptation* by H.A. Finney and Herbert E. Miller as a supplement to their conventional text, *Principles of Accounting*. (Introductory), Sixth Edition.

An example of a completely programmed linear text is *Principles of Accounting,* edited by Sidney Davidson. This text follows the conventional arrangement of elementary accounting texts, but it also incorporates the Skinnerian programming technique to insure that the student is actively engaged in the learning process by his responses and subsequent feedback during the study of the text. As is true with many programmed texts, Davidson's book includes a self review at the conclusion of each chapter to further test the student's understanding of the material.

Intrinsic (Scrambled) Programs

As was noted earlier in this paper, one of the first attempts at programmed instruction was the multiple-choice testing machine of psychologist S.L. Pressey in the 1920s. However, the work of Norman Crowder in military training during the 1940s and 1950s refined this technique into now what is known as the *intrinsic* or *scrambled* type of programmed instruction.

Briefly described, the "basic principle is to program multiple-choice questions throughout conventional prose material. The questions are primarily for diagnostic purposes as a periodic check upon student progress."[36] With intrinsic programs, unlike linear programs, "each student determines the sequence of frames by his responses to the multiple-choice questions contained in the frames."[37]

The typical intrinsic program allows for different student rates of learning by the following procedure. The student is directed to different pages, depending on his answer to the multiple-choice question. If he chooses an incorrect answer, he is given an explanation of his error and is instructed to return to the original question and try again. If he chooses the correct answer, he is instructed to proceed to the next frame. This technique is known as *branching*, i.e., the slower learners are exposed to additional material to aid in their comprehension of the subject matter, while the faster learner is able to move more rapidly and directly through the material. Branching is an essential characteristic of Crowder programs.

According to W. Lee Garner, the intrinsic program assumes that "Various paths provide opportunities to help special learners whose faculties or backgrounds vary. The only reinforcement needed for a superior learner may simply be going on to the next step. With slow learners, reinforcement may have to be words of praise or even material rewards."[38] The use of branching attempts to provide the best reinforcement possible; the paths taken may be of remedial content, enrichment material, etc., depending on the response made by the student to the multiple-choice question.[39]

Accounting: A Programmed Text (Revised Edition) by James Don Edwards, Roger H. Hermanson, and R.F. Salmonson illustrates the intrinsic or scrambled type method of programmed instruction. Compare the following multiple-choice question relating to the accounting cycle with the previous illustration using the linear technique. Also note the "scrambled" page numbers of the various multiple-choice responses in the text. (The superscript "3" indicates that the sections are from Chapter 3.)

(Section 13^3)
(page 99) Which of the following statements is *incorrect*?

1. The closing entries, earnings statement, and statement of financial position may be all prepared by looking only at the completed work sheet.   section 3^3

2. Transactions must be recognized, recorded, and alalyzed before entries can be made in the journal. section 24[3]

3. The regular journal entries and the closing journal entries can properly be made in the same journal and posted to accounts in the same ledger. section 36[3]

4. The open accounts are not the only ones shown on the post-closing trial balance. section 51[3]

(page 95) 3[3] You are wrong. The statement is true. It may be worth your while to go back and restudy Section 33[3] Then return to Section 13[3] and select another response.

(page 102) 24[3] You are wrong. The statement is true. You should verify this in section 13[3] and then choose another response.

(page 112) 36[3] You are wrong, but your error is somewhat understandable. This point has been implied but never covered specifically. The statement is true. Go back to Section 13[3] and try again.

(page 122) 51[3] Excellent. This is the false statement sought in Section13.[3] The open accounts are the only ones shown on the post-*closing* trial balance. The closed accounts have zero balances and therefore are omitted.

Continue with the glossary.

Several differences between the Skinnerian (linear, constructed response) technique and the Crowder (intrinsic, scrambled, multiple-choice response) technique are worth examining. Most evident is the difference in the theories of learning of Skinner and Crowder manifested by the contrasting construction of the frames, their sequence, and the responses required of the student. Skinner based his linear programs on the assumption that "learning takes place most effectively when a correct response is made and immediately reinforced."[40] He therefore constructed his frames and questions to induce the student to answer correctly.

Crowder's approach to programming was quite different. His intrinsic type programs usually presented much information prior to requiring a response from the student in the hope that the student could learn while reading the explanatory material of the frame. The response was designed to test whether or not the student had understood what he had read in the frame. Reinforcement took place when the student was directed to the proper location of his answer to the question and when he read the comments pertaining to his correct or incorrect response.

In more succinct terms, Garner describes this fundamental difference: "Whereas the linear program emphasizes closely controlled responses, uses the same stimuli for all learners and assumes that one optimum sequence can be determined, intrinsic programs emphasize the quality and variety of the stimuli, and use responses in part to discriminate amongst learners who follow separate paths to the end."[41]

Clearly, both methods are effective advances in educational technology; however, no conclusive research findings have proved either type to be superior to the other.[42] The choice of which method to use is more properly made by considering the type of subject matter that is to be programmed. "If the student must later recall the material verbatim and without any prompting, the Skinner approach is generally more appropriate."[43] However, the intrinsic program might be more suitable for material that requires the student to "recognize key responses from a number of alternatives," as well as in situations where the student must be able to discover new interpretations and relationships from material to which he has already been exposed.[44]

Other Types of Programmed Instruction Techniques

While the linear and intrinsic programs pioneered by Skinner and Crowder are the most widely used today, several other new programs are also being developed. Some involve modification of the above types, such as the incorporation of branching into linear programs. However, the *conversational chaining* style of J.A. Barlow, the *Ruleg* technique of J.L. Evans, R. Glaser, and L.E. Homme, and the *Methetics* programs of T.F. Gilbert offer new, yet somewhat unproved, additions to the emerging educational technology of programmed instruction.[45]

As an example of a program which exhibits characteristics of both linear and intrinsic programming techniques, consider the following illustration from Chapter 13 of another programmed text, *Managerial Accounting* by James Don Edwards, Roger H. Hermanson, and R.F. Salmonson. Note that the frame follows a linear presentation of text and questions; all students proceed through the same sequence of material. However, as is characteristic of intrinsic programs, the questions are designed to test the student's comprehension of the text material rather than to induce a correct response, as is the goal of linear programs. Note also the amount of text preceeding the questions and the explanatory comments in the answers—both characteristic of intrinsic programs.

FRAME 1:
The role of the accountant in information systems

In small organizations, the accountant often functions as both the director of the firm's information system and the chief financial officer. This often is due to the fact that the accounting system is the only formal information system in such a company. The organization is small enough so that personal, informed communication between individuals is easily accomplished. In addition, such a firm is concerned with a relatively small and well-defined market place in which individual executives are intimately familiar and actively involved. But much of present day business is carried on by very large and complex firms. The information needs of these large corporations cannot be fulfilled by the informal system that may be sufficient for smaller organizations. In many large organizations, the accounting system may be just one of the subsystems of the total information system. Many of these large systems require the use of electronic data processing equipment. As the total system is developed, the accounting system generally is one of the first to be computerized. Thus, the accountant will be deeply involved in the preparation and implementation of the data processing program. Yet, it must be noted that many of the large management information systems are the responsibility of non-accounting managers who report directly to top managment. Since the accounting system may be only a subsystem of this broader information system, the accountant must carefully define the accounting needs and controls that must be developed as part of the larger system. Indicate whether each of the following statements is true or false.

1. The accountant is generally the manager of large management information systems.

2. The management information system is usually considered to be a subsystem of the accounting system.

3. An information system may be either formal or informal.

Check your responses in ANSWER FRAME 1.

ANSWER FRAME 1 _____
_____
_____
_____.

1. False. Although the accountant might be the manager of the large management information systems, typically he is not. It is more likely that he will be the manager of the information system in smaller organizations.

2. False. The management information system is a broader concept than the accounting system. The accounting system may be a subset of the larger total information system or may be equal to the firm's information system in small organizations.

3. True. The information systems in small organizations may be rather informal, while the complexities of large organizations require more formal systems.

If you missed any of the above, reread FRAME 1, before proceeding to FRAME 2.

EMPIRICAL RESEARCH FINDINGS

Earlier, several advantages were listed in support of programmed instruction in accounting. They were:

1. Programmed instruction permits the student to participate actively in the education process.

2. Students are able to pace themselves through the program.

3. Greater individualism is achieved.

4. Students are highly motivated because of the immediate reinforcement they receive.

5. In general, students learn more material at a faster rate.

Several studies have attempted to provide evidence to support or refute these claims. In the study of Billy E. Askins, cited earlier, the following conclusions were made:

As compared with the conventional lecture-demonstration technique, the amount of time required to teach the example instructional unit can be reduced by approximately 25 percent, without sacrificing any loss on achievement test scores, by using the programmed textbook.

...More generally, the study is evidence that use of effective programmed material makes it possible to teach technical school subjects (and surely many phases of college level accounting, as well) in a shorter period of *time* and still attain the terminal objectives of the course including no loss in student achievement scores. Also, whether college or technical course, use of programmed materials, especially in conjunction with other instructional techniques or media, can greatly improve the *effectiveness* of instruction.[46]

The Committee on Multi-Media Instruction in Accounting of the American Accounting Association included the results of its own survey of programmed instruction in its 1972 Report. The committee stated:

Responses to ways in which programmed textbooks aid in the learning process included such expected items as pacing, individual learning, incremental steps, self-correcting, and immediate reinforcement. Among other cited benefits were:

"Rapid acquisition of basic concepts."

"Systematic coverage of subject matter."

"Low aptitude students accomplished more with programmed text than with traditional text."

"...It forces the student to learn the material when reading the text."

Some responses to the disadvantages of programmed textbooks were:

"Students find it a tedious process--uninspiring."

"Short retention period."

"Student is forced to master each 'step' before he can perceive the whole."

"Lack of availability of good material and relatively high cost."

"PT (programmed textbooks) cannot be used as reference books."[47]

The study concluded that "On the basis of the limited response, the committee is hesistant to draw inferences on the use of programmed textbooks in the whole field of accounting education."[48]

Another study, "Programmed Instruction in Elementary Accounting—Is It Successful?", by William Markell and Wilfred A. Pemberton stated:

After working with the text for a year, it seems to me that the text does what it is supposed to do and perhaps a little more. Students appear to learn somewhat better with the programmed text. We also found that the use of the programmed text stimulated discussion in the classroom. The difficulty of review must be considered as one of the major disadvantages of the text.

Based on our experience, the programmed text should certainly be considered as an alternative for the elementary course.[49]

CONCLUSION

Programmed instruction materials in accounting have made a contribution to accounting education and should continue to do so. Learning should be exciting, and any new technology available to instructors that gives the *learner* a greater opportunity to learn should be considered.

FOOTNOTES

[1] W. Lee. Garner, *Programmed Instruction* (New York, New York: The Center for Applied Research in Education, Inc., 1966), p. 8.
[2] *Ibid.*
[3] *Ibid*
[4] Wilbur Schramm, *What is Programmed Instruction* (California: Stanford University Press, 1964), p. 11.
[5] *Ibid.,* p. 12.
[6] Wayne Anton Johnson, *An Integration of Learning Theory and Accounting Education* (University of Illinois: Unpublished Ph.D. Thesis, 1965), pp. 25-6.
[7] J.L. Hughs, *Programmed Instruction for Schools and Industry* (Chicago, Illinois: Science Research Associates, 1962), pp. 2-3.
[8] *Ibid.,* p. 2.
[9] *Ibid.*
[10] *Ibid.*
[11] *Ibid.*
[12] *Ibid.*
[13] *Ibid.,* p. 8.
[14] *Ibid..* p. 10.
[15] Wilbur Schramm, *Programmed Instruction, Today and Tomorrow* (Fund for the the Advancement of Education, 1962), p. 4.
[16] G. Fred Streuling and Gary L. Holstrum, "Teaching Machines Versus Lectures in Accounting Education," *The Accounting Review* (October, 1972), p. 807.
[17] *What is Programmed Instruction?,* p.7.
[18] John W. Buckley, "Programmed and Non-Programmed Instruction: Integration Criteria in Curriculum Design," *The Accounting Review* (April, 1969), p. 391.
[19] *Ibid.*
[20] *Ibid.*
[21] *Ibid.*
[22] *Ibid.,* p.394.
[23] Billey E. Askins, "Determining the Effectiveness of Programmed Instruction—A Training Course Example," *The Accounting Review* (January, 1970), p.163.
[24] Garner, p.9.
[25] Hughes, p.9.
[26] Garner, p.10.
[27] *Programmed Instruction, Today and Tomorrow,* p.2.
[28] Garner, p.11.
[29] *What is Programmed Instruction?,* p.6.
[30] Garner, p.11.
[31] Hughes, p.34.
[32] *Ibid.*
[33] *Ibid.*
[34] *Ibid.*
[35] *Programmed Instruction, Today and Tomorrow,* p.2.
[36] Garner, p.16.
[37] Hughes, p.10.
[38] Garner, p.16.
[39] *Ibid.,* p. 17.
[40] Hughes, p.14.
[41] Garner, p.17.
[42] Hughes, p.15.
[43] *Ibid.*
[44] *Ibid.*
[45] *Ibid.,* p.17.
[46] Askins, p.163.
[47] Report of the Committee on Multi-Media Instruction in Accounting, American Accounting Association, Supplement to *The Accounting Review* (1972), pp. 118-19.
[48] *Ibid.,* p. 119.
[49] William Markell and Wilfred A. Pemberton, "Programmed Instruction in Elementary Accounting—Is It Successful?" *The Accounting Review* (April, 1972), p. 384.

Computer Usage in Accounting Education

Donald E. Stone
University of Massachusetts

Introduction

Computers and electronic data processing have had such a dramatic and pervasive impact on the environment into which most of our students are headed that it would be inconceivable (and irresponsible) if the accounting curricula had not been changed to keep accounting education current and relevant to our students' needs. Moreover, this powerful and flexible tool can augment and extend our effectiveness as accounting educators; computers can significantly enhance the learning environment in which accounting education takes place.

This paper focuses on ways in which the computer can augment and extend our capabilities as accounting educators. Considerably less attention is directed toward recommending changes in the subject matter of accounting that should be made because of the impact of computers on the practice of management and accounting. To oversimplify, this is a paper on teaching *with* computers rather than teaching *about* computers. However, since computers and electronic data processing are such an integral part of the subject matter of accounting, this separation is somewhat artificial and will not be strictly maintained.

This paper excludes applications dealing primarily with computers, programming, and data processing systems—courses about computers—and concentrates on "traditional" accounting courses—financial, managerial, cost, auditing, and tax. Many computer applications of the "real world" deal with problems covered in these "traditional" courses. The skillful integration of the computer into these courses can thus produce a synergy in which the student learns more both about the problem areas and about the application of computer power.

The majority of accounting educators involved in teaching the "traditional" accounting courses are not computer experts. Thus the material presented here does not deal with the technical aspects of designing and instituting course-oriented computer applications. Rather it surveys in a non-technical way some of the many potentials of contemporary computer technology for facilitating the learning process and it reviews the general types of course-oriented applications.

It is not necessary to be a computer expert to make effective use of the computer in the classroom. But one must view the computer as an ally, not a threat—and start making use of the growing body of literature on applications and implementation strategies. The purpose of this paper is to aid in this utilization.

The material presented here is based on the author's teaching experiences at Dartmouth College and the University of Massachusetts and a review of the literature related to educational applications of the computer, with special emphasis on accounting. In addition, it draws from an informal survey made by the author of computer usage in the accounting curriculum at 35 universities and colleges in the United States. Finally, the author benefited greatly from the review of a large number of manuscripts dealing with innovative computer applications in accounting which were submitted in response to the "call for papers" issued in connection with the publication of this book.

A few of these manuscripts have been included in the book's "Instructional Innovations: Techniques" section. They consist of:

1. "COMBUD: A Computer Simulation of the Budgetary Process of the Firm," by J. Timothy Sale, pp. 398-403. COMBUD is a computerized model which simulates the budgetary process of a business firm.

2. "A Computer Simulation Approach for Teaching the Evaluation of Internal Control," by David C. Burns, pp. 404-11. Here a realistic audit situation involving manufacturing inventories is described.

3. "Integration of the Computer into Systems and Auditing: A Team Approach," by Richard L. Cattanach and Glyn W. Hanbery, pp. 412-13. This paper describes the integration of the basic tenets of accounting systems and auditing with those of computer science.

COMPUTERS IN THE ACCOUNTING CURRICULUM—AN OVERVIEW

It may be of interest to examine the current state of computer usage in the accounting curriculum. The following statistics are drawn from the survey mentioned above. Included in the survey are schools from all sections of the country, both state and private schools, and schools ranging in size from very small to the largest in the country (as measured by size of the business school and the number of accounting majors).

All schools included in the survey had computational power available for educational use. Of the 35 schools included, 30 (86 percent) had time-sharing capabilities as well as batch processing available to their students, although not all were making use of the time-shared terminals.

A wide variety of languages are in use with FORTRAN still the most popular, followed by BASIC, PL-1, and COBOL. APL seems to be the most popular "new" language.

Thirty-two (92 percent) of the schools require a course in computer programming—as recommended by the AAA and AICPA studies,[1] but only 80 percent indicated these courses came prior to or concurrent with the introductory accounting course.

Formal computer usage—that is, applications specifically incorporated into the course design and syllabus—in the traditional accounting courses was reported by 77 percent of the schools responding. This "formal" usage was most often reported in the introductory managerial course and the cost course, and next most frequently in auditing and introductory financial accounting. Least frequently cited were the intermediate and advanced financial courses and the tax course.

Perhaps the most interesting and revealing response was in answer to the question: "How would you characterize the degree of success with which the computer has been integrated into your accounting curriculum?" Answers to this open-ended question revealed the following:

	Schools	Percent
Highly Successful	7	20 %
Moderately Successful	13	37 %
Low Success	10	29 %
No Success	5	15 %
	35	100 %

To summarize briefly, there is widespread awareness of the importance of integrating the computer in the accounting curriculum, and substantial efforts in this direction have been taken at most schools. However, as subjectively viewed by faculty at those schools, the degree and success of integration is not nearly so high or complete as might be desired. There is still considerable room for improvement, and considerable interest in taking the steps necessary to make that improvement.

Hopefully this paper and those on computer applications contained in the Instructional Innovations Techniques section of the book will help to further stimulate and provide some guidance in focusing this interest toward constructive curriculum development.

COMPUTER CHARACTERISTICS AND EDUCATIONAL OBJECTIVES

Even if narrowed to a discussion of selected computer characteristics relevant to *accounting* educational objectives, dealing with these topics in these few pages is presumptuous. But a failure to consider carefully general and specific educational objectives and the unique capabilities of computers in planning the integration of the computer into the accounting curriculum can result in substantial wasted effort—and applications which not only fail but may even have serious adverse effects.

When EDP first began to replace manual-mechanical systems in business, consultants advised against simply computerizing the existing manual systems because doing so would probably fail to achieve an optimal matching of the system output objectives with the capabilities of the computer. The same advice applies to the educational applications of computer power.

Much confusion exists when one thinks of the computer in relation to accounting education objectives because the computer is at once both an important part of the subject matter of accounting and a tool which can facilitate the learning process in a variety of ways. As subject matter (teaching about the computer) exposure to the computer and its actual and potential application to solving accounting and business problems is a legitimate part of the accounting educational output objectives. But in its role as an aid to learning experiences, computer usage is *not* an educational objective, but rather a *means* to achieving an objective—thus subject to testing and *rejection*; if some other means proves more efficient or effective. Often the two—computer as subject matter and computer as aid to education—overlap, but there are many instances where providing the student with exposure to applied computer power has been used to justify a forced integration of the computer into the classroom. Neither provides meaningful exposure to applied computer power nor is the most efficient approach to teaching the material. Some of the "computerized" practice sets may be an example of this confusion. The point to be made here is that when one considers a particular application of the computer for classroom use, he should have a clear understanding whether such use is intended to teach students *about* computers or if the computer is being used to teach some topic in accounting more effectively.

COMPUTER USAGE IN THE EDUCATIONAL ENVIRONMENT

A wide variety of computer applications is being suggested to enrich the learning experience of the student. It can even be argued that the availability of computer power, by itself and with no structure or guidelines provided by the instructor, enhances the learning environment. This is certainly true at a school like Dartmouth College where, by tradition and curriculum design, almost all students enter their advanced courses competent and confident in their ability to identify problems for which computer solutions are appropriate and to do their own programming to harness the computer's power. In such an environment, it is not surprising for the instructor to be *pushed* by his students who constantly *discover* new areas within the course where computer power can be applied. Such spontaneous, unplanned usage becomes contagious and makes for a highly stimulating environment.

In *planning* for integration of the computer into the curriculum, however, more structure and guidance are necessary. Some of the categories of "structured" or planned applications are discussed below to provide a framework for further discussion. Again, the emphasis is on the learning experience to be created and not on teaching about computers. The special capabilities of the computer simply make the experience possible. In many such instances, relatively little or even no computer capability is assumed or necessary on the part of the student. In others, the interaction with the computer by the student is more direct and the ancillary benefit of exposure and learning of the application of computer power to accounting problems is gained.

The following categories of educational applications of computer power will be discussed:

1. Canned Programs
2. Computerized Cases and Practice Sets
3. Games and Simulated Environments
4. Computer Aided Instruction
5. Data-Based Systems
6. Student-Developed Programs

Canned Programs

Canned programs are user-oriented computer programs designed to perform specific, well-defined analytical and computational tasks. Most commonly associated with time-sharing systems, these programs can be accessed by the user from a "systems library" and used with little or no modification to perform such operations as linear programming, present-value calculations, etc. Operating instructions are often contained within the program and available to the student as the program runs. On more complex programs, additional instructions and documentation are contained in hard copy user manuals as would be the case for canned programs used in batch processing systems. In many canned programs, the user must type his input data according to specific formatting instructions. In others, the operation of the program is more interactive and the student's inputs are solicited by the computer in a series of questions and answers.

Very similar in concept to canned programs are canned subroutines which are also pre-programmed packages designed to perform specific analytical or computational tasks but differ in that they are designed to be incorporated into student written programs.

A major advantage of canned programs is that they can place a considerable amount of analytical and computational power at the disposal of the student—without requiring that he or she have substantial background in computer programming or total mastery of the analytical technique. The availability of such programs can substantially augment the capability of the student to solve realistically difficult and data-rich problems. The student can spend more time doing in-depth analysis, explore more alternatives, and have more time to consider the conceptual and theoretical aspects of the problem than would be the case if such "packaged" computer power were not available. Canned programs are also very useful in motivating the student who is just beginning his exposure to computers—for the increase in computational power afforded by using such programs dramatically demonstrates to the student that the computer is a useful ally and not a threat. Because a large number of canned programs are readily available in many university computer systems, they offer a very attractive and easy way of integrating computer usage into a course for the first time.

Some instructors feel that canned programs can have undesirable effects because they can be used with little or no understanding of the theory and assumptions underlying the techniques contained in the program. This can lead to blind and unthinking dependence on the "black box" and serious misinterpretation of the results. There is some merit to this concern, but it can also be argued that such programs make exposure to more sophisticated analytical techniques possible where, without such programs, only very superficial exposure would be feasible. Students can learn much about the underlying concepts and assumptions simply by using the programs and interacting intelligently with the results.

Another problem often cited is the lack of canned programs specifically oriented towards accounting education. General business and mathematical-statistical programs are widely available and contain many applications which are adaptable to managerial accounting courses, but the availability of programs specifically designed or suitable for use in accounting courses other than managerial is not as great or widespread.

In an effort sponsored jointly by the American Accounting Association and Michigan State University, Professor James C. Lampe is compiling a Central Library for Time-Shared Computer Programs for use in accounting curricula, which will be made available to all interested users.[2] To date, Professor Lampe has compiled a list of over 70 potential non-managerial accounting applications in addition to the large number of programs now readily available in the managerial area.

Computerized Cases and Practice Sets

Computerized cases and practice sets are similar to canned programs in that they relieve the student of all or most of the programming effort, while making available the power of the computer. In effect, these are "special purpose" canned programs specifically related to case and problem materials in hard copy, which are given to the student.

A number of computerized practice sets and cases specifically designed for accounting courses are currently available in published form. (See bibliography for a listing.) Most of these materials provide full documentation, programming support, and guidance for the instructor so they represent an especially easy vehicle for integrating the computer into accounting courses where substantial computer expertise among the faculty does not exist. Most have been designed for use in the introductory course(s) and are compatible with the commonly used texts. They are designed as supplements, not replacements of the traditional teaching techniques and materials. Since these materials are designed to be used in batch processing mode in a variety of computer configurations, they are feasible for almost any school that has a computer center.

A second advantage claimed for these materials is that they have been specifically designed as *teaching* aids so that many contain such features as diagnostic feedback to aid the student in identifying and correcting his mistakes and the instructor in aiding the students and evaluating their performance. Also, by relieving the student of the tedious pencil pushing and propensity for mathematical error, it is argued that the student will maintain a higher level of interest and motivation in accounting, be able to focus more on conceptual understanding rather than procedural details, and cover more material in a given amount of time.[3]

The published computerized practice sets and case materials are not without their drawbacks. Even though the documentation and instruction provided in the instructor's manual makes their use possible by accounting instructors with little or no background in computers, their use requires careful advance planning and close cooperation between the instructor and computer center personnel. Lack of planning or poor coordination with the computer center can produce foul-ups and delays which negate the learning experience and destroy the motivation of the students (and the faculty). Also, some of the published materials are trivial and inappropriate applications of computer power—merely replacing pencil pushing with key punching and creating a misleading "exposure" to computer applications.

Some attempts have been made to develop computerized cases utilizing time shared computer capabilities,[4] adding the advantages that come with an interactive man-machine environment to those claimed for computerized practice sets and cases in the batch processing mode. However, there are additional limitations, including high initial cost (time to develop) and their tendency to channel the student's attention to what the computer covers, obscuring non-programmed decision-making alternatives.

Games and Simulated Environments

To teach inherently pragmatic courses as accounting and auditing to students is especially difficult and challenging for those who have had little or no business experience. Students can learn or memorize concepts and procedures but often fail to appreciate their full significance, their interrelationship with other aspects of business, or their pragmatic applications and justifications. The use of computer-driven simulations and business games are a promising way of bridging the gap between the real world and the classroom, and in doing so enhancing the educational environment by allowing the student to "discover from experience" these important dimensions of the accounting concepts being presented. Business games are more often associated with management, marketing, or business policy courses than with the accounting courses; however, their use in the accounting curriculum is increasing.[5]

Business games provide a controlled economic environment—economy, industry, individual firm, political subdivision, university, etc.,—within which the students either individually or in teams must function as decision makers and analysts (accountants) supporting decision makers. Often the setting involves competition among student teams within the simulated environment. While computer power is not essential to the use of business games, it makes possible the use of highly complex and realistically controlled environmental settings. Business games have been used in two somewhat different ways in the accounting curriculum. In games specifically developed for accounting applications or with a significant, specific accounting dimension, accounting students act as integral members of the student teams, simultaneously functioning as managerial accountants and managers. As the student performs accounting tasks— budgeting, financial statement analysis, etc.—he sees how these activities tie with management decision making in a natural and dynamic process.

The more complex games generally have a significant accounting dimension which makes students with accounting backgrounds in demand as team members, even though the course in which the game is used is often outside the accounting department. In addition, these more complex games have also been used to enhance advanced level accounting courses by having teams of students from the accounting or auditing courses function as auditors and/or technical consultants for the firms (student teams) actually playing the business game.

Simulated environments are similar to business games except that they usually involve only interaction between the student and the computer rather than competition among student teams. In the accounting curriculum, simulated environments can be used in a variety of ways to permit students to apply accounting and auditing concepts in situational contexts. Simulation models can also be used to permit students to explore the complex interrelationship between key variables in a business environment, to perform sensitivity analysis by altering variables, assumptions, decision rules, accounting measurement methods, etc., creating the valuable educational context of learning through self-discovery.

For example, in financial accounting a simulation model of a firm's accounting statements could be used in which the student could specify alternative accounting methods (LIFO vs. FIFO inventory costing, capitalize vs. expensing R&D, etc.) and see the impact of these changes on the financial statements. Similar applications, employing complex budgetary models of the firm, have been used in managerial and cost courses. In the auditing course, the various systems with which the auditor must interact in performing his audit tests can be simulated on the computer in ways which closely duplicate actual real world experience.

The use of games and simulated environments is, in the opinion of the author, the most exciting and promising type of computer application in accounting education—yet one whose potential for providing unique learning experiences (not possible without the computer) has barely been tapped.

Because of the relevance added by the simulated "real world" environment and the reinforcement value of learning by self-discovery, use of business games and simulated environments often has a very positive motivational effect on students. This motivation frequently spills over from the game or simulation itself into other aspects of the course. Teaching with the use of these learning tools is stimulating for the instructor as well as for the students.

Most business games and simulated environment applications do not require that the students using them have extensive computer programming capabilities; in fact, in many games the students have no contact with the computer, other than preparing their decision inputs on punch cards. While the development of business games and simulated environments requires extensive programming skills and considerable amounts of time, the non-computer oriented instructor can generally run a previously developed game or simulated environment in his course without much difficulty.

A major drawback to the use of these techniques in the accounting curriculum is the extremely high cost (in terms of time and computer programming talent) to develop, test, and debug a realistic business game or simulated environment. And overly simple games and models may give the student mistaken ideas about the "real world."

Relatively few published games or simulations specifically related to the accounting curriculum are available (see bibliography for some that are). However, a number of applications are being developed and used at various campuses across the country, and these along with other types of accounting education oriented computer applications, should soon become more accessible through the recently established Intercollegiate Clearing House for Computer Programs sponsored by the AICPA and Virginia Polytechnic Institute.[6]

Computer-Aided Instruction

Accounting instruction can be conducted directly between the student and the computer through the medium of computer-aided instruction (CAI). Segments or lessons on various aspects of accounting can be encoded, programmed, and loaded on a time-shared computer system to provide an interactive student-machine learning environment. CAI is basically an extension of learning concepts underlying programmed texts. (Sometimes CAI is nothing but a transplantation of a programmed text onto the computer—a rather inefficient and ineffective use of the computer's power and versatility.)

Most accounting applications involving CAI are found in the elementary courses and focus on the well-defined (procedural) portions of accounting and bookkeeping. CAI leads the student through the lesson material in short steps or frames with frequent student response and instantaneous feedback. In some versions, CAI is coupled with sophisticated audiovisual display systems to dramatize the concepts being presented with sound and visual effects as well as the printed word. CAI often is designed to provide the student with "hints" if he is encountering difficulty in a part of the lesson and to "diagnose" the student's problems based on the nature of his incorrect responses. The more sophisticated applications may attempt to recognize different learning capabilities[7] of the student users and move the more capable students through different paths and at faster pace than the weaker students. Also, many CAI applications are designed to record student performance for later recall and review by the instructor to facilitate evaluation of student performance and the CAI material.

The major advantage claimed for CAI in the accounting curriculum is that it facilitates individually paced instruction. It may also be an effective way to provide remedial instruction to students having difficulty in the traditional classroom course or having deficiencies in their accounting backgrounds. Also, while the development of any extensive set of CAI materials represents a sizable investment, if they can be used to serve a very large number of students,[8] significant reductions in instructional cost may be achieved.

A major drawback to CAI, other than its high cost of development, is a negative reaction to the concept by many accounting instructors and students who see CAI focussing on narrow "factual impartation" rather than meaningful learning. "Should students be educated or programmed?" is a commonly voiced challenge to CAI. As in most cases, it is much wiser to consider CAI and its positive and negative attributes and match these with specific educational objectives rather than to engage in blanket endorsement or condemnation. CAI has proven its effectiveness in other academic areas at the college level, and it can do so in certain parts of the accounting curriculum as well.

Another problem is that of availability of CAI accounting materials. To the author's knowledge, no publisher has yet been willing to take the risk of publishing CAI materials, and most CAI materials that have been developed are "hardware dependent," so each institution currently must develop its own. The Intercollegiate Clearing House for Computer Programs hopefully will encourage development and facilitate dissemination of accounting-oriented CAI materials.

Data-Based Systems

There are a number of commercially available data bases of particular relevance to accounting education and research, the most prominent of which is the COMPUSTAT[9] file of financial accounting and statistical data on major American corporations. Such data bases are generally available in machine readable form and can be used on a variety of computer configurations. Typically, they must be used in the batch processing mode by means of programs developed by the user to access the particular pieces of information needed and perform the desired computational and output operations. Such usage requires relatively advanced programming skills and is not feasible for educational applications in the elementary courses or advanced courses with large enrollments.

However, such data bases, when coupled with specially developed user-oriented languages and operating in an interactive mode[10] over a time sharing terminal system, offer impressive opportunities for a variety of educational applications. Such systems allow the student to interact quickly with a large volume of data, access the items needed, manipulate these data arithmetically, apply various statistical operations on them, and obtain processed information as output. The languages used are usually simpler to learn and use than regular programming languages, yet their power, when coupled directly with the data base, permits the student to conduct impressive problem investigations and research projects. A well-known example of such a system is Dartmouth's LAFFF system.[11]

Data based systems need not be restricted to commercially available data bases. Special purpose data bases have been developed "from scratch" for use in accounting courses.[12] Special purpose software is available in which almost any data base can be entered and subsequently manipulated and used by a general purpose user-oriented language through time-sharing systems.[13] The potential of such general purpose data-based systems coupled with data file generation capabilities of the computer audit system packages such as AUDITAPE suggest interesting possible developments of educational application in a variety of accounting courses at a reasonable cost in time, effort, and money.

Since this type of usage is what most systems designers envisage to be the way interactive management information systems in business and government should work, educational applications of data-based systems provide another good example of how the integration of computer power into the accounting curriculum can simultaneously improve the learning of accounting subject matter and provide realistic exposure to the potential of computer power in the business environment.

The major drawback is that for data-based systems to be effective with reasonably large enrollments, extensive time-shared computer capabilities are required. The basic concepts of data-based systems could be achieved in batch processing, but only with the *very significant loss* of the interactive feature.

Student Written Programs

At the beginning of this section, it was stated that merely having computer power easily available to students is a significant enrichment of the educational environment,—provided the students are capable and willing to make use of it. In fact, student written programs can provide a most flexible and powerful integration of computer power into accounting education.

The argument that accounting courses should focus on accounting and not programming is often advanced in opposition to having students write programs to solve accounting problems. While this argument has merit, on closer examination it is really more of an argument that the student in the accounting courses should possess reasonable programming skill *before* he enters the course, as recomded by both the AAA and AICPA. This is absolutely essential to the effective integration of computers into the accounting curriculum.

The act of reducing a set of procedures to an explicit set of operational statements can, in and of itself, significantly reinforce a student's understanding of the subject matter, and, as a fringe benefit, his understanding and command of computer power. Even greater potential benefit can be gained when the student discovers his own computer solutions to complex accounting problems. This step completes the marriage of accounting education and computer effectiveness and makes possible truly exciting projects and investigations in accounting courses.

Use of this approach can be encouraged or forced by the instructor by requiring that the student develop computer solutions to given problems. On some computer systems, student programs can be tested and evaluated by monitor programs controlled by the instructor,[14] which can significantly ease the instructor's burden of evaluating and grading student performance.

Requiring student written programs must be done with some careful thinking and planning or adverse results may ensue. It seems very simple to say to the student, "go write a program to compute sum-of-years'-digits depreciation." However, if the instructions are not sufficiently clear, the student will be frustrated. If the application is trivial,—that is, capable of manual solution faster than solution by programming,—the student will soon tire of this technique. The "gee whiz, I'm a computer programmer" euphoria is a short-lived phenomenon.

SUMMARY

There are a variety of ways in which accounting instructors can enrich students' learning experience and extend their effectiveness as educators by integrating the computer into the classroom. Those which have been discussed cover most of the current types of educational applications relevant to accounting education. As computer technology develops and our understanding of educational objectives and the learning process improves, new applications will surely develop. The computer is a powerful ally in the educational process.

Space limitations have precluded the presentation of specific applications. However, a number of specific applications have been included in the bibliography, and the interested reader is referred to those sources.

Even more important with respect to the development, publicity, and availability of computer-oriented materials for use in accounting education are the two new clearing houses cited in this section:

1. For time shared computer programs specifically oriented to accounting education applications, a program sponsored jointly by the American Accounting Association and Michigan State University, write: Professor James C. Lampe, 337 Eppley Center, Michigan State University, East Lansing, Michigan 48823.

2. For a full range of accounting-oriented computer applications (both batch and time sharing), a program sponsored by the AICPA and Virginia Polytechnic Institute, write: Intercollegiate Clearing House for Computer Programs, College of Business, Virginia Polytechnic Institute and State University, Blacksburg, Virginia 24061.

STRATEGIES FOR INTEGRATING THE COMPUTER INTO THE ACCOUNTING CURRICULUM

The informal survey of computer usage in the accounting curriculum revealed substantial progress by many schools in integrating the computer into the accounting curriculum. However, 23 percent of the schools surveyed had *no* such formal integration, and faculty respondents at 43 percent of these schools characterized the degree and success of computer integration as low or none at all. This suggests considerable room for improvement, and the need to develop sound strategies to guide and encourage such integration.

The results of the author's survey are consistent with other surveys covering computer usage at business schools.[15] Although the data are not sufficiently firm to make an irrefutable claim, it would appear, moreover, that in certain areas such as the use of games, simulations, canned programs, etc., that the accounting area is *lagging behind* other functional areas in utilizing the computer in educational applications.

In any event, improving educational effectiveness through the use of the computer and the removal of the problems that seem to retard integration of the computer into the curriculum are problems shared by all parts of the business school faculty, and should be approached jointly, not separately.

Factors Retarding Computer Usage

In the author's survey, respondents were asked to comment on "what barriers, problems, and constraints do you feel have prevented maximum utilization of the computer in accounting education at your school?" The responses, while not surprising to those who have considered the problem, are revealing. (Responses were open ended; the listing below is the author's condensation.)

Reasons for Inadequate Computer Utilization in Accounting Courses	Times Cited
Lack of faculty interest, support, and/or technical competence	16
Unavailability of suitable, prepared materials	8
Lack of time sharing facilities (and insufficient number of terminals)	7
Limited time of students	7
Limited time of faculty	5
Unreliable equipment, down-time, inadequate computer center	3
Cost constraints (especially for time-sharing)	2
Inadequate student computer training provide in prerequisite courses	2
Lack of encouragement by accounting instructors to use the computer in advanced level courses	1

One should not necessarily construe the number of times cited as a perfect measure of the seriousness or pervasiveness of the problem; it may measure the most obvious problems but more subtle problems may be equally important and receive little or no mention. For example, the two problems cited at the bottom of the list, inadequate prerequisite training and insufficient incentive to use computers in advanced courses, may have a significant behavioral impact on student computer usage.

Nevertheless, consistent with the *Computing Newsletter* survey,[16] the accounting faculty—their lack of interest in, support of, and competence in computers—is the major problem.

The approach to improving the integration of the computer in the accounting curriculum should begin with an analysis of these "barriers" to see which ones can be modified and to develop strategies for modification.

Of the problems cited in the author's survey, those for which it seems useful to generalize about solution strategies are: (1) lack of faculty interest, etc., and (2) availability of suitable materials. The other problems are either not subject to meaningful generalization or are functions of the first two and should resolve themselves accordingly.

Approaches to facilitating computer integration into the accounting curriculum should take place at three levels: the professional level (American Accounting Association—nationally and regionally, the AICPA, NAA, etc.), the school or department level, and the individual level.

Assistance from the Profession

The national professional accounting organizations, primarily the AAA and the AICPA, can and currently are assisting in improving computer utilization in the accounting curriculum. In the area of faculty development, special programs and workshops (similar to the AAA short courses on Quantitative Methods and Behavioral Science) should be established to help accounting faculty tool up their capability to use the computer,—with a special emphasis on *educational* applications as contrasted to business applications. Such a program for business faculty has been sponsored for several years now by the AACSB.[17]

In addition to these formal training programs, short workshops on specific educational computer applications should be conducted during the national and regional AAA meetings.

The AAA-sponsored Central Library for Time-Shared Computer Programs for use in the accounting curricula and the AICPA-sponsored Intercollegiate Clearing House for Computer Programs should help remove the unavailability of materials problem. The Clearing House is intended to serve as a repository for all types of computer aids which relate to accounting education. This includes simulations (both process and decision oriented), manipulative type programs, and specialized accounting applications, among others useful in an academic environment. The purpose of the Clearing House is to catalog and publicize the holdings and to distribute materials upon request to interested users.[18] These two organized efforts should provide both the vehicle to accumulate and distribute computer oriented materials for use in the accounting curriculum and the incentive to faculty to develop new materials. Moreover, the author's review of the published literature (see bibliography) reveals extensive amounts of available application-oriented materials. Certainly, if lack of available materials is a legitimate barrier today, it should only be a lame excuse in the near future.

One final strategy for the American Accounting Association—it should recognize the dual role of its members as professional accountants and professional educators and continue to extend its policy of encouraging research in *accounting education* as a topic of co-equal importance and merit with research in the subject matter of accountancy.

Assistance at the School and Departmental Level

The problem of faculty disinterest and lack of computer competence was recognized as far back as the 1964 AAA report on computers and accounting education. The problem is still with us and the solutions recommended then still seem appropriate:

1. Setting minimum standards by the American Accounting Association.

2. Including advanced EDP questions on the CPA examination.

3. Exerting administrative pressures (by heads of accounting departments).

4. Requring EDP competency for promotion.[19]

5. Granting released time to faculty for the purpose of attending formal EDP classes (coupled with 3 and 4).

Some additional strategies appropriate at the departmental level include:[20]

1. Assigning faculty members computer-oriented courses which permit them to upgrade their proficiency as part of their class preparation.

2. Providing faculty with computer-oriented courses which permit them to upgrade their proficiency as part of their class preparation.

3. Providing faculty with computer-oriented graduate assistants.

4. Providing faculty with free and unembarrassing (private) access to the computer—through time sharing terminals and getting them "on the machine."

5. Offering short in-house courses on computer topics.

6. Improving school library support—manuals, operating instruction, etc.

7. Conducting faculty seminars on computer applications.

8. Rewarding innovative educational developments (including computer oriented) on a basis equal to that of "scholarly research."

9. Emphasizing use of the computer to make teaching more effective, efficient, and fun rather than threats of professional obsolescence.

10. Examining what is being done with educational applications in other areas in and outside the school of business. It is not necessary to reinvent the wheel.

But faculty have often proved difficult to motivate by fellow faculty and administrators. There is another source of motivation which holds considerable promise—the students. The *Computing Newsletter* survey (1970) indicated the following suggestions under the caption, "Approaches for Students When Faculty Won't Retool."

1. Place indirect pressure on the instructors to introduce computer applications, through computer knowledgeable students.

2. Teach the students how to use the computer before they enroll in functional area courses. Then, students will utilize the computer, instead of less effective devices, for solving assigned problems.

3. Motivate students to pursue independent study of computers, through potential employers expressing desirability of computer-trained personnel.

4. Have quantitative instructors provide students with illustrations in functional areas, i.e., those examples that functional area professors should be providing.

5. "Tease" students with material in other courses; students then force laggard instructors to modernize.

6. Assign projects for computer courses related to a student's functional area.

7. Make extensive use in one or two functional area courses to generate student interest in using the computer in the remaining areas.

8. Prepare extensive library, preferably time sharing, for handling types of problems which students encounter in the functional areas. The library should be elaborately documented in a form which is easily understood.[21]

The author can attest from his personal experience that student interest is a powerful and vital motivating force, provided the computational power is sufficiently available to permit free and easy student access.

It is also important to consider computer usage from the student's viewpoint. It must be apparent to the student that utilizing the computer is clearly beneficial to himself, personally, or he (she) will be a reluctant user at best. Speculating on student behavior and motivation is a hazardous task, but talking with students about computer usage is quite revealing.

1. Trivial applications quickly bore and demotivate students. The

"gee whiz, I'm on the computer" euphoria is very short lived. Caution in this regard is urged regarding some of the published materials currently available.

2. If the student is using the computer to solve problems, both the problem and the computer utilization must seem relevant. It should be clear to the student that the computer permits better and faster solutions than would be possible without the computer.

3. Planning and facilities are very important. "Foul-ups" at the computer center, long turn around times, down time, and "aborts" of the time sharing system, long queues for time sharing terminals, unnecessarily ambiguous assignments, can all destroy student motivation even if the applications are relevant, interesting, and potentially fun.

4. Encouragement by example, of the peer group and the faculty, is important.

Self-Help—The Individual Faculty Level

Ultimately it is the individual faculty member, as a professional educator, who must take the initiative. Knowledge of the computer is necessary both because it is an integral part of the business environment and because it has the potential to augment the educator's effectiveness.

Assistance is available, as has been pointed out here and in the sources contained in the bibliography. For those who have yet to take the first step—take it the same way your students do. Get on the computer. Let *it* convince you.

SUMMARY

Integration of the computer into the accounting curriculum is *necessary* because of its pervasive and substantial impact on the *practice* of accounting and management. It is *desirable* because of the many ways in which the computer can enhance the environment in which accounting education takes place and augment our capabilities as accounting educators. Integration is underway in most schools and universities, but the degree of success of this integration varies widely from school to school, and even from course to course within schools. Significant interest in such development clearly exists; however, more coordination and support, such as this present effort and the sponsored programs mentioned here, should help to facilitate the successful integration of computers into the accounting curriculum.

This paper has reviewed several general categories of computer applications which can enhance the learning environment, including use of canned programs, computerized practice sets, games and simulated environments, computer-aided instruction, data-based systems, and student-developed programs.

Lack of faculty support and the unavailability of suitable course-oriented computer materials were identified as the major barriers to fuller and faster integration of the computer into the accounting curriculum. A number of programs and suggestions (some already implemented) were presented to mitigate or eliminate these barriers.

Finally, a selected bibliography of source materials dealing with course-oriented applications of the computer and published computer-oriented materials related to accounting follows this paper. Hopefully, this paper and these sources will help the reader more fully utilize the potential of the computer to enhance accounting education.

FOOTNOTES

[1] Most of the major reports and recommendations are summarized in "Report of the 1968-69 Committee on the Role of the Computer in Accounting Education." *The Accounting Review, Supplement to Vol. XLV, 1970, pp. 28-43.* The recommendations of the 1964 AAA Committee on Electronic Data Processing in Accounting Education are representative:

1. Concurrent with or prior to the introductory accounting course, students should receive instruction in a basic programming language, and should be able to write simple computer programs in that language.

2. Accounting instruction in a variety of subject-matter courses should incorporate some computer-oriented problems, where subject matter is conducive to formulation; but such instruction should convey the principles basic to the understanding of the profounder, non-technical issues to which computer solutions are being applied.

3. The traditional accounting systems course should continue to include a coverage of electronic data processing as one of the aids to accounting.

[2] Information on such programs may be obtained by writing to: Professor James C. Lampe, 337 Eppley Center, Michigan State University, East Lansing, Michigan 48823.

[3] Wilbur Pillsbury cites a 25 percent reduction in the time required to cover certain materials in the elementary accounting sequence due to computer assistance. *Collegiate News and Views* (October 1970), pp. 1-4.

[4] See David Hawkins and Brandt Allen, "Computer Assisted Case Analysis," *The Accounting Review* (October 1967), pp. 788-800.

[5] *Computing Newsletter for Schools of Business,* (October 1970), p. 5.

[6] For more details, see: Paul E. Dascher and Robert M. Strawser, "A Clearing House for Computer Programs Used in Accounting Instruction and Research," *The Journal of Accountancy* (April 1973), pp. 90-2.

[7] See: Zenon S. Zannetos, "Programmed Instruction and Computer Technology," *The Accounting Review,* (July 1967), pp. 566-71.

[8] Professor James C. McKeown of the University of Illinois reports that the PLATO-IV system, a CAI package for two-semester elementary accounting course, will ultimately be used over a 4,000-terminal statewide network using the capability of the system to display simultaneously slides and computer generated graphics.

[9] COMPUSTAT tapes are generated and distributed by Investors Management Sciences, New York (a subsidiary of Standard and Poors, Inc.).

[10] In the interactive mode the user "converses" with the data bank through the computer in a step-by-step fashion. The user gives questions or commands to the computer which immediately responds with answers or further instructions.

[11] See Richard S. Bower, Christopher Nugent, and Donald E. Stone, "Time Shared Computers in Business Education at Dartmouth," *The Accounting Review,* (July 1968), pp. 565-82; and Donald E. Stone, "Computer Simulation in Financial Accounting," *The Accounting Review,* (April 1973), pp. 398-409.

[12] See John J. Anderson, "Integrated Instruction in Computers and Accounting," *The Accounting Review,* (July 1967), pp. 513-88.

[13] For example, see Christopher E. Nugent et al., "User-Oriented Computer Modeling Language," *Computing Newsletter for Schools of Business,* (March 1972), p. 5.

[14] Bower, Nugent, and Stone, "Time Shared Computers in Business Education at Dartmouth," pp. 569-70.

[15] "Updating the Survey on Computer Uses and the Computer Curriculum," *Computing Newsletter for Schools of Business,* (October 1970), pp. 1-8.

[16] *Ibid.,* p. 6.

Factors Inhibiting Adoption of Computer Curriculum	(96 Schools Reporting)
Inhibitor	Weighted Value
Lack of interest by faculty	18.5
Restricted budget for computer use	12.7
Unavailability of proper type of computer	7.8
Lack of budget for training faculty	5.1
Lack of library routines	2.0
Lack of interest by administrators	1.9
Lack of interest by students	.7

[17] See February, 1973 *Computing Newsletter* for details.
[18] Dascher and Strawser, *The Journal of Accountancy* (April 1973), p. 90.
[19] 1964 American Accounting Association Committee on Courses and Curricula, "Electronic Data
[21] Processing in Accounting Education," *The Accounting Review* (April 1965), p. 426.
[20] Some of these ideas were "borrowed" from "Problems in Adoption of Computer Curriculum," *Computing Newsletter for Business Schools,* (October 1970), p. 6.
Ibid.

REFERENCES

General Background Readings

"Updating the Survey on Computer Uses and Computer Curriculum," *Computing Newsletter for Schools of Business,* (October 1970), pp. 1-8.

"Approaches to Introducing Computer Content into the Accounting Curriculum," *Computing Newsletter for Schools of Business,* (December 1970), pp. 1-5.

1964 American Accounting Association Committee on Courses and Curricula—Electronic Data Processing, "Electronic Data Processing in Accounting Education," *The Accounting Review* (April 1965), pp. 422-428.

Committee on the Role of the Computer in Accounting Education, "Report:...," *The Accounting Review, Supplement to Volume XLV (1970), pp. 28-43*.

Couger, J. D., *Computers and the Schools of Business* (Boulder, Colorado), Business Research Division, University of Colorado, 1967. A survey of practices at 11 leading U.S. schools of business. Contains good (but now dated) bibliography.

McKenney, J. L., and F. M. Tonge, "The State of Computer-Oriented Curricula in Business Schools 1970," *Communications of the ACM* (July 1971), p. 448.

Computing Newsletter for Schools of Business, J. Daniel Couger, Editor, Business Research Division, University of Colorado, Colorado Springs, Colorado 80907 ($18-year), since November 1967.

Applications—General

Proceedings of a Conference on Computers in the Undergraduate Curricula, Iowa City, Iowa: Center for Conferences and Institutes, University of Iowa, September 1970.

Proceedings of the 1972 Conference on Computers in the Undergraduate Curricula (Atlanta, Ga.: Southern Regional Education Board, 1972).

Barton, A., *A Primer on Simulation and Gaming* (Englewood Cliffs, N. J.: Prentice-Hall, Inc., 1970).

Bower, Richard S., Christopher E. Nugent, and Donald E. Stone, "Time-Shared Computers in Business Education at Dartmouth," *The Accounting Review* (July 1968), pp. 565-82.

Dyer, Charles A., *Preparing for Computer Assisted Instruction* (Englewood Cliffs, N. J.: Educational Technology Publications, 1972). A non-technical introduction to the design and use of CAI materials (not specifically related to accounting instruction) and bibliography.

Edwards, James B., "Should Accounting Students Write Computer Programs?" *The Accounting Review,* (January 1973), pp. 163-65.

McKenney, James L., *Simulation Gaming for Management Development* (Boston: Division of Research, Graduate School of Business Administration, 1967).

Porter, John C., et al., "The Use of Simulation as a Pedagogical Device," *Management Science* (February 1966), pp. B170-77.

Twelker, P. A., ed., *Instructional Simulation Systems* (Corvallis, Ore.: Continuing Education Publications, 1972).

Zannetos, Zenon S., "Programmed Instruction and Computer Technology," *The Accounting Review* (July 1967), pp. 566-71.

Applications—Introductory Accounting

Beams, Floyd C., "EDP and the Introductory Accounting Course," *The Accounting Review* (October 1969), pp. 832-36.

Bentz, William F., "Computer Assisted Algorithm Learning in Accounting," *Proceedings of the 1972 Conference on Computers in the Undergraduate Curricula* (Atlanta, Ga.: Southern Regional Education Board, 1972).

Dascher, Paul E., "EDP in Elementary Accounting Course," *Collegiate News and Views* (Winter 1972-73), pp. 11-15.

Downey, Lloyd D., "Integrating Accounting and Computerized Data Processing," *The Accounting Review* (April 1969), pp. 400-16.

Mastro, Anthony J., "EDP in One Elementary Accounting Course," *The Accounting Review* (April 1967), pp. 371-74.

Mecimore, Charles D., "Integrating EDP into the Elementary Accounting Course—One Approach," *The Accounting Review* (October 1969), pp. 837-39.

Neilsen, Gordon L., "The Computer in Accounting Education," *The Accounting Review* (October 1965), pp. 871-76.

Perritt, Roscoe D., "Innovations in an Elementary Accounting Program," *The Accounting Review* (July 1971), pp. 589-91.

Pillsbury, Wilbur F. "A Computer Augmented Accounting Course," *Collegiate News and Views* (October 1970), pp. 1-4.

Applications—Cost-Managerial

Anderson, John J., "Integrated Instruction in Computers and Accounting," *The Accounting Review* (July 1967), pp. 583-88.

Courtney, Harley M., "Remote Time-Sharing for Education in Business Planning and Control," in *Proceedings of the 1971 Conference on Computers in the Undergraduate Curricula* (Atlanta, Ga.: Southern Regional Education Board, 1972).

Frank Werner, "A Computer Application in Process Cost Accounting," *The Accounting Review* (October 1965), pp. 854-60.

Harris, John K., and Richard M. Halgetts, "A Quasi-Consulting Project Involving Accounting and Management Students," *The Accounting Review* (April 1972), pp. 375-80.

Prater, George I., "Time Shared Computers in Accounting Education," *The Accounting Review* (October 1966), pp. 619-25.

Sale, J. Timothy "Using Computerized Budget Simulation Models as a Teaching Device," *The Accounting Review* (October 1972), pp. 836-39.

Applications—Financial-Intermediate-Advanced

Allen, Brandt and David Hawkins, *Computer Models for Business Case Analysis* (Cincinnati, Ohio: South-Western Publishing Co., Inc., 1968).

Greynolds, Elbert B., Jr., "The Time-Sharing Computer and Elementary Accounting," *Proceedings of 1972 Conference on Computers in the Undergraduate Curricula* (Atlanta, Ga.: Southern Regional Education Board).

Hawkins, David and Brandt Allen, "Computer Assisted Case Analysis," *The Accounting Review* (October 1967), pp. 788-800.

Stone, Donald E. "Computer Simulation in Financial Accounting," *The Accounting Review* (April 1973), pp. 398-409.

Applications—Auditing

Arens, Alvin A., Robert G. May, and Geraldine Dominiak "A Simulated Case for Audit Education," *The Accounting Review* (July 1970), pp. 573-78.

Li, David H., "Audit-Aid: Generalized Computer-Audit Programs as an Instructional Device," *The Accounting Review* (October 1970), pp. 774-78.

McKeown, James C. "An Effective and Practical Tool for Conveying Test Deck Concepts," *The Accounting Review* (January 1973), pp. 172-74.

Myers, John H. and James R. Kinney, "A Computer Experiment in the Auditing Class," *The Accounting Review* (April 1972), pp. 399-402.

Walgenbach, Paul M. and Werner G. Frank, "A Simulation Model for Applying Audit Sampling Techniques," *The Accounting Review* (July 1971), pp. 583-88.

Published Computer Oriented Course Materials

Cadenhead, Gary M. and Wayne A. Label, *Using Accounting Information: A Simulation* (Encino, Cal.: Dickenson Publishing Co., Inc., 1972).

Couger, J. D., *FORTRAN for Schools of Business* (White Plains, N. Y.: IBM, 1969). An introduction to computing for faculty members, using programmed instruction approach. Second half of book provides sample problems which could be assigned to students. Flow charts and solutions to problems are provided.

Cunitz, Jonathan A., *Computer Cases in Accounting* (Englewood Cliffs, N. J.: Prentice-Hall, Inc., 1972). A collection of 10 cases related to topics covered in the introductory accounting course—"canned" computer programs provided to process student input data. No programming required by students.

Diehr, George, *Business Programming with BASIC* (New York: Becker and Hayes, Inc., 1972). A programming text containing some accounting-oriented computer problems; also suitable for faculty self-study.

Greenlaw, Paul S. and M. William Frey, *Finansim* (Scranton, Pa.: International Textbook Company, 1967). A computerized business game emphasizing corporate financial management and decision-making—includes full documentation and programming support.

Holmes, A. W., R. A. Meier, and D. F. Pabst, *Accounting Case with Computer Adaptability* (Homewood, Ill.: R. D. Irwin, Inc., 1968). Manual or computerized practice set; student prepares input data, processing program provided by publisher.

May, Philip T. *Programming Business Applications in FORTRAN IV* (Atlanta, Ga.: Houghton Mifflin Co., 1973). A programming text containing some accounting-oriented computer problems—suitable for faculty self-study.

McCoy and Anderson, *Computer Accounting Case* (New York: John Wiley & Sons, Inc., 1966). A computerized practice set—student "programs" the processing system in easy-to-learn special purpose language as well as preparing the input data.

McMillan, Claude and Richard F. Gonzales, *Systems Analysis: A Computer Approach to Decision Models* (Homewood, Ill.: R. D. Irwin, Inc., 1968). Advanced managerial text integrating computer usage, especially simulation techniques, into the study of quantitative decision models.

Mock, Theodore J. and Miklos A. Vasarhely, *APL for Management* (New York: Becker and Hayes, Inc., 1972). A programming text—contains some accounting-oriented computer problems—also suitable for faculty self-study.

Neilson, D. P. *Interactive Computerized Accounting Sets* (Homewood, Ill.: R. D. Irwin, Inc., 1972).

Perritt, Roscoe D. *PL/1 and FORTRAN IV: Computer Exercises, Accounting Problems and Practice Case to Accompany Financial Accounting and Managerial Accounting* (New York: The Macmillan Co., 1972). The annotation is provided in the title; designed for use with the financial and managerial texts by Bierman and Drebin.

Pillsbury, Wilbur F., *Computer Augmented Accounting CompuGuide I; CompuGuide II; CompuGuide III;* (Cincinnati, Ohio: South-Western Publishing Co., 1971, 72). Integrated package of computer-oriented materials (some canned programs, some involving student written programs) for use in introductory financial and managerial course.

Smith W. Nye, Elmer E. Estry, Ellsworth F. Vines, *Integrated Simulation* (Cincinnati, Ohio: South-Western Publishing Co., 1968). A business game or simulation which attempts to integrate the management disciplines of marketing, production, accounting, and finance. Programming support provided by the publisher.

Sweeney, Robert B. *The Use of Computers in Accounting* (Englewood Cliffs, N. J.: Prentice-Hall, Inc., 1971). A brief introduction to computers and programming (FORTRAN) with a set of accounting-oriented problems to be solved by student-written programs. Flow charting and solution programs for some applications included in workbook.

Wilkinson, Joseph W. *Accounting with the Computer, A Practice Case* (Homewood, Ill.: R. D. Irwin, Inc., 1969). A computerized practice set—student prepares input data; computer program to do processing provided by publisher.

Williams, Thomas M., James Wesley Deskins, and J. Stanley Fuhrmann, *Information Processing Simulation Model* (Homewood, Ill.: R. D. Irwin, Inc., 1968). A computerized practice set—student prepares input data; computer program to do processing provided by publisher.

Wohlh, Gerald, *Use of Generalized Packaged Computer Programs* (Homewood, Ill.: R. D. Irwin, Inc., 1967). Illustrates use of packaged programs in accounting. Student can do own programming or canned programs can be prepared by instructor from listings in the manual.

Bibliographies

van der Aa, H.J., *Computers and Education* (New York: Science Associates-International, 1970). An international bibliography on computer education; education about computers as well as the use of computers in education.

Graham, Robert G. and Clifford F. Fram, *Business Games Handbook* (New York: American Management Association, 1969).

Zuckerman and Horn, *The Guide to Simulation Games* (Information Resources, Inc., 1972).

Index to Computer Assisted Instruction (Boston, Mass.: Sterling Institute).

"Time-Sharing Programs Available from Dartmouth," *Computing Newsletter for Schools of Business,* (March 1973), pp. 7-8.

The Multi-Media Approach to Classroom Presentation

Clarence G. Avery
Florida Technological University

and

Donald F. Istvan
DePaul University

Introduction

The term "multi-media" does not mean just a "larger number" of media, but rather an entirely different approach to teaching. Through an integrated use of various media the speaker works to create a verbal experience addressed to the mind. The primary drawback to extended use of the multi-media approach is the professors' concern about his lack of competency in devising and using audio-visual materials. The authors point out this feeling is unwarranted because the multi-media approach is anything but a one-man show and experts in media design supply artistic talent to the team effort. A case history is used to illustrate how the typical "non-artistic" professor can utilize media design specialists in the preparation of classroom presentations.

The multi-media approach to teaching is not really an innovation at all. The illustration below clearly shows that a large number of media were available even in the horse and buggy days. On the other hand, modern technology has enabled the development of more sophisticated approaches which clearly fall under the heading of innovations.

Although in 1903 there were no slides and slide projectors, no transparencies and overhead projectors, no film strips and film projectors, the Public Schools of St. Louis were not without their "visual-aids."

Terminology

Aristotle has been quoted as saying "define your terms and I will argue with you." Before a case can be made here for greater use of the multi-media approach to classroom presentation the meaning of two key terms should be clarified:
1. Multi-media (approach).
2. Instructional technology.

The basic problem with the above terms is that they are used in different ways in the current literature:
1. Interchangeably at two levels.
2. The first can be used to encompass the second.
   or
3. The second can be used to encompass the first.

For this kind of confused usage there must be two definitions for each term—a narrow sense, and a broad sense.

The narrow meaning of multi-media is very literal. "Multi" refers to "a large number of" and media is simply the plural of medium. If medium is considered in our context as "an agency, means, or instrument" for audio-visual presentation, then multi-media can be defined narrowly as being "a large number of audio-visual materials."

The broad meaning of the term "multi-media" requires that the word "approach" or "method" be appended. The Commission on Definitions and Terminology appointed by the Department of Audio-visual Instruction of the National Education Association has presented a definition for "multi-media (approach)" as follows:

> Methodology based on the principle that a variety of audio-visual media and experiences correlated with other instructional materials overlap and reinforce the value of each other. Some of the material may be used to motivate interest; others, to communicate basic facts; still others to clear misconceptions and deepen understanding.[1]

Note that in this broad definition audio-visual media and materials are only one part of the total.

The two senses of the term "instructional technology" have already been reported by the AAA Committee on Multi-Media Instruction in Accounting. The following quotations were taken from their report.[2]

> Instructional technology can be defined in two ways. In its more familiar sense, it means the media born of the communications revolution which can be used for instructional purposes alongside the teacher, textbook, and blackboard... In order to reflect present-day reality, the Committee has had to look at the pieces that make up instructional technology: television, films, overhead projectors, computers, and the other items of "hardware" and "software" (to use the convenient jargon that distinguishes machines from programs). In nearly every case, these media have entered education independently, and still operate more in isolation than in combination.

> The second and less familiar definition of instructional technology goes beyond any particular medium or device. In this sense, instructional technology is more than the sum of its parts. It is a systematic way of designing, carrying out, and evaluating the total process of learning and teaching learning and communication, and employing a combination of human and nonhuman resources to bring about more effective instruction.

To recap the definitions presented above:

Narrow:

Multi-media—a large number of audio-visual materials.

Instructional technology—the media born of the communications revolution.

Broad:

Multi-media—methodology based on the principle that a variety of audio-visual media *and* experiences correlated with other instructional materials overlap and reinforce the value of each other.

Instructional technology—a systematic way of designing, carrying out, and evaluating the total process of learning.

When these definitions are set out one after the other it is easy to see that the old familiar chalkboards, texts, movies, transparencies, slides, etc., in the past referred to as visual aids, are often still called audio-visual materials but because they have increased so in number and variety a new term, "multi-media," has come into vogue. And because these devices are used in the instructional process and are the result of technology they are also designated as "instructional technology."

However, a new awareness of the power of these devices when used as an integral part of a total teaching system has brought about an expansion of the dimension of the meaning of both multi-media and instructional technology. It appears that although at present the two terms are often used interchangeably, "instructional technology" will more and more be used in the broadest sense and as such will encompass the "multi-media (approach)." This is the meaning which will be used for this paper.

Developing the Multi-Media Approach

The balance of this paper focuses on developing further the term "multi-media (approach)." Specifically it will:

1. Identify *what* media are available for use.
2. Discuss *why* we should use them.
3. Discuss *why* they are not used extensively.
4. Discuss *how* they can be implemented.

Identification of Media

The simple identification of the media available is really quite easy. All one need do is refer to Appendix B of the report of the aforementioned AAA Committee on Multi-Media Instruction in Accounting. There can be found a list of no less than 123 media classified under the following headings:[3]

Facilities
Source Material
Learning Activities
Supporting Media
Administrative Policies

This list is too extensive for the purpose of this paper partly because it includes computers, programmed texts, and games, which are the subject matter of other papers in this book, and partly because a smaller number will be easier to work with as we discuss "how."

The following diagram, adapted from Doyle Z. Williams, is one visualization of the more commonly employed aids to teaching:[4]

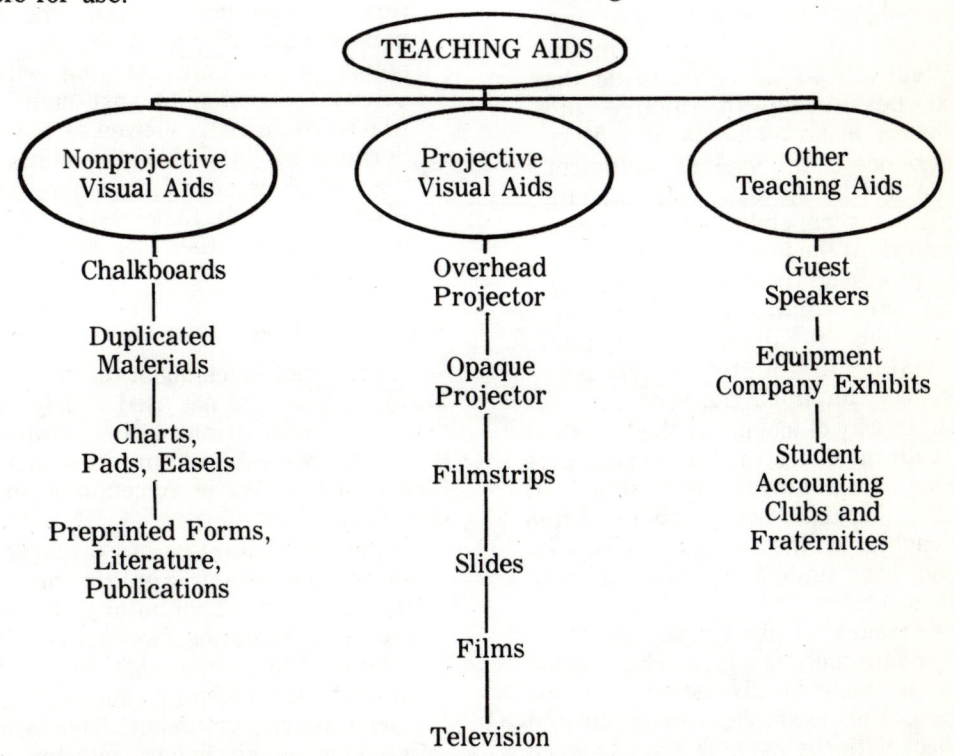

```
                        TEACHING AIDS
                             |
        ┌────────────────────┼────────────────────┐
   Nonprojective         Projective              Other
   Visual Aids           Visual Aids         Teaching Aids

   Chalkboards            Overhead              Guest
      |                   Projector            Speakers
   Duplicated                |                     |
   Materials              Opaque               Equipment
      |                   Projector         Company Exhibits
   Charts,                   |                     |
   Pads, Easels           Filmstrips            Student
      |                      |                 Accounting
   Preprinted Forms,       Slides              Clubs and
   Literature,               |                 Fraternities
   Publications            Films
                             |
                         Television
```

The only item listed in the diagram that may need explanation is television. According to one student of the subject:

> Television is difficult to categorize. It has been classified by many as an "aid" and by others as a "method." If TV is used only as an *occasional* means of presenting a part of a lecture, it would be considered as an "aid." On the other hand, if TV is used *exclusively* to give the entire lecture, it can be classified as a "method."

Why Multi-Media Should be Used

Dean Sidney Reisberg and Professor Terrell W. Bynum have this to say about the "why" of *mixed* multi-media presentations.

> When we speak of an "integrated mixed-media" introduction to the major issues of each topic, we mean that the slide, film, sound, or videotape segments are intimately woven into the fabric of ideas shared by the live professor and the class.
>
> The speaker works to create a verbal experience addressed to the mind. If, by some magic, the audience could sense the intended meaning via an actual life experience, right then and there, the speaker would ideally have accomplished his mission. We view the role of the different media strategically as an effort to do the next best thing—to involve the audience in an audio-visual sensory experience of the explicit statement made by the speaker, and thereby expand his capability of being understood. At the touch of a button, the host professor (or student or guest) calls forth audio playback, the projection of slides, film, and television on the three screens, telephone amplification, etc.[6]

Another way of looking at the "why" of using multi-media instruction is to examine a number of the advantages claimed for such use. "Virtually every article written by ... teachers on the subject of visual instruction lists time saved as the most important advantage."[7]

In the context of this discussion, "time saved" means more of a given class period can be devoted to discussion and explanation. For example, a consolidated worksheet with the opening trial balance can be put up on a screen in seconds as opposed to the considerable amount enhanced.

An extensive list of quotations in support of the use of multi-media could be presented. But the following quote from the previously mentioned AAA Committee will summarize:

> The signs are clear that great changes will occur in education within the decade of the 70s, and in truth have already begun. Too many pressures abound to see any other outcome, e.g., (1) the cry of individualism in learning, (2) the abundance of powerful technological tools which are massed on the borders of education waiting for signals to advance, (3) the need for greater flexibility in learning, including the growing belief that learning need not take place in a campus—let alone in a classroom—context; as well as the need for remote-access learning which is both occasioned and solved by our transportation complexes (4) the need to partition learning experiences into categories most conducive to various media, (5) the need to package information other than in standard course lots, (6) growing financial pressure to reduce the per person cost of education, (7) the notion of life-time learning which extends education to vast numbers who were formally viewed as having "graduated," (8) changing views of the role of persons as teachers, and (9) the need to make education a more integral rather than superficial part of life.[8]

Why Multi-Media is Not Used Extensively

There is not much doubt that the multimedia approach is not used widely in accounting education. The following statement by the AAA Committee on Multi-Media Instruction in Accounting makes this point:

> While the Committee has discovered some exemplary applications of Instructional Technology in accounting education, we are of the opinion that a thorough beginning throughout accounting education as a whole has not yet begun. This is not intended as an indictment—for ac-

counting educators are not uniquely ineffective or remiss in this regard—but rather as a call to action.[9]

A list of reasons why the multi-media approach has not been widely adopted might include:

1. Many teaching aids, like the overhead projector, require setup time and the preparation of the aids before class.

2. Some media, like the chalkboard or posters, and sometimes transparencies, cannot be effectively used in larger classes.

3. The use of teaching aids requires teacher-orientation to their use.

4. Some media require preparation time by the instructor and / or the office staff before they can be used in class.

5. Some forms of instructional media, such as slides and slide projectors, involve financial expenditures which make their feasibility questionable.[10]

From the University of Michigan Center for Research on Learning and Teaching we learn that:

> Teachers quite justifiably feel that they cannot afford the time and energy needed to make intelligent use of technological devices in their classrooms until academia responds to these efforts with the same promotions, salary increases, and esteem that go to the researcher.[11]

Perhaps the most telling reason for non-use of the multi-media approach is that it has not achieved status. There must be a reason why this is so. On the one hand very few professors deny that the use of the approach can have very beneficial results; on the other hand these same professors do not ascribe professionalism to the process of applying the approach. The University of Michigan memo goes on to say:

> Most affairs in teaching revolve about three basic responsibilities: (1) curricular decisions as to what students should learn, (2) classroom procedures, and (3) evaluation of student achievement. Good teaching requires coherence and consistency among these aspects of instruction, and the use of technological media does not alter this basic paradigm. Faculty members tend to give first priority to content in the sense that the message is more important than the medium; they spend a great deal of time, talent, and energy contributing to the substance of what should be learned.[12]

Multi-media instruction possibly and probably has been shunned by the teaching community because most professors feel a lack of competency in *devising* audio-visual materials to support their subject.

How Multi-Media Use Can be Implemented

While the authors were both at Northern Illinois University they were actively engaged in a multi-media instructional project. The procedures involved in preparing for a multi-media lecture were:

1. Select the topics for each lecture hour and set down, in writing, the instructional objectives for teaching the topics.

2. Set down, in writing, the teaching techniques or illustrations that might be used to accomplish each instructional objective.

3. Survey the various audio-visual media (slides, transparencies, films, etc.), that were available on campus for use in the lecture hall.

4. "Visualize" each teaching technique or illustration, and select the audio-visual medium that would best communicate it.

5. Prepare the audio-visual media.

6. Prepare a lecture outline that would coordinate the audio-visual media with the lecturer's oral presentation.

7. Coordinate the lecturer with the media in a rehearsal.

8. Deliver the lecture under multi-media mechanization.

9. Critique and revise the presented lecture.

Of the nine procedures, the authors, as professors responsible for the actual classroom presentations, were primarily involved in Steps 1, 7, 8, and 9, with heavy but not primary input into Step 2. Technical preparation of materials was accomplished by the university's graphic arts department.

The following short history of the

project points out that the teaching professor need not be, or become, a specialist in media design if he seeks out qualified assistance.

Just prior to the final decision to institute the multi-media approach the situation was as follows:

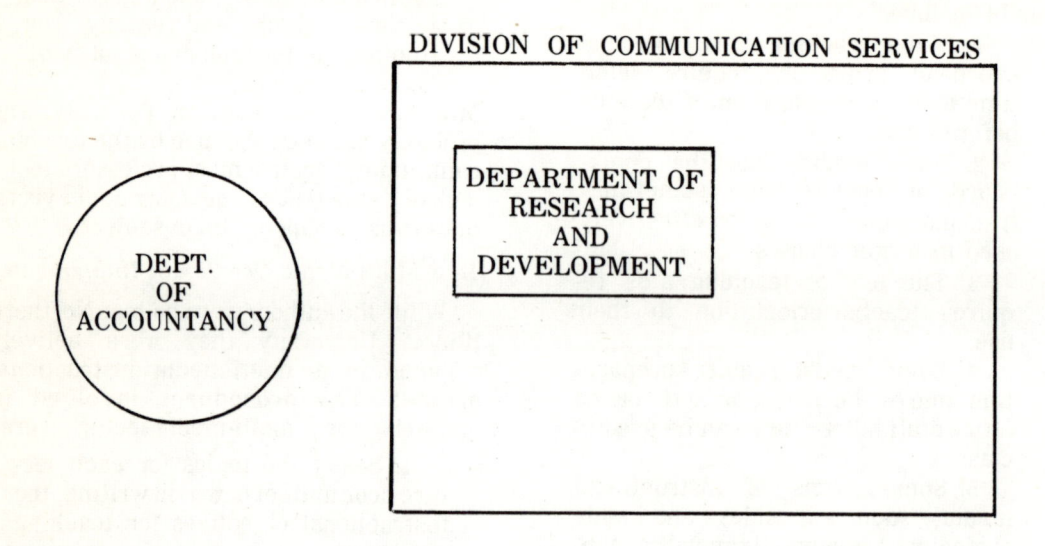

DIVISION OF COMMUNICATION SERVICES

DEPT. OF ACCOUNTANCY

DEPARTMENT OF RESEARCH AND DEVELOPMENT

The Department of Accountancy offered two required Elementary Accounting courses to all College of Business freshmen students, approximately 750 students per semester. Because of the shortage of qualified full-time instructors *and* because of the costs involved, the only feasible way to teach such a large number of students was to use graduate students as teaching assistants (T/A's). In order to mitigate the usual criticism leveled at the use of T/A's, the Department of Accountancy required that a mass-lecture be given by a full-time member of the department. The lecture was supplemented by three 50-minute laboratory sessions conducted by the T/A's.

The Research and Development Department of the Division of Communication Services had been working independently to develop for the University a multi-media lecture hall, had distributed a variety of informational brochures, and had presented several simulated demonstrations.

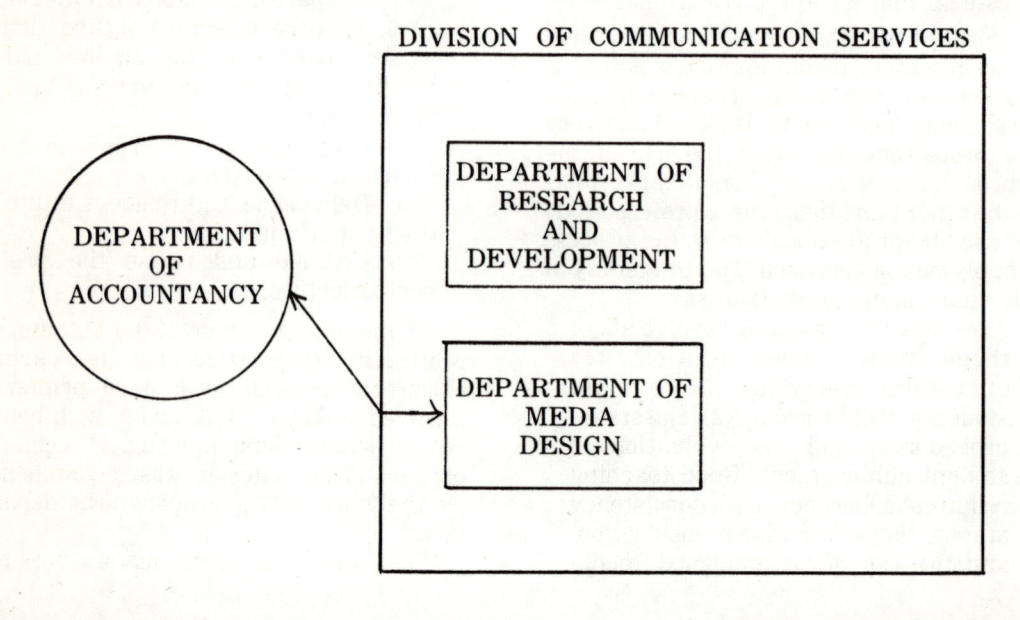

DIVISION OF COMMUNICATION SERVICES

DEPARTMENT OF ACCOUNTANCY

DEPARTMENT OF RESEARCH AND DEVELOPMENT

DEPARTMENT OF MEDIA DESIGN

The Media Design Department of the Division of Communication Services was primarily responsible for the liaison between the academic departments and the production departments of the Division. This liaison was accomplished by assigning a media designer to each project. Although the media designer assigned to the Department of Accountancy was not an accountant, he was a specialist in the principles of learning theory and the application of these principles to the various media.

Following initial selection of topics, teaching techniques, and illustrations by the professors (Steps 1 and 2), a consultation with the media designer resulted in the selection of appropriate audio-visual media and the design of the actual graphic material (Steps 3 and 4). Considerable flexibility was possible here because the lecture hall in use had three synchronized slide projectors, overhead projectors, live closed circuit television which could project materials shown on the podium, a 30 by 10-foot screen, a movie projector, and a sound system capable of playing background music while still amplifying the professor's voice. The auditorium seated 500.

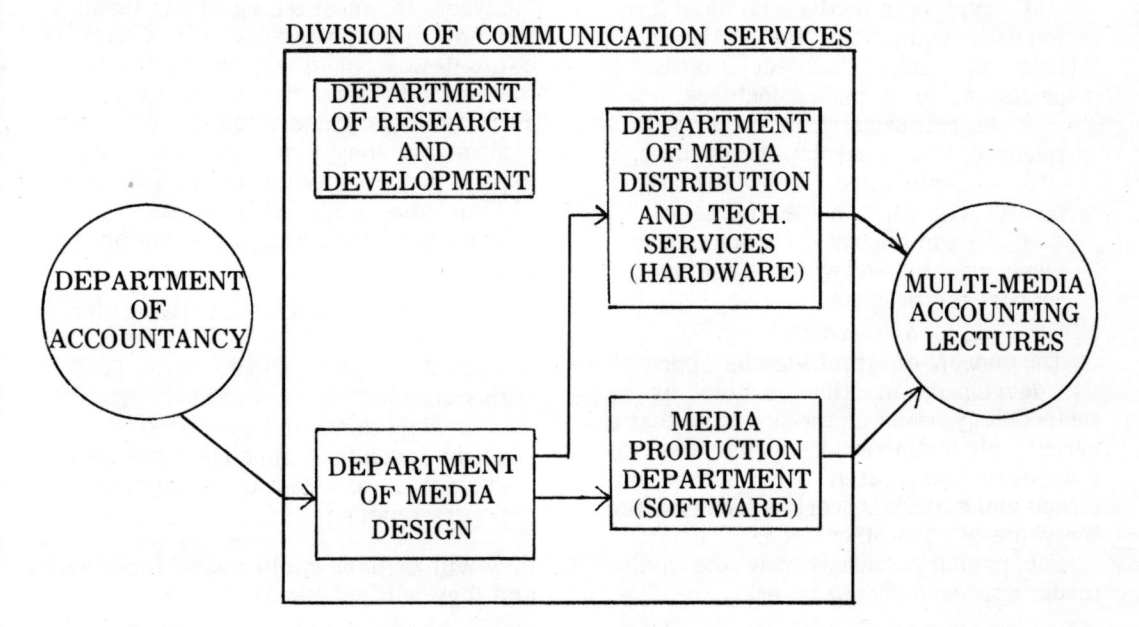

DIVISION OF COMMUNICATION SERVICES

[Diagram: DEPARTMENT OF ACCOUNTANCY → DEPARTMENT OF RESEARCH AND DEVELOPMENT and DEPARTMENT OF MEDIA DESIGN → DEPARTMENT OF MEDIA DISTRIBUTION AND TECH. SERVICES (HARDWARE) and MEDIA PRODUCTION DEPARTMENT (SOFTWARE) → MULTI-MEDIA ACCOUNTING LECTURES]

The Media Production Department was responsible for execution of art, original photography, slides, overhead transparencies, etc. While the professor and the media designer were frequently consulted, this (Step 5) was not their primary responsibility.

The Department of Media Distribution and Technical Services and the media designer would then set up the "sequence of events" and prepare an outline for the lecturer (Step 6). Because of the variety and number of visual aids, they would also arrange for a rehearsal to coordinate the lecturer and the media (Step 7). At this point (Step 8) the lecture was delivered under multi-media mechanization. The oral portion of the presentation remained, of course, the sole responsibility of the professor. Because it was possible to video tape the lecture, and because the visual aids were still available, post lecture critiques by a team consisting of the media designer, the professor who presented the lecture, and other interested colleagues, were especially valuable.

According to Reisberg and Bynum, the teaching professor does not need to be an expert in the use and development of various media:

In our view, media should be incorporated into the style of the professor—not replace him. However, it is unrealistic to expect the teacher to develop and integrate media materials on his own. In most cases he has no training in media at all, and the whole business is quite foreign to him. Thus, it is necessary to provide some bridge to the effective use of media, other than the usual technicians who are knowledgeable about the care and use of hardware. The necessary link consists of first-rate communicators who are at home in academic subject matter and able to help convert media technology into instructional art forms. To locate and attract such talents is not easy, but we found it very important to the success of the program.[13]

Clearly, the use of the multi-media approach is not a "one man show." Instead it is a team approach consisting of the following:

1. Experts in media who have the requisite equipment, materials and time to assist "subject matter" professors in preparing lectures.
2. An enthusiastic instructor with released time to develop the lectures.
3. An interested, knowledgeable faculty with faith in the approach.
4. An administration which is also knowledgeable and which is willing to support the program.

SUMMARY

The concept of a multi-media approach as developed in this article is a methodology based on the principle that a variety of audio-visual media and experiences correlated with other instructional materials overlap and reinforce the value of each other.

The primary reasons why the multi-media approach should be used are:

1. Communication between instructor and student is more effective.
2. Students are more likely to maintain attention to the lecture.
3. A sense of realism can be brought into the classroom.
4. Student motivation is greatly enhanced.

In spite of the rather lengthy list of reasons why the multi-media approach should be used, the research of the AAA Committee on Multi-Media Instruction in Accounting suggests it is not. After all the reasons why the approach is not used are analyzed, the most telling factor seems to be that most professors feel a lack of competency in devising audio-visual materials to support their subject. This situation can change when the professors realize that they personally need not be experts in media design anymore than each of them must write his own text.

Once the accounting professors become aware of:

1. *What* media is available for their use,
2. *Why* they should use such media, and
3. *How* they can be assisted in its use by specialists (much as a systems analyst is assisted by a computer programmer),

they will demand multi-media facilities—and they will get them!

FOOTNOTES

[1] Donald P. Ely (ed.), "Alphabetical Listing of Terminology," *Audio-visual Communications Review* Supplement 6, No. 1 (1963), p. 78.

[2] AAA Committee on Multi-Media Instruction in Accounting, "Multi-Media Instruction in Accounting," *The Accounting Review* Supplement to Volume XLVII, (1972), p. 111.

[3] *Ibid.*

[4] Doyle Z. Williams, "Teaching Methods and Aids," *American Accounting Association Guide to Accounting Instruction: Concepts and Practices* (Cincinnati, Ohio: South-Western Publishing Co., 1968), pp. 94-108.

[5] Carol A. Maruszak, *The Effectiveness of Multi-Media Lectures in Elementary Accounting Instruction: A Project Documentation* Unpublished Master's Thesis, Northern Illinois University, (1972), p. 56.

[6] Sidney Reisberg and Terrell W. Bynum, "Changing Instructional Patterns in the University: A Prototype," *AV Communication Review*, pp. 204-05.

[7] Frank L. McCormick, "Improving Instruction in Accounting Through the Visual Dimension of Accounting Instruction," *The Accounting Review* Volume XLII (1967), p. 53.

[8] *Op. cit.*, pp. 115-16.

[9] *Ibid.*, p. 115.

[10] Maruszak, pp. 88-89.

[11] Center for Research on Learning and Teaching, *Memo to the Faculty, No. 50*, The University of Michigan (1972), p. 2.

[12] *Ibid.*

[13] *Op. cit.*, p. 203.

Television Related Instruction

Robert W. Koehler
The Pennsylvania State University

Introduction

The objective of this paper is to disucss the problems and opportunities associated with televised instruction. To a large extent, the discussion is based upon the author's experience with the TV medium at The Pennsylvania State University. The critical issues of visual presentation, student-faculty communications, learning impact, student attitudes, and relative costs are highlighted. Other uses of televised instruction are considered, including television without laboratory sessions, prerecorded tapes, broadcasting over an educational network, and the use of television to support traditional instruction.

Television instructional systems are now and will continue to be a significant part of accounting education. Surveys indicate that accounting courses have been taught on television at about 40 schools[1]. Some very large accounting programs, among them Michigan State University and The Pennsylvania State University, have used television continuously for more than a decade. On the other hand, some schools have discontinued televised instruction after experimentation and, presumably, disillusionment. In early 1971, the American Accounting Association's Committee on Multi-Media Instruction in Accounting circulated a questionnaire on the use of television in accounting education.[2] Fourteen of the 42 schools responding had experimented with television; four of these had discontinued its use. The Committee concluded that: "While the use of television is limited at present, 75 percent of the respondents indicated a desire for increased experimentation and use of television."[3]

Therefore, in this spirit of pedagogical research, the remainder of this paper shall present some observations about the advantages and disadvantages of the TV delivery mode. The reader is warned, however, that the author has been an ardent participant in the "TV movement" so that a positive bias is likely to be present. Furthermore, the data which will be presented are mostly descriptive and specific to the Penn State case.

TELEVISION COMBINED WITH LIVE LABORATORY SESSIONS

Description of Method

TV has been used extensively at Penn State. During 1971-72, 16 different courses with an average enrollment of 340 were taught on television. This service is provided by three production studios and 11 cameras. The system transmits to six buildings, 70 classrooms, and up to 4,124 students simultaneously. The enrollment in the largest course is 1,200. In this (non-business) course, students view the lecture on screens 8 feet x 6 feet simultaneously in three large classrooms. In addition, some courses are taped for later use at 17 branch campuses.

The introductory financial and managerial accounting courses have been the only two business courses using television in recent years.[4] The author has taught the introductory financial accounting course on closed circuit television for two quarters and the introductory managerial accounting course during 13 quarters. Television lectures are transmitted to 18 viewing rooms in a single building. Each room has a capacity of 35-40 students. A senior accounting major is available in each viewing room to collect assignments, distribute handouts, proctor quizzes, and maintain order. Several graduate assistants supervise the operation. The professor conducts two live 75-minute televised classes per week.

A "talk-back" capability is provided by powerful microphones located at the front of each classroom. Students can answer or ask questions of the lecturer without leaving their seats or passing a microphone around. The lecturer in the TV studio and all the students in viewing rooms can hear questions and comments.

Televised classes are also taped and can be replayed anytime within a week. Replays are used by those who missed class or those who would like to review all or only a specific part. To economize on the number of tapes, they are erased after a week.

Master's candidates conduct one weekly 75-minute laboratory session for each viewing room section. The students have assignments consisting of both problems and theory questions which are discussed and frequently quizzes are given.

Visual Presentation

Television offers new possibilities for good visual presentations. Almost any type of visuals can be used: the blackboard, felt board, slides, movies, and overhead projector. Related to this, it is possible to display various kinds of exhibits, e.g., relevant newspaper clippings. Provided its details are clear, a small exhibit can be "blown up" to the desired dimensions.[5] Films also become more feasible. The per pupil cost of showing films is lower on TV (because of the large number of students) than it is in small classes. Moreover, note taking is easier because the viewing rooms need not be darkened.

Visual presentations are enhanced because the camera can zoom in on a specific detail and then zoom out to show that detail in its perspective (i.e., as part of a statement or schedule). The detail is clearer than it would be in a non-TV class, but the relationship to other parts of a problem is more difficult to illustrate. For this reason journal entries, schedules, and T accounts can be illustrated clearly; whereas columnar worksheets, special journals, financial statements, etc. are more difficult to illustrate. Accordingly, it is helpful to distribute a mimeographed format to the students and ask them to work along with the professor.

There are other visual restrictions. Visual material should be rectangular in shape with about 50 percent more on the horizontal than on the vertical. Unfortunately, visuals cannot always be adapted to fit this pattern. Obviously, visuals must be planned carefully in advance. Presentation and sequencing must be coordinated with the director and cameramen. If there are missed cues or technical difficulty, the professor may look foolish and his presentation will be weakened. Quite often the director can help in the effective use of visuals.

In general, visual presentation on television is effective only if the professor carefully prepares the materials, integrates them smoothly into his lecture, and coordinates his total presentation with the technical people. The risk of failure is higher than it is in a live class because the professor is dependent upon the cooperation of all the technical people working together as a team.

Student Reactions: The Penn State Case

Students in the televised classes have expressed their opinions via questionnaires distributed in eight quarters. The questions have covered various aspects of the courses, and the questionnaire has been modified several times as more specific information was desired. Responses to various questions are presented in conjunction with related topics throughout the paper.

Table 1 indicates that many students believe the visual presentation on television to be more effective than in large non-TV classes. For a live class of 300, more than twice as many responded that television visuals are better than responded that they are worse. The margin narrows for a class size of 125 with seven percent more still favoring television visuals over live class visuals. The preferences change considerably for classes of 35, but only half the students responded that television visuals are worse.

Table 1
Relative Effectiveness [a] of Visuals
on TV vs. Live Classes of
Varying Size [b]

Live Class Size	Better[a] Number	Percent	About the Same Number	Percent	Worse Number	Percent	Total Number	Percent
300	286	48%	174	29%	138	23%	598	100%
125	187	33	228	41	146	26	561	100
35	203	20	310	30	508	50	1,021	100

[a] Calculated by dividing the total number of "yes" responses from all quarters by the total number of responses rather than by taking a simple average of the percentages from each quarter.

[b] Since the questionnaire was changed over the four year period, not every question was asked each time.

The results of another study comparing student ratings of the visual presentation on television with a large lecture are available. During the fall of 1972 the introductory managerial accounting course was taught in a large lecture hall to 230 students. Eighty-four percent of these students had taken the introductory financial course on television from a different professor. Of these students 81 percent responded that the visual presentation on television was more effective, 11 percent preferred the visuals in the large lecture class, and 8 percent were indifferent.

The types of visual aids used are also important. Table 2 shows some student reactions for one term and one class. As always, student preferences vary but handout material is clearly the single most popular visual. Handouts allow the student to spend more time listening, watching, and thinking with less time required for copying and note taking. Some results are shown. For example, the newsprint pads are more popular than the blackboard. Also, the students have not been enthusiastic about overhead projectors. (For the television courses its use has been restricted solely to the laboratory sessions.) Finally, although a top selling textbook has been used, the least popular visuals have been the textbook illustrations. In a way, this response is encouraging because it shows that the professor is still important. He supplies the interest and meaning to the printed page. The reader is again cautioned that the results are relevant to a small, non-random sample, so that generalizability is very limited.

Table 2
Ranking of Visual Aids [a]

Type of Visual	Percent of Time Ranked as 1, 2, 3, 4, or 5					
	1	2	3	4	5	Total
Newsprint Pads	21%	28%	27%	14%	10%	100%
Blackboard	12	23	29	23	13	100
Overhead Projector	6	18	18	40	18	100
Textbook Illustrations	5	12	12	17	54	100
Handout Material	58	18	13	7	4	100

[a] 1 is *most* effective, 5 *least* effective.

Student-Faculty Communications

The most serious criticism that has been levied against televised instruction by both students and faculty is the lack of direct student contact. Half the students surveyed by the author have indicated that they feel they are missing a great deal because they do not have as much opportunity to know the professor as they would have in a class of 35.

While no data are available, it may be presumed that the faculty misses student contact when teaching on television. After having taught a course several times, the professor does not really need to see the students to know what topics and details need special emphasis. Professors, however, are reinforced by knowing the students personally, seeing their expressions, and hearing their responses to jokes. These rewards are absent in the television studio.

In an effort to counteract this unfavorable aspect of televised teaching, some professors prefer having a live class in the television studio. Such an approach is currently used in the first accounting course at Michigan State University.

Early experiments in televised teaching at The Pennsylvania State University were conducted with a class in the studio. This was dropped because the professors involved felt they were forced to divide their attention between the students in the studio and those in the viewing rooms. If the professor looked at the class in the studio, he appeared to be ignoring the students in the viewing rooms because he must look into the lens of the camera to achieve "eye-contact" with the television audience. But, if he looked into the lens of the camera, the students in the studio became observers who probably would be better off in a separate viewing room. It seems difficult to satisfy both groups by giving each group just enough attention to retain its interest.

In a related move, the author has had student participants on television to review material before an examination. Such sessions have been rehearsed. The majority of the viewers, however, seem to be indifferent to this attempt to induce student involvement. In part this is because the student participants are not experienced television performers nor teachers; they have a tendency to talk too fast and they sometimes fail to provide the proper emphasis.

For two quarters the author had five students in the studio for each lecture to provide some contact. They were selected from among those who in the first televised course were active participants in the laboratory sessions and in the talk-back system. They were encouraged to ask questions and volunteer information. Since the students in the viewing rooms could see and hear them, some variety was added to the class and the instructor was able to get to know some of the students. However, students in the viewing rooms were generally indifferent to this experiment. There appeared to be some feeling that these five were "teacher's pets."

Accordingly, the writer presently rotates the students with a different five in the studio each meeting. Since so many students are involved, the "teacher's pet" reaction has not developed. This still gives some immediate feedback, and the student participants enjoy seeing the activities in the studio.

Whatever the individual professor decides to do about having students in the studio, it is desirable to provide an opportunity for student-faculty interaction outside of the classroom. Graduate assistants and the professor hold special help sessions before examinations. With both groups holding office hours, there are about 15 hours per week outside of class when help is available. A graduate assistant has been stationed by a telephone during some evenings before class. This service was designed to provide quick answers to questions when students reached an impasse.

With the exception of well attended help sessions, students seem more hesitant to respond on a one-to-one basis when they do not know the professor personally. However, the professor's attitude may help to encourage student contact.

Although it may seem that the usual number of questions are being asked via the talk-back system, there are many more students involved, so the actual percentage of students participating is probably smaller. Table 3 shows that 76 percent of the students over four quarters felt freer to ask questions and volunteer information in live classes of 35 than they did to use the television talk-back system.

Table 3
Students Feeling Freer to Participate in Live Classes than to Use the Television Talk-Back

Class Size	Total Number of Respondents	More Participation in Live Classes Number	Percent
300	604	169	28 %
125	573	277	48
35	583	447	76

Thus, the talk-back system is not judged by the students to be as effective for discussion as a live class of 35. Students do, however, seem to be about as satisfied with it as with communication in a class of 125. Generally, they feel more comfortable with television talk-back than with participation in a class of 300. However, the evidence is mixed. In an introductory managerial accounting class of 230 students, taught in a large lecture, 34 percent of the students felt freer to ask questions in this lecture than to use a talk-back system, compared with only 30 percent who preferred to use the talk-back. The remaining 36 percent were indifferent. Again, such disparities in the data reflect the sampling biases which pervade such surveys.

During six different terms, students were asked how often they visited the professor's office in each of their courses for help or career oriented discussion. The results shown in Table 4 indicate that many students do not take advantage of office hours.

Table 4
Frequency of Office Visits

Response	Number	Percent
Never	289	27 %
Seldom	469	44
Occasionally	281	26
Frequently	36	3
	1,075	100 %

However, with a televised course, students visit even less often. Table 5 shows the percentage responses to the question "Compare your frequency of office visits during a television course with such visits in a conventional course."

Table 5
Comparison of Office Hour Visits in Television Course with Those in Conventional Course

Response	Number	Percent
More Often	35	3 %
About the Same	462	45
Less Often	534	52
	1,031	100 %

Several tentative explanations may be suggested for the responses in Tables 4 and 5. Some students are not interested in getting to know their professors. Many are shy and lack the confidence to initiate social contacts with an "older" generation. Television students at Penn State are sophomores, whereas juniors and seniors are likely to show more interest in their professors because they have gained more self-confidence and have a need for career information and recommendations for jobs and graduate schools.

At the end of one quarter, 190 students were asked to rank four services in order of importance to them and to indicate those they had used. Table 6 suggests that the laboratory instructor's office hours are slightly more important to the students than the professor's and that they were used by more students. Even so, office hours were not widely used. The telephone answering service was not considered to be important to the students. Unfortunately, the questionnaire omitted the help sessions before the exams; about three-fourths of the students attend these.

Table 6
Student Ranking of Various Services [a]

	\multicolumn{5}{c}{Percentage Ranking}	Percentage Using Service
	1	2	3	4	Total	
Professor's Office Hours	29	34	22	15	100	7 %
Laboratory Instructor's Office Hours	34	37	21	8	100	10
Television Replays	25	13	28	34	100	14
Question Answering via Telephone	14	16	28	42	100	5

[a] 1 indicates most important, 4 least important.

The students' overall reaction to the tape replays is not enthusiastic. Only about 1 percent use them regularly, another 3 percent occasionally, about 10 percent rarely, and the remaining 86 percent never use them. The structure of the course no doubt contributes to their infrequent use. Homework assignments are collected and announced quizzes are given in about one-fourth of the classes. Thus, students are discouraged from missing regularly scheduled classes. They are not required to be present to receive credit for homework, but it has to be submitted prior to class. While no data are available, it is possible to speculate that the quiz policy keeps attendance high and that those who cut class will not have the incentive to attend replays either. Students who want to review a point they do not understand usually seem to prefer asking questions directly in class or during office hours to replaying the tape. However, these are only conjectural on the part of the author.

During one term when the television class met at 8:00 a.m., more students took advantage of the replays. Seven percent used them regularly, 18 percent occasionally, 10 percent regularly, and 66 percent never used them.

The replays are an example of an educational device that most students seem to want to have available whether or not they personally use it. Seventy percent of the students in the introductory managerial accounting course taught by the large lecture method felt that the replays presented a significant advantage of televised instruction over the large lecture method. However, most of these students never used the replays.

Effect on Learning

The writer's intuitive and undocumented feeling is that students have done about as well on examinations in his televised courses as they would have done in a live class of 35. However, such studies have been conducted by others who have published comparative statistics from common examinations.

Perhaps the first such experiment (1956) was conducted by Woolsey. Comparative results of his final examination were as follows:

	Television Class	Regular Class
Median Score	69	68
Arithmetic Mean of Sources	65.3	67.8
Percent Failing	19.3 %	7.5 %

He concluded that: the better students can do as well or better in TV classes as they could in normal classes, but the poorer students get hopelessly lost in television classes, probably because they are not personally supervised.[6]

An experiment at Michigan State University compared two television classes and three live classes of conventional size. One of the live classes was taught by the professor who taught both televised classes; the other two live classes were taught by instructors with at least five years teaching experience. On common examinations, the professor's "live" students performed slightly lower on the first and second tests and slightly better on the final than his television students. However, the average television score was higher on all tests than the average score for all live classes combined. The second test was the only one resulting in a significant difference at the .05 level.[7]

Another study at the University of Miami resulted in higher averages in the conventional sections; however, Mr. Reyna concluded that these differences were *not* statistically significant.[8]

Finally, Bowling Green State University used five different approaches to teaching introductory accounting during 1964. These included different amounts and sequences of instruction time and programmed instruction as well as television. These different approaches "had *no significant effect* on the students' ability to perform on an examination of the type used in this study"[9] (50-minute multiple choice questions).

Similar results have been reported on comparisons in disciplines other than accounting. For example, Mr. Greenhill has said: "At The Pennsylvania State University 32 comparisons in seven different courses were made in terms of student achievement, between televised and face-to-face instruction with the same instructors teaching by each method. In 30 of the 32 comparisons, no significant differences in achievement were found"[10]

In his research Mr. Kumata has learned that there have been at least sixty studies aimed at answering the general question whether the mode of communications makes a difference, and, with very few exceptions, the answers are that there are "no significant differences."[11]

These findings may run counter to what many would expect. The author asked his students if they thought they were learning as much from the televised presentation as they would learn in live classes of various sizes. Table 7 shows that the majority thought they were learning as much as they would in a large class while only a third thought they were learning as much as they would in a class of 35.

Table 7
Students Who Think They Learned as Much from the Television Presentation As from Live Classes of the Specified Sizes

Class Size	Total Number of Respondents	Think They Learned as Much from TV Number	Percent
300	619	419	68 %
125	597	325	54
35	1,056	352	33

Some would argue that there are phases of learning that cannot be measured by an examination and that the *quality* of learning is less in a televised class than in a class of 35, even though the examination scores are not significantly different. This paper does not address that question.

Student Attitudes

The questionnaires used at Penn State have asked students to indicate whether they prefer non-televised classes of various sizes to television instruction. Virtually all of the students had taken large lecture courses so they had a basis of comparison. Their preferences are summarized in Table 8. The significant factor is that in no term did a majority of the students indicate a preference for "large" classes to television. Not surprisingly, their preferences for non-televised classes increased as the class size decreased. On the average, 11 percent of the students even preferred television to a class of 35.

Table 8
Students Preferring Non-Televised
Classes of Various Sizes to
Televised Instruction

Class Size	Total Number of Respondents	Preferring Non-TV Classes Number	Percent
300	608	74	12 %
250	734	217	30
125	587	246	42
35	614	544	89

Interestingly, the students' preferences were unaffected by the grades they expected to receive. Tests of statistical significance failed to reject a "no relationship" hypothesis.

The author has received informal confirmations of these findings from other teachers who have indicated that their students also preferred television to large lectures in approximately the same proportions as indicated in Table 8.

As an experiment during 1971, two classes were held in a large classroom instead of being televised. The experiment was repeated for one class in 1972. These occasions were timed for classes which did not involve heavy visual presentation, which is more difficult in a large lecture. The professor made a special attempt to establish favorable rapport with his students during these live meetings. While it is impossible to generalize from such limited evidence, the student preferences shown in Table 9 are meaningful because the students were comparing two instructional approaches with the same professor. Table 9 shows that less than one-fourth of the students preferred these large lectures to television.

Table 9
Comparison of Large Lectures to
Television Conducted During the Same Course

	Quarter Fall 1971	Spring 1972
Class Size	150	200
Number of Live Lectures Held	2	1
The Live Lectures (Not Televised) were:		
More Effective	22 %	23 %
About the Same	22 %	44 %
Less Effective	56 %	33 %
	100 %	100 %

The following reasons (in decreasing order of frequency) were given by the students who felt that the large lectures were less effective. Note the emphasis on physical facilities as opposed to other features.

1. General disturbance resulting from too many people in one room (i.e., students whispering, shuffling their feet, coughing, etc.).
2. Inability to see lecturer or visual aids adequately.
3. Inability to hear adequately.
4. Room too hot. (The room assigned to the fall class was especially overheated, probably accounting for the larger percentage who responded less effectively in that class.)
5. Poor classroom design.

Another experiment also supports the use of television for large classes. Recall that 84 percent of the 230 students who took the introductory managerial accounting course in the large lecture in 1972 had taken the introductory financial accounting course on television from a different professor. Of these students, 66 percent preferred televised instruction, 24 percent preferred the large lecture method, and 10 percent were indifferent. In this case, the large class could have been more attractive. This professor made many improvements during the course. He started using a microphone, and he changed classrooms three times until he found the one most suitable for showing his visual aids. By starting out with these improvements in a future term, he feels that more students would favor the large class approach.

Teaching is very much a matter of individual style. Some professors are probably much more effective in a large lecture than they would be on television. On balance, a professor must use the method that is comfortable and effective for him. Nevertheless, the studies just cited indicate that students prefer television to large lecture classes.[12] In an earlier study at The Pennsylvania State University involving eight televised non accounting courses, "the students have, on the average, chosen televised instruction over large-group instruction (with the same teachers) in a proportion of 6 to 4."[13]

The students do, however, want to retain the laboratory sessions. The percentage of students who feel that these labs are a vital part of the course has varied over four quarters from 66 percent to 93 percent. This variation is probably due to the relative capabilities of the particular graduate students involved. The mean is 79 percent.

Cost Analysis

Mr. Greenhill has reported on a methodical cost analysis that was conducted at The Pennsylvania State University many years ago (1956-57).

> Four well-established courses were selected for the cost analysis: Psychology, Accounting, Sociology, and Air Science (ROTC). Comparisons were made between actual costs of televised instruction and the costs that would have been incurred in the courses had they been taught in the usual way in sections averaging 45 students. This cost analysis showed a saving in favor of televised instruction totaling almost $40,000 annually for the four courses. Projection of the cost curves showed that the cutting point in cost for televised instruction in groups of 45 came at about 200 students per course. The savings described above would almost pay for the cost of the television system in one year.[14]

The actual costs of television instruction included salaries and wages for all television personnel, cost of spare parts, depreciation of original cost (spread over 5 years), a percentage for television administration, and a percentage of professional salaries based on the estimated time that they devoted to television instruction. The costs that would have been incurred had the courses been taught in sections of 45 were the estimated professorial salaries that would have been involved assuming that a sufficient number of professors would have been available to teach these sections. The system in operation at that time had an equipment cost of $45,000.

Unfortunately, there has been no update of this cost analysis. Obviously, salaries for television personnel and professors would be considerably higher today. Interestingly enough, much of the same equipment is still in operation.

In the past there was very little variety in the type of equipment that could be used for closed circuit television. Today there are wide differences in the type of equipment that is available, and some of it is relatively inexpensive. However, the salaries of the television personnel and maintenance crew still must be covered.

The cut-off of 200 students is still used as a general guide for deciding whether to offer a course on television. However, since the system is in operation, fewer students are needed to cover the out-of-pocket costs. Moreover, some courses with lower enrollment are televised because that presentation is judged to be more effective. For exampe, Table 8 showed that an average of only 42 percent of the students preferred a lecture class of 125 to television.

Obviously, subjective judgments must be combined with cost analysis in arriving at a decision. If a sufficient number of professors could have been hired to teach in sections of 45, it may have been worth the additional $40,000 if that approach would have resulted in a better learning situation for both professors and students.

It should be emphasized that this study compared the cost of television instruction with the cost of teaching sections of 45. Courses could generally be taught in large lectures less expensively than on television. If, however, the enrollment in a course is so large that additional faculty would be needed to teach additional large lecture sections, television which could reach all of the students simultaneously likely would be less expensive. However, the introductory accounting courses at Penn State could be taught in large lectures without a greater time commitment than that devoted to television. Just the out-of-pocket costs of televised instruction are larger than the cost of the large lecture approach. Therefore, television must be justified on the basis of greater effectiveness than can be gained from large lectures.

Advantages

To summarize, the most important advantage of television is that a large number of students seemingly can be accommodated without adverse effects on their learning. There is some tentative evidence that students prefer it to large lectures (size 125 and above). It is important, however, that about 80 percent of the students have felt that the laboratory classes are a vital part of the course. The labs have another advantage in that they give the graduate students an opportunity to teach with some supervision. [15]

In the area of communications, the talkback system generally seems to result in more class participation than is generated in large lectures. This is obviously dependent upon the extent to which the professor encourages questions. The graduate student involvement makes it possible to offer a large number of office hours at different times. One graduate student can be assigned to answering questions by telephone at designated hours so that students can receive help while preparing their assignments. Although most students have not responded to the availability of many different office hours, they are important to those that do. On the other hand, help sessions before the examinations were appreciated by the students and were well attended.

The tapes benefit those who miss a class or would like to review a lecture. They also help the professor evaluate his teaching style, including his ability to emphasize, articulate, gesture, and time his presentation. The writer was shocked the first time he review his own tape, e.g., he discovered that he laughed at his own jokes. Although some habits are hard to break, he feels that he has been able to improve his teaching as a direct result of replaying these tapes.

The tapes also add flexibility when it is necessary to be away from campus. However, on these occasions it can be good experience to give one of the graduate assistants the opportunity to conduct the television class.

The visual presentation generally is more effective on television than it would be in a large class.

One professor has written that televised instruction encourages the self-development of students:

The greatest unused resources for educational achievement in America are the brains of our students. In this connection it seems possible that television might be used as an instrument to help wean students away from immature dependency upon their instructors and to encourage their initiative, self-discipline, individual effort, and unique personal development.[16]

Professor Ruswinckel believes that television's "strongest selling point is the ability to provide *uniform* instruction by an experienced instructor to a great many students."[17] While many would not share his enthusiasm for uniformity, it is clear that there are wide ranges of abilities of instructors to conduct the whole course.

Disadvantages

The major disadvantage is the lack of direct student contact. Alternative opportunities through increased office hours, special help sessions, etc. are not satisfactory substitutes for having the students in the classroom. The author's own experience indicates that this may be more of a disadvantage to the professor than to the student. Televised teaching is a lonely experience. Therefore, one's teaching should not be restricted to television although it can be difficult to break away. Since there is so much preparation time involved in developing the course and the visual material, there are naturally strong incentives to get as much as possible from the initial preparation.

Loneliness results from the lack of psychological support that one gets from student reactions. Attempts at humor are better when one sees the smiles and hears the laughs and without these, teaching becomes mechanical and opportunities for humor are bypassed. A degree of spontaneity helps to establish a favorable rapport with students. When a professor feels relaxed and comfortable with his students, spontaneity comes naturally. Even with students present, it is difficult to achieve the same degree of spontaneity in a television studio that arises in a small class. There are just too many details to keep in mind. In addition to having a command of his subject matter, the television professor must remember not to devote too much time to the students in the studio at the expense of losing the attention of the television viewers. When using visual aids, he must watch the television monitor to be sure that the cameraman is focusing on the appropriate details and that there is optimum timing on each aspect of the presentation, since at any given time the viewer sees only the small part of a problem that the cameraman is directed to show. Even though the professor is accustomed to working in the studio, he will probably be too concerned over such details to be completely relaxed.

Another disadvantage is that many faculty are unwilling to teach on television. Once the department becomes committed to its use, the responsibility must often be shouldered by a few. Perhaps, the most important reason for discontinuing television is the "unwillingness of other department members to share the load"[18] when present TV teachers desire other teaching experiences with non-TV courses.

The heavy preparation time is also a disadvantage. However, since the TV medium reaches so many students, it should not be difficult to justify a reduced teaching load to provide time for preparation. Of course, it is rewarding for the professor to develop a high quality course.

The time commitment is not limited to the technical aspects of the course. The television professor must be a good administrator who can coordinate his work with director, cameramen, and graduate assistants. This means arriving at the studio well before class. It means having a sense of humor when a cameraman shows the wrong visual or when the sound goes off; maintaining composure when a cameraman is late; preparing outlines for the graduate assistants; and visiting the labs periodically.

There are some other disadvantages. Studio lights get very hot. And students seem to have a shorter attention span than they do in a live class, resulting from lack of direct contact and inability of the professor to observe and prod daydreamers. The TV lecturer in accounting has subtle forms of competition. Students watch a great deal of television at home for several hours, and these programs are of great variety. For example, on the news programs, different people announce weather, sports, national news, etc. Commercial programs have full-time professional writers, directors, lighting experts, etc. To a certain undetermined extent, the television instructor is competing with these programs without the benefit of the same professional help. One way to avoid the comparison is to be as natural as possible, including making some intentional arithmetic errors. Students seem to delight in using the talk-back system to make corrections. Similarly, one student said that he had never seen anyone sneeze on television before.

The television instructor's physical movements are limited. Those who like to pace the classroom would feel very restricted. One cannot move around too much and must look into the lens of the camera to achieve "eye contact" with the viewers.

Some evidence points to a potentially serious disadvantage. Students' evaluations of courses seem to be adversely influenced by the size of the class and the level of elementary courses. On several occasions, the writer has taught intermediate and advanced accounting to classes of 35 during the same term that he taught on television. While the course material was different, his general style was the same except that perhaps he was more spontaneous in the live classes. Certainly, he spent more time preparing for the television class. The evaluation from the students was based on 50 multiple choice questions. Each faculty member who elected to participate received a percentile ranking. No distinctions were made between the sizes or levels of the courses evaluated. Recall that previously cited surveys indicated that students prefer television to large lectures. Nevertheless, the authors ranking for his television classes is normally 50 percent lower than his ranking for the live classes at higher levels which have a higher percentage of accounting majors. The results are confounded with class size, course level, and medium (TV vs. live), and require more study, but such findings may deter some.

Finally, some professors may be inhibited by the "fish bowl" feeling. They never know when the president, dean, or state legislator may be watching.

OTHER USES OF TELEVISED INSTRUCTION

Live Television Without Labs

Some schools use television without live laboratory sections. Those who believe that uniformity is an advantage would favor this approach because all instruction is handled by the professor. However, as previously indicated, about 80 percent of the students sampled at Penn State thought that the labs were helpful. Moreover, they provide an opportunity for the graduate student to teach. Their support and cooperation contributes to the success of the course and their involvement in teaching (rather than just proctoring and paper grading) enhances their cooperation.

Pre-Recorded Tapes

The major advantage of pre-recorded tapes is that they can be repeated whereas, if the live presentation is used, each lesson is usually given only once. The use of tapes, then, can circumvent scheduling conflicts.

However, other problems arise in taping. For example: since the resulting tapes are expected to be used for several course offerings, everyone wants to have as foolproof a presentation as possible. This means that several hours can be spent in preparing one "script." The "script" is produced, the resulting tape reviewed, and then probably remade to correct some *faux pas* that occurred during the taping.[19]

Thus, the faculty time is initially very heavy for taping. Furthermore, it is not necessarily true that faculty time in subsequent terms can be substantially reduced. Often, "other parts of the course need supervision and any course with enough enrollment to justify CCTV requires more than a normal amount of supervision."[20] The performing professor would have to review each tape in subsequent terms to recall the specific concepts and problems covered so that he could help students during office hours. Then too, there are examinations, grading, and graduate assistants to be supervised.

Pre-recorded tapes create other complications. It may be difficult to change the textbook or vary problem assignments from term to term. There is also a question concerning the rights the professor has to the tapes. Finally, the tapes themselves are expensive in the quantity needed for a whole course.

Some schools may need to conserve professors for upper-level courses. Accordingly, they may purchase tapes for the elementary courses from another institution. For some non-business courses at Penn State, tapes are prepared on the main campus for use at branch campuses. In either case, instructors still hold office hours, answer questions, and prepare and grade examinations. It would seem difficult in such situations to gain the full cooperation of the instructors who may feel that they are qualified to teach the course on their own. There is, of course, the counter argument that some instructors do not enjoy lecturing. When freed from the preparation of lectures, they have more time to spend with students on an individual basis. Also, some specialized courses or mini-courses could be taped. In this manner students at small schools and branch campuses could receive courses that would otherwise be unavailable. Arrangements could be made to have questions answered by mail, telephone, or occasional visits from whomever prepared the tape.

Michigan State University has used prerecorded tapes to capture "the personality, ideas, etc. of notable individuals for ... future local use and for distribution to other universities for graduate courses in accounting."[21] This appears to be an excellent use of pre-recorded tapes. Another supplementary use would involve preparation of tapes on certain topics that students may want to review in future courses. For example, students in intermediate accounting may find it helpful to review the principles of adjusting entries.

Television to Support Traditional Instruction

Relatively low cost portable cameras and recorders are now available which allow television to be used to support traditional instruction.[22] For example, oral student reports can be taped. The replay permits the student to evaluate his own performance and makes the professor's critique more meaningful because the student can observe his own strong and weak points. Likewise, class discussions and interviews can be taped so that those involved can better review their techniques. Student teachers can tape their classes for self-review and to enable one supervising teacher to handle several student teachers simultaneously. Recorders cost betwen $400 and $600. Two cameras would be needed at a cost of between $400 and $600.[23] If extensive use is to be made of this supporting television, students could be taught to operate the equipment, thereby eliminating the cost of the technical people. This approach has been used at Penn State in courses in speech, education, physical education, psychology, and other courses which focus on oral communications.

Television to Resolve Some Logistics Problems

The sprawling growth of many campuses has created some difficulties in traveling from one class to another during the allotted break. At one time, closed circuit television courses at Penn State could be received in the dormitories. This was especially helpful when students were ill. However, because of the large number of handouts, some unannounced quizzes, and the absence of talk-back equipment, it was never used much by accounting students. The logistics problem could be reduced by having the viewing rooms scattered around the campus for maximum student convenience. However, administrative problems may be encountered in enrolling the students into their appropriate sections. Moreover, additional fixed costs are incurred for each building serviced with a talk-back system. (This problem is not encountered with commercial telephones which are used for talk-back equipment such as at Michigan State. There is, however, the inconvenience of having to pass the telephone around when a student wishes to speak.) Finally, coordination of proctors and distribution of handout materials is complicated when the viewing rooms are in different buildings. Each user school must determine for itself whether the advantages of scattering the viewing rooms outweight the drawbacks.

There have been some experiments in live television transmittal between the main campus of Penn State and some of its branch campuses. The introductory financial accounting course was received by microwave at its Altoona Campus (50 miles from the main campus). Because there was no talk-back system, the approach was not popular with the Altoona Campus students. Since there was a qualified instructor available, this approach was discontinued after one term. Also, some non-business graduate courses have been conducted between the main campus and its Capitol Campus 100 miles away. The small number of students have been in the Capitol Campus studio where they could be seen as well as heard by the professor. The professor visited the Capitol Campus for one session every two weeks. However, this has been discontinued because the low usage could not justify the annual $38,000 telephone line rentals.

CONCLUSION

Televised instruction involves a substantially larger time commitment from the "performing professor" than does face-to-face instruction. Because of coordination with the technical personnel, graduate assistants, and proctors, this involvement is even greater than it would be for a large lecture. It is essential that schools planning to adopt television recognize this greater time requirement. The professor must be given some released time from other responsibilities so that he can conduct a quality course.

On the favorable side, television offers opportunities for the effective use of visual aids. Evidence indicates that students perform about the same on examinations as they do in a conventional size class of about 35. While most students prefer face-to-face instruction in small classes, research conducted in the accounting courses at Penn State over a four-year period indicates that they prefer televised instruction to large lectures.

No decision is ever clear cut. A departmental decision to offer one or more courses on television should be accompanied by a group of professors who are willing to use this medium occasionally. No professor should be required to have continous involvement. Those faculty who teach on television will miss the direct student contact. While talk-back systems are important, even vital, to the success of televised courses, they are a poor substitute for face-to-face instruction. This relates to the satisfaction of the teaching-learning situation more than to the quantity and quality of learning that actually takes place.

To the extent that student evaluations of courses are used to determine raises, promotion, and tenure for faculty, allowances should be made to consider the following likely outcomes:

1. Required elementary courses in which a high percentage of non-majors are enrolled will result in lower evaluations for a given professor than higher level courses taken for the most part by accounting majors.

2. Evaluations will be lower as the class size increases regardless of whether the course is taught by face-to-face instruction or on television.

In courses with continuous enrollments over 200 there may be four alternatives:

1. Use graduate assistants to teach the entire course in sections of about 35.

2. Teach the course in a large lecture.

3. Teach the course on television with one laboratory class per week conducted by a graduate assistant.

4. Teach the whole course on television.

Variations of these alternatives are possible. For example, the large lecture could be accompanied with a laboratory period. If television is used, the classes could be live or taped.

Few schools have enough graduate assistants to adopt the first alternative. Furthermore, many believe that their own graduate courses are too demanding for these students to accept full responsibility for teaching a course of their own. Nevertheless, this could be a viable alternative for some institutions, particularly those that could use upper-level graduate students. According to the surveys cited in this paper, television combined with the labs is preferred to large lectures of 125 and above.

FOOTNOTES

[1] Dorothy Weeks Black included a list of 37 schools in her 1970 proposal for a Doctoral Dissertation at The Pennsylvania State University. These colleges (including one junior college) and universities were either using or had used television to teach accounting. She developed her list from 15 volumes of the *Compendium of Televised Education*, compiled and edited by Lawrence E. McKune, Continuing Education Service, Michigan State University, East Lansing, Michigan. Publication of the *Compendium* was suspended in September, 1968.

[2] Committee on Multi-Media Instruction in Accounting, Committee Report, *The Accounting Review* (Supplement, 1972), pp. 121-122.

[3] *Ibid.*, p. 121.

[4] Business law, economics, and transportation have been offered on television. They were changed to large lecture sections because of changes in departmental policy and difficulties in persuading faculty to teach a televised course. In fact, the introductory managerial accounting course has also recently been taught with fairly large lectures, both an experiment and because of faculty reluctance to teach on television.

[5] Arthur H. Reede and Roland K. Reed, *Televising Instruction in Elementary Economics*, Industrial Research Bulletin No. 5, (Bureau of Business Research, College of Business Administration, The Pennsylvania State University, University Park, Pennsylvania 16802), p. 59.

[6] Sam M. Woolsey, "Teaching Accounting by Television," *The Accounting Review* (January, 1957), p. 121.

[7] John W. Ruswinckel, "Closed Circuit TV: 1967," *The Accounting Review* (January, 1967), p. 140.

[8] Ramon Jose de Reyna, II, "Accounting Achievement in Conventional and Television Classes at the University of Miami," *The Accounting Review* (July, 1965), p. 655.

[9] Lloyd D. Doney and Richard C. Neumann, "Teaching Approaches to Elementary Accounting," *The Accounting Review* (July, 1965), p. 655.

[10] Greenhill, p. 5.

[11] Report of a Conference sponsored jointly by the Committee on Television of the American Council on Education and The Pennsylvania State University at University Park, Pennsylvania, October 20-23, 1957, *College Teaching by Television* (American Council on Education, Washington, D. C., 1958), p. 84.

[12] These are the only two alternatives at The Pennsylvania State University where there are too few graduate assistants to teach the complete course with classes of 35.

[13] Leslie P. Greenhill, "Closed-Circuit Television for Teaching in Colleges and Universities," mimeographed at The Pennsylvania State University (1966), p. 8.

[14] *Ibid.*, p. 14.

[15] Teaching is an important part of the educational experience at the graduate level. Those who do well and enjoy it often enroll in a Ph.D. program and become teachers. Those that do must start their teaching somewhere. Over the years there have been few complaints from students regarding the teaching of the labs. Some schools have experienced good results by having graduate assistants teach most of the elementary sections whereas other schools have not been happy with this approach. For example Professor Ruswinckel from Michigan State University has been quoted as saying, "Often graduate assistants teaching live sections of an elementary accounting course are not prepared at all times. Hence their students may be at a disadvantage when compared with other sections. CCTV (closed circuit television) avoids this." [a]

[a] "Starring An Accounting Professor," *Management Accounting* (May, 1970), p. 55.

[16] C.R. Carpenter, *College Teaching by Television*, p. 16.

[17] Ruswinckel, p. 136. (Emphasis supplied.)

[18] H. Milton Jones and Vernon E. Pontius, "Survey of Accounting Teaching via Television," *The Accounting Review* (October, 1965), p. 864.

[19] Ruswinckel, p. 135.

[20] American Accounting Association, *A Guide to Accounting Instruction: Concepts and Practices* (South-Western Publishing Co., 1968). Section from pp. 103-08 written by John W. Ruswinckel, p. 105.

[21] Ruswinckel, *The Accounting Review* (January, 1967), p. 135.

[22] John H. Joseph, *A Survey of the Use of Television to Support Classroom Instruction at The Pennsylvania State University* (Unpublished Master's Thesis, The Pennsylvania State University, December, 1972), 76 pp.

[23] *Ibid.*, p. 18.

REFERENCES NOT CITED

Periodicals

Earnest, Ernest, "Must the TV Technicians Take Over the Colleges?" *American Association of University Professors Bulletin* (September, 1958), pp. 582-588.

Kane, Howard H. and Donald F. Ungurait, "Accounting Telecourse: A Case History," *Collegiate News & Views* (March, 1968), pp. 1-4.

Malinosky, A. T., "Television, Televised Instruction, and Teaching Accounting by Television," *Illinois CPA* (Spring, 1969), pp. 34-39.

Meyer, Richard J., "A Critical View of Television and Higher Education," *American Association of University Professors Bulletin* (May, 1970), pp. 108-111.

Murphy, Judit and Ronald Gross, "The Unfulfilled Promise of ITV," *Saturday Review* (November 19, 1966), pp. 88-89, 103-105.

"Statement on Instructional Television," *American Association of University Professors Bulletin* (March, 1969), pp. 88-90.

Research Studies

American Council on Education, *Credit Courses by Television* (Washington, D.C.: American Council on Education, 1955).

―――――, *Teaching by Closed Circuit Television* (Washington, D.C.: American Council on Education, 1956).

Costello, Lawrence F. and George N. Gordon, *Teach with Television* (Hastings House Publishers, New York, 1961).

Crosby, Andrew and John Lucas, *Survey of Student Attitude Toward TV Instruction* (Office of Institutional Research, University of Tennessee, 1966).

Dwyer, Francis M., *Improving Instructor Effectiveness on Television* (University Division of Instructional Services, The Pennsylvania State University, 1967).

Ford Foundation, *Teaching by Television,* (New York: Fund for the Advancement of Education and the Ford Foundation, 1959).

Leyden, Ralph C., *Ten Years of Closed Circuit TV at Stephens College 1955-1966* (Office of Educational Development, Stephens College, 1966).

Reid, J. C. and D. W. MacLennan, *Research in Instructional Television and Film* (Washington, D. C.: U. S. Government Printing Office, 1967).

Schramm, Wilbur, "What We Know About Learning from Instructional Television," *Educational Television: The Next Ten Years* (Stanford: Institute for Communication Research, 1962).

Stock, G. C., *Changes in Attitudes Towards Educational Television Through Experience* (Office of Institutional Research, State University College of New York, 1967).

Weber, LaVerne William, *A Study of the Uses of Closed Circuit Television in the State Supported Institutions of Higher Education in Michigan* (a doctoral dissertation, The University of Michigan, 1970, Ann Arbor, University Microfilms, 1971).

The Case Method in Accounting

Robert N. Anthony
Harvard Business School

Introduction

Instructors who are interested in the case method, but who have not actually experienced it, undoubtedly have a great many questions about it. In the first section of this paper, some of these questions are framed and answered. The second section discusses an actual case. The third section lists some new developments in the use of cases.

QUESTIONS AND ANSWERS

The Nature of the Case Method

Q. *What is the case method?*

A. It is a learning method in which emphasis is placed on the preparation for and classroom discussion of a situation that is described in a case. It can be contrasted with what might be called the textbook problem method, in which the emphasis is on memorizing and understanding material contained in a text and working out the numerical solution to problems or exercises.

In preparing a case for class discussion, the student must decide what the issue is, make numerical calculations, identify and assess the strength of the arguments bearing on the issue, and reach a conclusion. In some schools students meet in small groups to develop this analysis, often dividing up the work among members of the group. In class the student explains his position, defends it, appreciates and evaluates the statements made by his colleagues, and modifies his own position if he is convinced that this is the right thing to do.

In the case method, the focus is on students learning through their cooperative efforts, rather than on the instructor conveying his own views.

Q. *What is the difference between a case and a problem?*

A. A problem as used here has a correct solution; a case does not. In solving a problem, the student usually works by himself and applies the knowledge he has learned from the text or from his instructor. In attacking a case, the student analyzes the situation described and reaches a conclusion about it. In order to do this, he must exercise judgment, and it is because individual judgments differ that there is no unique correct solution to a case.

Many materials that are labelled "cases" are actually "problems" as the term is used here; the nature of the material, rather than the label, is governing.

Q. *Will you say more concretely what a case is?*

A. The typical case describes a real business situation on which a real manager had to reach a decision. The case gives quantitative and qualitative information that is, or may be, relevant to that decision. There are several types of cases:

1. The *issue* case is the prototype. In this case, the issue to be resolved is fairly obvious (e.g., should Company A buy machine X or not?), the student is given facts relating to this issue, he makes numerical calculations, he makes judgments about the relative importance of various considerations, and he reaches a conclusion.

2. In an *appraisal* case, a system or

practice is described, often with an account of its historical evolution. The student is asked to analyze the system or practice and recommend improvements in it. In another variation, the solution to an issue and the reasoning behind that issue is described, and the student is asked to appraise the soundness of this reasoning.

3. In a *blind* case, the issue is not clear. A situation is described, and the student's task is to identify what issues, if any, exist and what should be done to resolve them.

4. In an *iceberg* case, only a little relevant information is given, and the student must decide what information should be collected and how it can be obtained.

5. In a *series* case, the student is given several different problems that occurred in the same general setting. Often these problems are sequential in that the student's decision on one problem affects his analysis of the next one.

Cases can also be classified by source as armchaired, published source, or field. An *armchaired,* or generalized experience, case is created by the author. It is especially useful for simple, well-defined issue situations, such as those in elementary accounting. Writing a realistic armchaired case is more difficult than one might think. A *published source* case is derived from an annual report, a magazine article, or other published material. A *field* case is written from information in company records and from interviews. It must be released by the company. It may be disguised; that is, fictitious names may be used, and the data may be altered.

Q. *Are business cases like law school cases?*

A. A law school case quotes or summarizes an actual court decision. It is, therefore, the same as an appraisal case, as defined above, but it is not an issue case.

Q. *Does it follow that a "case-method" course in accounting uses only cases?*

A. By no means. Thirty years ago some accounting courses did use only cases, but this was found to be an inefficient way of learning. For some purposes, expository material (e.g. lectures, text, articles, programmed material, audio-visual material) is best; for other purposes, problems are best. A case-method course, therefore, has both expository material and problems in addition to cases. A case-method course emphasizes cases.

Q. *Could you illustrate the place of each of these learning methods?*

A. Take the first course in financial accounting as one example. There might be a case on the first day to create interest and to serve as a vehicle for introducing the subject. In the next segment, in which the accounting structure, terminology, and principles are being taught, the emphasis would be primarily on expository material and on the solution of problems with perhaps an occasional case. After this foundation has been laid, the relative proportion of cases would increase. In a second semester course, there might well be a case discussion in most of the classes, but in some classes a fraction of the hour would be spent on expository material, and in other classes the emphasis would be on the solution of problems.

Q. *Could you characterize the function of the textbook-problem approach and of the case approach, respectively?*

A. Education has three general objectives: (1) to impart knowledge, (2) to develop skill, and (3) to change attitudes. A text is a more efficient way of imparting knowledge than is a case. A problem is the more efficient way of developing certain types of skill. A case is best for developing other skills, such as integrating knowledge and building problem identification and attack skills, and for changing attitudes.

Q. *In what subjects is the case method appropriate?*

A. Except for bookkeeping, the case method can be, and is, used in any accounting course. In a bookkeeping course in which the objectives are to impart knowledge and to develop highly routinized skills, the case method is inappropriate. Some believe that the case method should not be used in a first course unless it is likely that advanced courses will also use the case method; otherwise, students may perceive the advanced courses as being artificial and dull.

Q. *Isn't it true that the case method is appropriate only for mature, experienced students?*

A. Not at all. Cases have been used in high schools. The situations discussed in many Sunday School classes are, in fact, cases. In the present stage of development, there is indeed a tendency for the use of cases to vary with the maturity and experience of students; that is, cases are used in almost all executive development programs, they are widely used in graduate schools, and they are less widely used in undergraduate schools. There is no inherent reason why undergraduate schools could not make much more use of cases than they do, however, and there does seem to be a rather sharp increase in the use of cases in undergraduate schools in recent years. The student's educational environment is much more important than his age or experience.

Q. *What do you mean by "environment"?*

A. It is difficult to teach a case method course if it is the only such course that the student has. For best results a student must develop a certain attitude toward the analysis and discussion of cases, and it is helpful if this attitude is reinforced by his experience with cases in more than one course. It is possible to teach a lone case course, but the instructor has a more difficult job because he has sole responsibility for creating the necessary attitude.

Q. *Why is text material important in a case-method course?*

A. From the text the student acquires knowledge. In part he learns this knowledge simply because he will need it on his job. In part he uses it as factual background for the analysis of cases. In general it is inefficient to induce generally accepted principles, terminology, or practices of accounting from cases. To do so would be to re-invent the wheel. It is, however, useful to have a few cases that focus on the development of principles, for these help the student to understand that accounting principles are man-made and subject to debate.

Q. *What are the advantages of the case approach?*

A. There are several. First, educational psychologists tell us that knowledge is learned more thoroughly and retained more completely if the student is actively involved in the learning process. Using knowledge in the analysis of a case is one way of encouraging student involvement. (So is solving a problem.) Knowledge "sticks" better when the student has used it in his analysis of a case than it does when he is merely asked to read and memorize text material.

Analysis and discussion of a case helps the student to appreciate the fact that textbook knowledge does not provide a complete solution to real world problems, except those of a trivial nature. The real world is messier than the text admits. Issues are not black and white; they are many-hued. The student begins to appreciate the relative importance of material that can be learned from a text and of judgments, estimates, and intuition that cannot be so learned. The student begins to realize there is no single acceptable procedure in the real world but rather there is a set of concepts and principles which are broadly accepted within which there is much room for variation and differences in treatment. A classic article on the case method is appropriately titled "Because Wisdom Can't Be Told."

Preparation of a case teaches a student to reason, to apply knowledge to the solution of problems. If the student prepares as a member of a group, he learns interpersonal skills, how to divide up work, to use the work done by others, and to interact cooperatively.

Class discussion gives the student practice in communication. The results of an analysis are ineffective unless action results. In order to get action, those involved must be made to understand and must be persuaded. The executive vice president of a large company said recently: "The technical job of decision making is easy. The really tough job is communication." Class discussion increases this skill.

A case discussion tends to be more interesting to students and also to the instructor than either a discussion of a text or a recitation of the solution of a problem. The class is dealing with real-life problems, and the discussion of these problems often becomes quite heated.

Especially in graduate and executive programs, the interraction of students with various backgrounds is a valuable learning experience. Engineers and those with similar quantitative orientation learn that numbers do not tell the whole story, and students who are majoring in behavioral subjects learn that quantitative techniques are in fact helpful.

Q. *But aren't you overdoing it a bit? Do you claim that a student cannot learn from a textbook-problem approach, or that such an approach is necessarily dull?*

A. Not at all. Students can learn from a text, and a good instructor can make any subject interesting; however, these objectives tend to be easier to achieve with a case approach.

Q. *You make it sound like a panacea. Are there any weaknesses to the case approach?*

A. Frankly, there are. Students, particularly those who have not been exposed previously to the case method, tend to feel frustrated. They want "the word." They think that somewhere there must exist a set of rules which, if carefully memorized and followed, will lead them to the correct solution. They are unhappy about the fact that in their cases different terms are used for the same thing, whereas a text tends to use a single set of terms consistently throughout. Cases are messy and disorderly.

The feeling of frustration arises especially in the area of accounting principles. Students who take an elementary course in accounting taught by the textbook-problem approach often come away with the impression that there is a fairly well-defined body of principles to which there are relatively few exceptions. When they subsequently start a course that uses cases, it takes them some time to get over this notion.

Q. *This sounds like a pretty serious weakness. Can't something be done about it?*

A. No one has discovered a way of avoiding an initial feeling of frustration. The fortunate thing is that after the students become accustomed to a discussion of cases, the feeling gradually disappears of its own accord, and students accept the fact that in real life there is no simple, rigid route to a solution. Students should appreciate that they are fortunate that everything cannot be reduced to a set of rules, for if this could be done, the rules could be programmed into a computer and there would be no need for human managers.

Students should also appreciate the fact that they are better off to become acquainted in the classroom with the uncertainties and frustrations of life rather than waiting until exposure to real-life situations teaches them that life is not as the textbook implies.

Q. *Isn't it true that the case method requires more student preparation time than the textbook-problem method?*

A. There is much difference of opinion about this. The fact is that preparation time varies greatly. At one extreme a student can spend 20 or 30 hours on many cases and still not exhaust all the possibilities. At the other extreme, a facile student can carry on a classroom discussion after merely skimming the case. In practice what seems to happen is that a "norm" is established, and students tend to spend about this amount of time on the case. This resembles the situation in the real world; businessmen could spend much more time on practically any problem then they actually do spend. They must limit themselves to the time that is available.

Q. *You have discussed the student preparation time. What about the instructor?*

A. Somewhat the same situation exists for the instructor. For the same case one instructor may make 15 pages of notes, whereas another instructor may go to class after 30 minutes of preparation. On the average, preparation for case discussion probably does require more time than preparation for a textbook-problem class. Even when a good "teacher's guide" for the case exists, the instructor usually will not agree with it completely; he will want to work out his own analysis. Many cases raise factual questions not covered in the text, and the instructor needs to anticipate these questions and find out the answers to them. Moreover, a thorough review is desirable each time a case is used; the instructor can't simply dust off last year's notes.

Q. *Isn't it true that a case discussion is an inefficient way to acquire knowledge; that is, less pieces of knowledge per minute of class time can be acquired with a case discussion than with alternative instructional techniques?*

A. Definitely. This is why a "pure" case-method approach is rarely used. Certain class periods or portions of class periods are used to impart knowledge. Case discussions reinforce this learning process, but they are not a substitute for it.

Q. *Does it follow then that a student acquires a greater quantity of knowledge in a textbook-problem approach than in a case-method course?*

A. In a literal sense this is probably true,;

that is, in the textbook-problem approach the *breadth* of knowledge can be greater. The *depth* of knowledge is, however, probably less in a textbook-problem course. There is an optimum balance between learning a great many things some of which are quite unimportant, and learning fewer things but learning them well and learning how to apply them.

Q. *You admitted earlier that a case discussion is disorderly. Isn't that a disadvantage?*

A. In addition to being disorderly, cases and case discussion are also ambiguous and contradictory. This does make it difficult for the student to sort out and assimilate what he has learned. Part of almost every case discussion was in retrospect a waste of time, but such waste is inevitable.

Q. *It has been said that the case method is "nonscientific." Is this so?*

A. This assertion stems from the *Encyclopedia Britannica* article by C. West Churchman on management science. In Churchman's view the only scientific methods are those that arrive at a conclusion by a rigorous process of either induction or deduction. Unfortunately, the information available as a basis for deciding most important real-world issues is so incomplete and ambiguous that such scientific methods cannot be applied. The trouble is with the real world, not with the cases which attempt to mirror the real world.

The techniques of management science are of some help in solving certain real-world problems, and the use of these techniques in solving classroom problems is a valuable intellectual exercise to the student. They do not, however, equip the student to cope adequately with real-world problems, any more than a knowledge of anatomy equips a student to become a physician.

Q. *It has been said that since cases report what practice actually was, they perpetuate the past rather than teach new developments.*

A. It would be most unfortunate if schools taught only what current practice is. New ideas are often introduced via armchaired cases, or in a case describing the first application of the idea. If, as time goes on, practical examples of the use of a new idea do not turn up in field investigations, this fact raises legitimate doubts about the usefulness of the new idea. The first cases in linear programming, for example, were armchaired because linear programming was taught in the classroom prior to its use in practice; numerous real-life linear programming cases now are taught. By contrast, there are few if any practical applications of game theory. The designer of a course has to guess which of the new ideas are likely to be fruitful and which are not.

Designing a Course

Q. *Suppose an instructor has decided to teach a case-method course. How does he obtain the cases?*

A. He has three choices. He can select a printed casebook, he can assemble a selection of cases written by others, or he can write his own cases. A printed casebook has the advantage that the author has already done much work. He has selected what he believes to be the most appropriate cases from the vast quantity of those available, he has probably edited some of these cases, and he has prepared a teacher's guide. On the other hand, an instructor may not find a printed casebook that contains cases on the topics that he wants to cover, or one that has the right level of difficulty. He then will assemble his own collection.

Q. *How does he find out about available cases?*

A. The most complete source is the *Bibliography*, published approximately biannually by the Intercollegiate Case Clearing House, (Morgan 23, Soldiers Field, Boston, MA 02163). From the brief description published in the *Bibliography*, he can decide which cases sound useful and request free sample copies. Often, free teaching notes for individual cases are available from the same source. Public accounting firms have collections of cases written for use in their own educational programs that they sometimes are willing to make available to accounting instructors.

Q. *What about the third possibility in which the instructor writes his own cases?*

A. In addition to adding to the inventory of cases, the act of writing a case is a valuable experience in itself. It is, however, more time consuming than most people realize. It is unlikely that an instructor could write all the cases needed for a course.

Q. *What is the optimum section size?*

A. People have strong opinions, but there is very little hard evidence. Some schools have sections of 80 to 100 students, but most instructors regard these sections as large. Other schools have section sizes of 15, 25, 50, or 75 students. As is the case for most pedagogical questions, there are no good empirical data.

Q. *What should the instructor do in class?*

A. There is a great deal of variation among instructors and also a great deal of variation in what a given instructor does on various days. Teaching styles vary in case discussions just as much as they do in other pedagogical approaches. Most people agree that as a minimum the instructor should do two things: (1) keep the discussion on the track, and (2) summarize what has developed. A few do not agree with these two points; they expect students to discipline other students who wander too far from the main point, and they expect students to provide their own summarizes.

Q. *What else might the instructor do?*

A. Depending on his personal preference, he might do any or all of the following:

1. Stimulate student interest in the case and in the accounting issue by a description of its importance and relevance.

2. Provide additional facts or clear up ambiguities in the case.

3. Correct misstatements of facts, and, conversely, praise particularly good points made by the students.

4. Set up an outline of the topics to be discussed, and keep the discussion to this outline.

5. Provide his own analysis of the case, or of some aspect of the case.[1]

Q. *Can you generalize about the fraction of class time that the instructor should use?*

A. Unfortunately, no. One very successful instructor typically opened the class with the question: "Who wants to start the discussion?," and said not one word more during the class except to designate the next speaker. Few people are comfortable with this approach, although in general the instructor talks much less in a case discussion than in a textbook-problem course.

Q. *Shouldn't the instructor take an active role in encouraging students to participate in the discussion?*

A. Yes, probably he should. A call list is a simple device for doing this. It is also helpful if the instructor establishes by his attitude that when a student ventures an opinion, the opinion will not be belittled; that is, that neither the student's personal integrity nor his right to an opinion will be ridiculed. In such an atmosphere, even timid students are willing to speak out, especially when they come to realize that the penalty for trying out a wrong idea or a wrong approach in class is much less severe than it is in the real world.

Q. *What about the opposite problem, the student who takes more than his fair share of the available time?*

A. Sometimes the class exerts social pressure by shuffling of feet, obvious yawns, and the like. Although not all would agree, most instructors believe that it is desirable to cut off such a student so as to keep the discussion moving, realizing that this runs the risk of antagonizing not only the student concerned but also (if the instructor has misjudged the irrelevance of his remarks) the class as a whole.

Q. *Suppose the discussion runs out of steam before the end of the period?*

A. Instructors who are new to the case method worry about this quite a lot and prepare supplementary "lecturettes" so as to be ready to fill the gap. The fact of the matter is that the problem is invariably the reverse; that is, to cut off the discussion at the end of the period.

Q. *Is it a good idea to prepare an outline of the main topics that should be covered in the discussion and the time that should be allotted to each?*

A. Yes, this is an excellent idea provided that the instructor is willing to be flexible in the use of such an outline. It is particularly useful when the case is complicated and when there are controversial numerical calculations. In alternative choice cases, it is desirable to limit the discussion of the quantitative aspects to perhaps half the class period, so that adequate time is available for the judgmental aspects. In order to do this, the instructor may be fairly arbitrary in insisting on a single set of numbers, even though the class does not agree with his numbers and would like to discuss them further. If the case involves a series of accounting transactions, it is usually desirable to predetermine the amount of time to be allotted to the discussion of each transaction.

Q. *Should students be graded on the basis of their participation in class?*

A. Generally, yes, although it is by no means easy to record a grade and keep track of the discussion at the same time. Students are motivated to participate if they know they will be graded, especially if they are promised that the classroom grade will be a "plus factor" and that the final grade will be higher than the grade on written work if class participation is strong, but not lower than the grade on written work if class participation is weak or nonexistent. Under such a ground rule, students can't lose anything by participating in class. Participants in management development programs usually are not graded.

Q. *Should the instructor give his own "solution" to the case?*

A. It depends. If part of the case involves a numerical calculation to which there is a correct answer, such as the calculation of differential costs, it is perfectly appropriate to give this calculation by overhead transparency or on the chalkboard, even if the class has not arrived at it through its own discussion. It is not sound pedagogy for students to leave class with erroneous impressions on factual matters. On judgmental matters, the question is more difficult. When the class has floundered around and is nowhere near a solution, it does appreciate knowing how the instructor analyzes the problem. This provides individual students with a useful check on their own thinking (which may not have come out in class). If, however, this practice is overdone, the class will tend to sit back and wait for the "school solution," and not do hard thinking for themselves. They will then take away the erroneous impression that there is *a solution*, and that other solutions are incorrect.

A similar problem arises when the instructor knows what the people involved in the case actually decided. Students are, of course, interested in learning what actually happened, but they should not get the impression that what the company did was necessarily correct. The important point is the analysis, not the solution.

Q. *Does this mean that you don't care what solution the students arrive at?*

A. No, it does not. It is important that the recommended course of action be consistent with the analysis, and even more important, that the students arrive at *some* recommendation, rather than merely listing a set of pros and cons. They must learn that in the real world a decision must be made, even though the available information is less than one would like to have.

Q. *What if the case does not actually contain enough facts to arrive at a reasonable solution?*

A. In order to make the point that in the real world decisions must be made, the instructor sometimes underplays the importance of evidence that is missing from the case, or of case facts that are ambiguous. Sometimes he asks the students to proceed on the basis of any reasonable assumption as to the missing or ambiguous fact. In the real world, there may be time to seek out missing facts and clarify ambiguities, but the classroom is not exactly like the real world. No case catches all of the nuances that the real world decision maker appreciates. There is not time nor is it generally possible in the classroom to acquire missing information. The classroom is enough like the real world so that a classroom discussion is valuable, but students should never get the impression that the real world is exactly like the classroom.

Q. *Can a case be assigned for more than one day?*

A. Yes, provided that there is a new issue to be discussed on the second day. If the second day is merely a continuation of the first, the discussion tends to be less lively.

Q. *In assigning a case, should the instructor assign specific questions to be answered?*

A. Questions are more likely to be used early in a course than later on. If the issue in the case is not fairly obvious, questions are a useful way of guiding the student's preparation. In class, however, the discussion does not necessarily involve answering these questions. Class discussion may be quite different from student preparation.

Q. *Should all students prepare the case each day?*

A. Practice varies, and variations are highly desirable as a change of pace. An instructor may assign a small group of students to prepare a case thoroughly; other students are expected to have only a general knowledge of it. Or an instructor may assign some students to represent the viewpoint of one party or faction in the case and other students to represent an opposing party or faction.

Examinations

Q. *What about examinations?*

A. Generally, in a course which involves considerable discussion of cases, the final examination should include one or more cases. The examination may also include objective questions. Quizzes can consist of objective questions.

Q. *Aren't such examinations difficult to grade?*

A. They are obviously more difficult to grade than an examination consisting of true-false or multiple-choice questions, but the latter type of examination is also much more difficult to prepare because of the difficulty of framing unambiguous questions. A case examination involves approximately the same grading problem as does an essay examination, although a four-hour examination can consist of one or two cases whereas a four-hour essay examination typically consists of many more questions.

Q. *Isn't this another disadvantage of the case method?*

A. Some people regard it so. Most instructors dislike grading of any type. The ideal world would be either one in which there were no examinations or one in which someone else designed objective questions that could be machine graded. To the instructor reading examinations, the case method is less boring than the use of essay questions because the variety of approaches tends to be greater.

AN ILLUSTRATIVE CASE

There is space here for only a relatively short case. I have selected the Birch Paper Company, which is quite widely known and, in fact, has been discussed in *The Accounting Review.* [2] The case is reproduced in its entirety below.[3]

"If I were to price these boxes any lower than $480 a thousand," said Mr. Brunner, manager of Birch Paper Company's Thompson division, "I'd be countermanding my order of last month for our salesmen to stop shaving their bids and to bid full cost quotations. I've been trying for weeks to improve the quality of our business, and if I turn around now and accept this job at $430 or $450 or something less than $480, I'll be tearing down this program I've been working so hard to build up. The division can't very well show a profit by putting in bids which don't even cover a fair share of overhead costs, let alone give us a profit."

Birch Paper Company was a medium-sized, partly integrated paper company, producing white and kraft papers and paperboard. A portion of this paperboard output was converted into corrugated boxes by the Thompson division, which also printed and colored the outside surface of the boxes. Including Thompson, the company had four producing divisions and a timberland division, which supplied part of the company's pulp requirements.

For several years each division had been judged independently on the basis of its profit and return on investment. Top management had been working to gain effective results from a policy of decentralizing responsibility and authority for all decisions except those relating to overall company policy. The company's top officials felt that in the past few years the concept of decentralization had been successfully applied and that the company's profits and competitive position had definitely improved.

Early in 1957 the Northern division designed a special display box for one of its papers in conjunction with the Thompson division, which was equipped to make the box. Thompson's package design and development staff spent several months perfecting the design, production methods, and materials that were to be used; because of the unusual color and shape, these were far from standard. According to an agreement between the two divisions, the Thompson division was reimbursed by the Northern division for the cost of its design and development work.

When the specifications were all

prepared, the Northern division asked for bids on the box from the Thompson division and from two outside companies, West Paper Company and Erie Papers, Ltd. Each division manager normally was free to buy from whichever supplier he wished and even on sales within the company, divisions were expected to meet the going market price if they wanted the business.

Early in 1957 the profit margins of converters such as the Thompson division were being squeezed. Thompson, as did many other similar converters, bought its board, liner or paper; and its function was to print, cut, and shape it into boxes. Although it bought most of its materials from other Birch divisions, most of Thompson's sales were to outside customers. If Thompson got the order from Northern, it probably would buy its linerboard and corrugating medium from the Southern division of Birch. The walls of a corrugated box consist of outside and inside sheets of linerboard sandwiching the corrugating medium.

About 70 percent of Thompson's out-of-pocket cost of $400 a thousand for the order represented the cost of linerboard and corrugating medium. Though Southern division had been running below capacity and had excess inventory, it quoted the market price, which had not noticeably weakened as a result of the oversupply. Its out-of-pocket costs on both liner and corrugating medium were about 60 percent of the selling price.

The Northern division received bids on the boxes of $480 a thousand from the Thompson division, $430 a thousand from West Paper Company, and $432 a thousand from Erie Papers, Ltd. Erie Papers offered to buy from Birch the outside linerboard with the special printing already on it, but would supply its own inside liner and corrugating medium. The outside liner would be supplied by the Southern division at a price equivalent to $90 a thousand boxes, and would be printed for $30 a thousand by the Thompson division. Of the $30, about $25 would be out-of-pocket costs.

Since this situation appeared to be a little unusual, Mr. Kenton, manager of the Northern division, discussed the wide discrepancy of bids with Birch's commercial vice president. He told the commercial vice president, "We sell in a very competitive market, where higher costs cannot be passed on. How can we be expected to show a decent profit and return on investment if we have to buy our supplies at more than 10 percent over the going market?"

Knowing that Mr. Brunner had on occasion in the past few months been unable to operate the Thompson division at capacity, the commercial vice president thought it odd that Mr. Brunner would add the full 20 percent overhead and profit charge to his out-of-pocket costs. When he asked Mr. Brunner about this over the telephone, his answer was the statement that appears at the beginning of the case. Mr Brunner went on to say that having done the developmental work on the box, and having received no profit on that, he felt entitled to a good markup on the production of the box itself.

The vice president explored further the cost structures of the various divisions. He remembered a comment the controller had made at a meeting the week before to the effect that costs that for one division were variable could be largely fixed for the company as a whole. He knew that in the absence of specific orders from top management, Mr. Kenton would accept the lowest bid, namely that of the West Paper Company for $430. However, it would be possible for top management to order the acceptance of another bid if the situation warranted such action. And though the volume represented by the transactions in question was less than 5 percent of the volume of any divisions involved, other transactions could conceivably raise similar problems later.

Questions

1. Does the system motivate Mr. Brunner in such a way that actions he

takes in the best interests of the Thompson division are also in the best interests of the Birch Paper Company? If your answer is "no", give some specific instances related as closely as possible to the type of situation described in the case. Would the manager of other divisions be correctly motivated?

2. What should the vice president do?

Comment

Presumably, the first thing the student should do with this case is to work out the differential costs and revenues of the three alternatives. In assigning the case, it is probably desirable to state this requirement specifically. This part of the analysis is a problem in the sense in which the term is used in this paper; that is, it has a correct answer. The facts needed to arrive at this answer are scattered throughout the case, and the student, therefore, gets practice in finding and interpreting the relevant facts which he does not get with a typical problem; generally in a problem only relevant facts are given. With some intellectual effort and relatively simple arithmetic, the student should arrive at the conclusion that the differential costs to Birch Paper Company for having the boxes made in the Thompson Division are lower than those for either of the other alternatives, and also that the Thompson Division would report a higher divisional profit if it manufactured the boxes and sold them at $430 a thousand, assuming the Thompson Division is not operating at capacity.

If this were a problem rather than a case, the discussion would end when this conclusion had been reached. Since it is a case, the students are supposed to go on to a recommended course of action. Some will reason that this course of action is obvious: choose the alternative with the lowest differential costs. But others may call attention to the first sentence of the case in which Mr. Brunner argues against this course of action. Mr. Brunner is on the scene, and he has access to the same figures that the students have used. Is he not able to make the same calculations that the students have just completed? Presumably, he can. Why, then, is he apparently willing to reject what the figures show to be the best course of action for him?

As soon as the students start thinking about this question, they see that much more is involved than a simple calculation of differential costs. Mr. Brunner is trying to implement a new pricing strategy. If he accepts this order, his action might undermine this strategy. There are good, possibly conclusive, arguments for the position he has taken.

All of this is background for the real issue of the case, which is an appraisal of the system of transfer prices used in this company. Students should be asked to evaluate this system and to recommend improvements in it if these are desirable. In order to do this, they should apply the transfer pricing criteria that they have presumably learned from a text, and in particular, the idea of goal congruence. Goal congruence means that a system should be such that the actions it motivates a manager to take in his own best interests are also in the best interests of the company. This is a slippery concept to understand, and thinking about it in the context of this case facilitates such an understanding. In my own opinion, the system is fine as it stands, especially since managers are permitted to negotiate transfer prices with one another (and this point helps to drive home the importance of negotiation in a transfer price system). Other instructors and students disagree with this conclusion and recommend, for example, a system that identifies the variable costs.

Regardless of the final conclusion (and it is important that the class come to *some* final conclusion), the discussion of this case produces the following results:

1. It gives practice in calculating differential costs, thus helping to solidify an understanding of the concept of differential costs.

2. It gives practice in finding and using relevant facts that are not clearly stated and that are scattered among some irrelevant facts.

3. It gives practice in applying the criteria for a transfer price system, and thus aids in understanding and remembering these criteria.

4. It requires the student to analyze a situation, to arrive at a conclusion, and, if he participates in the class discussion, to defend it.

Although this is a short case, it has been used successfully for two class periods, the first period focusing on differential costs, and the second on the transfer price system. This is a rich case, and it should be noted that a rich case is not necessarily a long case.

RECENT DEVELOPMENTS

The case method itself is a teaching innovation, for although it has been around for fifty years or more, its widespread use is a fairly recent development. The method continues to evolve, and some of the new developments are described briefly below. Additional information can be obtained from the persons listed.

Computer-Assisted Cases

For a few accounting cases, and for a number of finance cases that are sometimes used in accounting courses, interactive computer programs have been developed that make possible a much more sophisticated analysis than is possible with the usual manual method. One type of case in which the computer is helpful is that involving the preparation of a budget or of a cash forecast. A great deal of pencil pushing is involved in such a case, and the computer program eliminates most of this work and permits the student with little effort to find the effect of various assumptions. Cases involving alternative accounting practices, especially those that affect several accounts, also have programs that permit the effect of using various alternatives over a period of years, and under various cyclical assumptions, to be found quickly. These programs can be used only when computer terminals are available, however. Further information can be obtained from Professor David Hawkins, Harvard Business School.

Prior Agreement on Assumptions

Professor John K. Harris of the University of Nebraska-Lincoln, assigns a group of three or four students to present the case to the class. This group formulates and distributes in advance to the class as a whole a list of assumptions that they propose to make in analyzing the case. Other students use these assumptions in preparing the case. In class, the first order of business is to discuss the necessity and reasonableness of these assumptions. Professor Harris finds that this practice tends to focus the discussion and to place a premium on logic and reasoning because all students are proceeding from the same set of facts and assumptions and are not spending time arguing about them. In particular, it simplifies the discussion of numerical calculations. It also highlights the importance of making reasonable assumptions and only those assumptions that are necessary to a discussion of the issue.

Grading Group Discussions

Professor Charles E. Yeager divides his class into groups of five or six students. One group is assigned to present a case. Members of that group grade each other on such factors as cooperation, writing skills, statistical skills, administrative ability, and willingness to work. The instructor grades the overall case discussion, and this becomes the average grade for the group. Grades of individual group members vary around this average according to the rankings made by group members and by the instructor.

An Incident Process Approach

Professor Earl A. Spiller, Jr., of Washington University, has developed materials that are designed to teach students to ask the right questions. He assigns a case in which the issue is whether or not a company should purchase a new executive airplane, but the case itself has few facts. Students are divided into teams and are told that the instructor will provide additional information upon request. The instructor has considerable additional data on the characteristics of the airplane under consideration and on the company. He provides this information if, but only if, it is requested. He also points out the irrelevance or unobtainability of other questions that are asked. After obtaining the additional data, each team prepares its analysis of the case.

CONCLUSION

A basic premise of the case method is that one learns best by doing. It follows that the best way to learn about the case method is to give it a try and observe what happens. It can be a stimulating, rewarding experience both for the instructor and for the student.

FOOTNOTES

[1] For a longer list see "Two Dozen Ways of Handling Cases," Harold W. Fox, *Collegiate News and Views*, (Spring 1973), pp. 17-20.

[2] R.L. Virgil et al., "A Classroom Experience in the Behavioral Implications of Accounting Performance Measurements," *The Accounting Review* (April 1973), pp. 410-18.

[3] Copyright © 1960 by the President and Fellows of Harvard College. Used by permission.

Team Teaching

Kenneth W. Perry
University of Illinois

Introduction

This paper discusses the pros and cons of an instructional concept which emphasizes the utilization of the best talent at the most opportune time and which appears to offer many possibilities for an interdisciplinary approach to the teaching of accounting.

Team teaching, as the term implies, is a method of instruction by which a number of individuals work together in a concerted effort to perform related teaching activities in the pursuit of common educational objectives. When applied to accounting education, as indicated by the American Accounting Association's Committee on Multi-Media Instruction in Accounting, team teaching is basically a method of organizing groups of students for instructional purposes so that they may receive the benefit of instruction from the most capable teacher in a particular area and also receive the benefit of increased intellectual stimulation as the result of contact with several personalities rather than with only one teacher.[1] Implicit in the team concept is the belief that the desired educational objectives can best be achieved through the coordinated joint effort of a group of instructors rather than through unrelated individual efforts, and a willingness of the various members of the team to cooperate in forming an integrated system of instruction as a means of achieving these objectives.

Ohm suggests the following rationale for team teaching. Although his comments are directed primarily toward the pre-college level institution, they are equally apropos to institutions of higher learning.

The word "team" suggests a type of working relationship among individuals that does not presently exist in most schools. The nature of this relationship requires some arbitrary definition if a useful distinction is to be made between teams and other forms of cooperative working relationships between members of the school staff. It is based on the assumption that one of the major functions of teaching is the control and direction of the necessary and sufficient variables that form, or directly influence, the teaching-learning process.

A team relationship occurs when a group of teachers and students as an organized unit, accept and carry out decision-making responsibilities for a set of instructional variables such as time, space, group size, group composition, teacher assignment and resource allocation. In addition to the variables normally under control of the teacher, the team unit permits delegation to the instructional team, decisions usually made by smaller, single-teacher class unit or organization. The value of team teaching will be determined by the extent to which team organization permits effective coordination of a larger number of variables important to the achievement of higher levels of teacher and student performance.[2]

HISTORICAL PERSPECTIVE

Team teaching has been rather widely employed in elementary and secondary schools throughout the United States since the mid-to-late nineteen fifties. The team approach has been used in one form or another in a number of colleges and universities since the late nineteen forties. However, based on the limited discussion of its philosophy and methodology in the educational literature dealing with higher education, team teaching does not appear to have received widespread acceptance at the college and university level.

Team Teaching at the Pre-College Level

At the pre-college level team teaching often has been employed to utilize master teachers as team leaders, allowing them to teach larger groups of students than normally would be feasible. At the same time, by the utilization of teaching aides and assistants, small-group instruction can center on materials presented by the master teacher in his lectures.

Another kind of team arrangement used at the pre-college level is the so-called "associate" type which consists of several teachers joined together to form an instructional bloc. For example, a team from an elementary school may consist of teachers in complementary skills, such as an expert in reading, one in social studies, and one in mathematics and science. At the secondary level teachers of a single subject such as English may develop specialties within that subject and become experts in grammar, literature, language, or other disciplines.[3]

Since 1957 when the team teaching explosion began on the pre-college level, there has been an extensive series of experiments with the method. Many of these experiments have been supported by grants to the Commission on the Experimental Study of the Utilization of the Staff in the Secondary School, which was appointed by the National Association of Secondary School Principals and supported by the Fund for the Advancement of Education. The common features and results of many of the various experiments are ably reported in issues of the National Association of Secondary School Principles *Bulletin*. Many of the schools involved in the experiments are associated with colleges and universities such as the University of Chicago, Claremont Graduate School, Harvard, Stanford, the University of Wisconsin, and the University of Maine. The school systems of Concord, Lexington, and Newton, Massachusetts, for example, joined Harvard University in the School and University Program for Research and Development. Commonly referred to as SUPRAD, this alliance is responsible for many of the original projects in the team-teaching area. The Harvard-Lexington Program is given considerable credit for having developed many of the distinguishing features of the team approach which currently is being used with variations throughout the country.

The Claremont Graduate School in Claremont, California, has assisted in the development of teaching teams in a number of schools in southern California. Aided by grants from the Ford Foundation and the Fund for the Advancement of Education, the so-called Claremont Plan, which includes several California schools working cooperatively with the Claremont Graduate School, presently is using a team-teaching setup that practically amounts to "a school within a school." The Claremont Graduate School projects are considered by many educators as representative of the best team-teaching efforts in the country.

Team Teaching at the College and University Level

Although team teaching is not yet widely employed at the college and university level—or if so it is not officially recognized as such—it nevertheless has been used in several institutions of higher learning to achieve a wide variety of educational objectives. As an example, team teaching has been instituted in some schools as a method of teaching highly selected superior students, highly selected marginal students, and students of relatively limited ability. This method also has been used to teach such diverse subjects as nursing, marketing, statistics, dentistry, cybernetics, history, chemistry, and philosophy, among others. The following subjects and related universities are illustrative:

Cybernetics—University of Florida
Dentistry—University of Kentucky
Philosophy—Florida State University
Statistics—Hofstra University

Regarding the study of cybernetics at the University of Florida, a team approach was initiated when a new course entitled "Cybernetics and Society" was inaugurated in 1967. This course, the objective of which is to acquaint the student with the role of computer technology in the collecting, processing, and disseminating of information, was developed by five instructors who represented the areas of social sciences, the humanities, and mathematics in the general education core curriculum. During the first quarter in which the course was offered, these five instructors as a team taught only seven students, providing an unusual opportunity for effective course development. Eventually the course was taught on a rotational basis by three of the original team of five, and consisted of three weekly lectures and one weekly two-hour laboratory session. The five-quarter-hour course explores the historical development of computers, introduces the student to computer operations and programming, discusses the present applications of computers, and concludes with a consideration of the philosophical and social impact of computer technology.[4]

In 1956 the Ford Foundation and the Fund for the Advancement of Education under a program administered by the Committee on Utilization of College Teaching Resources funded a group of experiments to demonstrate a series of comprehensive approaches to general education. Experiments have been conducted at Antioch College, Yellow Springs, Ohio; Austin College, Sherman, Texas; Goddard College, Plainfield, Vermont; Hofstra College, Hempstead, New York; the University of Kentucky, Lexington, Kentucky; and Wayne State University, Detroit, Michigan. Using team teaching in various ways, the respective institutions have attempted to revise their curricula, promote independent study, provide large-group instruction, and bring into college and university instruction a wider use of modern teaching technology.

ORGANIZATIONAL STRUCTURE

The way in which a specific team is organized will vary with the institution in which it operates, with the particular educational objectives for which it is designed and with the human, financial, and technological resources upon which it depends. Organizational patterns will range all the way from the simple to the very complex and from the informal to the formal, with the number of team members varying from two or three to several. Regardless of the particular organizational structure in a given situation, the faculty group generally is organized with one faculty member functioning as the "in-charge" or primary instructor, and the other faculty members sharing in the teaching responsibilities by utilizing their particular expertise in all possible areas.

Simple Structure

A prime requisite for the successful operation of any team teaching program, as is true of any other successful method of instruction, is that it be free from unnecessary and restrictive administrative control. When a team consists of only two or three members, the organizational structure can be both simple and informal and still allow the presentation of instructional material to be as broad and varied, as each instructor's knowledge and ability complements that of the others. When operating in an informal environment, autonomous self-directed teams are ordinarily, and normally more or less spontaneously, formed by the various faculty members involved, rather than by formal administrative action. For example, an accounting course in which the author is usually the primary instructor contains several sessions on income taxes which are taught by a colleague who is eminently qualified in this area. This course is a popular one in the accounting curriculum at the University of Illinois, and without a doubt the team approach, in this case both informal and on a small scale, has contributed greatly to its success.

Complex Structure

Whereas the organizational pattern of many teams may be simple and informal, other team setups are considerably more complex. Stephens College, Columbia, Missouri, for example, combines general education and team instruction with a house plan by which a large group of students, normally about one hundred, take the same general education courses and live in the same dormitory. Instructors in the courses—in this case Communications, Basic Beliefs in Human Experience, General Humanities, and Contemporary Social Issues— have their offices in their students' dormitory and also meet their classes in an instructional suite there.

The team system can be the pivot of an entire two-year college program. This is true of Boston University's College of Basic Studies, which has used a team system from the very beginning of its existence in 1952. Originally, the team approach was introduced as a means of helping faculty members integrate the various subjects in the curriculum; later it was retained not only because it proved indispensable to this end, but also because it strengthened and individualized relationships between students and teachers and enabled students to progress more rapidly.

Faculty Mix

On a given team, the faculty makeup (mix) is influenced by such factors as balance, personality, personal preferences, and the overall needs of the academic program. Proper balance suggests that inexperienced team members are best assigned to teams of predominantly experienced personnel. (As will be noted later, the well-organized and properly conducted team teaching program may well be one of the best vehicles available for the training of the new and inexperienced faculty member.) Other factors influencing team balance include rank and leadership ability. Sometimes a five-member team will function better and retain continuity of effort if at least two or three of its personnel are reassigned to the same team for several consecutive quarters or semesters. Needless to say, with the passage of time realignment of team members will take place as a result of the normal process of attrition within a faculty as well as in response to changes in the overall academic requirements of the program and the professional needs and desires of the individual faculty members. One excellent means of insuring the availability of qualified team teachers is to train such faculty in a continuing teacher-training or internship program.

POTENTIAL BENEFITS OF TEAM TEACHING

Ideally, an educational team is composed of a group of teachers and students united in a common effort to overcome obstacles to learning, to share jointly in the educational process, and to reach higher levels of understanding and self-fulfillment. However, almost any innovation is likely to have both good and bad effects on many aspects of the social system into which it is introduced, and team teaching is no exception. For example, the introduction of team teaching into a given educational system may eventually affect areas ranging all the way from the utilization of physical facilities to the normative beliefs and sentiments (e.g., attitudes toward autonomy and academic freedom) of the faculty.

Potential benefits to be derived from team teaching include:

    1. Provision for in-service training.

    2. An integrated approach to the acquisition of knowledge.

    3. Interdisciplinary development of Faculty.

In-Service Training

As Ohm suggests, the instructional team may well have few peers as a form of in-service training.[5] In the same vein, James B. Conant in his book, *The Education of American Teachers,* proposes that team teaching be used as a means of inducting the new teacher into the teaching of his subject. Conant suggest a four-member team consisting of two senior teachers, a third or fourth year probationary teacher, and a beginning teacher. He argues for a four-year period of induction into the teaching profession and notes that during the first year the beginner is a very junior member of the team, while by the fourth year he has become a senior junior so to speak and almost on a par with the teacher who holds a permanent appointment. Conant's contention is that the beginning teacher is being both educated and evaluated during this probationary period, and that in the event he is not successful, the program will serve as a weeding out device.

Although Conant's comments are directed primarily to the pre-college teacher, his views apply equally as well to the instructional staffs of institutions of higher education. As indicated by LaFauci and Richter, team teaching by its very nature and the manner in which it operates has special significance for training college faculty. They contend that the opportunities for creative involvement in cooperative curriculum development, for concurrent exposure to many broad disciplines and their methodologies, for direct participation in both team and departmental activities, and for close personal contact with both faculty and students make teaching internships particularly suitable to a team-teaching situation.[6]

Too often the beginning teacher at the college level is placed in a classroom situation without ever having adequately prepared a lesson or rehearsed a presentation. He must "swim or sink" on his own, and, as is well known, the first impression of a new teacher is also often the lasting one. To assume automatically that because an individual has been granted an M.A. or Ph.D. degree, he is by edict a good teacher is of course absurd. Without a doubt, the failure to train the new college teacher adequately before placing him in a classroom situation has been one of the most expensive follies ever thrust upon the educational process. Not only are the students shortchanged, but the taxpayers and the whole of society eventually suffer.

As pointed out by Polos, the new teacher often dwells in a world of confusion, anxiety, and urgency.[7] However, the team, if properly structured, provides a highly organized framework within which he can master the mysteries of the art of teaching. Here the neophyte finds some form of security and flexibility, an opportunity to learn to share in planning, time for preparation, and the opportunity to observe the methods of experienced colleagues. He learns how to avoid the pitfalls that often plague the inexperienced teacher and receives valuable advice and guidance on matters such as grading and discipline. In short, the properly structured team provides a foundation upon which the beginning teacher can stand firmly and confidently.

While the preceding comments have been directed primarily toward the beginning teacher, the in-service growth advantages of a team-teaching situation also can be of great assistance to the poor and average teacher who has experience in the field.

The poor teacher who recognizes his own weaknesses and is sincerely interested in improving has many opportunities in a team-teaching situation. (Obviously, the poor teacher who cannot or does not wish to improve does not belong in the classroom.) If a less than able teacher is willing to learn, he can profit from the intimate contact with fellow teachers. In a team-teaching situation individual shortcomings are readily apparent; thus, in self-defense the poorly prepared teacher will add strength to his teaching repertoire. At the very least he can imitate the more capable members of the team.

The average teacher likewise can improve his competence and classroom skills through his association with other team members. Many average teachers are average only because they never have been encouraged or inspired to overcome mediocrity. When opportunity is provided for intellectual discourse with fellow teachers, latent talents are likely to flourish.

If maximum in-service training benefits are to be derived from a team-teaching situation, it perhaps goes without saying that the "in-charge" teacher must possess a high degree of self-acceptance as well as the wisdom to recognize the strengths and weaknesses of other members of the team. In addition, he must have the ability to implement this knowledge, with purposeful performances. In a team situation which has an effective "in-charge" leader, team members will encourage and assist each other both to improve their classroom competence and to develop new instructional techniques for meeting the continuing challenge of contemporary events.

Integration of Knowledge

In general, institutions of higher learning are designed to seek, extend, and transmit knowledge. But as Say implied over one hundred years ago when he said, "A knowledge of facts, without a knowledge of the affinities which bind them together, is of no more value than the crude information of a public clerk...,"[8] knowledge is more than mere information. It is the awareness which the individual experiences as he reflects upon his environment. Information about people, places, things, and processes is essential. However, while much of this may be learned atomistically by studying various subject areas, if a student is to gain real knowledge, these parts must be integrated to form a whole.

For many institutions of higher learning, the general education offerings constitute the only visible attempt at integration of knowledge, and in these cases it must be assumed that the student not only is capable of, but will actually achieve, the necessary integration himself. Needless to say, this is a rather bold assumption. A general education requirement composed of a set of courses taken from the humanities, the physical sciences, and the social sciences does not necessarily carry with it the requisites for integration.

Although currently we are not optimizing the integration of knowledge in our educational institutions, it must be admitted that our institutions of higher learning do possess all the resources necessary for such integration; they need only to commit themselves to this purpose. While team teaching in and of itself will never provide a panacea for all or even most of the problems higher education is facing, it does appear to offer excellent opportunities for integrating knowledge.

Unfortunately, as all knowledgeable educators recognize, educational institutions are more often than not very unwieldy. It is one thing to express "the integration of knowledge" as one of the chief objectives of an institution but quite another to charge the faculty with its implementation. Ideally, each faculty member would participate in such a way as to maximize his contribution to this purpose. Furthermore, there would be combined faculty action designed to enhance the overall program.

An excellent example of what an institution can do along this line by the utilization of team teaching is the humanities program at Scripps College in Claremont, California. The dominant feature of the curriculum is the sequence of courses in the two-year humanities program which is captioned, "The Ancient World to America in the Contemporary World." The unusual organization of the curriculum integrates five broad fields of interest: literature, the arts, social studies, science and psychology, philosophy and religion. This type of curriculum, taught by highly trained faculty members operating as a team, makes possible, as Polos has pointed out, "...an appreciation of the continuity and wholeness of learning." [9] Stated another way, the knowledge of the five fields is synergistic—that is, an understanding of the five together is more than just a summation of the knowledge of the five individual fields.

Regarding accounting education and the integration of knowledge, as is repeatedly stressed throughout the AICPA's *Horizons for a Profession* (generally referred to as "The Common Body of Knowledge"), accounting exists within a socio-economic environment, and since it interrelates with other disciplines it is not readily subject to isolation from its environment. For example, accounting measurements, analyses, terminology, and statement format are intrinsically financial. Thus, to understand accounting properly, one necessarily must have been exposed to the study of finance. Likewise, an understanding of the relationship of accounting to the broad field of economics is an important one for the student of either accountancy or economics. For example, accounting for private business is socially justifiable only if the entire economic structure itself is justifiable. Accounting, being an integral part of the business and economic structure of a nation, must stand or fall with that structure. Unfortunately, the actual interdependence of educational disciplines, of human life, and of nations normally far surpasses the individual's awareness of it, and perhaps still more importantly his arrangements for cooperation. Wisdom is largely the perception of this interdependence.

As indicated by Polos, "Team teaching is an excellent vehicle for interdisciplinary combinations of knowledge."[10] Of particular significance is the potential of team interdisciplinary instruction for meeting more directly and more completely the concerns of today's students. As is generally well known, the contemporary college student not infrequently decries the lack of relevance and existential meaning of the traditional curriculum.[11] Team instruction permits a group of instructors representing diverse fields to construct and present a program which has a coherent pattern, a meaningful structure of interrelated concepts and ideas. As students come to expect their instructors to point up relationships among various areas, they begin to develop a sense of the interrelatedness of concepts, ideas, and facts. In this way they can gradually, if not instantaneously, realize that there is a wholeness and a coherence to real education.

Interdisciplinary Development of Faculty

While team teaching allows instructors

to share their knowledge and teaching techniques in dealing with a comprehensive and complex field, interdisciplinary instruction by its very nature presents continuing challenge to the team teacher. To be successful he must constantly broaden his scholarly interests and learn more of the content of all the courses in the curriculum in order better to be able to find points at which cooperative effort is most likely to be fruitful. As his knowledge of the curriculum increases, his ability to contribute to the development of an integrated program is strengthened and the role he plays as a team member becomes more valuable.

As indicated by Gordon and Howell in their well-known and often quoted *Higher Education for Business,* too many faculty members in schools of business view their own areas of interest both too narrowly and too superficially and are too little concerned with what has been called "the intellectual foundations of professional work."[12] Since the businessman of the decades ahead will need a higher order of analytical ability, a more sophisticated command of analytical tools, a greater degree of organizational skill, a greater capacity for dealing with the external environment of business, and more of an ability to cope with rapid change than has been true in the past,[13] it is perhaps obvious that the successful business teacher of the future will possess an interdisciplinary orientation.

In the past the classroom teacher was trained to perform more or less as an individual, and in the self-contained classroom a premium was placed upon independence. Since team teaching provides for an integration of knowledge and an openness that could never be obtained in the self-contained classroom, there is a great possibility that in the future educational emphasis will be placed not upon individual teaching performances but upon the collective abilities of a group of teachers operating as a team. In this event interdependence will take precedence over independence, making an interdisciplinary approach almost mandatory.

By working with a team composed of instructors from several areas and disciplines, the individual teacher inevitably finds that his own knowledge of and interest in his colleagues' areas and fields are increased. Many artificial academic barriers such as departmental or divisional boundaries are readily penetrated and bridged by the physical proximity, continuous communication, and common commitment inherent in a team-teaching program. In order to understand the various perspectives from which his students view other courses, the successful team teacher must strive continually to broaden his own knowledge, thereby increasing his effectiveness both as a team teacher and as a teacher in his own specialized field.

POSSIBLE BARRIERS TO TEAM TEACHING

As is true of all other methods of instruction, team teaching is not without its possible drawbacks or weaknesses. As indicated by LaFauci and Richter, some of the more important barriers to a good team teaching program are:

1. Lack of understanding and commitment.
2. Multiplicity of demands placed on faculty.
3. Resistance to change.
4. Absence of available research.[14]

While no one drawback is unsurmountable in and of itself, these weaknesses taken as a whole can combine to impair the overall effectiveness of a system.

Lack of Understanding and Commitment

Since one of the chief objectives of the team-teaching concept is the integration of subject matter from several areas or disciplines, each member of the team, to be an effective participant, must possess a broad knowledge of the principles, concepts, and methodologies of several areas of study. This means that he must constantly broaden his understanding and find new points at which meaningful relationships among the various areas may be developed or reinforced.

Team teaching also presupposes a willingness to participate in a cooperative effort, to share in joint decisions, and to compromise when necessary. In spite of the potential benefits to be derived from the team approach, on occasion some instructors are either unable or unwilling to follow team consensus in decisions which may affect their autonomy as teachers of a specific subject. Needless to say, an instructor who is unwilling to use an interdisciplinary approach in his teaching or is unwilling to work cooperatively with others toward common goals is not likely to be very happy or successful in a team-teaching program.

Miltiplicity of Demands Placed on Faculty

Faculty members frequently find it difficult if not impossible to accept the many roles which they must assume as members of a team in order that the team may function effectively. The demands made upon them as scholars, teachers, counselors, department members, and members of a college faculty and university community are constant and sometimes excessive. Thus, it may not be unusual for a faculty member in a team-teaching program to find one of his roles in conflict with another. For example, a conflict between the demands of the department and the requirements of the team may sometimes lead to a division of interest on the part of an instructor, reducing his total contribution to the program and thereby threatening his welfare and security as a faculty member. Likewise, a teacher may find that the demands of his role as a member of a team, which require the constant broadening of his scholarship, will gradually weaken his command of his special field.

Resistance to Change

As is the case with individual instruction, one of the greatest challenges a team may encounter is that of retaining maximum effectiveness in the face of changing conditions. As the distinguished educator and author Howard Mumford Jones so aptly put it in his work entitled *Education and World Tragedy*:

> One difficulty with educational programs is that they are never built for time but are always built for eternity. Each pedagogical reformer, convinced that he has found at last a changeless and enduring way of educating human nature, announces his program as a series of timeless absolutes. Every curriculum has an air of being built upon the impregnable rock of holy scripture; and, since academic institutions are highly conservative, the new curriculum, once alive and vital, when it becomes moribund, either changes slowly or changes not at all. Thus in the British Isles a curriculum for the public schools that had real vitality for the Renaissance lingered spinelessly into the eighteenth and nineteenth centuries, nor could all the wit and wisdom of persons as gifted as Sydney Smith, Thackeray, John Stuart Mill and Thomas Huxley easily affect a change. So in American schools and colleges what has been, by sheer power of endurance, takes on a patina of wisdom and must, in the minds of teachers, forever be.

As we all know, change frequently disturbs our complacency—that comfortable feeling that all's right with the world. When this comfortable state is threatened, the normal reaction is to counterattack. Thus, it perhaps is only normal that many faculty members tend to resist change, resting content with programs and teaching methods which bear their own or their colleagues' imprints and which already reflect their own academic interests, their considered compromises, and their overall educational philosophies.

Change, by its very nature, implies criticism. Every method, every procedure was devised by someone else or grew under someone else's supervision. When changes are recommended, those individuals closely related to the previous method or procedure often feel their ideas and efforts are being criticized.

In the face of such built-in opposition, innovators may find it difficult if not impossible to install new programs, especially if, as is the usual case, new proposals must undergo committee review and recommendation, departmental scrutiny, and ultimate vote by the faculty. Progress toward change often moves very, very slowly. Modern educational programs must be responsive both to the past and the present and, if change cannot at times be brought about speedily, education will tend to lose its relevance. Obviously, if team teaching is to be successful, the teachers involved must have more than a passing superficial interest in change, and their interest must run deeper than a mere psychological involvement in change for its own sake. The change should be directed toward breaking the undesirable locksteps of tradition for the sole purpose of improvement of the learning process.

Unfortunately, the recognition of a need for change in the educational process is often associated with the young instructor and the resistance to change with the older faculty member. In a given situation, as any astute observer of a modern educational system recognizes, nothing could be further from the truth. The "curiosity age" of the instructor is important, not the chronological age. Any instructor, young or old, experienced or inexperienced, whose outlook is flexible with regard to change, experimentation, and variation has the potential to become an effective team teacher. As the eminent English educator Charlton Laird so fittingly puts it: "Good teachers are good teachers because they have brains, great learning, engaging personalities, and enough experience to learn what to do with themselves."[16]

Absence of Available Research

Another drawback to team teaching is presently found in the lack of precise knowledge of how it affects learning and the extent to which subsequent success can be attributed directly to the processes of team instruction. Most of the research which has attempted to evaluate recent experiments in team teaching indicates that currently there is little concrete evidence that improved learning results from this method of instruction. Much of the enthusiasm for team teaching seems to stem from subjective elements such as "testimonials," which do not lend themselves to precise measurements.

In sum, research in the area of team teaching is limited, and, at present, conclusions which will yield satisfactory guidelines for new team-teaching programs are not available. As a result, each new program must stand on its own and proceed more or less by trial and error, without the benefit of careful research which would ease the way and provide some degree of assurance for attaining desirable outcomes. The problem of determining the degree of effectiveness of each of a team's functions and the extent to which each variable in a specific program contributes to the student's eventual success will be solved only after more time, energy, and financial resources have been devoted to research on team instruction.

CONCLUSION

Students throughout the world are expressing dissatisfaction with contemporary educational institutions. This is particularly true in higher education. In addition to other grievances, today's college students complain that academic bureaucracy and impersonality are shortchanging the educational process, if not actually thwarting their opportunities to learn; that college faculties are more concerned with maintaining the status quo by transmitting traditions than with restructuring society; that college and university administrators preach democratic involvement while they practice authoritarian control; and that many of our best institutions of higher learning have become mere handmaidens of the industrial, military, and political complex. The militants among them are alienated and often reject the educational system in its entirety, while the conformists indicate by their passive acceptance the failure of the system to provide the necessary stimulation and challenge.

Recent unrest among students has made it unmistakably clear that in attempting to meet the needs of modern youth, we as educators cannot rely solely on one method of instruction such as Mark Hopkins' log, B. F. Skinner's teaching machine, or the case method. Somehow a way must be found to restructure the educational process so that a lively and meaningful dialogue between students and teachers takes place with each and every encounter. Fortunately, college and university faculties and administrators now are being compelled to reexamine their educational theories and practices in order to understand the causes of student unrest and to seek new and positive means of dealing with them. The author believes that team teaching provides one relatively new and highly promising approach to many of the problems currently faced by higher education, because by its very nature it promotes close personal relationships, invites continuous student involvement, and, perhaps most importantly, respects the autonomy and integrity of each student as an individual. Even though there is an absence of conclusive experimental data to support in detail its methodology, team teaching appears to offer sufficient observable advantages to both faculty and students to warrant its continued utilization and growth while the necessary research is being carried out. As educators we must recognize we are in a "twilight zone" of team teaching education and only time will present us with a better understanding and a more refined image of it.

FOOTNOTES

[1] American Accounting Association, Committee on Multi-Media Instruction in Accounting, *The Accounting Review*, Supplement to Vol. XLVII, (1972), p. 154.

[2] Robert E. Ohm, "Toward a Rationale for Team Teaching," *Administrator's Notebook*, Vol. IX, March (1961), p. 1.

[3] Judson T. Shaplin and Henry F. Olds, editors, *Team Teaching*, (New York: Harper & Row, 1964), p. 18.

[4] Horatio M. LaFauci and Peyton E. Richter, *Team Teaching at the College Level*, (New York: Pergamon Press, 1970), p. 10.

[5] Ohm, *op. cit.*, p. 4.

[6] LaFauci and Richter, *op. cit.*, p. 36.

[7] Nicholas C. Polos, *The Dynamics of Team Teaching*, (Dubuque, Iowa: Wm. C. Brown Company, 1965), p. 106.

[8] J.B. Say, *A Treatise on Political Economy*, (Boston: Wells and Lilly, 1821), p. 27.

[9] Polos, *op. cit.*, p. 47.

[10] *Ibid.*, p. 104.

[11] LaFauci and Richter, *op. cit.*, p. 43.

[12] Robert Aaron Gordon and James Edwin Howell, *Higher Education for Business* (New York: Columbia University Press, 1959), p. 355.

[13] *Ibid.*, p. 127.

[14] LaFauci and Richter, *op. cit.*, p. 113.

[15] Howard Mumford Jones, *Education and World Tragedy* (Cambridge, Massachusetts: Harvard University Press, 1946), pp. 88-89.

[16] Charlton Grant Laird, *And Gladly Teche; Notes on Instructing the Natives in the Native Tongue* (Englewood Cliffs, New Jersey: Prentice-Hall, Inc., 1970), p. 6.

Instructional Innovations:
Techniques

A Method for the Integrated Use of Learning Resources in Education*

John F. Rockart
Massachusetts Institute of Technology

Introduction

Educational literature has recorded many individual advances in technique over the past few years. Self-study courses have been developed. Programmed instruction has been used. Interactive computer programs have been developed. Professors have changed dry lecture techniques to more stimulating class discussion. However, in most cases, these advances have been applied one *at a time. The results of an* integrated use of available learning *methods and* resourses *in an accounting course are reported here. Measurable increases in student performance on examinations, course quality (as expressed by students), and academic productivity are noted.*

It is no secret that the cost of education has risen much faster in recent years than the cost of living as a whole. At the same time, quality appears to have fallen off—or at least *perceived* quality has been reduced. Students complain about the size of classes, the dedication of the faculty to research rather than teaching, the dullness of some classes, and many other things.

All of these symptoms (despite the recent dropoff in student strikes and other dramatics) may be indicative of what some have termed an "educational crisis." At the very least, they are symptoms of a productivity problem in a labor-intensive industry. While technology has done much to raise output per man in many other industries, it has done little, if anything, in education. A lack of increased productivity not only causes increased costs, it also eliminates the possibility of increasing quality at equivalent cost. Under these conditions, resources are most often strained to merely "keep the system going."

It is clear that the productivity problem in education and other knowledge-based industries now is of extreme importance. As Drucker has pointed out, "The bulk of tomorrow's employment will be in service trades, knowledge jobs—in health care, teaching, government . . . and the like. And no one knows much about knowledge work, let alone how to improve it."[1]

Drucker may overstate the case somewhat. This perceived need has certainly called forth a spate of research. In the education area alone (with which we are concerned in this paper), there has been a significant amount of research into new teaching methods. These have ranged from the development of paper programmed instruction textbooks,[2] to computer-assisted instruction,[3,4] to computer-assisted homework,[5] to computer-managed instruction, to on-line modeling of significant decision processes.[6]

Other efforts have turned their back on the utilization of new technology and instead focused on the behavioral aspects of

---

* The course (illustrated as a specific example in this paper) won the 1971-72 Western Electric Fund Award for Educational Innovation in Higher Education for Business Administration of the American Association of Collegiate Schools of Business. The author is grateful for the assistance of Colin Lay, now an assistant professor of the University at Ottawa, in the course's development. This paper is a slightly reduced version of an article which was published in the *Journal of Higher Education* in April 1973, and is reprinted here with the permission of that journal.

the learning process. Chief among these has been self-paced, self-study learning, one of whose chief and earliest advocates was Keller. Working from Skinnerian principles, Keller in 1965 ran a successful application of self-study.[7] Since then, self-study has grown and flourished, although in universities almost entirely on the undergraduate level.[8,9]

In addition to these two major trends—computer assistance and self-study—a host of other efforts have taken place. These include the use of video tape, pass-fail courses, smaller classes, larger classes, student teaching, etc.

All of the above are efforts to satisfy a felt set of needs which might be enumerated as follows:

1. To increase productivity in the educational process.

2. To achieve "higher quality" of learning (although the definition of quality is unclear).

3. To "take the heat off the student" by allowing him to learn material at his own pace.

4. To individualize instruction to the needs of the particular student.

5. To provide the student with more autonomy by allowing him to study in depth those subjects which are of great interest to him while achieving an unpenalized minimum standard only in other courses.

One major failing of these efforts has been the lack of good controlled studies to determine what has been accomplished. In the main, most courses involving new techniques such as self-study have been composed of student volunteers willing to take the educational risks of experimental situations. In addition, many of the new courses are based on techniques which explicitly do not allow comparisons with control groups. Yet, there is an evident need to evaluate new forms of education.

Perhaps most interestingly, most educational innovations have focused on the use of a single technique at a time as a particular instructor has become enamored with computer-assisted instruction, self-paced study, or some other individual method.[10,11] This has been perhaps *the* major failing of the process of innovation in education. Despite much jawboning to the contrary, very seldom has a very detailed look been taken at the existing courses in today's curricula (especially at the graduate level). If this were done, the rudimentary fact would be noted that most courses are composed, and rightly so, of diverse types of material which meet multiple learning objectives. It follows, then, that diverse learning methods should be applied in each course to enable students to best comprehend the diverse material. This paper reports on an experiment in the integration of available methods "delivered" by varying resources to meet the requirements of diverse learning objectives and the resulting diverse materials in a single course.

The objectives-material-methods-resources development process of an experimental course is illustrated in the next major section of this paper. Much has been written about the need for clear course objectives, the decision process with regard to course material, and the pros and cons of different teaching (or learning) techniques. This background is presented in only as much detail as necessary to illustrate the development of the particular course in issue, which in turn is done primarily as an illustration of the major point of this paper. That point is simply that it is necessary to define carefully the role of each major resource (professor, student, and technology) so that it is compatible with the prior choices of course objectives, type of material, and learning methods. The second major section of the paper presents the resulting course design, and the final section reviews the results obtained with regard to this course design in a controlled experiment.

A FRAMEWORK FOR COURSE DEVELOPMENT

Objectives of the Course

The course with which we experimented was entitled "Information and Decision Systems I" taught to both undergraduate and graduate students at the Sloan School of Management at MIT. The subject is a core course in both curricula. It is intended to provide students with an in-depth grounding in the principles and application of accounting for management decision-making purposes. It introduces financial and cost accounting systems as one major segment of corporate information systems.

The course has several objectives. It is felt that the student should learn:

1. The principles which underlie the development and use of accounting data.

2. The general process of management decision-making in which accounting data is used.

3. The accounting system and the detailed knowledge necessary to actually perform journalizing, adjusting and closing entries, to the corporate books.

4. The process of cost distribution, the use of accounting data for product pricing, performance analysis, and capital budgeting.

5. The concepts underlying "management planning and control," the other area of major use of accounting data.

6. The subjectivity and imprecision inherent in much of the cost and financial data used by management.

7. The basic concepts concerning data collection and the "fit" of the accounting system within a model corporate information system.

Pedagogic Groupings of Course Material

With regard to the learning process, the course objectives were operationally translated into teaching material which divided fairly clearly into the following six types of material:

1. *Material illustrating the management process, especially the decision-making process.* The target course is the initial "functional" course in management for most of the Master's candidates. (Most of the other courses taken in the first term are disciplinary courses.) Some idea of the management process must be depicted. Emphasis is placed on the primary role of decision making.

2. *Motivating material.* Accounting methodologies, no matter how important, can be dull. There is a need to insert material which illustrates the absolute need for managers to understand cost and other financial data.

3. *Material concerned with the "language", "principles", and "procedures" of accounting.* Making up the bulk of the course, this material is well described, although in highly varying ways, by diverse authors.[12] Although far from "cut and dried," this material is clearly set forth in understandable form. It varies in content or form only slightly from year to year.

4. *Material on which the student can test his detailed knowledge and understanding of accounting techniques.* This is "practice" material, best popularly exemplified by "homework."

5. *Material highlighting "grey areas" or "major issues" which face developers and users of financial information.* The language and procedures of accounting leave a great deal of latitude to the individual company accountant in the development of financial results for any period and in the development of cost data. While it is important that the student understand the basic postulates and principles underlying accounting and the results they produce, it is perhaps more important that he understand the "failings" of these manmade principles. It is important that he have a deeper knowledge of the material for the student to ponder such notions as replacement-cost depreciation, the results in product costing of various methods of overhead distribution, etc.

6. *Material which is "timely," has changed during the period of the course, or which offers new perspectives on the process.* In general, this is material which cannot be (or has not been) put into writing prior to the start of the course. It is material, however, which often adds greatly to student understanding of the course, or which makes the course material "live" through relating it to current events or to ideas which the professor has recently developed and is excited about.

Available Learning Methods

The material above is diverse. It therefore demands diverse treatments. At the very least, it demands a careful matching of the way that each type of material can best be assimilated against the repertoire of teaching techniques available. If the learning process were better understood, instead of being a coin-flipping process for the theory which one wishes to select, an unambiguous material-to-technique matching process could take place. Unfortunately, it is not that simple. Today each professor must employ his own rules of thumb to select techniques for each type of material to be learned.

A learning method may be defined as a procedure, process, or technique by which material is presented to a student with the expectation that the student will gain in the knowledge, understanding, or skill encompassed by the material. Many learning methods are available. Use was made in the new course of eleven of the most ubiquitous methods. These eleven learning methods—and some of their cardinal attributes from our point of view—are as follows:

1. *Listening to lectures.* Excellent for communicating new or ill-defined material. Very poor for the transmission of well-understood facts which are available in books, since reading speed is several times faster than verbal communication rates.

2. and 3. *Case discussion or class discussion of readings.* Excellent for the involvement which they provide, the requirement which they place on the student to "think through" the material—no matter how cloudy the issue—and the need this method poses for the student to determine his own position, and to defend it. Good for the absorption of all sides of major issues and for the exposition of all sides of "grey areas." Poor for learning "facts," because of the inefficiency (verbosity and nondirectedness) of presentation.

4. *Reading of textbooks.* Excellent for the transmission of facts and well-understood, well-digested material because of comprehension speed and efficiency of presentation.

5. *Reading of programmed instruction (paper).* A first-rate alternative for some students to traditional textbooks, for the transmission of facts. Some students consider this a highly efficient method of learning.[13]

6. *Following instructional modules.* As developed for self-study courses, modules are "instructor's guides" to sets of materials. When well-written, they provide directions as to how to go about the efficient assimilation of material provided by others of the above learning methods.

7. and 8. *Performing homework and taking marked (but ungraded) quizzes.* These can allow the student to test his knowledge of each segment of the work and get feedback on his degree of knowledge.

9. *Taking part in question sessions."* (These are class sessions in which the professor is present but which are designed to be "run" by the students who introduce the topics for discussion. Only those topics, which meet the needs of the students at the time, are discussed. The agenda is the student's—not the professor's.) (Our view on these sessions has been shaped by feedback from students, most of whom cite the major value of these sessions as "tutorial" in the sense that they allow the removal of specific learning "blocks," i.e., they allow students to clear up difficult points or misconceptions and to continue the learning process.)

Very poor, to date, as a replacement for textbooks or paper programmed instruction for original learning of most material on a cost-benefit basis. Highly worthwhile, if the programs are well-developed, in allowing students to test their understanding of material or explore the effects of certain choices in a simulated world represented by a computer model.[14]

11. *Self-paced, self-study.* This—incorporating many of the above techniques—is excellent for the transmission of facts and techniques which are well understood and where the material or adequate guidelines to its comprehension can be adequately presented in written form. Self-study suffers, however, in areas where many views must be heard to illustrate the multiple facets of an important issue.

As previously noted, there are additional learning methods not discussed just above. And we have only begun to scratch the surface in developing the multiple attributes of some of these methods. The prime point, however, is that diverse learning methods do have diverse strengths and weaknesses. These attributes of each method must be matched against the attributes of each type of material to be presented within each particular course. To expect that one learning technique can be stretched to cover all types of material is to deny students the benefits of the application of the correct tool at the correct time. It is similar to a dentist who uses a single cutting bit, or a golfer playing with only his five iron. The task can be accomplished, but with far less than optimal results—both in terms of output and aesthetics.

From Methods to Resources

Interestingly, the eleven teaching methods just presented can be broken down into three major classes along the lines of the three major resources available today to the learning process. The methods fall into classes of those that are professor dominated, those that are heavily dependent on the student for attainment in the learning process, and those in which technology plays a major part. The initial class, which we term *professor-intensive,* is characterized by class sessions in which the professor takes the responsibility for delivering the material or shaping the discussion. In *student-intensive* learning, to the contrary, the professor is either not present at the learning site, or merely acts as a resource for the learning student. In *technology-intensive* learning the prime actor guiding the process is some form of technology—today usually a computer.

From a resource point of view, a curriculum developer can then selectively utilize the strengths of these three major actors. In sum, one can choose among:

1. *Professors*—whose major comparative advantage is not sheer "information transfer" but rather in the development of motivation, in the leading of discussions of issues to which there are no "right answers" but whose significance must be comprehended, and in the guiding of the student's learning process through intelligent interaction with students.

2. *Students*—whom it has been shown are capable of "active" learning of well-understood, well-documented material on their own when properly directed and relieved of the need to sit "passively" in class.

3. *Technology*—which, it is believed, can take the place of previous professor or student-intensive methods where patient "answer checking," exploration of a simulated environment, or simple tutoring assistance is necessary.

SPECIFIC COURSE DESIGN

The traditional method of teaching the course described earlier had been 24 class meetings of 1.5 hours each based on both lecture and class discussion techniques. As a result of the above-described process, the new course structure was developed and can be summarized as shown in Table 1. This exhibit illustrates the matching of the types of material (material sets) to be presented in the target course (rows) with learning methods (columns) and with major resources (groups of columns). It is a sparse matrix since only the *most* applicable learning methods (the methods used) are noted for each type of material. Following the resource lines shown in Table 1, the new syllabus was divided into two basic types of pedagogy. These were a *classroom-oriented set* of lessons (professor-intensive), and a *self-study set* (student-and technology-intensive) as shown at the top of Table 1 and described below.

1. *A classroom oriented set of sessions.* To take best advantage of the professorial resource, eight classroom sessions remained "required." These sessions (four at the start of the course, two in the middle, and two at the end) were timed and designed to make maximum use of professorial skills. The start-of-the-course sessions were used to motivate the students with regard to the material, to provide examples from the instructor's background of the material's importance to managers, to provide an "overview" of the course, and to develop the decision-making setting in which the material is utilized by managers. Basically, the initial sessions were used to provide the students with a "feel," from a managerial viewpoint, of the material they were about to master. The later

TABLE 1
Specific Course Design

	Classroom-Oriented Sessions			Self-Study Sessions					Technology Intensive
	Professor Intensive					Student Intensive			
Learning Methods	Lecture	Case Discussion	Class Discussion	Text Books	Programmed Instruction	Instructional Modules	Home-work	Feedback Quizzes	Question Sessions	Computer Models
Types of Material										
(1) Decision making and managerial process		X								
(2) Motivational		X	X							
(3) Language Principles and Procedures of Accounting				X	X					
(4) Material to test understanding of (3)						X	X	X	X	X
(5) "Issues," "grey areas"	X	X	X							
(6) Timely, changing material	X									

classroom sessions were utilized to discuss case situations, providing further perspective on basic material previously learned, as well as linking the material to other areas of management knowledge.

All of these classroom sessions were designed around the instructor's comparative advantage over other learning media. In particular, instructors—as previously noted—have advantages in terms of motivation of material; providing students with insights into "issues" in the course; exposing "grey areas" in the material; and, finally, in making managerial case situations "live," therefore further explicating and providing depth to the material. Material sets 1, 2, 5, and 6 from Table 1 were therefore taught in this manner.

2. *Self-study oriented sessions.* The remaining two-thirds of the scheduled course time was devoted to a self-study mode. Material sets 3 and 4 were included here. As noted below, all of the student-intensive and one form of technology-intensive learning methods were utilized in this section of the course.

It is relevant to note that self-study was utilized—not self-paced self-study. The students were paced by the course examinations. It is felt that in their coming professional world, the students will be paced by externally imposed deadlines which they will have to meet by working on their own. There is good reason to provide them with experience in doing exactly this in the academic setting.

For these sixteen self-study sessions, students were expected to study the basic course material on their own. This self-study was assisted, however, by the following:

a. *Nine written guides to the instructional modules.* (averaging approximately ten pages each) which provided information as to the particular concepts to be learned, reading to be done of particular material in the texts, (both required and optional), the instructor's comments concerning the material (which ranged from such things as putting stress on particularly important aspects of the reading to further explanation), and homework to be handed in and/or other exercises to be performed such as on the computer.

b. *Optional attendance at "Question Sessions."* Replacing sixteen class sessions which would ordinarily have been held were Twelve "question sessions" at which the instructor was present solely to answer student questions on the assignments and to respond to any other questions concerning management in general which the students wished to discuss. Attendance at these sessions averaged 25 percent of each class (approximately ten students per session). Some two-thirds of each session turned out to be concerned with questions on the material. The remaining third varied widely over general management subjects, reflecting particular student interests.

c. *Homework.* This was marked by the instructor and by teaching assistants. The teaching asistants, traditionally used in this course, also answered student questions during their office hours.

d. *Feedback examinations.* These were brief, informal, marked but non-graded "quizzes" which students could take after completing modules 2, 4, 6, and 8 to allow them to gauge their progress in the course. The exams were immediately marked and could be discussed with the teaching assistants.

e. *An interactive computer program—CLOSE.* This on-line computer program allowed the student to review, whenever he wished to do so, the complete material of the first half of the course. The accounting cycle (the major material of the first half) breaks down into a simple posting-adjusting-closing chain of events. Using computer graphic-capability on a cathode ray tube screen, students were able to test their ability to perform financial accounting entries throughout this entire cycle. The interactive program assisted them by performing arithmetic, displaying for them the up-to-date status of the books, and by tutoring whenever a mistake was made. (In this last "tutor" mode, the program indicates each entry which is made in error—pointing to the exact part of the entry in error. In addition, it provides hints to the student to enable him to derive the correct answer, but only if the student asks for help. Many other similar features of the program provide it with an ability to reasonably replicate the actions of a human tutor.)

The most important point about the program, however, is that it enables a student to thoroughly test his ability to actually perform all of the accounting functions which he has learned in one relatively short session at the computer console. In this way the student can check his detail and overall understanding of the material in a short session with the computer. The student can test and retest his knowledge by himself, at the time of his own choosing, with or without tutoring assistance.

The material included in the original version of CLOSE was simple for the best students—but of greater challenge to the less well prepared students to whom it is most particularly addressed. A version with advanced subject material has been prepared.

Process Objectives for the Experiment

The experimental course was designed with five process objectives clearly in mind. These were:

1. To improve academic productivity by making optimum use of the strengths of all of the resources available to the learning (not teaching) process.
2. To increase student satisfaction with the learning process by allowing pupils greater flexibility in the use of their time and greater initiative in the learning process through the above methodology.
3. To increase the quality of the learning process by providing, for those students who desired it in the particular subject, more meaningful access to the professor. (It is felt that not all students want, or can handle, great depth in all courses—but greater depth and breadth should be available to those who desire it in any particular course.)
4. To allow (and encourage) the students to feel a greater responsibility for their own education by putting the emphasis, through self-study and optional learning feedback mechanisms, on active learning on the part of the student, rather than on passive classroom-based absorption of material.
5. To thoroughly test the validity of the innovative course by both quantitative and qualitative means. Measures of success were therefore designed and control sections run so that sound experimental results could be derived.

RESULTS OF EXPERIMENTATION WITH THE PROGRAM

The course was run for the first time in the fall term of 1971. There were seven sections of the course. Four sections were taught in the "regular" fashion—a combination of lecture and class discussion. Three of the sections utilized the innovative program (hereinafter these sections are referred to as self-study or "SS," with regular sections sometimes referred to as "REG").

Students selected particular sections in accordance with their schedules. Notification of which sections would be self-study was not given ahead of time. In addition, every attempt was made to play down the "experimental" nature of the course. Although there is undoubtedly some Hawthorne effect in every innovation, it is felt that there was as little as possible involved in the experimental results.

In order to check the value of the program in an objective, quantitative manner, the three self-study sections and the four regular sections were given the same midterm and final examinations. In addition, a questionnaire was distributed to all students in both the self-study and regular sections at the end of the course to determine their subjective feelings about the course.

Results, both in terms of relative performance of SS versus REG sections on the examinations and in terms of student "feelings" about the course as noted on the seventy-question questionnaire, suggest that the objectives-material-methods-resource matching approach to the course was a definite success. The results were as follows:

TABLE 2
Relative Performance: Mid-Term Exam

		Regular Sections		Self-Study Sections
Undergraduate	Mean	42.27	Mean	52.02
	Std. Dev.	9.62	Std. Dev.	11.28
	N	(67)	N	(23)
Graduate	Mean	51.54	Mean	52.09
	Std. Dev.	8.84	Std. Dev.	10.56
	N	(60)	N	(82)
TOTAL	Mean	46.65	Mean	52.08
	Std. Dev.	10.22	Std. Dev.	10.67
	N	(127)	N	(105)

TABLE 3
Relative Performance: Final Exam

		Regular Sections		Self-Study Sections
Undergraduate	Mean	87.66	Mean	101.55
	Std. Dev.	19.48	Std. Dev.	21.36
	N	(57)	N	(21)
Graduate	Mean	102.17	Mean	105.10
	Std. Dev.	20.1	Std. Dev.	25.45
	N	(57)	N	(82)
TOTAL	Mean	94.91	Mean	104.37
	Std. Dev.	21.02	Std. Dev.	24.61
	N	(114)	N	(103)

Objective Evidence from Examination Results

All students in the course, both REG and SS, took the same two examinations (midterm and final) at the same time. The results were as shown in Tables 2 and 3.

The objective evidence from the examinations, both midterm and final, is clear. The self-study sections outperformed the regular sections. There is no reason to suspect that the two groups were not homogeneous in mental ability and background at the start of the course. Teaching ability undoubtedly makes some unmeasurable differences, but the average number of years of teaching experience in this course of the instructors for both SS and REG sections was approximately the same.[15]

The differences for the *Total* (both undergraduate and graduate) scores of SS versus regular (52.08 vs. 46.65 on the midterm and 104.37 vs. 94.91 on the final) is highly significant at the .01 level on a t-test. On both examinations, SS undergraduates and graduates outperformed their REG counterparts. But the difference is most striking with regard to undergraduates. However, when a group of graduates who took the course in a "regular" section as an *elective* (and who therefore might be expected to be more motivated toward the material) is removed from the data, the examination results show a significant difference in the graduate ranks in favor of self-study, also! (Ed. Note: A two-way analysis of variance would more clearly reveal the role of the undergraduates in achieving the high level of significance and the possible interaction effect of treatment and class level.)

Subjective Evidence from Questionnaires

In the free-form section of the course, self-study students provided some logic behind the above results. Some of the ideas frequently expressed were:

> I felt the responsibility for learning the material had been transferred, under self-study, from the professor to me.
>
> Self-study is a lot more productive. I didn't have to waste time in class on things I already understood . . . or spend time in class when I was too far behind for the class to do me any good.
>
> The computer program enabled me to check on my own learning of the entire first half of the course when *I was ready to do so*. That's great. You ought to have a program for the second half, too, if you can design one. It helps to be able to review *all* the material—for integrated understanding—in two to three hours on the computer.

The instructors liked it, too. One self-study instructor summarized his views by saying:

> I've never enjoyed teaching so much. I taught only those things which require a professor. Self-study removed the "transmission" of a lot of the dreary details which can be learned from a book. The question sessions, above all, were challenging and fun. Only those students who were motivated to come showed up—and our discussions were always lively.
>
> We got to discuss, in addition to the strict course material, things like management in general, and philosophies of life—both mine and theirs. These were things one would hesitate to tie up a class of forty on but with ten to twelve interested students, these discussions came naturally.
>
> The variety of possible questions, some of which I could not answer (students could ask *anything*) somehow made me appear more human, I think . . . a bit less the "authority" and a bit more an "assistor in the learning process." This is the only way to teach.
>
> The students who *want* personal contact get more attention than they would otherwise get (ten people in question sessions vs. forty). Those who are satisfied merely with picking up the basic knowledge alone in this particular course are left alone to do so most easily and efficiently.

More quantitative assessments of these "feelings" are available from the course questionnaire data. Student answers to nine of the questions tell much of the story.[16] (Fig. 1).

The course design and the materials for implementation purposes required approximately four man-months of effort. As noted below, the resulting increase in academic production can quickly amortize this investment.[17]

Old System (2 sections)	
Sections	= 2
Class sessions	= 24
Hours per session	= 1.5
(2 x 24 x 1.5)	= 72 class hours

New System (3 sections)	
Lecture sections	= 3
Lecture class sessions	= 8
Hours per session	= 1.5
3 x 8 x 1.5)	= 36 class hours
Question sections (At 15 students per session average)	= 2
Question sessions	= 12
Hours per session	= 1.5
(2 x 12 x 1.5)	= 36 class hours
Total load (36 + 36)	= 72 class hours

Question Number

1. "For learning the material in this course, self-study is a preferable mode."

	Strongly Agree	Uncertain	Strongly Disagree
SS	71	21	8
REG	41	42	17

Chi Square Significance Level .005

2. "This course will be more useful to me in the future—compared with other courses."

	Strongly Agree	Uncertain	Strongly Disagree
SS	50	40	10
REG	35	49	16

Chi Square Significance Level NS *

3. "During the course my knowledge of management techniques changed considerably."

	Strongly Agree	Uncertain	Strongly Disagree
SS	70	28	2
REG	49	46	5

Chi Square Significance Level NS

4. "During the course my knowledge of management principles changed considerably."

	Strongly Agree	Uncertain	Strongly Disagree
SS	59	35	6
REG	49	45	6

Chi Square Significance Level NS

5. "In this course the professor stimulates students to think about the issues."

	Strongly Agree	Uncertain	Strongly Disagree
SS	46	51	3
REG	19	56	25

Chi Square Significance Level .005

6. "Professor has a clear plan for the semester's work."

	No	Uncertain	Yes
SS	4	16	80
REG	25	42	33

Chi Square Significance Level .005

7. "Class sessions are always interesting."

	No	Uncertain	Yes
SS	25	50	25
REG	49	49	2

Chi Square Significance Level .005

8. "Professor motivates students interest in the material."

	No	Uncertain	Yes
SS	7	44	48
REG	46	49	5

Chi Square Significance Level .005

9. "Professor is available for outside assistance."

	No	Uncertain	Yes
SS	13	34	53
REG	28	57	15

Chi Square Significance Level .01

* Not Significant

FIG. 1. Significant Questionnaire Results
(A Pertinent Set of 9 out of the 70 Questions)

Relationship to Academic Productivity

The course allows a 50 percent increase in academic productivity. One instructor can now handle three sections instead of two. This statement concerning productivity is based on the conclusion that the average number of students in each *question session* can be increased from ten to fifteen with little effect. Thus, one instructor can "lecture" three sections and combine them into two for "question session" purposes, providing an exactly equivalent teaching hour load for the instructor as in the past with a 50 percent increase in sections taught.

During this term there was evidence that the increase in students in the question sessions from an average of ten to fifteen was highly feasible. A very few sessions, did, in fact, have fifteen students. These sessions were felt in no way to be inferior.

Relationship to Educational Quality

It is felt that this course has increased the quality of education in several ways. First, students in the question sessions had a chance to follow their agenda. They could inquire about what interested them—whether or not it was part of the strict curriculum. And the students took advantage of it. Questionnaire data reflect their belief that the course was better planned and better orchestrated for them. Second, and perhaps most important, the individual students who most wanted exposure to the instructor in this particular course received it in the self-study group. In the questionnaire, "access to the instructor" was seen to be significantly greater (.01 level) in the self-study sections than in the regular sections (Figure 1, No. 9). Some students noted that the computer program allowed them to get an integrated understanding of that section of the material which they felt was not available in previous courses they had taken.

This particular course deals with basic material. Its decreased need for faculty time will also provide faculty availability to teach more professor-dependent material in later courses in smaller sections. Alternatively, greater faculty time will be available for curriculum development to introduce new concepts and material.

SUMMARY

The educational literature has recorded many advances in technique over the past few years. Some have stressed technology. Others have stressed more awareness of human potential and psychology in the learning process. Unfortunately, most of these advances have been applied one at a time.

This paper suggests that the strengths of each of the three major available resources in the learning process must be clearly understood and the use of these three resources carefully orchestrated in each course. The exact use of each resource will depend on previously defined course objectives, the transformation of these objectives into relevant classes of materials, and the methods which are chosen to best transmit each type of material. We know a great deal about this process, but it is far from a science at present. An illustration of the recommended process as performed for a particular course has been given.

Of some importance is the fact that this educational change is *implementable* in today's universities. It is not a radical departure, yet it goes far toward meeting some of the currently felt needs in education as noted in the first several paragraphs of this paper.

FOOTNOTES

[1] P.F. Drucker, "The Surprising Seventies," *Harper's Magazine* (July 1971), p. 39.

[2] See for example, J. Dearden, *Essentials of Cost Accounting* (Addison-Wesley Publishing Company, 1969).

[3] B.J. Nordman, "Teaching Machines and Programmed Instruction: An Introduction and Overview," Report No. 260 (University of Illinois, 1962).

[4] R.E. Grubb, "Learner-Controlled Statistics," *Programmed Learning* (January 1961), pp. 38-42.

[5] J.W. Wilkinson, *Accounting with the Computer: A Practice Case* (R.D. Irwin, Inc., 1969).

[6] Z.S. Zannettos, et. al., "The Developments of an Interactive Graphical Risk Analysis System," Working Papers 502-70 (Sloan School of Management, Massachusetts Institute of Technology, 1970).

[7] F.S. Keller, "Good-bye Teacher...," *Journal of Applied Behavior Analysis*, Vol. 1, No. 1 (Spring 1968), pp. 78-89.

[8] B.A. Green, "A Self-paced Course in Freshman Physics", Occasional Paper No. 2 (Education Research Center, Massachusetts Institute of Technology, 1969).

[9] C.D. Ferster, "Individualized Instruction in a Large Introductory Psychology Course", unpublished manuscript (Georgetown University, 1968).

[10] M.S. Scott-Morton, "On Educational Technology," unpublished paper (Sloan School of Management, Massachusetts Institute of Technology, 1970).

[11] E.D. Schein, *Professional Education: Some New Directions* (McGraw Hill, 1972), pp. 97-98.

[12] Since it was wished to illustrate varying views, as well as to take the best from each author, various sources: R.N. Anthony, *Management Accounting* (Richard D. Irwin, Inc., 1970), C.T. Horngren, *Accounting for Management Control* (Prentice-Hall, Inc., 1970), M.J. Gordon and G. Shillinglaw, *Accounting: A Managerial Approach* (Richard D. Irwin, Inc., 1964) were utilized in different parts of the course.

[13] Z.S. Zannetos, "Programmed Instruction in the Light of Anticipated Computer Technology," *The Accounting Review* (July 1967).

[14] Although some would challenge them, Professors Z.S. Zannetos, M.S. Scott-Morton, and this writer have found these comments on computer assistance to learning to be true in our work in this field. See, for example, John F. Rockart, M.S. Scott-Morton, and Z.S. Zannetos, "Associative Learning Project in Computer Assisted Instruction," *Educational Technology* (November 1971) and Z.S. Zannetos and M.S. Scott-Morton, "Efforts Toward an Associative Learning Instructional System," *Proceedings of the IFIP Congress 68* (Sloan School of Management, Massachusetts Institute of Technology, 1968).

[15] Still, one suspects that the teaching factor may have played a definite role since significant differences in results caused by learning method alone are almost impossible to find in the literature. See H. Guetzkow, E.L. Kelley, and W.J. McKeachie, "An Experimental Comparison of Recitation, Discussion and Tutorial Methods in College Teaching", *Journal of Educational Psychology*, Vol. 45, No. 4 (April 1954), pp. 193-207 and L.P. Grayson, "Costs, Benefits, Effectiveness: Challenge to Educational Technology," *Science*, Vo. 175)March 1972), p. 1219.

[16] Seven point scales were used. For clearer exposition, and to allow Chi Square analysis, the points were grouped to a three point scale.

[17] In addition, some course redesign takes place each year. Therefore, the four months of curriculum development effort is not all "extra" effort.

A Games Approach to Introducing Accounting

Marvin L. Carlson
Southern Methodist University
and
J. Warren Higgins
University of Connecticut

Introduction

The technique of introducing accounting through a game in which students make judgments about the relative positions and incomes of two individuals is described in this article. The game is played during the first two class sessions (before the students have had any other introduction to the concepts of financial position and income.) Playing the game provides students with a broad overview of accounting—an overview which focuses on the nature of the balance sheet and income statement, the social role of these reports, and the problems inherent in their preparation. The authors have found that, with this overview, the student has a workable context in which to view the more detailed course exposition which will follow. In addition, the game stimulates student involvement and fosters a favorable initial impression regarding the study of accounting.

Many students approach the first course in an unfamiliar discipline with considerable trepidation. The first chapter in typical introductory accounting texts frequently is found by students to be extremely general and sometimes unexciting. This is understandable since it is a Herculean task to describe adequately the nature of accounting to readers who may know very little about business in general and nothing about the terminology of financial statements. The authors have constructed a game designed to supplement text material during the first several sessions of the introductory course. The game assumes no previous knowledge of accounting. It is based on a barter economy and is designed to illustrate many of the objectives of accounting as well as many of the problems which confront its practitioners. The game is played by dividing the class into groups of five or six students, each group electing one of its members to serve as the reporter of the group's solution. Each reporter puts his group's solution on the board, and the various solutions are then compared and analyzed. By playing Part I of the game, students find that by using their intuition they are quite capable of preparing a form of balance sheet even though they have never seen one and do not know the definition of the term "balance sheet." In Part II the student explores the income concept.

An advantage of the games approach is that most students become intensely interested in the debates which take place within their groups. This interest leads to participation which in turn usually demonstrates to the student that he has an intuitive concept of welloffness which he can apply, with considerable success, to an accounting entity. Thus, at a very early date in the course students develop a sense of confidence in their ability to deal with the problems of the field. The motivational impact of the game, as observed in the authors' classes, has been most encouraging: the level of student involvement is high and student reaction to the study of accounting is generally quite favorable, with students frequently expressing, sometimes with obvious amazement, the impression that accounting can be fun and relevant.

Generally the entire first class period is devoted to Part I of the game which is shown below.

The Sheepherders
An Accounting Game
Part I

In the high mountains of Chatele, two sheepherders, Deyonne and Batonne sit arguing their relative positions in life, an argument which has been going on for years. Deyonne says that he has 400 sheep while Batonne has only 360 sheep. Therefore, Deyonne is much better off. Batonne, on the other hand, argues that he has 30 acres of land while Deyonne has only 20 acres; then too, Deyonne's land was inherited while Batonne had given 35 sheep for 20 acres of land 10 years ago, and this year he gave 40 sheep for 10 acres of land. Batonne also makes the observation that of Deyonne's sheep 35 belong to another man and he merely keeps them. Deyonne counters that he has a large one-room cabin that he built himself. He claims that he has been offered three acres of land for the cabin. Besides these things, he has a plow, which was a gift from a friend and is worth a couple of goats; two carts which were given him in trade for a poor acre of land; and an ox which he had acquired for five sheep.

Batonne goes on to say that his wife has orders for five coats to be made of homespun wool, and that she will receive 25 goats for them. His wife has 10 goats already, three of which have been received in exchange for one sheep just last year. She has an ox which she acquired in a trade for three sheep. She also has one cart which cost her two sheep. The Batonne's two-room cabin, even though smaller in dimensions than Deyonne's should bring him two choice acres of land in a trade. Deyonne is reminded by Batonne that he owes Tyrone three sheep for bringing up his lunch each day last year.

Objective

By studying the situation carefully, see what solution you may be able to offer these men. Specify any assumptions which you find it necessary to make.

While this game is clearly not one for which a single correct answer can be identified, a tenable solution is provided in the appendix to this paper.

In class, after the group solutions have been recorded on the board, the instructor can comment upon them in a manner which allows him to identify many major accounting concepts by pointing to their role in this particular game. Examples follow.

The Entity Concept
When the question at issue concerned the welloffness of each man, why did some groups include (exclude) the assets of Batonne's wife?

Realization
Why did some groups include (exclude) the value of orders received but not yet completed?

Were any groups concerned with possible changes in the quality of the herd (due to changes in age, weight, etc.) rather than only with the number of animals?

Choice of a Valuing Agent
Why did some groups choose sheep (goats) as the unit of measure? What are the limitations of sheep (goats) as valuing agents? If money had been the valuing agent, would all of these problems have been avoided?

Valuation Principle
Why did some groups value land at its actual historical exchange price while others valued it in terms of its replacement cost (most recent exchange price?)

Limitations of Financial Statements
What dimensions of welloffness have not been quantified in each group's solution, e.g., age, state of health, capacity for enjoying life, etc.?

The second meeting in the term is devoted to solving Part II and, in the process, to gaining some understanding of the income concept.

The Sheepherders
An Accounting Game
Part II

A year has elapsed since you solved Part I of the Sheepherders Game. After studying your solution to Part I, Deyonne and Batonne grudgingly accepted your opinion as to their relative wealths at the end of last year. The passage of time has not diminished their penchant for argument, however. Now they're arguing about who had the largest *income* for the year just ended.

Deyonne points out that the number of sheep which he personally owns at year end exceeds his personal holdings at the beginning of the year by 80, whereas Batonne's increase was only 20. Batonne replies that his increase would have been 60 had he not traded 40 sheep during the year for 10 acres of additional land. Besides, Batonne points out that he exchanged 18 sheep during the year for food and clothing items; whereas Deyonne exchanged only seven for such purposes. The food and clothing has been pretty much used up by the end of the year.

Batonne is happy because his wife made five coats during the year (fulfilling the orders she had at the beginning of the year) and received 25 goats for them. She managed to obtain orders for another five coats (again for 25 goats)—orders on which she has not begun to work. Deyonne points out that he took to making his own lunches this year; therefore he does not owe Tyrone anything now. Deyonne was very unhappy one day last year when he discovered that his ox had died of a mysterious illness. Both men are thankful, however, that none of the other animals died or was lost.

Except for the matters reported above, each man's holdings at the end of the current year are the same as his holdings at the end of last year.

Objective

What solution can you offer the two men as to which had the greatest income for the year?

A Note on the Income Concept

The concept of income refers to how much one has improved his welloffness (wealth) during a period of time. J.R. Hicks, an economist well known for his definition of income, has defined income as the amount a man could consume (or otherwise distribute) during a period of time and still be as well off at the end of the period as at the beginning.

Two approaches to the solution of Part II are illustrated in the appendix to this paper.

Classroom discussion of the groups' solutions to Part II can be used to introduce important concepts in income measurement. Examples follow:

Alternative Views of the Income Concept
> Income may be viewed either as a "change-in-net-worth" concept or as a flow concept (revenues minus expenses). The alternative solutions to Part II illustrate the validity of both views of income.

Depreciation
> Most groups will give the same weight to the cabin, carts, and plow at the end of the year as at the beginning. This gives the instructor the opportunity to introduce the notion of depreciation.

Recurring Income vs. Extraordinary Items
> The possibility of treating the ox's death as an extraordinary item might be discussed.

When taken together, Part I and Part II give the student an early glimpse at the relationship between the income statement and the balance sheet. He then has an overview of the accounting process before examining its parts in detail.

The use of the game approach generates greater student involvement in the learning process and better prepares the student for the study of accounting than do the traditional first lectures in accounting. This approach also gives the student a much better framework for evaluating later discussions on differences in accounting methods, and it helps to explain many of the "why's" of accounting.

APPENDIX OF TENABLE SOLUTIONS

Solution To Part I

Balance Sheets
(All items stated in sheep-equivalents)

Assets	Deyonne	Batonne
Sheep	400	360
Land	80	120
Cabin	12	8
Carts	4	2
Plow	$2/3$	0
Ox	5	3
Goats	0	$3 1/3$
Total assets	$501 2/3$	$496 1/3$
Liabilities		
Sheep belonging to others	35	
Payable to Tyrone	3	
Total liabilities	38	0
Net worth	$463 2/3$	$496 1/3$

Solutions to Part II

Part II can be solved in two ways. The first views income as a "change in net worth" concept; the other views it as the result of certain flows of resources taking place during the period. The first method translates Hick's definition of income into algebraic form. Hick's definition implies that income for an individual is equal to the change in net worth during the period plus that period's consumption, or,

$$Y = NW_1 - NW_0 + C$$

where Y = Income
NW_1 = Net worth at the end of the period
NW_0 = Net worth at the beginning of the period
C = Consumption during the period

"NW_1" is computed below:

Balance Sheets
Date of Part II
(All items stated in sheep-equivalents)

Assets	Deyonne	Batonne
Sheep	480	380
Land	80	160
Cabin	12	8
Carts	4	2
Plow	$2/3$	0
Ox	0	3
Goats	0	$11 2/3$
Total assets	$576 2/3$	$564 2/3$
Liabilities		
Sheep belonging to others	35	0
Net Worth	$541 2/3$	$564 2/3$

Income for Part II can now be computed.

Income Computation
"Change In Net Worth" Approach

$$NW_1 - NW_0 + C = Y$$

Deyonne $541 2/3 - 463 2/3 + 7 = 85$
Batonne $564 2/3 - 496 1/3 + 18 = 86$

The income numbers derived above can also be derived by basing the computation on the inflows and outflows of resources during the period. Most students will find that this flow-based computation illuminates further the understanding of income which they acquired from study of the change in net worth method.

Income Statements
Flow Approach

	Deyonne	Batonne
We became better off by Acquiring animals:		
Sheep		
Net increase in sheep herd	80	20
Plus: Sheep traded during the year		
For consumer goods	7	18
To pay Tyrone	3	0
To purchase land	0	40
Total sheep traded	10	58
Gross increase in sheep (identical with number of sheep born during the year)	90	78
Goats		
Goats received for services (stated in sheep-equivalents)	0	$8\frac{1}{3}$
Total animals acquired during the year	90	$86\frac{1}{3}$
We became worse off because of animal deaths:		
Death of ox (stated in sheep-equivalents)	(5)	0
Net income	85	$86\frac{1}{3}$

The Use of Dynamic, Interacting Business Simulations for Accounting Instruction

Howard D. Leftwich
Oklahoma Christian College

Introduction

Business simulations offer teaching and learning possibilities that are not present in the traditional lecture and problem-solving techniques. Learning resulting from behavior which leads to a reward or reinforcement is superior to learning that results from behavior which is primarily a response to given facts. Participation in business simulations provides the former. Business simulations provide realism because they are dynamic, they encourage the development of interpersonal relationships, and they require integration of all of the functions of a business in decision making. They can be implemented in an accounting curriculum in several ways to augment the more traditional teaching methods.

Accounting educators have made little change in their approach to teaching over the past few decades. Little evidence is available to indicate that the teaching techniques of lecture and problem assignments are any different from twenty years ago. These methods have turned out many good accountants (or at least they did not prevent them from becoming good accountants); however, educators have an obligation to explore and develop methods that will accelerate and improve the quality of learning.

Most practitioners and educators would agree that accounting students do not really learn accounting until they do it. The problem-solving approach was developed to attempt to recognize this fact. There have even been sporadic ventures into providing internships for students in "real live businesses." Guest-lecturers who are practitioners are used to partially close the gap between classroom and practice. These and other techniques have chipped away at the problem but the gap between classroom and practice is still large enough to warrant the use of additional techniques.

This paper shows how the use of dynamic, interacting business simulations can overcome some of the shortcomings of other common methods of attempting to bring realism into the classroom as an aid to learning. Business games, as they are sometimes called, add dimensions to teaching and learning accounting that are not present in traditional techniques.

SOME CONCEPTS ABOUT LEARNING

Bass and Vaughn define learning as..."a relatively permanent change in behavior that occurs as a result of practice or experience."[1] In the field of accounting, this change in behavior hopefully would involve the ability to perceive the need for certain accounting techniques as well as the skill for applying them. In static problem solving, the facts and the need for applying the technique are accepted as given, and the behavior is concentrated on applying the skill.

Hilgard and Bower discuss two basic processes of learning in their *Theories of Learning*. "Classical conditioning" refers to the formation of an association between a conditioned stimulus and a response. Learning through "instrumental conditioning," on the other hand, is the result of the individual operating on the environment with his behavior being instrumental[2] in obtaining a reward or reinforcement. With respect to "classical conditioning" the individual is passive in his response once the conditioning has taken place. The response is virtually automatic. It has no real purpose beyond providing the "correct" answer. An application of such behavior to accounting would be the computation of the break-even point of an organization from a given set of data. The response is related to the given data rather than to making use of the answer. "Instrumental conditioning" as a type of learned behavior is characterized by the reward or reinforcement to which it leads rather than the stimulus which elicits it. An accountant deciding to prepare a cost-volume-profit analysis for guidance in management decisions illustrates this type of learning. The stimulus that will automatically call forth this kind of response is hard to find.

"Modeling" (patterning our behavior after another), "mediation" (communication of knowledge from one to another), and "trial and error" (response in an attempt to obtain a reward) are ways of behaving that result in learning. The latter behavior necessitates recognizing a problem, then calling forth whatever ingenuity and knowledge is available to find possible solutions. Modeling and mediation may teach this process, but most evidence points to the value of letting the learner himself delineate the complex problem he faces and then create and try out his own solutions. Bass and Vaughn observe that this emphasis on personal experience and discovery as the most profitable basis for the learning of complex meanings is particularly important if the long-term retention of learning is our concern.[3]

The premises of the remainder of this paper are that the most predominantly used methods of teaching accounting, i.e., lecture and problem-solving, involve the "classical conditioning" process of learning and the "modeling" and "mediation" types of learning behavior. All of these learning characteristics tend toward the "rote learning" extreme of a continuum which has "idea learning" at the other end. On the other hand, dynamic, interacting business simulation involves "instrumental conditioning" and "trial and error" learning behavior which tend toward the "idea learning" end of the continuum. Bass and Vaughn note further that there are other means of absorbing ideas but discovery seems to be the most effective and most lasting of them all.[4]

BUSINESS SIMULATIONS IN GENERAL

Business simulations, or business games, are used commonly enough to make it unnecessary to describe their characteristics in detail. Those involving sufficient quantitative data to make them appropriate for accounting applications consist of a mathematical model of a simulated industry consisting of several firms. The model contains a number of variables that can be manipulated to reflect management operating decisions by the student-team managers of each firm. The simulated industry is dynamic in that (1) total industry results reflect the decisions of each firm's student-team management and (2) individual firm results reflect the interaction of that firm's management decisions with those of other firms. Industry and firm results are provided to participants for each operating period (usually quarters) in the form of balance sheets and income statements for each firm as well as other statistical and quantitative data. This data is the stimuli which must be evaluated and used as raw material for trial and error responses in the form of various financial and accounting analyses. "Instrumental conditioning" is at work in that the stimulus to which the response leads (future successful management decisions) is the reward or reinforcement.

Livingston labeled such actions as "operant behavior" involving "...finding problems and opportunities, initiating actions, and following through to attain desired results...," as opposed to "respondent behavior," the ability to analyze and solve problems already defined and described.[5] Although case studies may not define a problem completely, they still lack the motivation that comes from knowing that the correctness with which a problem is defined and a solution tried will have a bearing on future results which must also be dealt with.

McKenney observed that game playing is an iterative process and if the participant feels that he can control the success of his firm in the game environment, he will accept the feedback information on how he has performed and will attempt to learn from his mistakes.[6]

Following is an example of the cash budgeting process that can occur in a business simulation with a comparison of teaching the process through lecture and static problem solving:

> A business simulation provides for the hypothetical business obtaining cash in the normal manner through operations as well as through borrowing or obtaining new equity capital. The student-team management is not required to make any decisions affecting its cash balance directly but if the net result of its other decisions causes it to run out of cash it will incur an automatic loan at a high rate of interest. On the other hand, if the resulting cash balance is abnormally high, its return on investment percentage will suffer and the team faces having to justify to simulation administrators, this inefficient use of assets. The combination of the possible unfavorable results and the inherent challenges of having a favorable return on investment and planning the desired cash balance provides the rewards or reinforcements characteristic of "instrumental conditioning." This combined with the resulting trial and error behavior in using the available data to plan the optimum cash balance is the process of discovery which results in learning of a lasting nature.
>
> Traditional methods of teaching cash budgeting involve a combination of reading material and lecture explaining the need for cash budgeting and illustrating the techniques. The assignment of static problems for solution follows. The individual student is the only participant in solving the problem and the only reward for a correct response is the satisfaction of hitting a stationary target (not a moving one) and the possibility of a good grade. The facts of the problems are not the result of any decision making by the student and the answers obtained have no ongoing significance. In short, there is no overall business context for the entire process.

THE DYNAMIC NATURE OF BUSINESS SIMULATION

Solving problems in the "real business world" may be compared to shooting at a moving target. Decisions are made based on facts, some of which must be estimated, some of which are uncontrollable, and most of which are constantly changing. A business simulation can provide all of these realistic characteristics. Static problems which consist of a set of given facts suggest to the student that all of the facts are knowable, controllable, and constant. This suggestion is inherent in the instructions which require the correct answer. Even then, the real importance of the answer, whether right or wrong, may escape the student because there is no context in which to use it. The reward or reinforcement is limited to the satisfaction of making a correct calculation and a high grade.

A business simulation is dynamic in several respects. The absolute size of the industry market may grow or decline from period to period depending upon economic activity indexes as well as the management decisions made by the firms in the industry. Each firm's operating results are not within complete control of the student-team management because of uncontrollable fluctuations in the total market and because their market share is determined by pitting all of the marketing decisions of each firm against all of the decisions of all of the other firms in the industry. This characteristic of problem solving in the framework of a business simulation promotes the greatest benefits of trial and error behavior—learning that lasts. The simulation participants deal with some facts which must be estimated, some which are uncontrollable, and some which are constantly changing.

THE INTERACTING NATURE OF BUSINESS SIMULATIONS

Accountants need to be well informed with respect to the necessity for integration of the financial function with other functions, and skilled in interpersonal relationships with other specialists. One of the more important benefits that accounting students can derive from business simulation is the preparation of accounting and financial analyses as part of an interdisciplinary team that must be vitally concerned with marketing, production, and research and development decisions. Dill concluded that simulations provide a setting which develops skills including an understanding of relationships between specialized jobs in the firm and a willingness to work responsibly and effectively with others.[7] The accountant who is part of a student-team management that must balance an array of marketing, production, financial, and research and development management decisions in order to achieve success for his firm in the simulated industry will develop sympathy for the viewpoints of the other specialists. At the same time he will perceive the need for persuasiveness when he concludes that a financial restraint must override an otherwise attractive alternative in another functional area.

IMPLEMENTATION OF BUSINESS SIMULATIONS IN AN ACCOUNTING CURRICULUM

Business simulations cannot replace lecture and traditional problem solving because it is impractical for them to touch on all of the accounting theory and techniques that must be covered. The simulation can be used to call forth knowledge, techniques, and skills under circumstances that are the most favorable for sustained learning. Existing business simulations make evident the need for and provide the data required for operating budgets, cash budgets, capital budgets, inventory and production management, financial structure management, cost-volume-profit analysis, cost accounting, financial statement analysis, financial reporting, auditing, and systems development. The degree of sophistication expected in applying these techniques in a given simulation depends on the academic level of the students involved. The very inability of a lower level accounting student to cope with some of the required decisions satisfactorily is learning in itself. He is more likely to see the value of a theory or technique presented in a traditional manner if he has previously seen the need for the result in a simulation.

The following methods have been used for involving accounting students in simulations:

1. As an outside project related to a specific course, similar to a term paper or a research project.
2. As a specific segment of basic course content.
3. As a seminar or for independent study credit.
4. Participation in intercollegiate business simulation competition.
5. Interdisciplinary programs in cooperation with other business disciplines where each discipline provides staff specialists to a simulation team.

Combinations of two or more of these methods are also appropriate.

Harris and Hodgetts reported on the results of a research project bringing accounting and management students together in a business simulation. The management students formed the simulation teams and the accounting students formed consulting teams serving purely staff roles in the decision making. The management students reported that the accountant-consultants contributed by applying analytical tools involving cash flow analysis, inventory control, pricing, trend analysis, and contribution margin techniques. The accountants were also credited with eliciting valuable ideas and providing fresh and objective viewpoints.

The accountants reported that they had gained these insights:

1. Even though they were assigned staff roles, they could informally have significant influence on decision making.
2. They must consider interrelationships of various management functions.
3. They must integrate many factors which had previously been studied as isolated subjects.
4. Dynamic relationships or conditions of uncertainty were more vividly illustrated than in textbooks.
5. Accounting data can only improve the quality of decision making as opposed to the static problem implication that there is a "correct" solution.[8]

Large computer systems are not required to process simulations containing these potential accounting applications. A school that has no direct access to computer facilities can use various forms of data transmission for both input and output and have the computer scoring done by a computer service center. Some quite successful intercollegiate business simulations are handled by transmitting data between the host school and competing schools.

Simulations are published by many of the major business publishers as well as smaller ones. In most cases a booklet or packet containing game instructions and other necessary data for participants is available along with instructors' manuals which contain the computer programs and other technical data necessary to operate and administer the simulation. Examination copies of the simulations with sufficient technical data to determine computer hardware requirements will generally be made available by publishers. Several bibliographies of simulations have been published, including one edited by Twelker, and one by Zuckerman and Horn.[9,10]

The educator interested in using the simulation technique should be able to select a simulation that will suit his needs from one of these sources.

CONCLUSION

Accounting educators have the obligation to continue to attempt to initiate methods that will accelerate learning and improve its quality. Problem solving, internships, and other methods have been used to attempt to close the gap between classroom and practice but part of the gap remains.

Learning theory suggests that behavior which leads to a reward or reinforcement is superior, with respect to learning, to behavior elicited primarily by stimuli which is provided in advance of the response. For this purpose learning is defined as a relatively permanent change in behavior that occurs as the result of practice or experience.

Business simulations provide a framework within which accounting theory and techniques can be applied under circumstances of "instrumental conditioning." The reward or reinforcement for an accurate response calls forth problem delineation activity and "trial and error" responses. Traditional problem solving is characterized by "classical conditioning" which results from "modeling" or "mediation" learning techniques. Trial and error responses result in more permanent changes in behavior.

Problems presented by business simulations are realistic because of their dynamic characteristics. They may be thought of as moving targets whereas static problems may be compared to stationary targets. The business simulation provides a context within which the answer to a problem can be used rather than the answer being an end in itself.

Business simulations evoke an appreciation for the problems of other functional specialists because the student-team management is making an array of decisions which it hopes will be balanced for the overall benefit of the firm. Interpersonal relationships are sharpened by the necessity for the functional specialists to agree on this array of decisions.

There are several ways that the use of business simulations can be implemented in an accounting curriculum. Simulations elicit the use of many of the more important accounting theories and techniques. Further, it is not necessary to have direct access to a computer to use business simulations.

Bishop and Keys concluded that business simulations offer possibility for experience in virtually every functional area of management; that they allow the compression of lifelike business experiences into a much shorter period than on-the-job training; and most importantly, they allow a manager or student to fail and to learn from his failure without suffering long-run consequences.[11]

FOOTNOTES

[1] Bernard M. Bass and James A. Vaughn, *Training in Industry: The Management of Learning* (Belmont, Calif.: Wadsworth Publishing Company, Inc. 1966), p. 8.

[2] Ernest R. Hilgard and Gordon H. Bower, *Theories of Learning* (New York: Appleton-Century-Crofts, 1966) pp. 48-72.

[3] Bass and Vaughn, p. 38.

[4] *Ibid.*, p. 53.

[5] Sterling Livingston, "Myth of the Well-Educated Manager," *Harvard Business Review*, (January-February, 1971), pp. 79-89.

[6] James L. McKenney, *Simulation Gaming for Management Development* (Boston: Division of Research, Graduate School of Business Administration, Harvard University, 1967), p. 3.

[7] William R. Dill, "What Management Games Do Best," *Business Horizons*, (Fall, 1962), pp. 55-64.

[8] John K. Harris and Richard M. Hodgetts, "A Quasi-Consulting Project Involving Accounting and Management Students," *The Accounting Review*, (April, 1972), pp. 375-380.

[9] Paul Twelker, *Instructional Simulation Systems* (Corvalis, Oregon: Continuing Education Publications, 1969).

[10] David W. Zuckerman and Robert E. Horn, *The Guide to Simulations-Games* (Lexington, Mass.: Information Resources, Inc., 1973).

[11] Doyle Bishop and Bernard Keys, "New Hope for the Well-Educated Manager", *Conference Proceedings—"Games Executives Play,"* held at Oklahoma Christian College and Central State University, December 4 and 5, 1970 (Norman, Oklahoma: Bureau for Business and Economic Research, University of Oklahoma, 1972), p. 10.

The Use of Role Play Simulation in Accounting Education

Lawrence A. Tomassini
The University of Texas at Austin

Introduction

This paper proposes the use of role play simulations as an effective mode of accounting education. In this proposal the nature of an rationale for role playing are discussed, and the means of conducting such exercises are described. Finally, the potency of utilizing this method in a variety of contexts is demonstrated through actual case illustrations.

Experiential learning has become increasingly popular in contemporary education. This reliance upon "learning by doing" is, in part, a response to the growing demand for relevance and pragmatism in education, and reflects trends in both the employment market and social values.[1]

Various modes of experiential learning are used in business education, including internships, field studies, simulation games, and role play simulations. The last, the subject of this paper, can be defined as a contrived exercise in which individuals assume the role and behavioral patterns of other people and simulate their experience of real world problems.

In view of this role playing theme, the purposes of this paper are threefold:

1. To discuss the educational rationale for utilizing role play simulations in accounting education.

2. To enumerate and describe the specific procedures which constitute the role play implementation process.

3. To demonstrate the potential applicability and benefits of role playing in accounting education through actual case illustrations.

EDUCATIONAL RATIONALE FOR ROLE PLAYING

Volumes have been written which describe the rationale underlying the use of role playing in educational and other settings. Much of this work appears in the educational, psychological, and sociological literatures since it is primarily within these disciplines that the use of role playing has been developed.[2] Chesler and Fox, speaking of the inherent use of role playing in human socialization, placed it in an educational perspective:

> Human maturation is more than a process of learning 'things;' it involves the gradual creation of a 'role,' a unique and accustomed manner of relating to 'others'—persons, things, situations outside the self that will determine and characterize all of a person's social behavior. Part of growing up is the learning and developing of this role, not solely as a factor of social status or social identification but also as a matter of personal identity. A person's role is not only his patterned way of evaluating and behaving toward the world of others; it is also his way of evaluating and behaving toward himself. In these terms all behavior is

the reflection of a role, and all social interaction is a continuous sequence of interacting roles, or role-playing episodes..[3]

Their view suggests that an educational process which merely provides for comprehension of concepts or techniques, independent of the personal affect (feeling) of the learners, is really inadequate.

Using this reasoning accounting educators might infer that students need to have experiences where the learning of traditional materials is integrated and internalized with personal referents which will continue through the person's entire maturation process. The role playing technique described here is an effective mechanism for facilitating this critical aspect of the educational process.

Role playing is useful on at least three levels. On the first level, participants can acquire an understanding or "appreciation"[4] of an individual's behavior in a particular role set,[5] where the role set is defined by the various forces in his work environment. As an example, one might argue that learning concepts and techniques of auditing are of little practical use until these cognitive elements become associated with an appreciation of the auditor's experiences at an affective level. Presumably, then, when students role play the application of auditing skills, they develop a better understanding of the auditor's work environment.

On a second level, role play participants can experience and develop skills in interpersonal relationships. Since roles, by definition, imply interdependencies of people's tasks, feelings, and actions, the study of business topics should consider the importance of roles and interpersonal relationships. In learning about budgeting, for example, students should become aware of the inherent feelings (including role conflicts)[6] of the management parties involved in the budgeting process. Role playing can be an effective means of experiencing, rather than merely discussing, this interaction.

On the third and final level, participants can gain an understanding of broader social phenomena among individuals or organizations. For example, such large scale problems as analyzing the presidential information system can be fruitfully explored through role playing, as described later in this paper. Learning, at this level, usually focuses upon the phenomenon rather than the personal or interpersonal affect of the parties involved.

On all of these levels, then, role playing actively engages students in the simulation of real world decision making, providing a relevant and creative framework for motivating students in the contemproary educational scene.

VARIANTS IN ROLE PLAYING

Prior to a description of the means of implementing role play simulations, certain possible variations should be mentioned. Common variants are scale (size and time), topical focus, educational purposes, and role playing techniques.

Scale (Size and Time)

Role playing can be effectively utilized with an individual or with an entire class of 30 to 40 students. For larger groups, simultaneous duplication of the role play with smaller sub-groups may be advantageous. The time consumed often depends upon the scale size and can vary from a few minutes to several hours.

As previously indicated, the focus of a small scale simulation is usually an event which helps individuals experience the feeling of a particular personal situation. In contrast, the very large scale simulation engages the participants in the critical roles of an organization-wide series of activities.

Topical Focus

A great variety of topical foci can be adapted to the role play method as the needs of the instructor and participants require. Among the topical applications with which this writer has had experience, both financial and managerial accounting have been central themes. In addition, these excercises emphasized the behavioral and information system aspects of accounting, two areas of particular contemporary interest.

Educational Purposes

Several general educational purposes can be served by utilizing role playing. These include:

1. The development of problem-solving skills, especially those involving interpersonal data gathering processes.

2. The creation of a common data (experience) base with which other course material can be related and intergrated.

3. The demonstration of the relevance through their application in a realistic work environment.

Role Playing Techniques

A number of specific techniques can be used in the conduct of role playing exercises—for example, role reversal, imitation (or mirroring), and the "wheel" feedback method.[7] One or more of these techniques are usually chosen by the instructor-coordinator in accord with the foregoing variants of scale, topical focus, and educational purpose.

PROCEDURAL IMPLEMENTATION OF ROLE PLAYING

Although role plays have numerous variations, the operational procedures discussed here apply predominantly to full scale simulations. Those instructors who have less complex educational needs for the role play technique can omit or alter certain procedures to fit their particular circumstances.

A complete course of action for implementing the role play technique would include:

1. Identifying the educational needs and defining the objectives for using a role play simulation.
2. Acquiring and organizing simulation facilities and equipment.
3. Acquiring or devloping the necessary background materials and the scenario.
4. Determining complementary reading material, if necessary, to enhance the role play exercise.
5. Organizing "simulation central," the role play management group.
6. Preparing input and output forms.
7. Briefing non-participant observers.
8. Holding a pre-simulation briefing for participants in which materials, roles, and schedules are distributed.
9. Executing the role play exercise.
10. Conducting the post-simulation debriefing and feedback session.

Each of these procedures is discussed in the sections which follow.

Identifying Needs and Objectives

An essential beginning point for applying role playing (or any pedagogical technique, for that matter) is the identification of the cognitive and affective needs[8] of the concerned parties—students and instructor(s)—and the subsequent formation of concrete educational objectives.[9] In accord with these objectives, the nature and scope of the role play should be specified in order to give direction to the remaining implementation procedures.

Acquiring and Organizing Facilities and Equipment

Having set the nature and scope of the role play, the coordinator should next determine what facilities and equipment are necessary to administer it. In some cases, the regular classroom can be utilized, and little or no special equipment is needed. For more sophisticated applications, however, the use of special laboratories with video and audio communication equipment adds reality and enriches the total learning experience.

Acquiring or Developing Background Materials and a Scenario

The core of the role play technique consists of background materials and the simulation scenario, the script which structures the exercise. Several combinations of options are available for gathering or developing these materials. Generally, however, only two strategies are used. First, the materials and the scenario can simply by purchased in package forms which have been developed and tested for general marketability.[10] These can be useful where time constraints are great or where large numbers of students are to participate.

A second strategy is the development of a scenario with the assistance of colleagues or student assistants while participants acquire the background materials through extensive research. This can be quite a time-consuming procedure, but it can enrich the participants' experience through involvement.

Determining Complementary Reading Materials

While the bulk of the participants' preparation comprises familiarization with roles and with information about the simulated context, the use of complementary reading materials is often beneficial. This may be the case, for example, where the participants are unfamiliar with some terminology that is used in a pre-packaged scenario which, although applicable, is somewhat advanced for the participants. Here a handout or assigned reading of articles is appropriate complementary preparation for the role play.

Organizing "Simulation Central"

One of the most critical ingredients in the successful implementation of role playing, particularly on a large scale, is a well-prepared management group, usually called something like "simulation central" or "SimCen" to indicate the core function it performs. Normally headed by the coordinator of the role play, this group is primarily responsible for the scenario development or adaptation and for solving the logistical problems associated with the simulation. An example of its coordinating role is the function SimCen plays as a receiver and transmitter of messages and data which are products of the exercise. The group should be well versed in the objectives of the role play, the boundaries within which the scenario is intended to operate, and the possible interrelationships of the roles portrayed in the simulation.

Preparing Input and Output Data Forms

A typical means of initiating and documenting communication in the simulation is by some type of written message or form. The input messages are usually prepared in advance when the scenario is developed (during the organization of SimCen). Forms for documenting interaction during the role play are also useful, particularly in subsequent analysis for educational or research purposes. Generally, the type of documentation needed can be anticipated, and the forms can be structured prior to the actual simulation.

Briefing Non-Participant Observers

Where the interaction process (and subsequent reporting of such) is a major element of the simulation's purpose, it is most helpful to use one or more means of observing the events which take place during the role play. While videotape facilities are particularly effective, they are often restrictive or simply unavailable. Consequently, the use of non-participant observers is commonplace.[11] The coordinator must prepare these people well so that they may attune themselves to the types of processes which fit the objectives of the particular learning experience. Ideally these observers operate unobtrusively, such as behind one-way viewing mirrors in communication laboratories. Subsequent to the role play, the observers should participate in feedback and debriefing sessions so that their observations can be shared with the participants.

Briefing the Participants

Before beginning the role play, a briefing session should be held. At this time, the participants should be told about the nature of the simulation (or reminded of it, in the event that they have worked on gathering materials), be given any general reading materials that are required for preparation, and be given roles and some verbal material regarding the roles, so that each person can begin living or experiencing the particular focus and value system which he is to assume. A time schedule for the simulation is usually distributed at this meeting, and it is helpful to deal with questions and clarifications at this briefing so that the actual simulation can operate without interruption.

Executing the Role Play

The culmination of the preparation described above is reached in the actual execution of the simulation. Student participants exert most of their efforts during this phase of the implementation process and usually find it an exciting, involving experience. The coordinator should remember, however, that the key factor in the success of the exercise is adequate planning and preparation.

Conducting a Feedback and Debriefing Session

Either immediately following the actual role play or as soon after it as is feasible, the instructor-coordinator conducts a debriefing session with all participants, organizers, and observers present. The debriefing portion of the session is intended to elicit feelings and observations which help to clarify the role play experience and the educational points encompassed in the simulation's objectives. The feedback portion of the session usually focuses upon feelings about the experienced worth of the simulation—likes, dislikes, and suggestions for future use. This last step in the implementation process is critical to students and instructor alike and should not be omitted.

SPECIFIC ILLUSTRATIONS

To demonstrate the variations of role playing and the flexibility of this method in different accounting education contexts, three actual case illustrations are presented:

Auditing (Client Relations)

The first illustration concerned the performance of a financial audit. Here a small number of students were assigned tasks similar to those encountered by audit staff personnel in a CPA firm. One student, for example, was assigned the task of verifying Accounts Receivable and the Allowance for Bad Debts. In doing so, he was required not only to determine the proper sources of the information but also to encounter others who played the roles of client personnel.

The objectives of this exercise were:
1. To develop interpersonal problem-solving skills required for audit engagements, particularly regarding means of data collection and interpretation.
2. To enable students to apply textbook concepts and techniques by performing actual audit tasks in a more realistic setting than traditional practice sets allow.
3. To force participants to experience the inherent role sets and conflicts which exist in auditor-client relations.

Budgeting for a Personnel Department

The second case illustration focused upon the evaluation of a proposed operating budget for the personnel department of a manufacturing firm.[12] In an exercise conducted prior to the beginning of a course in managerial planning and control, students were assigned roles which varied among levels of the organization and among functional areas. After a series of committee and department meetings, the simulation culminated in a presentation of the final budget proposal to a simulated Board of Directors, played by five faculty members. Some of the major advantages of this application of role playing were:

1. A common, relevant base was provided with which students could associate other course readings or discussions.
2. The biases, influences, and interdependencies of managers in different organizational capacities were experienced and discussed.[13]
3. The components of an operational budget were easily learned through the analysis required by the assigned tasks in the role play.

Management Information Systems (MIS)

Various information systems can be simulated through role playing exercises. While most applications of this variety in accounting education would deal with *management* information systems, it is not necessary to simulate the operations of a private sector organization to achieve the MIS educational objectives. The third case illustration exemplifies this point.

In this case, students and faculty simulated the information system for the President of the United States in regard to foreign policy matters.[14] This particular instance required a great deal of logistical planning and preparatory research into the system and the roles of the individuals involved. Three critical days in the life of the President during a foreign policy crises were simulated, including various interactions of staff and advisors in analysis and action-taking. A number of key aspects of information systems were made explicit by the simulation and the feedback session which followed, including:

1. The differences between the formal and informal information systems in an organization.
2. The fact that information systems are created in accordance with such factors as:
   a. Key personnel in the organization.
   b. The organization structure.
   c. The organization's explicit and implicit goals.
3. The influence on decision making of:
   a. Data presentation order.
   b. Interaction and information exchange frequency.
   c. Information filtering.
   d. Feedback mechanisms utilized.

This last case demonstrates that, by using role playing a variety of interesting contexts are available for the study of information problems in accounting education.

SUMMARY AND CONCLUSION

Utilizing role playing simulations in accounting education is an effective means of satisfying demands for relevant and pragmatic education. This approach elicits personal affect (feeling), which is as necessary as cognitive elements to learning, on at least three levels: personal, interpersonal, and organizational (or societal).

As a concluding note, potential users of the role play methodology are cautioned to consider its disadvantages and limitations. Role playing, like other experiential techniques, can be costly and time-consuming. Perhaps more importantly, this method should not be expected to be useful in every educational setting. Educators should be encouraged to utilize this technique, but they should be certain to integrate it carefully within the framework of their own instructional needs and objectives.

FOOTNOTES

[1] Two particularly insightful views of these trends and their implications can be found in: John W. Gardner, *Self Renewal: The Individual and the Innovative Society* (New York: Harper and Row, 1963); and Donald J. Hart, "An Outsider Looks at the Accounting Curriculum," *The Journal of Accountancy* (March 1969), pp. 87-9.

[2] See for example, Mark E. Chesler and Robert Fox, *Role-Playing Methods in the Classroom* (Chicago: Science Research Associates, Inc., 1966); Raymond J. Corsini, Malcolm E. Shaw, and Robert R. Blake, *Role Playing in Business and Industry* (New York: The Free Press of Glencoe, Inc., 1961); and Bruce J. Biddle and Edward J. Thomas (eds.), *Role Theory—Concepts and Research* (New York: John Wiley and Sons, Inc., 1966). Excellent annotated bibliographies are included.

[3] Chesler and Fox, p. 5

[4] Sir Geoffrey Vickers, *The Art of Judgement* (New York: Basic Books, Inc., 1965), pp. 39, 40 and 47.

[5] Edgar H. Schein, *Organizational Psychology*, Second Edition (Englewood Cliffs, N.J.: Prentice-Hall, Inc., 1970), p. 111.

[6] *Ibid*.

[7] Corsini, Shaw, and Blake, pp. 81-100, gives detailed descriptions of these and other techniques.

[8] "Cognitive" needs encompass proficiency, comprehension, and other levels of "knowing;" "affective" needs include arousal, attitudes, and other forms of "feeling" toward the subject.

[9] For a detailed discourse on this matter, see: Benjamin S. Bloom (ed.), *Taxonomy of Educational Objectives: The Classification of Educational Goals, Cognitive Domain* (New York: David McKay Company, Inc., 1956); and David R. Krathwohl (ed.), *Taxonomy of Educational Objectives: The Classification of Educational Goals, Affective Domain* (New York: David McKay Company, Inc., 1964).

[10] Two excellent series are produced in inexpensive paperback form by Science Research Associates, Inc., Chicago, Illinois and by MacMillan Comapny (Creative Studies Simulations), New York, New York.

[11] See, for example, Dorwin Cartwright and Alvin Zander (eds.), *Group Dynamics*, Third Edition (New York: Harper and Row, 1968), pp. 170, 471-72, and 527-29.

[12] Jay J. Zif, Arthur H. Walker, and Eliezer Orbach, *The Personnel Department* (New York: Creative Studies, Inc., The MacMillan Company, 1970).

[13] For those who are unfamiliar with these and similar concepts a good basis can be gained from: Harold J. Leavitt, *Managerial Psychology,* Third Edition (Chicago: The University of Chicago Press, 1972), especially pp. 71-86, 208-20, 259-65, and 305-10.

[14] This simulation was produced and supervised by Professor Eric Flamholtz with a group of graduate students and faculty at the University of California, Los Angeles.

Cooperation vs. Competition

R.E. Shirley
Oregon State University

Introduction

In order to simulate the group decision-making processes encountered by the student in the real world, it seems appropriate for accounting classes to facilitate group discussion and other forms of group interaction.

Competition in the classroom seems to be a way of life for the typical college student.

Competition has its recognized advantage in stimulating students to their best efforts. And, indeed, the real world requires healthy competition. However, students should also learn to cooperate as they prepare for the real world.* For example, auditing work, which is largely a team effort, requires cooperation. Perhaps accounting students need more training and experience working together as teams in a spirit of cooperation.

To foster cooperation and minimize competitiveness, an accounting class can be group or team oriented with a substantial part of grades determined by cooperative effort and accomplishment. Accounting students need to get experience working together and solving problems operating in small groups, and this should be simulated in the classroom. A brief outline of such an approach is given below:

1. At the beginning of the term the class is divided into teams of three students using a random number basis of selection. Each team sits together and works together for the entire term. Student teams should organize themselves and select their own chairmen or leaders and the teams should be encouraged to rotate chairmen.

2. All homework assignments are prepared by the teams together and one solution reported. Dissenting minority reports can be attached and identified by name.

3. Examinations are given to groups and each group prepares its joint solution and all members of the same team receive the grade given to the team. Examinations are analytical in nature, such as a case study requiring accounting tools of analysis, or essay questions regarding concepts of the course. If large classrooms are available, examinations can be taken by groups during the regular class period. However, this may not be feasible for small classrooms or for large classes. Where facilities are small and for classes over 30-40 students take home examinations may be necessary in order to retain group evaluation. An alternative would be to hand out tests at the beginning of the class period; have groups go to other rooms and complete the test and return it to the instructor at the end of the class period.

4. Classroom performance consists of as much discussion as possible with specific questions directed to groups and requiring a group answer.

5. Students are assigned a team research project and asked to prepare a team report. If they wish, parts of the report written by individual

---

*For references dealing with cooperative vs. competitive concepts and research findings, see "Cooperation vs. Competition" of "Interpersonal and Social Environment" of "A Conceptual Overview of Learning for Accounting Educators," pp. 151-2

students could be identified by the writer's name. The group should report areas of responsibility assigned to each member, such as data gathering, evaluating, and summarizing.

6. Short workshops are also utilized in class with short cases or problems assigned to groups of students for a team solution, with class discussion of the results.

7. The chairman of each team is asked to attach a confidential rating of the members of his team with each written report turned in during the term. This report should rate each team member on the quality of his or her performance on that particular project. The ratings could be as follows:

    a. Above average contribution.
    b. Average contribution.
    c. Below average contribution.

As an alternative, this check list could be expanded into more specific work behaviors and attitudes so evaluations would be more empirically based. Individual ratings simulate the practice followed by auditing firms of rating individual performances on each audit engagement. This stimulates individual contribution to the team and does not change the basic orientation of the team effort. By rotating the chairman of each group, each member of the team would rate the other team members the same number of times.

8. The instructor rates all work turned in as one numeric team score. However, members of the team can receive bonus points or minus points based upon a summary of individual ratings as to the quality of contribution they have made to the group effort. For example, a particular group may have received an instructor's grade of 88 percent with individual ratings as follows, made by fellow team members:

	Team Score	Summary of Student Ratings	Bonus or Minus Points
George	88	average contribution	0
Gloria	88	above average	+10 percent
Bob	88	below average	-10 percent

In the above example, total scores for the course would be as follows:

George	88 percent
Gloria	97 percent
Bob	79 percent

9. An added feature of the team effort is that any team may call in a consultant (who must be another student in the class). The consultant will receive 5 percent of the total points earned by the team on this particular project and this comes off the total points awarded for the project.

Depending upon both the instructor's and students' preferences, the team approach used in the classroom may include some or all of the nine features described above.

The team approach is particularly appropriate for advanced accounting seminars such as accounting theory, auditing, and advanced cost accounting. However, the approach also can be used successfully for the principles course, and it may well be the catalyst which adds interest and enthusiasm to students who are first exposed to accounting. It could be a way of attracting many more new students to the field of accounting.

Financial Statement Content and Use: A Classroom Simulation

James J. Benjamin
Virginia Polytechnic Institute
and State University
and
Robert H. Strawser
Texas A & M University

Introduction

The purpose of this paper is to describe a simulation exercise which may be used in the classroom in order to provide students with "hands on" experience in the use of financial statements, financial statement analysis, and the effects of proposed changes in financial reporting. The exercise, described herein, which can be completed in two class periods, deals with published forecasts. The basic methodology described, however, may be used to illustrate the potential effects of any alternative reporting practice.

Among the objectives of many accounting courses is providing the student with an understanding of both the uses and the limitations of accounting information. Most courses which are primarily concerned with financial accounting attempt to include a discussion of the currently accepted principles of accounting and the implications of proposed improvements in accounting principles and practices as well. In addition, efforts are usually made to provide the student with at least a basic understanding of the content of published annual reports as well as the ability to analyze and interpret financial statements.

One problem which is often encountered in the traditional financial accounting course is the limited opportunity for the student to obtain "hands on" experience in the use of actual financial statements. In an attempt to overcome this and other related problems, a simulation exercise has been adapted and used in conjunction with the financial statement analysis section of both the introductory and intermediate accounting courses. As statement analysis was discussed in these courses, it was emphasized that each student would be required to make his own analysis of a complete corporate annual report. In addition to the analysis of financial statements, the exercise included a proposed change in reporting practice—use of published forecasts.

Basically, the exercise employs an actual report to shareholders which, by means of successive modifications, was developed into the following series of annual report packages:

1. *An unmodified annual report.* The basic report package was developed from the 1971 annual report of a medium-sized manufacturer. The report used was eight pages in length and included: financial highlights, president's letter, a ten-year summary, statements of earnings and retained earnings, balance sheet, statements of changes in financial position, footnotes, and the auditor's opinion.

2. *An annual report modified to include forecasted financial statements from the prior year and for the forthcoming year where the prior year forecast was relatively accurate (i.e., within five percent).* A section was added to the report package described in (1) above indicating both the purpose for disclosing forecast data and the methods used in devel-

oping the forecasts. The forecast from the prior year predicted an earnings per share (EPS) of $.93 while the actual EPS for that year was $.89. A section was added to the president's letter which mentioned the relative accuracy of the prior year's forecast.

3. *Same as (2) above except that the forecasts were attested to by a CPA.* A paragraph was added to the auditor's report which extended the opinion to include attestation as to the accuracy of the compilation of the forecast and appropriateness of the accounting principles employed.

4. *Same as (2) above except that the forecast for the prior year was inaccurate.* The forecast from the prior year predicted an EPS of $1.25 as compared with the actual EPS of $.89 for that year. A section was added to the president's letter which indicated that the inaccuracy of the forecast data was primarily due to factors beyond the control of management, i.e., an unexpected downturn in the economy.

5. *Same as (4) above except the forecast for the prior year was attested to by a CPA.*

The five report packages were randomly arranged and distributed in class. The students were unaware that the reports differed in any way. Based on his analysis, each student was asked to make a point estimate of the expected earnings per share for the next year and, in addition, an estimate of the range within which EPS would be likely to fall. After collecting these predictions, the students whose report packages included forecasts were asked to respond to several questions regarding the importance of forecast data in their analysis, the ability of management to develop financial forecasts, and, in general, the reliability of forecasts. The remaining students were given a questionnaire similar in appearance so that the fact that different reports were used was still not apparent. (The questionnaires appear in the Appendix.) Experience has shown the exercise can easily be completed in a single fifty-minute class period, thus preventing the students from working together and/or discovering that the report packages used differed in any way.

As an assignment for the next class period, each student was asked to prepare a brief report which summarized the analytical techniques which he employed in making his predictions. The overall results of the predictions and questionnaires were tabulated and reported to the students during the following class period. Each student also received his own report, predictions, and questionnaire.

Each time the exercise has been used, the inclusion of forecasts in the annual report had a noticeable effect on the students' predictions of the next year's EPS. Both the extension of the auditor's opinion to include the published forecast and the relative accuracy of the prior year's forecast were also found to have a noticeable effect on predictions for every class. The differences in predictions among the various report sets were highlighted and provided the basis for a lively (and often heated) discussion of the issues involved. The students were somewhat divided as to the specific question of whether forecasts should be included in published annual reports. This division emphasized the difficulty of introducing significant changes in financial reporting practices. The various techniques used by the individual students in their analyses were also discussed in detail, again emphasizing the different approaches employed as well as the relative strengths and weaknesses of each.

The authors feel that the use of this exercise relieves some of the drudgery which is often associated with the traditional textbook approach to financial statement analysis and provides students with exposure to a somewhat realistic decision-oriented situation. Student comments support this opinion and also indicate that the more seriously the student approached the exercise, the more interesting the material became to him.

The issue of including forecasts in annual reports was selected for use because of the attention it has recently received. The basic methodology described above could, of course, be used to illustrate the potential effects of any alternative reporting practice.

Individuals interested in obtaining a copy of the complete set of report packages for their own use may do so by writing: Professor James J. Benjamin, Department of Accounting, College of Business, Virginia Polytechnic Institute and State University, Blacksburg, Virginia 24061.

APPENDIX

Questionnaire

1. On the basis of your analysis of the annual report of Eastern Publishing Company, what is your prediction for next year's earnings per share? $ _____
2. What is the approximate range for the next year's earnings per share for which you feel reasonably confident that the actual EPS will fall within this range. $_____ to $_____
3. What kinds of information would you like to have in this annual report which are not presently included? List on the reverse of this sheet and indicate your assessment of the relative importance of each item.
4. Please rank the items given below by the importance you give to each in your analysis of the firm.

	VERY IMPORTANT	IMPORTANT	SOMEWHAT IMPORTANT	OF LITTLE IMPORTANCE	OF NO VALUE
A. ACTUAL:					
Sales	( )	( )	( )	( )	( )
Rate of Change in Sales	( )	( )	( )	( )	( )
Net Income	( )	( )	( )	( )	( )
Earnings Per Share	( )	( )	( )	( )	( )
Rate of Change in EPS	( )	( )	( )	( )	( )
Working Capital	( )	( )	( )	( )	( )
Change in Working Capital	( )	( )	( )	( )	( )
Common Equity	( )	( )	( )	( )	( )
Depreciation	( )	( )	( )	( )	( )
Total Assets	( )	( )	( )	( )	( )
*B. FORECASTED:					
Sales	( )	( )	( )	( )	( )
Net Income	( )	( )	( )	( )	( )
Assets	( )	( )	( )	( )	( )
Earnings Per Share	( )	( )	( )	( )	( )

5. On the basis of your analysis, how would you assess the general capability of management? (Please circle one.)

    no capability   little capability   somewhat capable   capable   very capable

*6. In making your prediction of earnings per share, how important was the forecasted data relative to the rest of the annual report? Please indicate your answer by allocating 100% between the forecasts and the other parts of the report.

    FORECASTS _____% + OTHER PARTS OF REPORT _____% = 100%

*7. On the basis of your analysis, how would you rate the ability of management in the development of financial forecasts? (Please circle one.)

    no ability   little ability   somewhat able   able   very able

*8. How would you rate the reliability of the financial forecasts included in the reports? (Please circle one.)

    no reliability   little reliability   somewhat reliable   reliable   very reliable

*Questions 4B, 6, 7, and 8 were omitted from the questionnaire given to the students that had reports with no forecasts.

A Teaching Machine Application In a Basic Tax Course

G. Fred Streuling
The University of Texas at Austin

Introduction

This paper presents a discussion stressing the usefulness of a teaching machine as a supplemental alternative to classroom lectures. Emphasis is given to the development and production of programs for a teaching machine. Excerpts from a program written for a basic tax course are presented. The paper concludes with an enumeration of the possible benefits which can be achieved through the adoption of a teaching machine.

When competing for students' attention in the age of electronic gadgets, standard classroom lectures often run a distant second compared to technological communication innovations such as audiovisual slide and/or tape presentations. Although audio-visual aids are certainly available for adoption by instructors, budget constraints and a lack of technical know-how needed in the preparation of teaching aids often act as a deterrent to abandoning the standard lecture approach.

Modern equipment and teaching techniques have been used in training centers of the Internal Revenue Service. With the permission of the Service, the author used both software and hardware on a temporary basis. But the Internal Revenue Services' software was not adaptable to a basic tax course. The alternative was to improvise and to experiment with the creation of an appropriate program for tax courses. This experience eliminated, at least for this writer, the erroneous misconception that the production and adoption of suitable teaching aids can only be achieved with extensive budgets and considerable technical experience.

HARDWARE

Understandably, audio tapes and color slides, when used alone to supplement classroom lectures, represent a superb teaching aid. However, their effectiveness can be further enhanced when used in conjunction with a teaching machine. Teaching machines vary greatly in degree of sophistication. Capabilities of simple units may be limited to the transmission of students' true-false responses which are registered by a panel of lights on the instructor's control unit. The equipment experimented with is one of the more complex machines available today and features a number of interesting options:

1. A response unit capable of accommodating multiple choice questions with up to four options, as well as true-false questions.
2. An instructor-control panel with a capability of supplying:
   a. An immediate percentage breakdown of the total class response to each question, i.e., 70 percent chose option (A), 5 percent chose option (B), etc.

b. A cumulative total of correct responses for each individual student.
3. A tape deck for prerecorded audio programs.
4. A feed-in for movie or slide projectors to enable synchronization with the audio program.
5. A dial which enables the instructor to call back, for replay, specific segments of the program.

The variety of these features provided a considerable amount of flexibility for use in the classroom.

SOFTWARE

Initially, the relatively complex topic of capital gains and losses was selected as subject matter for a prerecorded programmed lecture. The lecture was supplemented with appropriate color slides and organized into small segments. Excerpts of one such segment from the program are presented below. Note that the segment is further divided into four parts consisting of (1) discussion of the main idea (slides 1 through 3), (2) appropriate illustrative examples (slides 4 through 7), (3) a series of multiple choice questions (slides 8, 10, and 12), and (4) a correct response to each question (slides 9, 11, and 13).

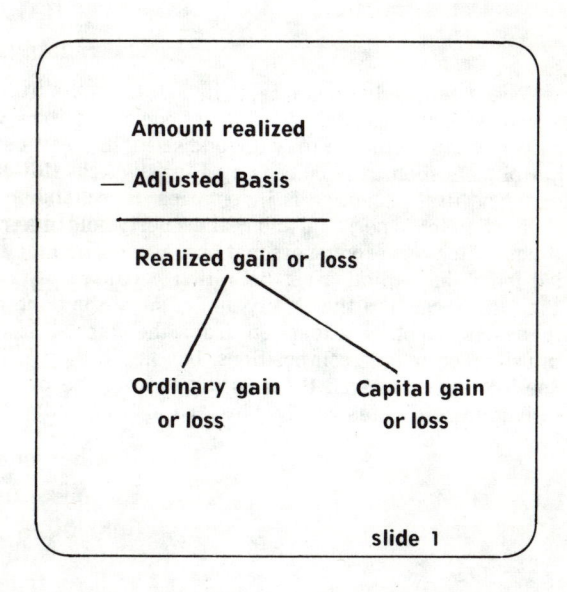

```
        Amount realized
      — Adjusted Basis
        _____
        Realized gain or loss
           /        \
          /          \
    Ordinary gain   Capital gain
      or loss         or loss

                        slide 1
```

For Slide 1
The basic formula used to determine the gain or loss in a transaction involving a sale or exchange of property consists of the amount realized less the adjusted basis resulting in either a realized gain or loss. Such gains or losses fall into one of two categories. They are either ordinary gains or losses or they are capital gains or losses. The distinction between ordinary and capital gains and losses is important since special rules and preferential tax rates may apply to capital gains and losses.

> **A capital asset is property held by the taxpayer except —**
>
> (a) Inventories
>
> (b) Personal property ⎫ used in a
> ⎬ trade or
> (c) Real property ⎭ business
>
> (d) A copyright, literary, musical, or artistic composition held by the creator
>
> (e) Accounts or notes receivables
>
> slide 2

For Slide 2
The Internal Revenue Code specifies that a capital gain or loss results from the sale or exchange of a capital asset. Exactly what is a capital asset? The Code states that basically all assets are capital assets. This rather broad definition may include sizeable objects such as a building or a ship as well as smaller objects such as a shotgun or a wristwatch. However, some specific exceptions are mentioned. The first exception is inventories, merchandise which a businessman holds for resale. Another exception is personal and real property held in a trade or business. Thus, machinery and equipment which represents personal property or a factory which constitutes real property are excluded from the capital asset definition because they are used in a trade or business. However, the family car and the family home, since they are not used in a trade or business, are capital assets. Another exception from the capital asset definition includes copyrights, literary, musical, or artistic compositions, but only if they are held by the creator of such property or if the taxpayer received them as a gift from the person who created them. Finally, accounts receivables and notes receivables are also excluded from the capital asset definition.

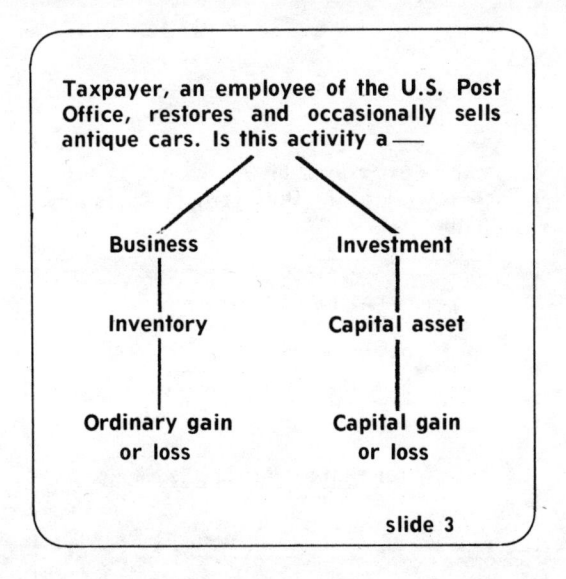

```
┌─────────────────────────────────────┐
│  Taxpayer, an employee of the U.S.  │
│  Post Office, restores and          │
│  occasionally sells antique cars.   │
│  Is this activity a —               │
│                                     │
│        Business    Investment       │
│           |            |            │
│        Inventory   Capital asset    │
│           |            |            │
│       Ordinary gain Capital gain    │
│        or loss       or loss        │
│                                     │
│                          slide 3    │
└─────────────────────────────────────┘
```

For Slide 3
While apparently very exact, the definition of a capital asset, or more specifically what a capital asset is not, contains several ambiguities which have resulted in controversies between taxpayers and the Internal Revenue Service. For example, a taxpayer who is employed by the United States Post Office purchases and restores antique cars as a sideline. Periodically he sells some of the restored cars to provide capital for the purchase of additional antique cars. In this example, does the taxpayer's sideline constitute a business? If so, the restored cars would represent inventories and the gain or loss from their sale would result in ordinary gains or losses. If on the other hand, the taxpayer engaged in his sideline activities for investment purposes only, the sales transaction would result in capital gains and losses. Situations like the foregoing often end up in the courts to determine their status.

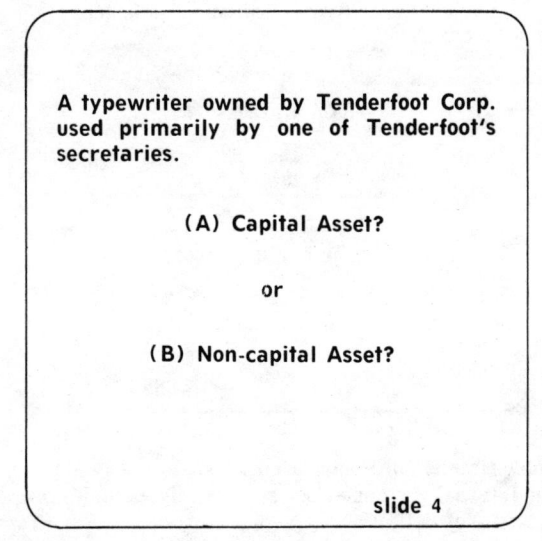

```
┌─────────────────────────────────────┐
│                                     │
│  A typewriter owned by Tenderfoot   │
│  Corp. used primarily by one of     │
│  Tenderfoot's secretaries.          │
│                                     │
│            (A) Capital Asset?       │
│                                     │
│                   or                │
│                                     │
│            (B) Non-capital Asset?   │
│                                     │
│                                     │
│                          slide 4    │
└─────────────────────────────────────┘
```

For Slide 4
Here are less controversial situations. In the following cases let us see whether a typewriter is in each instance a capital or a non-capital asset. First, the typewriter is owned by Tenderfoot Corp. and is used by one of Tenderfoot's secretaries.

```
┌─────────────────────────────────────┐
│                                     │
│   Donny Carter used his typewriter  │
│   in his school work at the         │
│   University of Texas at Austin.    │
│                                     │
│                                     │
│         (A) Capital Asset?          │
│                                     │
│                                     │
│                  or                 │
│                                     │
│                                     │
│         (B) Non-capital Asset?      │
│                                     │
│                                     │
│                           slide 5   │
└─────────────────────────────────────┘
```

For Slide 5
Next, Donny Carter a student at The University of Texas at Austin uses the typewriter in his school work.

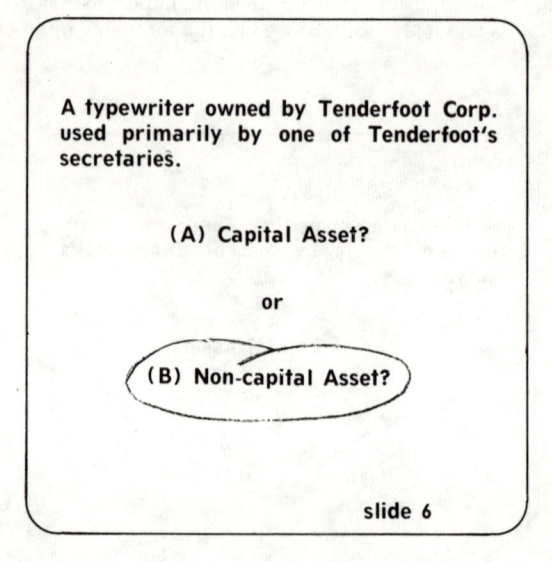

```
┌─────────────────────────────────────┐
│                                     │
│   A typewriter owned by Tenderfoot  │
│   Corp. used primarily by one of    │
│   Tenderfoot's secretaries.         │
│                                     │
│                                     │
│         (A) Capital Asset?          │
│                                     │
│                                     │
│                  or                 │
│                                     │
│                                     │
│        ((B) Non-capital Asset?)     │
│                                     │
│                                     │
│                           slide 6   │
└─────────────────────────────────────┘
```

For Slide 6
In the first case, the typewriter is not a capital asset since the typewriter is used in a trade or business. Sec. 1221 of the Internal Revenue Code specifically excludes property used in a trade or business from the capital asset definition.

A Teaching Machine Application in a Basic Tax Course

> Donny Carter used his typewriter in his school work at The University of Texas at Austin.
>
> **(A) Capital Asset?** *(circled)*
>
> or
>
> (B) Non-capital Asset?
>
> slide 7

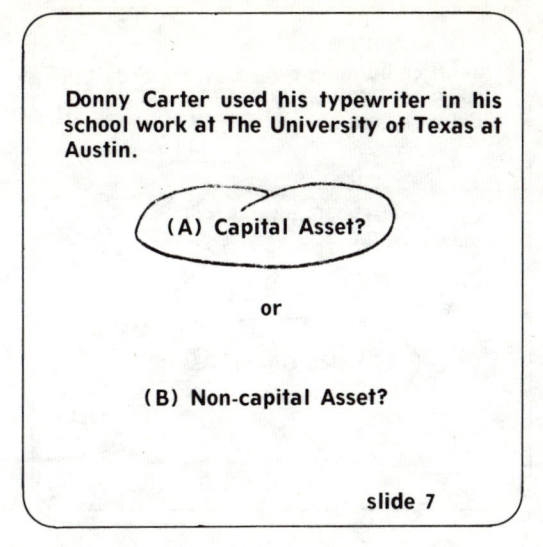

For Slide 7
Donny Carter's typewriter represents a capital asset. A typewriter used by a student is not specifically excluded from the capital asset definition.

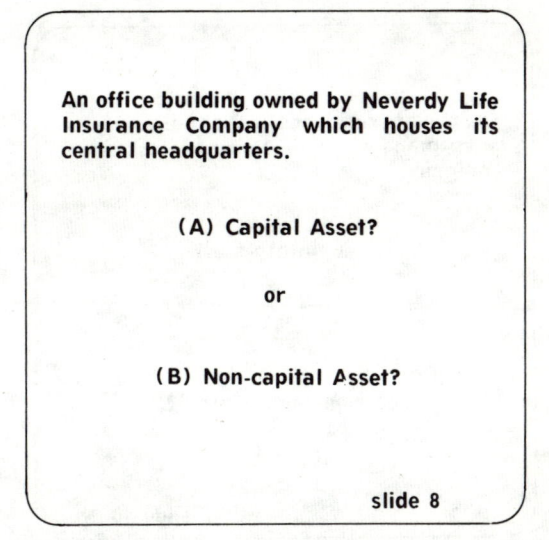

> An office building owned by Neverdy Life Insurance Company which houses its central headquarters.
>
> (A) Capital Asset?
>
> or
>
> (B) Non-capital Asset?
>
> slide 8

For Slide 8
Here are some questions for you to test your understanding. In each case choose either (A) Capital Asset or (B) Non-Capital Asset. An office building owned by Neverdy Insurance Company which houses its central headquarters.

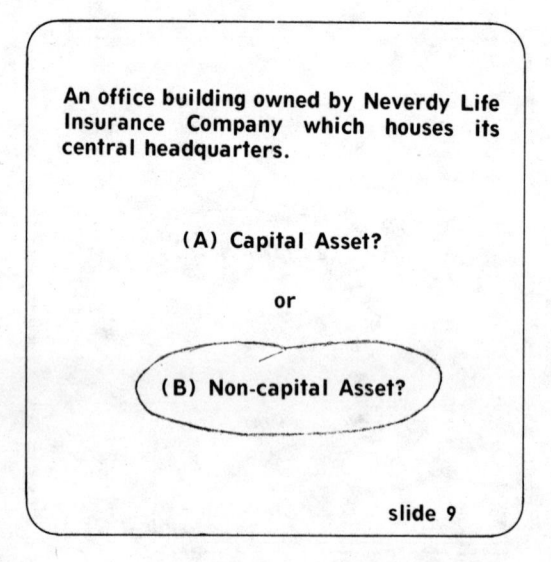

```
┌─────────────────────────────────────┐
│                                     │
│   An office building owned by Neverdy Life
│   Insurance Company which houses its
│   central headquarters.             │
│                                     │
│                                     │
│         (A) Capital Asset?          │
│                                     │
│                 or                  │
│                                     │
│        ((B) Non-capital Asset?)     │
│                                     │
│                                     │
│                           slide 9   │
└─────────────────────────────────────┘
```

For Slide 9
The correct answer is (B) Non-capital Asset. Since it is used in a trade or business, it is specifically excluded from the definition of a capital asset.

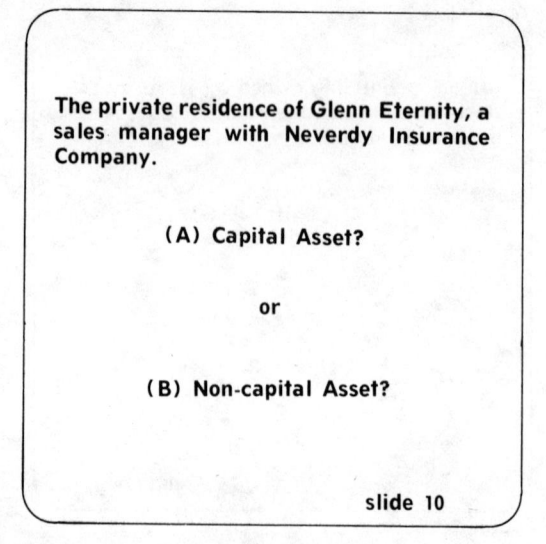

```
┌─────────────────────────────────────┐
│                                     │
│   The private residence of Glenn Eternity, a
│   sales manager with Neverdy Insurance
│   Company.                          │
│                                     │
│         (A) Capital Asset?          │
│                                     │
│                 or                  │
│                                     │
│         (B) Non-capital Asset?      │
│                                     │
│                                     │
│                           slide 10  │
└─────────────────────────────────────┘
```

For Slide 10
The private residence of Glenn Eternity, a sales manager with Neverdy Life Insurance Company.

A Teaching Machine Application in a Basic Tax Course   395

> The private residence of Glenn Eternity, a sales manager with Neverdy Insurance Company.
>
> (A) Capital Asset?
>
> or
>
> (B) Non-capital Asset?
>
> slide 11

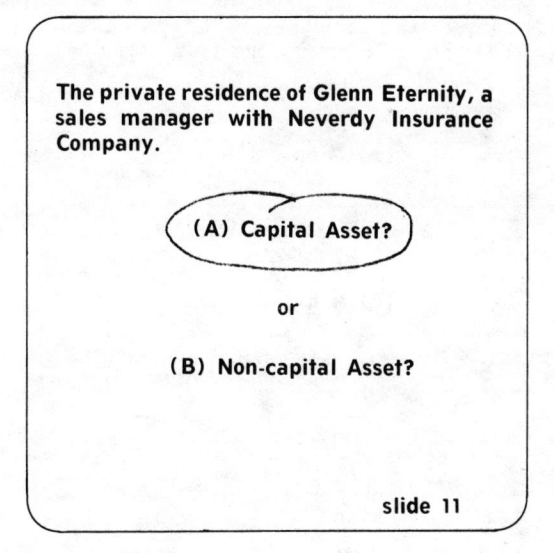

For Slide 11
The correct answer is (A). The Internal Revenue Code does not exclude from the capital asset definition a private residence.

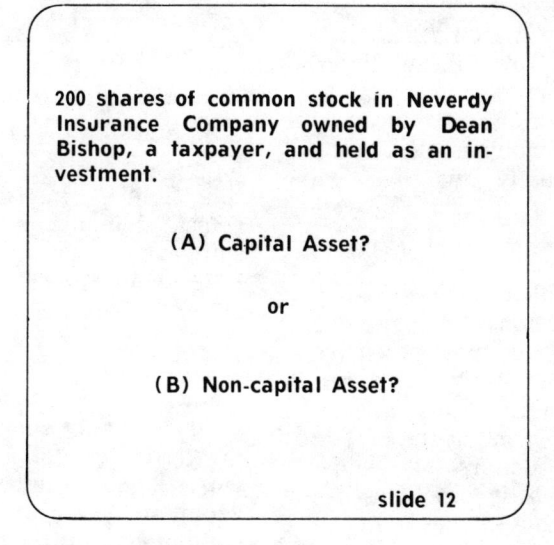

> 200 shares of common stock in Neverdy Insurance Company owned by Dean Bishop, a taxpayer, and held as an investment.
>
> (A) Capital Asset?
>
> or
>
> (B) Non-capital Asset?
>
> slide 12

For Slide 12
Two hundred shares of common stock in Neverdy Insurance Company, owned by Dean Bishop, a taxpayer, and held as an investment.

> 200 shares of common stock in Neverdy Insurance Company owned by Dean Bishop, a taxpayer, and held as an investment.
>
> (A) Capital Asset?
>
> or
>
> (B) Non-capital Asset?
>
> slide 13

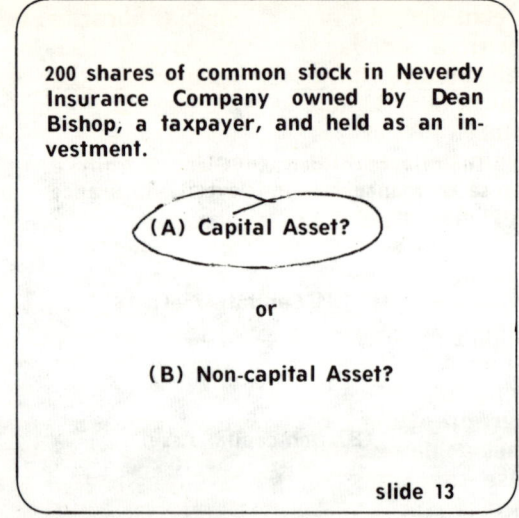

For Slide 13
The correct answer is (A). The Internal Revenue Code does not exclude stock held as an investment from the capital asset definition.

PRODUCTION AND COSTS

Audio Tapes

Experimentation showed that an average speaking voice will produce an acceptable product. Recording in a carpeted room or facilities which resemble a recording chamber improved the quality of the sound. Because of a better tone quality, reel-to-reel tape recorders are usually preferable to casette machines. Cost of the tapes is minimal, usually less than two dollars per reel.

Video Slides

Because of the author's unfamiliarity with available processes, color slide production proved to be the most expensive undertaking of the entire project. Utilization of type-setting and special photographic methods brought the cost to approximately three dollars per slide. However, much less costly processes are available. For example, slides can be produced through a photographic process for approximately twenty-five cents and through a heat (thermofax) process for about five cents. All slides fit a carousel-type projector.

Teaching Machines

A teaching machine similar to the IRS equipment, complete with carousel projector and tape deck, would require an investment of approximately three thousand dollars. However, machines with less sophisticated features suitable for 30-40 student terminals have been produced for as little as one hundred dollars. Of course, the slide projector and tape recorder would constitute an additional expense.

Availability of Software and Hardware

Software programs dealing with tax topics are not commercially available at this time.[1] Instructors should be encouraged in the production of their own software.

Teaching machine equipment may be obtained from companies such as Visual Educom, Inc. or Electronic Measurement, Inc. However, instructor control panels and student response units can easily be produced by the college electronics shop or by graduate students in the engineering department. Undoubtedly, the college department responsible for audio-visual equipment can render valuable assistance in supplying needed equipment for experimentation with new teaching methods.

POTENTIAL OF TEACHING MACHINES

The main purpose of a teaching machine is to implement learning processes which reach beyond just hearing and seeing a lecture. Since each student is required to communicate through a response unit with the instructor, the active participation of the class as a whole is considerably increased in comparison with a standard lecture method. Although studies have shown that immediate recall of information gained through the lecture method is greater when compared with the teaching machine method, retention of the material learned is greater under the teaching machine approach.[2]

Furthermore, the instructor may set a predetermined success quotient for accurate responses. For example, assume the instructor only feels satisfied if 70 percent of the students can correctly answer each question included in a program segment. If this success quotient is not achieved, the instructor may wish to use supplemental lectures, replay segments of the program, or assign additional learning material from outside sources. Of course, consistent low scores on some segments of a program might tell him that portions of the program require revision.

Another advantage of a teaching machine is the immediate feedback feature for both the students and the teacher. Students benefit from seeing and hearing the correct answer instantaneously after each of their responses. This either reinforces correct thinking processes or could change a wrong reasoning method, since the program usually explains the underlying logic of the correct response. In addition, the instructor becomes aware relatively early of specific individuals who consistently give incorrect responses. Such knowledge enables the instructor to give greater personal attention or to assign additional work to assist the student with his deficiency. Teaching machines can also be an aid in giving short quizzes since the results are immediately available at the completion of the exam.

Perhaps one of the most notable potentials of teaching machines lies in the area of self instruction in laboratories or special libraries. Use of a machine in the classroom usually infers an incorrect assumption that learning speeds of all students are equal. However, on an individual basis the student can adjust the program to his own speed. Undoubtedly, in the near future when enough programs become available, students will be able to study their lessons using home television sets with video tape adapters. Such equipment is now commercially available.

Another benefit which became apparent during the experiment is the larger quantity of material which can be covered in a given time period via the machine as compared to the lecture. Research disclosed a time saving of approximately 20 percent with the machine approach.[3]

The general attitude of the students towards the teaching machine was good. Favorable comments far outnumbered the negative responses. The major criticism was directed towards the inability of the students to take notes during the program. This limitation can easily be overcome, however, by furnishing students with copies of the program script.

SUMMARY

To improve teaching methods and enhance the learning efficiency of students, instructors might consider the adoption of various audio and visual equipment together with teaching machines. Budget constraints and limited experience in the preparation of programs should not overly discourage ventures into experimentations with teaching machines and related programs. Adoption of a trial and error approach by instructors with communication media should be encouraged. Perhaps an increased demand for audio and visual programs will lead to the establishment of more and better equipped communication aids facilities on departmental and/or college levels.

FOOTNOTES

[1] However, two well-known publishing companies have produced multi-media programs for adoption in an elementary accounting course. The Charles E. Merrill Publishing Company is marketing its product under the title "Accounting Principles: A Multimedia Program." Prentice-Hall advertises its program as "ALEX (Accounting: A Learning Experience)." Both can be adapted for use with a teaching machine.

[2] G. Fred Streuling and Gary L. Holstrum, "Teaching Machines Versus Lectures in Accounting Education: An Experiment," *The Accounting Review* (October, 1972), pp. 806-810.

[3] Ibid.

COMBUD: A Computer Simulation of the Budgetary Process of the Firm

J. Timothy Sale
University of Cincinnati

Introduction

COMBUD is a computerized model which simulates the budgetary process of a business firm. This model is an exercise and comprehensive budgeting on a short-term basis which illustrates the interrealtionships between the budgets prepared by the firm and the relationships between the variables included in the budgetary process. The student provides input data for the 15 decision variables included in the COMBUD model on 10 punched cards and the computer prepares 12 budgets and three estimated financial statements for the firm. Since the model is computerized, the student can experiment with alternative sets of values for these decision variables and study the behavior of the budgetary process under a variety of conditions. This paper provides a general description of the COMBUD simulation model and discusses experiences using this computerized model in the classroom. COMBUD is representative of computerized models of the budget simulation type.

The traditional method for teaching the budgetary process of a firm is to assign a highly simplified problem which requires the student to prepare the various budgets of a firm using one set of predetermined values for the decision variables. The level of sophistication of these problems is generally quite low since they are usually solved manually and any degree of sophistication would make them impossible to solve in any reasonable amount of time. As a result of this needed simplicity, such problems cannot adequately illustrate the concept of comprehensive budgeting.

Through the use of computer simulation, however, this basic limitation can be overcome. The elements of the budgetary process of a firm can be defined in mathematical terms and programmed to construct a computerized budget simulation model. By simulating the simultaneous interaction of the large number of variables included in the budgetary process, such models can make the following contributions to accounting education:

1. They can provide a feasible method for studying how the budgetary process will react to changes in values for specific variables.

2. They can provide valuable insight into the interrelationships of the variables included in the budgetary process.

3. They can provide a tool for experimentation with alternative sets of values for these variables.

A computer simulation model with the acronym "COMBUD" has been developed for classroom use at the University of Cincinnati. The model simulates the budgetary process of a hypothetical, but very realistic firm. The purpose of this paper is twofold:

1. To give a general description of this computerized budget simulation model.

2. To describe experiences using this computerized model in the classroom.

COMBUD SIMULATION MODEL

The COMBUD simulation model was designed to be used as an exercise in comprehensive budgeting on a short-term basis. It is a computer simulation which approximates the interaction between a large number of variables in an actual budgeting system and has the capability of predicting how the system will react to specific changes in these variables.[1]

The COMBUD model simulates the budgetary process of a hypothetical firm which produces soap products and is accompanied by a manual which contains information which the participant needs to select values for the decision variables included in the simulation.[2] The budgetary process of the hypothetical firm follows the basic pattern shown on Figure 1. This figure indicates the order of preparation of the firm's budgets and projected financial statements and illustrates their interrelationships. For example, the sales budget is developed first, followed by the production budget. These two budgets are interrelated, however, and if the sales and production budgets are not compatible, a stockout condition exists and the sales budget is adjusted accordingly.

Given the information in the COMBUD manual relative to both the past history and the future expectations of the firm, each participant is required to select values for the decision variables shown in Figure 2. The hypothetical firm in the COMBUD model, for example, uses a regression model to forecast the annual sales of its products. The annual sales forecast for each product includes two steps:
1. A projection of industry sales.
2. A projection of the company's share of the total industry sales.

Industry sales for each product are a function of four variables:
1. Gross National Product.
2. Market area population.
3. Consumer expenditures for durable goods.
4. The prior year's sales for the industry.

The company's share of these industry sales for each of its four products is a function of:

1. The selling price for each product.
2. Advertising expenditures for each product.
3. The firm's credit policy.

The participant, therefore, must estimate values for six of these seven variables to determine the sales for the budget period. As indicated in Figure 2, the participant must also select expected values for the other nine decision variables included in the COMBUD model:

1. Desired production-inventory policy.
2. Expected direct material prices.
3. Expected direct labor rate.
4. Estimated minimum cash balance.
5. Expected purchases of short-term investments.
6. Expected sales of short-term investments.
7. Expected repayments of short-term debt.
8. Expected dividend payments.
9. Expected purchases of property, plant, and equipment.

Once the values for these decision variables have been estimated, the data must be key-punched into ten input cards in accordance with the formats indicated in the COMBUD manual. Processing these input cards produces the twelve budgets and three estimated financial statements shown in Figure 1. If a particular set of values selected for the decision variables fails to produce an acceptable result, then the attempted budget plan should be reviewed and other values selected. After several alternative sets of data have been processed, a pattern usually develops which will provide the participant with an indication of which combination of values will produce an acceptable profit plan for the budget period. The relationships between the budgets prepared by the firm and the variables included in the budgetary process can be very effectively illustrated.

FIGURE 1

BUDGETARY PROCESS OF HYPOTHETICAL FIRM IN COMBUD MODEL

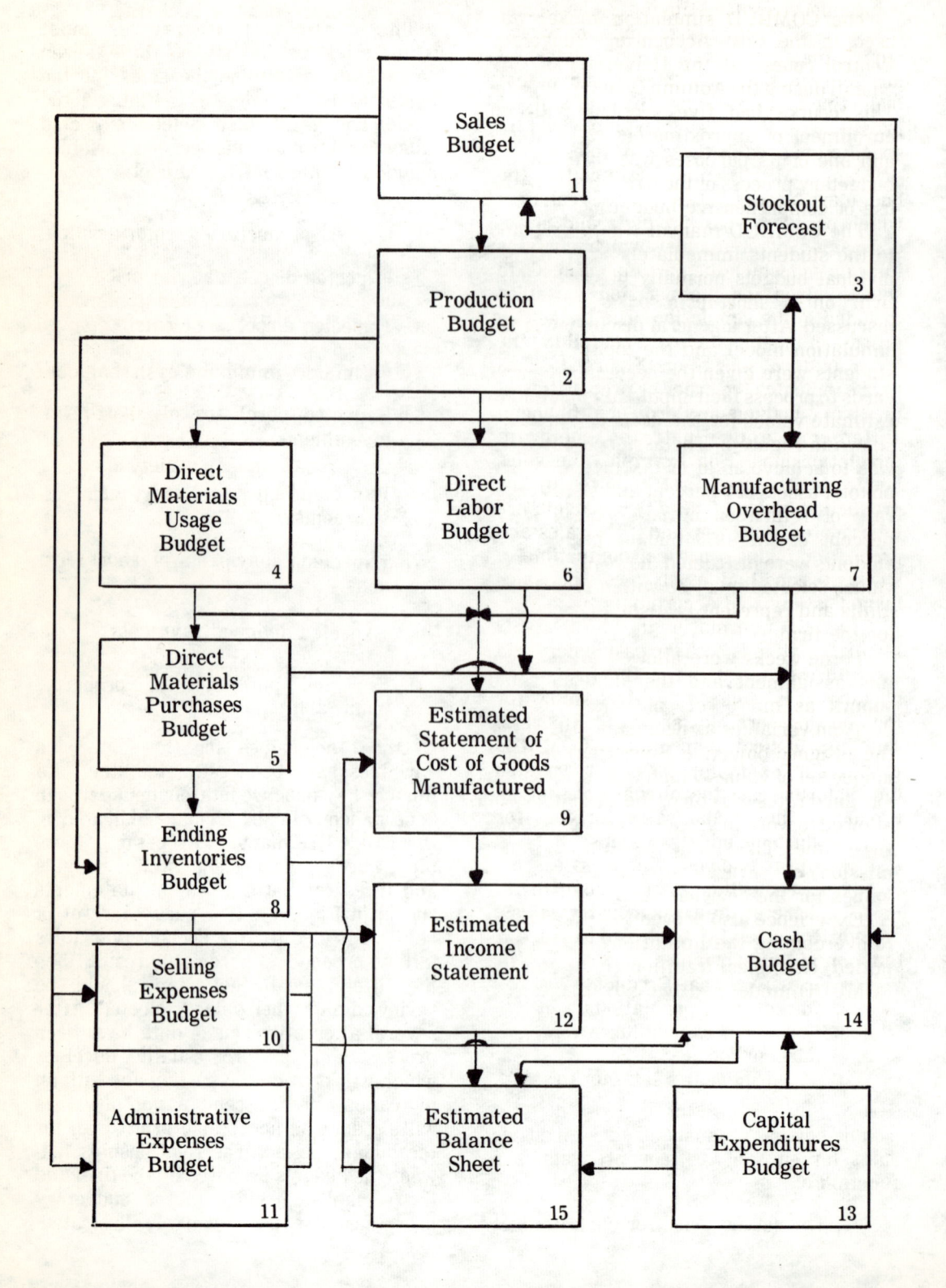

EXPERIENCES USING COMBUD MODEL

The COMBUD simulation model was used in the Cost Accounting Budgetary Control course at the University of Cincinnati during the Autumn Quarter, 1972-73. This course had five sections with an enrollment of approximately 120 students and one of its purposes was to teach the budgetary process of the firm stressing the use of comprehensive budgeting.

The COMBUD manual was distributed to the students immediately after the individual budgets normally prepared by a firm on a short-term basis had been discussed. After a general discussion of the simulation model and the input data, the students were given the necessary control cards to process their input data and told to estimate values for the decision variables shown in Figure 2. The assigned objective was to achieve an after-tax rate of return on total assets of 7 percent and an after-tax rate of return on owner's equity of 11 percent of the 1973 budget period. The students were instructed, however, that the values selected must be within reasonable limits and represent realistic expectations for the firm.

Three weeks were allowed to complete this assignment and the students could submit as many sets of values for the decision variables as necessary to achieve the assigned objective. Since there is not a unique set of values which will result in the assigned rates of return, the students were allowed to work in groups of two or three to save time. This made possible the submission of several alternative sets of values for the decision variables.

Experience also proved that in addition to overcoming the limitations of the simplified examples traditionally used, the COMBUD model had two advantages:

1. It brought all of the classroom discussion of the various budgets prepared by the firm together in one comprehensive problem that illustrated to the students the real meaning of comprehensive budgeting.

2. It demonstrated to the students how the computer can be an effective tool for comprehensive profit planning by simulating an actual business situation.

SUMMARY

Computerized budget simulation models can make an important contribution to accounting education. By simulating the budgetary process of the firm, they can:

1. Provide a feasible method for studying the behavior of the budgetary process under a variety of conditions.

2. Provide valuable insights into the interrelationships of the variables included in the budgetary process.

3. Provide a valuable tool for experimentation with alternative sets of values for these variables.

To allow accounting students an opportunity to appreciate the potential of such computerized simulation models, a computerized model with the acronym "COMBUD" has been developed for classroom use. The use of this simulation model illustrates to students the real meaning of comprehensive budgeting and the effectiveness of computer simulation as a tool for comprehensive profit planning.

FIGURE 2

DECISION VARIABLES INCLUDED IN COMBUD MODEL

Sales Budget:
Inputs to forecast industry sales
1) Estimate of Gross National Product for 1973 _____
2) Estimate of market area population for 1973 _____
3) Estimate of consumer expenditures on durable goods for 1973 _____

Inputs to forecast company's share of market
1) Estimated selling price for 1973:
   Product A _____
   Product B _____
   Product C _____
   Product D _____
2) Estimated advertising expenditures for 1973:
   Product A _____
   Product B _____
   Product C _____
   Product D _____
3) Desired credit policy for 1973 (Select one number)

   loose ⟵ 1 2 3 4 5 ⟶ tight

Production Budget:
Desired production inventory policy for 1973
(Select one number)

Completely
Stable
Inventory
Production ⟵1 2 3 4 5 6 7 8 9 10⟶ Inventory
                                              Fluctuates
                                              With Sales

Direct Materials Purchases Budget:
Expected changes in direct material prices for 1973
1) Expected price for Material V _____
2) Expected price for Material W _____
3) Expected price for Material X _____
4) Expected price for Material Y _____
5) Expected price for Material Z _____

Month of expected price change (Jan.=01, Feb.=02, etc.)
1) Month of price change in Material V _____
2) Month of price change in Material W _____
3) Month of price change in Material X _____
4) Month of price change in Material Y _____
5) Month of price change in Material Z _____

Direct Labor Budget:
Expected changes in direct labor rate for 1973 _____
Month of expected rate change _____

Cash Budget:
Estimated minimum cash balance for 1973 _____

Expected purchases of short-term investments for 1973

Month	Amount	Month	Amount
January		May	
February		June	
March		July	
April		August	

Month	Amount
September	
October	
November	
December	

Expected sales of short-term investments for 1973

Month	Amount	Month	Amount
January		May	
February		June	
March		July	
April		August	

Month	Amount
September	
October	
November	
December	

Expected repayments of short-term debt for 1973

Month	Amount	Month	Amount
January		May	
February		June	
March		July	
April		August	

Month	Amount
September	
October	
November	
December	

Expected dividend payments for 1973

Month	Amount
March	
June	
September	
December	

Capital Expenditures Budget
Expected purchases of property, plant, and equipment for 1973

Month	Amount	**Month**	Amount
January		May	
February		June	
March		July	
April		August	

Month	Amount
September	
October	
November	
December	

FOOTNOTES

[1] The COMBUD simulation model is not currently being sold commercially, but for those who are interested, the manual describing the model and the necessary input data as well as a sample of the computer output can be obtained at no charge by writing Dr. J. Timothy Sale, Assistant Professor of Accounting, Department of Accounting, College of Business Administration, University of Cincinnati, Cincinnati, Ohio 45221. A copy of the computer program for the model, written for an IBM 370-165 system, is available at the nominal cost of reproduction.

[2] The first section of the manual contains a general description of the company's organization structure, products, and manufacturing process, and the previous year's actual financial statements. This section is followed by individual sections for each of the twelve budgets and three estimated financial statements prepared by the firm. These individual sections include the following: (1) a discussion of the techniques used by the company to forecast the information included in the particular budget or financial statement; (2) the data necessary to select values for the variables upon which the particular budget or financial statement is based; and (3) a copy of the particular budget or estimated financial statement for the previous year. The section for the sales budget, for example, includes discussions of the techniques employed by the company to forecast sales, the effects of the company's advertising expenditures and credit policy on the sales forecast, and the seasonality of the company's sales, as well as historical data for the variables used to forecast sales and a copy of the sales budget for the previous year. Following these individual sections, the manual contains instructions for the preparation of the input data cards to be key-punched by the student. The manual also contains technical appendices which discuss the use of regression and correlation analysis to forecast sales and expenses, the use of matrix algebra to allocate overhead costs, and the use of present value analysis to evaluate investment opportunities.

A Computer Simulation Approach for Teaching the Evaluation of Internal Control

David C. Burns
Naval Postgraduate School

Introduction

This paper describes how a computer simulation model supported by certain class handout materials can be used in the auditing classroom to create a realistic audit situation involving manufacturing inventories. The audit situation requires the students to study a set of prescribed inventory procedures and controls, design an appropriate audit program of tests of compliance, carry out certain tests of compliance, and evaluate inventory related internal controls. This simulation teaching approach can be employed by most auditing instructors. It does not require any particular expertise in the area of computers. Upon written request, the author will supply the interested reader with a package of materials necessary to implement this teaching approach.

The second generally accepted auditing standard of field work states:

> There is to be a proper study and evaluation of existing internal control as a basis for reliance thereon and for the determination of the resultant extent of the tests to which auditing procedures are to be restricted.[1]

Furthermore, when the auditor performs his study and evaluation of internal control, he is expected to comply with Statement on Auditing Standards No. 1. This statement requires that the auditor concentrate his efforts on those accounting controls which could have an important bearing on the reliability of external financial statements.[2]

When the auditor evaluates internal control, using the evidence which is at his disposal, he must make two interrelated decisions:

1. He must decide how any existing weaknesses in accounting controls (disclosed thus far by his examination) affect the amount of reliance he can place on the system of internal control.
2. He must further decide (in the light of point 1 above) the resultant extent of the tests to which further auditing procedures are to be restricted.

In making these two decisions, the auditor must assess the potential effect that existing weak controls could have on the reliability of the accounting records.[3] This assessment permits the auditor to determine the materiality of the potential threat posed by existing weak controls. The materiality of this potential threat is one of the chief factors which determines the amount of reliance that the auditor should place in the existing system of internal control. Consequently, this materiality determination (and the related reliability assessments) can have a significant impact upon the auditor's decisions concerning the design of other auditing procedures necessary in the circumstances.

The auditor's evaluation of his internal-control-related evidence is one of the most important phases of the contemporary audit. However, the primary emphasis of most current auditing courses (and auditing texts) appears to be on gathering internal control audit evidence, not on evaluating it. As a result, the typical auditing student is not well trained in how to approach an evaluation of this type of evidence. Consequently, many students leave the classroom believing that any weakness in internal accounting control is *prima facie* evidence that extended other auditing procedures are necessary.

The remainder of this paper describes a computer simulation model based teaching approach that has proved to be a valuable tool for exposing auditing students to some of the complex problems that can arise in connection with an evaluation of internal control audit evidence. This approach seems most effective when it is employed simultaneously with material which deals with the study and evaluation of internal controls related to inventory. This approach seems to be particularly effective in helping to improve the students' understanding of:

1. The purpose and nature of the auditor's study and evaluation of internal control.
2. The potential dynamic behavior of complex accounting systems.
3. The audit concept of accounting record reliability.
4. How to perform an assessment of the potential effect that existing controls could have on the reliability of an accounting record.
5. How to carry out audit sampling procedures.
6. How the results of the evaluation of internal control can affect the auditor's reliance upon the system and the design and timing of the other necessary auditing procedures.

The teaching approach described later in this paper is based upon a computer simulation model of a manufacturing inventory accounting system. A brief narrative description of this computer simulation model (or program) is given in the following section. This description should give the reader a basic understanding concerning both the purpose of the model and how the model operates. Following this description is a further explanation of how the model should be used in the auditing classroom. This explanation includes several brief descriptions of the various types of class handout materials which are necessary to carry out this simulation teaching approach. Interested readers can obtain from the writer a "package of materials" containing copies of all the items necessary to employ the simulation teaching approach described in this paper[4].

DESCRIPTION OF THE SIMULATION MODEL

The key to the teaching approach described later is a computer simulation model (or program). This program consists of approximately 725 FORTRAN statements and is written for the Control Data 6600 FTN compiler. This computer program requires approximately 130,000 words of core storage and can be easily converted to run on IBM equipment. Most university computer centers could make a conversion of this program from Control Data to IBM in one or two days. A listing of this program will be included in the "package of materials" mentioned above. This version of the program requires less than one minute of processing time on the Control Data 6600 computer.

The computer simulation model represents the system to be audited by the students. The model is designed to simulate the detailed manual inventory accounting processing activity of a hypothetical manufacturing firm over a time period which can be specified by the instructor. A manufacturing inventory accounting system was selected in favor of other types of systems because such inventory systems typically involve a greater number of different types of interrelated transactions than do other types of systems (e.g. direct labor inputs, direct material inputs, etc.). Consequently, inventory systems usually present a wider variety of audit problems than do other types of systems (e.g., direct where internal control evaluations are concerned.

The scope of the simulation model is restricted to the accounting activity related to four products which are produced using four raw materials. The model assumes the use of standard costs, and all productive activity related to these four products is assumed to take place in two manufacturing departments. The model is further designed so that the instructor may establish the total volume of accounting activity to be processed by the firm during the simulation time period by specifying the following three items:

1. The number of units of each type of raw material to be received by the firm.
2. The number of units of each type of product to be produced by the firm.
3. The number of units of each type of product to be sold by the firm.

The computer program listing, available to interested readers (see footnote 4), is already set up to run for a nine month accounting time period. Values for the three activity measures listed above have also been specified in this listing. The reader is cautioned against changing any of these factors, since the supporting class handout material supplied with the computer program listing is based upon the values of these factors specified by the writer. However, when the reader becomes familiar with the entire teaching package, he may wish to change some of these computer program values and appropriately modify the supporting class handout material.

The major portion (or "framework") of the computer simulation program is devoted to the accounting operations and reporting processes necessary to account for raw materials, work in process, and finished goods inventories. In this sense, the framework of the model constitutes no more than an abstract version of a standard cost inventory accounting computer program. In fact, the major part of the framework section of the program probably could have been obtained from an actual business firm.

There is, nevertheless, one major difference which distinguishes the framework of the program from the typical inventory accounting computer program found in actual practice, and this necessary difference prompted the writer to design his own framework section. The framework of the program is designed to maintain two separate, but parallel, sets of inventory account balances: (1) a *Reported* set of balances, and (2) a *Control* set of balances. The framework is designed to process each inventory accounting transaction (or data input) twice: once for the purpose of updating the Reported records, and a second time for the purpose of updating the Control records. The need for these two records will become clear later.

Several short specialized computer routines were written and either spliced into or appended to the model's framework. Some of these routines generate all of the necessary input data which the framework of the model is designed to process. These input data are as follows:

1. Data representing the firm's receipt of individual incoming raw material shipments. The quantity of material contained in each shipment is treated as a normally distributed random variable.
2. Data representing individual production reports for the production orders manufactured. The quantity of units produced on each production order is also assumed to be a normally distributed random variable.
3. Data representing individual raw materal requisitions.
4. Data representing the transfer of completed production orders from work in process to finished goods inventory.
5. Data representing sales and finished goods withdrawals.

The specialized routines mentioned above generate one set of detailed external input data and feed this data set to the framework of the program for processing. The program uses the computer's random number generator to drive these external input generating processes. As was explained, the framework processes this single set of input data twice.

Several weaknesses in internal accounting controls were assumed in designing the simulation model. These weaknesses were further assumed to permit processing errors, committed at random by various accounting operations of the system, to remain undetected. The remainder of the specialized routines previously mentioned are designed to simulate these erroneous accounting operations. These routines cause the framework of the model to commit at random (but with a specified frequency rate which may be changed by the instructor) various types of processing errors.[6] Since individual transaction sizes vary (e.g., normally distributed production counts), the magnitude of most errors depends almost entirely upon chance (e.g., a pricing error). However, these special error routines are only spliced into the Reported record segments of the program framework. Hence, these random errors only affect the reliability of the Reported ending inventory balances generated by the model. No errors occur in processing the same transactions (i.e., input data) for the purpose of updating the Control records.

At the conclusion of the simulation run, the Reported balances contain some resultant amount of processing error. These Reported balances are the balances to be audited. The total amount of the error contained in these Reported balances is a complex random variable, because it depends upon all of the random elements of the model.[7] However, the ending Control balances contain no error and consequently represent the amounts that should have resulted as Reported balances, had no processing errors occurred during the time period simulated.

The following list describes the different types of random error processes which are designed into the simulation model:

1. Misstatements of a specified magnitude occur in the receiving and inspecting counts on a specified percentage of the incoming raw material shipments.

2. Inappropriate material price standards are applied to a specified percentage of the raw material purchases vouchered. The model selects all inappropriate standard costs at random from lists of standards (i.e., both appropriate and inappropriate) which are fed to the program as parameters.

3. Misstatements occur in the production counts of good units produced on a specified percentage of the production reports and raw material requisitions processed.

4. Inappropriate physical and price standards are applied in costing out a specified percentage of the production reports and raw material requisitions processed.

5. Misstatements occur in the unit counts on a specified percentage of the completed production orders transferred to finished goods.

6. Inappropriate unit standard costs are applied in costing out a specified percentage of the transfers to finished goods.

The simulation program uses the computer's random number generator to drive each of the six random error processes described above. Thus, the specific occurrence of each error depends upon the random number selected by the simulation program.

The simulation model is further designed to generate several detailed print-out listings of accounting information. This information is assumed to represent all of the accounting documents either processed or prepared by the assumed firm in generating the erroneous ending Reported balances. Hence, some of the information is in error. For example, two of these listings contain information which is assumed to represent the calculations used to cost out production reports. Some of the production reports which appear on these listings are costed out with inappropriate standards. The students can discover these costing errors by referencing the standards used in the erroneous cost calculations to proper standards supplied in the supporting case material. This supporting case material is described later.

The computer print-outs supply enough information so that a detailed audit of them would disclose every error committed by the system in generating the ending Reported balances. However, a simulation time period of nine months is long enough to cause these listings to be voluminous enough to make such a detailed audit approach a hopeless task. (The simulation model is a computerized paper mill.)

Of course, some of the errors committed by the model could only be detected in actual practice by visual observations and test counts (e.g., receiving and inspecting count errors and production count errors). The detailed listings are, therefore, designed to disclose both the Reported and Control information related to these processes. This permits the students to discover errors in these processes by making comparisons of the relevant detailed Reported and Control information. Thus, the students must be instructed to restrict the scope of their tests of these processes to a realistic level.[8]

DESCRIPTION OF THE SUPPORTING WRITTEN CLASS HANDOUT MATERIAL AND THE SUGGESTED CLASSROOM TEACHING APPROACH

The "package of materials" (see footnote 4) includes one copy of a detailed written description of the assumed inventory accounting system. This system description has been prepared in a format which resembles that of an auditor's permanent file work papers. A correct standard cost build-up for each product is included in this description and the description is cross-referenced to a complete set of inventory accounting document flow charts. Copies of this material should be distributed to the students on the first day they begin the simulation audit. The students should be instructed to perform an internal control review of the assumed system using the descriptive handout material. In connection with this review, the instructor should assume the role of the client's controller and answer any questions which arise. Obviously, students cannot perform single purpose tests (walk-through tests), but the instructor can fill in this gap by talking through various hypothetical transactions with them. The instructor can also fill in the gap, caused by a lack of an audit opportunity to make visual observations, by telling the students what such observations might have disclosed in the assumed circumstances. These explanations can be based upon the instructor's inside knowledge concerning the errors generated by the simulation model. This verbal question and answer process should take one or two 50 minute class periods. During this time, the class should identify some of the more obvious weaknesses in internal controls, evident from the system description handout.

At the close of this question-answer process the students should be instructed to prepare (outside of the classroom) an audit program for testing the assumed system's actual compliance with prescribed controls. At a later class period, the instructor should hold discussions with the students concerning the strengths and weaknesses of their audit programs. During this session, the instructor should guide the students toward unanimous agreement on one "ideal" audit program. At a minimum, this "ideal" audit program should include tests which will disclose each *type* of error committed by the simulation model. A list of these *necessary tests* is included as part of the "package of materials."

When the class has reached unanimous agreement on an audit program, the instructor can run the previously described simulation model on the computer. Most university computer centers can arrange to generate multiple copies of the output listings by simple adding an additional control card to the simulation program deck.

Copies of the detailed output listings generated by the model should be distributed to the students. The instructor should also give the students both the accurate beginning inventory levels used to initialize the model and the Reported ending inventory balances generated by the model. The proper Control ending inventory balances should not be disclosed to the students at this point in the case.

Next, the students can be instructed to carry out their "ideal" audit program on the detailed data listings generated by the model. However, the simulated data will not permit the students to carry out two very important types of audit tests that will be contained in their programs:

1. Tests which involve the examination of transactions for proper approval and authorization.
2. Tests which are aimed at determining the existing system of segregation of duties.

To remedy this shortcoming of the model, another handout document has been prepared. This document is assumed to represent a portion of the memorandum of another colleague auditor who has already carried out the two types of tests mentioned above. This memo accurately points out those weaknesses in accounting controls that such tests should have disclosed.

Copies of this memorandum should be distributed to the students. Then, the students should be instructed to carry out the remaining steps of their "ideal" audit program. These remaining steps primarily involve dual purpose tests of accounting transactions for accuracy. The students can employ these tests on samples of data included on the detailed listing print-outs. Since these listings are quite extensive, many students may elect to use statistical sampling procedures in employing the dual purpose tests.

When the students complete the tests described above, the instructor should review their work papers. In reviewing the students' work papers the instructor should make sure that each student resolves any shortcomings in his tests at this point. When each student completes this testing phase of the case, he should have developed audit evidence which indicates the following factors:

1. Each weakness in internal accounting controls which directly or indirectly affects the reliability of the Reported balances.

2. An accurate indication of how each weakness affects the reliability of the Reported balances.

At this point the students should be instructed to evaluate their audit evidence for the purpose of deciding how much reliance they would place in the assumed system and the Reported account balances generated by it. In addition, the students can be asked to answer the following questions in the light of their evidence thus far.

1. Should this client be urged to take his annual physical inventory at the close of his fiscal year? Why?

2. If the client insists on taking his physical inventory at an interim date (say at the close of the 10th month), will extensive audit tests of interim inventory transactions be necessary? Why?

3. How extensive should physical inventory audit procedures be? Why?

4. Should tests of transactions be extended through the remaining three months of this fiscal year? Why?

5. Which of the weaknesses in accounting controls pose the greatest threat to the reliability of the inventory records? What other auditing procedure should be employed as a consequence? Why?

As the reader has probably surmised, this internal control evaluation poses a difficult problem for the students. The model is designed so that the potential independent effect of each accounting control weakness on the reliability of the Reported balances appears to be relatively immaterial. However, the potential combined (or joint) effect of all of these weaknesses can have a material impact upon the reliability of the Reported balances. This latter point is perhaps the most important factor which the model illustrates to the students.

When the students have completed their evaluations, the instructor should supply the proper Control ending inventory balances. These Control balances disclose the accuracy of the Reported balances. However, in performing their evaluations the students will have assessed the *potential* reliability of the Reported balances. This reliability assessment will have necessitated that the students consider the range of the total error that might exist in each Reported ending inventory balance. Hence, knowing the accuracy of the Reported balances may not provide them with conclusive proof concerning the correctness of their reliability assessments and, hence, their evaluations of internal control.

The simulation model permits the instructor to provide the students with an objective illustration of how the existing weaknesses in the system's accounting controls *could have* jointly affected the reliability of the Reported balances. Only two major modifications of the previously described model are necessary to provide this information:

1. A loop (or DO) statement must be added to the beginning of the previously described program.

2. All of the print statements must be removed from the program except those connected with the Reported and Control ending inventory balances.

The modifications described above cause the model to replicate the simulation process, previously described, time and time again.[9] Each time the model replicates this simulation process, it selects a different set of random numbers. Since random numbers drive the random processes of the model, this causes processing errors of different magnitudes to occur on different combinations of

FIGURE 1

PLOT OF THE PROBABILITY DISTRIBUTION OF
THE ERROR IN THE W.I.P. INVENTORY
COMPUTED BY THE SYSTEM SIMULATION MODEL

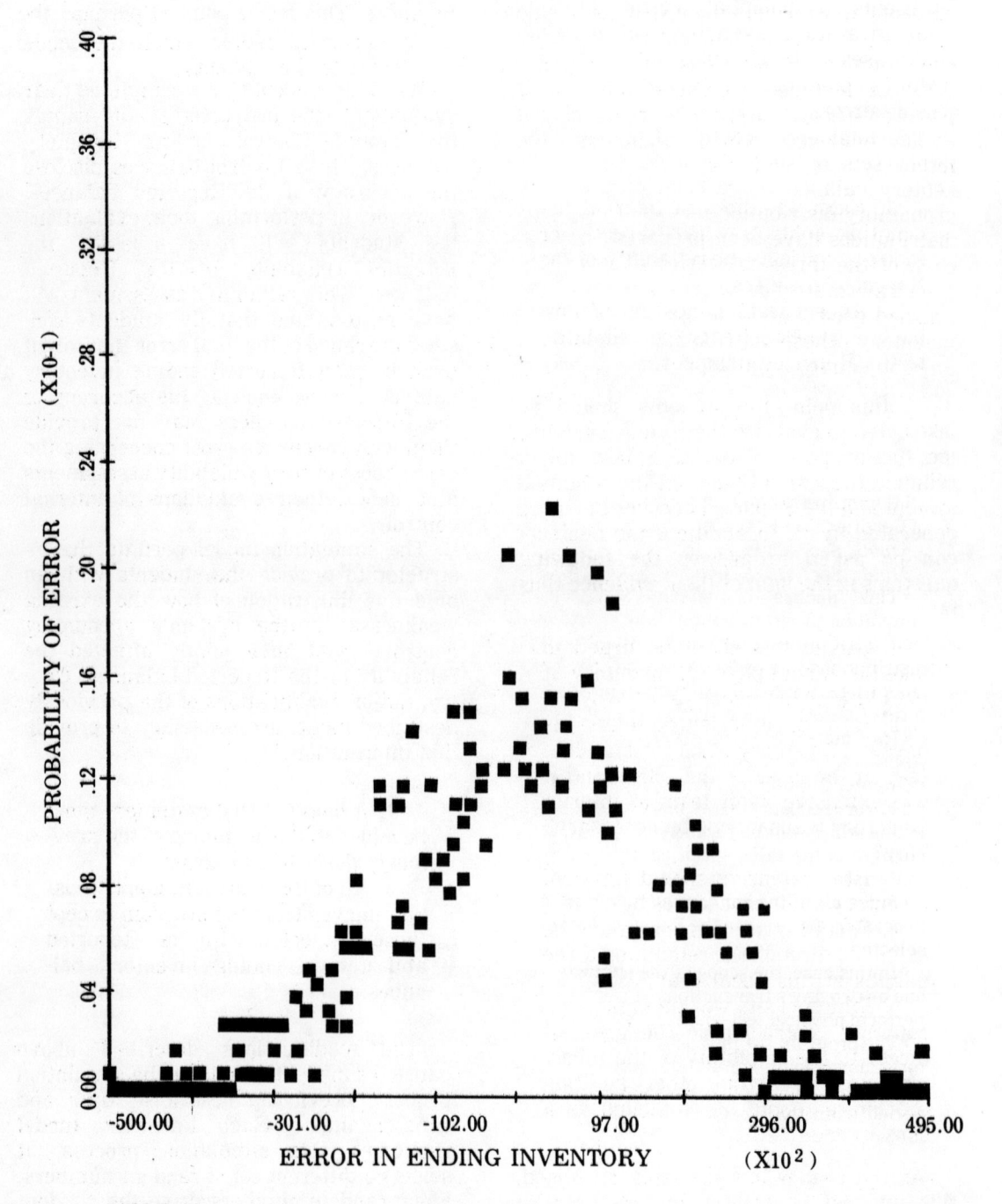

LEGEND
  TOTAL BUSINESS ACTIVITY - 9 MO.
  PLOTTED AFTER 1,500 ITERATIONS
  FREQUENCY INTERVALS OF 500

transactions during each replication of the model. Consequently, the Reported balances differ at the conclusion of each replication, because they contain a different amount of total error. Each of these different sets of Reported balances represents a potential result of the assumed system given both the existing weaknesses in the internal control and the system's potential for committing processing errors.

The total error contained in 1,500 different sets of such Reported ending inventory balances have been plotted in a probability distribution format. Four such distributions have been prepared; one for each of the three categories of inventory (i.e., raw materials, work-in-process and finished goods) and one for the combined inventory. These distributions disclose, in an objective matter, the *potential* reliability of the Reported ending inventory balances assuming both the existing weaknesses in the hypothetical system's internal accounting controls and the system's potential for committing errors. An example of one of these distributions is given in Figure 1.

The simulation audit can be concluded effectively by distributing copies of these distributions to the students. These distributions provide the students an objective portrayal of the potential reliability of the Reported ending inventory balances and hence the adequacy of internal controls. One copy of each of these distributions will be included in the available "package of materials." Of course, these distributions are only valid with respect to the simulation program as supplied and set up by the writer.

FOOTNOTES

[1] Committee on Auditing Procedure, *Statement on Auditing Standards No. 1*, (American Institute of Certified Public Accountants, Inc., 1973), Sec. 320.01, p. 13.

[2] *Ibid.*, Sec. 320.11, p. 16.

[3] *Ibid.*, Sec. 320.65, p. 30.

[4] This "package of materials" includes one copy each of the following items: a computer simulation program listing, flow charts of the computer simulation program, systems description, a list of necessary audit tests of compliance, an audit memorandum, and four probability distributions. The package may be obtained by writing: Professor David C. Burns, Department of Operations Research and Administrative Sciences, Code 55, Naval Postgraduate School, Monterey, California 93940. A price of $5.00 is requested to cover duplicating and handling costs.

[5] Raw material shipments and production counts were generated using the Monte Carlo "Direct Approach" described in Thomas H. Naylor, Joseph L. Balintfy, Donald S. Burdick, and Kong Chu, *Computer Simulation Techniques* (John Wiley and Sons, Inc., New York, New York, 1966), p. 95.

[6] Error frequency rates have been specified by the writer and incorporated into the program listing which will be furnished to the interested reader. Again, the reader is cautioned that any changes in the rates specified by the writer will necessitate changes in the supporting handout material.

[7] Since all of the random elements of the model are driven by the computer random number generator, the error in the Reported balances depends upon the specific string of random numbers selected.

[8] In this case, the scope of the students' tests should probably be restricted to the equivalent of one or two day's transactions. A restriction of this nature assumes that it would be practicable to perform physical test counts to this extent in an actual situation.

[9] The program listing (included in the materials described in footnote 4) is already set up to run for a nine month simulation time period. Hence, one replication of the modified model would constitute a nine month time period, unless the instructor decides to change the simulation time period from that specified by the writer.

Integration of the Computer into Systems and Auditing: A Team Approach

Richard L. Cattanach
and
Glyn W. Hanbery
University of Denver

Introduction

Retention of basic concepts of one course can be reinforced by examination of such concepts in other courses and other contexts. This objective may be accomplished by adopting a multi-disciplinary approach involving the undertaking of projects with the participation of students and faculty from a variety of courses. This paper describes the application of such an approach wherein the basic tenets of accounting systems and auditing are integrated with those of computer science.

The advantages of reinforcement and feedback have long been recognized in educational theory. Retention of basic concepts, once learned, is far greater when the concepts are reexamined in other courses and perhaps in other contexts. Cognizance of this particular educational theory in business curricula has manifested as the "systems" approach. Whenever the basic concepts of several courses are to be applied in concert, a new "capstone" course often is proposed.

Frequently, however, the addition of one business course requires deletion of another due to constraints placed upon business curricula such as those prescribed by the American Association of Collegiate Schools of Business. And proliferation of courses likely will not provide the best means for offering new concepts as well as integrating established ones.

PROPOSED APPROACH

Accordingly, an approach must be adopted which recognizes the need for a multi-disciplinary approach, but which also recognizes present curricula constraints. Specifically, such an approach might involve undertaking projects with the participation of students and faculty from a variety of course. In this manner, the basic tenets of each discipline could receive due consideration, and the project could represent a broadening educational experience for all persons involved.

One area to which this whole issue may be easily related is the computer curriculum, because if students are to benefit most from their exposure to computers, other courses must familiarize them with indigenous computer applications. However, computer ap-

---

*For example, the authors have required students in accounting systems, advanced data processing, and auditing classes to participate in designing a relatively complex, computerized payroll system for a manufacturing concern. Thus, in addition to computing and accounting for deductions, the system must be designed to allocate labor costs to the functions of selling, production, and administration.

For maximum educational benefits, the authors believe that the least information possible should be revealed in the case. Accordingly, our case reveals only the company's principal products, divisional structure, personnel assignments, bases for remunerating personnel, and information about payroll deductions apart from those required by Federal and state statutes. The students must determine on their own what deductions are necessary according to Federal and state statutes. Additionally, and more importantly, they must determine what types of information must be retained under Federal and state laws.

plications in many courses are discussed only on a conceptual basis, if at all considered. Techniques do exist for integrating computer technology with most areas, but this approach usually incorporates the concepts of but two courses. Surely better results could be achieved by integrating the concepts of several courses.

For this reason, the authors utilize an approach involving the participation of several different courses, namely: accounting systems, advanced data processing, and auditing. First, students in accounting systems design a relatively complex, computerized system. Basic constraints and other pertinent data about the system are presented to the students in a case.* Once designed and described in a formal report, the system is programmed by advanced data processing students to promote maximum efficiency regarding computer usage and data processing. Finally, the system is evaluated by auditing students for its ability to provide information for external reporting and for incorporation of proper elements of internal control. Also, auditing students are asked to determine proper measures for auditing the system.

DERIVED BENEFITS

The benefits accruing to the students depend principally on the course in which they are enrolled. Accounting systems students gain an appreciation of the problems involved in designing even minor subsystems and the need to incorporate flexibility into a system so that the proposed "paper" system can undergo the inevitable redesigning prior to final implementation. This appreciation results from providing these students with only a general overview of a particular organization and the system to be designed. With these limited facts, each student is required to define the needs and objectives of the organization, and design the proposed system, complete with documentation, internal controls, and report formats. Then, in conjunction with data processing students, accounting systems students refine and purge their systems of errors or deficiencies.

Data processing students, who program the system, are presented the opportunity to apply their knowledge to a realistic situation. This requires of the students both proficiency in program language and an understanding of the consequences of the various features of the designed system so that they can point out omissions or potential weaknesses. Additionally, they are exposed to concepts of internal control which, while essential, necessarily constrain achievable efficiency. Students are faced with the problem of devising a program that will not only meet the needs of management but will do so at least possible cost and in the most efficient manner practicable. Once the program is operational, the data processing students receive feedback from auditing students regarding the program's internal controls and its ability to provide required information. So, not only are their experiences broadened by exposure to new horizons, but they also receive relatively prompt feedback on their interpretation of perhaps totally foreign concepts, i.e., internal control and financial reporting standards.

Like the data processing students, auditing students are given the opportunity to apply recently acquired knowledge. They are offered the opportunity of evaluating the integrity of a realistic computerized subsystem and of developing appropriate measures for auditing it. Each student receives his own system to evaluate and is required to prepare a report for management on the system's ability to provide desired information and another for his audit supervisor on the reliability of the information and the efficiency of the system.

PROBLEMS OF IMPLEMENTATION

Like most multifaceted projects, this approach has some serious problems and limitations. First, and perhaps foremost, cooperation and coordination among the faculty is essential. Courses must be structured and subject matter arranged with a view toward scheduling each part of the project. This may require presenting some material in class before it otherwise would be. In auditing, for example, internal controls for electronic data processing systems and resultant effects on auditing procedures must be covered early in the semester and out of their natural context. Yet, this seems to create no difficulties for student participants. Also, the case, which must be general but sufficiently detailed, must be agreed upon well in advance of a semester to consider such factors as computer limitations, programming requirements, etc.

Another serious limitation is the tight schedule which must be developed to successfully complete the project. In a fifteen-week semester, each class was allowed four weeks to conclude its section of the project. Project evaluation was scheduled for the last three weeks, but an emergent problem necessitated utilizing even this time for further system's design.

The emergent problem was that students responsible for designing the system failed to provide sufficient instructional detail for those responsible for programming it. Accounting systems students assumed too much knowledge of accounting systems on the part of the programming students. Although anticipated by the professors, this assumption and resultant deficiency was not corrected in the early stages of the project, for allowing students to discover this kind of problem is a corollary benefit of the approach.

Finally, a problem directly related to the scheduling limitations involved feedback and evaluation of the students' efforts by the professors. The accounting systems class was expected to develop a relatively sophisticated system within only the first four weeks of a course designed to devote the entire semester to covering that very subject. In addition, final evaluation of the project was delayed until the end of the semester to avoid influencing programming and auditing students; consequently, feedback in terms of a grade for accounting systems students came so long after completion of their part that its value was diminished. This same problem applied to data processing students, but was virtually nonexistent for auditing students.

There appear to be two possible solutions to this problem. One method consists of forming teams composed of students from accounting systems, data processing, and auditing. Each team would be responsible for designing and implementing a system with the full participation of all team members. Through faculty evaluation, feedback could be made available continually throughout the term. Incidentally, this method also seems most appropriate for the initial implementation of this approach, for the design-evaluation-feedback cycle is completed in one term for all student participants. The other possible solution requires two terms for completion of that cycle. Here, students in accounting systems and data processing would be allowed one complete term for designing and programming their systems. Additional feedback could be obtained by requiring each student to evaluate another team's proposed system. Auditing students then would evaluate these systems the following term.

EXTENSION OF THE APPROACH

Of course, other disciplines also could be involved, depending on the project selected. For example, suppose the project required designing a computerized information system for the inventory of a manufacturing concern. In this instance, additional information needs must be satisfied for such functions as marketing, production, finance, and personnel. The accounting systems class, which would be principally responsible for designing the system, must first establish the specific needs of each of the several functions through consultations with representatives from classes in marketing, finance, and production and personnel management.

CONCLUSION

In conclusion, this proposal offers benefits beyond the traditional approach where concepts of each discipline are studied almost in isolation. Admittedly, the various subsystems, i.e., production, marketing, finance, accounting, etc., may have received recognition as a group, traditionally, but only conceptually because of the complexity of an entire system. Consequently, students often advance beyond an area uncertain of their ability to apply their knowledge of that area and unaware of the interrelationships among the subsystems. Reinforcing their confidence in their abilities and providing them with the experience of designing an acutal computerized system can be accomplished by this proposed approach. It not only reinforces student confidence, but in many respects mirrors situations which they can reasonably expect, once employed.

An Illustration of Four Price Level Approaches to Income Measurement

Harry I. Wolk
Drake University

Introduction

General price level changes and specific price changes have created an enormous problem relative to accurate and meaningful income measurement. Using a simple set of data, this article illustrates and compares general price level adjustment and three specific or current value approaches to income measurement. In addition, capital maintenance and the calcalculation of general and specific purchasing power gains and losses arising from this holding of monetary assets and liabilities are demonstrated.

Problems of financial statement presentation under conditions of changing price levels have probably been the most recurrent single topic appearing in the accounting literature of the post World War II era. However, price level adjustments and replacement cost accounting are presently outside the scope of generally accepted accounting principles in the United States.[1] We are faced with the paradox of an extremely important problem which is, nevertheless, beyond the pale of accounting orthodoxy. Consequently, accounting teachers may desire to introduce the topic in advanced accounting theory or contemporary issues courses and yet spend a minimum of time on the subject. If this task is to be accomplished, the extensive diversity of solutions to the changing price level problem must be effectively synthesized.

The comparative illustration shown here was developed for an advanced accounting theory class with these considerations in mind. In a short period of time, students can be exposed to four important price level approaches to income measurement, their underlying relationships, and theoretical rationales.

This illustration is closely tied to the excellent and extensively researched article by Stephen Zeff.[2] Students should read it prior to working with the illustration. Zeff discusses in depth two of the four methods shown here and has a very lucid explanation of general and specific price indexes. Since an understanding of the three types of price movements is essential, each is quickly reviewed.

Type A price movements refer to changes in the prices of all goods and services throughout the economy. Because of the totality of the concept, the reciprocal of a Type A price movement for a particular period of time would be the change in the general purchasing power of the monetary unit.

Specific price movements are for particular segments of the economy and may be very broad or narrow in scope. Specific price indexes, in Zeff's terminology, are called Type C indexes. The key to remember is that Type C movements are automatically affected by changes in the general level of prices (Type A movements) as well as price changes arising from real changes in demand or supply for the goods and services comprising the particular segment of the economy covered by a specific price index. These real changes in price are called Type B movements. Specific price indexes, then are an amalgam of general (Type A) and real (Type B) prices.

Specific price changes occurring between two points of time, t_0 and t_1, can be expressed as an equation when the three types of price movements are expressed as percentage changes from their respective beginning of period (t_0) levels:

$$C_{t_1-t_0} = A_{t_1-t_0} \pm B_{t_1-t_0} \qquad (1)$$

and, by subtraction, the percentage of the B type change can be shown as a residual:

$$C_{t_1-t_0} - A_{t_1-t_0} \pm B_{t_1-t_0} \qquad (2)$$

In this example, historical cost adjusted by a Type C index is used as a substitute for replacement cost (actual specific cost of individual factors) valuation of services used during the period. However, specific index adjustment can be used in conjunction with replacement cost in order to determine obsolescence cost of fixed assets.[3]

With these relationships in mind, the hypothetical income illustration and the attendant price level ramifications can now be examined.

ILLUSTRATION

The accompanying example has been intentionally simplified in order to minimize class coverage time. Simplicity also enhances conceptual clarity and comparability among approaches. For this latter reason, discussion of purchasing power gains and losses arising from holding monetary assets and liabilities is withheld until the following section.

The balance sheet of TUV Company (historical cost basis) on December 31, 1971 is shown in Figure 1.

Figure 1
Balance Sheet
TUV Company
December 31, 1971

Assets		Liabilities and Equities	
Cash	$15,000	Bonds Payable	$10,000
Merchandise Inventory	15,000	Capital Stock	20,000
Fixed Assets (net)	20,000	Retained Earnings	20,000
	$50,000		$50,000

An income statement for the year 1972 (historical cost basis) is shown in Figure 2. Assume that there are no other transactions during the year nor any income taxes.

Figure 2

Income Statement
TUV Company
Year Ending December 31, 1972

Revenues		$15,000
Cost of Goods Sold	6,000	
Depreciation	4,000	10,000
Operating Income		5,000
Bond Interest		500
Net Income		$ 4,500

General and specific indexes for 1970-72 are shown in Figure 3. We assume that the fixed assets were acquired in 1970 and that the merchandise inventory was acquired during 1971. In order to avoid further complexities, the index figures are averages for each year.[4]

Figure 3

General and Specific Price Indexes

PRICE INDEX	YEAR		
	1970	1971	1972
General price index	100	105	110
Specific price index applicable to firm's merchandise inventory	100	102	105
Specific price index applicable to firm's fixed assets	100	110	120

A brief description of each method follows, accompanied by illustrations from our previous data. The various price level multiples used in the income statements can be easily traced from Figure 3.

Adjusted Historical Cost Income (Figure 4.)

The purchasing power of the dollar has not been stable over time. Consequently, income determined by unadjusted historical cost measurements results in the combining of dollars of different purchasing power because the dollars represented in an income statement have been expended over a range of time. Hence from the standpoint of constant purchasing power of the monetary unit, there is a very real question of validity relative to unadjusted historical cost income statements.[5] Moreover, since individual income statements are not uniform in terms of constant purchasing power of the dollar, serious questions arise relative to comparability among income statements for the same period of time as well as over time. The adjusted historical cost method attempts to correct this situation by stating all costs and revenues in terms of dollars of constant purchasing power. This is accomplished by adjusting historical cost dollars for income statement items by the change in general purchasing power from acquisition or receipt date to a common date such as the close of the current operating period (or, as here, average for the current year). The method does not attempt to derive a current value for expense flow during the year but simply to adjust for disparity of general purchasing power of dollars expended over a significant range of time.[6] Hence the method is viewed as both an improvement over and a natural extension of historical costing.[7]

Figure 4
Adjusted Historical Cost Income Statement
TUV Company
Year Ending December 31, 1972

		Historical x Type A Multiple	= Adjusted Historical Cost
Revenues	$15,000		$15,000
Cost of Goods Sold	6,000	110/105	6,285
Depreciation	4,000	110/100	4,400
	10,000		10,685
Operating Income	5,000		4,315
Bond Interest	500		500
Net Income	$ 4,500		$ 3,815

Disposable Income (Figure 5).

Current value of assets and services consumed (Type C measurement) is matched against revenues.[8] The method is intended to indicate managerial efficiency. Real holding gains and losses (Type B changes), the offsetting elements arising from increases or decreases in value of assets consumed, are not considered to be elements of income. In addition to indicating managerial efficiency, disposable income is intended to show the maximum possible distribution of dividends consistent with maintaining the same scale of operations as that existing at the start of the period.[9]

Figure 5
Disposable Income Statement
TUV Compaay
Year Ending December 31, 1972

		Historical x Type C Multiple	= Current Value
Revenues	$15,000		$15,000
Cost of Goods Sold	6,000	120/110	6,545
Depreciation	4,000	105/100	4,200
	10,000		10,745
Operating Income	5,000		4,255
Bond Interest	500		500
Net Income	$ 4,500		$ 3,755

Realized Real Holding Gain Income (Figure 6).

This method goes one step further than disposable income. Realized real holding gains and losses are considered to be a non-operating element of income.[10] The traditional realized-unrealized distinction of conventional accounting is maintained. Thus for cost of goods sold and depreciation expense applicable to the current period, the Type B holding gains are added back to income. Since realized real holding gain and loss elements are included in income, the Type B portion of current value of assets and services consumed is offset in the final calculation of income and the final result is exactly the same as the adjusted historical cost approach. However, the organization is different because the separation of current operating costs and holding gains enables us to get the same measure of managerial efficiency with disposable income as an intermediate income figure. Realized real holding gain income is thus closely related to both of the preceding measures of income.

Figure 6

Realized Real Holding Gain Income Statement
TUV Company
Year Ending December 31, 1972

	Historical	x Type C Multiple	or Type B = percent [a]	Current Value
Revenues	$15,000			$15,000
Cost of Goods Sold	6,000	120/110		6,545
Depreciation	4,000	105/100		4,200
	10,000			10,745
Operating Income	5,000			4,255
Bond Interest	500			500
Net Income Before Realized Holding Gains	$ 4,500			$ 3,755
Realized Holding Gains: Cost of Goods Sold	6,000		4.34 %	260
Depreciation	4,000		-5 %	-200
Net Income				$ 3,815

[a] The Type B percent was determined as a residual in accordance with Equation (2):

	C	−	A	=	B
Cost of Goods Sold	109.1%(120/110)	−	104.76% (110/105)	=	4.34 %
Fixed Asset	105%(105/100)	−	110% (110/100)	=	-5 %

Earning Power Income (Figure 7).

Earning power income goes one step beyond realized real holding gain income. All real holding gains, whether realized or unrealized, are closed to income. By eliminating the realized-unrealized dichotomy, the underlying intention is to recognize the change in specific demand as shown by the appropriate specific indexes. The method is thus intended to give us a signal relative to future earnings trends.[11] Final net income would have little utility as a gauge relative to dividend payments because of the unrealized holding gains component.

Figure 7

Earning Power Income Statement
TUV Company
Year Ending December 31, 1972

	Historical	x	Type C Multiple	Type B Multiple[a]	Current Value
Revenues	$15,000				$15,000
Cost of Goods Sold	6,000		120/110		6,545
Depreciation	4,000		105/100		4,200
	10,000				10,745
Operating Income	5,000				4,255
Bond Interest	500				500
Net Income Before Holding Gains	$ 4,500				3,755
Holding Gains: Inventories	$15,000			4.34%	651
Fixed Asset	20,400			-1.82%	-371
					280
Net Income					$4,035

[a] Holding gains would be computed annually on the currently adjusted beginning net book value of fixed assets. Hence $20,000 \times \frac{102}{100} = \$20,400$. The Type B part would then be based on the current year's changes: $\frac{105}{102}(C) - \frac{110}{105}(A) = -1.82\%$.

PURCHASING POWER GAINS AND LOSSES ON MONETARY ASSETS AND LIABILITIES

Unlike historical cost accounting, all of the methods exhibited here assume either a changing general or specific purchasing power of the monetary unit. Consequently, it is proper to include within income purchasing power gains or losses from holding net monetary assets or liabilities (assets and liabilities requiring specific and fixed amounts of money for their settlement, including cash itself).[12]

Since the adjusted historical cost and realized real holding gain approaches arrive at final income in terms of general purchasing power adjustments, a Type A adjustment would be applied to the net monetary assets on hand at the beginning of the year.[13] The relative change in general purchasing power is arrived at by dividing the 1971 general price level into the corresponding 1972 figure. Since the index has increased, general purchasing power has declined. The calculation for our simple example would be

$$\left[A_1 - L_1\right] \frac{P_2}{(P_1 - 100)}$$

where A_1 and L_1 are the stock of monetary assets and liabilities existing at the end of Year 1 and P_1 and P_2 are the general price level index averages for the respective years. Substituting, we have

($15,000 - $10,000) (110/105 - 100) = $238

Final net income ($3,815 - $238 $3,577), including the loss from holding net monetary assets, shows the maximum amount of dividends that can be paid consistent with maintaining the same general purchasing power of owners' equity at the end of the period as existed at the beginning of the period.[14] This can be shown by deducting net assets at the beginning of the period from net assets at the end of the period after adjusting all items to 1972 general purchasing power. Results are shown in Figure 8.

Figure 8

Change in General Purchasing Power of Owners' Equity (Net Assets)

	(1)	(2)	(3)	(4)	(5)	(6)	(3) - (6)
							Difference in
		Type A	1972		Type A	1971	1972
	12/31/72	x multiple =	adjusted	12/31/71	x multiple =	adjusted	purchasing power
Cash	$29,500[a]		$29,500	$15,000	110/105	$15,714	$13,786
Inventories	9,000	110/105	9,429	15,000	110/105	15,714	-6,285
Fixed Assets	16,000	110/100	17,600	20,000	110/100	22,000	-4,400
Total Asset			56,529	10,000		53,428	3,101
Bonds Payable	10,000		10,000		110/105	10,476	+476
Net Assets			$46,529			$42,952	$ 3,577

[a]Assume all sales are for cash. Monetary assets and liabilities are, by definition, stated in terms of current purchasing power in the current period. Since 1971 assets are being adjusted to 1972 purchasing power, monetary items in the 12/31/71 balance sheet must be adjusted.

For the earning power and disposable income approaches, purchasing power gains and losses on net monetary assets might well be related to the specific purchasing power represented by the type of assets used by the firm. As long as all indexes have a common base period, a weighted average of index numbers can be constructed for each year. This is done by weighting current year specific index figures for both years t_2 and t_1 by the respective specific assets at the end of year t_1 stated in base year dollar amounts, adding the products and dividing by the sum of the specific assets stated in base year dollars. The change for the current year will be the difference between the two weighted average index figures.[15]

In formula terms, this can be expressed as:

$$I_2 - I_1 = \frac{\sum_{i=1}^{k}(p_{oi}\, q_{ni})}{\sum_{i=1}^{k}(p_{oi}\, q_{ni})} - \frac{\sum_{i=1}^{k}(p_{oi}\, q_{ni})\, I_{1i}}{\sum_{i=1}^{k}(p_{oi}\, q_{ni})} \quad (3)$$

where

I_2 = weighted average specific index for the later year (1972 in our example)

I_1 = weighted average specific index for the earlier year (1971 in our example)

p_{oi} = price of the i-th commodity in the base year (1970 in our example)

q_{ni} = quantity of the i-th commodity at the n-th period (end of 1971 in our example)

I_{2i} = specific index for the i-th commodity for the later year (1972 in our example)

I_{1i} = specific index for the i-th commodity for the yearlier year (1971 in our example)

Substituting from our data, we would have:

$$I_{72} - I_{71} = \frac{(\$20{,}000 \times 1.05) + (\$15{,}000 \times \frac{100}{110} \times 1.20)}{\$20{,}000 + (\$15{,}000 \times \frac{100}{110})} - \frac{(\$20{,}000 \times 1.02) + (\$15{,}000 \times \frac{100}{110} \times 1.10)}{\$20{,}000 + (\$15{,}000 \times \frac{100}{110})} = 5.84\% \quad (3.1)$$

The extra adjustment factor for the inventory of 100/110 is brought about in order to convert it into base year prices because the inventory was acquired in 1971.

The specific purchasing power loss due to holding of net monetary assets would be $5,000 x 5.87% = $293. As with adjusted historical cost and realized real holding gain income, a reconciliation of income with capital maintenance could be made for both earning power and disposable income methods.

SUMMARY

With this comparative example, four of the more important proposals for the problem of changing prices can be quickly illustrated, tied together, and their underlying rationale discussed. The individual teacher can, of course, modify the presentation of supplementary issues discussed here such as demonstrating capital maintenance and calculating the specific purchasing power loss on net monetary assets.

If desired, other proposals such as current cash equivalent can be compared and contrasted with these systems.[16] Also, the student should be able to begin to assimilate offshoots of these basic systems without becoming engulfed by the diversity of approaches. Certainly actual solutions to the problem such as the replacement value system used in the Netherlands can be understood and appreciated more after getting a basic grasp of the many facets of price level accounting.[17]

FOOTNOTES

[1] The Accounting Principles Board has recommended that general price level information may be presented in addition to historical cost statements but not as the basic statements. See Paragraph 25 of Accounting Principles Board Statement No. 3, *Financial Statements Restated for General Price-Level Adjustments* (New York: AICPA, 1969). The January 1973 issue of *Financial Executive* was devoted entirely to the topic of fair value accounting.

[2] Stephen A. Zeff, "Replacement Cost: Member of The Family, Welcome Guest, or Intruder," *The Accounting Review* (October 1962), pp. 611-25.

[3] See Harry I. Wolk, "Current Value Depreciation: A Conceptual Clarification," *The Accounting Review* (July 1970), pp. 544-52.

[4] Gynther advocates averages for the year rather than year end index figures for income statements to avoid adjustment of the individual expense and revenue items when price levels change relatively slowly. R.S. Gynther, *Accounting for Price Level Changes: Theory and Procedures* (Oxford: Pergamon Press, 1966), pp. 174-77.

[5] For a graphic discussion see W.A. Paton and W.A Paton, Jr., *Corporation Accounts and Statements* (The MacMillan Company, 1955), pp. 523-25.

[6] Three general types of indexes have been proposed: Consumer Price Index, Wholesale Price Index, and the GNP Implicit Price Deflator. For extensive discussion see William H. Hannum and W. Wasserman, "General Adjustments and Price Level Measurements," *The Accounting Review* (April 1968), pp. 295-302.

[7] See Paul Rosenfield, "The Confusion Between Price-Level and Value Accounting," *The Journal of Accountancy* (October 1962), pp. 62-8 for an extensive discussion of differences between general price level adjustment and current valuation methods.

[8] One of the issues of specific price index adjustment is whether to use a single all-encompassing index or multiple indexes more closely tailored to the firm's individual asset composition. See Eldon S. Hendriksen, *Accounting Theory* (Homewood: Richard D. Irwin, 1970), pp. 224-28 and Charles A. Tritschler, "Statistical Criteria for Asset Valuation by Specific Price Index," *The Accounting Review* (January 1969), pp. 99-124.

[9] Zeff, op. cit., p. 618. See also Jean St. G. Kerr, "Three Concepts of Business Income," *Australian Accountant* (April 1956), pp. 139-46 reprinted in S. Davidson, D. Green, C. Horngren, and G. Sorter, eds., *An Income Approach to Accounting Theory* (Englewood Cliffs: Prentice-Hall, Inc., 1964), pp. 40-8.

[10] This method has been advocated and discussed in great detail by Edgar O. Edwards and Philip W. Bell, *The Theory and Measurement of Business Income* (Berkeley: University of California Press, 1961). A particularly graphic example of the approach is given in Edgar O. Edwards, "Depreciation Policy Under Changing Price Levels," *The Accounting Review* (April 1959), pp. 267-80 and reprinted in Stephen A. Zeff and Thomas F. Keller (eds.), *Financial Accounting Theory* (New York: McGraw-Hill, 1964), pp. 167-82.

[11] Predictive uses of income are discussed by W.H. Beaver, J.W. Kennelly, and W.M. Voss, "Predictive Ability as a Criterion for the Evaluation of Accounting Data," *The Accounting Review* (October 1968), pp. 675-83 and Joseph G. Louderback, "Projectability as a Criterion for Income Determination Methods," *The Accounting Review* (April 1971), pp. 298-305.

[12] The definition of monetary items is discussed by Lloyd C. Heath, "Distinguishing Between Monetary and Nonmonetary Assets and Liabilities in General Price-Level Accounting," *The Accounting Review* (July 1972), pp. 458-68.

[13] See Accounting Research Study No. 6, *Reporting the Financial Effects of Price Level Changes* (New York: AICPA, 1963), pp. 137-52 for an extended discussion and illustration of purchasing power gains and losses on monetary items.

[14] For an extensive discussion of capital maintenance measurement see R.S. Gynther, "Capital Maintenance, Price Changes, and Profit Determination," *The Accounting Review* (October 1970), pp. 712-30.

[15] The weighted average of index numbers is covered in Lee H. Smith and Donald R. Williams, *Statistical Analysis for Business: A Conceptual Approach* (Belmont: Wadsworth Publishing Company, 1971), pp. 678-81.

[16] See Raymond J. Chambers, *Accounting, Evaluation and Economic Behavior* (Englewood Cliffs: Prentice-Hall, 1966).

[17] See Morton Backer, "Valuation Reporting in the Netherlands: A Real-Life Example," *Financial Executive* (January 1973), pp. 40-50.

A Visual Comparison of Direct Costing Versus Absorption Costing Income Effects

H. Milton Jones
California State University, Los Angeles

Introduction

The income effects of direct costing versus absorption costing can be illustrated by means of a simple chart. With changes in inventory levels, the amount of fixed factory overhead to be match against revenue under each product costing concept can be visually compared. As a result, students can readily comprehend the difference between direct and absorption costing.

Accounting students often have difficulty understanding the significance of direct costing. They usually have no trouble understanding that direct or variable costing means that product costs consist of variable manufacturing costs only. They can also readily comprehend the meaning of contribution margin. Even the notion that fixed factory overhead is a period expense under direct costing can usually be grasped by students. However, they find it difficult to understand why a firm's net income for a period determined by direct costing differs from what it would be if the absorption costing method were used. The general conclusion that direct costing net income fluctuates with sales while absorption costing net income fluctuates with production is often a mystery to them.

Most of the literature on direct costing attempts to provide a comparison of direct and absorption costing results. Cost accounting textbook coverage of direct costing commonly consists of a series of income statements prepared by both the absorption costing and the direct costing methods.[1] These statements illustrate that in periods when production and sales are equal there is no difference in net income under either method. They also reveal that when an inventory build-up occurs, absorption costing net income is greater than direct costing net income. That the reverse is true when inventories are depleted is also shown. Such illustrations are good. The only difficulty is that this type of illustration utilizes six income statements—three under each method. When consideration is also given to the complexity of each statement, even in its simplest form, it is no wonder that a full understanding of the causes of the net income differences is usually grasped by only the most persevering and analytical students.

A more rapid and deeper comprehension of the significance of direct costing can be obtained by exposing students to a simpler illustration comparing direct and absorption costing income results. Since the difference between the two approaches to income determination centers on the timing of the

---

* The typical textbook presentation ignores the effects of differing inventory costing methods. In fact, the generalized statements in this paper and in most textbooks hold true only under the LIFO and standard cost methods of inventory costing. For a detailed presentation of the various results of using different inventory costing methods, see Yuji Ijiri, Robert K. Jaedicke, and John L. Livingston, "The Effect of Inventory Costing Methods on Full and Direct Costing," *Journal of Accounting Research,* Spring 1965, Vol. 3, No. 1, pp. 63-74. This article points out that the results under FIFO and average cost are more complex than those considered in this paper and therefore do not apply.

A Visual Comparison of Direct Costing

Comparison of Fixed Overhead Matched Against Revenue in Three Equal Time Periods

Time Periods

	Period I Sales = Production (No Inventory Change)	Period II Production > Sales (Inventory Increase)	Period III Production < Sales (Inventory Decrease)
Absorption Costing Fixed Overhead Matched	■■■■■■■	■■■■	■■■■■■■■■■
Direct Costing Fixed Overhead Matched	■■■■■■■	■■■■■■■	■■■■■■■
Net Income Comparison	No Difference	Absorption Costing—Greater Net Income	Direct Costing—Greater Net Income

matching of fixed expenses against revenue, a simple illustration of the relative amounts to be matched against revenue in each time period can readily be charted.

The chart shows that a full period's fixed factory overhead is matched against revenue in each period under direct costing, because fixed factory overhead is treated as a period expense. However, in any one period the relative amount of fixed overhead to be matched against revenue under absorption costing is determined by the relationship of production to sales. Under absorption costing, fixed factory overhead is first a product cost and is matched against revenue only in the period when it is sold. This means that an inventory build-up causes the amount of fixed factory overhead to be matched against revenue to be less than the amount incurred in that period. An inventory reduction causes the amount of fixed factory overhead released against sales to be greater than the amount incurred in that particular time period.

The chart readily shows that net income comparisions can be made for each time period. If no change in inventory levels occur, the net income will be the same under either method. However, net income will be greater under absorption costing during periods of inventory build-ups and less under this method when inventory levels decline. Since inventory levels are a function of both production and sales, one can readily see that changes in the relationship of production to sales can affect net income under absorption costing. Under direct costing, this does not happen since fixed overhead is always a period expense. If sales are constant from period to period, all other things being equal direct costing net income is constant. This is not true under absorption costing. The chart also reveals that the amount of difference in profit between the two methods can be computed by multiplying the absorption costing fixed overhead rate times the units of inventory change. For example, if the fixed factory overhead rate is $5.00 per unit and the inventory increase is 10,000 units in period II, the profit under absorption costing will be $50,000 greater than under direct costing. This is because of the deferring of some of period II's fixed factory overhead ($50,000) to the next period. If period III's inventory level decreases by 10,000 units, the the absorption costing profit will be less by $50,000 than it would be by using the direct costing method.

Teaching Economic Order Quantities In a Price Break System

Edward B. Deakin
The University of Texas at Austin

Introduction

Quantity discounts are frequently offered in the commercial environment. However, the traditional economic order quantity model does not offer a method for analyzing when to take advantage of these quantity discounts. This paper presents a method for such an analysis by simply extending the initial economic order quantity analysis to include implicit foregone dscount costs.

One of the major problems in inventory cost control deals with the determination of how much to order from a supplier. Traditionally, students have been taught to use an economic order quantity formula in solving this problem. This equation may be expressed:

$$E = \sqrt{\frac{2AP}{S}}$$

Where E is the optimal or "economic" order quantity;
  A is the annual usage in units,
  P is the cost to place an order, and
  S is the cost to carry one unit in inventory for the year.

However, this approach has been criticized on the grounds that it does not provide for the situation where a supplier offers a discount for quantity purchases nor when discounts on transportation or handling costs will occur when bulk quantities are ordered (for example, unit freight rates are much lower for a full carload than for a fraction of a carload). These situations will be referred to as price break systems.

So far there have been few attempts to present a simplified approach to this aspect of the EOQ problem[1]. The solution to the optimal order size problem under a price break system can be developed from the basic EOQ model. Geometrically, the economic order quantity is shown by the graph in Figure 1. The order cost line is defined by the equation $\frac{A}{E} \times P$; carrying costs are defined as $\frac{E}{2} \times S$. The total cost line is the sum of these two equations. Symbolically this is represented as

$$TC = \frac{A}{E}P + \frac{E}{2}S.$$

Figure 1 is, of course, dependent upon the assumption that there are no quantity discounts.

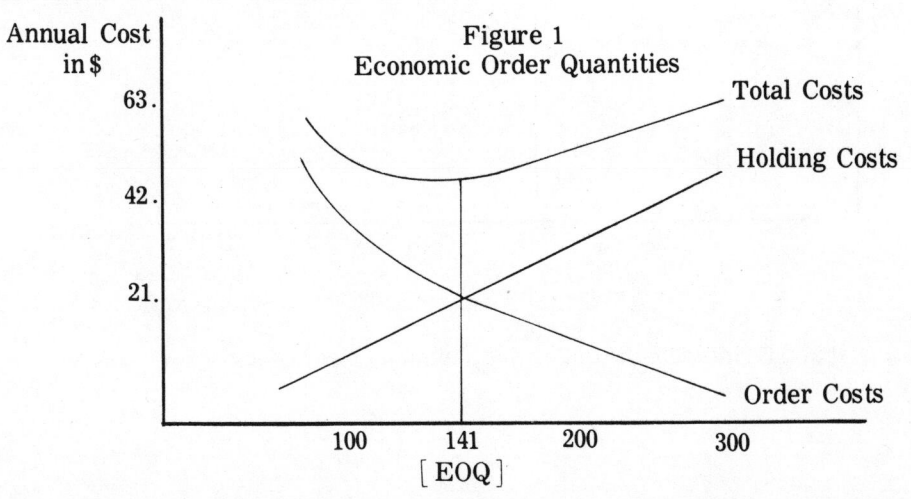

Figure 1
Economic Order Quantities

Any order quantity less than that for which the maximum discount is offered is made with the understanding that unit costs will be higher than they would be at the maximum discount quantity. The difference between unit cost at the smaller order size and unit cost at the maximum discount quantity can be referred to as a foregone discount cost (F). For example, if a supplier charges $2.05 per unit for orders of one to ninety-nine units and $2.00 on orders of one hundred units or more, then the foregone discount on all orders of ninety-nine units or less is ($2.05-$2.00) or $.05 per unit. The annual foregone discount cost will simply be the unit foregone discount cost times the annual usage (F x A). If this cost is added to the graph in Figure 1, total costs will be shown as in Figure 2.

Two significant observations result from Figure 2. First, since total costs are decreasing up to the EOQ point, it will not be possible to obtain an optimal order policy at any order size less than that derived by calculating EOQ without regard to foregone discounts. Thus, an optimal order quantity must be found at either the initial EOQ or at some larger order quantity. Second, the shape of the total cost function in Figure 2 to the right of initial EOQ illustrates the set of points that can result in an optimal order policy. Since each segment of the total cost line to the right of EOQ increases continuously, it is apparent that the minimum of each line segment must occur at the extreme left of that segment. This point corresponds to the lowest order quantity required to earn a particular discount.

Thus, the set of points from which an optimal order policy can be found is defined as the initial EOQ point and the minimum quantities needed to earn each of the higher discount levels. The two possible points in Figure 2 are labeled A and B.

Figure 2

Economic Order Quantities Considering Price Breaks

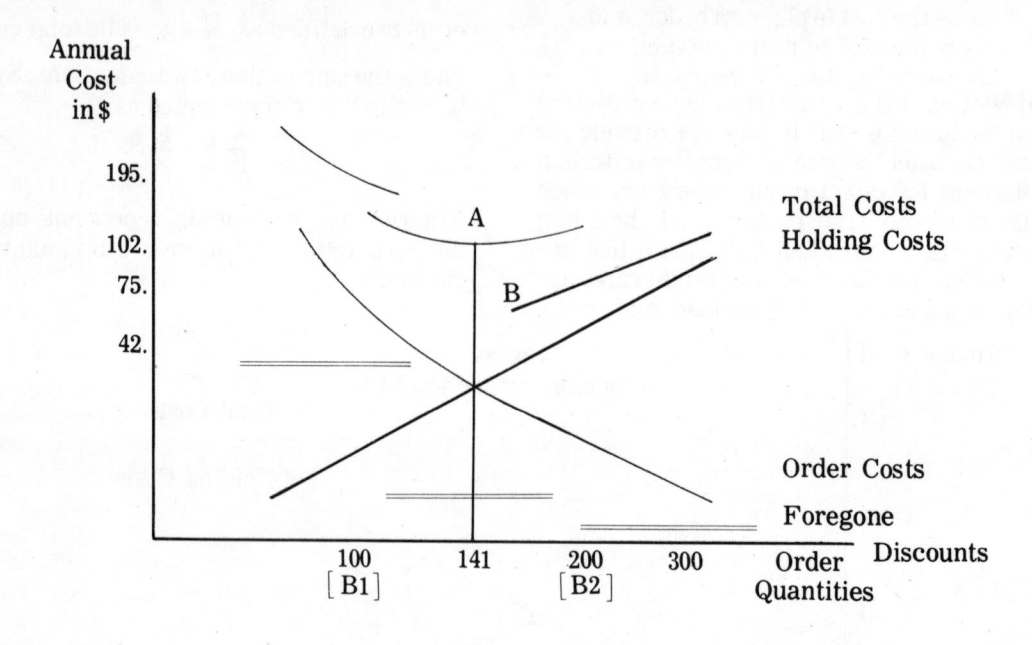

B1 and B2 indicate the quantities at which price breaks occur.

Teaching Economic Order Quantities In a Price Break System 429

From this a simple procedure may be derived to find the optimum order quantity:

1. Determine EOQ without regard to foregone discounts.
2. Determine the total of order costs, $(\frac{A}{E} \times P)$, carrying costs $(\frac{E}{2} \times S)$, and foregone discount costs $(F \times A)$ at the EOQ point.
3. Determine the total of order costs, carrying costs, and foregone discount costs for the minimum purchase required for each higher discount

$$\left[TC = \frac{A}{E} \times P + \frac{E}{2} \times S + (F \times A) \right].$$

4. Repeat step 3 and stop after determining the total costs when foregone discounts equal zero.
5. Select the minimum total cost and the order quantity associated therewith.

An example of the use of this procedure follows:

Assume a supplier offers the following price schedule for Product X:

Order Size	Price per Unit
1 - 99	$2.05
100 - 199	2.02
200 - 499	2.01
500 and over	2.00

Unit foregone discount costs are then:

Order Size	Unit Price	Price at Maximum Order Size	Foregone Discount
1 - 99	$ 2.05	$ 2.00	$ .05
100 - 199	2.02	2.00	.02
200 - 499	2.01	2.00	.01
500 and over	2.00	2.00	.00

If annual usage is 3,000 units, order costs $1.00, and carrying costs $.30, then the initial EOQ will be:

$$EOQ = \sqrt{\frac{2 \times 3,000 \times \$1.00}{\$.30}}$$

$$= \sqrt{20,000}$$

$$\approx 141$$

Total annual costs at EOQ will equal the order costs, plus carrying costs, plus foregone discount costs. $\frac{A}{E} = \frac{3,000}{141}$ or 21.27 orders per year. At $1.00 per order (P), the order cost will equal $21.27. $\frac{E}{2} = 70.5$ which when multiplied by the unit carrying cost (S) of $ .30 results in an annual cost of $21.15. Foregone discounts will equal $.02 per unit times the 3,000 units (A) or $60.00. At the initial EOQ, then, total annual costs are $102.42 ($21.27 plus $21.15 plus $60.00).

According to the procedure, the next step is to look at the total cost for the minimum quantity needed to earn the next discount. This occurs at an order size of two hundred. At this order size, order costs are $15.00 ($\frac{3,000}{200} \times \$1.00$); carrying costs equal $30.00 ($\frac{200}{2} \times \$.30$); and foregone discounts are $30.00 ($.01 x 3,000). At this quantity, total annual costs are reduced to $75.00 ($15.00 plus $30.00 plus $30.00) which is $27.42 less than at the initial EOQ.

The third trial for this problem is a test of total costs at the final discount level—500 units. Here order costs will equal $6.00 ($\frac{3,000}{500}$ x $1.00); carrying costs, $75.00 ($\frac{500}{2}$ x $ .30), and foregone discounts are $0. Total costs are $81.00 which is $6.00 greater than at the 200 order size level. Since foregone discounts are now equal to zero, the process stops.

The results of this procedure are summarized in Table 1. The minimum total cost occurs at an order size of 200 units, thus, the optimal policy will be to place orders for 200 units. This order size is greater than the EOQ found by the traditional approach. Also, the procedure takes all relevant costs (both actual and implied) into account. Thus, it is possible to evaluate the reduction in foregone discounts against the increase in the total of order and holding costs. In the example, the benefit from the discount reduction for 500 units was insufficient to overcome the increase in other relevant costs.

By noting the specific points at which optimal order quantities can occur in a price break system, we can extend the traditional EOQ formulation to cover those cases where price breaks are available. Likewise, by developing a simple iterative procedure for solving this problem, we facilitate demonstration of the solution in the accounting classroom.

TABLE 1
Computation of Total Costs

Quantity Ordered (E)	Holding Costs ($\frac{A}{E}$ x P)	Carring Costs ($\frac{E}{2}$ x S)	Foregone Discounts (A x F)	Total Costs
141	21.27	21.15	60.00	102.42
200	15.00	30.00	30.00	75.00 *
500	6.00	75.00	0	81.00

*Optimal

A Pictorial Discussion of Corporate Tax Reorganizations

D. Larry Crumbley
University of Florida

Introduction

The presentation of complex tax laws in a logical fashion can improve the communication skills of a tax instructor. The use of a pictorial approach can provide a student with a generalized tax knowledge of the combinatory and divisive reorganization areas. This paper provides pictorial diagrams, which may be used as transparency projections or as mimeographed handouts, for A, B, C, D, split-up, split-off, and spin-off types of reorganizations.

An understanding of corporate tax reorganizations is important for an accounting student who intends to move into a corporate position or public accounting. Yet the tax reorganization provisions are very complex and a great deal of class time is traditionally needed to adequately cover this important subject. Due to this complexity and lack of time, tax reorganizations are often omitted from the first tax course. Similarly, only the brave and/or foolhardy tax instructor includes a discussion of reorganizations in the second tax course. This omission is unwise if one considers the importance of this subject to the careers of many accounting students. For example, much of the tax work of many of the largest CPA firms involves some phase of reorganizations. The "urge to merge" appears to be here to stay.

An accounting instructor can give a student a generalized knowledge of the combinatory and divisive reorganization areas in a short period of time with the use of a pictorial approach. The teaching of reorganizations can be greatly aided by logical diagrams of the various types of transactions. The use of the following diagrams either as transparency projections or as mimeographed handouts can improve the communication skills of a tax instructor.

REORGANIZATIONS

The four major nontaxable reorganizations available to combining corporations are as follows:[1]

1. A statutory merger or consolidation (type A).
2. An acquisition by one corporation (in exchange solely for all or part of its voting stock) of the stock of another corporation if, immediately after the transaction, the acquiring corporation controls 80% or more of the stock (type B).
3. An acquiring corporation obtains, solely for all or part of its voting stock, substantially all of the assets of another corporation (type C).
4. A corporation (the transferor) shifts all or part of its assets to another corporation which is controlled thereafter, and either the transfer corporation is liquidated or the controlled corporation stock is distributed in a divisive transaction (type D).

If a transaction falls within the bounds of the tax law's definition of reorganization, then no gain or loss is recognized by the acquiring corporation, the acquired corporation, or to the shareholders of the acquired corporation.

The transferor's tax basis for the consideration received is the same as his tax basis of the transferred property. In essence, any gain or loss is deferred until the transferor disposes of the consideration he received in the combination. Also, the transferee "steps into the shoes" of the transferor's tax basis. If the transferor's assets have appreciated in value, the acquirer cannot recognize this appreciation for tax purposes and must continue to use the transferor's tax basis in any future transactions (e.g., depreciation purposes). The basic theory underlying a tax-free reorganization is that the new enterprise or the new corporate structure is a substantial continuation of the old one still unliquidated.[2]

If a combination does not meet the specific requirements of a reorganization, then the seller must recognize a gain or loss for tax purposes. Such gain or loss is measured by the difference between the amount of consideration received and the tax basis of the stock or assets surrendered. Obviously, a seller normally prefers not to have a taxable reorganization. But the purchaser receives a new tax basis for the assets he receives. If such assets have appreciated in value, the buyer is able to recognize this increment for tax purposes. For example, this step-up in basis would mean a greater depreciation deduction for the fixed assets.

In most cases when a firm decides to purchase another business the buyer will ask the IRS for a ruling as to whether the contemplated combination is taxable or nontaxable. After the ruling is known, the purchasing firm must decide whether or not to proceed with the acquisition. Of course, once the tax nature of the combination is known, the buyer must decide which accounting method must be used—purchase or pooling.[3] The criteria for tax treatment and accounting treatment of combinations are not identical. Suppose we now proceed with a discussion of the four major nontaxable reorganizations.

Statutory Merger or Consolidation

A statutory merger or consolidation is classified as a type "A" reorganization. The combining of these corporations must merely conform to the corporate laws of any state (or states) that has jurisdiction over the proposed combination.

A merger occurs where one corporation absorbs the corporate structure of another corporation with the resulting liquidation of the acquired enterprise. Figure 1 indicates the general type of "A" merger. Note that the flag on corporation A indicates that this corporation is liquidated. Also, B corporation may or may not be a subsidiary.

Figure 1

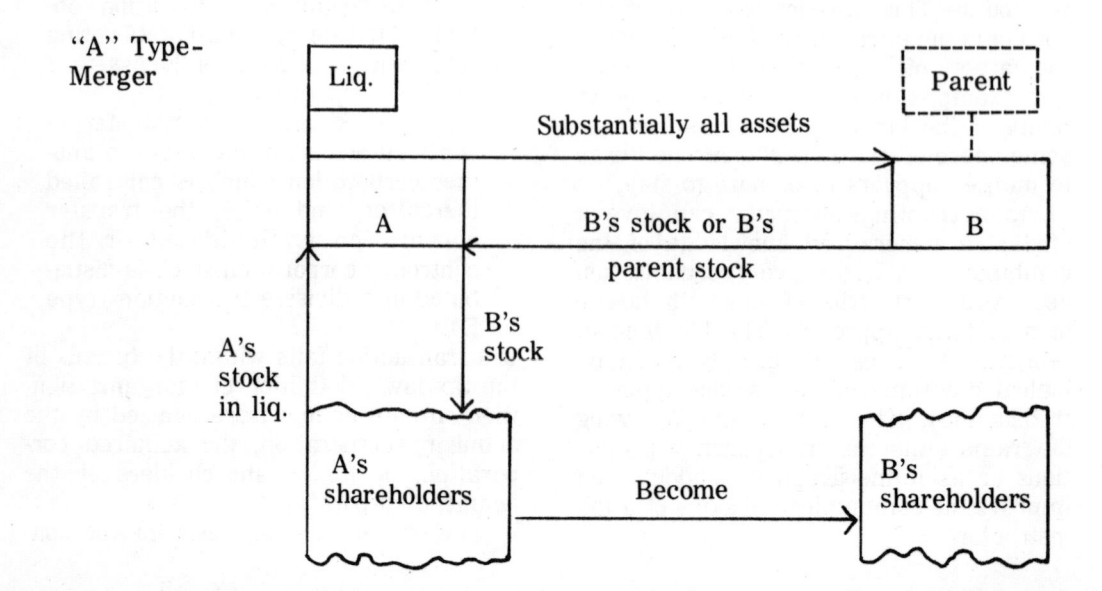

Since October 21, 1968 a triangular "A" type merger is feasible. Under this special type of merger corporation B can use stock of its parent to pass to A corporation (but not a combination of B's stock and parent's stock). Three requirements must be met in order to qualify as a triangular "A" type merger:

1. The merger must have qualified as an "A" reorganization if the merged corporation (the liquidated corporation A) had been merged into the parent corporation instead of the subsidiary corporation.

2. The subsidiary (corporation B) must *not* issue any of its own stock.

3. The subsidiary must acqire substantially all of the assets of the merged corporation.

Figure 1 can be used to demonstrate this special type of merger.

Beginning January 12, 1971, Section 368 (a) (2) (E) permits a tax-free statutory merger of a controlled subsidiary into an unrelated corporation using the voting stock of the controlled subsidiary's parent—a reverse triangular "A" merger. Notice that the unrelated corporation (corporation A in Figure 1) is the surviving corporation in the merger and B corporation goes out of existence. Remember, under prior law the unrelated corporation had to be merged into the existing subsidiary. Two requirements must be met in order to qualify for this reverse triangular "A" merger:

1. The surviving "A" corporation must hold substantially all of its properties and those of the merged corporation.

2. 80 percent stock control of the acquired corporation must be obtained in the merger.

A consolidation is also an "A" type of reorganization. A consolidation occurs where two or more corporations are combined into a *new* corporation, with the old corporations going out of existence. A consolidation may be diagrammed as in Figure 2. Note that both A and B corporations are liquidated, and only AB corporation remains in existence.

Figure 2

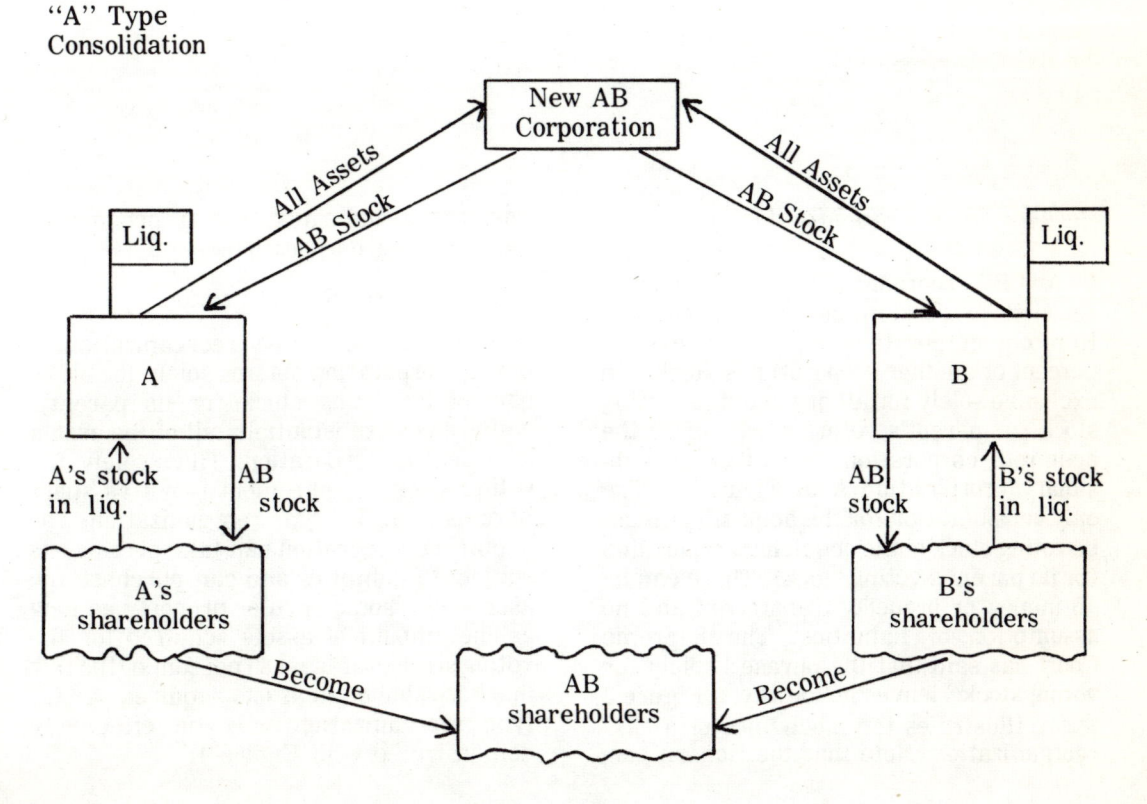

"A" Type Consolidation

Figure 3

'B" Type

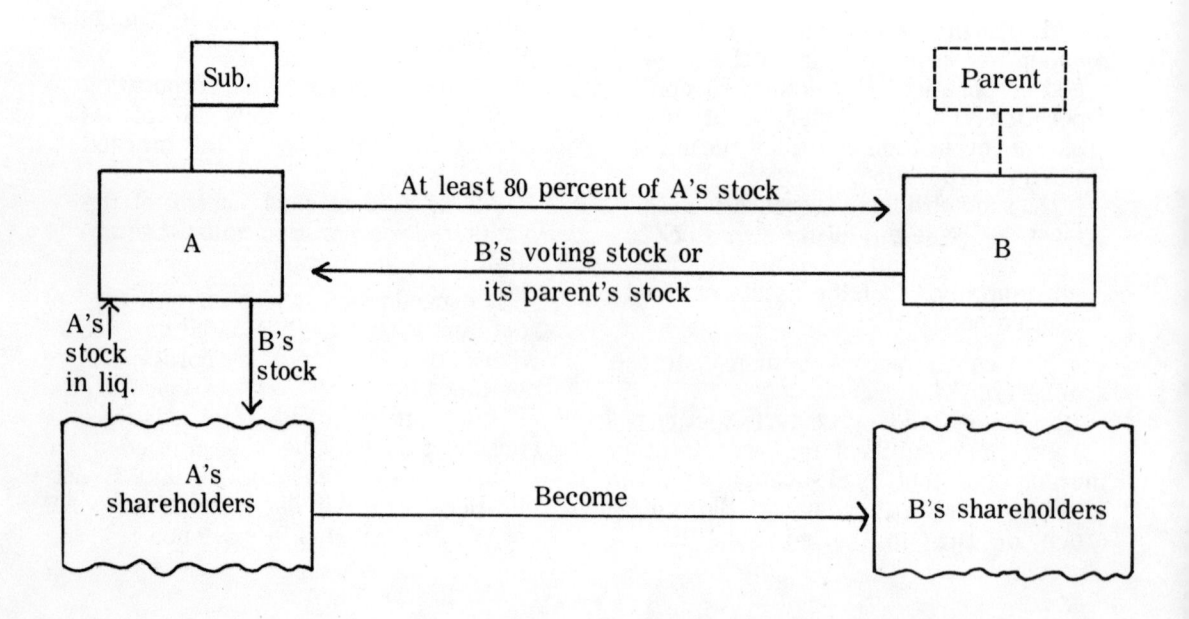

Stock-for-Stock Reorganization

A "B" reorganization is frequently selected to consummate a combination. Here one corporation acquires at least 80 percent of another corporation's stock [4] in exchange solely for all or part of its voting stock (or parent's voting stock), with the acquired corporation becoming a subsidiary (corporation A in Figure 3). The only consideration for the acquisition must be voting stock of the acquiring corporation (or its parent's voting stock). There can be no money or property transferred and no assumption of liabilities. The Supreme Court has said that the phrase "solely for voting stock" leaves no leeway.[5] Figure 3 above illustrates the mechanics of a "B" reorganization. Note that the flag on corporation A indicates that it becomes a subsidiary of corporation B.

Stock-for-Asset Reorganization

Under a "C" type reorganization a buying corporation obtains solely for all or part of its voting stock (or its parent's voting stock) substantially all of the assets of a second corporation. The "solely for voting stock" requirement is not as strict here as in a "B" type reorganization. The acquiring corporation can take over assets subject to liabilities and can purchase the assets with some cash or property as long as the amount of assets acquired for the voting stock is at least 80 percent of the fair market value of all assets acquired. A "C" type reorganization may be effectively demonstrated with Figure 4:

A Pictorial Discussion of Corporate Tax Reorganizations

Figure 4

"C" Type

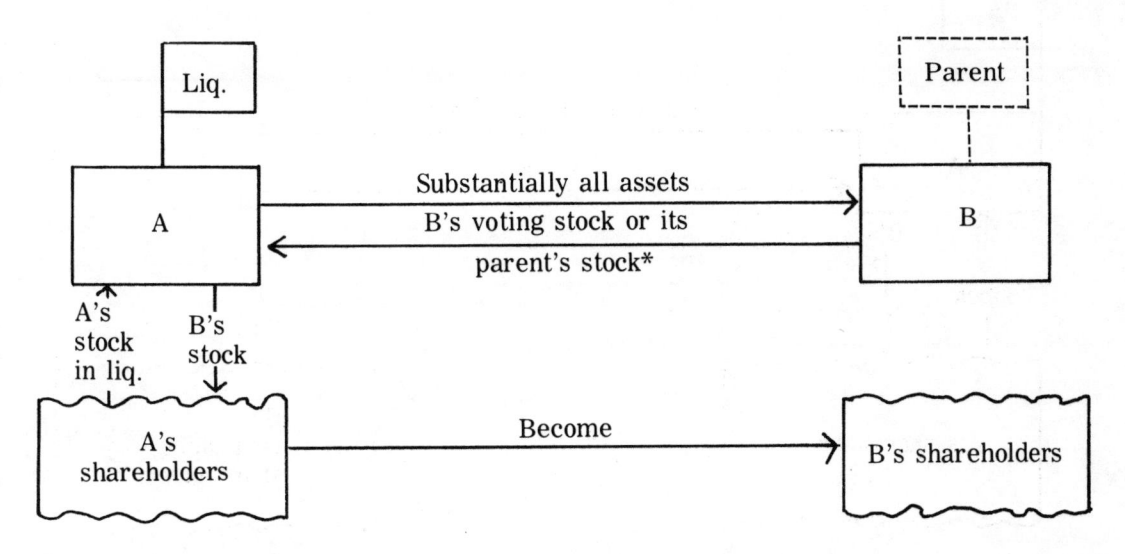

*Plus a limited amount of money and/or property.

Transfer of Assets to a Controlled Corporation

A "D" type of reorganization requires two major characteristics. First, a transferor corporation (corporation A in Figure 5) shifts all or part of its assets to another corporation (the transferee) and immediately thereafter the transferor or one or more of its shareholders (or a combination thereof) is in control of the transferee. Control refers to the holding of 80 percent or more of the voting stock and 80 percent or more of all other classes of stock. Second, as part of the "D" reorganization plan, the stock or securities of the transferee corporation must be distributed in a transaction which qualifies under Sections 354, 355, or 356.[6]

There are generally two types of "D" reorganizations:

Type No. 1—A transferor corporation shifts substantially all of its assets to a controlled corporation, followed by a complete liquidation of the transferor corporation. In other words, any remaining assets of A corporation and B's stock is transferred to A's shareholders who become controlling shareholders of B corporation. Figure 5 demonstrates the mechanics of a "D" reorganization. Note that a "D" reorganization differs from a merger or consolidation in that the transferor's shareholders become controlling shareholders of the surviving corporation. Also, if a transaction is both a "C" reorganization and a "D" reorganization, the transaction is treated as a "D" type reorganization.[7] But a transaction will be a type "F" reorganization if the reorganization qualifies both as a type "D" and type "F" transaction.[8]

Type No. 2—A transferor corporation shifts part of its assets to a controlled corporation, followed by a distribution of the controlled corporation's stock in a split-

Figure 5

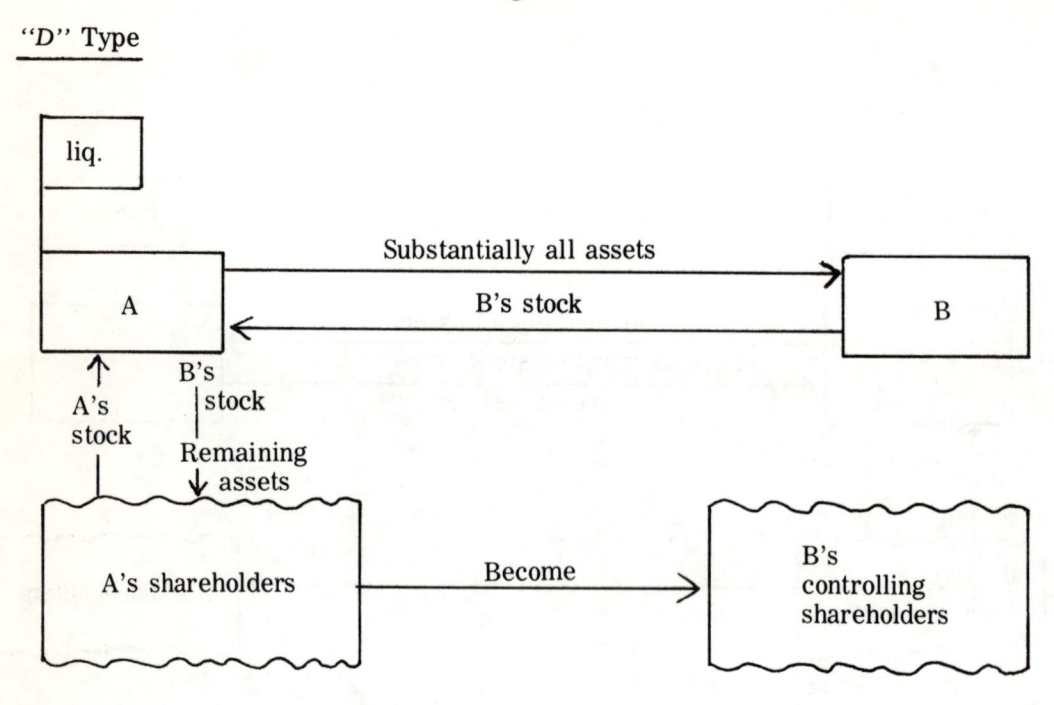

"D" Type

[Figure 5: Diagram showing "D" Type reorganization. Corporation A (with "liq." notation) transfers "Substantially all assets" to Corporation B, receiving "B's stock" in return. A's shareholders give A's stock and receive B's stock and Remaining assets. A's shareholders "Become" B's controlling shareholders.]

up, a split-off, or a spin-off. Figure 5 can be combined with Figures 6, 7, or 8 in order to illustrate this second type of "D" reorganization.

DIVISIVE REORGANIZATIONS

Corporate organizations may wish to participate in the converse of a combinatory transaction. For any number of reasons, a corporation may wish to sell or split-off a division, a subsidiary, or a corporate segment. In other words, management may wish to split-up their investment into several corporate entities through a divisive transaction. Under the normal rule when property is sold or exchanged, the entire amount of any gain or loss is recognized for tax purposes. For example, suppose an enterprise wishes to dispose of a substantial part of its assets. If the business sells the assets and distributes the proceeds, the corporation must pay a tax on any gain and the shareholders will probably have to pay another dividend tax on the distribution. It is possible to avoid this double tax with the use of a divisive reorganization under Section 355. There are three types of divisive transactions—split-up, split-off, and spin-off.

If a transaction falls within the divisive reorganization provisions, no gain or loss is recognized to a shareholder who receives *only stock or securities* (i.e., receives no boot). However, a gain is recognized to the extent the shareholders receive boot.[9] "Boot" refers to everything other than stock or securities, such as money or other property.

Split-up

A split-up occurs where a corporation is split into two or more new smaller corporations and the stock of the new corporations is distributed to the shareholders of the old corporation who in turn surrender the stock of the old corporation. This divisive exhange can be presented as in Figure 6 following:

A Pictorial Discussion of Corporate Tax Reorganizations

Figure 6

Split-up

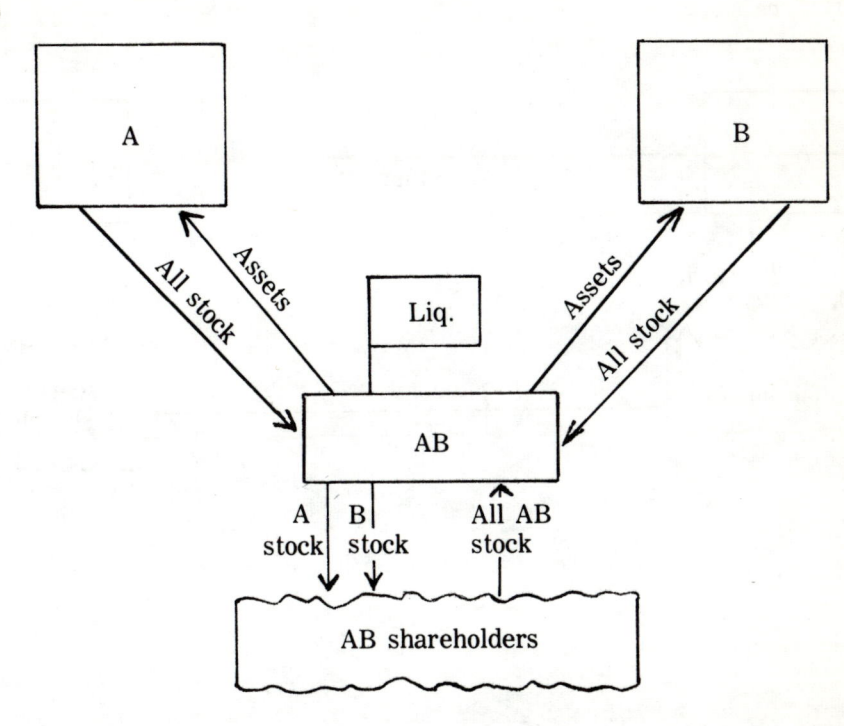

Split-off

There are two distinctive types of split-offs. Under a type "No. 1" exchange a corporation transfers part of its assets to a new corporation in exchange for stock of the new corporation. The original corporation then distributes this same stock to its shareholders who in turn surrender part of their stock in the original corporation. A type "No. 1" contraction may be illustrated as follows:

Figure 7

Split-off: *Type No. 1*

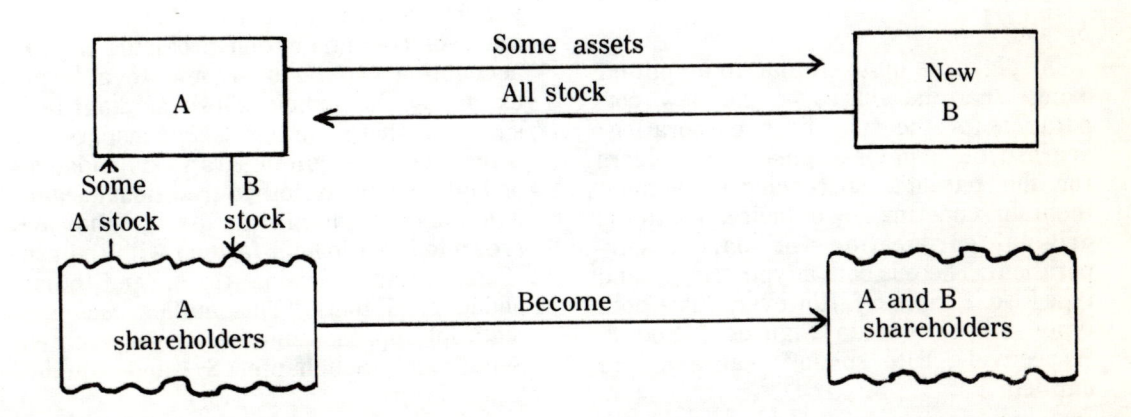

Figure 8

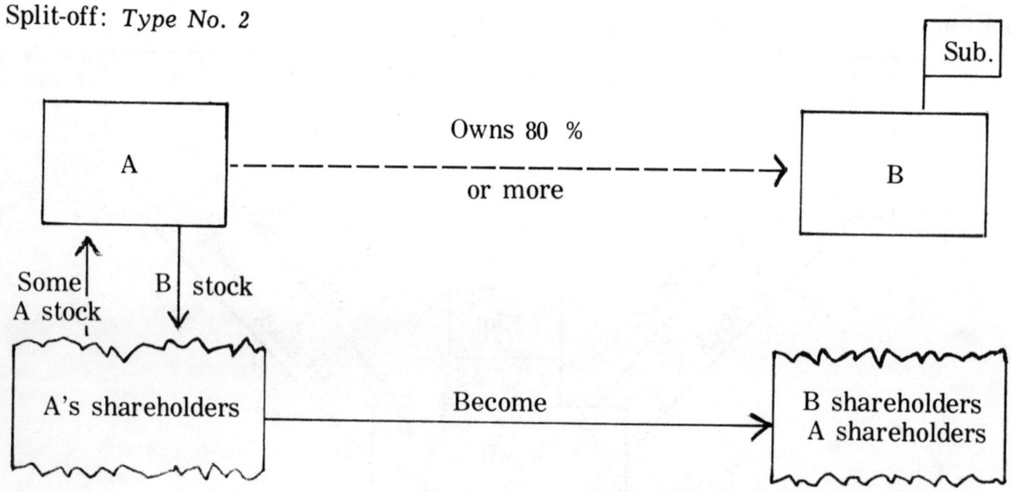

Split-off: *Type No. 2*

[Diagram: Corporation A owns 80% or more of Corporation B (which has a Sub.). A transfers B stock down to A's shareholders, who give back Some A stock. A's shareholders Become B shareholders / A shareholders.]

A type "No. 2" contraction occurs when a parent company transfers stock of a controlled corporation to its stockholders in redemption of a similar portion of their stock. "Control" refers to the ownership of 80 percent or more of the corporation whose shares are being distributed. A type "No. 2" split-off can be illustrated with Figure 8:

Spin-off

A spin-off is quite similar to a split-off except that the shares of the new corporation (or the subsidiary corporation) are distributed to the original shareholders (or the parent's shareholders) without them surrendering any of their stock in the original corporation (or parent corporation). There is both a type "No. 1" and type "No. 2" spin-off. However, since both types are similar to Figures 7 and 8, respectively, both spin-off diagrams are omitted.

CONCLUSION

Taxation offers numerous complex concepts, the teaching of which can be greatly aided by logical diagrams. Obviously, the pictorial diagrams presented in this paper do not indicate the grotesquely complex provisions and nuances present in the reorganization area. However, the maze of communication problems in tax accounting can be overcome to a large extent by the judicious use of diagrams such as these, either as transparency projections or as mimeographed handouts, or both. Similarly, other traditional legalistic gobbledygook in the tax law may be presented in a logical fashion with the use of diagrams, decision trees, and other pedagogical tools.[10] This author uses the pictorial approach in other areas, such as Section 351, Subchapter S,[11] and liquidations.

FOOTNOTES

[1] Two other reorganizations, Types E and F, are omitted since they are merely changes in or rearrangements of a corporate structure.

[2] Reg. 1.368-1 (b).

[3] It is beyond the scope of this short paper to discuss the accounting treatment, but an instructor can easily incorporate a discussion of purchase versus pooling into his tax lecture. Similarly, an instructor teaching business combinations could use these diagrams to introduce his students to the tax side of reorganizations.

[4] "Control" is defined in Section 368 (c) as the ownership of stock possessing at least 80 percent of total combined voting power plus at least 80 percent of the total number of shares of all other classes of stock.

[5] *Helvering* v. *Southwest Consol. Corp.*, 315 US 194 (1942).

[6] If the securities are not distributed, the transaction is not a reorganization, but it still might be nontaxable under Section 351.

[7] IRC Sec. 368 (a) (2) (A).

[8] Rev. Rul. 57-276, 1957-1 C.B. 126.

[9] In the case of a split-off or split-up, the taxable gain is the lesser of (1) actual realized gain, or (2) fair market value of the boot. As for a spin-off, any boot is treated as ordinary income to the extent of any earnings and profits of the corporation.

[10] For an example of a decision tree approach with the child care expense deduction, see Crumbley, "Child Care Expense Deduction—A Decision Tree Application," *The Accounting Review,* Vol. 45, (January, 1970), pp. 143-144; updated in Crumbley and Flanagan, "Child Care Expense Deduction," *The Journal of Accountancy,* Vol. 135 (April, 1973), pp. 88-89.

[11] See Crumbley and Davis, *Organizing, Operating, and Terminating Subchapter S. Corporations,* Tucson: Lawyers and Judges Publishing Co., 1971, pp. 56, 159.

Section V
Evaluation of Performance

EVALUATION OF PERFORMANCE: AN OVERVIEW

This section is concerned with certain aspects of accountability in accounting education. Accountability is a fundamental concept in business, government, and society in general; and it is a concept that is receiving increasing attention in the university community.

The evaluation of performance is an important element of accountability. It is this particular topic that is emphasized in Section V. This section contains articles which discuss the evaluation process specifically from the perspective of evaluating faculty and student performance.

There are a host of issues related to the evaluation of faculty and student performance. A sample of questions which have been and are being raised include: What constitutes effective teaching? What is the proper mix between faculty teaching and research effort? What are the appropriate criteria for determining faculty promotion? Should students be allowed to participate in the faculty evaluation process? Of what value are student rating forms? What are the purposes of grades? Should a Pass-Fail system of grading be adopted? What type of tests best measure student performance?

The eight papers which follow discuss many of these and other related issues. Obviously, the papers do not contain answers to all of the questions. They do, however, present interesting viewpoints, and in several instances provide empirical evidence as to possible answers. Unquestionably, they should stimulate the reader's own thinking about the issues discussed, topics that are specific and relevant to accounting educators.

The first selection by Lumsden lays the groundwork for the remaining articles in the section. Lumsden's paper provides an overview of the accountability issue as it relates to the college setting.

Articles two through four are all related to the evaluation of faculty. One of the specific issues they raise is the value of student ratings of faculty performance. Robert Wilson, a research psychologist, draws upon extensive research experience in discussing the evaluation of teaching at the college level. A significant portion of his article summarizes the results of a study conducted in connection with the University of California - Davis and includes the evaluation instruments developed which are now being used by over 150 universities and colleges in the United States. The Crooch and Krull article represents a specific application and description of the experience of one school in developing a student rating instrument for use in evaluating faculty teaching. The Centra paper also draws upon the results of extensive research in describing the potential impact of student ratings in modifying certain aspects of academic life.

The next two articles both deal explicitly with faculty evaluation models. The Skousen article presents case illustrations of actual approaches which are being used by departments or schools of business to evaluate faculty productivity. The Read article demonstrates a technique and a methodology for presenting the results of such evaluations. This technique could be used, with some modification, by almost any data based faculty evaluation model.

The last two papers in this section deal with the evaluation of student performance. The Turppa article provides both an overview of testing and grading as well as a description of a specific technique which some educators may want to consider for their own grading purposes. The concluding paper, written by another research psychologist with considerable research experience, presents an interesting point of view. Warren notes that many of the reasons for grades are not relevant from the educators' viewpoint. Furthermore, from the accounting profession's viewpoint (not the individual recruiter's) the predominant ABCDF grading system may not be necessary nor desireable.

Accountability in Accounting Education

Keith G. Lumsden
Stanford University

Introduction

A typical dictionary definition of "accountability" is "the quality or state of being responsible or answerable." In universities and colleges in the accounting field, as in any other, a legitimate question follows: who is responsible to whom for what? In this article an attempt is made to demonstrate that there is no unique answer to the question. The goals of the interested parties may be only slightly less numerous than the number of players in the game; which game is being played may not even be universally recognized and when agreement is reached on the appropriate game, there is little assurance that all players will abide by the same rules. The reasons for this state of affairs are not hard to find. In an attempt to bring some order from the chaos, it might prove useful to view the accounting department as a subset of a school which in turn can be thought of as a subset of a university or college. The university shall be the starting point.

Complexity of the University

Educators have not been particularly helpful in providing a theory of the university which is both realistic and also useful for policy implementation. Traditional theories of optimizing behavior, of equating marginal social benefits with marginal social costs, are theoretically valid but of little practical significance for university administrators. Indeed, most of the scholars concerned with efficiency problems in general have avoided efficiency studies in the higher educational industry since that which is to be maximized cannot be agreed upon by a majority of the diverse interested parties.

Until recently research on the economics of higher education has been addressed largely to the question of what is the proper allocation of resources between higher education and alternative uses. This question has been approached from several points of view, each of which provides at best an ambiguous answer and none of which begins to address the problems relating to the internal efficiency of the higher education system.

The most widely adopted research approach has been to estimate from data on differences in individual's incomes and educational attainments, the rate of return to investment in additional years of higher education. Whether society would make better use of its resources by allocating more or less of them to higher education would depend upon whether the rate of return on investment in higher education exceeded or fell short of that on alternative investment opportunities.

Another approach has been to measure the aggregate, cumulative educational investment embodied in the labor force for different years, and to infer from time series data on aggregate output, labor, physical capital, and the stock of educational capital, the contribution that a marginal addition to the stock of educational capital would make to the production of national output. Again, given the costs of adding to educational investment, it is possible to calculate a rate of return to educational investment to be compared to the rates of return on alternative forms of investment with obvious implications for resource allocation.

A third approach has been to calculate average educational attainments of employees in different skill and occupational categories and, on the basis of forecasts in manpower requirements, to determine what resources must be devoted to higher education if the required numbers of employees with different qualifications are to be forthcoming. Clearly, if the resources available to higher education fall short of the needs calculated in this way, then according to the model it would pay to eliminate the gap.

Each of these three areas of research has been marked by serious limitations resulting from inadequacies in the available data and untested restrictive assumptions in the theory. Even if the research objectives could be fully attained, they would provide only a limited basis for educational policy, since they fail to suggest how resources allocated to higher education can be most effectively used. The full complexity of what is involved in the rational planning of higher education is only apparent when the problems in allocating resources between higher education and other economic activities are considered jointly with those relating to internal efficiency. It seems to be an unwise research strategy to consider the first set of problems and ignore the second, when the elimination of substantial internal misallocations could have a profound influence on the optimum share of resources to be devoted to higher education.

In traditional theory it is assumed that forces operate to induce firms to utilize resources in an efficient fashion over time. Firms which fail to take advantage of technological progress and ignore marginal equivalency conditions will be forced to change their behavior or go out of business unless they are sheltered from these market forces. There is good reason to believe that such assumptions are realistic for many sectors in our economy. Unfortunately, such forces are either nonexistent or extremely weak in the education industry. The argument is perhaps best expressed diagrammatically.

The curve OA is a locus of points relating maximum output (Q) to different amounts of a variable input (X)[1] Technological advances would be demonstrated by upward shifts of the curve OA. For a given amount of input X_1 there exists an infinite number of outputs (q_0 to q_{max}), two of which q_1 and q_2 are noted in Figure 1. In discussing efficient resource allocation all non-frontier points (i.e., all non q_{max} on curve OA) are ignored. Now in the education industry if, for most or all institutions of higher learning, the outputs observed are the q_1's and q_2's, then research approaches, such as these enumerated above, and resulting policy choices and implications essentially have little to say about efficiency. Consequently not much can be said about the optimum allocation of resources to education. For conventional educational firms, i.e., universities, in contrast to competitive

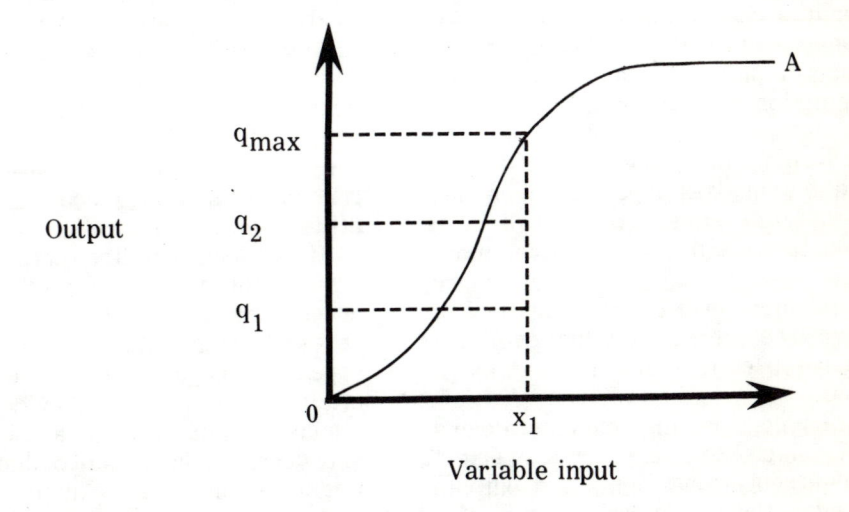

Figure 1. Production Curve

firms, the assumption that each strives to reach the frontier curve OA is invalid; not only is OA seldom if ever reached (existing resources are not used efficiently) but new technologies capable of shifting OA upwards are adopted with reluctance[2].

The reasons for the inertia are not hard to find; few incentives exist for individual faculty members or departments to become more efficient since the benefits from increased efficiency are unlikely to be enjoyed by either. If an accounting professor, for example, could produce at least the same amount of learning (and course satisfaction) in his students with a substantial reduction in resources (e.g., reducing his own class time and simultaneously incurring no additional costs to the university), obviously everyone concerned could benefit from such a course of action.

The reason why such adoptions are not eagerly embraced is perhaps best shown by example. Last academic year in a certain business school a professor taught a basic accounting course to first year MBA's in four, sixty man sections, i.e. on teaching days, he held the same class four times. To the extent that many class sessions involved class participation and discussion, a case could well be made for having no more than sixty students in one class. For those portions of the course, however, which comprised almost all lecturing, substantial evidence exists to support the contention that no loss of learning would occur in either a two hundred and forty man live class or in a class utilizing a televised or videotaped lecture. If we assume, though many accountants might quibble with such an assumption, that one half of the basic accounting course is amenable to the large lecture format, the professor could have reduced his in-class input by over one third; the time saved could have been allocated to an additional elective, more research, closer student contact, more consulting, more leisure or combinations of the above. The main point is that everyone *could* have benefited and no one made worse off.

But now consider the academic dean's position. Since he has very imperfect knowledge concerning inputs and outputs in the educational process, he typically stipulates for each faculty that a certain number of hours will be allocated to teaching. Thus, any professor saving hours in one course can expect to find himself allocating those hours to another course so that "equity" is preserved among the faculty. If an innovating faculty member could appropriate a significant portion of the gains from more efficient teaching, he would be motivated to become more efficient. Furthermore, if a department (e.g., all the accountants in a school) could appropriate such gains, innovations would undoubtedly occur.

Unfortunately, the most likely outcome of the accountants telling the dean that they could effectively teach next year's students with two or three fewer faculty members because they were teaching more efficiently is that the dean would increase accounting electives or allocate fewer resources in the future to the accountants. Thus, while it undoubtedly is in the "university's" interest to become more efficient, it is highly unlikely, under normal existing institutional arrangements, for an individual entity, which cannot appropriate the gains from more efficient teaching practices, to adopt them; indeed, strong disincentives exist to do anything other than preserve the *status quo*.

In short there is an absence of a proprietary group with the customary contractual prerogatives of shareholders. In addition, even if an individual faculty member or department were motivated for altruistic reasons (or for university welfare), data regarding which technologies or pedagogies to adopt are practically nonexistent. Without such information institutions are unlikely to adopt new technologies, or, if they do venture into new pedagogies, they are likely to use them along with established practices. The net result may well be no increase in output, a rise in costs, and a continuing negative attitude toward innovation.

If we consider the entire university system, the inefficiencies multiply; many accountants across the country teach more or less the same thing each year and many repeat large parts of their courses year after year. The use of videotapes and televised lectures, for example, could not only decrease the amount of duplication but might also increase the quality of lectures, on average. Again, the incentive problems which discourage internal university efficiency likewise discourage efficiency on a university-wide basis.

What may force change in universities is the type of crisis which rocked higher education during the past decade. Dissatisfaction of taxpayers, antagonism of students, rising costs, and dwindling resources have forced educational decision makers to reassess their position and come up with new solutions. The measure of merely increasing class size is unlikely to provide little more than a temporary respite on the teaching front. The time may be ripe to reexamine the whole of the higher education industry and to concentrate research on internal university efficiency.

University Outputs

Research on higher education must find a way to deal with the fact that output produced by the contemporary university includes numerous and diverse components, whose quantities and prices are difficult to measure. The present lack of meaningful quantitative information creates serious difficulties for educational decision makers, both within and outside universities. Unless techniques for measuring these variables can be found or methods of rational decision making that do not depend on this information can be devised, the prospects for significant increases in efficiency will remain poor.

A list of the various components of university output would include at least the following broad categories:

1. Educational output—increases in students' knowledge and skills, both cognitive and social, which may add to their productivity and thereby enhance their ability to earn income

2. Informational output—the reporting of students' attributes and educational attainments to students themselves and to prospective employers, which may facilitate more rational career choices and hiring decisions

3. Research output—increases in empirical knowledge, development of new logical concepts, and creation of new works of art, which may directly or indirectly increase the economy's productive capacity.

The fact that university output is multidimensional is not in itself the source of the analytical difficulty. If the components of university output were like other goods, it would be a relatively straightforward matter to apply the calculus of optimizing behavior to the allocation problem and find a reasonably efficient solution. The fact that university decision makers do not have reliable measures of the quantities and prices of university outputs is the principal reason why they cannot readily apply a simple model. To clarify this point, it is useful to raise an issue that has been debated on many campuses recently—namely, whether resources should be reallocated away from research toward undergraduate education. To assess the benefits from such a reallocation it would first be necessary to determine what changes in educational and research outputs would result.

What is clear, however, is that the adoption of technologies which produce no less output than previously but which do so with fewer inputs can benefit all parties concerned.[3] Resources that are freed can be used to admit more students, offer more classes, provide more student-faculty contact, additional research time or any combination of the above. New media in higher education, while not producing substantial gains in student performance, seldom show evidence of loss[4] and roughly the same output could be produced with a substantial saving of resources especially when economies of scale are capable of being exploited.

One of the more striking examples of this situation is the United Kingdom's Open University[5] where teaching costs per student equivalent are approximately 60 percent of conventional universities. Of course it is true that the conventional universities are not teaching efficiently but there is evidence that the Open University also could reduce costs without loss in output and that the potentiality for economies of scale has not been fully exploited.

There is, however, a relatively subtle argument for preserving the *status quo* in higher education. For various reasons associated with the nature of public goods, of which research output is one, existing resource sources produce a suboptimal quantity of research. Inefficient teaching practices provide additional resources to help fill the gap. Faculty implicitly collude to avoid "efficient" teaching since it would result in a decrease in resources for research.

How little is really known about the nature of the education process is made evident by considering two of the broad components of university output listed previously: educational output and informational output. What is the relative importance of these two types of output generated by the educational process? The traditional view of university education is that it provides students with productivity-raising additions to human capital in the form of increases in knowledge and skills. An alternative view is that university education consists of a series of obstacle courses, designed to provide information on students' capacities or potentials to perform certain tasks. While these two views are not mutually exclusive, which view is more accurate is of great significance for educational policy. With respect to the internal efficiency of universities, it is safe to presume that the organization of activities that would be best for human capital formation would be suboptimal for providing labor market information.

In general, it is clear that what seems appropriate for increasing efficiency from one extreme point of view can reduce efficiency from the other extreme point of view. A proper mix of these two types of output can be selected only when it becomes possible to assess both the extent to which university education adds to human capital and the value of information on the productive talents of students that university selection and assessment procedures generate. The principal reason why it is now difficult to make these assessments is that it is practically impossible to determine from available data how much of the difference between the incomes of persons with and without a university education is due to what the graduates gained from having attended a university and how much is due to the greater motivation and ability of those who are admitted to, and graduate from, a university. Until data are collected which make it possible to observe and control for inherent factors influencing productivity, there is no point in making rate of return calculations that are based on the assumption that most or all of the difference in average income between graduates and non-graduates is due to the additional human capital provided to graduates by a university education.

University planners, given the present form of organization in higher education, are severely hampered in making resource allocation decisions by the lack of quantitative information about the educational process. Not only does this lack of information obscure the consequences of any planning decision, but it even makes it difficult to define a useful criterion for success.

Accountability in the University

What emerges from the above discussion is that the functions of the university are several; the output choices of the university, for all practical purposes, are infinite; prices of many of the output elements are not readily available; the underlying engineering production functions have seldom been identified; and current institutional arrangements discourage actions which could lead to less inefficiency. An additional complicating factor is that the interest groups the university serves are many, making the accountability problem complex.

Outside interest groups include governments, foundations and private donors, professional associations, firms and households. Inside interest groups include students, faculty, administration, librarians, and other university staff. From these lists the accounting professor is forced into several roles and often encounters conflicting goals. For example, as a member of the American Accounting Association should he be concerned with maintaining professional standards in publications or in teaching and examining students? Or should he be responding solely to the demands of governments and firms for qualified accountants? Does "qualified" imply maximizing the amount of accounting that students know or making sure that those certified are capable of learning once employed in a government or private office? In the university should the accounting professor be concentrating on writing esoteric articles which will meet the acclaim of his peers, appear in journals, and be rewarded with salary and advancement, or should he be allocating more of his time to his students in the class-

TABLE V

Dependent Variable: Overall Evaluation of the Instructor

Independent Variable	(20) B	t	(21) B	t	(22) B	t	Independent Variable	B	t	B	t
1. Constant term	-1.14	-12.5	-1.84	-11.6	-1.05	-6.9	18. PhD candidate	-.26	-3.5		
Opinion of extent instruction:							19. Years in program	.01	0.3		
2. Imports enthusiasm***	.24	20.6	.24	21.2	.23	18.8	20. Years of full-time work	-.04	-7.7		
3. Knows subject***	.14	8.2	.13	8.0	.14	8.0	21. Years in military	-.03	-6.1		
4. Is well prepared***	.12	8.1	.12	8.3	.13	8.3	22. GSB GPA	*	.8		
5. Has practical know. of subject***	.09	6.6	.09	6.6	.09	6.0	23. No GPA	.10	.8		
6. Presents materials clearly***	.26	17.5	.26	18.1	.26	17.3	*Instructor Characteristics*				
7. Speaks clearly***	.03	1.9	.02	1.7	.02	1.3	24. Age			**	-.1
8. Uses visual aids well***	.05	4.5	.05	4.6	.06	5.0	25. Full professor			-.04	-.6
9. Avoids being sidetracked***	.06	6.1	.06	5.9	.06	6.0	26. Associate professor			-.05	-.8
10. Makes useful comments on h.w.***	.03	2.9	.03	2.9	.02	2.4	27. Assistant professor			-.13	-2.3
11. Is available outside class***	-.01	-.5	**	-.3	**	-.4	28. Years since PhD			**	-.2
12. Was int. in stud. as person***	-.03	-2.5	-.03	-2.3	-.03	-2.6	29. Has PhD			.12	2.3
13. Sensitive to stud.'s needs***	.02	1.4	.02	1.9	.02	1.6	30. Years at Stanford			**	-.5
14. Respects student opinion***	.20	16.2	.18	14.6	.21	16.4	31. Outside activities			-.01	-.4
Student Characteristics:							32. Times taught course before			**	-.1
15. Time spent on course			.06	4.3			33. Teaching other sections			-.07	-2.3
16. Age in years			.02	8.4			34. Time for res. last yr.			*	.5
17. MBA candidate			-.15	-3.6			35. Time for res. this yr.			*	.5
R^2	.73		.73		.75			.73			

* Between 0 and -.005   ** Between 0 and .005

***To control for the fact that some students in some courses did not give a response for these independent variables, dummy variables were included in the regressions. When one of variables 2-14 took on a value of 0, the corresponding dummy variable took on a value of 1; otherwise, the dummy variable took on a value of 0. The mean values for the dummy variables corresponding to variables 2-14 are .01 for 2, .01 for 3, .02 for 4, .02 for 5, .01 for 6, .02 for 7, .07 for 8, .06 for 9, .22 for 10, .41 for 11, .37 for 12, .05 for 13 and .08 for 14. The regression statistics for these variables are not shown in the table.

room, holding more office hours, and responding to student demands? Should he be concerned with student evaluations of his courses and his teaching performance and should he be rewarded by such evaluations in contrast to the opinions of his peers in his research?[6] Should he be working to promote internal efficiency within his department, school or university or should he be persuading the American Accounting Association to tackle the problems of efficiency on a national basis?

It may prove of little comfort to know that other disciplines are no further forward than the accountants. Under present institutional arrangements, the accounting professor may wear one of many hats, and make a strong case for his personal choice.

FOOTNOTES

[1] The case of multiple outputs and inputs introduces some complexities but does not violate the general principles.

[2] See, for example, M. Woodhall, and M. Blaugh, "Productivity Trends in British University Education 1936-62." *Minerva,,* 1965, Vo. 3, and, J. O'Neal, "Productivity Trends in Higher Education" in Radner and Froomkin (eds.) *Education as an Industry* NBER and Columbia University Press, forthcoming.

[3] See, for example, Richard Layard, "The Cost-Effectiveness of the New Media in Higher Education" in Lumsden (ed) *Efficiency in Universities, The La Paz Papers,* forthcoming, and Jamison, Suppes, and Wells, "The Effectiveness of Alternative Instructional Media: A Survey," Stanford University, February, 1973.

[4] See, for example, D. Jamison and K. Lumsden, "Improving Efficiency in Business Education—Assessment of the Potential"—Stanford University, 1972 and "Television and Efficiency in Higher Education", Stanford University, 1973.

[5] See, for example, Keith G. Lumsden, "The Open University, A Survey and Economic Analysis" unpublished paper, September, 1972.

[6] Readers interested in student evaluations of courses and instructors might like to read this author's paper "The Information Content of Student Evaluation of Faculty and Courses," Research Paper No. 157, Graduate School of Business, Stanford University, May, 1973. The regressions in the table below, (Table V in the paper containing three regressions (20, 21, & 22) attempt to explain student overall opinion of the instructor in terms of the evaluations of individual qualities of the instructor (20). In regression (21) student characteristics and in regression (22) instructor characteristics are included as additional explanatory variables. The data comprised approximately 5,000 responses of students in all Stanford's Graduate School of Business courses in 1970-71.

In all these regressions, the opinion of how clearly the instructor presents his materials, and the extent to which he imparts enthusiasm have the largest coefficients. Having respect for student opinion, knowing his subject, being well prepared, and demonstrating a practical knowledge of the application of course material have sizable and significant coefficients. The instructor's use of visual aids, ability to avoid being sidetracked, and willingness to provide useful comments on homework have small but statistically significant coefficients. Speaking clearly, being available outside of class, and being sensitive to students' needs had no significant effect on the overall evaluation of the instructor, while being interested in the student as a person had a significant negative impact on the overall evaluation.

Regression (21) indicates that given a student's evaluation of the instructor's individual qualities, the more time the student spends on the course, the older he is, and fewer years spent in full-time work or the military, the higher will he rate in instructor overall. Furthermore, MBA and Ph.D students tend to be significantly harsher in their overall evaluation of the instructor. Since a significant number of non-Graduate School of Business students take Graduate School of Business courses, this finding suggests that teaching performance, as evaluated by these students, is substantially better in the Graduate School of Business than in the remainder of the University. Regression (22) suggests, again given the evaluation of the instructor's individual qualities, an instructor who is an assistant professor and or who does not have a Ph.D. and who is teaching more than one section of the same course will fare significantly worse in this overall evaluation.

Evaluation of College Teaching

Robert C. Wilson
University of California, Berkeley

Introduction

Professor Wilson's paper has two main purposes: (1) to define and describe effective teaching characteristics so that accounting educators can improve individual teaching efforts; and (2) to present information, research results, and test instruments useful for incorporating the evaluation of teaching into college advancement procedures. If valid and reliable evaluation and reward systems can be developed, the incentive will be present to increase the status and the quality of teaching.

The most common conception of college and university teaching among legislators and the general public is that of a professor standing at the front of a classroom lecturing to a group of students for six to twelve hours a week; in short, a view of the teacher as a "talking textbook" and "dispenser of knowledge". Those who are more familiar with academic life recognize that classroom teaching is only the most visible part of teaching, that classroom teaching is based upon a great deal of much less visible activity and that much of teaching takes place outside the classroom.

There have been a number of workload studies of college teachers which indicate that they average between 50 and 60 hours of work per week. Nevertheless, the very damaging public image of the college teacher's 6 to 12 hour work-week exists and has contributed greatly to the hostile and punitive actions which several state legislatures have taken against public higher education.

Teachers, perhaps, should share some of the blame for having contributed to this image. Even though there are many activities in which teachers must engage, they generally do not talk about them when discussing teaching assignments and workload distribution. Because classroom hours are convenient units in which to think, teachers and administrators tend to consider them as being equivalent to each other and also as being the most meaningful units to use in distributing the teaching resources of college campuses. The lack of real equivalence receives some acknowledgement, however, in the way assignments are made. The number of courses calling for different preparations is sometimes taken into account, and workload credit may be given for the supervision of theses and independent study.

Ways need to be found to assign and report teaching workloads which reflect the real breadth of direct and indirect teaching activities. The following is a sample of teaching-related activities engaged in by many college teachers in order to facilitate student learning.

1. *Classroom teaching activities*—lecturing, leading discussions, suggesting reading references, making assignments.

2. *Preparatory classroom activities*—reading assigned books, preparing notes, constructing reading lists, devising assignments, preparing laboratory demonstrations, securing equipment for studio classes.

3. *Associated housekeeping activities*—making problem sets, preparing quizzes and examinations, reading and grading quizzes and examinations, reading term papers, evaluating class projects.

4. *Course planning activities*—reconsidering the needs and interests of students, evaluating the state of the

discipline, reviewing possible textbooks, planning course sequences.

5. *Out-of-class teaching activities*—talking with students about classroom discussions, clarifying assignments, helping students plan and prepare term papers or projects, holding conferences about papers or examinations, discussing intellectual matters with students, helping students learn how to study, supervising independent study.

6. *Teaching through advising and counseling*—helping students with their vocational aims and plans, advising about academic programs, discussing students' problems, acting to help students with difficulties.

7. *Teaching through extracurricular activities*—advising student organizations, attending student functions, discussing campus issues with student groups.

8. *Keeping one's teaching up-to-date*—reading books and journals in one's specialty, reading in related fields, attending professional meetings to learn of recent developments, selecting books for the library.

9. *Keeping informed about campus issues which affect students and teaching*—discussing issues with colleagues, members of committees, and administrators; reading or composing memos, position papers and planning documents which affect the curriculum teaching and learning.

10. *Graduate teaching activities*—supervising graduate students, preparing, administering and evaluating graduate examinations, serving on thesis committees.

The above is a lengthy but not exhaustive list of activities in which college teachers engage. Not all faculty members perform all of these activities. Each activity listed, however, is directly or indirectly related to effectiveness in teaching when it is broadly conceived. Clearly, teaching involves a complex of activities, only a few of which occur within the familiar confines of the classroom.

Alternative Measures of Teaching Effectiveness

Considering the diversity of activities which may be considered part of a professor's teaching duties, how should one go about measuring his teaching effectiveness (the goodness or badness of his performance of these duties)? What should be the criteria of a good or bad performance? What kinds of performance evidence are acceptable?

First, it is apparent that "effective" is a value term, a judgment rather than a description. This means that the same teaching activity may be judged differently depending upon the values of the persons making the judgment. It is also apparent that people differ about the kinds of data or information they are willing to accept as evidence of teaching effectiveness. Much of the controversy about teaching effectiveness and how to measure it boils down to disagreement about the adequacy or acceptability of different kinds of information. Evaluation, then, involves obtaining information and making judgments about the meaning of that information, usually in relation to some decision. In the evaluation of college teaching, the information may take a number of forms. It may be useful, at this point, to list some of the types of information which have been proposed for use in judgments about teaching effectiveness.

1. *Information from teachers*

This source has the virtue of allowing the person closest to the situation, the teacher, to provide information. Since he is largely responsible for designing and teaching courses, he may be in the best position to assess progress toward his own objectives. The major limitations of this approach lie in the fact that many teachers do not know how effective their teaching is; they may be so involved in the teaching process that they cannot assess their effectiveness accurately. However, this is one source of information which can b used in conjunction with other information.

2. *Information from measures of student achievement or change*

On the surface this source of information appears to be the most directly relevant and valid of all, for is not the proof of good teaching found in the actual achievement of students? If possible, this is the kind of criterion which most people would like to use. However, there are several problems which have hampered widespread use of this approach. First, people disagree as to what kinds of achievement or change should be measured; second, there are real difficulties in developing achievement tests which are sufficiently sensitive to give reliable measures of change; third, there are many important kinds of change in students not easily measured with the kinds of tests presently available. However, considerable experimentation with this approach is currently underway.

3. *Information from alumni*

Sometimes students do not really appreciate what they have learned from a teacher until they have been out in the real world for a while. However, in the few studies that have been made of information from alumni, agreement with student judgments is generally high. Major limitations of this approach arise from faculty turnover and also the fact that junior faculty members were probably not on campus when the alumni were.

4. *Information from colleagues*

While colleagues are often asked to give information about teaching, the evidence they use is generally indirect. A few institutions have made use of classroom visitation with some success, but it requires a school or department in which there is a good deal of mutual confidence and trust. The classroom visitation approach is also time-consuming and expensive, particularly when the number of teachers involved is large. An interesting description of this approach is presented by Eastman (1969).

5. *Information from students*

Student input continues to be one of the most controversial sources of information despite the fact that there has been fifty years of research which supports the usefulness of student evaluations of teaching. Despite the controversy, a recent survey of 669 colleges and universities by the American Council on Education (Creager, 1973) indicated that 65 percent of the responding institutions made use of student evaluations of teaching effectiveness in all or nearly all departments. This percentage is a substantial increase over the figures reported by Astin and Lee (1966).

Many readers will have heard of the controversial science article by Rodin and Rodin (1972) entitled *Student Evaluations of Teachers*. The authors concluded that students rate most highly those instructors from whom they learn least and that "good teaching is not validly measured by student evaluations in their current form." Detailed critiques of the article may be found in Gessner (1973), Wilson (1973), Doyle and Whitely (1972). Only a few of the article's most obvious inadequacies will be mentioned here. The sweeping generalization asserted in the conclusion is based on a study of 12 teaching assistants, using a one question evaluation of their teaching. The students who "learned least" earned a B+ average on the examinations. It is obviously ridiculous to generalize from a single teaching situation involving 12 teaching assistants to all teaching situations involving 500,000 faculty members. The single evaluation question that Rodin and Rodin used certainly does not generalize to all "student evaluations in their current form". The range of grades used as a measure of learning goes only from 3.1 to 3.6 raises some doubts. Performance at the B+ level is a rather high level of "learning least."

Summaries of the considerable body of research on the use of student evaluations can be found in McKeachie (1969), Costin, Greenough, and Menges (1971), Trent and Cohen (1973). At the present time, in the absence of performance based measures of teaching effectiveness, the use of systematically gathered data from students can serve as a useful adjunct to whatever other sources of data are available.

Student and Colleague Perceptions of Teaching Effectiveness

Perhaps it might be useful to summarize the procedures and results of a three-year study of university teaching carried out at the Davis campus of the University of California in collaboration with Milton Hildebrand, professor of Zoology and Chairman of the Academic Senate Committee on Teaching. The objectives were to identify and describe effective teaching and to develop more valid and reliable means of incorporating teaching evaluation into advancement procedures.[1]

Three surveys were conducted in the first year and one in the second year. Initially, 338 students (including 60 graduate students) identified the "best" and "worst" teachers they had during the previous year, and answered 158 questions about the teaching of each. Second, 119 members of the faculty identified the best and worst teachers among their colleagues, and answered 103 questions about the teaching and other academic activities of each. Third, 162 faculty members reported how often they had performed various academic pursuits during stated time periods. Finally, a validation survey was made in which 51 classes were selected to include, in about equal numbers, those instructors previously identified as best teachers by three or more students or colleagues, those instructors previously identified as worst teachers, and other instructors not previously named either best or worst. The 1015 students in these classes answered questions about the teaching of their respective instructors.

The principal results of this study are as follows:

1. There is excellent agreement among students, and between faculty and students, about the effectiveness of given teachers.
2. Best and worst teachers engage in the same professional activities and allocate their time among academic pursuits in about the same ways. The mere performance of activities associated with teaching does not assure that the instruction is effective.
3. After performing an item-analysis, 85 items emerged that characterized best teachers as perceived by students, and 54 items that characterized best teachers as perceived by colleagues. All items statistically discriminate best from worst teachers with a high level of significance.[2]
4. A factor analysis of the items characterizing best teachers as perceived by students produced five scales, or components of effective performance. (Table 1) These may be summarized as follows:

   A. *Analytic/Synthetic Approach*
   Has command of the subject, presents material in an analytic way, contrasts points of view, discusses current developments, and relates topics to other areas of knowledge.

   B. *Organization/Clarity of Presentation*
   Makes himself clear, states objectives, summarizes major points, presents material in an organized manner, and provides emphasis.

   C. *Instructor-Group Interaction*
   Is sensitive to the response of the class, encourages student participation, and welcomes questions and discussion.

   D. *Instructor-Individual Student Interaction*
   Is available and friendly toward students, is interested in students as individuals, is respected as a person, and is valued for advice not directly related to the course.

   E. *Dynamism/Enthusiasm*
   Enjoys teaching, is enthusiastic about his subject, makes the course exciting and has self-confidence.

5. A factor analysis of the items characterizing best teachers as perceived by colleagues produced five scales of components (Table 2) which may be summarized as follows:

   A. *Research Activity and Recongnition*
   Is well known and highly regarded for his scholarly activity, publications, and research. Confers with colleagues about research and keeps abreast of recent developments in his field.

   B. *Intellectual Breadth*
   Has broad knowledge both within and beyond his field. Is sought out by students and colleagues for information and academic advice.

   C. *Participation in the Academic Community*
   Attends and participates in campus lectures, social functions, and student-oriented activities. Maintains a congenial relationship with colleagues.

   D. *Relations with Students*
   Maintains an informal and congenial relationship with students beyond the classroom. Is consistently available to students for consultation about personal and academic concerns.

   E. *Concern for Teaching*
   Expresses concern for teaching and consults with colleagues about issues related to teaching.

The majority of the colleague scales are mainly concerned with activities that take place outside the classroom. This is because the majority of our respondents had not observed the person they nominated (as best or worst) in the classroom. However, when colleagues do observe in the classroom, scales similar to the student scales can be used.

6. As most investigators have found students' ratings of teachers show only negligible correlations with the academic rank of the instructor, class level, number of courses previously taken in the same department, class size, required versus optional course, course in major or not, sex of the respondent, class level of the respondent, grade-point average, and expected grade in course.

7. Students evaluated the positive contributions made to their lives by the best teachers in six areas: knowledge imparted, counsel given, objectives clarified, values developed, incentive elicited, and skills developed. Correlations of mean scores for these areas with mean scores for the components of effective teaching and with overall ratings of effectiveness of teaching were high.

8. The scales derived from the characterization of effective teaching by students provide conceptual understanding of the components of such teaching. Having been developed from items to which most students of a large random sample could respond, the student scales are applicable to most kinds of college-level teaching. Attention to the scales helps to assure that the major components of effective performance are considered when teaching or evaluating teaching. This helps to direct attention to the multidimensional nature of effective teaching and helps to overcome the rather simplistic idea that a teacher is either good or bad. Only a rare teacher rates high on all five dimensions of teaching.

KEY DECISIONS IN PLANNING FOR PROGRAMS OF TEACHER EVALUATION

The purposes and resources of individual colleges and universities vary, and the committees and individuals charged with teacher evaluation on particular campuses usually want to put their own unique imprints on whatever programs are used at their institutions. Because of this, a single prepackaged product for teacher evaluation is generally not acceptable.

Nevertheless, whatever the variations in local options, there are some key decisions which must be made in developing a successful program of teacher evaluation. It has become evident that the chief sources of disillusionment with programs for teacher evaluation arise from the failure to develop sufficiently detailed plans which spell out key decisions and anticipate realistic difficulties and possible controversies.

The following outline is intended to assist planners by spelling out a number of tasks to be undertaken and options to be considered in implementing an evaluation program.

PURPOSES

Feedback to instructor for self-improvement
Data for making salary, promotion, and tenure decisions
Information to assist students in choosing courses and instructors
A combination of the above

SCOPE

Number of Teachers
Small number (e.g., all of one department)
Medium number (e.g., all eligible for tenure)
Large number (e.g., all in the institution
Number of classes
One per instructor per advancement period
One per instructor per year
Each once per advancement period
Each every other year, or every year
Number of students
Random sample of X students (large classes only?)
X percent of class (large classes only?)
All (but with minimum of X returns to qualify for interpretation?)
Kinds of courses
Undergraduate credit courses
All except seminars and field research courses
All (including noncredit and extension?)

FORMS

Style
Structured check-off items
Open-ended essay items
Coverage
Teaching only
Teaching and course
Teaching, course, and student data (demographic, objectives, values)

Format
Optical scanning sheets
Mark sense sheets
Porto-punch cards
Duplicated questionnaire with key punch
Duplicated questionnaire with hand tally
Length
Short (1-25 items)
Medium (26-50 items)
Long (greater than 50 items)
Sources
External (for example, another campus, Center for Research and Development in Higher Education, Berkeley.)
Local committee (faculty, administrative, student, combination)
Instructor
A combination of the above

ADMINISTRATION AND DATA GATHERING

Time of distribution
Early in course
Late in course
With final examination
After course
Method of distribution
Instructor
Student representative
Administrative representative
With registration packets
Method of return
Collected by instructor
Collected by student representative
Collected by administrative representative
Mailed to a central office.

DATA REDUCTION

Persons involved
Instructor
Department
Committee (student, faculty, administrative, combination)
Central office
Method
Summarization by computer, with norms and variances
Hand-tabulation and individual case study
Summarization of open-ended data

INTERPRETATION OF DATA

Persons involved
Instructor
Department
Committee (student, faculty, administrative combination)
Central office
Basis
Individual case study
Department norms
College or school norms
Campus norms

PROVISION FOR CHALLENGE

None
By instructor
By student or department
Procedures

DISSEMINATION AND REPORTING

To instructor only
To instructor, and departmental chairman or committee
To instructor, department, and administration
To university community at a central location
To university community by sale or general distribution.

The outline of program decisions presented above lays out many of the options which should be considered in gathering information about teaching effectiveness, making judgments as to its meaning and making decisions. As indicated, the choice of options must ultimately be determined by local conditions, including economic, political, and humanistic concerns.

SUMMARY

In fulfilling teaching responsibilities, college teachers are involved in numerous activities, both in and out of the classroom. The significance of these activities suggests that a multi-dimensional approach is needed in evaluating teaching effectiveness. However, the establishment of an evaluation system that is accurate and equitable is not without difficulties.

An evaluation program which gives attention to the characteristics of effective teaching, as perceived by students and faculty colleagues, will help accounting educators sharpen individual teaching efforts. Reference to the outline of key decisions in planning for teacher evaluation programs should assist in the development of such a program.

TABLE 1. COMPONENTS OF EFFECTIVE TEACHING AS PERCEIVED BY STUDENTS

SCALE 1. ANALYTIC/SYNTHETIC APPROACH

	Factor coefficient
1. Discusses points of view other than his own	.70
2. Contrasts implications of various theories	.66
3. Discusses recent developments in the field	.64
4. Presents origins of ideas and concepts	.60
5. Gives references for more interesting and involved points	.53
6. Presents facts and concepts from related fields	.53
7. Emphasizes conceptual understanding	.46

SCALE 2. ORGANIZATION/CLARITY

8. Explains clearly	.78
9. Is well prepared	.63
10. Gives lectures that are easy to outline	.62
11. Is careful and precise in answering questions	.61
12. Summarizes major points	.51
13. States objectives for each class session	.50
14. Identifies what he considers important	.47

SCALE 3. INSTRUCTOR-GROUP INTERACTION

15. Encourages class discussion	.70
16. Invites students to share their knowledge and experiences	.65
17. Clarifies thinking by identifying reasons for questions	.64
18. Invites criticism of his own ideas	.62
19. Knows if the class is understanding him or not	.58
20. Knows when students are bored or confused	.57
21. Has interest and concern in the quality of his teaching	.48
22. Has students apply concepts to demonstrate understanding	.43

SCALE 4. INSTRUCTOR-INDIVIDUAL STUDENT INTERACTION

23. Has a genuine interest in students	.74
24. Is friendly toward students	.71
25. Relates to students as individuals	.69
26. Recognizes and greets students out of class	.68
27. Is accessible to students out of class	.65
28. Is valued for advice not directly related to the course	.64
29. Respects students as persons	.60

SCALE 5. DYNAMISM/ENTHUSIASM

30. Is a dynamic and energetic person	.80
31. Has an interesting style of presentation	.76
32. Seems to enjoy teaching	.74
33. Is enthusiastic about his subject	.65
34. Seems to have self-confidence	.64
35. Varies the speed and tone of his voice	.63
36. Has a sense of humor	.53

TABLE 2. COMPONENTS OF THE ACTIVITIES OF EFFECTIVE TEACHERS AS PERCEIVED BY COLLEAGUES

SCALE 1. RESEARCH ACTIVITY AND RECOGNITION

	Factor coefficient
1. Does work that receives serious attention from others	.69
2. Corresponds with others about his research	.69
3. Does original and creative work	.64
4. Expresses interest in the research of his colleagues	.55
5. Gives many papers at conferences	.55
6. Keeps current with developments in his field	.49
7. Has done work to which I refer in teaching	.48
8. Has talked with me about his research	.38

SCALE 2. INTELLECTUAL BREADTH

9. Seems well read beyond the subject he teaches	.66
10. Is sought by others for advice on research	.60
11. Can suggest reading in any area of his general field	.59
12. Knows about developments in fields other than his own	.51
13. Is sought by colleagues for advice on academic matters	.43

SCALE 3. PARTICIPATION IN THE ACADEMIC COMMUNITY

14. Encourages students to talk with him on matters of concern	.60
15. Is involved in campus activities that affect studenns	.58
16. Attends many lectures and other events on campus	.47
17. Has a congenial relationship with colleagues	.39

SCALE 4. RELATIONS WITH STUDENTS

18. Meets with students informally out of class	.58
19. Is conscientious about keeping appointments with students	.57
20. Meets with students out of regular office hours	.57
21. Encourages students to talk with him on matters of concern	.55
22. Recognizes and greets students out of class	.37

SCALE 5. CONCERN FOR TEACHING

23. Seeks advice from others about the courses he teaches	.70
24. Discusses teaching in general with colleagues	.60
25. Does not seek close friendships with colleagues (Negative)	.47
26. Is someone with whom I have discussed my teaching	.45
27. Is interested in and informed about the work of colleagues	.44
28. Expresses interest and concern about the quality of his teaching	.40

APPENDIX A. CHARACTERIZATION BY STUDENTS OF EFFECTIVE TEACHERS

CHARACTERISTICS OF A MAJORITY OF BEST TEACHERS AND OF A MINORITY OF WORST

Course content and presentation

† * 1. Contrasts implications of various theories
    2. Presents origins of ideas and concepts
  * 3. Presents facts and concepts from related fields
    4. Talks about research he has done himself
    5. Emphasizes ways of solving problems rather than solutions
    6. Discusses practical applications
    7. Explains his actions, decisions, and selection of topics
†   8. Seems well read beyond the subject he teaches
  * 9. Is an excellent public speaker
† 10. Speaks clearly
 * 11. Explains clearly
   12. Gives lectures that are easy to outline
   13. Reads his lectures or stays close to his notes (Negative)
   14. Assigns text as background, but lectures include other topics
 * 15. Makes difficult topics easy to understand
   16. Summarizes major points
   17. States objectives for each class session
   18. Identifies what he considers important
 * 19. Shows interest and concern in quality of his teaching
   20. Gives examinations requiring creative, original thinking
   21. Gives examinations having instructional value
   22. Gives examinations requiring chiefly recall of facts (Negative)
   23. Gives interesting and stimulating assignments
   24. Stresses the aesthetic and emotional value of the subject
 * 25. Is a dynamic and energetic person
† * 26. Seems to enjoy teaching
† 27. Is enthusiastic about his subject
† 28. Seems to have self-confidence
   29. Varies the speed and tone of his voice
   30. Has a sense of humor

Relations with students

   31. Is careful and precise in answering questions
† 32. Explains his own criticisms
   33. Encourages class discussion
 * 34. Invites students to share their knowledge and experiences
 * 35. Clarifies thinking by identifying reasons for questions
 * 36. Invites criticism of his own ideas
† * 37. Knows if the class is understanding him or not
   38. Knows when students are bored or confused
   39. Has students apply concepts to demonstrate understanding
† * 40. Keeps well informed about progress of class
   41. Anticipates difficulties and prepares students beforehand
   42. Has definite plan, yet uses material introduced by students
   43. Provides time for discussion and questions
 * 44. Is sensitive to student's desire to ask a question
   45. Encourages students to speak out in lecture or discussion
† 46. Quickly grasps what a student is asking or telling him
   47. Restates questions or comments to clarify for entire class

48. Asks others to comment on one student's contribution
49. Compliments students for raising good points
50. Doesn't fully answer questions (Negative)
51. Determines if one student's problem is common to others
52. Reminds students to see him if having difficulty
53. Informs students of coming campus events related to course
54. Encourages students to express feelings and opinions
55. Relates class topics to students' lives and experiences
† 56. Has a genuine interest in students
57. Relates to students as individuals
58. Recognizes and greets students out of class
* 59. Is valued for advice not directly related to the course
60. Treats students as his equals

CHARACTERISTICS OF A MAJORITY OF BEST AND WORST TEACHERS, BUT MORE TYPICAL OF BEST

61. Discusses points of view other than his own
62. Discusses recent developments in the field
63. Gives references for the more interesting and involved points
64. Emphasizes conceptual understanding
65. Disagrees with some ideas in textbook and other readings
66. Stresses rational and intellectual aspects of the subject
67. Stresses general concepts and ideas
68. Seems to have a serious commitment to his field
69. Is well prepared
70. Gives examinations stressing conceptual understanding
71. Gives examinations requring synthesis of various parts of course
72. Gives examinations permitting students to show understanding
73. Is friendly toward students
74. Is accessible to students out of class
75. Respects students as persons
76. Is always courteous to students
77. Gives personal help to students having difficulty with course
78. Has an interesting style of presentation

RESULTS TYPICAL OF TAKING A COURSE FROM A BEST TEACHER AND NOT FROM A WORST

† * 79. Have developed increased appreciation for the subject
* 80. Have learned new ways to evaluate problems
81. Have worked harder than in most other courses
82. Know how to find more information on the subject
83. Have studied a topic from the course on own initiative
84. Plan to take more courses on the subject
85. Have gained self-knowledge

* Descriptive of 75% or more of best teachers and 25% or less of worst teachers

† Descriptive of 95% or more of best teachers and 45% or less of worst teachers

Items are not listed in rank order

APPENDIX B. CHARACTERIZATION BY COLLEAGUES OF EFFECTIVE TEACHERS

CHARACTERISTICS OF A MAJORITY OF BEST TEACHERS AND OF A MINORITY OF WORST

1. Does original and creative work
2. Expresses interest in the research of his colleagues
3. Gives many papers at conferences
4. Has done work to which I refer in teaching
5. Has been consulted by me about my research
6. Has consulted by me about problems in his field
7. Discusses students' work with colleagues
† 8. Spends much time planning and preparing for his teaching
9. Seems well read beyond the subject he teaches
10. Is sought by others for advice on research
† 11. Can suggest reading in any area of his general field
12. Is sought by colleagues for advice on academic matters
13. Encourages students to talk with him on matters of concern
14. Is involved in campus activities that affect students
15. Attends many lectures and other events on campus
16. Enjoys controversy in discussion and may provoke opposing views
† 17. Comes to departmental or committee meetings well prepared
18. Meets with students informally out of class
19. Meets with students out of regular office hours
20. Encourages students to talk with him on matters of concern
† 21. Seems to have a congenial relationship with students
† 22. Seems to have a genuine interest in his students
* 23. Seeks advice from others about the courses he teaches
† 24. Discusses teaching in general with colleagues
25. Does not seek close friendships with colleagues (Negative)
26. Is someone with whom I have discussed my teaching
27. Is interested in, and informed about, the work of colleagues
28. Expresses interest and concern about the quality of his teaching
† 29. Seems to enjoy teaching

Further characterization if speech or seminar was attended

† 30. Gives a well organized presentation
* 31. Is an excellent public speaker
32. Summarizes major points at the end of a presentation
* 33. Uses wit and humor effectively
† 34. Uses well chosen examples to clarify points
† 35. Communicates self-confidence

Further characterization if classroom teaching was attended

36. Encourages students to express feelings and opinions
* 37. Clarifies thinking by identifying reasons for questions
38. Presents facts and concepts from related fields
* 39. Anticipates difficulties and prepares students beforehand
† 40. Quickly grasps what a student is asking or telling him
† 41. Is careful and precise in answering questions
42. Presents origins of ideas and concepts
† 43. Emphasizes ways of solving problems rather than solutions

CHARACTERISTICS OF A MAJORITY OF BEST AND WORST TEACHERS, BUT MORE TYPICAL OF BEST

44. Invites discussion of points he raises
45. Is careful and precise in answering questions
46. Keeps current with developments in his field
47. Has talked with me about his research
48. Knows about developments in fields other than his own
49. Has a congenial relationship with colleagues
50. Is conscientious about keeping appointment with students
51. Recognizes and greets students out of class
52. Is enthusiastic about his subject
53. Does work that receives serious attention from others
54. Corresponds with others about his research

---

* Descriptive of 75% or more of best teachers and of 25% or less of worst teachers

† Descriptive of 95% or more of best teachers and of 45% or less of worst teacher

Items are not listed in rank order

Evaluation of College Teaching

STUDENT DESCRIPTION OF TEACHERS

(1-3)

Instructor _____ Department _____ (4-6)

Course number or title _____ (7-9)

I. The following items reflect some of the ways teachers can be described. For the instructor named above, please circle the number which indicates the degree to which you feel each item is descriptive of him or her. In some cases, the statement may not apply to this individual. In these cases, check *Does not apply or don't know* for that item.

	Not at all Descriptive			Very Descriptive		Doesn't apply or don't know
1. Discusses points of view other than his own	1	2	3	4	5	( ) (10)
2. Contrasts implications of various theories	1	2	3	4	5	( )
3. Discusses recent developments in the field	1	2	3	4	5	( )
4. Presents origins of ideas and concepts	1	2	3	4	5	( )
5. Gives references for more interesting and involved points	1	2	3	4	5	( )
6. Presents facts and concepts from related fields	1	2	3	4	5	( )
7. Emphasizes conceptual understanding	1	2	3	4	5	( )
8. Explains clearly	1	2	3	4	5	( )
9. Is well prepared	1	2	3	4	5	( )
10. Gives lectures that are easy to outline	1	2	3	4	5	( )
11. Is careful and precise in answering questions	1	2	3	4	5	( )
12. Summarizes major points	1	2	3	4	5	( )
13. States objectives for each class session	1	2	3	4	5	( )
14. Identifies what he considers important	1	2	3	4	5	( )
15. Encourages class discussion	1	2	3	4	5	( )
16. Invites students to share their knowledge and experiences	1	2	3	4	5	( )
17. Clarifies thinking by identifying reasons for questions	1	2	3	4	5	( ) (26)

	Not at all Descriptive				Very Descriptive	Doesn't apply or don't know
18. Invites criticism of his own ideas	1	2	3	4	5	( ) (27)
19. Knows if the class is understanding him or not	1	2	3	4	5	( )
20. Knows when students are bored or confused	1	2	3	4	5	( )
21. Has interest in and concern for the quality of his teaching	1	2	3	4	5	( )
22. Has students apply concepts to demonstrate understanding	1	2	3	4	5	( )
23. Has a genuine interest in students	1	2	3	4	5	( )
24. Is friendly toward students	1	2	3	4	5	( )
25. Relates to students as individuals	1	2	3	4	5	( )
26. Recognizes and greets students out of class	1	2	3	4	5	( )
27. Is accessible to students out of class	1	2	3	4	5	( )
28. Is valued for advice not directly related to the course	1	2	3	4	5	( )
29. Respects students as persons	1	2	3	4	5	( )
30. Is a dynamic and energetic person	1	2	3	4	5	( )
31. Has an interesting style of presentation	1	2	3	4	5	( )
32. Seems to enjoy teaching	1	2	3	4	5	( )
33. Is enthusiastic about his subject	1	2	3	4	5	( )
34. Seems to have self-confidence	1	2	3	4	5	( )
35. Varies the speed and tone of his voice	1	2	3	4	5	( )
36. Has a sense of humor	1	2	3	4	5	( ) (45)

(Additional items may be presented by the instructor and/or department)

37.	1	2	3	4	5	( )
38.	1	2	3	4	5	( )
39.	1	2	3	4	5	( )
40.	1	2	3	4	5	( )

Evaluation of College Teaching

	Not at all Descriptive			Very Descriptive		Doesn't apply or don't know
41.	1	2	3	4	5	( )
42.	1	2	3	4	5	( )
43.	1	2	3	4	5	( )
44.	1	2	3	4	5	( )
45.	1	2	3	4	5	( )
46.	1	2	3	4	5	( ) (55)

II. 1. How does the instructor of this course compare with other teachers you have had at this school?

Among the very worst			About average			Among the very best	(56)
1	2	3	4	5	6	7	

2. How does the instructor of this course compare with other teachers you have had in this department?

Among the very worst			About average			Among the very best	(57)
1	2	3	4	5	6	7	

You are invited to comment further on the course and/or effectiveness of this instructor especially in areas not covered by the questions.

Developed by Robert C. Wilson and Evelyn R. Dienst, Center for Research and Development in Higher Education, University of California, Berkeley. Form SMF.

REFERENCES

Astin, A. W. and Lee, C. B. T. "Current Practices in the Evaluation and Training of College Teachers." *The Educational Record,* 1966, pp. 47, 361-375.

Costin, F., Greenough, W. & Menges, R. "Student Rating of Colllge Teaching: Reliability, Validity and Usefulness." *Review of Educational Research,* 1971, pp. 41, 511-535.

Creager, J. A. "Selected policies and practices in higher education." Washington, D. C.: American Council on Education, 1973. Cited in *The Chronicle of Higher Education.* October 15, 1973, 8 (4).

Doyle, K. O. & Whitely, S. E. "Student evaluations revisited: A reply to Rodin and Rodin." Measurement Services Center, University of Minnesota, 1972.

Eastman, A. M. "How visitation came to Carnegie-Mellon University." *Bulletin of the Association of Departments of English,* May, 1969.

Gessner, P.K. "Evaluation of instruction," *Science,* 1972, pp. 180, 566-569.

Hildebrand, M., Wilson, R. C. and Dienst, E. R. *Evaluating University Teaching,* Berkely: University of California, Center for Research and Development in Higher Education, 1971.

McKeachie, W. J., "Student ratings of faculty." *AAUP Bulletin,* 1969, pp. 55, 439-444.

Rodin, M. & Rodin, B. "Student evaluations of teachers: Students rate most highly instructors from whom they learn least." *Science,* 1972, pp. 177, 1164-1166.

Trent, J. W. & Cohen, A. M. "Research on teaching in higher education." In R. M. W. Travers (Ed.), *Second handbook of research on teaching.* Chicago: Rand McNally, 1973. pp. 997-1071.

Wilson, R. C. Generalizing from 12 teaching assistants to 500,000 faculty members: A critique of the Rodin and Rodin *Science* article on student evaluation of teaching. Teaching Innovation and Evaluation Services, University of California, Berkeley, 1973.

FOOTNOTES

[1] A more complete description of the study is presented in M. Hildebrand, R. C. Wilson and E. R. Dienst, *Evaluating University Teaching,* Berkeley: University of California, Center for Research and Development in Higher Education, 1971.

[2] Complete lists of these items may be found in the Appendices A & B.

An Improved Instrument for Measuring Teaching Effectiveness

G. Michael Crooch
and
George W. Krull, Jr.
Oklahoma State University

Introduction

This article reports the results of an attempt to prepare an improved, student-completed rating scale for evaluating teaching effectiveness. Included is a brief discussion of the need for teaching evaluation, a description of the instrument's development and administration guidelines, a summary of some observed benefits of student evaluations, and a presentation of the evaluation instrument.

With increasing frequency, academic administrators must justify the quality of teaching currently available within our nation's colleges and universities. Pressures for greater educational accountability originate with two primary sources—the general public and enrolled students. The general public is being asked to supply additional revenues to support burgeoning public education enrollments and accompanying costs. Commensurate with this added request for funds has arisen the demand for improved accountability of expenditures. Evidence of this pressure can be found in an emerging trend of less emphasis on research and more on teaching. Many state legislatures are passing laws which dictate a minimum number of classroom contact hours. At the same time, higher education governing bodies are increasingly scrutinizing the availability of faculty for counseling and advisement. In addition, students are expressing dissatisfaction with several aspects of the educational process and are demanding increased involvement in the appraisal of classroom teaching performance. As a result, the academic community will be required to demonstrate active participation in the measurement and improvement of teaching effectiveness.[1] This paper reports the result of efforts of the Department of Accounting faculty, Oklahoma State University, to create an instrument which will measure teaching effectiveness and, at the same time, provide an avenue for bringing about improved instruction. The report is divided into:

1. a description of the development of the instrument
2. guidelines for its administration and use
3. a discussion of the expected benefits from employing the instrument
4. experience with its use
5. a presentation of the instrument

Developing the Instrument

The search for a scaling instrument to measure and improve faculty teaching effectiveness began with an examination of the literature to determine if the research of others had developed techniques which would fit the needs of Oklahoma State University. Not surprisingly, much research has been done attempting just what these authors had set out to do, and many quality papers have been written on the subject. By far the best condensations of past research on student evaluation of teaching effectiveness are found in an article by Kent [2] and a more recent one by Costin, Greenough, and Menges.[3]

Many interesting aspects of evaluating teaching performance have been substantiated by past research. A few of these include:[4]

1. Student ratings of teaching effectiveness are infrequently used by administrators when recommending faculty for salary adjustment, promotion in rank, or tenure.
2. Well-prepared rating scales of teaching effectiveness may be used to improve course content and individual instructor's teaching effectiveness.
3. Student ratings of teaching effectiveness are valid, reliable measures.
4. Student ratings correlate highly with administrator's ratings of teaching effectiveness.
5. Most studies indicate that the relationship between the grade expected in a course and a student's evaluation of the instructor's teaching effectiveness show little positive correlation.
6. Student ratings of teaching effectiveness are not significantly influenced by an elective or required course, course difficulty, major or non-major course, grade point average, class size, and student's or teacher's sex.
7. Two factors, student's class rank and faculty's academic rank, bear strong relationship to student ratings of teaching effectiveness.
8. Student ratings are less critical than most faculty and students would expect.

In addition, the literature contains numerous sample instruments which profess to accurately measure teaching effectiveness. However, none of the instruments examined seemed to be in a form directly amenable to use in undergraduate accounting courses. As a result, the decision was made to create a new instrument incorporating the best parts of previously tested rating scales and the ideas of our faculty and students concerning the attributes which must be isolated to accurately measure teaching effectiveness. The development process included the following steps: First, an initial draft of the rating scale was prepared using a Purdue Rating Scale by Brandenberg and Remmers as a guide. Second, the initial draft was distributed for individual faculty comments and suggested changes. Third, a second draft was prepared and distributed for additional faculty comments. Fourth, a third draft was distributed among several large accounting classes and student feedback was obtained as to the adequacy of the instrument. Specific comments were elicited concerning the comprehensiveness of the instrument and suggestions for deletions and additions were noted. Fifth, a fourth draft was prepared and distributed to additional classes for comment and suggestions. The finalized instrument was administered in all undergraduate accounting classes (not participating in the drafting process) to evaluate teaching effectiveness and to take a final reading of the students' feelings concerning the adequacy of the instrument. No changes were necessary as the result of this final step.

The result of the above steps is an improved scale for measuring accounting teaching effectiveness. The instrument contains a total of eighteen items. Items one through eleven gather information using a modified semantic differential format with eleven gradations. Items twelve through fourteen rank both the instructor and the student with respect to his peers, and items fifteen through eighteen are essay questions which allow the student to elaborate upon the scaled responses.[5] The final instrument gathers information about the quality of all items which appear to affect the level of teaching effectiveness and, at the same time, gives the instructor some measure of his relative performance. The areas covered are:

1. Course organization.
2. Instructional materials.
3. Subject matter presentation.
4. Grading basis.
5. Intellectual motivation.
6. Interest in subject.
7. Self-reliance and confidence.
8. Sense of proportion and humor.
9. Attitude toward students.
10. Personal attributes.
11. Appearance.
12. Relative ranking of teaching in the course.
13. Cumulative grade point average.
14. Expected course grade.
15. Principal teaching strengths.
16. Principal teaching weaknesses.
17. Impact of class size and/or room.
18. Suggestions for improvement.

Guidelines for Administration and Use

Several decisions must be made concerning administrative procedures before efficient application of the instrument can be accomplished. Decisions concerning the timing and frequency of administration, the method of summarizing the results, and the use of the results are very important to the success of the evaluation effort.

Generally, student evaluations of teaching effectiveness are elicited at or very near the end of the course. The disadvantages of this practice are that the evaluating students do not have the opportunity to benefit from their suggestions, and that students who drop the course usually must do so prior to a designated final-drop date and are not present to evaluate the course. Therefore, student evaluations should be collected at an optimum time, which at Oklahoma State appeared to be sometime during the eleventh or twelfth week of a sixteen-week semester. This timing appears to be far enough along in the semester for the student to be able to evaluate the instructor's teaching effectiveness and, at the same time, does not involve the above disadvantages.

Great care must be taken to preserve student anonymity. The fact that the instructor does not know who completed an evaluation is equally important with the fact that students feel their answers will not be held against them. Each instructor should reassure his class that anonymity will be maintained, and he should emphasize the instruction on the form that the student make no attempt to identify himself. Ideally, the instructor will not be in the room while evaluations are being completed.

A critical step in properly analyzing the student evaluations lies in the proper summarization of the results. Care should be taken to emphasize the concentration of ratings to the exclusion of any extreme responses. Some students may have a strong emotional reaction to the instructor which impairs the objectivity of their evaluation. The possibility of such a reaction can be alleviated by minimizing the impact of any extremely high or low ratings.[6] We believe the most useful measure for interpreting the evaluations is the statistical median supplemented with the range of the second and third quartiles. The median and quartile measures have the advantage over the more frequently used mean and standard deviation in that they are not significantly affected by extreme values and allow concentration on the desired information.

The decision concerning who should receive a summary of the results must, in the final analysis, rest upon the ultimate use intended for the results. Several possible uses of the summarized results include: (1) as evidence of student satisfaction or dissatisfaction with teaching effectiveness (2) as an aid in self-improvement of teaching (3) as evidence to concerned parties of efforts to improve teaching effectiveness (4) as support for merit salary increases (5) as evidence to consider in granting promotions and tenure (6) as proof of doctoral candidates' teaching abilities.

The Department of Accounting presently believes the evaluation results may best be utilized in aiding the self-improvement of teaching effectiveness, as support for merit salary adjustments, and as evidence for promotions in rank. With such utilization as a guide, the following steps are taken. The completed forms are first summarized and reviewed by the instructor for his immediate benefit. The summarized results and all completed forms are then forwarded to the Department Head for review. After careful review, the faculty member and Department Head discuss the results. The instructor then returns to his classes, discusses the findings, and, hopefully, begins to alleviate any critical deficiencies. The completed forms remain the joint property of the faculty member and the Department Head and are retained for comparison with subsequent evaluation results.

The final decision which must be made regarding the administration of the instrument concerns how frequently an instructor should be evaluated. Under normal circumstances, maximum benefits are gained by evaluating every instructor once per year in each course. For the most conscientious instructors, the evaluation results will highlight only a few, if any, areas which need immediate attention. Where no serious deficiencies exist, teaching effectiveness will not be substantially impaired even if no adjustments are made. Therefore, a subsequent evaluation sooner than one year does not appear warranted. However, where serious impairments to teaching effectiveness are discovered, a strong argument can be made for requesting an evaluation each term until the deficiencies are corrected.

Benefits

Student evaluation has the potential to contribute many benefits to instructional efforts and faculty-student relationships. Some of these benefits are obvious and require little discussion. Therefore, only a few of the major benefits gained from the adoption of this improved instrument are discussed below.

The instrument's format allows evaluation of results by adopting the exception principle. An individual evaluating the results need only concentrate upon those teaching effectiveness attributes ranking below an acceptable range. Several of the items allude to more than one factor affecting teaching effectiveness. In case of a low rating on an item, the various factors may be considered to ascertain desirable corrections. The establishment of an acceptable range is an area requiring careful faculty and administrator consideration. In the final analysis, each institution must determine the minimum level of performance which will attain the desired quality of teaching effectiveness.

As with any project requiring the expenditure of scarce resources, an attempt was made to develop an improved instrument which maximizes the benefits attained while minimizing the required faculty and student time commitment. The use of the modified semantic differential format requires a minimum amount of time for administration while allowing the student to evaluate a broad range of teaching effectiveness attributes. The limited number of essay questions obtains student elaboration on very favorable or very unfavorable responses and those few attributes which cannot be fitted into the modified semantic differential form. Experience suggests the instrument requires no more than fifteen minutes to administer. For the benefits gained, this time seems a small price to pay relative to the overall commitment of time and resources to the educational process.

Summarizing the results is easily accomplished due to the numerical gradations of the format. Further, since the bulk of the data is in numerical form, computer processing may be used to summarize and provide initial comparisons for further analysis.

Since many accounting departments rely on doctoral candidates to teach lower-division courses, the improved instrument may be of additional benefit in at least two ways. First, frequent evaluation allows the department to carefully supervise the candidates and maintain a desired quality of instruction. Second, doctoral candidates seeking permanent employment may gain from objective evidence of their teaching abilities. In any case, prospective employers need (and probably desire) such evidence to adequately appraise a future employee's potential. By requiring doctoral candidates to obtain evaluations each term, data is readily available for each of these purposes.

Experience

Only subsequent improvements in teaching effectiveness and faculty-student rapport can demonstrate the benefits derived from implementing a student-completed rating scale. Unfortunately, the rating scale has not been in use a sufficient period to adequately assess its long-run benefits. Preliminary results, however, should indicate the rating scale's positive characteristics. To this end, preliminary reactions of the faculty and teaching assistants were obtained by circulating a brief questionnaire designed to gather attitudes and specific comments concerning the validity and usefulness of the rating scale's results. Questionnaire results were divided into:

1. faculty reactions
2. faculty perception of students' reactions.

The faculty and teaching assistants reacted favorably toward using the rating scale to measure teaching effectiveness and to indicate areas requiring improvement. Evidence supporting these favorable attitudes is based on three questionnaire responses. First, eighty-one percent replied that the rating scale responses were an approximate measure of their teaching effectiveness. The remaining respondents felt the scale *overstated* their teaching effectiveness with the exception of one who believed students were not able to determine the effectiveness of certain teaching methods for producing the best long-range results. Second, eighty-eight percent replied that the rating scale provides valid inputs for improving their performance. Those questioning the instrument's validity based their observations upon the belief that responses are a function of student motivation and upon the belief that certain items examined on the scale are not subject to change at will. Finally, significant changes have been made in teaching methods as a result of student criticisms. Among the changes which appear to have improved teaching effectiveness were:

1. Attempting to be more sympathetic toward students feelings and suggestions.

2. Introducing and discussing new material before requiring written problem assignments. (Previously, problems were due the meeting new material was introduced.)

3. Reducing examination ambiguity and length while better matching examination coverage with class discussion and assignments.

4. Changing textbooks.

5. Adopting a more modern dress code.

One change was made which did not appear to improve teaching effectiveness. Students complained about being required to submit written assignments daily. Changing the policy resulted in decreased class participation and an apparent decline in examination performance so the change was discontinued.

Little can be said at this point concerning student reactions to the rating scale. The rating scale's form and content continue to receive favorable acceptance by students interested in evaluating teaching effectiveness. Evaluation difficulties result more from student indifference toward the evaluation process than from the rating scale itself. While a small percentage of students appears indifferent, the vast majority appears to appreciate opportunities to evaluate teaching effectiveness.

SUMMARY

Student evaluations provide a formal communication channel in which students may express their feelings concerning the effectiveness of accounting instruction. This paper reports the results of an attempt by the Accounting Department of Oklahoma State University to prepare an improved, student-completed rating scale to evaluate teaching effectiveness. In an age when students and parents frequently complain about the lack of faculty and student interaction, a student expression concerning teaching evaluation is a welcome addition to the communication process without being a significant added burden to faculty and student. Of course, the degree to which the rewards of student evaluations may be reaped depends upon the extent of commitment of the participants. Without this cooperation, the project is doomed before it begins.

The definite trend toward greater educational accountability may ultimately result in mandatory student evaluation. If mandatory evaluation becomes a reality, the accounting department which has had the foresight to implement an instrument specifically designed for accounting courses will be in a position to account for its teaching effectiveness.

OKLAHOMA STATE UNIVERSITY
Department of Accounting
Rating Scale for Teaching Effectiveness

Instructor———————————— Room———————— Course————————

This rating is to be as impersonal as possible. Do not sign your name or make any mark which may serve to identify you.

Circle one of the numbers on the line which indicates your judgment of the teaching effectiveness in this course.

1. COURSE ORGANIZATION:

10 9 8 7	6 5 4 3	2 1 0
Clear statement of expectations, assignments, attendance policy, grading basis; closely follows assignment time budget	Imprecise as to expectations; class work usually lags behind assignments in course work	Little attention as to work of students; erratic progress

2. INSTRUCTIONAL MATERIALS:

10 9 8 7	6 5 4 3	2 1 0
Textbook, readings, problem and case material at appropriate level	Usefulness of instructional material varies quite a bit	Assignment material too difficult or too simple

3. SUBJECT MATTER PRESENTATION:

10 9 8 7	6 5 4 3	2 1 0
Clear, definite, forceful, and relates to assigned material	Sometimes mechanical and monotonous; often class presentation is unrelated to assignments	Indefinite, involved, monotonous and class presentation is rarely related to assignments

4. GRADING BASIS:

10 9 8 7	6 5 4 3	2 1 0
Tests are fair and related to course material; grading basis explained	Tests discriminate somewhat as to course achievement and grading basis varies	Test questions are ambiguous, unrelated to class material grading basis unexplained

5. INTELLECTUAL MOTIVATION:

10 9 8 7	6 5 4 3	2 1 0
Motivates students to considerable intellectual effort; arouses interest in the subject	Occasionally motivating and interesting	Destroys interest and does not motivate

6. INTEREST IN SUBJECT:

10 9 8 7	6 5 4 3	2 1 0
Appears keenly interested in subject; has enthusiasm	Seems mildly interested and has moderate enthusiasm	Subject seems boring to him

7. SELF-RELIANCE AND CONFIDENCE:

10	9	8	7	6	5	4	3	2	1	0

Sure of himself; meets difficulties with poise   Fairly self-confident; occasionally disconcerted   Hesitant, timid, uncertain

8. SENSE OF PROPORTION AND HUMOR:

10	9	8	7	6	5	4	3	2	1	0

Keeps proper balance; nor overly critical not over-sensitive   Fairly well-balanced   Over-serious; no sense of relative values

9. ATTITUDE TOWARD STUDENTS:

10	9	8	7	6	5	4	3	2	1	0

Courteous and considerate   Tries to be considerate but finds it difficult at times   Unsympathetic and inconsiderate

10. PERSONAL ATTRIBUTES:

10	9	8	7	6	5	4	3	2	1	0

No distracting mannerisms   More than a few annoying mannerisms   Repulsive mannerisms (identify in No. 16)

11. APPEARANCE:

10	9	8	7	6	5	4	3	2	1	0

Well-groomed   Somewhat untidy   Slovenly

12. Mark an "X" through the number which in your judgment best ranks the effectiveness of teaching in this course compared to other courses you have taken.

   (5) highest fifth   (4) next to highest   (3) middle fifth   (2) next to lowest   (1) lowest fifth

13. My cumulative grade point average is:

   ( ) 4.0-3.6   ( ) 3.5-3.1   ( ) 3.0-2.6   ( ) 2.5-2.1   ( ) 2.0 or less

14. The grade I expect in the course is: A   B   C   D   F

15. What were the most effective aspects in the *teaching* of this course?

16. What were the principal weaknesses, if any, in the *teaching* of this course?

17. What impact, if any, did the class size and/or the room have on the effectiveness of the teacher?

18. Please list below any suggestions to improve the effectiveness in the teaching of this course.

FOOTNOTES

[1] Recently one state's Higher Education Governing Board instituted a requirement that recommendations for merit salary adjustment or promotion in rank must be supported with evidence of classroom teaching effectiveness. Failure or hesitance of the administration to submit evidence will require that state's Board to take more direct means to ensure that measurements of classroom teaching effectiveness are collected.

[2] Laura Kent, "Student Evaluation of Teaching," *The Educational Record.* XLVII (Summer, 1966), pp. 376-406.

[3] Frank Costin, William T. Greenough, and Robert J. Menges, "Student Ratings of College Teaching: Reliability, Validity, and Usefulness," *Review of Educational Research,* XXXXI, No. 5 (December, 1971), pp. 511-535.

[4] See Kent; Costin, Greenough, and Menges; and James W. Pattillo, "The Student Evaluates the Instructor," Chapter Eight in Committee to Prepare a Revised Accounting Teachers Guide, *Accounting Instruction: Concepts and Practices* (2nd. ed.; Cincinnati: South-Western Publishing Co., 1968).

[5] The complete instrument appears as the last section of this paper.

[6] Committee to Prepare a Revised Accounting Teacher's Guide, p. 188.

The Student as Godfather?
The Impact of Student Ratings on Academia*

John A. Centra
Educational Testing Service—Princeton

Introduction

This paper is addressed to the important question: "What is the ultimate impact of student evaluations on teaching and learning?" The article presents evidence and observations concerning the effects of student ratings on the individual instructor, on teaching generally, on students, on the administration, and on the college unit. Substantial documentation is incorporated in the references cited.

There are some who fear the college student, by virtue of the apparent increasing emphasis on student ratings of professors, could become the "Godfather" of the academic community. More exactly, they fear too much emphasis could be put on these ratings and that, generally speaking, the power that students might acquire would not be in the best interest of the academic community.

These individuals can, in fact, point to the medieval universities as an example of unreasonable student influence over teachers. As Hastings Rashdall states in his writings about the medieval European universities, students at the University of Bologna not only paid teachers a "collecta" or fee (which apparently was determined by a teacher's ability to haggle), but they also could report teacher irregularities to the rector. For example, law texts were divided into segments, and each instructor was required to cover a particular segment by a specified date; to enforce this statute, the rector appointed a committee of students to report on dilatory professors, who were then required to pay a fine for each day that they had fallen behind.

While few people would take seriously the possibility that students are on the verge of assuming the role they played in medieval days, some do question the ultimate impact of student evaluations on teaching and learning. Some of their reservations will be made more specific later in this paper. In addition, evidence of the positive effects of student ratings will be discussed, and finally, since the impact of student ratings on certain aspects of academic life is not totally known, some possible consequences are presented.

Comments have been grouped within five categories: the impact or possible impact of student ratings on the individual instructor, on teaching generally, on students, on administrators, and on the college.

The Individual Instructor

The person the ratings are meant to influence most is the individual teacher. There has been a good deal of skepticism over how much effect the ratings actually have on changing or improving in-

---

*Paper presented at the First Invitational Conference on Faculty Effectiveness as Measured by Students, Temple University, April 1973.

struction—particularly when the results are seen only by the individual teacher. Faculty conservatism, when it comes to educational changes, has been a well-known tendency, although there are signs that it may be less true now than in the past. For example, according to the responses of some 2800 college teachers to the question, "When did you last make changes in the teaching methods you are using?", about a fourth indicated that they had never made changes. On the other hand, about half said that they *had* changed their methods during the past two years. Thus, it looks as if all college teachers should not be indicted with the time-worn stereotypes of stodginess and traditionalism. Many apparently are willing to change their methods.

The question, though, is what causes teachers to change and, more germane to the topic, can ratings by students lead to any noticeable changes among college teachers? While a few investigators have noted that the ratings that teachers receive seem to improve over time, one cannot assume a cause and effect relationship. Those changes could have been caused by any number of factors other than the initial student feedback.

One of the best ways to investigate the effects of student ratings on an instructor's practices is to employ an experimental design in which random groups of teachers receive feedback from students while other teachers—those in the control groups—do not. This writer recently completed such a study within the past year with the cooperation of over 400 faculty members at five colleges. The details of that study are presented elsewhere (Centra, 1972), and are not repeated here, but the results are worthy of further consideration. The major conclusions of the study were, first, that changes in instruction (as assessed by repeated student ratings) occurred after only a half semester for instructors whose self-evaluations were considerably better than were their student ratings. If, in other words, teachers were especially "unrealistic" in how they viewed their teaching—unrealistic relative to their students' views, that is—then they tended to make some changes in their instructional practices, even though they had only a half semester to do so. Furthermore, such variables as the subject area of the course, sex of the instructor, and number of years of teaching experience did not distinguish which instructors made changes; or to put it another way, none of the subgroups of teachers formed by these variables were more likely to change. The second conclusion was that a wider variety of instructors changed if given more than a half semester, and if they had some minimal information to help them interpret their scores. Consider the implications of each of these findings.

Starting with the first result, why were changes in teaching procedures related to the discrepancy between self-evaluations and student ratings? Actually this result was predicted at the outset of the study because there was fairly good reason to expect it, based on social psychological theory. Several similar theories help explain the finding. Most are referred to as self-consistency or equilibrium theories whose central motion is an individual's actions are strongly influenced by his desire to maintain a consistent cognitive condition with respect to his evaluations of himself. When student ratings are much poorer than an instructor's self-ratings, a condition of imbalance (Heider, 1958), dissonance (Festinger, 1957), or incongruency (Newcomb, 1961; Secord & Backman, 1965) is created in the instructor. In an attempt to become more consistent, or in more theoretical terms to restore a condition of equilibrium, the instructor changes in the direction indicated by his students' ratings.

These theories assume most instructors place a high value on collective student opinion and instructors know how to go about making changes. Undoubtedly some teachers merely write off student judgment as unreliable or unworthy, and for these individuals, changes are unlikely even though they may be called for. At least the changes are unlikely if the only motivation comes from within the individual teacher. Increasingly, however, student ratings of professors are becoming public information, and in these instances there is undoubtedly a good deal of social pressure to change. In fact, not only is there social pressure, but in some instances there is economic pressure, since the ratings may be used in salary and tenure deliberations. But as already stated, it is not always clear to the teacher how to change, if indeed he or she believes the change would be an improvement. This leads to the implications of the second finding from the five-college study.

With additional time and with some interpretative information, the ratings for a more diverse group of teachers had changed in a positive direction. Not surprisingly, many teachers need more time to change their procedures, particularly in those areas that cannot be quickly altered (clarifying course objectives, for example). Yet if student ratings are to have *maximum* impact, more needs to be done in interpreting the results for instructors and in helping them improve. One of the reasons that instructors need help in interpreting their ratings is that the ratings are typically skewed in a positive direction. Most teachers do not realize this. On a five-point scale, the teacher may view his mean score of 3.6 as above average, when actually it may well be only average or even below average if compared to other teachers. Parenthetically, instructor self-ratings, not surprisingly, are skewed even more positively than student ratings. And faculty peer ratings based on classroom visits, according to some data recently collected by this writer, are also generally more favorable than student ratings. In any event, some kind of normative or comparative data is important for interpreting student ratings, and, perhaps, the more the better. The instructor might be given the choice of comparing his students' responses to those of other teachers at his institution, or to those of members of his department; or perhaps he may prefer a more cosmopolitan comparison—such as to instructors from a sample of other institutions, or perhaps to a national sample of teachers in his field. A variety of comparisons might be made available to the instructor so that he can decide which are most meaningful.

Some of these comparison data are already being made available to instructors, though not always with the variety suggested above. But unfortunately that does not totally solve the problem. There will still be some instructors who need special help, and for this reason Kenneth Eble (1971), for one, has suggested that individual instructional counseling be made freely available. A teacher counselor might not only help instructors interpret their student evaluations but could, of course, also suggest particular ways in which to improve. A few institutions are already doing this, but in these times of tight money this will probably remain a limited endeavor.

Another possibility now being pursued by the writer might therefore be considered. In place of an individual counselor the next best thing might be substituted: the computer. One of the remarkable feats of the computer is that it can be programmed to produce a verbal interpretation of a numerical summary. Rather than means, standard deviations, or percentile ranks, each professor could instead get several paragraphs of prose telling him how he differs from his own expectations and how he differs from some predesignated group, such as other teachers in his field. The number-leery professor need not worry about whether his scores are significantly different—the computer will make that interpretation. Moreover it would even be possible to refer the instructor to specific materials, books, or even video tapes pertinent to his weaknesses. For example, if students indicated that the course objectives were not made clear, or if they rated the quality of examinations poorly, there would be several excellent references dealing with these topics suggested to the instructor. In fact, there's really no need to rely on the computer to produce these suggestions—that ought to be done right now.

Before discussing other categories, one last point regarding the effects of student ratings on the individual teacher might be made. With the emphasis generally put on mean scores or percentile ranks of scores, the individual teacher may be influenced to see his class only as a homogeneous glob. Anyone who has taught knows that quite frequently there are several types of students in the typical class, each of whom may be reacting a little differently to the teacher and the course. These different types and their various viewpoints do not mean that the ratings are unreliable in the sense that there is a great deal of fluctuation or inconsistency in student responses. Student ratings *are* reliable as indicated by the numerous intraclass reliability studies reported. But are there identifiable subgroups of students who differ systematically in their ratings? Is there, in short, some rhyme or reason to the diversity of viewpoints that may exist in the typical class?

One way to investigate this question is to use factor analytic techniques that allow one to group individuals rather than items as is usually the case (see Tucker & Messick, 1963). One study that looked at this question investigated students' general notions about types of teachers, rather than their specific ratings of individual teachers (Rees, 1969). Other analyses—first with three large classes separately and then across a larger sample of courses—indicate there are frequently three or sometimes four points of view represented in a single class. Each of these groups sees various aspects of the course or the instruction they are receiving somewhat differently then the other groups. One group, for example, may have rated the instructor as generally ineffective, but at the same time indicated that the instructor was well organized and usually accessible; another group might have rated the instructor as ineffective and inaccessible. Unfortunately, there is not currently enough information about student characteristics in this study to describe the groups. Ultimately, however, the individual teacher may detect relevant subgroups or points of view in the class; these points of view might be identified by student characteristics information, or they might be identified by patterns of ratings. Until then, teachers should be encouraged to look at the distribution of student responses to the items on their rating form—and not only at the mean scores. While no one expects instructors to please all of their students all of the time, they ought to be aware of how they interact with different segments of the class.

Impact on Teaching Generally

Closely related to the effects of student ratings on the individual teacher is the possible impact that they have on teaching generally. The critics of student ratings claim that an undue emphasis on the ratings, such as using them to assist in decisions on faculty promotions, can have adverse effects on instruction. What are some of these adverse effects? First, some critics claim that the ratings do not allow for individual styles of teaching, that they instead force everyone to be measured on the same yardstick. According to one skeptic of student ratings, few people would try to assess artists or composers on the same yardstick. That skeptic goes on to say, in an article in *The American Scholar*, that:

> The art critic need not evaluate portraits painted by Picasso, Whistler, and Rembrandt in terms of criteria for effectiveness common to all three. He finds it possible to examine each artist's work in terms of the artist's own goals, or to identify the strengths and weaknesses of an individual painting in terms of relations of parts to the whole (Kossoff, 1972, p. 89).

Even though teaching and art are not entirely comparable, we know enough about teaching to know that individuals can have quite different styles, and that they should probably develop the style that best fits their personality and approach.

A second adverse effect of student ratings, according to the same critics, is that they encourage traditional modes of teaching. Most rating forms are indeed directed at classes taught in some combination of lecture-discussion, but logically so—that happens to be the way most courses have been taught and the forms are merely reflecting what is typically the case. The question is, however, are other methods such as student-centered learning, or nondirective teaching, or team teaching being stifled by the typical student rating forms? Probably so if an institution does not allow some flexibility in the application of student ratings. For some courses, and this is still a relatively small number on most campuses, supplementing or disregarding items in the traditional rating forms may be required.

Flexibility in the employment of student ratings is extremely critical. Many of the widely used forms have been developed through what might be called the consensus approach. In other words the developers have asked samples of faculty members (or faculty members and students) to identify specific characteristics that are important in teaching. Those areas or items for which there was the greatest consensus were then included in the rating instrument. Generally speaking, the items have centered around such factors as course organization, teacher-student interaction, and communication or verbal fluency. This approach does not produce an instrument that reflects any particular theory of teaching. And that probably has made good sense because no college faculty is likely to agree on a single theory of teaching.

While most forms allow individual instructors to add their own items to a basic set, there are other ways in which the rating forms can be even more flexible. If the items are to be used in making decisions on faculty members, then the individual teacher might be allowed to eliminate those items that are not relevant to his style. Better yet, a system might be implemented which allows teachers to both choose and weigh in advance the items which they feel most adequately reflect their style of teaching and what they are trying to accomplish in the course. At least one institution is now working on such an approach.

Impact on Administrators

Another group that student ratings influence—albeit more indirectly than previous groups—are college administrators. Two observations are offered regarding this. First, where the ratings are used in making decisions on promotions, the dean or department chairman's job should become a little easier.

National surveys frequently reveal the judgments of one or more administrators are relied on to assess teaching effectiveness, particularly at smaller colleges. Not many people would defend this as a very wise or valid approach. If evidence provided by student evaluations means not only wiser decisions but also ones that are more easily defended, then students' evaluations make the administrators' jobs easier and more effective. Some would undoubtedly debate this point.

Student evaluations may well be contributing to what seems to be a current groundswell for administrator evaluations by faculty members. Instruments to evaluate administrator performance are frequently requested from the Educational Testing Service. If faculty can be evaluated by their constituents, then so can (and are) administrators. For example, the trustees of the State University of New York announced in January that the presidents of the 29 colleges operated by the state will have to undergo intensive evaluation of their records every five years. But it is not definite that a handy-dandy machine-scored instrument could be developed that would measure reliably and validly an administrator's performance. More likely the change is for administrator accountability in which an individual is accountable not only to his superiors but also to his subordinates.

Impact on Students

According to the results of the ACE 1972 annual survey of freshmen, students feel generally that faculty promotions ought to be based in part on student ratings. The opinion was endorsed by three-quarters of the students from the 373 institutions in the survey and comes as no surprise. The past decade has, of course, been a time when students have demanded a greater role in institutional decision-making, and the evaluation of teaching would appear to be an area in which they feel they can make a unique contribution. Where student ratings have been incorporated into faculty evaluation procedures, the impact on students is likely to be quite positive; at least each of them can feel that he or she is helping the institution make important educational decisions. This is not to be taken lightly. While in the past teachers and administrators have been willing to give students a say in such areas as the establishment of student personnel policies and regulations, they have been more reluctant to relinquish their hold on academic decision-making.

Aside from this, probably the major impact of student ratings on students is provided by published course and teacher critiques. While some institutions make public the results of college-sponsored student evaluations (and some publish course guides based on detailed descriptions provided by the instructor), most of the critiques are based on surveys that are student initiated and conducted. As might be suspected, these student-produced critiques vary considerably in quality from one institution to another; in fact, they may vary from year to year at single institutions, depending upon those involved. The worst of the critiques have been based on poor samples and frequently border on sensationalism by highlighting the juiciest of criticisms. These critiques do neither the teachers nor the students much good. But what about the better publications; what about the critiques based on thorough methodology and which, as in some instances, also give the teacher an opportunity to respond to his student evaluations? Do they have a suitable reason for being? One might argue that they provide information that the college catalog or other publications do not provide and this would seem to be a valid purpose. Nevertheless there are many faculty members who object strongly to student conducted course ratings. Their objections have been delineated by Kerlinger in a 1971 article in *School and Society*. He argues that student initiated ratings result in "instructor hostility, resentment, and distrust," and thus alienate faculty members from their work. He goes on to suggest that ratings are legitimate only if conducted voluntarily by professors and used for self-improvement. Obviously then, not only is there concern for who initiates and conducts a student rating of instruction program, but also to what end the results are to be used.

A major study of the effects of student ratings is needed where ratings are used to assist in promotion decisions. There are a number of questions that such a study might investigate. For example, to what extent do faculty become alienated? Which types become most alienated? Does it encourage traditional teaching and limit teaching styles, as already discussed? Does it erroneously reinforce the notion in students that the instructor is largely responsible for how much students learn in a course? This last point may be true regardless of how student rating results are used and in spite of the fact that many of the rating forms ask students about their own effort and involvement in the course. But the major question to be answered by such a study is whether more defensible promotion decisions are made when student evaluations are included as part of faculty assessment.

Impact on the College

Changes that take place among individual teachers—or at least among some teachers—have already been discussed. But can an institution, or perhaps the departments within an institution, learn something about themselves from student evaluations? A corollary question is: "What can the institution or department then do about what they've learned?"

Starting at the department level, a seldom mentioned though seemingly worthwhile use of student ratings is that of providing departments with information about the effectiveness of their offerings as seen by students. To do this it would be necessary to combine the ratings of all members in a department, and items dealing with specific as well as general course objectives should be included in the assessment. In addition to these course-instructor evaluations, a major field questionnaire might be given to seniors. Princeton University, for one, has been using a major field or department questionnaire. While not the typical application of student evaluations, the assessment of departmental offerings would seem to be worth consideration by other institutions.

Another point that might be made concerning the departments is that there are some interesting variations in the evaluations that teachers in different subject fields receive. Among a group of some 450 teachers, for example, the writer found that courses in the natural sciences, relative to those in humanities, social sciences, and education and applied subjects, were seen by students as having a faster pace, as being more difficult, and as being less likely to stimulate student interest. In addition, students perceived the natural science teachers in the sample as less open to other viewpoints. Humanities teachers, in comparison to those in the other three general subject areas, were likely to inform students of how they were to be evaluated, and there was less agreement between the announced objectives of humanities courses and what was actually taught.

The obvious question is whether it is the subject matter itself that produces these differences or the types of individuals within each of the subject areas. It may well be a combination of both. At any rate, patterns of ratings would indicate that subject fields or departments might focus on certain apparent weaknesses (for example, humanities professors might attend workshops on improving their evaluation procedures).

The whole notion of focusing on weaknesses highlighted by student evaluations could be applied at the college level even more generally. If a college is able to compare itself to other colleges—that is, if the aggregate ratings of all teachers can be compared—then it may be possible to identify specific weaknesses. Workshops in that particular aspect of instruction might then be offered to assist in faculty improvement.

CONCLUSION

This paper has attempted to discuss the effects or possible effects of student evaluations on academia. Throughout the discussion the major effects are, to a large extent, dependent upon how the ratings are used. Their primary uses can perhaps be summarized best by adapting Michael Scriven's (1967) terms for the two major functions of tests: formative and summative evaluation. Tests used formatively, according to Scriven, give the instructor periodic feedback on his students' progress, this telling the instructor what needs to be stressed in the future. The summative function of tests, as the term implies, is a way of providing a summative evaluation of each student at some point in time.

When student ratings of instruction are used formatively—that is, when they are used by instructors as a source of feedback on their teaching—the evidence indicates that some changes are made by the instructor. And most likely, better interpretation of the ratings will help bring about even more improvement. The effects of using student ratings in a summative way—that is, in making administrative decisions on faculty—is a little more difficult to assess. As a researcher it is easy to argue that more needs to be known about the side effects. But department chairmen and deans are faced with increasingly tougher tenure-promotion decisions; and many faculty members feel that their teaching is not being rewarded with current evaluation systems. These other views must also be considered. Certainly student evaluations are no less trustworthy than other methods now available to assess teaching performance, and when combined with other methods, they probably contribute to a fair judgment.

Students, through student ratings, are not likely to become a Mario Puzo type of Godfather to the academic community. But this is not to say they might not function in a limited way as proper Godfathers. Traditionally, of course, a Godfather has had a much more positive image; he essentially is one who helps provide guidance and direction to those in his charge. While this is not to suggest that students are the new saviors of academia, or that college teachers must rely on the guidance of their students, a well-designed student ratings program can do more to benefit than to harm the academic community.

REFERENCES

Centra, J.A. "The Utility of Student Ratings for Instructional Improvement." *Project Report 72-16*. Princeton, N.J., Educational Testing Service, 1972.

Eble, K. *The Recognition And Evaluation Of Teaching: Project to improve college teaching*, Salt Lake City, Utah, 1971.

Festinger, L. A. *Theory of Cognitive Dissonance*. Evanston, Ill.: Row, Peterson, 1957.

Heider, F. *The Psychology of Interpersonal Relationships*. New York: Wiley, 1958.

Kerlinger, E. "Student Evaluation of University Professors." *School and Society*, October, 1971, pp. 353-356.

Kossoff, E. "Evaluating College Professors by 'Scientific' Methods." *The American Scholar*, Winter 1972, pp. 79-93.

Newcomb, T.M. *The Acquaintance Process*. New York: Holt, Rinehart and Winston, 1961.

Rees, R.D. "Dimensions of Students' Points of View in Rating College Teaching." *Journals of Educational Psychology,, 1969, 60*(6), pp. 476-482.

Scriven, M. "The Methodology of Evaluation." American Educational Research Association monograph series on curriculum evaluation, No. 1, *Perspectives of curriculum evaluation*. 1967.

Secord, P.F., & C.W. Backman, "An Interpersonal Approach to Personality." In B.A. Maher (Ed.), *Progress in Experimental Personality Research*, Vol. 2. New York: Academic Press, 1965.

Tucker, L.R. & S. Messick, "An Individual Difference Model for Multi-dimensional Scaling." *Psychometrika*, 1963, *28*(4), pp. 333-367.

Some Approaches to Faculty Evaluation

K. Fred Skousen
Brigham Young University

Introduction

This paper presents the result of a survey conducted to provide information concerning the extent and nature of formalized models currently being used to evaluate faculty performance in schools of business. Five case illustrations are presented. The cases incorporate a variety of ideas and procedures which may be of interest to those contemplating instituting or modifying a data based faculty evaluation model.

Previous articles in this section repeatedly mention the increasing demand for accountability of university administrators and faculty. If faculty performance will be evaluated more carefully in the future than in the past, then more definitive, objective, effective methods and standards should be developed for carrying out this important function. This paper presents some of the approaches currently being used to evaluate the faculty of schools of business at several universities. Various forms, where pertinent, unique, or generally representative, are also provided in the appendices. Hopefully the ideas and illustrations included will stimulate thinking and action toward improving faculty evaluation procedures.

A Survey

In order to gain some appreciation of "current practice" of faculty evaluation, a letter was sent to the deans of schools of business at 13 universities. These schools represent large and small, private and state universities, and are geographically located throughout the United States. All but two of the deans responded. (The respondents and their respective schools are listed in Appendix 1.)

For most schools in the sample, an attempt is being made to measure and quantitatively assess faculty productivity in much the same sense that professors try to quantify a judgment of student performance for grading purposes. As with any evaluation the subjective element is present.

Before proceeding with the case illustrations resulting from this limited survey, some of the issues involving evaluation generally and faculty evaluation specifically are briefly discussed.

Faculty Evaluation Issues

Questions relating to faculty evaluation are numerous. Many of the issues have been raised and discussed in some detail in earlier papers in this section. In the specific context of faculty evaluations, an important consideration is the purpose for which the evaluation is being conducted. Possible reasons include:

1. for hiring, retention, promotion, and tenure decisions.

2. for annual salary adjustment decisions

3. for feedback to the faculty member to assist him in correcting weaknesses and in improving strengths.

(In a normative ordering of importance, the reasons listed probably should be reversed; unfortunately, the order given probably is more in conformance with practice, with little emphasis on (3).)

Another basic question concerns what is being evaluated. Is it the teaching effectiveness of the faculty member, his research, his academic or professional service, the degree of his personal professional development, or some combination of these important aspects of faculty productivity? The likely answer is the evaluation of total productivity (total performance). However, to accomplish this requires careful specification of individual criteria for excellence in teaching,[1] research, and service. Because research productivity is most easily quantified, too often it becomes the sole measure for judging total faculty performance.

Differing viewpoints and associated behavioral problems are still other factors to be considered. For example, younger faculty members want to know explicitly what is expected of them. Exactly what are the rules of the game? What does it take to make associate or full professor? Will developing a particular course curriculum offer as much potential for reward as publishing an article or serving on a university committee?

Older faculty members have valid concerns also. They worry about the rules being changed mid-way in the ball game, or perhaps retroactively. Research and other variables given considerable current emphasis may be of little interest to certain faculty members.

These difficulties are compounded because many evaluation systems are not well-defined, are shrouded in secrecy, provide few opportunities for prior explanation of what is expected, or furnish little feedback as to the results of the evaluation process. Consequently, the direction and magnitude of the desired effort of faculty members is not maximized, and university administrators are less successful than they might be in utilizing faculty resources.

Finally, what are the alternative evaluation methods that should be considered, and how effective are they, collectively or singly? Obviously, there are a variety of methods for evaluating faculty performance. They range from the single assessment of a department chairman to the combined judgment by an evaluation committee. The latter may be comprised of representatives from the department, the college, the university at large, and perhaps students. The evaluation process may be based upon little data, accumulated haphazardly, or upon an organized system of interviews and detailed reports which summarize faculty activity for the year. Student evaluations relating to teaching performance may play a prominent role or be non-existent.[2] Classroom visits by department chairmen or others to check on teaching effectiveness, or feedback from alumni, may or may not be used. The extent of usage of peer group evaluations or self-appraisals also may vary considerably. The illustration of how some of these methods are applied in practice is the subject of the next part of this paper.

A second part of the evaluation question, how effective are the evaluation techniques, is difficult, if not impossible, to answer. The following quote, while specifically related to teaching effectiveness, seems applicable to the evaluation of total faculty performance:

> The inadequacies of our present procedures for evaluating and recognizing teaching effectiveness are most apparent where decisions are being made about retention, promotion, and tenure. The decision for or against tenure is critically important both for the young teacher and the institution, but in thousands of instances each year this decision is made on the basis of extremely tenuous information about his teaching ability; a limited amount of student response, usually informal, undiscriminated, and distorted by successive reporters; judgments by deans, chairmen or colleagues deriving from social conversations and corridor exchanges; and guesses about classroom effectiveness based on the faculty member's performance of quite different institutional duties.[3]

A carefully developed and properly implemented system of faculty evaluation, while not without difficulties, can be a significant and positive step forward, at least for those faculty and administrators who are seeking positive motivation through a merit-reward system and improved performance through evaluative feedback.

Illustrations from Selected Approaches

The following discussion of five cases incorporates most of the ideas that are being used by the schools surveyed. The particular elements described in this section were not selected because they are necessarily considered the "best" nor the "worst", *but because they are representative of the impressive variety of procedures being tried.* Obviously, only a brief summary of the essential or unusual elements of each illustration can be presented here. Also, the actual mechanics of implementing these ideas, while an important aspect, are not dealt with to any great extent.

University of Washington. The approach used in the School of Business and in the Graduate School of Business Administration (SBA) at the University of Washington is based upon an annual review of performance of all faculty members by senior faculty in their respective departments, by department chairmen, and by the dean. Teaching and research are the major factors considered; service, while of significance, is of lesser importance. The five department chairmen in the SBA serve as an advisory committee to the dean in reviewing all evaluations. This committee presents the results of their combined judgments to the dean, expressed in terms of dollar amounts for merit salary increases and for promotions in rank. A "Performance Record" form[4] is used so that relatively uniform information is available for all faculty members. This form is to be completed by the faculty by the end of the calendar year, and the review process occurs during the winter quarter and early spring quarter. The "Performance Record" form is supplemented by a complete bibliography of publications for each faculty member, and student evaluations of teaching.

Two particular points are of interest concerning the University of Washington approach. First, is the strong emphasis on student ratings of teaching. The University of Washington has had an Office of Student Ratings for at least twenty-five years, although, historically, utilization of this service was optional for individual faculty members, and the results of evaluations were sent to department chairmen and deans only upon authorization by the instructors who had been rated. In 1969 the Faculty Senate passed a resolution endorsing regular student ratings for all classes. Further, the Faculty Council of the SBA voted to make the practice mandatory for all faculty in the SBA; many faculty opt to have the survey results sent to department chairman and or the dean. The evaluation questionnaire currently being used is a university wide form. (See Appendix II.)

Second, is the experience of the SBA at Washington concerning the quantitative weighting of variables in evaluating faculty performance. Several years ago an attempt was made to assign weights to individual items on the "Performance Record." They found the use of weights tended to be confusing, lead to lengthy debates and nit-picking, and that equitable decisions regarding merit increases were not contingent upon the utilization of quantitative weights or measures. The subjective nature of many items made it difficult, if not impossible, to assign weights which would be regarded by the faculty as fair and just. This experience is contradictory to the University of Georgia approach described later.

University of Utah. A basic, and perhaps unique, element in the faculty evaluation system used by the College of Business at the University of Utah is a pre-promotional conference. A professor who considers himself ready for promotion meets with his department chairman and the Departmental Advisory Committee on Promotions, the preeminent group who eventually will decide on his promotion, to discuss his future programs and plans. In effect, the professor selects from among various channels[5] and pre-determined criteria for promotion those best suited to his situation, and then has an opportunity to receive an opinion *in advance* as to whether or not his program would appear to qualify him for the promotion he seeks. He avoids two common traps in evaluation and promotional systems. First, he does not expend a year or two of effort on a program which is subsequently described as being inadequate. Second, the standards are mutually understood, and both the people who are to make the promotional decision and the person seeking the promotion are in basic agreement, *in advance,* on what is expected.

Another interesting feature of the

system used at the University of Utah is the Annual Goals Conference. At this conference, each member of each department outlines his personal and professional teaching, research, and service objectives for at least the coming year. In the instance of those people who aspire to promotion, these statements of personal goals and plans are an important ingredient.

Although, as expected, Utah's experience with the above procedures has exposed some ambiguities and difficulties in implementation, by and large, the program is considered successful. It has also relieved a great deal of tension and unhappiness that is frequently associated with faculty evaluation, specifically as it relates to academic promotions.

University of Illinois. The evaluation model used by the Department of Accountancy at the University of Illinois is based upon both peer group evaluation and student evaluation inputs. The peer group evaluation consists of a quantitative rating for each faculty member by his colleagues. There are seven areas considered in this evaluation: instruction; service to the profession; service to the university, college, and department; special assignments for the Department; publications; delivery of professional papers; and retention factor. For each of these variables a measure is assigned as follows:

1 = outstanding
2 = better than average
3 = average
4 = below average
5 = unsatisfactory

An overall average is then computed for each faculty member.

Guidelines for the evaluation areas are included in the following policy statement:

Instruction obviously includes consideration of teaching loads and effectiveness as a teacher. It also includes such factors as to whether the man keeps his courses up-to-date.

Service to the profession. Since education for business has strong professional connotations, participation in professional organizations is important. Election to offices, participation in technical programs, committee activity, and attendance at meetings of professional groups representative of the field of the faculty member, are considered in faculty advancement.

Recognition of faculty members by professional organizations through awards, achievement citations, special appearances on important programs, and general recognition of special competence are important considerations in faculty advancement.

Editorships and service on editorial boards of well-known publications provide important evidence of professional competence and recognition.

Special assignments would include the development of new courses or the substantial improvement of existing courses.

Publications. While the quantity of publications is important, the quality as reflected by its import or significance obviously must be the preeminent consideration. The caliber of the journal accepting the publication certainly is one factor in judging the merit of a publication. The ultimate hope from the Department's standpoint is that publications will reflect credit upon the Department and influence favorably its position in national rankings of accounting departments and the business schools of which they are a part.

The *retention factor* may reflect many things but certainly consideration must be given to the market factors, to such personal qualities as attitude, appearance, etc. Market factors include consideration of the general rise in offer price for new assistant professors, difficulty in recruiting replacements because the specialized compentency is in such high demand, the man's attractiveness to other universities, etc. On the matter of attitude, the following factors are germane: Lack of integrity; inability to fit into the work situation; extreme emotionalism in dealing with faculty, students, and administration; lack of perspective relative to the objectives of the University and the College; downgrading of the University, College, and other faculty; inadequate attention to personal appearance; negative attitude in general with respect to administrative matters that are essential; negative attitude toward assignments given by Departmental functions; negative attitude toward other disciplines; lack of tact and respect for the viewpoints of others; and holding grudges and taking personal affront, from discussions and disagreements on academic and adminstrative matters.

In addition to this rating by the teacher's own peer group, a College Executive Committee, elected by the College, evaluates each faculty member once a year. This review is thorough and comprehensive.

Finally, professors are encouraged to use the Self-Evaluation Questionnaire (See Appendix IV). The Academic Vice Chancellor has also indicated that student completed teaching ratings, must be prepared for each professor and be retained for later reference.

Oklahoma State University. Although not formally adopted, the College of Business Administration (CBA) at Okalahoma State has been considering a set of guidelines for faculty evaluation that recognize the need for flexibility according to variations in academic load (the mix of teaching, extension, research, public service, etc.). The total evaluation system includes, among other items, a teaching evaluation program as well as the evaluation of research undertaken and completed.

In terms of the teaching evaluation, three broad alternative classifications are identfied. All three contain the following common criteria:

1. Maintenance of high standards of effectiveness in classroom teaching and in faculty-student rapport.
2. Faculty contributions to the extension program, consistent with individual capabilities, as well as the needs of the State of Oklahoma.
3. The principle that faculty rank is based upon academic qualifications and productivity[6]

Alternative I applies to faculty ordinarily teaching 12 hours, normally undergraduate courses with a maximum of three different preparations. Alternative II is applicable to a 9 hour teaching load, generally involving both graduate and undergraduate courses. This alternative includes expected demonstration of research competence through publication as well as thesis supervision. Alternative III applies to faculty ordinarily teaching 6 hours of graduate or undergraduate courses, with an expectation of increased performance relative to research output. Incidentally, this alternative is not open to administrators.

Other than for the adjustments in teaching loads identified above, reductions are given only for service as:

1. a department head (6 hour reduction)
2. a coordinator of a department's graduate program (3 hour reduction)
3. by specific authorization of the College of Business Administration Executive Committee.

University of Georgia. Perhaps the most detailed faculty evaluation system of the schools surveyed is the one being used by the College of Business Administration, University of Georgia. (To show the extent of detail and quantitative orientation of the University of Georgia's system, a complete set of forms used in that system is provided in Appendix V.) The model has been operative for two years after several years in the development stage. It is the result of a search for procedures that permit quantitative comparison of faculty with greatly differing mixes of contributions.

The model has three components- *teaching, research,* and *professional activities and service.* In measuring teaching effectiveness, structured evaluations by both students and department heads are used (see Appendix V, Exhibits A-E, for illustrated forms). Initially, student evaluations are being conducted quarterly until the number of evaluations for each faculty member is sufficiently large to provide a sound basis for analysis. Thereafter, student evaluations will be conducted annually.

The department heads evaluate teaching competence by use of a structured, three-part evaluation. One part covers classroom or instructional competence (Appendix V, Exhibit C), another part relates to counseling and advising aspects (Appendix V, Exhibit D), and the third part deals with program contribution (Appendix V, Exhibit E).

Raw scores are developed for both sets of evaluations (by students and by the department head); they are then converted into standard scores so that the two evaluations can be combined. Equal weight is given to student and department head evaluations. Feedback concerning the results of this analysis, as well as other evaluations, is communicated to individual faculty members. (See Appendix V, Exhibit F.)

In evaluating research productivity, different types of research and publications are given various assigned weights. The form used to obtain research and publication data and the types and weights assigned are shown in Appendix V, Exhibits G. and H, respectively. (The criteria for categorizing journals and periodicals is shown in Appendix V, Exhibit I.) Again, raw scores are developed and converted into standard scores to enable the combining of teaching, research, and service components.

The same approach described above is used for the professional activities and services variable. The weights assigned to particular activites in this area are illustrated in Exhibit J of Appendix V.

Finally, the raw scores and standard scores indices for all three variables are summarized (See Appendix V, Exhibit K). These data are reported for lifetime production as well as on a current basis. The current data permit identification of those who are continuing to contribute and those who have stopped-temporarily or permanently.

While there have been, and continue to be, problems in applying this model, the overall reaction by the administrators and faculty members involved seems positive. Administrators are allowed to "put the reward where the productions is," and provide goals and objectives to an extent far surpassing previously used procedures. Additional important by-products are the insights provided concerning the relative performance of departments within the college, and the increased credibility of the college with respect to the university administration.

CONCLUSION

The illustrations described in this article are attempts by several schools to resolve some of the problems of evaluating faculty performance. While improvement is needed, these illustrations should prove useful as examples of procedures currently being tried. Generalizing from a relatively few individual applications is hazardous, and the ideas presented here will need to be adapted to particular purposes and individual circumstances to be most effective.

Regardless of the form or particular details of the system, an effective approach to faculty evaluation should be based upon carefully established evaluation criteria, should provide for orderly accumulation of data relevant to the evaluation criteria, and should include a periodic and thorough review of the evidence in judging faculty productivity. The results of this annual assessment, including both positive and negative feedback, should be explicitly communicated to individual faculty members.

Appendix I

A Survey of Approaches to Faculty Evaluation

Respondents

Dean Weldon Taylor
Dean Lawrence Fouraker
Dean Richard Poole
Dean L. J. Andrews
Dean William Flewellen, Jr.
Dean Robert Lanzillotti
Dean Vernon Zimmerman
Dean Wendel Smith
Dean George Kozmetsky
Dean George Odiorne
Dean Kermit Hanson

Sample Schools

Brigham Young University
Harvard University
Oklahoma State University
University of California (Davis)
University of Georgia
University of Florida
University of Illinois
University of Massachusetts
University of Texas (Austin)
University of Utah
University of Washington

Total requests	13
Total responses	11
Rate of response	85 percent

Appendix II
Illustration of the University of Washington Questionnaire

UNIVERSITY OF WASHINGTON
SURVEY OF STUDENT OPINION OF TEACHING

Rev. 11/71

Instructor _____
Course _____ sect _____ date _____

STUDENT CHARACTERISTICS

Major	Class	Age	Cum GPA	Sex	Course	Grade expected
☐ This department	☐ Freshman	☐ 18 or under	☐ Below 2.5	☐ Female	☐ Required	☐ A
☐ Social science	☐ Sophomore	☐ 19-20	☐ 2.5-2.9	☐ Male	☐ Elective	☐ B
☐ Natural science	☐ Junior	☐ 21-22	☐ 3.0-3.4			☐ C
☐ Humanities	☐ Senior	☐ 23-24	☐ Above 3.4			☐ D
☐ Other (incl pre)	☐ Graduate	☐ over 24				☐ Fail or E
	☐ other					☐ Pass

USE PENCIL ONLY. Mark one space for each item. Please do not make stray marks on this answer sheet. Additional comments may be made on the back of this sheet. Many instructors make the statistical report of these surveys available to students in the department office and to their chairman and dean.

STUDENTS MAY RETURN THIS QUESTIONNAIRE UNANSWERED WITHOUT PREJUDICE TO THEM.

Rating scale: Outstanding / Superior / Competent / Only fair / Of less value

1. Abstract ideas and theories were clearly interpreted.
2. Takes an active, personal interest in the class.
3. My skills in thinking were increased.
4. Helped broaden my interests.
5. Stressed important material.
6. Made good use of examples and illustrations.
7. Motivated me to do my best.
8. Inspired class confidence in his knowledge of subject.
9. Gave me new viewpoints or appreciations.
10. Clear and understandable in explanations.
11. Teaching sessions gave viewpoints and info text did not contain.
12. Material enthusiastically presented in teaching sessions.
13. Material presented in a well-organized fashion.
14. Helpful to individual students.
15. Integration of material into coherent whole was.
16. Text clear in presentation of concepts.
17. Text's overall rating.

---

18. How much was your interest in the subject changed by this course? .... More interested ☐ ☐ ☐ ☐ ☐ Less interested
19. What level of student sophistication was assumed in teaching sessions? .... Very high ☐ ☐ ☐ ☐ ☐ Very low
20. Were students free to ask questions, disagree, express their ideas, etc.? .... Encouraged ☐ ☐ ☐ ☐ ☐ Discouraged
21. Has improved my problem-solving methods. .... Very much ☐ ☐ ☐ ☐ ☐ Not at all
22. Did test questions cover the material emphasized in the text and teaching sessions? .... Very well ☐ ☐ ☐ ☐ ☐ Very poorly
23. Would you recommend this course by this instructor to majors in this dept? .... Very highly ☐ ☐ ☐ ☐ ☐ Never
24. Would you recommend this course by this instructor to non-majors? .... Very highly ☐ ☐ ☐ ☐ ☐ Never

25.
26.   QUESTIONS 25-27 WILL BE ON THE CHALKBOARD IF THE INSTRUCTOR WANTS TO USE THEM.
27.

(25.) _____ ☐ ☐ ☐ ☐ ☐ _____
(26.) _____ ☐ ☐ ☐ ☐ ☐ _____
(27.) _____ ☐ ☐ ☐ ☐ ☐ _____

Appendix III

Illustration of the University of Utah "Channels"

Promotion will be based upon one of the following alternative channels:

	Teaching	Publications	Administration	Service
1.	Excellent	Adequate	-------	Adequate
2.	Adequate	Excellent	-------	Adequate
3.	Good	Good	-------	Adequate
4.	Adequate	Good	-------	Adequate
5.	Good	Adequate	-------	Adequate
6.	Excellent	Excellent	-------	-------
7.	Excellent	-------	Excellent	-------
8.	Excellent	-------	-------	Excellent

A ninth channel may be added to the above alternatives. A faculty member in conjunction with the promotions advisory committee of his department may define well in advance [1] of his petition for promotion his preferred objectives (if other than those eight channels specified above). Upon departmental committee approval, the College Council will give special consideration to such a proposal. If the Council and the departmental committee agree by majority vote, then this special channel will be available to that faculty member in that particular department for that specific promotion. [2]

---

[1] The College Council realizes that during this initial year, it is not possible for a faculty member to define this ninth channel "well in advance."

[2] The Council views this ninth channel as being especially appropriate for faculty members who are now eligible for promotion or will be eligible soon and who may feel it is unfair for them to be subject to a new and different set of guidelines.

Appendix IV

Illustration of the University of Illinois • Teacher Self-Evaluation Questionnaire

UNIVERSITY OF ILLINOIS INDIVIDUALIZED QUESTIONNAIRE   FORM-51

INSTRUCTIONS

This will help you assess your use of some types of self-evaluation tools. Darken one of the following for each question. Use pencil only.

A. Have used and found valuable in the last three years.
B. Have used but NOT found valuable in the last three years.
C. Might be interested in trying.

TOOLS FOR TEACHER SELF-EVALUATION

Ray H. Simpson, Professor of Educational Psychology, University of Illinois, Urbana, Illinois 61801

1. Teacher-constructed self-evaluation check list.
2. Written teacher evaluation after each class.
3. Yearly written recap and evaluation of strong and weak aspects of own teaching activities.
4. Comparative check on own efficiency using one teaching approach vs. another.
5. Follow-up of former students in graduate work.
6. Structured test to check achievement against objectives.
7. Comparison of student achievement with norms on standardized or teacher-made tests.
8. Departmental oral, written, or performance examinations of students.
9. Invited cooperating colleague near end of semester leads discussion evaluating your class.
10. Workshop to construct teacher evaluation instrument.
11. Observation and evaluation of classes by invited colleague.
12. Questionnaire constructed by faculty committee.
13. Interaction through team or panel teaching.
14. Use of guidance specialist to help analyze teacher-student social-emotional climate.
15. Exchange of material with colleagues or instructors in other institutions.
16. Visiting in a colleague's class for ideas for evaluating and improving your classes.
17. Voluntary and continuing colleague discussions or seminars by instructors of a particular course.
18. Regular luncheons to discuss evaluations of own and others' teaching.
19. Planned meetings with colleagues for evaluating your own and others' teaching.
20. Soliciting the help of administrators or supervisors in evaluating one's teaching.
21. Adaptation of evaluative processes from industry or noneducational occupations.
22. Self-constructed evaluative questionnaires or check lists to be filled out by your students.
23. Open-ended relatively unstructured written evaluation by students.
24. Comparative ratings by students on specified dimensions of your instruction vs. that of other instructors.
25. Student evaluation committee to provide feedback to the instructor.
26. Published teacher evaluative instruments given to students.
27. Nonclass member who is an advanced student observe and evaluate all class sessions.
28. Informal discussions with small groups and individual students.
29. Reaction sheets given students after each class during selected parts of the term.
30. Class-constructed evaluation instrument.
31. Use of student self-evaluation as one check on teacher efficiency.
32. Class evaluation of its own progress.
33. Eliciting judgments of bright or "reliable" students.
34. Faculty observations of student reactions.
35. "Keeping ear to the ground" for evidences of student reaction.
36. One class session devoted to course evaluation and planning for the following year.
37. Tape recording of an evaluative class session where course's strengths and limitations are listed.
38. Role playing with student assuming role of instructor to help the latter assess student perception of him.
39. A different student each day assumes role of class evaluator.
40. Evaluation instrument prepared by student council or university student committee.
41. Individual conference with poor students to determine causes of weaknesses.
42. Tape or TV recording or regular class sessions and then self feedback analysis.

DIRECTIONS:
1. Print instructor's last name here
2. Complete identification information to the right.
3. Respond to the items presented frankly and completely - one response per item. (See sample mark and response code)
4. Use pencil only. Do not use pen, ballpoint or ink of any kind.

Appendix V

Forms Used in Implementing The University of Georgia Faculty Evaluation Model

EXHIBIT A

1971-72 STUDENT EVALUATION OF TEACHING*

Part A-Mark appropriate answer on separate answer sheet.

1. My major is:
   (1) Finance (2) Accounting (3) Management (4) Marketing (5) Economics

   or

2. My major is:
   (1) Insurance (2) Real Estate (3) General Business (4) Other

3. My cumulative grade point average is:
   (1) Below 2.5 (2) 2.5 to 3.0 (3) 3.0 to 3.5 (4) Above 3.5

4. I transferred to the University of Georgia:
   (1) Yes (2) No

Each of these statements describes a basic component of teaching. Give the instructor an overall rating for each component.

	Low Score				High Score
5. Has command of the subject, presents material in an analytic way, contrasts points of view, discusses current developments, and relates topics to other areas of knowledge.	1	2	3	4	5
6. Makes himself clear, states objectives, summarizes major points, presents material in an organized manner, and provides emphasis.	1	2	3	4	5
7. Is sensitive to the response of the class, encourages student participation, and welcomes questions and discussion.	1	2	3	4	5
8. Is available to and friendly toward students, is interested in students as individuals, is himself respected as a person.	1	2	3	4	5
9. Enjoys teaching, is enthusiastic about his subject, makes the course exciting, and has self-confidence.	1	2	3	4	5
10. Considering everything, how would you rate this teacher?	1	2	3	4	5
11. What grade do you expect in this course?	1 (F)	2 (D)	3 (C)	4 (B)	5 (A)

*Adopted with permission from the Student Evaluation Questionnaire developed by the Center for Research & Development in Higher Education, Berkeley.

EXHIBIT B
INSTRUCTOR EVALUATION

Part B is designed to solicit your comments regarding the instructor and the course. Write your responses after each question. Do *NOT* give your name.

PART B

1. What do you especially like about this person as a teacher?

2. How could this teacher improve himself to become a better teacher?

3. What weaknesses do you find in the course as it is set up and what do you suggest for eliminating these weaknesses?

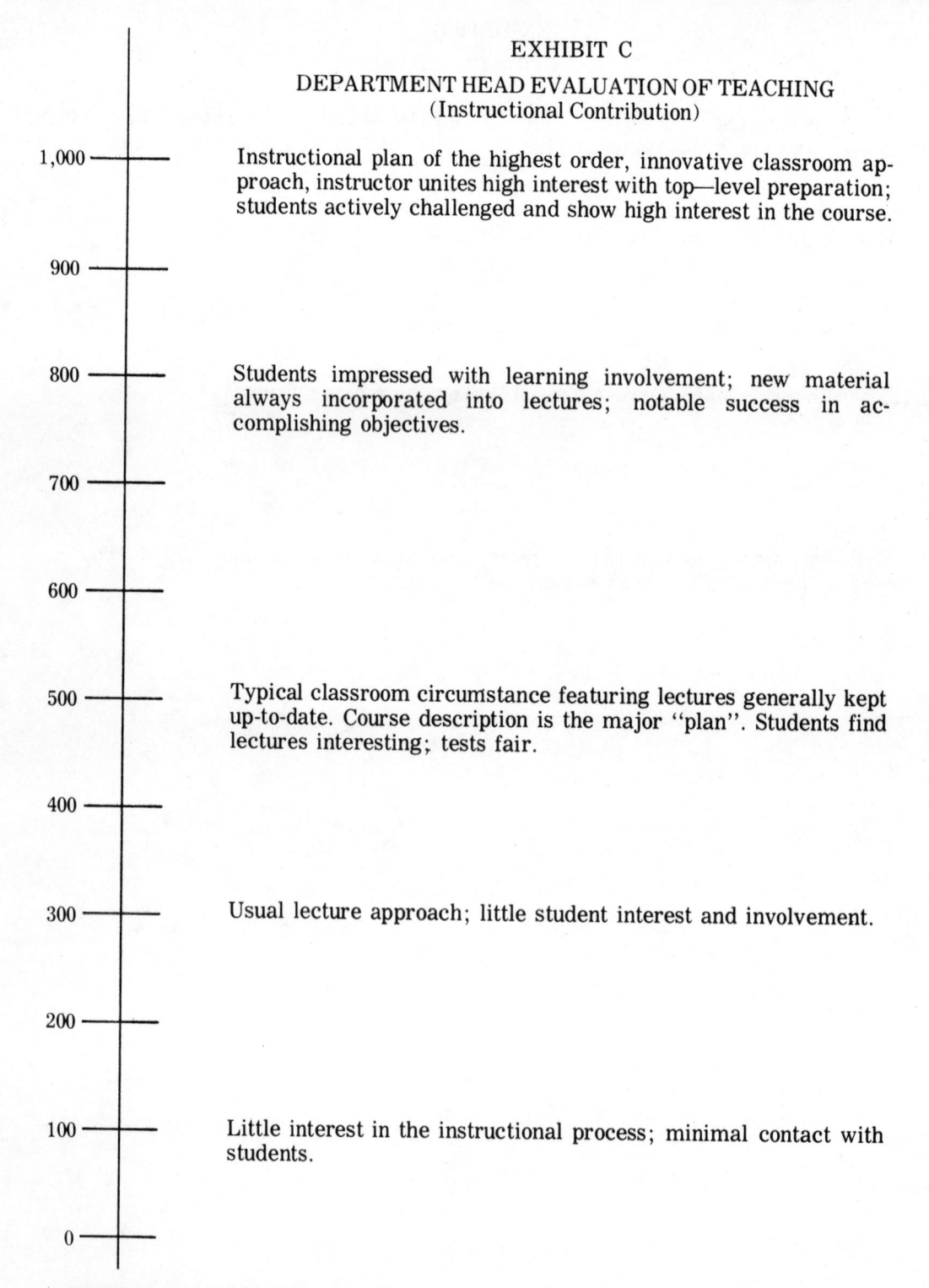

EXHIBIT C
DEPARTMENT HEAD EVALUATION OF TEACHING
(Instructional Contribution)

1,000 — Instructional plan of the highest order, innovative classroom approach, instructor unites high interest with top—level preparation; students actively challenged and show high interest in the course.

900 —

800 — Students impressed with learning involvement; new material always incorporated into lectures; notable success in accomplishing objectives.

700 —

600 —

500 — Typical classroom circumstance featuring lectures generally kept up-to-date. Course description is the major "plan". Students find lectures interesting; tests fair.

400 —

300 — Usual lecture approach; little student interest and involvement.

200 —

100 — Little interest in the instructional process; minimal contact with students.

0 —

INSTRUCTIONAL CONTRIBUTION
   Evaluates classroom focused activities, particularly holding that preparatory, innovative and presentation aspects are the best proxy measures of contribution.
   How well the individual develops course objectives, prepares his approach and such support activities as carefully developed tests or class handouts, and uses innovative techniques to prompt active learning situations—these are manifestations.

EXHIBIT D
DEPARTMENT HEAD EVALUATION OF TEACHING
(Counseling-Advising)

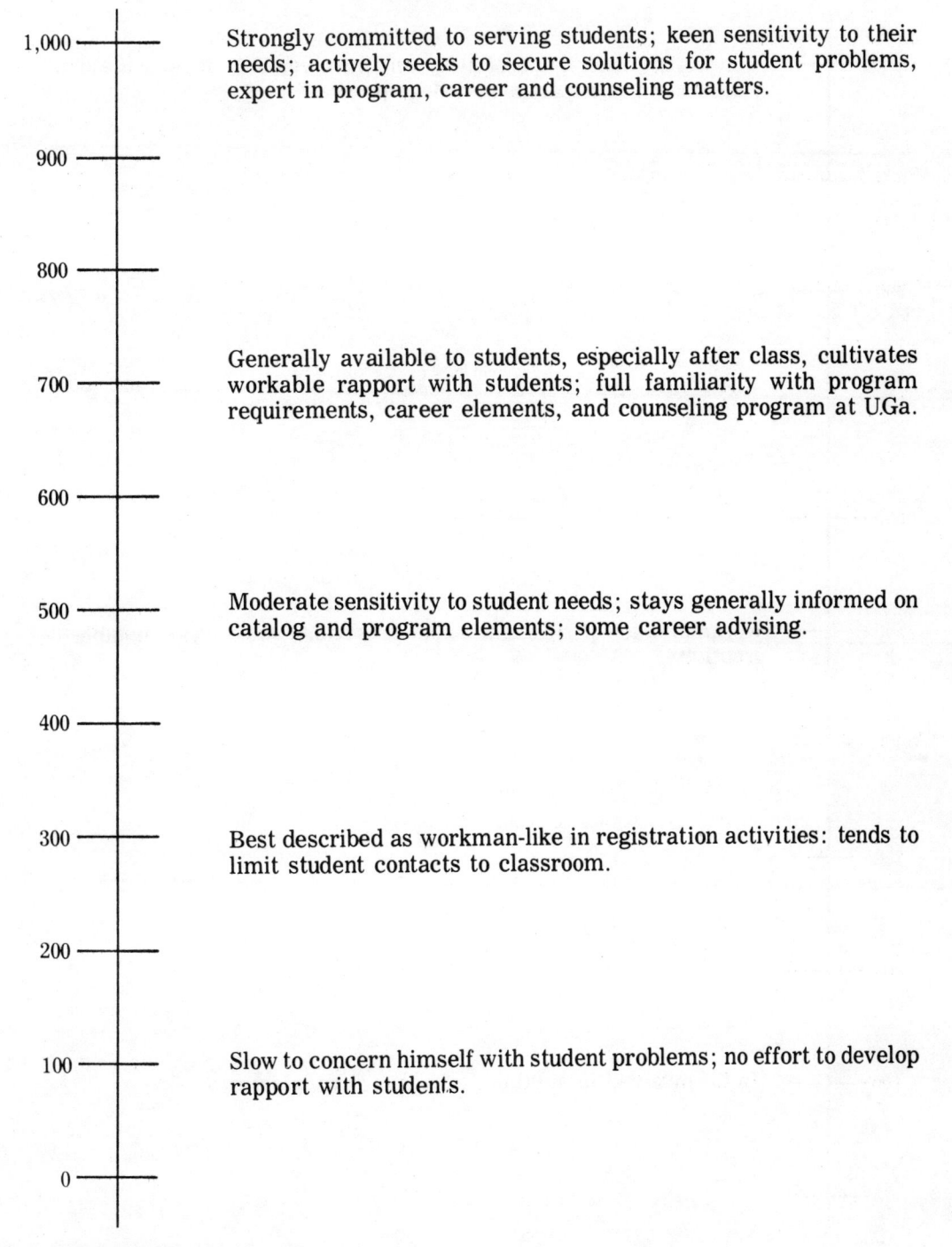

Scale	Description
1,000	Strongly committed to serving students; keen sensitivity to their needs; actively seeks to secure solutions for student problems, expert in program, career and counseling matters.
900	
800	
700	Generally available to students, especially after class, cultivates workable rapport with students; full familiarity with program requirements, career elements, and counseling program at U.Ga.
600	
500	Moderate sensitivity to student needs; stays generally informed on catalog and program elements; some career advising.
400	
300	Best described as workman-like in registration activities: tends to limit student contacts to classroom.
200	
100	Slow to concern himself with student problems; no effort to develop rapport with students.
0	

COUNSELING-ADVISING

Evaluate performance (actions) which reflect the sensitivity to student needs; interest in helping them achieve solutions; knowledge and-or capacity to help effect satisfying answers in both program and career aspects.

EXHIBIT E
DEPARTMENT HEAD EVALUATION OF TEACHING
(Program Contribution)

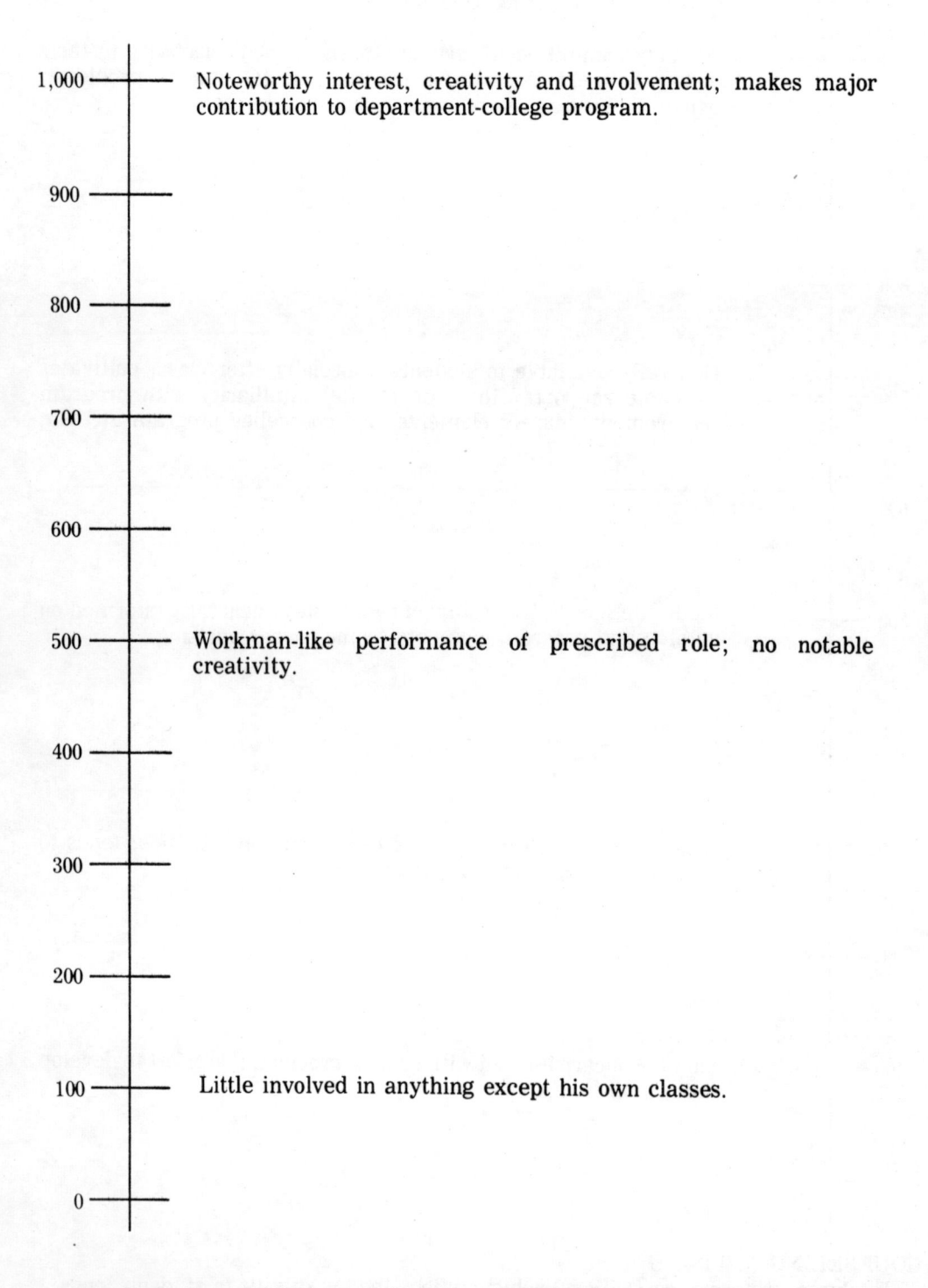

1,000 — Noteworthy interest, creativity and involvement; makes major contribution to department-college program.

900 —

800 —

700 —

600 —

500 — Workman-like performance of prescribed role; no notable creativity.

400 —

300 —

200 —

100 — Little involved in anything except his own classes.

0 —

Evaluate those activities not directly oriented to specific classes, such as supervising doctoral teaching assistants; coordinating teaching of principles sections; course development; curriculum development; faculty development activity; etc.

EXHIBIT F

FACULTY EVALUATION PROFILE, CBA

SCORE   140   160   180   200   220   240   260   280   300   320   340   360   380   400

5. ABILITY TO GET STUDENT COOPERATION & ATTENTION

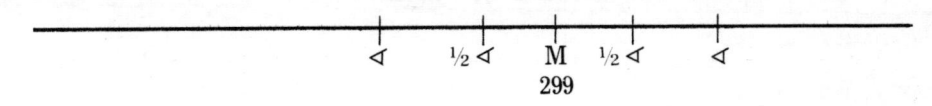

◁   ½◁   M   ½◁   ◁
         299

10. FAIRNESS IN GRADING AND DEALING WITH STUDENTS

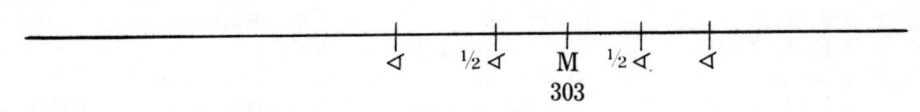

◁   ½◁   M   ½◁   ◁
         303

14. INTEREST AND ENTHUSIASM

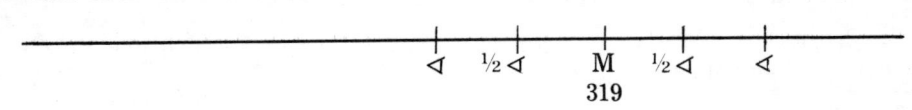

◁   ½◁   M   ½◁   ◁
         319

16. ABILITY TO PLAN & ORGANIZE EFFICIENTLY

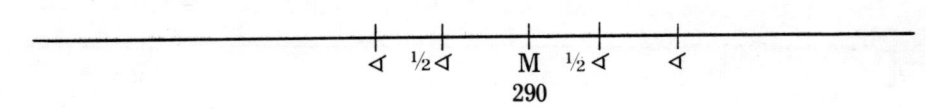

◁   ½◁   M   ½◁   ◁
         290

18. KNOWLEDGE OF SUBJECT MATTER

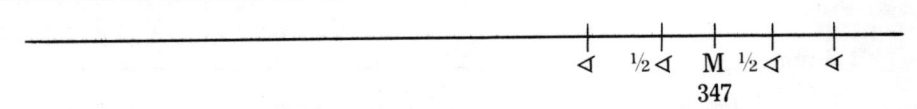

◁   ½◁   M   ½◁   ◁
         347

24. OVERALL TEACHING ABILITY

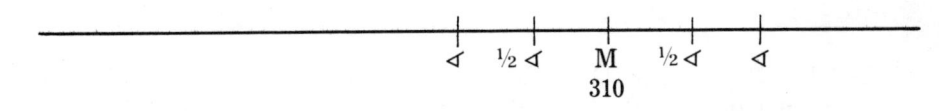

◁   ½◁   M   ½◁   ◁
         310

EXHIBIT G

FORM A (FOR RESEARCH DATA)
A PUBLISHED OR REPUBLISHED WORK

FORM A

Fill out a form for each piece of work. Put an "NA" in blanks that are inapplicable. Check ( ) appropriate boxes. If unknown, leave blank.

NAME L_____, F_____, MI_____ S.S.No._____

WORK TYPE ( ):

( ) Abstract	( ) Chapter	( ) Handbook	( ) Selection
( ) Annotated biblio.	( ) Collection	( ) Letter to editor	( ) Synopsis
( ) Article	( ) Comment	( ) Monograph	( ) Text
( ) Bibliography	( ) Communication	( ) Note	( ) Translation
( ) Book	( ) Compilation	( ) Occasional paper	( ) Working paper
( ) Bulletin	( ) Condensation	( ) Book review	( ) Paper in proceedings
( ) Business game	( ) Discussion	( ) Research report	
( ) Case	( ) Other		

STATUS ( ): ( ) Published ( ) Accepted for publication ( ) Republished alone ( ) Republished in a collection

Please PRINT or TYPE information about this work as it would appear in a bibliographical listing. List additional names and roles on back.

[L_____ F_____ MI__][L_____, F_____ MI__]
  ( ) Author ( ) Editor   ( ) Co- ( ) Jr. author ( ) Co- ( ) Jr. ed.

L_____ F_____ MI_____ _____
  ( ) Co- ( ) Jr. author ( ) Co- ( ) Jr. ed.   Title of work

Edition _____

Journal, periodical, or collection, name   Publisher
Place_____ Vol., no., & series_____ Publication date_____ No. pages_____

If case-where catalogued _____

YOUR ROLE IN PREPARATION ( ): ( ) Sole investigator ( ) Principal investigator ( ) Contributor ( ) Participant ( ) Director of research activities ( ) Co-director ( ) Coordinator ( ) Other

SUPPORT SOURCE ( ): ( ) University ( ) Government ( ) Foundation ( ) Assn. ( ) Business firm ( ) individual ( ) Self ( ) Other

SUPPORT TYPE ( ): ( ) Grant ( ) Contract ( ) Consulation fee ( ) Released time ( ) Summer research ( ) Extra compensation ( ) Other

IF FUNDED: Amount $_____; Sponsor _____

( ) WORK HAS RECEIVED WRITTEN PROFESSIONAL RESPONSE OR RECOGNITION (provide specifics on back).
( ) ABSTRACT OR BRIEF DESCRIPTION OF WORK (optional; use back):
Date _____ Signed _____

EXHIBIT H

RESEARCH WORK TYPES AND WEIGHTS

	Work Type	Brief Description	Weight
1.	Book	Original work of book length and comprehensiveness—not of the nature of a textbook	1500
2.	Book of readings	Book composed primarily of original works by the author	900
3.	Textbook	A text composed primarily of original work by the author of the book. This work type contrasts with a collection of readings. Published by a non-captive publisher	900
4.	Book	Republished or revised book of non-text nature	375
5.	Article I	Article of two or more pages published in a Category I journal or periodical	300
20.	Business game	Package of game materials including manuals, published by a non-captive publisher	200
25.	Syllabus	Of major importance, developed for use in a course of national or regional appeal	200
30.	Comment	Less than two pages in a Category I journal or periodical	150
50.	Annotated bibliography	Comprehensive bibliography on a subject with notations about or abstracts of contents of the individual entries	80
71.	Technical report	Report of technical matters or of a technical nature, published by a captive publisher	75
79.	Book review	Critical review of a book authored by someone else	40
80.	Case	Case catalogued with a case clearing house but not yet published in a book or collection	40
91.	Abstract	An abstract or a published work, including abstracts by the author of the work abstracted	20
108.	Advertisement	Design and development of an advertisement published by a non-captive publisher	10

EXHIBIT I

CRITERIA FOR CATEGORIZING JOURNALS-PERIODICALS

A *CATEGORY I* journal or periodical must have:

(A) circulation of 10,000, or national distribution, or a significant part of the intended market.

(B) authors list mostly of persons with national reputations.

(C) a board of editors or referees whose reputations are generally comparable to those of the authors.

Two or more of the following criteria must also be met. That is, a

Category I journal or periodical also must have:

(D) professional society sponsorship and-or

(E) professional format and-or

(F) research presented in at least ½ of its pages and-or

(G) indexing by the principle indexing services.

A *CATEGORY II* journal or periodical must have:

(A) circulation of 5,000-10,000 or regional distribution, or a significant part of the intended market.

(B) authors list mostly of persons with regional reputations. Exceptions may be made for this criterion of the periodical is excellent in other areas.

(C) a board of editors or referees whose reputations are generally comparable to those of the authors. Exceptions may be made for this criterion if the periodical is excellent in other areas.

Two of the criteria listed above as (d), (E), (F) and (G) must also be met.

A *CATEGORY III* journal or periodical includes all not listed in Category I and Category II above.

EXHIBIT J
WEIGHTS FOR FACULTY EVALUATION IN PROFESSIONAL ACTIVITIES AND THE SERVICE AREA

1. Consultantships and business appointments—10 points per item listed (number of years not taken into consideration)

2. Professional association activity

   A. Memberships—5 points for being a member at any time

   B. Committee appointments, board of directors and officer (except president). Note: work on planning of annual meetings is included as a committee assignment category.

	State	Regional	National
a. First year	10	25	50
b. Each subsequent year	2	5	10

   C. President (at the national level a subjective judgement will determine actual points awarded)

	State	Regional	National
	25	50	100-200

   D. Member of editorial board

	State	Regional	National
a. First year	10	25	50
b. Each subsequent	2	5	10

   E. Correspondent (no distinction between state, regional or national)

a. First year	10
b. Each subsequent year	2

3. Public service (major)—at the national level a subjective judgement will determine actual points awarded

State	Regional	National
25	50	100-200

4. Local community organization and charitable service (credit given once for belonging and once for being current) 2

5. College and University services

   A. Committee appointments (other than ex-officio)—credit given for each year faculty member is on the committee 10

   B. Sponsor or faculty representative of a student academic organization—credit given for each year faculty member serves 10

EXHIBIT J (Continued)...

	Local State	Regional National
6. Participation in *academic programs* at other universities and *professional associations*		
A. Major speaker or lecturer (credit given for each program)	20	40
B. Chairman, panelist, discussion leader (credit given for each program). Note: Participant means panelist if shown a specific time less than the length of the conference.	10	20
C. Attendee at seminar and workshop (credit given for each program)	4	10
D. Speaker at a banquet (paper type of presentation, not an after-dinner speech). Note: This activity is not limited to academic programs or professional associations. Generally, this will be a speech for a particular company at a banquet.	20	40
7. Special professional development activities of one month duration or longer (credit given for each program)		
A. Internships, extended training program, post-doctoral work (based on 15 points per quarter) credit given for each program	15 to	60
8. Service programs at University of Georgia Center and other centers for continuing education or training programs at other locations aimed at a particular business group or firm.		
A. First time on a particular program (same type of program but for a different company will be considered as the first time).	15	30
B. Subsequent appearances on the same type of program (Same program for same company but at a different time or general public program).	3	6
C. Academic Director (each program)		
a. First year		25
b. Subsequent years		12
9. Addresses to practitioner groups (non-academic)		
A. A speech imparting technical or professional information	20	40
B. A speech mainly for entertainment (after-dinner) or to a very general audience (school, PTA, etc.). This would normally be a speech where the group invites the faculty member because of his ability to speak well or because of his reputation (man's stature).	15	30

EXHIBIT K

SUMMARY—FACULTY EVALUATIONS

NAME: _____

RANK: _____ DATE _____

DATE OF APPT., UGA _____

BUDGETED ASSIGNMENT: SALARY: 1971-72 _____
                                                                1970-71 _____
                                                                1969-70 _____

     TEACHING _____   1968-69 _____
     RESEARCH _____
     SERVICE _____
     ADMIN. _____
     COUNS.

---

1. *Lifetime Scores*

	Raw	Index
Teaching	____	____
Research	____	____
Prof. Act. & Service	____	____

   Combined Score _____   Rank Order _____

2. Lifetime (Research and Service)

	Index
Research	____
Prof. Act. & Service	____

   Combined Score _____   Rank Order _____

3. *Current Score*

	Raw	Index
Teaching	____	____
Research	____	____
Prof. Act. & Service	____	____
Combined		____
Groupings		____

4. Other Factors:

FOOTNOTES

[1] Eble points out that most college teachers are not aware of the significant number of scholarly studies which have tried to identify teaching effectiveness. Furthermore, there he asserts that there is substantial agreement as to what constitutes effective and ineffective teaching. The reader is referred to *The Recognition and Evaluation of Teaching,* Kenneth E. Eble, (Project to Improve College Teaching; The American Assocation of University Professors, One Dupont Circle, Washington, D.C. 20036, especially Chapters 2 and 5.)

[2] For a good summary of some of the arguments for and against student evaluations, see Eble, *The Recognition and Evaluation of Teaching,* pp. 17-19.

[3] Ibid., p. 16.

[4] The "Performance Record" form contains information on (1) teaching (courses taught, new course developments, innovative teaching techniques, supervision, and-or work with MBA, MA, and DBA students, and other such information); (2) Research and Publications (including current year and past year's publications as well as current research projects in progress); and Service (membership in professional organizations, including committee assignments, editorships, visiting professorships, University, College, or Department committees, etc.).

[5] The College of Business has established an explicit set of alternatives (channels) through which a faculty member may excel and be promoted, (See Appendix III.)

[6] Indications of academic qualifications and productivity include: effective classroom teaching, participation in professional organizations and projects, community service relating to the faculty member's discipline, research, publication, professional development, innovation in curriculum development and teaching techniques, and time spent in advising and working with students in academic pursuits. Certain non-academic activities are worthwhile and are rewarded through salary rather than faculty rank, e.g., administrative assignments, non-academic committee service, non-academic speeches to civic clubs, and work with student groups in university related activities that are not academic in nature.

A Technique for Summarizing and Presenting Data Relative to Faculty Performance

R. R. Read
Naval Post Graduate School

Introduction

Professor Read's paper introduces a methodology for summarizing multiple opinions concerning the performance of faculty, and illustrates a technique for convenient presentation of such data. The methodology is both simple and general. It can be used with many differing forms of raw data collection. It can be used over time, and can be applied to courses and other related entities as well.

Many instruments are available for the gathering of student opinion on courses and instructors (see, for example, [1] and [2]). Their value is directed largely toward the improvement of instruction. Through their use a teacher can gain some insight into his performance. Especially useful are comparative data summaries such as those that accompany the use of the Student Instructional Report (SIR), available from the Educational Testing Service, Princeton. This allows a teacher to compare his results with the results of others.

What role these instruments play in the administrative review of faculty is not clear. An institution professing high quality teaching as one of its important criteria for advancement should make that claim credible [1]. Moreover, there is a need to account for the effects that concomitant variables (e.g., variability of students, nature of course, class size) may have on an instructor's rating. The methodology presented here is a simple and useful tool for understanding the nature of these questions and helping in their solution. It is a technique that can accept many kinds of input, and while not restricted to the summary of evaluation of instruction data, is particularly adaptable for that purpose.

This general methodology is especially useful for the administrative review of university faculty. The key point is that such review is often broadly based. Ratings of faculty may be obtained from students, or from a reasonably sized group of peers. The main advantage is to present the data summary in a two dimensional visual display that seems more meaningful than a set of mean ratings, paired with the corresponding standard deviations, and yet is comparable in its simplicity.

The comparison of faculty is especially delicate because each person is an individual with a particular specialty, a unique professional who pursues his quest of excellence in his own way and often does so rather independently of others. Thus, broadly based review is appropriate since it helps to smooth out the effects of selectively applied subjective bias.

The standards by which faculty are compared are variable and often qualitative [1]. Furthermore, there is controversy over the question of how finely each faculty member or each characteristic of faculty members can be measured (or the meaningfulness of such measurements). There seems to be little disagreement, however, (see [4]) in the ability of an observer to make course classifications into three bins such as above average, average, and below average, or superior, adequate, and inferior. The choice of adjectives can have an effect, but such distinctions are not important in understanding the proposed methodology. Only the use of three bins for each observer need be accepted.

The set of observers cannot be expected to match up with the set of faculty members in any balanced way. That is, each observer will not be in a position to judge all faculty (in a department or other comparison group), nor will all observers be judging the same number of faculty. Likewise, each faculty member will not be rated by the same set or the same number of observers. The difficulties of making comparisons in these circumstances are discussed and illustrated in [3] and [4]. While these difficulties may not be overcome through use of the proposed methodology, it can serve as a probing tool to research the effects of unbalance as well as other effects. Application to well selected subsets of observers and faculty may provide benchmarks useful for extending the interpretations or for extrapolation purposes.

The methodology is presented first in abstract form and then illustrated with some real but simple data. Other applications and extensions are then discussed.

The General Methodology.

Suppose there are k faculty labeled $T_1,...T_k$ under comparative review. Let n_i be the number of observers who rate T_i for $i = 1,...k$. Each observer places each of his subset of faculty into one of three bins, either directly or indirectly (e.g., by filling out a questionnaire which is later used to group faculty). For convenience of terminology, the bins are labeled "above," "center" and "below." These data are then reorganized by faculty. The triplets (x_i, y_i, z_i) representing the total number of observers who rate T_i as "above," "center," and "below" respectively are collected. The components of the triplet will be nonnegative integers whose total is n_i.

To simplify the notation, let us drop the subscripts. Normalization of the vector (x,y,z) by n produces a vector (p,q,r) whose components represent proportions (i.e., $p = x/n$; $q = y/n$; $r = z/n$). Doing this for each faculty member produces a set of k vectors each of whose components is nonnegative and they sum to unity. The set of all possible such points in three spaces is an equilateral triangle (called the simplex) with vertices (1,0,0), (0,1,0) and (0,0,1). Thus the scatter plot of the k vectors (p,q,r) can be displayed in two dimensions and are contained by an equilateral triangle. The mathematical details of plotting are presented in Appendix A.

An Illustration

Moving immediately to an application will illustrate how such a scatter plot may come about. The data in hand are limited to student opinions of the teaching capabilities of faculty. The details of the original experiment are contained in [4]. Only the following aspects were used for the present illustration. Each student (observer) was asked to rank each of his teachers on a rating scale of one to fifteen, with one representing the very worst and fifteen the very best. Most of the students used essentially the full scale so their data were widely dispersed. Quite arbitrarily, the "upper seven faculty members with ties" and the "lower seven with ties" were assigned each scale to represent the bins "above" and "below," with the remainder designated as "center." Most of the students rated 20 to 22 teachers so this choice approximated a division into equal thirds. Note the forced choice nature of this rule. A more direct approach could allow the observer to decide how many of his subjects were "above," "center," or "below."

Next, the (x,y,z) counts (number of "above," "center," and "below" votes) were made and divided by n. The results of plotting the vectors (p,q,r) for all teachers whose $n \geq 19$ (19 was a convenient breakpoint in the distribution of (n)) appear in Figure 1.

The position of the rating summary vector (p,q,r) of a given T in relation to the three vertices bears picturesque witness as to how T is viewed by his observers. If all his observers place him in the same bin, his vector will plot on the corresponding vertex. If all place him in one of two bins, then his vector will fall on the leg of the triangle connecting the appropriate two vertices. If they use all three bins, his point

A Technique for Summarizing and Presenting Data

FIGURE 1.

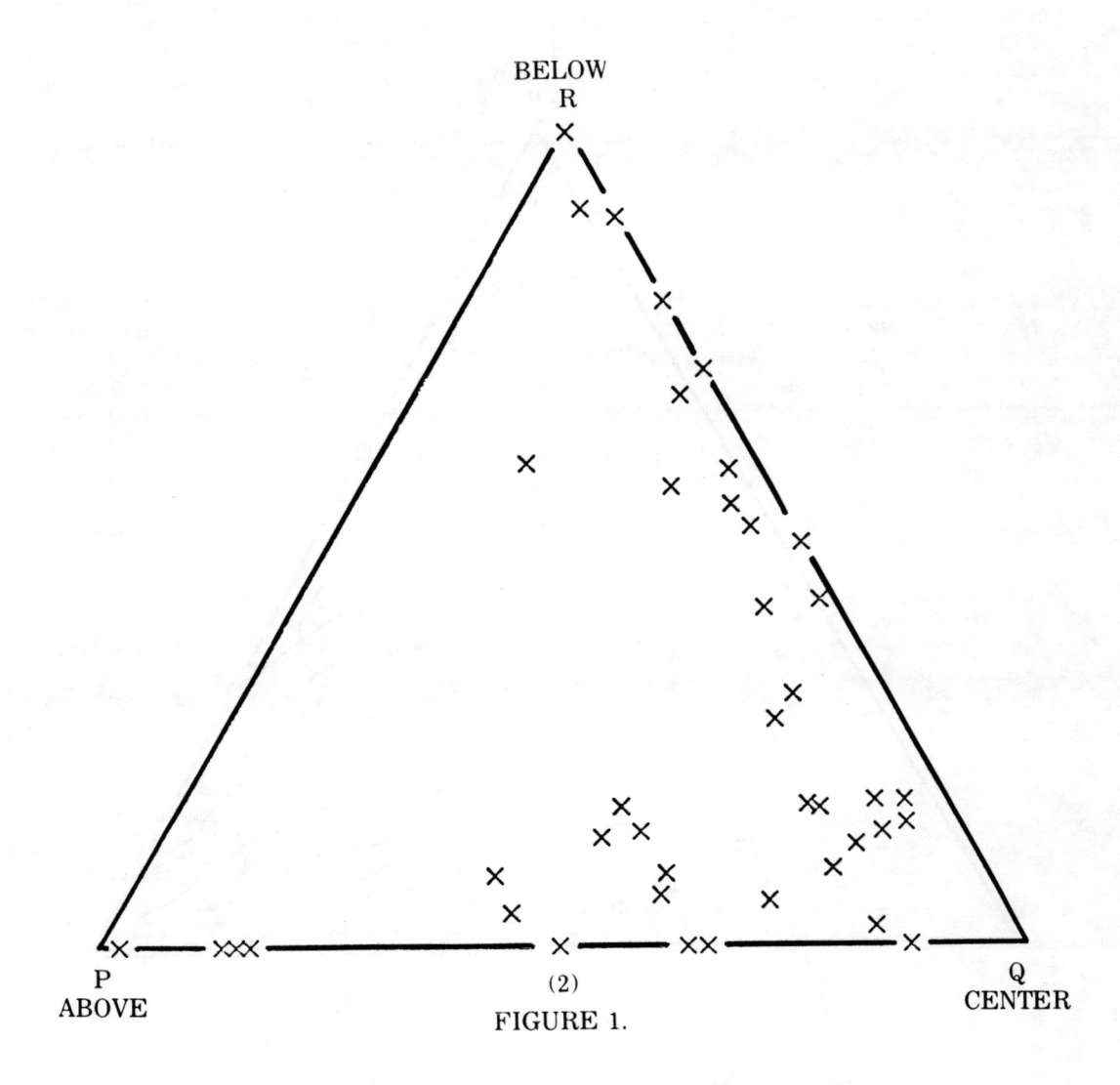

SCATTER PLOT OF (p, q, r) VECTORS OF THE
FORTY ONE FACULTY WITH n $\geq$ 19

FIGURE 2.

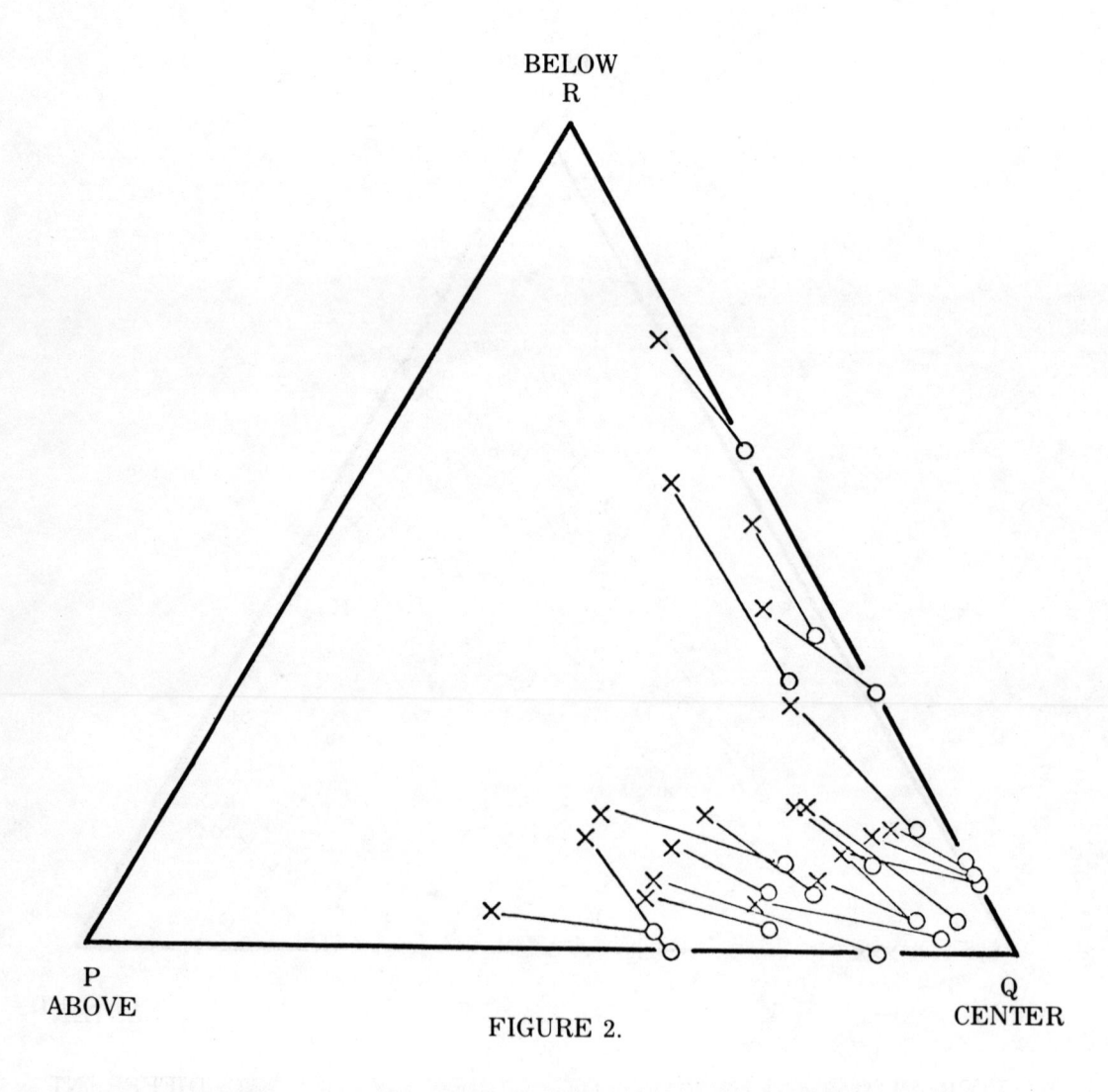

MOVEMENT OF SELECTED POINTS WHEN CRITERIA FOR "ABOVE" AND "BELOW" ARE MADE MORE STRINGENT. ($n \geq 19$)

X — LESS STRINGENT DEFINITION OF EXTREMES

O — MORE STRINGENT DEFINITION OF EXTREMES

FIGURE 3

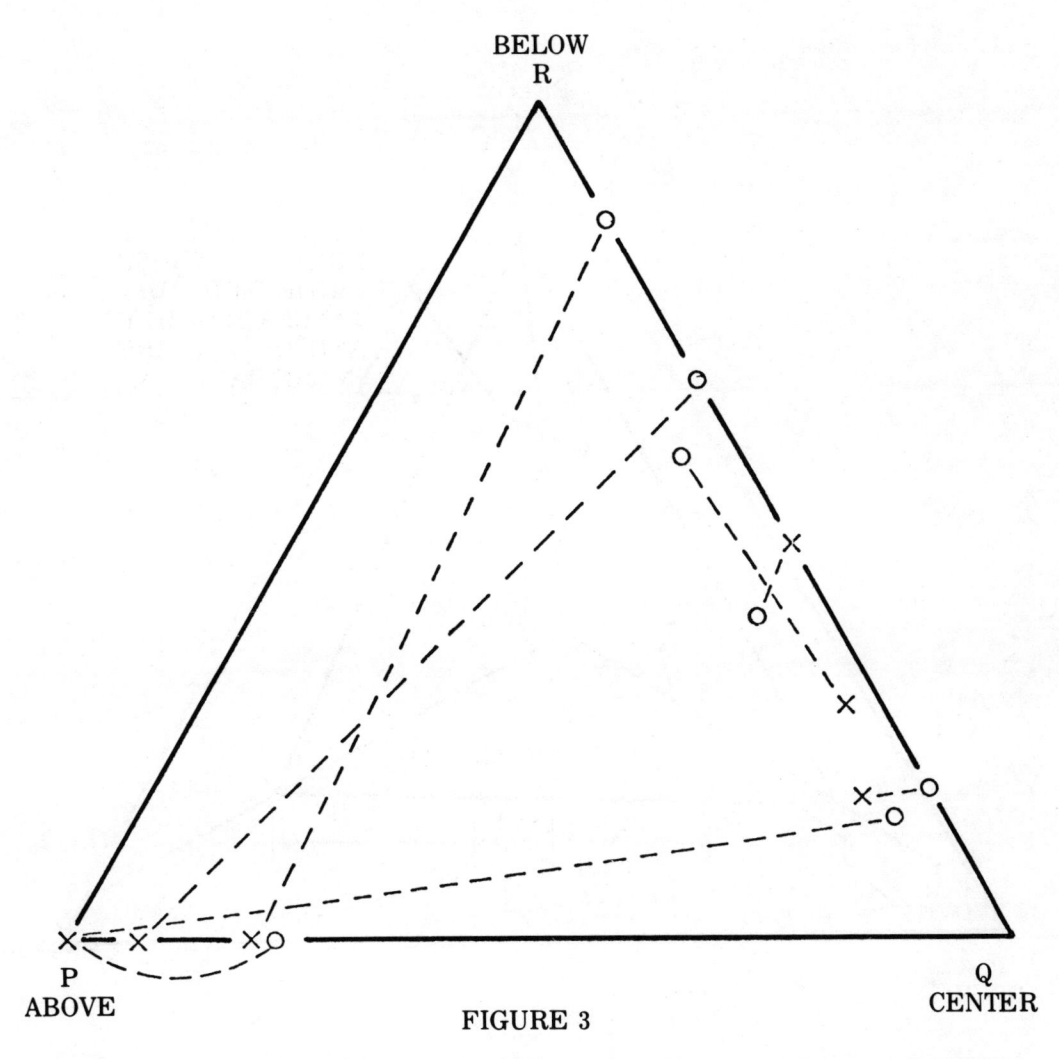

SCATTER PLOT OF REACTIONS OF STUDENTS FROM TWO DIFFERENT CURRICULA TO SEVEN TEACHERS THAT THEY HAD IN COMMON

O RATING BY THE FIRST CURRICULUM
X RATING BY THE SECOND CURRICULUM

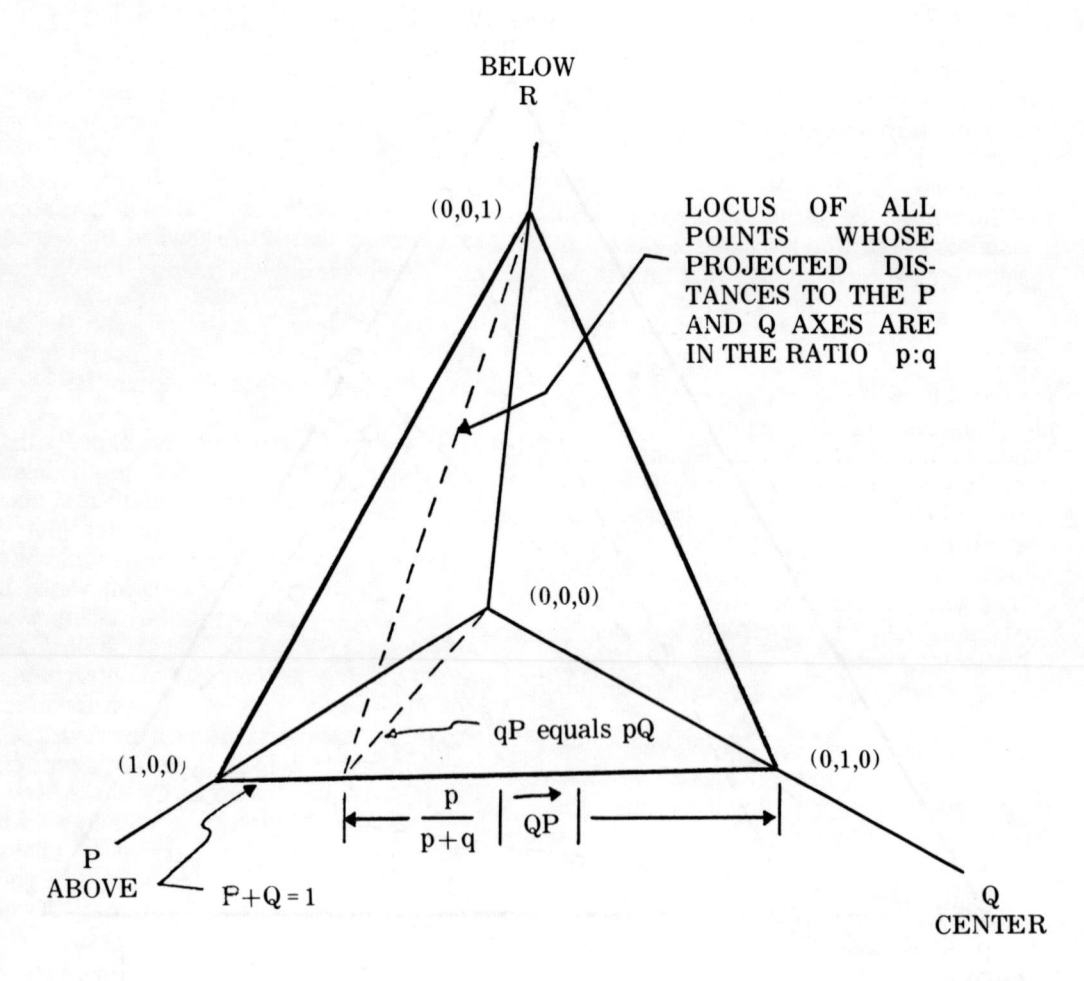

FIGURE 4

THREE DIMENSIONAL RELATIONSHIPS USEFUL IN
LOCATING POINTS ON THE SIMPLEX

will fall within the triangle's interior.

The variability of reaction to T can also be interpreted visually. The most controversial faculty will fall near the midpoint of the leg connecting the vertices "above" and "below." Faculty whose points fall close to the vertex "center" will not have elicited much extreme response from their sets of observers. A point that falls near one of the other two vertices represents a more extreme reaction, with variability increasing with distance from the boundaries. How both distance and direction must be used in making comparisons is illustrated later. Also, one must account for both when clustering the points on the scatter plot into groups of faculty with common characteristics.

Finally, the distribution of the points on the triangle deserves comment. If there is no disagreement concerning the bin to which each faculty member belongs, then the points will pile up on the three vertices. At the other extreme, let us suppose that each observer throws his subset of faculty into the bins totally at random. Then the points will be uniformly distributed over the triangle. The distribution expected represents a situation intermediate to these two extremes. The highest density of points should fall near the vertex "center" with moderate tailing off toward the two other vertices. (This tailing off should be symmetric for the data in hand because the forced choice porportions for "above" and "below" are equal.) A more rapid decline of density should occur as one moves toward the midpoint of the opposite leg. This reflects the idea that the frequency with which observers disagree (regarding an individual) over the bins "above" and "below" should be less than the frequency of disagreement over the other two pairs of bins. This situation is observed to occur in Figure 1, indicating that the students possessed discriminating power but were not in uniform agreement.

Further Applications.

In order to understand better the behavior of the methodology, the definition of "above" and "below" is changed to "upper five with ties" and "lower five with ties." This approximates the division of the psychological scales according to the proportions upper sixth, center two-thirds, lower sixth. Having turned up the "dial of stringency," it is interesting to note how the points move. This is illustrated in Figure 2. To reduce cluttering, only teachers in Figure 1 from a selected department and only interior points were used. Of course, all points that move under this change must move somewhat toward the Vertex Q, but not necessarily in a straight line, nor at the same speed. Points on the legs PQ and QR must move along those legs. Interior points that move on a straight line toward Q are shedding "above" and "below" votes at the same rate. Points that move toward the leg PQ are shedding "below" votes faster than "above" votes, and the opposite effect occurs for points moving toward the leg QR. Points that move short distances are less affected by the change than those that move long distances.

It seems reasonable to expect that administrators using this methodology would confer with their faculty and show them their vector on the scatter plot. It follows that the administrators should be to say what movements of a point would be regarded as improved performance, what movements would be degradations, and what would be considered no change. Contours or regions of equi-performance should be indicated. More experience will be required to help in these decisions, but the notions illustrated in Figure 2 are a beginning. In turn, the teacher who strives to improve may have to choose exactly how he might achieve a higher fraction of "above" ratings. Frank discussion may help him decide. This particular aspect emphasizes the need for understanding what variables are important to the students. (See [1], [2].)

The effects of unbalance and other concomitant variables can also be examined using this methodology. For example, type of course taught, class size, and variability of the students are important variables that are usually not within the control of teachers.[1] In some cases, it may be possible to plot all teachers who teach the same thing on the same display. This would provide a bench mark for that course or subject. Some teachers regularly teach a narrowly based set of courses. Perhaps they should be viewed differently from those who do not. The viability of this effect on an instructor's rating could be examined on the scatter plot. Advanced elective courses may be considered the more desirable teaching assignments and better teaching performance may be a reasonable expectation. Again, the identification of such points using the display technique may assist in measuring this effect.

The question of variability in students, based upon data from [4], will serve to illustrate. The students involved came from two different curricula and the resultant two groups observed seven teachers in common, but not in common classes. Their individual reactions to these seven teachers appear in Figure 3, using the first rule (upper seven and lower seven). It is seen that the two group reactions to the same people were vastly different. This result remains unchanged when the stringency rule is increased. In the most extreme case, the two groups took the same course (nominally).

The discovery of phenomena such as these should be very important, and deserving of careful study and interpretation. The great discrepancies in the above case emphasize the importance of the comparison group being used.

CONCLUSION

The applications illustrated earlier suggest other uses for the proposed technique. One could chart how a teacher changes with time by tracking him on a display. Several characteristics of good teaching such as organization of courses or lectures, ability to field questions, and rapport with students, could be charted separately. Opinions concerning a faculty member's research and other activities also could be summarized on these triangles.

The three bins do not have to be ordered among themselves, but they must be exhaustive. For example, at the higher levels of review one might compartmentalize the activities of faculty as being "teaching," "research," and "service." Each observer could place each faculty he is rating into exactly one of these bins as representing the observer's perception of the faculty member's most prominent activity. However, it might be better if the observers divided, say ten points over the three bins. A productive researcher who divides his remaining energies equally between teaching and service activities might receive a (2,6,2) rating. A person who devotes equal effort to teaching and research but does nothing else may receive a (5,5,0) score. The (p,q,r) vector for a faculty member is developed by averaging as before (but in this case the score must be divided by ten to place it on the simplex). The distribution of points would no longer peak near the Q vertex, but would reveal how faculty devote their energies as perceived by the observers. (Note there is no discrimination according to productivity or "organizational worth.")

Deeper understanding could also evolve from analysis such as this. Suppose faculty members are placed into groups of comparable experience, or of comparable total productivity. Then a triangle scatter plot for each group would contribute to the understanding of how the system operates. The de facto effect of past promotion and tenure policies would be revealed picturesquely by looking at these layers of triangles and identifying those points that are moving through the system successfully. Faculty could see themselves in relation to others and make a judgement concerning the advantage of their position in the current environment.

The use of figures other than triangles (such as squares or pentagons) is possible, but in so doing one would have to make some compromises. Distances from vertices would not produce unique points (i.e. each point would be a convex combination of the extreme points and such representations can no longer be unique). The four dimensional simplex is a regular tetrahedron and a two dimensional picture of it could be a square. Points projected onto this square would fail to reveal relative depth. A side view would serve this purpose, but the simplicity of presentation would be lost.

APPENDIX A

Mathematical Details of Plotting

Any widespread use of the methodology requires ADP (Automatic Data Processing), and the analytical technique used may vary with the equipment. One way to plot the point (p,q,r) is to compute its distance from each of any two vertices. The two circles (of appropriate radius) will intersect in two points, but only one of the points will be in the triangle and that will be the solution (p,q,r). The distance from vertex P for example is $[(1-p)^2 + q^2 + r^2]^{1/2}$

A second plotting technique is more difficult to describe but simpler in its execution. It involves located points in convex sets. Let us return to three space and recognize that the leg PQ is on the line P = 1 - Q in the PQ (i.e. R = 0) plane, the leg QR is on the line Q = 1 - R in the QR plane, and the leg RP is on the line R 1 - P in the RP plane. The situation is illustrated in Figure 4.

The locus of all points whose projections to the P axis and the Q axis are in the ratio of the given p:q is a plane through the R axis which intersects the PQ plane in the line (through the origin) q P = pQ. Intersecting this line with the line P = 1 - Q implies that the point (p,q,r) must lie on a line connecting the R vertex to a point on the opposite leg of the triangle which is p/(p+q) of the distance from the vertex Q to the vertex P; having this line, we need only intersect it with another line similarly constructed from another vertex. Thus, we could connect the vertex Q to the leg opposite it on the triangle by finding the point which is p/(p+r) of the distance from R to P along that leg. The intersection of these two constructed lines is the point (p,q,r) in the triangle.

FOOTNOTES

[1] Formal significance tests for these effects can be performed by partitioning the triangle into cells, counting the number of observations in each cell for each attribute. (e.g., type of course, or class size interval) and using the Chi squared contingency table technique.

REFERENCES

[1] Eble, K.E., *The Recognition and Evaluation of Teaching*, American Association of University Professors, One Dupont Circle, Washington, D.C., 1971.

[2] Hildebrand, M., R.C. Wilson, and E.R. Dienst, *Evaluating University Teaching*, Center for Research and Development in Higher Education, University of California, Berkeley, 1971.

[3] Pelz, D.C. and F.M. Andrews, *Scientists in Organizations: Productive Climates for Research and Development*, Wiley, New York, 1966.

[4] Read, R.R. and H.J. Zweig, "On the Quantification of Teacher Performance Using Student Opinion," NPS55REZW72031A, Naval Postgraduate School, March, 1972.

*Accounting Education: Problems and Prospects,
AAA, Education Series No. 1, 1974.*

Testing, Grading, and Evaluation of Student Achievement

William J. Turppa
Georgia State University

Introduction

As a basis for considering the measurement of student achievement in accounting education, this paper outlines some general notions that underlie testing, grading, and evaluation. In addition, Professor Turppa describes an evaluation technique which he has found particularly useful.

Part I Some General Considerations

A. *The Functions of Testing*

Tests provide the essential means of satisfying administrative requirements related to final course grades. However, there are other functions which, depending upon the individual teacher, may carry even greater significance both to the teacher and to the student.

Generally the student essentially considers a test grade as a short-run measure of short-run goal attainment. Only an unusual student is able to overcome his immediate ego-involvement and consider long-run implications which may also be a part of his test grade. Long-run implications include his ability to organize thoughts, to demonstrate an analytical ability, to integrate the bits and pieces of his knowledge, and to recognize subtleties of meaning and significance. These long-run implications are important to him in terms of his future academic achievement as well as in forming some of the dependent variables relating to his prospective professional success.

For the student, a test should provide a means for determining the degree of attaining a level of knowledge which he has prescribed for himself. The implication here is that a student may select a desired level of achievement independent of the desires of the accounting instructor. Certainly professors may influence his decision as the course progresses, but the student is the one who selects his own attainment goal. A student may enroll in an accounting course for the purpose of obtaining a limited background (perhaps representative of a "C" grade). This is a purely rational and intellectual decision on his part. We typically teach more about the "elephant" than the student may *want* to know. Periodic tests throughout the course provide the student with an opportunity to measure his progress in attaining his achievement goal.

For the teacher, tests should provide a means for determining the strengths and weaknesses of his students for the purpose of selecting those items of "wisdom" which need to be re-taught, stressed, or amplified as the course of study develops. Often few accounting instructors take these purposes of an examination into consideration in planning their teaching. This condition may be partially explained by the structuring of accounting courses, where one course contains prerequisite learning for other courses or where the course syllabus is so highly structured that the additional time which might be taken in re-teaching would necessitate elimination or inadequate coverage of other, equally important, topics. Nevertheless, attempts should be made to stress again those concepts which have been shown to be in need of repair.

A few years ago a bill was introduced in the legislature of the State of Illinois which would have required a sign to be posted in every classroom in the public schools of that state. The sign was to read, "If the student hasn't learned, the teacher hasn't taught." During that session one of the decisions which the legislators could look upon with satisfaction was defeat of the bill. But the event does serve to point out another function of testing—the opportunity for the teacher to evaluate his teaching. Self-evaluation on the part of the teacher regarding his teaching methods, presentations, classroom bearing, and testing techniques can only result in improved teaching.

However, one should not be too quick to ascribe an ultimate value to testing in this regard. The typical test is an incomplete device, at best only a poor and unsophisticated statistical sample of achievement. A test is not given in advance of learning and therefore cannot be used to guide the learning. Grading, typically, is not standardized and both student and teacher confidence in the resulting grade is tenuous. Hence, many teachers evaluate a student by taking into account other, perhaps more subjective, measures such as class attendance and participation.

Tests are largely for purposes of measuring achievement, but perhaps it would be useful to indicate what functions a test does not (or should not) serve. For example, some teachers believe that tests should be used as motivational devices.

Generally, when a teacher indicates he uses tests to motivate his students, he may be admitting to the use of a "threat system," rather than a motivational system. "You must study this material because I shall test you on it," is an empty statement. Notwithstanding this, to some extent we must yield to reality. The "typical" student *is* motivated by the realization that he will be tested. Some studies have sought to determine whether a student learns as much or as thoroughly given the absence of directed evaluation. The results of these studies have been mixed and are not conclusive. Perhaps this is because motivation may be a function of the ability of individual teachers to stimulate students in ways other than tests. (Selected bibliographies of research relating to testing and student behavior and to test construction and grading are presented in Appendix A and Appendix B respectively.)

What one should consider is the difference in the meaning and intent of the terms motivation and threat. Motivation is positive in nature and based on pragmatic understandings of the reasons for learning, whereas threat is negative in nature, even though occasionally also based on pragmatic understandings.

B. *A Brief Examination of Alternative Types of Test Items*

There is a sizeable amount of literature available relating to objective and essay test items, and the purpose here is merely to review some basic notions regarding their use. However, little has been written regarding problem-type test questions and following the review of objective and essay questions, five basic types of problem-oriented test items are considered.

True-False. The true-false question best serves the testing of specific and unassailable facts. However, this seemingly innocuous statement presumes that such facts can be explicitly stated and, more importantly, placed in a question framework which does not detract from the function of true-false questions.

For example, consider the following question:

An individual who has subscribed and partially paid for 100 shares of XYZ Corporation capital stock, and who subsequently defaults on his subscription contract, is subject to a loss equal to the total payments he has made.

The best answer to this question would be "it depends." Although some state corporate codes may provide for such an ultimate effect, not all do. Additionally, the phrase "is subject to" requires some interpretation—does this mean immediately upon default or after certain other legal options have been satisfied?

The example given above is representative also of another consideration: a true-false question should incorporate some standard which the student may use as a means of judging its truth value. How true does a statement have to be before it should be marked true?

One last warning regarding true-false items, though perhaps obvious, should be stated. One must resist the temptation to adopt a verbatim statement from textbooks or other assigned material or to make the statement false by including some negative terms in the item. Such practices encourage students to merely memorize text material.

Multiple-Choice. Multiple-choice questions are true-false questions in a different setting. This type of question is not limited to statements of fact, but can be used to test the students' ability to discriminate among alternatives. A multiple-choice question embodies a standard to be used as a means of judging truth value by virtue of allowing the student to make comparisons among the alternatives, while knowing that one response must be "better" than the others.

The requirement that verbatim statements taken from assigned materials must be avoided is perhaps even more important in a multiple-choice context. A student's recall of a phrase or sentence noted in his reading may result in distracting his attention from what is being asked in the question and lead him to select a response which simply appears familiar to him.

The multiple-choice test item is believed to be the most objective means of testing the achievement of the learner. Significantly, objectivity is granted not so much from the point of view of the individual taking the test but rather from a grading frame of reference. Each question has but one "right" response for all students and the grader is not able to interject his personal predispositions in an evaluation of individual student responses without also grading all students on the same basis.

Furthermore, multiple-choice questions provide the instructor with the opportunity to evaluate the examination in terms of test reliability (i.e., the possibility that differences in scores among students are due to factors other than chance) and test validity (i.e., the discriminating power of the right answer versus all of the other alternatives). The purpose here is not to examine these concepts but rather to point them out as significant advantages to a multiple-choice test. The reader may find useful insights in Wood (21) and Tuttle (8). Additionally, many schools now have available a computer analysis using mark-sensing answer sheets, which performs not only the scoring but also provides an analysis of test reliability and validity in a single package.

Many accounting instructors are not disposed to using multiple-choice questions for accounting tests. They reason that accounting is problem oriented, and since problems are the primary learning tools, problems should be used in testing. Although there is no disagreement with the reasoning, there is disagreement with the implication that multiple-choice test items cannot be framed in a problem setting. For example, a test question from an elementary accounting examination is given:

Assume a company has three product lines, all produced in one factory. Management is considering dropping product Z. The present earnings statement, by product-lines is given:

	X	Y	Z	Total
Sales	1,000,000	800,000	200,000	2,000,000
Variable costs	590,000	560,000	150,000	1,300,000
Nonvariable costs	330,000	180,000	90,000	600,000
Net Earnings	80,000	60,000	(40,000)	100,000

Assume that the only alternatives are to drop Product Z or to continue with Product Z. Assume further that the total assets invested will not be affected by the decision. Finally, assume the only change in non-variable costs realted to Product Z which will occur as a result of dropping the product is the elimination of $20,000 in supervisory salaries.

The decision should be:
a. To drop the product line, because a loss of $40,000 is occurring.
b. To keep the product line, because the total earnings would drop by $30,000 if the product were discontinued.
c. To drop the product line, because the salaries of $20,000 will be saved thereby reducing the loss to only $20,000.
d. To keep the product line, because the added revenue of $200,000 is greater than the nonvariable costs of $90,000.
e. To keep the product line, because there is a contribution margin of $50,000 and all nonvariable costs are irrelevant in this decision.

This test question was analyzed, by a computer program known as "MERMAC—Test Analysis and Questionnaire Package," (19) with the results indicating a high degree of item reliability:

Score on the examination as a whole	Percent of each quintile with correct response to this question
upper 1/5	.93
next 1/5	.89
next 1/5	.80
next 1/5	.62
lower 1/5	.38

A problem format for multiple-choice questions can be developed at any level of complexity. However, the individual developing the items should have considerable teaching experience and should be prepared to spend a significant amount of time in constructing and analyzing the finished product. The reason for specifying the need for teaching experience is that in constructing problem formats, it is necessary to anticipate the types of student errors that might be made and provide a possible answer among the choices based on these errors. If five choices are allowed for each question, the right response cannot be obvious to the student merely by inspection.

The advantages of developing a file of reliable test questions will, in the long run, exceed the disadvantage of the time required in developing the file. These advantages will eventually include:

1. Less time in constructing the test, in that previously used and analyzed questions may be re-used.

2. The instructor's confidence in the reliability and validity of a testing device can be measured.

3. The student's attitude toward the testing experience is improved by virtue of a recognized objective grading technique.*

Essay. The objective of essay questions, including those referred to as "short answers," is to test the ability of the student to organize his thoughts around a given theme. An essay question should not test specific facts unless the question has been developed in the context of larger problem. In this case, the objective would be to determine the depth of understanding about the underlying considerations which the student, perhaps impliedly, employed when solving the mechanical aspects encompassed in the problem.

Here is an example of an essay question used on a final examination in intermediate accounting which led the students to think about the answer within a narrow framework rather than being open ended!

Accounting deals primarily with questions related to:
1. The selection of events to be recognized in the accounting system (model).
2. The selection of the time at which the event should be recognized.
3. The selection of a means for measuring the event.

Though all these problems "hang together," they are generally dealt with separately.

REQUIRED:
1. Which of these problems cause accountants the greatest difficulty? Briefly explain.
2. Describe an accounting problem which demonstrates your answer to requirement No. 1.
3. Provide a solution to the problem you noted in requirement No. 2. (It need not be "generally accepted.")

Another format for essay questions may be referred to as an open-end essay. Again, from an intermediate examination the following is given:

REQUIRED:
Select one accounting concept, technique, or principle currently accorded "general acceptability."
 a. Criticize its use.
 b. Defend its use.

(Allow yourself time for thought before committing yourself to writing. The point of this question is for you to exhibit your depth of understanding on a question which you feel you can be most authoritative.)

Accounting Problems. As mentioned earlier, most accounting professors have reservations about giving tests which include only objective or essay questions. The following statements are guidelines which may be used in the construction of problem-oriented test items:

1. As far as possible, the problem should be one-dimensional. This means that the solution to one part of the problem should not be a function of the solution to another part of the same problem. A simple example will illustrate:

Requirement No. 1 -
Make the journal entries required by the following set of transactions related to stockholders' equity. (A set of transactions follows.)

Requirement No. 2 -
Calculate the book value per share of common stock.

The solution to requirement No. 2 is dependent upon the solution to requirement No. 1, and unless the grader is willing to make a host of alternative satisfactory solutions based on each student's responses to No. 1, there is no way to determine whether or not the student knows how to calculate book value per share.

2. Ordinarily the data necessary to solve the problem should be given in an orderly fashion. This is not to say that extraneous (non-relevant) data may not be included as a means of determining the student's ability to discriminate between relevant and irrelevant data. The requirement relates most directly to the types of accounting problems where the sequence of events is of importance in analyzing the data provided.

3. The requirements of the problem should be clearly spelled out and given prominence so that the student is able to determine what is required of him even before noting what data are available for the solution. This gives the student perspective when considering the available data.

4. Problems should be constructed in a fashion which clearly indicates to the student what type of response and what level of sophistication is expected of him. There are five basic types of problems and it would be desirable for each type to appear in a given examination. Though the types are treated here separately, it is likely that they may be combined in an actual test. (Appendix C presents examples of each of the problem-types which have been developed for an intermediate accounting course.)

a. *Specific items*—the majority of test problems are likely of this sort, and usually require an entry or calculation of some kind as an answer.

b. *Related items*—a series of transactions which test the comprehensive understanding of a single topic, such as accounting for the cost of goods sold, and may include entries for a set of inventory transactions, valuation of ending inventory, adjusting and closing entries for cost of goods sold items, and perhaps the preparation of a partial income statement. The objective to be satisfied in both specific and related-item problems is to test the student's ability to *do* accounting.

c. *Alternative treatments*—this type of problem has the objective of testing the student's awareness of alternative solutions which can be given to the same set of data, and perhaps the underlying justifications which support the alternative treatments. It is at this point that problems and short-answer responses begin to be useful in combination. Though this involves some conceptual ability, it is not truly a test of a student's ability to organize his thoughts conceptually, in that the test item still allows for the likelihood of rote memorization of specific fact.

d. *Accounting analytics*—it is at this point that a student is tested on whether he can "think" accounting. A distinction is made between straightforward, relatively uncomplicated responses as required in A, B, and C, above, and the more complex and possibly unfamiliar presentation of data. A representative problem requiring accounting analytics would be one which requires a correction of errors or which requires a student to consider various effects of errors. At a lesser level of sophistication, the effects of a single transaction on various financial statement or decision model values may also be considered within this category.

e. *Accounting concepts*—this type of problem requires the use of accounting abstractions (concepts) but the problem is constructed so as to place the student in an essentially unfamiliar setting. Very often the problem would pertain to an unsettled controversial issue in accounting. Though conceptual ability is probably tested best by means of essay questions, problems may be designed which call for an entry or set of entries whereby the student is led by the nature of the questions to a reasoned response. There is little doubt that this is the most difficult kind of question to construct as well as to grade.

Part II. A Case Study of a Testing, Grading, and Evaluation Technique

Rather indirectly, Part I of this paper has indicated that testing, grading, and evaluating of student achievement may be viewed as three separate dimensions of a single problem. Testing serves many objectives, grading is subject to alternative interpretations, and evaluation implies an even greater level of subjectivity. Over the past few years the author has experimented with alternative techniques of accomplishing these different, yet related, tasks. Although the system presented here is in a developmental stage, it has already yielded greater personal confidence that the end result is more rational and objectively determined than any system previously employed by the author. Perhaps a more important advantage is the favorable student reaction to the method.

A. *Underlying Judgments*

Any student evaluation system should be based upon certain predispositions which the evaluator believes to be congruent with the nature of his discipline, juxtaposed with an understanding of the strengths and weaknesses of the testing techniques available to him. The following enumeration of underlying judgments is presented in order to allow the reader to more completely consider the adequacy of the method described.

1. Accounting is not deterministic but rather abstract in nature. Admittedly this does not appear to be a true statement if one views accounting as a debit-credit, forced balance, closed system. However, the concepts underlying the accounting model are difficult to formalize and subject to multiple interpretations with varying degrees of intensity; frequently, the interpretation is dependent upon who is stating a position and the context in which the concept is employed. (For example, the justification for a given accounting technique (LIFO) depends upon the relative strength of balance sheet or income statement objectives as seen by the individual stating his position.)

2. Accounting tests should reflect the abstract nature of accounting.

3. Grading points assigned to each part of a test are useful devices for evaluating student responses, but are primarily for the convenience of the grader and may not be significant in any other respect.

4. The use of fractional points belies the nature of accounting and may mislead the student by appearing as though the grading

carries absolute values. (How often have you had a student argue for the addition of a single point to his raw score?)

5. Each test may or may not accumulate to a possible total of 100 points. The total points are a function of the points assigned, for grading convenience, to the individual parts of the test. Therefore, total points vary and may be more than or less than 100 points for any given test.

6. A summation of grading points may not be indicative of the relative merit of the student's responses taken as a whole, in that the points may not be indicative of the relative weights of importance among the parts of a given test. At best, a summation of points may only be a position from which to begin an interpretation of the meaning of a raw score.

7. An evaluation of achievement requires an evaluation of the student's *relative* performance on each part of the test— *relative* meaning pertaining to other students performance, instructor expectation, and to the test as a whole.

8. Given the difficulty of assigning significance to a raw score, letter grades (A, B, C, D) are preferred as a means of indicating over-all performance.

B. *Test Construction*

Although the usefulness of multiple-choice test questions has earlier been emphasized, the purpose here is to continue the examination of the problem-oriented accounting test. The statements which follow are consonant with earlier sections of this paper and continue to be versed in a normative fashion.

1. Each test should employ as many of the different types of accounting problems as is possible within the time constraint allowed. The sequence of the problem-types given earlier approximates a range of difficulty from easiest (specific items) to most difficult (accounting concepts). On each test, there should be "something for everybody" so that even the poorest prepared student may find *some* success and *all* students will be challenged. Any test where a student earns 100 percent may be considered a poor test in that every student did not have the opportunity to clearly demonstrate his real academic superiority.

2. Each part of the test should cover a single unit (often a chapter) of instruction, e.g., accounting for bonds, accounting for trade receivables.

3. Each part of the test should be roughly of equal importance. (This requirement occasionally is not possible.)

4. Enforced time demands should be avoided if at all possible. To those instructors who believe that a timed test is desirable for students planning to take the CPA exam or is more "realistic" in terms of on-the-job experience, it can be argued:

a. The student is in a learning situation. A well-designed test is a learning experience as well as an evaluational device. More will be said about this later.

b. An examination period is not, and cannot be, "realistic." Problem data are abstracted from a larger set of available data, the student is without supervision, there is no mechanism to monitor his progress or correct his errors, and the intense ego-involvement of an examination is unlike the day-to-day operations encountered on-the-job.

However, if there is an enforced time constraint, great care must be given to the construction of the test if one wishes to avoid behavioral dysfunctions on the part of the student.

C. *Test Administration*

A well constructed test can fail to accomplish the desired objectives if careful consideration is not also given to the administration of the test.

1. Students should be informed of the type of test questions to expect, the test materials they will need to bring to the test, and any other information which will tend to remove the mysteries associated with the testing technique. For this purpose, it is worthwhile to give to the students a copy of an earlier test for whatever use they may wish to make of it. If possible, it may be desirable to file old tests in the school library reserve section to insure the availability of this information to all students.

2. The classroom to be used for the testing period should be checked to insure the suitability for the intended usage. It should be large enough to provide spacing between students in hopes of avoiding the possibility of academic misconduct and to

allow the instructor to move about the room without disrupting the concentration of the students.

3. The test should be given a careful review by the instructor prior to the testing period so as to allow for changes or corrections to problems prior to starting the test. No questions or answers about the test should be allowed once the test has started. The interruptions caused by student queries, instructor responses and the general commotion caused by making changes in the problem data after the test has started is extremely distracting to students.

4. The student should provide his solutions to the problems on separate paper and should be allowed to keep the test when he is finished. Requiring the student to provide his solutions on separate paper (typically accounting analysis paper) amplifies an instructional objective in using problems as learning tools, whereby the student considers not only a solution but also a means of presenting the solution. The test is merely a continuation of that objective.

The reason for allowing the student to keep the test questions is a pedagogical one. A test is conceived of as a learning tool. As a learning device, a test should be given and graded immediately (see Wood, 21). This thought is behind programmed instruction and response displays in lecture halls whereby the lecturer may electronically obtain student responses to the lecture material presented. Typically, an accounting test cannot be graded immediately; however one may approximate the objective by allowing the students to keep the test questions. The ego involvement of the student will frequently cause him to consider his solution in light of the course materials upon leaving the classroom. He accomplishes this both as an individual as well as a member of a group.

Unusual students cannot gather immediately after a test to review one another's responses and determine what they, as a group, consider to be a "right" answer. Occasionally the author has been permitted to sit in on this post-test review and has wished that he might able to create a similar attitude and atmosphere in the classroom--it has been a truly rewarding experience.

5. Lastly, and in conformance with the points raised above, the test should be graded immediately, returned to the student and reviewed during the next regular class period. Admittedly this may not be possible at times, but if the instructor wishes to gain educational value from the testing process this requirement is of paramount importance.

D. *Grading a Test*

There are few absolute statements for consideration related to the philosophy or techniques of grading. Nearly every accounting professor "does his own thing" in this area; a "model" grading technique is presumptious. Each instructor must determine a method which satisfies his own testing objectives. However, the statements which follow represent a technique employed by the author which are consistent with the arguments presented throughout this paper:

1. A solution, including grading points, should be made out before giving the test to the students. This solution would represent the answers that the professor believes to be "ideal" and forms the basis for assigning relative weights to the problems or parts of problems. This then provides a standard by which to compare student responses as well as for judging the relative difficulty of the test as a whole. Succinctly, the students should not be allowed to set the grading standards.

2. A preliminary statement of expected performance for "A" and "F" extremes is made based on a subjective evaluation of the level of difficulty of the test, not a preconceived notion of a "curve." The use of a curve would be feasible given a large enough distribution of grades and a test which has been standardized. Neither requirement is likely in a typical accounting class. Additionally, there has been no "curve" developed which is unique to various levels of accounting instruction. It would seem that elementary accounting might come close to conforming a standard grading curve since the population is relatively heterogeneous and the course of study is generally viewed as "general education."

The first course in intermediate accounting would not likely conform to a standard curve because it is the first "professional" exposure to the discipline with which the student is confronted. Secondly, students may have developed a preconceived notion of what accounting is and the intellectual demands required, which may not be accurate. And thirdly the course is generally designed as a filter for screening candidates for the accounting major.

One would expect that courses following intermediate accounting would have a "curve" skewed toward A, B, and C grades, especially if the screening process has been successful.

3. Approximately five responses should be tentatively graded before definitely setting a grading standard. This gives recognition to the fact that though the professor knew what he was testing, the problem may have been constructed to include distractors which will not yield the intended results. This technique is merely a check of the professor's ideal solution.

4. Each problem should be graded in its entirety for each student rather than grading the entire examination of an individual student. This provides for greater consistency in grading each student on a similar standard.

5. Each problem should be graded at one sitting. The grader should not begin to grade a problem unless he is sure he has enough time to finish that problem for the entire set of examinations. It is too easy for the grader to change his evaluation if his efforts are interrupted in the process of grading.

6. During the grading, a test analysis form (Exhibit A, page 21) is developed using the number of grading points lost (columns 1, 3 and 5). An abbreviated example for five students on a three-part test is given. This form is discussed later in greater detail.

7. The grader should sample his grading for consistency upon completion of the set of problems. This may be accomplished by comparing the last five solutions graded to the first five graded. Also, during the grading process, the instructor may find it useful to accumulate grading notes which can be used both as a means of maintaining a consistent grading standard as well as reference material when reviewing the test with students.

E. *Interpretation and Evaluation of Results*

At one time it was common to find published departmental standards for interpreting results. A typical approach was to use a point system which, when accumulated, was to fit into a predetermined scale, such as:

percent	
93	A
85	B
77	C
70	D

Such inflexible scales no longer seem to be widely used, and for good reason. Each instructor, in order to satisfy the scale, was forced to construct tests (or to grade them) so as to yield a "legitimate" distribution of grades. Certainly, such constraints limit the usefulness of tests (as described earlier) by emphasizing the single purpose of satisfying administrative requirements.

The "absolutes" in accounting instruction have been diminishing in significance over the years. The emphasis of pure bookkeeping mechanics has been reduced with greater stress being placed on the abstractions embodied in the accounting model. As a result, accounting tests represetative of the changing emphasis in accounting instruction are more difficult to grade objectively and the interpretation of the grade is more difficult to generalize.

A raw score (summation of grading points) needs to be interpreted in terms of the relative level of difficulty of the test as whole, as well as the standard selected by the instructor in grading individual responses. For example, if an instructor uses an "ideal" solution and conscientiously grades student responses in this manner, he should anticipate a lower raw score than if he has employed a "loose" standard of grading. That is, on the same test, it is entirely plausible that a raw score of 73 percent for one grader would be equivalent to an over-all performance of a "B," whereas for another grader a score of 73 percent may be a "C." It is worthwhile to note that the interpretation of grading points in the manner described here can be viewed as a one-dimensional interpreta-

Test Analysis Form
Exhibit A

COLUMN NUMBER	(1)	(2)	(3)	(4)	(5)	(6)	(7)	(8)			(8a)	(9)	(10)
POSSIBLE PTS.	(30)		(42)		(25)		(97)						
	PART NO. 1		PART NO. 2		PART NO. 3		TOTAL POINTS LOST	PART RANKS			RANKS WEIGHTED	TENT. GRADE	TEST GRADE
STUDENT NAME	POINTS LOST	RANK	POINTS LOST	RANK	POINTS LOST	RANK		+	0	−			
ADAMS	4	0	6	0	2	+	12	1	0	0	8	B	B
BROWN	13	−	3	+	1	+	17	2	2	1	8	C	B
CATES	18	−	20	−	10	−	48	0	0	3	0	F	F
DORN	9	0	5	0	6	0	20	0	3	0	6	C	C
ESTER	0	+	3	+	1	+	4	3	0	0	12	A	A
ACCEPTABLE AVERAGE RANGE	3-9		5-9		4-6								

tion, in that no consideration is given to the grading of various parts of the test. It should be noted that this author uses a two-dimensional interpretation of grading in an effort to provide not only an interpretation of the grading but also an *evaluation* of the student's relative achievement.

Completion of the test analysis form (Exhibit A) requires the grader to:

1. Sum points lost on each problem for each student (column 7).

2. Assign a "tentative grade" (column 9), based on the preconceived acceptable ranges as noted above. In the example, the maximum allowable points deducted for each letter grade are as follows:

$$A = -8$$
$$B = -16$$
$$C = -24$$
$$D = -32$$

3. Rank the score on each part, for each student, in accordance with an "acceptable average." An acceptable average is the instructor's evaluation of a point range in which he would expect a "C" student to fall. If one were to determine an arithmetic mean for each problem and use this as a center position for an acceptable average, he would tend to develop a nearly perfect grading curve as a net result of this technique. However, to do so would be to allow the students to set the standard of achievement in a class that either by lack of class size or lack of test standardization does not truly exhibit the prerequisites for "normal" distributions. In the example "+" represents above average on that problem alone, "O" represents about average, "—" represents below average (columns 2, 4, 6).

4. Sum problem rankings according to the number of +, 0,— for each student (column 8).

5. Assign rank weights and sum. In the example, + = 4; (0) = 2; (—) = 0 (column 8a).

6. Verify tentative grade with rank weights. In the example, note the results for Adams and Brown; though 5 points separate their raw score, with Adams falling within the "B" range and Brown falling within the "C" range, their rank weight is equalized at 8. This would imply that these students should be earning roughly the same grade. Further inspection of the scores would indicate that Brown "blew" the first part, but has scored better on two of the three parts than Adams. Incidentally, greater confidence in the results of this technique are achieved when there are four or five parts on each test, with all parts carrying the same relative importance. (However, it is not necessary that the grading points assigned to each part be weighted evenly.)

7. Determine the test grade. The relationship between the tentative grade based on raw score and the rank weights yields the test grade (column 10). Each instructor may impose additional qualitative requirements. For example, one may interpret an "A" as superior performance and that no student may earn an "A" on a single test who has ranked below average on any part of that test, even though based on a purely raw score he may "fit" into the tentative grade range of "A."

F. *Final Student Evaluation*

A final evaluation of student performance in the course is made using an approach similar to that indicated for a single test. An analysis form for this purpose is given in Exhibit B. The illustration assumes that three tests, consisting of four parts (12 total parts), have been given in the course. If the instructor gives tests or term papers which have variable weights, the technique requires weighted averages for points lost and part ranks, just as would be employed in any other evaluation technique.

Exhibit B indicates that although the tests carried equal relative weight, they were not equal in total possible grading points. Again, points are determined on the basis of grading convenience. The "curve" for each test in this illustration is the same for each examination, but it need not be. In the example, the implication is that since the points decreased with each test (97-84-65) and the "curve" based on points remained the same, each test was progressively more difficult. However, this relationship need not be the case. Each instructor must subjectively evaluate each test's difficulty and derive an acceptable curve. The "range based on points" in Exhibit B, Part II, is nothing more than a summation of individual test curves established at the time of each test.

Student Evaluation—Course Grade
Exhibit B—Part I

POSSIBLE PTS.	(97) TEST NO. 1				(84) TEST NO. 2				(65) TEST NO. 3				(246)					
STUDENT NAME	POINTS LOST	RANKS +	RANKS 0	RANKS −	G R	POINTS LOST	RANKS +	RANKS 0	RANKS −	G R	POINTS LOST	RANKS +	RANKS 0	RANKS −	G R	Σ POINTS LOST	TOTAL PART RANKS + / 0 / −	WEIGHTED RANKS	TENT GRADE	FINAL GRADE
FRANK	12	2	2	0	B	14	2	2	0	B	17	2	1	1	C	43	6 / 5 / 1	34	B	B
GREEN	18	3	0	1	B	16	2	2	0	B	15	2	2	0	B	49	7 / 4 / 1	36	C	B
HARVEY	48	0	1	3	F	32	0	2	2	D	34	0	1	3	F	114	0 / 4 / 8	8	F	F
IBSON	20	1	3	0	C	14	2	2	0	B	26	0	2	2	D	60	3 / 7 / 2	26	C	C
JONES	4	4	0	0	A	8	3	1	0	A	8	3	0	1	B	20	10 / 1 / 1	42	A	A

Grade Ranges—Course Evaluation
Exhibit B—Part II

Grade	Test No. 1	Test No. 2	Test No. 3	Range based on Σ points	Range based on Weighted Ranks
A	8	8	8	0-24	48-42
B	16	16	16	25-48	41-32
C	24	24	24	49-72	31-22
D	32	32	32	73-96	21-12

Tentative grade based on Σ points   Final grade based on weighted ranks.

The "weighted ranks" for the 12 parts of the three tests have been determined, as before, on the basis of (+) = 4 points; (0) = 2 points; and (-) = 0 points. The grade instructor's subjective measure of acceptable performance in each grade category. For example, the lower limit of the "A" achievement level (42), represents the following possible achievement on the twelve parts.

(+) above average	(0) average	(—) below average	weighted ranks
9	3	0	42
10	1	1	42
10	2	0	44
11	0	1	44
11	1	0	46
12	0	0	48

The remaining grade categories can be determined in a similar manner; it is a matter for each instructor to select his own achievement standards.

Notice that the only unusual result in the exhibit is for Green, who, on the basis of points, would have earned a "C," but on the basis of ranks has earned a "B."

G. *Advantages of this technique*

Ranking the individual parts of each test provides information to the instructor regarding individual student weaknesses as well as class weaknesses. This information satisfies the need to know what instructional units need to be reconsidered in future classroom activities. Additionally, the information on an individual basis can be used to design remedial activities for the individual student.

From the point of view of evaluating achievement, the two-dimensional approach provides for a more realistic measure in that the evaluation is not subject to material errors caused by the weighting of individual parts of a test which may be disporportionate when the test is considered as a whole.

In terms of grading, the instructor is not forced to assign points or to grade the test in a manner that will "beef up" the raw scores.

Student reaction to the technique is favorable. It indicates to them that the instructor is attempting to evaluate their performance, rather than to merely grade the test.

Perhaps the single greatest advantage to this technique is the requirement that the instructor explicitly determine acceptable levels of performance that may have been previously subjugated by a simple point system. Once the standards** have been stated and uniformly applied to all students, it is possible to refer to the evaluation technique as "objective," even though the test items themselves cannot similarly be referenced.

---

*As an aside, it seems that a question bank composed of multiple-choice questions adequately catalogued by topic and course level, which have been developed and tested for reliability and validity and made available to teaching members, would be a worthwhile educational project of the American Accounting Association.

**The standards are also two-dimensional. Recall that an "acceptable average range" must be stated for each part; secondly, it is necessary to state acceptable performance ranges when relating the over-all weighted ranks to a grade level.

Testing, Grading, and Evaluation of Student Achievements

Student Evaluation—Course Grade
Exhibit B—Part I

POSSIBLE PTS.	(97)			(84)			(65)			(246)					
	TEST NO. 1			TEST NO. 2			TEST NO. 3			Σ POINTS LOST	TOTAL PART RANKS		WEIGHTED RANKS	TENT. GRADE	FINAL GRADE
STUDENT NAME	POINTS LOST	RANKS + / 0 / -	GR	POINTS LOST	RANKS + / 0 / -	GR	POINTS LOST	RANKS + / 0 / -	GR		+ / 0 / -				
FRANK	12	2 / 0 / 0	B	14	2 / 2 / 0	B	17	2 / 1 / 1	C	43	6 / 5 / 1		34	B	B
GREEN	18	3 / 0 / 1	B	16	2 / 2 / 0	B	15	2 / 2 / 0	B	49	7 / 4 / 1		36	C	B
HARVEY	48	0 / 1 / 3	F	32	0 / 0 / 2	D	34	0 / 1 / 3	F	114	0 / 4 / 8		8	F	F
IBSON	20	3 / 0 / 0	C	14	2 / 2 / 0	B	26	2 / 2 / 2	D	60	3 / 7 / 2		26	C	C
JONES	4	4 / 0 / 0	A	8	2 / 1 / 0	A	8	3 / 0 / 1	B	20	10 / 1 / 1		42	A	A

Grade Ranges—Course Evaluation
Exhibit B—Part II

Grade	Test No. 1	Test No. 2	Test No. 3	Range based on Σ points	Range based on Weighted Ranks
A	8	8	8	0-24	48-42
B	16	16	16	25-48	41-32
C	24	24	24	49-72	31-22
D	32	32	32	73-96	21-12

Tentative grade based on Σ points
Final grade based on weighted ranks

527

Appendix A
Selected Bibliography on the Effects of Tests on Student Behavior

1. Boyd, G.R., "Tests As Instructional Tools," *Improving College and University Teaching,* 18:217-218, Summer, 1970.
2. Clifford, M.M. *et al.* "Effects of Emphasizing Competition In Classroom-testing Procedures," *Journal of Educational Research,* 65:234-238, January, 1972.
3. Hakstian, R., "Effects of Type of Examination Anticipated On Test Preparation and Performance," *Journal of Educational Research,* 64:319-324, March, 1971.
4. Marso, R.N., "Classroom Testing Procedures, Test Anxiety, and Achievement," *Journal of Experimental Education,* 38:54-58, Spring, 1970.
5. Proger, B.B., "Test Anxiety and Defensiveness Experimentally Induced By Four Conditions of Testing Arousal," *Journal of Experimental Education,* 39:78-83, Summer, 1971.
6. Schutz, R.D., "Role of Measurement In Education: Servant, Soulmate, Stoolpigeon, Statesman, Scapegoat, All of the Above, and-or None of the Above," *Journal of Educational Measurement,* 8:141-146, Fall, 1971.
7. Terranova, C., "Relationship Between Test Scores and Test Time," *Journal of Experimental Education,* 40:81-83, Spring, 1972.

Appendix B
Selected Bibliography on Test Construction and Grading

8. American Accounting Association, *Accounting Instruction: Concepts & Practices,* Chapter 6, "Testing," by Roy Tuttle, South-Western Publishing Company, Cincinnati, 1968.
9. Alker, H.A. *et al.* "Multiple-Choice Questions and Student Characteristics," *Journal of Educational Psychology,* 60:231-248, June, 1969.
10. Arnold, J.C., "On Scoring Procedures for Multiple-Choice Tests," *Journal of Experimental Education,* 38:9-12, Fall, 1969.
11. Baker, E.L., "Effects of Manipulated Item Writing Constraints on the Homogeneity of Test Items; Teacher-made Tests," *Journal of Educational Measurement,* 8:305-309, Winter, 1971.
12. Costin, F., "Optimal Number of Alternatives in Multiple-Choice Achievement Tests: Some Empirical Evidence for a Mathematical Proof," *Educational and Psychological Measurement,* 30:353-358, Summer, 1970.
13. Davis, R.A., "Planning Teacher-Made Tests," *Journal of Education,* 46:155-158, November, 1968.
14. Ebel, R.L., "How to Write True-False Test Items," *Educational and Psychological Measurement,* 31:417-426, Summer, 1971.
15. Gorth, W., "Tape-Based Data Bank From Educational Research or Instructional Testing Using Longitudinal Item Sampling," *Educational and Psychological Measurement,* 29:175-177, Spring, 1972.
16. Lee, Y.B., "Computer Procedure For the Item Analysis of a Multiple-Choice Test," *Educational and Psychological Measurement,* 32:203, Spring, 1972.
17. Marso, R.N., "Test Item Arrangement, Testing Time, and Performance," *Journal of Educational Measurement,* 7:113-118, Summer, 1970.
18. Olson, L.A., "Item Analysis, Measurement, and Instruction," *Improving College and University Teaching,* 16:163-164, Summer, 1968.
19. Educational Tests and Measurement Division—University of Illinois, *MERMAC— Test Analysis and Questionnaire Package,* University of Illinois at Champaign-Urbana; Urbana, Illinois, (Unpublished). (Other schools have developed similar computer packages. For example, the Testing Division of the Student Counselling Center at Georgia State University, Atlanta, Georgia, has developed a program entitled "Test Scoring and Analysis Program.")
20. Wofford, J.C., "Effects of Test Construction Variables Upon Test Reliability and Validity," *California Journal of Educational Research,* 20:96-106, May, 1969.
21. Wood, D.A., *Test Construction,* Charles E. Merrill Books, Inc., Columbus, Ohio, 1961.

Appendix C
Examples of Accounting Problem-Type Test Items

A. Specific Problem

Patent Amortization

On September 1, 1969, Wright Company purchased a patent from a competitor for $19,200. The patent was on a product known as "Exacto," which is similar to one sold by Wright Company. The purpose in acquiring the patent was to remove "Exacto" from the market, thereby leaving Wright Company's product (known as "Neero") free of competition.

REQUIRED:
Record the adjusting entry as of December 31, 1969, for the amortization of the patent. The legal life remaining on the patent acquired (Exacto) was 10 years. The estimated useful life remaining on the patent covering "Neero" is 8 years.

B. *Related Items*

Stock Options

REQUIRED:
Prepare the necessary entries related to employee stock options as noted below. If no entry is needed for the event described, write *no entry.*

On January 1, 1970, the stockholders of DEF Corporation adopted a plan whereby each executive may acquire rights to purchase up to 1,000 shares of common stock at $51 per share. Par value of the stock is $50. Current market value is $52.

On February 1, 1970, options were granted to ten executives to purchase 1,000 shares each. The plan required the executives to have been employed by DEF Corporation for 5 years before they could exercise the options. In addition, after satisfying this condition each executive was required to exercise his options within 6 months of the date he became eligible. The market value of the stock on this date was $55.

On April 1, 1970, five of the executives became eligible. The market value on this date was $56.

On April 15, 1970, four (4) of the executives exercised their options. The market value of the stock on this date was $58.

On August 2, 1970, the options held by the fifth executive had expired. The market value of the stock on this date was $60.

C. *Alternative Treatments*

Bond Refunding

Eggsacto Co. is confronted with the decision to refund an existing bond issue. Data which may be relevant have been accumulated by your assistant (he doesn't know how to calculate the expected discount on the new issue.)

	Old Issue	New Issue (Pro-forma)
Face Value	100,000	100,000
Annual Interest (Stated Rate)	(5 percent)	(4 percent)
Initial Life	20-years	10-years
Remaining Life	10-years	10-years
Call Premium	2,000	3,000
Unamortized Discount	2,500	?

(The new issue can be sold to an underwriter at an effective interest rate of 5 percent.)

REQUIRED:
1. Provide evidence to support the decision to issue or not to issue the new bonds.
2. Without regard to whether it is a rational decision:
   a) Record the sale of the new issue at a yield of 5 percent.
   b) Record the call and retirement of the old issue. (Assume the date of call is on an interest date and that the values indicated above are "up-to-date.")
   c) Record the first payment of annual interest on the new bond issue. Compounded interest amortization should be used for Bond Premium or Discount.
3. Present two different treatments which may be given to the "Unamortized Discount & Call Premium" arising from the call of the old bonds.
4. Of the two methods in (3), which do you find "most acceptable?" Why?
5. As between the "compound interest" and "straight-line" methods of amortizing Bond Premium or Discount, which do you find to be most theoretically elegant? Why?

D. Accounting Analytics

Accounting Changes

The Delta Company had constructed a building at the beginning of 19A which cost $40,000 and was estimated to have no salvage value and a 10-year useful life. At the beginning of 19E the company realized that a $6,000 charge made during the construction period to an expense account, should have been capitalized as a part of the cost of the building.

In addition at the end of 19E, the company, with the approval of their auditors, has determined that the building should have been depreciated on a 12-year basis with a $6,000 estimated salvage value.

Net Income for 19D was reported as $50,000. All adjusting entries have been prepared for 19E, but the books have not been closed. Net Income prior to any necessary entries to account for these changes was $60,000. *You may ignore tax effects.*

Retained Earnings at 1-1-19E had a $100,000 credit balance.

REQUIRED:

1) Make all necessary entries at the end of 19E to account for the above changes and errors in accordance with APB No. 20. (Hint: Account for the error *first.*)

2) Delta plans to present comparative statements for 19D and 19E. Calculate the balances which would appear as follows:

	19D	19E
Building		
Accum. Depreciation		
Retained Earnings—Beg.		
Net Income		
Prior Period Adjustment		
Retained Earnings—End.		

E. Accounting Concepts

Pensions

Part I. Short Answers

The pension problem can be posed in a fashion similar to other problems encountered in financial accounting:

1. *What* events need to be recognized in the accounts?
2. *When* should the events be recognized in the accounts?
3. *How* should the events be measured?

REQUIRED: (Be brief, to the point, and cogent!)

A. As the proponent of a pay-as-you-go approach to pension accounting, provide answers to each of the above questions.

B. As the proponent of APB No. 8, provide answers to each of the above questions.

Part II.

A company has initiated a pension plan at the beginning of the current year. They have agreed to fund normal cost as periodically determined and past service cost over a 10-year period. Past service cost is being amortized to expense on a 20-year basis.

REQUIRED: Using any amounts you wish:

1) prepare an entry in the first year of the plan.
2) prepare an entry in the 11th year of the plan.

Grading Systems and the Purposes of Grades

Jonathan R. Warren
Educational Testing Service—Berkeley

Introduction

Grading procedures have tended to evolve over time. In this paper, Mr. Warren discusses some of the newer grading systems being proposed, including the pass-fail option. The discussion also emphasizes the purposes and problems of grades, generally and as specifically related to the accounting profession.

The past eight or ten years have been a period of widespread tinkering with grading procedures in higher education. Several such periods have occurred since grades first came into general use about a hundred years ago. They have in the past produced such shifts as moving from grading on a scale of 100 to the currently dominant ABCDF system. Little more than vestiges of the 100-point system remain, and they are mostly in areas outside higher education. Examples are Civil Service, CPA, and bar examination procedures, where 70 or 75 out of a possible 100 is often established as a passing score as though it had some intrinsic significance rather than being an arbitrary point on an arbitrary scale. Only one of the recent changes in grading practices seems likely to have any pervasive or lasting effect.

The Decline Of Negative Grades

The change in grading practices with the best promise for a long and healthy life is the abandonment of use of failing grades. More precisely, it is the abandonment of the use of the failing grade to highlight failure, an approach which may have negative consequences which go beyond a simple absence of advancement in the absence of achievement. The more accurate term for the abandoned part of the grading system is a negative grade rather than a failing grade since it applies to both D's and F's and is associated with the common practice of requiring a specified grade-point average for graduation, with D's and F's contributing negatively to that average. A student's failure to achieve the level of accomplishment expected in one course forces him to perform higher than an acceptable level in another course to compensate for the D or F in the first course. This policy treats failure to achieve as a transgression for which atonement must be made, while the same lack of achievement in a student who did not enroll in the course requires no such atonement.

A growing number of colleges and universities, following the early examples of Brown and Stanford, have abolished D and F grades, treating absence of achievement in the same way whether it accompanied enrollment in a course or not. Academic credits and graduation are based on positive achievement. Failure to achieve has no negative consequences other than the absence of academic advancement. Most of the institutions that have abolished negative grades have retained the three ABC grades plus optional Pass grades. Practices still differ in the way failure to achieve an acceptable level of performance is treated even when no grade below a C is possible. Some institutions do not retain a record of courses students have taken and not passed. Others record the fact that a course was taken with no grade awarded; the course does not affect the student's grade-point average.

The abandonment of D's and F's is not a radical departure from common current practices. Distributions of grades in a number of colleges and universities show D's and F's together constituting no more than about 10 per cent of all the grades awarded. Today's undergraduate grade distributions have their centers much closer to a B than a C, with B having become the most common grade and C regarded as a moderately poor grade. Thus most institutions with traditional ABCDF systems are not far from the new ABCX system (where X indicates either no record or no effect on the student's grade-point average). The policy of requiring academic atonement for poor performance is applied relatively rarely.

Other Grading Innovations

The alternative to the customary five-level system in use at the largest number of institutions is Pass-Fail grading (Burwen, 1971). In spite of its wide use, it is rarely the primary system at any institution (AACRAO Survey, 1971). Usually it is offered as an option, with several limitations on its use. Typically only one course per term can be taken Pass-Fail and that one cannot be in the student's major field. Fears of graduate and professional schools that Pass-Fail grading would seriously affect student selection process are therefore exaggerated. Few students present transcripts with more than 10 per cent of their grades as Passes, and those will rarely be in the student's major field.

Pass-Fail grading has two drawbacks that make it unlikely to retain even the limited popularity it has reached in the last few years. First, the F is still a negative grade that can put students in a worse position than they would be in if they had not taken the course at all. Second, many students, faculty members, and those who use grades in selection for further education or employment, value the distinctions among several levels of acceptable performance that a Pass hides. Both these objections are met by the ABCX system.

At some institutions that have adopted the ABCX system, similar to those usually placed on Pass-Fail options. In keeping with the non-negative aspects of the ABCX system, a course taken on a Pass basis and not passed does not enter the student's record. Thus a Pass-No Record option is replacing Pass-Fail. (The University of California at Santa Cruz, for example, a leader in the move to Pass-Fail grading, has recently shifted to a Pass-No Record system, which is really a supplement to a descriptive grading system, as described below.)

Institutions that are sometimes thought of as having complete Pass-Fail grading systems such as Sarah Lawrence College, the University of California at Santa Cruz, and Goddard College, really use Pass-Fail as an adjunct to a descriptive grading system. The results of faculty members' evaluations of students are reported in descriptive prose. Any aspect of student performance considered pertinent can be described. Different strengths and weaknesses in the same student can also be reported in whatever detail is desired. Grading is not limited to a single general dimension of overall achievement.

When grades are to be used for selection to higher levels of education or other intellectual activities, the details of achievement provided in descriptive grading can be quite valuable. Different selection situations may have different requirements. The elements of achievement important in one situation may be secondary considerations in another. Descriptive grading permits such distinctions to be made in selection procedures.

The major problem with descriptive grading is the time and effort required to write the descriptions and to read and use them in comparing a large number of applicants in selection decisions. Comparisons are difficult when the persons compared are described in different terms. Yet academic performance is not a one-dimensional attribute. Forcing it onto a single scale of performance by combining a variety of judgments into one statement of achievement makes comparisons mechanically simpler by ignoring distinctions in achievement that may be important. With the development of procedures for convenient and efficient handling of descriptive grades and with advances in computer processing of prose, the use of descriptive grades may become more widespread.

A grading procedure that compromises between the unlimited diversity in judgments that can be accommodated in descriptive grading and the ease of handling one-dimensional grade symbols has been suggested by Elbow (1969). He proposes that a list be compiled of those aspects of student performance considered important by the faculty. Each faculty member then would select the elements of performance pertinent to his course and rate his students with respect to each of them, using a pre-prepared rating scale. Students in different courses would probably be rated on somewhat different combinations of attributes, and different students in the same course may also be rated with respect to different kinds of achievement. Having each faculty member work from the same master list of qualities of performance makes possible the cumulation and summary reporting of a number of ratings of the same student by different faculty members. As with descriptive grading, persons using grades for selection could base their selection on whatever achievement dimensions were important in that particular selection situation.

A method of grading that avoids a problem typical of most grading systems is the use of student portfolios. This approach permits the grading decision to be made by the person or agency making the selection decision. Representative samples of the student's work are collected in a portfolio that can be examined by anyone considering that student in a selection process. This procedure has the distinct advantage of placing the responsibility for evaluating achievement on those who will use the results of that evaluation. In all the other procedures, the professors evaluating student performance may not hold the same views as those who will later rely on those evaluations in selection decisions. The obvious drawback of portfolios as reports of achievement is their cumbersomeness. If a large number of applicants are to be considered, reviewing individual portfolios may be impractical.

The Basic Problem

Grades serve primarily as a selection device. Their other functions are distinctly secondary. They are used as bases for decisions about who is to be permitted to advance educationally through the undergraduate years and into and through postgraduate study, and at times for decisions about who is to be employed. The basic problem underlying every aspect of the grading controversy is whether grades, in whatever form, lead to a sensible and fair selection process. (For a more detailed discussion of grades in selection, see Warren, 1971.)

The employment decisions in which college grades enter most strongly occur in those fields where a close relationship exists between education and occupation. These are dominantly the applied fields-- accounting, engineering, pharmacy, nursing, and to some extent the physical sciences and business administration fields other than accounting. Yet even in these fields college grades have typically not been associated to any substantial degree with performance on the job (Berg, 1970; Hoyt, 1966). The kinds of academic performance required by college professors differ in substantial ways even in applied fields from the requirements of the occupations to which those fields lead.

The use of grades in occupational selection rests on one of two premises. One is that the kinds of accomplishment indicated by grades are similar to the requirements of a particular occupation. This is rarely the case if the relationships found between college grades and job performance are to be accepted. If graduates of applied college programs such as accounting have acquired the basic capabilities necessary for effective job performance, and then grade and job performance differences are due to other attributes such as interest, dependability, commitment, or interpersonal qualities, grades and job performance would be expected to show the low relationship that is typically observed. This would imply that the information useful to employers is the general content of the courses the applicant has passed without regard to his level of performance.

The alternative premise in using grades for occupational selection is that grades indicate general levels of intelligence and industriousness that are indicative of performance in a broad range of activities.

Again, the relationships observed show this to be true only to a small extent. More specific indicators of occupational performance appropriate to the demands of a particular occupation are likely to be far superior to college grades as criteria for job selection.

The new and promising ABCX system illustrates the problem of selecting which students are allowed to advance educationally. The major criticism raised against the ABCX system is that some students may fail to pass large numbers of courses, making very slow progress toward a degree while occupying space in classes and otherwise using educational resources that might be better used by more effective students. Yet this is not inherent in the system and can be avoided. A student-faculty committee at the University of California at Davis, while recommending adoption of the ABCX system, recognized the use of grades as a culling device and also recommended that students be required to maintain a minimal pace in the accumulation of credits toward a degree. If that pace were not maintained, the student would not be permitted to re-enroll and his place in the university would be given to someone else (Committee on Educational Policy, 1972). Brown and Santa Cruz have adopted such a minimum-progress requirement. This practice shifts the decision process concerning educational advancement from the grading system to the credit system. It does not solve the problem of determining how limited educational resources are best used or whether the selection process is consistent with that use.

Limiting access to college and university resources to students able to use them effectively seems sensible and justifiable as long as those resources are limited. Yet no adequate determination of effective use of educational resources has been made. The assumption that a student who has taken a course without being able to pass it has not benefited from the course may not be defensible. Students who get an A in a course the second time through after failing it the first time, an event that can be observed, demonstrate that learning does occur while failing a course, as reflected in the following A. A situation can be imagined in which a student would complete a college degree in eight years after taking every course twice. The same expenditure of educational resources would produce two people with bachelor's degrees if the two had been adequately prepared at entry to college. To assume that the production of two bachelor's degrees represents a better use of educational resources than the production of one bachelor's degree in a person initially poorly prepared for entry into college requires that education be viewed as a production process designed to turn out as many people as possible at a prescribed educational level, not as a process intended to bring people the greatest possible intellectual growth. Whether effectiveness in the use of educational resources is or is not defined in terms of the number of graduates produced, that is the definition assumed in most present grading policies.

Except in a few junior colleges that use the ABCX grading system with no limit on the number of times a student can repeat a course, grades and rate of progress are used to select those students permitted to continue educationally. During the undergraduate years that selection process directly eliminates a relatively small number of students, as indicated by the small proportion of D's and F's awarded. The dominant use of grades as selectors occurs between the undergraduate years and graduate school. The major function of the four-year process of assigning and recording grades occurs at the transition between undergraduate and graduate education. A pertinent question is whether the benefits justify the cost.

If selection is the primary function grades serve, the choice of a grading system ought to be based on the purposes of the selection process. Graduate and professional schools need to determine the number of students they will commit themselves to, the kind of students most appropriate for their programs, and the ways they can best identify the most appropriate from among their applicants. The grading system adopted by undergraduate colleges should be designed to satisfy those graduate school needs. Whether undergraduate schools should commit the required time and effort to serving graduate school needs is a question that seems never to have been seriously asked. Yet that is the primary function present grading systems serve.

The secondary selection function of grades—eliminating poorly performing undergraduates to make room for better students—affects only small numbers of students. Its major effect is probably on the composition of upper-division enrollment, particularly in areas where junior colleges are well established. As is the case with graduate schools, selection based on grades provides students the faculty will be most satisfied with. Yet faculty satisfaction with their students and effective use of educational resources may not be totally congruent. The institution's obligations to society may be better met through a different selection process.

Selection applied in licensing or certification is usually intended to deny licensure or certification only to those not minimally qualified for the pertinent tasks. Distinctions in performance above the minimum level are not needed. In selection for employment or for postgraduate education, on the other hand, the highest level of accomplishment among the persons available is desired. Whichever type of decision is to be made, the most effective grading system will be one designed for that particular selection purpose. If only minimum competence is to be required, a comprehensive list of clearly defined capabilities should be established and a Pass-No Report grading system would be most appropriate. Only if particularly high performance in one area could reasonably compensate for performance below the minimum in another area would the measurement of several levels of acceptable performance be necessary. In short, the purposes that the selection process grades are to serve should determine the nature of the grading system used.

Other Purposes Of Grades

The major opposition to Pass-Fail or Pass-No Report grading comes from graduate and professional schools. They want several levels of acceptable achievement reported so as to be able to select a limited number of students from among all those who successfully complete an undergraduate program. Some students also prefer a system with several levels of successful performance because of the recognition and sense of accomplishment at the highest level that grades can provide. Some faculty members like a multiple-level system because it gives them a set of rewards they can distribute to students, a set of "motivators" they can use to assure student responsiveness. While their dominant function is in selection, grades also act therefore as rewards and incentives.

One function commonly attributed to grades that they do not fill is as aids to instruction. The contention is made in support of grades that evaluation of performance is essential to good instruction. That contention is sound, but it pertains to evaluation rather than to grades. Evaluation of learning, and of students' progress is important to instruction, but evaluation occurs independently of grading. Grading is the process through which the results of an evaluative process are translated into some form of report to a person or agency other than the evaluator. Instructors report evaluative results to their students in a wide variety of ways—through the give-and-take of classroom discussions, through informal verbal comments, through comments written on papers, reports, or other student products. Students usually know before receiving an end-of-term grade how well they have learned the material of the course, and they effectively differentiate what they have learned into various components, only some of which are reflected in grades.

Grades are reports of the results of an evaluative process. As such they are communicative devices. But their messages are for people other than the instructors and students involved in the learning, primarily selection agencies that want some kind of evaluative report on the student. The primary function of grades is therefore entirely outside the instructional process.

In professional fields such as accounting, in which the major preparation is at the undergraduate rather than graduate level, faculty members feel a strong responsibility to assign grades in such a way that the students passed will be competent members of the profession. Grading in these fields, then, has some of the elements of licensure. When that is the case, grading may well take a Pass-No Record form if a Pass indicates acceptable performance in a required aspect of the profession. Graduation, or semi-licensure, would then be based on the passing of a selected number of specified professional requirements. The minor functions of grades—acting as sources of recognition to students or of control of students for professors—might lead to the adoption of an ABCX system. But the requirements of the profession would be satisfied by Pass-No Record.

REFERENCES

The AACRAO Survey of Grading Policies in Member Institutions. Washington: American Association of Collegiate Registrars and Admissions Officers, 1971.

Berg, I. *Education and Jobs: The Great Train Robbery.* New York: Praeger, 1970.

Burwen, L.S. *National Grading Survey.* Office of Institutional Research. San Francisco State College, San Francisco, California, January, 1971.

Committee on Educational Policy. *Report on the Grading System.* University of California, Davis, California, March, 1972.

Elbow, P.H. More Accurate Evaluation of Student Performance. *The Journal of Higher Education,* 1969, *40,* pp. 219-230.

Hoyt, D.P. College Grades and Adult Accomplishment. *Educational Record,* 1966, *47,* pp. 70-75.

Warren, J.R. *College Grading Practices: An Overview.* Report 9. ERIC Clearinghouse on Higher Education, Washington, D.C., March, 1971.

Section VI
Research in Accounting Education

Research on Teaching Innovations in Accounting

Thomas R. Hofstedt
Stanford University

Thomas R. Dyckman
Cornell University

It is both lamentable and typical that accounting educators have allocated relatively little research effort to understanding and improving their own activities in the classroom. There has, of course, been substantial innovation (as the contents of this book may indicate), but it has not been subjected to rigorous, organized study. The reasons why such a dearth of research is lamentable should be obvious: for most professors, 90 percent of the time is spent in classrooms and 10 percent in research; but, that time spent on research is allocated 10 percent to pedagogical research and 90 percent to "substantive" research.[1] The lack of proportion is glaringly obvious. Such a failing is typical of those involved in education, as observed by a prominent Dean:[2]

"In our hurry to purvey or consume it (Education) we pause infrequently to question what we are up to. We are alternately too brash and too reactionary and always, it seems, too busy to decide which and why. More importantly, we are too caught up with pressing numbers and immediate crises to decide what we should be doing in the first place. So we stumble on, giving and receiving schooling without full reflection on the truly sophisticated and ethical practice it involves."

In accounting circles, pedagogical research is often viewed as second class research. It is segregated from "real" research in the *Accounting Review*; it is unacceptable as thesis material at a number of institutions granting Ph.D.'s; it is difficult to obtain funding and so on. The effects of this treatment are, first, the relative neglect mentioned above and, secondly (and even more unfortunate), a self-fulfilling set of complaints. Pedagogical research often is second-class research in terms of techniques and sophistication. All in all, the deficiencies in accounting education must be attributed to the educators—including those who have done (bad) research and those who have discouraged (any) research. Accounting educators should pay heed to the phrase on a popular ecology poster, "We have met the enemy and he is us."

Objectives

The purposes of this paper are:
1. To motivate good pedagogical research;
2. To discuss certain prominent methodological features of educational research;
3. To present and evaluate the four case studies of accounting educational research which comprise the remainder of this section.

The first objective permeates the entire book, including this section, and will not be dealt with any further.[3] The next two objectives are, of course, about methodology. We shall not attempt nor pretend to be comprehensive. The following sections only highlight certain problems endemic to educational research. Specific critical comments follow each of the individual papers. The intent is that this section of the book be akin to a workshop.

The Choice of the Problem

An educational environment, whether university, classroom or a teacher-student dyad, is a functioning (or dysfunctioning) social system. Therefore, it is amenable to the full range of social science techniques and measurements. The sociologist, the psychologist, the teacher, the administrator, the student and myriad others may study groups, individuals, attitudes, performance, motivation, learning, structures and any of a thousand other variables. The richness of the educational environment mirrors that of society at large. The point is that educational research is simply applied social science, and this fact accounts for both opportunities and problems.

However, since this volume is for accounting educators, it seems reasonable to focus on *teaching* research. The remainder of this paper—and the set of papers included in this section—will assume that the researcher is concerned with the process by which certain parties (call them "students", for convenience) change their behavior ("learn") as a result of environmental manipulations (say, "teaching"). Note, by the way, that the traditional terms, such as "student", are automatically suspect.[4]

Evaluating Research on Accounting Education

Four major questions may be posed against which any educational research project may be evaluated. These criteria are not an exhaustive or mutually exclusive set; nor are clear-cut, yes-no answers easily arrived at; nor can the erstwhile researcher guarantee equally satisfactory outcomes on all four dimensions. Nevertheless, the four questions do provide a simple organizing perspective as a starting point for evaluation.

1. *Relevance.* Is the researcher attacking an important problem in a manner that promises some eventual practical payoff? Clearly, the problems we study reflect our values and, since values are so diverse, our perceptions of relative importance will surely differ. Nevertheless, it is possible to make preliminary judgments. For example, all of the papers included in this section have "student attitudes" as a major variable. Certainly, such a choice is in the mainstream of today's needs and values. At the other extreme, it is all too easy to find studies of very global behavior attributes (e.g., teacher "firmness") *or* very micro bits of behavior (e.g., "number of declarative statements made by the teacher during a class session"), without any real attempt at operationalizing or relating those variables to the context of the classroom.[5]

Eventually, the teacher must and will ask, "How should I behave in the classroom?" Unless research provides some benchmarks—even if they are highly tentative—it has failed to be relevant. On this point, note that purely descriptive research is of little help.

2. *Literature Review.* Educational research (if not accounting applications thereof) has a reasonable long and prolific history.[6] The literature is huge and diverse.[7] Furthermore, the more basic social sciences all have something to say about attitudes, learning, motivation and all of the other basic behavioral processes involved in teaching and learning. For accountants to do educational research without consulting the relevant literature seems either an extremely naive or extremely arrogant strategy. A hopeful corollary of this large body of extant knowledge is that accountants could proceed to do highly specific, applied research, relying on the underlying disciplines and/or schools of education to provide "basic" research. The obvious point needs to be made that a surfeit of research is hardly a guarantee of success, as borne out by the current and endemic debate about the sorry state of educational affairs.[8]

3. *Internal Validity.*[9] The next two criteria are methodological in character. Internal validity, as a criterion, basically asks the question: has the researcher eliminated rival explanations for his results? Can he make causal inferences? Internal validity is a function of *control* and *comparison*. In educational research, numerous variables are at work in the classroom. Each of them

must be manipulated, suppressed or judged to be irrelevant before the research results may be judged internally valid.[10] Obviously, this is a harsh test.

4. *External Validity.* External validity is derived from the researcher's ability to extend, extrapolate and predict based on his finding. Can the results be used to predict behavior in a different class, with different teachers, different courses? *Representativeness* and *randomization* are key tactics in achieving external validity.

The interplay between internal and external validity and the research technique being employed is subtle and complex. Basically, different methods (e.g., experiments vs field studies) display different tradeoffs between internal and external validity. The important feature is that there *are* inevitably tradeoffs. Nevertheless, different techniques for different purposes, as shown in the approximate breakdown below:

Figure No. 1

TYPES OF RESEARCH AND THEIR RELATIONSHIP TO EDUCATIONAL INNOVATION [11]

	Analytic	*Descriptive*	*Experimental*
Purpose	To derive relationships within a deductive system	To describe existing conditions	To test causal relationships
Methods	Deductive, mathematical, historical, philosophical, legal, linguistic	Correlations, surveys, case studies, direct observation, cross cultural, growth studies	Comparison of experimental and non-experimental groups by systematically varying conditions
Relation to Innovation	Points out assumptions and possible consequences of proposed changes; useful in establishing criteria	Describes currently existing conditions so that they can be modified later	Shows the effects of a proposed innovation

In terms of the tradeoffs between different techniques, Figure No. 2 captures some of the major shifts in a single diagram.[12] Eight techniques are shown, each of which falls somewhere on each of two spectrums: generality-concreteness, obtrusive-unobtrusive research. All are available to the educational researcher (with the possible exception of "judgment tasks"), and his choice inevitably will reflect his own sense of immediacy about these two dimensions.

Figure No. 2
A FRAMEWORK FOR COMPARING SOME MAJOR RESEARCH STRATEGIES

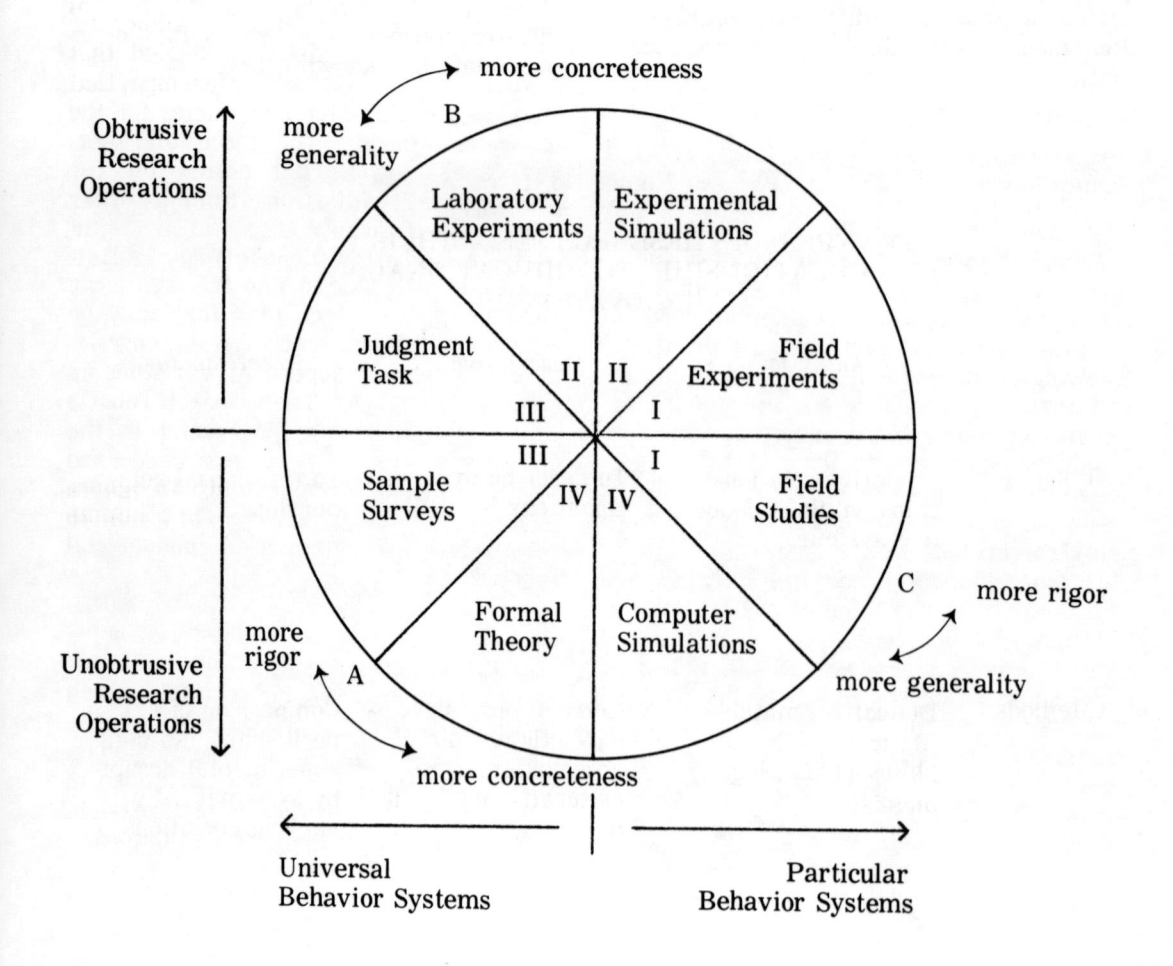

(Circular diagram divided into eight sectors)

- Obtrusive Research Operations ↑
- Unobtrusive Research Operations ↓

Sectors (clockwise from top-left):
- Laboratory Experiments (II)
- Experimental Simulations (II)
- Field Experiments (I)
- Field Studies (I)
- Computer Simulations (IV)
- Formal Theory (IV)
- Sample Surveys (III)
- Judgment Task (III)

- B: more concreteness / more generality (top)
- A: more rigor / more concreteness (bottom-left)
- C: more rigor / more generality (right)

← Universal Behavior Systems | Particular Behavior Systems →

I. Settings in natural systems.
II. Contrived and created settings.
III. Behavior not setting dependent.
IV. No observation of behavior required.

A. Point of maximum concern with generality over actors.
B. Point of maximum concern with precision of measurement of behavior.
C. Point of maximum concern with system character of context.

Another excellent listing and evaluation of alternative research strategies is provided by Campbell and Stanley.[13] They evaluate a dozen or more techniques on each of several sub-criteria of internal and external validity.

Again, the point in this paper is not to discuss these techniques at length, but instead to emphasize that each technique carries with it certain obligations, opportunities and limitations and it is incumbent on the educational researcher to be aware of these. His critics will.

Research in the Accounting Classroom: Some Constants[14]

If one is studying or evaluating educational innovation (as are most of the papers in Section (VI), then certain facts, assumptions and plausible conditions come into play. To a greater or lesser extent, the following conditions will affect the results and, therefore, should affect the research design. As before, no assumptions about exhaustiveness or mutually exclusiveness are made, but these points do reflect the folk wisdom and collective experiences of many researchers in the classroom.

1. *Individual differences affect learning situations.* Students and teachers are different. A class is not an amorphous mass of homogeneous globs; it is a collection of individuals. A superb lecturer may be a lousy case teacher. The "Quiz Kid" mentality may be an appropriate learning objective for one student, but completely antithetical to another. An accounting course that "soars" for an MBA class may "bomb" with undergraduates and vice versa. The differences are pervasive and situation specific. The implications for research are compelling: One must be concerned with individuals, not the mythical "average student".

2. *Learning is ubiquitous.* Some kind of learning is occurring in the classroom, although it may not be the kind that the instructor desires or the researcher is measuring. Students may be learning facts, processes, problem-solving or simple coping behavior. They are being socialized, professionalized (or deprofessionalized) and sometimes indoctrinated. So is the professor. If an innovation is introduced, then the researcher must be concerned with the kind of learning that it induces. It seems inadequate and shortsighted to observe "No improvement in performance as measured by the AICPA, Level I test" and stop there. The implication is that the researcher and his research design should be sensitive to the emitted behavior, whether or not it is "relevant".

3. *Feelings are real, always present and relevant for learning.* The success of an innovation depends on its acceptance and the attitudes of the students. The autocratic style which once existed pretended that feelings were not relevant for learning, that students were passive receptacles for the teacher's wisdom. The force and pervasiveness of liberal education for professional education, among other things, have largely dispelled that impression, so that student feelings and attitudes are attended to, and are legitimate variables for research (and they may be either independent variables in correlational studies or dependent variables in laboratory studies). The research reports which follow indicate one trend in the educational research: all are concerned with feelings to some extent. To ignore feelings is to be both callous (in a human sense) and casual (in a methodological sense).

4. *Learning includes content, skills, attitudes and values.* A comprehensive education goal set would attend to all four categories of learning. For example, much of the criticism by professionals of the college accounting classroom centers on its failure to inculcate favorable attitudes in the students (See Section II of this book, particularly the papers by Mautz and Langenderfer). On the other hand, an overconcern with the psyche of the student can lead to a skill deficiency which may become serious (Again, see Section II, particularly the papers by Trump and Bartholomew). For the erstwhile researcher, it is probably safe to assume that one kind of goal can be emphasized only by deemphasis of some other goals. Of course, such deemphasis has implications for generalizability.

5. *Specific learnings and results are likely to be transitory.* By extreme specialization, the teacher can induce achievement on a well-defined skill. For example, students may become quite facile with double entry bookkeeping through extended drill. However, such learning occurs more or less at the expense of other

things, say, concept mastery or theoretical knowledge, and its duration is uncertain. For the researcher, the import of this psychological assumption is that behavior change or learning should be assessed over different dimensions and extended time periods.

6. *Some learning is involuntary.* The student defending a point of view in class is learning to "think on his feet" as well as, hopefully, learning his and others' viewpoints. A case method applied to the transfer pricing problem must convince the student that there is a large element of subjectivity and human relations in transfer pricing as well as imparting certain technical skills. The moral is that the researcher who focuses on overt, direct forms of observed learning may be missing a significant part of the behavioral change. Yet another implication is that attitudes, while they are important, are not the sole determinants of learning.

7. *Students are motivated to seek as well as to reduce tension.* In a sense, this is the Theory Y concept applied to the classroom. Students like problems, can become aroused and intellectually stimulated. Much of the movement called "educational innovation" consists of attempts to arouse the student to be curious. The researcher-teacher who views the classroom as more like a filling station than a frontier outpost is likely to fail to stimulate significant happenings in the classroom and will overlook them even if they are inadvertently created.

8. *Students can introspect about their own acts, feelings and needs.* Most educational research involves tacit collusion between the researcher and the student. In most situations, either before, during or after the research has run its course, it seems desirable to ask the students how and why they acted as they did. This also is a learning process for both parties. Research on teaching often involves the study of essentially qualitative phenomena with strictly quantitative techniques. Data and numbers must be tempered with less rigorous checks; in many cases, data is made sensible only by insights gained in a debriefing.

9. *Self-examination is learnable, uncomfortable and resisted.* Many experiments, including some described in this book, have introduced "liberalizing" features into the classroom, only to have the experimenter dismayed at the outright hostility engendered by the change. Students and professors all have some unconcious investment in the status quo. Since most kinds of educational research involve some perceptible change being inflicted on the objects of the research (and "change" includes being included in a "control" group while others are receiving some active experimental manipulation), it is natural to expect some transitional problems. That is, the researcher should expect to find reactivity in his study. The power of this assumption has probably been experienced by those teachers who have seen themselves on video tape.

10. *Learnings are promoted by feedback.* This most elementary fact hardly deserves additional emphasis, although the form of the feedback and its frequency may be legitimate objects for research; and it may be useful and surprising to inquire into what kind of learning is being promoted. For example, the *withholding* of explicit feedback may be an important element in self-directed, inquiry-oriented types of accounting courses. Furthermore, some kind of feedback is always occurring.

11. *Small groups make more complex and frequent feedback possible.* It is trivial to note that individualized instruction (i.e., customized feedback) becomes more feasible as class sizes become smaller. Group size is an important and often overlooked intervening variable in educational research. What is the optimal class size for learning bookkeeping? Theoretical concepts? Solving CPA problems?

12. *Teachers are models for students.* An inexorable fact of educational life is the pervasive influence of the teacher. This is particularly troublesome for the teacher who is concurrently researcher, since he may find his subjects-students to be distressingly cooperative (or intransigent). Teachers and students are expected to live up to a complex set of expectations, and simple intuition tells us that the attitudes and aura of the teacher shape the students just as surely as what he teaches. If the professor is disdainful of accounting practice (theory), then the student will most likely be equally disdainful. The teacher cannot abdicate this influence, but he can, through research, seek to un-

derstand it and channel it in deliberate directions.

13. *One major goal of accounting education is to impart the ability to learn.* This assertion seems unchallengeable. But this is a kind of learning that is rarely measured in educational research. (Why not give an ATGSB test before *and* after the completion of a graduate education?) Many vacuous statements are made, much lip service is paid to this objective, and many curricula are redrawn with this in mind, but there is yet remarkably little research directed at measurement of such learning.

It would seem that the above set of assumptions and semi-facts leads to some generalizations for the erstwhile innovator in the accounting classroom. First, self-awareness (on the part of all people involved, students and faculty) is a prerequisite to change. Second, the change agent must be explicit about his goals and possible incompatibilities between them. Third, the type of change is constrained by the resources available. Fourth, the program of change must have a built-in feedback mechanism. It must be systematic and automatic. Fifth, the change agent and/or researcher must plan on disappointment and be prepared for repetitions, acclimatization and longitudinal studies. There must be a durable commitment. As John Gardner observed,

"The roller coaster of aspiration and disillusionment is amusing to the extreme conservative, who thought the aspirations silly in the first place. It gives satisfaction to the left-wing nihilist, who thinks the whole system should be brought down. It is a gold mine for mountebanks willing to promise anything and exploit any emotions. But it is a devastating whipsaw for serious and responsible leaders."

The papers which follow were selected so as to meet four basic criteria. First, they must involve research on teaching. "Research" may be operationally defined as a paper which contains some theory and some data. Second, each paper is representative of a different type of research technique. They are: a case study (Newton et al.), a pre-test/post-test design (Buehlman), a non-equivalent control group design (Berry), and a Solomon 4-Group Design (Sanders). Third, each paper deals to some extent with methodology. Fourth, the authors have been willing to expose their papers to published criticism.

Concerning that criticism, it is our intention to be relatively severe, with the pious hope that better research efforts will result. We shall attempt to stress both the strengths and the limitations of the techniques.

The concerned reader is invited to apply the framework and assumptions discussed in the preceding pages to each of the studies which follow. It is clear that all of the papers are less than ideal in terms of that framework, but, then, so is the criticism.

FOOTNOTES

[1] The exact proportions are arguable, but the relative time spent on the two types of research is clearly in favor of "substantive" research. For example, approximately 15 percent of the space in the *Accounting Review* is allotted to educational topics.

[2] Theodore R. Sizer, Foreword to *Graduate Study of Education: Report of the Harvard Committee.* (Cambridge, Mass.: Harvard University Press, 1966).

[3] Concerning the motivations to do psychological research, see Wilse B. Webb. "The Choice of the Problem" *American Psychologist.* Vol 16 (1961),

[4] Who is the "student" in a case course? In a Ph.D. seminar? Who "learns" in a classroom dialogue? If learning is adaptation of behavior, then mandatory course evaluations are a teaching device, and so on.

[5] For a reasonable overview of the range of variables, see A. Morrison and D. McIntyre (Eds.) *Social Psychology of Teaching.* (Baltimore: Penguin Books, 1972).

[6] Gilbert Sax, *Empirical Foundations of Educational Research.* (Englewood Cliffs, New Jersey: Prentice-Hall, 1968) Chapter 2.

[7] For example, skim the table of contents of the *Journal of Educational Research,* the *Journal of Educational Psychology,* or other journals. An excellent starting point would be the *Handbook of Research on Teaching.* N.L. Gage (Editor), (Chicago: Rand-McNally, 1963) and its more recent

companion volume *Second Handbook of Research on Teaching*. Robert M. W. Travers (Editor). (Chicago: Rand-McNally, 1973).

[8] Jacques Barzun, *House of Intellect* (New York: Harper, 1959), or Charles Silberman, *Crisis in the Classroom* (New York: Random House, 1970), or Philip Runkel, Roger Harrison & Margaret Runkel (Eds.) *The Changing College Classroom* (San Francisco: Jossey-Bass, 1969).

[9] An excellent book directed at precisely these issues in educational research is Donald Campbell and Julian Stanley, *Experimental And Quasi-Experimental Designs for Research* (Chicago: Rand-McNally, 1963).

[10] See H.M. Blalock, Jr. *Casual Inference in Non-experimental Research* (Chapel Hill: University of North Carolina Press, 1961) for a sympathetic review of this dictum.

[11] Adapted from Sax, p. 36.

[12] Philip J. Runkel and Joseph E. McGrath, *Research on Human Behavior*. (New York: Holt, Rinehart & Winston, 1972) p. 85.

[13] Campbell & Stanley, *op. cit.*

[14] This section, especially the listing of assumptions, borrows heavily from Leonord M. Lansky. "Changing the Classroom: Some Psychological Assumptions", in Runkel, Harrison & Runkel (Eds.), p. 290-30.

[15] John Gardner, *No Easy Victories*. (New York: Harper & Row, 1968). p. 4.

A Case Study of Comprehensive Educational Innovation

James D. Newton, Dallas M. Cullen,
Ray V. Rasmussen and Eugene Swimmer
University of Alberta

Introduction

Universities are in a state of crisis. The crisis can be traced to many social problems and can be identified under many catagories. In particular, soaring costs, declining enrollments, decreasing employment opportunities, and demands for alternate forms of post-secondary education have become facts of life in the university environment. Coupled with all of these problems, and perhaps at the root of many of them, is the "crisis in the classroom". This paper discusses the crisis, cites some of the reasons which may be behind the problems, and proposes changes for the design of undergraduate curricula, and (in Part II) describes an organized attempt to implement those changes.

PART I: PROBLEM DIAGNOSIS

Learning to Learn

The educational process involves the intellectual and personal development of the individual. As a result, education is a lifelong process. Formal education in an institutional setting provides a focus for this development. While an increase in factual knowledge is an obvious goal of such formal education, it is not and should not be the only goal. More important than providing students the opportunity to obtain an increased factual awareness of certain bodies of knowledge, formal education should provide an opportunity for the individual to "learn how to learn", so that his or her intellectual and personal development can continue after formal schooling has been completed.

Learning is not just the acquisition of information; it is also the ability to integrate and utilize old and new information in both familiar and unfamiliar situations. The individual who is a goldmine of information is not capable of functioning effectively unless he or she is also capable of utilizing this information in a variety of situations. The person who has learned how to learn will always be able to handle new situations.

Learning to learn can be defined in problem-solving terminology. That is, it consists of training in problem recognition (inadequacy of information, lack of understanding), problem clarification (determination of the specific area of information inadequacy), construction of alternative solutions (management development programs, self-study), and so forth. While these steps seem self-evident, it nevertheless is true that the knowledge of university trained individuals often becomes obsolete, and that such obsolescence would be greatly diminished if these individuals were taught how to learn as well as being taught facts. Learning to learn is dependent on the individual developing his own learning goals and methods and thus is significantly different from the normal university classroom situation.

The importance of the ability to continue to learn is nowhere more important than in the accounting profession. Accountants, and accounting instructors in particular, have recognized this fact for some time. Most university accounting programs today stress a large measure of conceptual considerations, often to the exclusion of procedural aspects of the field, but in any case with the recognition that the student must not be taught only today's practice and procedures. The emphasis must be such that the graduate accountant will be capable of growing with a rapidly changing field, or perhaps of leading that growth. To that end, many changes have been made in the approach to various accounting topics, and many more to the relative emphasis of various topics.

Virtually all of the changes in accounting curricula which are designed to permit the accounting graduate to cope with the "real world" in which he will find himself after graduation have the goal of teaching the student how to learn. Likewise, virtually all of these modifications and innovations, as in most subject areas in the university, have dealt with factual rather than attitudinal changes. Today's accounting graduate from a major university is well equipped with knowledge of various accounting models and how they relate to various criteria for judging the usefulness of financial statements. The question remains whether students have learned how to learn from the changing environment. Are they responsive, active and involved (the characteristics of people who are learning) or do they parrot responses concerning a particular accounting model (with much attendant complaining about the irrelevance of it all)? Are we really attaining the goal of educating accounting students to cope with change, or are we simply providing them with a different set of facts which are memorized and fed back to the professor on command?

The Problem of Student Attitudes

Many university students seem to be slipping through their years at the university untouched by their coursework. We observe ourselves and our colleagues lecturing and grading; we observe our students reading, doing projects, and writing exams. The question is whether this activity is productive and relevant to learning. Are professors and students colluding to ignore the question, "Is anyone learning anything?"

Formal education in our society is often a very structured and controlled process. Students are directed through a rigid and standard curriculum at a set rate, with the teacher as the directing force, defining for the student what, where, when, why, and how to learn. Moreover, the teacher, through exams and grades, defines for the student whether or not "learning" has occurred and how well it was demonstrated. As a result, the student is given little or no opportunity to exercise any choice as to what or how he or she learns.

Through elementary, junior high and high schools, the same process is repeated again and again. The teacher tells the student what material to learn, measures (by exams) whether or not learning has occurred and certifies the extent of this learning with a grade. By the time students enter university they believe that the grade, rather than true learning, is the important thing, and that the professor is responsible for the feelings (boredom or interest) they experience.

In fact, what the student learns, other than the course content, is that the learning process is controlled by others. The teacher is seen as the source of knowledge about both the subject matter and mastery of this subject matter. Many students feel the goal is not the acquisition of knowledge for intellectual stimulation or the personal satisfaction of learning, but the grade. Since there is no individual choice in the learning process, there is little motivation for the student to become actively involved. Furthermore, since many grades are largely based on the memorization and regurgitation of discrete bits of information, there is little opportunity or incentive for the student to attempt to integrate material from various courses or to explore new subject fields.

This does not imply that evaluation and grades are unnecessary; nor does it imply that professors do not have a responsibility for the quality of the courses they teach. It *does* argue that meaningful learning and teaching do not, and cannot occur when students see the grade as their one and only goal, and refuse, or are unable to assume some of the responsibilities of the learning process. These impressions are supported by studies of student behavior in the college classroom. Through the use of interviews, questionnaires, and observations of classroom behavior, Mann *et al.* at the University of Michigan (1971) identified eight distinct types of student characteristics. Descriptions of the students in each type are presented in Table 1.

TABLE 1

TYPES OF STUDENT BEHAVIOR AND ATTITUDES*

Type	Number of Students	Characteristics
1. Compliant	12 (5 men; 7 women)	Trusting of authorities; willing to go along with what teacher wants; focus on understanding material rather than criticizing it or formulating own ideas.
2. Anxious-dependent	28 (12 men; 16 women)	Very dependent on what authorities think of them; doubtful of own intellectual competence; anxious about exams and grades.
3. Discouraged workers	4 (3 men; 1 woman)	Intelligent; hardworking; intellectually involved; chronically depressed; personally distant.
4. Independent students	12 (9 men; 3 women)	Self-confident; interested; involved; identify with teacher; see teacher as colleague; older than average.
5. Heroes	10 (10 men)	Intelligent; creative; involved; resentful of authorities; ambivalent toward teacher; erratic in performance.
6. Snipers	10 (7 men; 3 women)	Rebellious; defensive; less creative than students in Type 5; uninvolved and indifferent toward class; stress fact they were required in some way to take course.
7. Attention-seekers	11 (5 men; 6 women)	Social, rather than intellectual orientation; want to be liked and get good grades.
8. Silent students	20 (8 men; 12 women)	Speak in class only when sure teacher will approve.

* From Mann et. al. (1971, p. 47)

At best, it could be said the students in types 3, 4, and 5, a mere 24 percent, are involved in intellectual quest. The others seem to be more involved in pleasing the instructor, gaining social acceptance, striking out at the instructor, or are not involved at all.

Similar data were obtained on the University of Alberta campus. In the spring of 1971, a survey was conducted of a random sample of students enrolled in the Faculty of Business Administration and Commerce. The final results showed that only 44 percent of the sample were interested in their courses; 72 percent were bored by lectures; and 82 percent did not work to their full capacity. Furthermore, the student's work was inefficient and ineffective; 75 percent did little work between exams and "crammed" just before an exam, with the result that 61 percent did not remember after the exam what they had learned. Students blamed this shortcoming on the professors—78 percent agreed that if the course was boring or poorly structured, it was the fault of the professor. Given this, it is not surprising that 76 percent wanted to get out of university as soon as possible.

In February 1972, similar results were obtained in a survey of first-year business administration students. Almost 75 percent of the students reported an overall negative reaction to their university experiences. Of the remaining 25 percent who reported positive feelings about university, such feelings were positive only to a slight degree. The writers' experiences at a number of major universities [1] suggest that these results reflect the feelings of students in most universities.

It should be emphasized that this situation exists not because of student perversity or faculty incompetence. Rather, it exists because of the flawed structural format of educational institutions, and the effects this format has on the attitudes about the educational process developed by students.

Of particular concern is the response to questions asking students whether they perceived channels for change. To the contrary, most indicated that they thought it best to "tell the professor what he wants to hear" and "to show an interest in the course." Few indicated that they perceived channels through which they could act to change the situation.

Changes in University Structure

Over the last four decades, there has been a massive amount of research concerned with the impact of various pedagogical styles on learning. Many individual instructors, as well as entire faculties and colleges, have attempted innovations involving greater student choice and participation in the design of the learning process. Often, though, these innovative efforts have been less than successful (Runkel, Harrison and Runkel, 1969). A major reason for this failure has been that most innovative attempts have only changed the structural aspects of the teaching environment. For example, lectures have been replaced by discussion groups, grades have been based on term papers rather than exams, various class sizes have been used, and so on.

Structural changes of this type ignore the problem of student attitudes. No attempt has been made to change the attitudes, so that students still look to the professor as the primary (or sole) guide to the discussion, and "what to do to get the grade" is still the main concern. Such student questions as "How many pages does the paper have to be?" provide evidence of student attitudes in this regard. Small wonder that, having conducted an examination of research into such structural changes, Dubin and Taveggia (1969) conclude: "These data demonstrate clearly and unequivocally that there is no measurable difference among truly distinctive methods of college instruction when evaluated by student performance on final examinations."

University faculties, then, have made changes in an attempt to improve the learning environment in the classroom. The lack of success in these endeavors can be traced to the lack of attention paid to the vital factor of attitude change. In addition, other learning process variables impinge upon these attempts at change.

Student Attitude

The known facts and assumptions lead to the conclusion that in order to change learning behaviors, attitudes of students must be changed along with pedagogical structures. As a demonstration of this argument, consider again the various behavioral responses of students in the Mann et al. study. The compliant students (type 1), as an example, are characterized as trusting of authorities, as willing to go along with what the teacher wants, and as focused on understanding material rather than evaluating it or formulating their own ideas. It appears reasonable to suggest, first, that the compliant students' behaviors are reflective of their attitudes. (e.g., throughout the educational experience, they have been positively reinforced for following the lead of the classroom authority) and, second, that short-run structural changes are not going to affect these attitudes to any great degree. These students will be trusting, willing to go along, and uncritical whether in a large or small class, whether in lecture or seminar format, and so on. A seminar format may have characteristics leading to changes in these behaviors, but with just one class, change is not likely. A similar argument may be advanced for each of the student types. A reasonable conclusion, then, is that an attitude change approach must be a component of any program designed to increase student motivation to learn, and that long-run rather than short-run programs are necessary.

Choice

A second key hypothesis is that the forced nature of the educational system has led students to hold negative attitudes toward learning, and that structural changes which remove the element of force have potential for re-involving the student in the learning quest. Thelen has elaborated this point:

> The schools "socialize" children, shaping them into the role of organization man and student. But the schools do not "educate" children because the process of education is a quest, voluntarily entered into, after meaning, and there is nothing voluntary about participation in most classrooms. (Thelen, 1965)

In support of this, researchers have found evidence that "sense of control over the environment" shows a significant relation to achievement. (Schmuch and Miles, 1971).

However, the simple removal of force is not enough to reinvolve students. Students who hold mainly negative attitudes about the educational system are most likely to move away from it when given the freedom to do so (as an example, visualize student type 6). In addition, students who have been brought up to be dependent on the classroom authorities to make choices for them are likely to experience some frustration when first asked to make their own choices (as examples, visualize the response of student types 1, 2, and 3).

The conclusion is that structural changes which bring about new freedoms must be accompanied by attitude change and by active preparation for dealing with the emotional stress, which is likely to arise initially from increased choice.

Relevance

The authors believe that the learning process is enhanced if the skills and knowledge to be learned are acquired in situations like those in which they are to be used. One author of this paper has developed an application of the concept of situational relevancy to the teaching or organization behavior (Miles et al., 1970). In this approach, large scale organizations are simulated through a variety of techniques and student members are asked to validate course constructs in the situation which they are experiencing directly. This approach is similar to that of the physical sciences where students are regularly required to move from the classroom to the laboratory so that they may validate course constructs through controlled experiments. Similarly, executive development programs are often more successful than undergraduate programs because of the increased relevance perceived by the participants.

Educational change in the accounting context could benefit directly from increased situational relevance. Often, accounting concepts, particularly in the managerial area, are difficult to discuss because students have little or no organizational experience as a basis for understanding. The existence of an organization in which students could directly experience some of the concepts (for example, means of control and evaluation) should enhance the learning of these concepts.

Feedback

An observation of present classroom practice is that little is done to promote the development of feedback about the learning process. We emphasize here that feedback is useful to the designer of the course as well as to the learner. Feedback which is evaluative or "grade-oriented" tends to suppress other kinds of vital information (e.g., direct statements as to whether the student feels he is understanding the material) and often comes too late to allow for changes in the learning design.

It is our belief that the development of an open feedback system will bring about a number of other important benefits; namely, tendencies to reduce the role barriers between professor and student, to enhance the learning experience since students will move beyond emotional learning blocks if they have the opportunity to do so in a supportive environment.

Transition

Change has been shown to cause stress. Movement to a new educational structure likewise causes these reactions, though such reactions can be reduced through adequate preparation for the transition to the new environment.

Consider, for example, educational innovations which have simply turned course and grading control over to students. The students in such a circumstance are being given free choice to participate in the educational experience and opportunity for involvement in the design of their learning experience, both important components of educational change, but they are also being asked to do a variety of other complex and difficult tasks, specifically:

1. To deal with the emotional shock of moving into a system of learning completely unlike their prior experience
2. To build and maintain a complex learning organization composed of members with a variety of needs and attitudes
3. To accomplish a learning task (i.e., the curriculum)
4. To move through behavioral as well as attitudinal changes.[2]

A quick changeover in structure without proper preparation asks the student to do too much too fast in too many areas. It is not surprising that some of these programs have ended in confusion and frustration, and in an unwillingness to continue.

Therefore, transition must occur gradually, or it must be accompanied by careful planning and involvement of students, or both. An attempt at transition to an improved set of classroom dynamics is described in the following section.

PART II: IMPLEMENTATION

An innovative undergraduate business administration program was started in the fall term of 1972-73 at the University of Alberta. This program involves 60 student volunteers and five professors, one each in economics, accounting, statistics and two in organization theory. The program will be continued during the 1973-74 school year with a new group of student volunteers. The previous section discussed the conceptual issues which gave rise to the program; this paper will discuss the program itself, its organization, objectives, and some of the results which have been realized.

Program Objectives

The purposes of the program are several: to bring about a mastery of typical undergraduate business subjects, to develop interpersonal competence in problem-solving and decision-making in teams, and to develop skills in learning (e.g., to help students develop their abilities to select and clarify learning goals, to design action steps for the achievement of those goals, and to measure and evaluate their progress). The program encompasses a shift in emphasis from the present undergraduate program which focuses primarily on the first purpose, mastery of subject matter, and not at all on the latter two. The program is based on the premise that both attitudinal and structural factors must be changed if changes in learning behavior are to be expected. In the following paragraphs we will explore some of the innovative structural and attitudinal change factors which have been introduced.

Figure 1 presents a model of the

FIGURE 1

DETAILED MODEL OF THE PROGRAM AND ITS OUTCOMES

PROGRAM COMPONENTS

- Changed Attitudes
- Organizational Skills
- Increased Choice
- More Informative Feedback
- Relevant Learning Situations

→ Increased Motivation and Involvement
→ Increased Ability to Perceive and Utilize Available Choices

PROGRAM OUTCOMES

- Better Learning of Second Year Material
- Better Learning of Third and Fourth Year Material
- More Effective Independent Action

Program Inputs
{ Faculty Characteristics
  Student Characteristics }

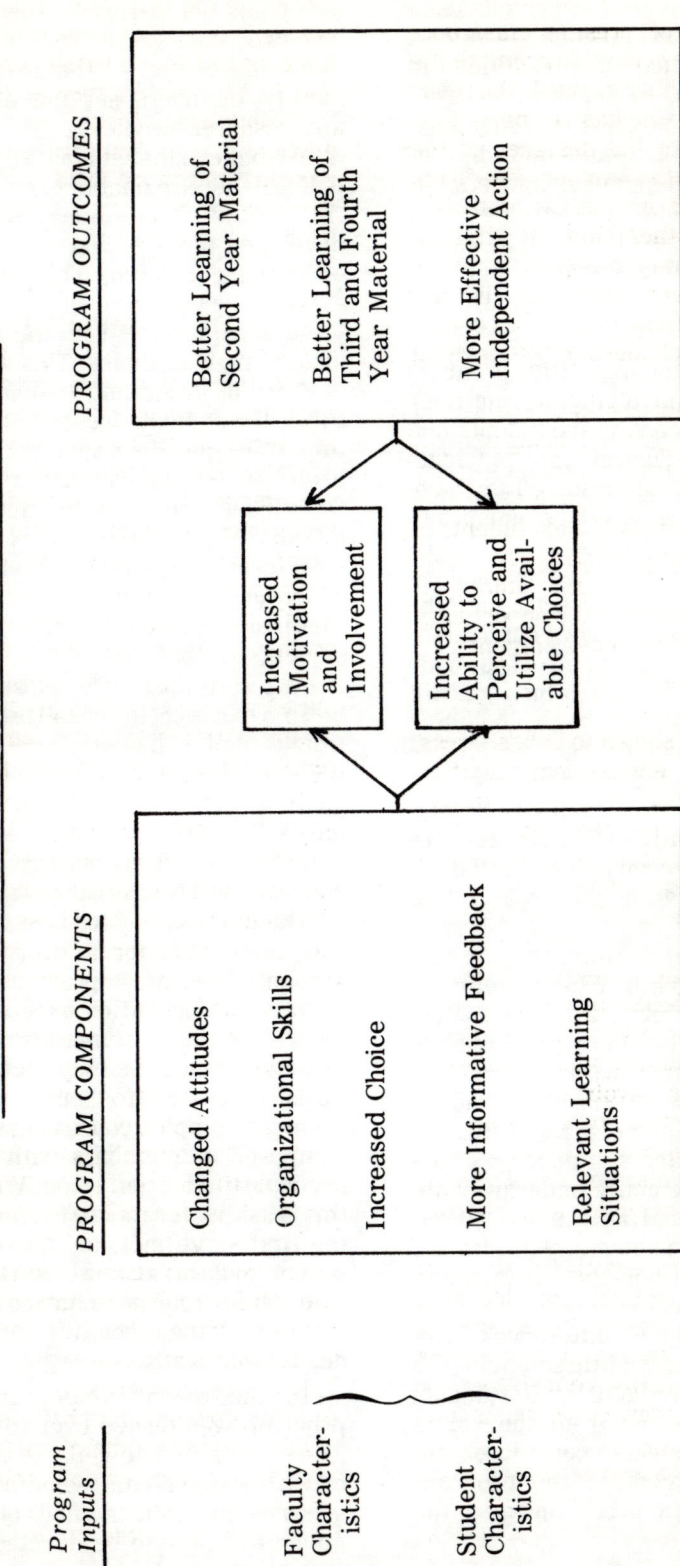

NOTE: Increase in one stage will feedback and strengthen changes in previous stages.

program and its expected outcomes. The features of the program—changed attitudes, improved organizational skills, increased opportunity to choose methods of learning, more open feedback and a relevant learning situation—should lead to greater motivation to learn, increased ability to utilize various learning methods, and better retention and understanding of the various academic subject matters. In addition, there should be a greater and more effective range of action in third, fourth and post-graduate years.

Program Organization

The first year of the innovative program is a pilot project involving a relatively small number of second year students and faculty members. Second year students were chosen for several reasons. They have had one year in the standard university format and will have two years after the program year in which both they and the faculty can evaluate effects of the program. The second year curriculum contains mandatory elements of a wide range of course offerings which permit innovation in a number of ways, including integration of subject matters which are traditionally separated. The courses involved include introductory financial and managerial accounting, intermediate micro and macro-economics, statistics, computer programming, and organization theory.

Both faculty and students in the program are volunteers. While volunteers may affect results obtained (since they would presumably be more motivated to make the program work), the experimental nature of the program made it necessary to use volunteers. Nevertheless, the student volunteers appear to be representative of the entire undergraduate business administration student body. Their high school and university grades are the same as those of non-participants, and tests have not revealed any major personality or attitudinal differences. Approximately 40 percent of those eligible to participate volunteered and the 60 students were randomly selected from the volunteers. Women students constitute approximately 10 percent of the program participants, the same proportion as in the regular program.

The first year of the program consisted of two stages. The first stage was designed to instigate attitude changes and to serve as a transition period for the second stage. The second stage involved students assuming control of the community, with faculty members serving as consultants and resource people.

We believe that students do indeed want to learn, but are unable to do so because of the attitudes and behaviors they have developed through past experiences in the educational system. Therefore, the first stage of the program was designed to allow them to explore, understand and hopefully change their attitudes. This was done with a series of group and individual projects. First, the students focused on a number of important questions such as: what are the goals of an educational system? What techniques are used to measure the efficiency of a human system? What are the structural characteristics of the present educational system? What are the attitudinal and behavioral responses of students to that system?

As a result of this focus, students should be in a position to visualize their own attitudes and behaviors, and to articulate their own educational goals. Hopefully, students also gain useful insights into the effect of organizational structures on behavior, as well as ideas about alternative educational structures.

The other major focus of the first stage was to provide for a transition into the second stage. Most previous attempts at large-scale innovation have simply turned control of the learning process over to students without helping them develop the skills necessary for building and maintaining a complex educational organization composed of members with a variety of needs, attitudes and so on. We believe that this is asking too much, too fast. Therefore, the first stage included an opportunity to learn organizational skills such as leadership, interpersonal communication, team building, conflict resolution and negotiation skills.

In the second stage, control of the program was turned over to the students. They were allowed to design the educational system, including the specific areas of study, the methods of learning, the amount of time to be devoted to learning, and the method of evaluating this learning (that is, the assessment and grading system—either pass-fail, the normal system, or some other method).

It should be emphasized that giving students the opportunity to choose areas of study, etc., does not mean that, for example, prospective accountants are able to ignore crucial aspects of introductory accounting. Since students must re-enter the normal program in their third year and are presumably motivated to eventually complete their university degree, they still have to master the subject material necessary for success in later courses. However, they are free to explore specific areas in more depth if they wish, and do the minimum required in other areas. The role of faculty members is to serve as resource people for the student groups, by presenting brief lectures or seminars, assisting in the design of projects, and so on.

Assessment of the Program

At the time of writing, the program for 1972-73 is just ending and plans are underway for continuation of the program in 1973-74. Volunteers for the subsequent program have been selected, but no other significant contact has been established. The professorial group has collected data of various types during the year and has formed many opinions, judgments and evaluations of the results of the first year. Some of these data can be analyzed statistically, but we believe that there is now and will continue to be for some time a Hawthorne effect surrounding the participants in the program. Elimination of this effect requires that some of the results of the program be collected surreptitiously during the third and subsequent years of each student's academic and post-academic career. Data on retention, improved communication skills, better ability to deal with the university environment, greater independence, and so forth, must await subsequent developments in the students' lives.

As an example of the types of data which will be collected, plans call for observing ways in which the program students respond to the courses and instructors in their third and fourth years—their contacts with their professors, their attempts to change course requirements (e.g., requesting substitute assignment topics, etc.), the amount of "extra" work done in courses, and so on—in other words, their involvement in restructuring the learning process. Grades will of course be of interest, although there is no certainty that grades will improve. Since they presumably will be less grade-oriented, their grades may remain the same or even drop slightly as they may do the minimum required for a course while pursuing their own learning goals. However, since they will also be more motivated and better able to learn, their grades may improve. We also expect that, because of their greater interest in the entire learning process, they will become more involved in other activities at the university such as student government, clubs, and so on.

At the end of the fourth year, students' future plans will be of interest—whether they go on to graduate school or seek a job, the types of jobs they want, the number of job offers they receive, etc. Eventually, plans call for following the progress of students in their jobs (say, two to three years after graduation), examination of their current positions, promotions received or expected, current salaries, job satisfaction and long-range plans. This follow-up contact should not be difficult to establish. Personal relationships formed during the program are such that most participants should retain a continuing interest in the activities and well-being of the others in the program. This is a sign of a meaningful learning experience for both faculty members and students.

Simple testing of a given student's knowledge of a particular topic at this time is difficult because of both examiner bias (though all professorial participants teach the same or similar topics in the regular second year program) and because of the Hawthorne effect. As a result of these factors, much of the evaluation which can be made at this time must be based on impressions, anecdotal material and feedback from the students themselves as to their feelings toward the program. It must be emphasized that the professorial group intends to pursue program evaluation using statistical tools, and to publish these results as soon as such evaluation can be carried out. Such rigorous evaluation is not possible at the present time, however. Consequently, the following discussion is based primarily on the opinions and judgments of the professorial group.

Discussion of the results of the program must necessarily be combined with plans for improvement during the next and subsequent years. As a result, the following material refers back to objectives, discusses the degree to which objectives (as measurable at this time) were realized, and refers forward either to new approaches to the original objectives or to revised, more realistic new objectives.

Changed Attitudes

Figure 1 identified the components of the program. One of these components is a changed attitude or attitudes on the part of the students. Certainly it can be said that attitudes changed as a result of the student-student, student-professor, and professor-professor contact. Initially, it now appears, students thought that learning in the program would be easy and fun. Professors thought that, as a result of the motivational preparation and organizational skills acquired by the students, the class would consist of eager learners. The expectations of both groups were wrong. Students discovered that learning is difficult and even somewhat painful, regardless of the motivation to learn. Professors discovered that the students' new-found motivation did not necessarily lead them to seek the particular information which the professor thought they should know.

Nevertheless, attitudes did appear to be significantly altered as a result of the program (the precise causes of alteration are not clear; we can only say at this point that attitudes were changed, though analysis of taped interviews with each student individually, done by an independent trained interviewer, will hopefully provide part of the answer). Students' apparent hostility toward faculty members is now virtually nonexistent. They appear able to evaluate learning opportunities now open to them with much clearer ideas of their own goals and how the university experience can aid those goals. Interestingly, though their hostility toward faculty seems to have disappeared, their apparent tolerance for boring, dull, or poorly presented classes seems to have declined. This is shown by their willingness to report to the professorial team such things as "I was bored in class" individually and in private. There was no apparent need to snipe at the professor in class, nor was there a need to seek safety in numbers when reporting complaints.

Of even greater interest is the relative lack of altered behavior as a result of altered attitudes. Conventional social-psychological dicta state that changed attitudes should result in changed behavior. The experience of the program indicates that this is difficult to demonstrate. Several examples suggest themselves.

During the early stages of the program, students were exposed to numerous motivational exercises and to development of organizational skills. These inputs changed student attitudes toward themselves and their roles in the classroom. They wanted to have control over their environment, to design their own learning experience, to choose the level at which they would approach each topic. Their attitudes clearly were different from those encountered in other second year students. Yet upon gaining control of their situation, and with the standing offer of aid from the professorial group, they found themselves unable to proceed with the design of the remainder of the year. The attitude called for self-determination, but experience and ability were not equal to the task. It became necessary for the professors to provide a great deal of guidance in this phase.

Later in the year, students began to discuss the desirability of taking a number of their third year classes together. Their belief was that as individuals, even with increased awareness and understanding of the traditional system and the possibilities for change, they would be somewhat ineffective in changing the process they encountered in large classes. As larger groups, they could affect the class discussions and perhaps even the tone and direction of the classes. At the very least they could work and study together and thus avoid the alienation of large classes with few or no familiar faces. While they believed this to be a desirable course of action, they were unable to develop the necessary strategy to accomplish the goal.

The behavior simply did not follow the attitude. Plans were developed only after professors took an active role in encouraging the plan.

These and a number of other incidents suggest that a program of this type must not only seek to change student attitudes, but must provide the guidance necessary to develop altered behavior patterns as well.

This insight will provide a different approach to the whole area of attitude change in subsequent years.

Organizational Skills

A considerable amount of time was devoted to discussion and practice of improved organizational skills. Students were given specific training in communication skills (e.g., learning to more effectively listen to the other person's point of view), understanding group processes, and effective group decision-making.

The problems encountered in this area are similar to those encountered with changed attitudes. Students recognized the value of the skills, but had difficulty utilizing the skills in situations other than training exercises. For example, while recognizing that it hinders the communication process to interrupt other people in mid-statement, they continued to do so during group decision-making times, particularly when the decision situation was perceived as being one of greater importance to their personal well-being. This type of problem also contributed to the frustrations encountered by students in attempting to design their own learning environment.

In spite of the difficulty in operationalizing all of the concepts learned in this area, the training did carry over into the students' personal lives. A number of them reported that their relationships with other people in their lives changed as a result of the focus on understanding of self and others which resulted from the attitude change and organizational skills training. Moreover, many found themselves truly involved in the educational process and were astonished to discover that a "good day" in class produced a good feeling out of class, or that a "bad day" continued to affect them after class. In this sense the learning was continuous.

Increased Choice

One of the prime goals of the program is to give students increased choice, both in terms of learning format and in terms of subject matter. Certainly the program was successful in this area, though several interesting developments have implications for the program for 1973-74.

At the beginning of the year, attention was focused on developing communication skills, on instilling a sense of community among all participants (both students and professors), and on preparing the students to take over their own learning environment. The assumption was that, having both the skills and the motivation to structure the situation to meet their individual needs, students would opt for a wide variety of learning modes, with the majority of the students seeking small group or individual study for at least a portion of their work. Surprisingly, many if not most of the students were initially unable to utilize the wide availability of learning modes possible.

There may be several reasons why students failed to design and implement these learning programs at the outset. At least two of the reasons appear to be directly related to the structural relationships of the program itself, and as such are susceptible to change. The first of these involves the degree of understanding possessed by students at the time they were expected to make decisions about learning modes. The professorial group had spent considerable time explaining the nature of the various course contents, the minimum time or effort necessary to adequately cover each, and the possible approaches to each. With this knowledge, it was expected that students could decide how deeply they wished to delve into each topic and the method of approach they wished to employ. In fact, they were unable to make these decisions, and the reasons now appear to be that they simply did not adequately understand the range of possibilities, and particularly did not grasp the nature of the subject material adequately enough to enable depth-of-coverage decisions to be made.

The implications for subsequent programs are clear. Along with the communications and decision-making training in the early phases of the program, students must be introduced to the subject material in a substantive manner, such that subsequent decisions can be based on adequate knowledge. The amount of such knowledge required for these decisions simply had been underestimated.

The second problem which arose within the program was that students perceived that in a democratic organization it was necessary to obtain 100 percent concurrence within the group before any decision could be implemented. This misunderstanding was cleared up when the students were made to realize that various interests and needs must be considered and dealt with in the context of group decision-making, but total agreement was neither necessary nor possible.

A third class of problems revolving around the free choice parameter was somewhat unexpected. The professorial group, as noted, had expected that, given a free choice environment, most students would choose learning modes significantly different than those normally encountered in the university (i.e., lecture/discussion, with the class essentially run by the professor). When, in the early stages, the students seemed unable to structure a satisfactory learning environment, the professors offered to give lectures for those students who were so inclined. Note that students didn't ask for lectures on certain portions of the course material (the anticipated situation). Yet when such lectures were offered, a large number of students used the opportunity to attend.

The lecture sections were nominally much like those in a regular classroom. Professorial control, however, was considerably attenuated by comparison with the normal classroom. Feedback was much more immediate, student participation much greater, and professor-student rapport greatly heightened. Nevertheless, students appeared to need a more structured format than had been anticipated. This appears to be due to personal characteristics of the students themselves; certain "types" of students were desirous of the lecture format, certain were not.

Finally, it must be noted that as the year progressed, fewer students used the available lecture formats and more used individual or small group formats. Apparently there was growth toward greater independence and greater trust of themselves to direct their own learning. This is, of course, a primary goal of the program.

More Informative Feedback

The goal expressed by the foregoing title is based primarily on the perceived need to make feedback to students consist of more than marks on exams and term papers, and to make feedback to professors more than regurgitation of lecture or textual material. The goal is to permit students and professors to develop relationships in which students perceive and understand the motivating factors behind professorial learning goals and have greater understanding of professors' values than is possible in a normal classroom setting. Similarly, teaching excellence is a very elusive goal when the only feedback available to the professor is the performance which he observes on exams. Ideally, students should receive continuous feedback concerning their progress in a particular subject or behavioral area, and professors should receive continuous feedback concerning their success in imparting knowledge and positive learning behaviors.

Feedback in the innovative program goes a long way toward accomplishing the goals stated above. For example, students were encouraged early in the program to construct small signs which they could flash to the professor during a lecture. These signs said, STOP, CONTINUE, SLOW DOWN, COFFEE BREAK, or other messages which the students wanted to convey but were hesitant to express aloud because of many years of taboos about such behavior. Such signs are infinitely superior to glazed eyes, yawns, silence, restlessness and similar manifestations of student inattention which the professor can only hope to occasionally decipher. Interestingly, students soon found it unnecessary to use the signs because the ice was broken and they felt more comfortable about simply expressing their feelings about the progress of a particular class.

One factor which may be essential in improving feedback is the removal of grades as an instrument for professor control. Where students fear that their frank remarks will be used to their detriment, or where they perceive that their remarks can influence the professor in their favor, honesty is severely limited.

Simply saying that class participation will or will not influence final grades may be inadequate to remove the influence of grades on classroom feedback. The authors' experience both in and out of the innovative program suggests that where feedback is tied to grades, in students' minds, the benefits of improved feedback will be difficult to achieve.

Where the class atmosphere, or student-professor rapport out of the class, is such that open communication can occur, the benefits are enormous. Students freely inform the professor as to their current level of understanding, so that time is spent on only those elements which are not yet understood. Time wastage is thus minimized. At the same time, the instructor discovers which of his techniques are valuable to students and which are not. He learns which problems, examples, and procedures are effective and which are less so. Most important, hostility is greatly reduced and a genuine cooperative effort can be undertaken because none of the participants are obliged to continue with ineffective or inefficient methods. All receive immediate rewards for their progress, rather than the traditional reward or a grade at the end of the term.

Relevant Learning Situation

A problem which continually bothers university level instructors is the lack of experience which their students can bring to bear on the discussion of a given topic. Nowhere in the university is this problem more acute than in a business school. Discussion of organizational structure, resource allocation decisions, or problem solving in an organizational context often falls on extremely infertile ground because students simply have no experience to which they can relate the discussion. In a similar way, accounting is sometimes difficult to relate to human problems in the organization, and the informational content of financial statements may not be relevant for the student because he is unable to visualize the investor's situation.

There are at least two components necessary in making the learning situation more relevant. One of these involves integration of the various topics so that the management situation is seen as an integrated whole rather than a series of separate topics. Business schools have long attempted to accomplish this goal, but it is difficult where students attend a class labelled accounting and another labelled finance and they are not specifically shown that they are learning about different aspects of the same managerial problems. Such integration is possible in a program such as that described herein. This is true because students and professors work as a team to investigate the various aspects of the administrative sciences, and the team has the freedom to integrate these investigations to a much greater extent than is possible in the normal situation.

Even more important than the possibility of topic integration is the ability of the professorial group to present concepts in such a way that they can be demonstrated in the context of the program community organization itself. For example, organizational principles may appear abstract to a student when they are presented in an article or lecture. Where they can be related to occurrences in the group organization, they become much more relevant because the student has the actual experience. Such experiential learning is a primary goal of the program, though it has proven more difficult than at first believed to discover situationally relevant means to demonstrate accounting and economic principles. Changes in the program structure for the 1973-74 program should greatly increase the opportunity to use these learning techniques, specifically through the use of a token economy. The details of such an economy have not been completely defined, but the purpose is to provide immediate feedback to both faculty and students through the use of "tokens". The existence of the tokens provides many opportunities for teaching accounting and economics in the experiential mode.

Program outcomes, as defined by Figure 1, include better learning of academic material in the program year, better learning of material in subsequent years, and more effective independent action. Many of the program outcomes have been alluded to in the preceding discussion. While these statements are not in any way conclusive, nor are they scientifically supportable (at this time), they do provide some insights into the operation of an innovative program of the type described. In addition to these insights, some reactions to such an experience on the part of the professorial group may be instructive.

Sense of Community

One of the most pervasive feelings about the program is the sense of community which developed during the year. While this feeling had been anticipated by the professorial group, the extent to which it developed, both among students and between students and faculty, was a surprise. While there were periods during which members of the group became unhappy with group decisions, the general warmth and closeness surrounding group activities was unprecedented for virtually all faculty and students involved. There remains a feeling at year end that we have been part of something special, and that this aspect of the program has produced benefits which have not only influenced the objectives of the program, but which have been valuable in their own right.

Intellect vs. Basic Values

A program of the sort described has many frustrating elements. These frustrations are to be expected, and some of them are described in greater detail below. The situations and factors which give rise to these frustrations, however, also produce other feelings which are not necessarily expected and not necessarily understood when they occur. A specific example of this may be informative.

In the early phases of the program, as noted, students were introduced to many of the communication, decision-making and organizational skills necessary to enable them to design their own learning programs for the remainder of the year. They were then given the freedom to accomplish this design and to proceed with the program which they had developed. Unfortunately, they seemed unable to accomplish this task. Much time (actually, a month at most and more nearly two and a half weeks) went by during which they argued and planned and struggled with directions, goals and methods. The professorial group offered aid, if requested, but carefully avoided giving the impression that they wanted to exert influence over the decisions. In reality, the students were unable to act because of their impression, previously mentioned, that one hundred percent agreement was necessary for implementing a workable design.

During this period faculty members experienced not only frustration but a somewhat painful recognition that their intellectual commitment to free choice and student control was in conflict with their values which argued that "something had to be done." Many solutions were proposed, some only half-humorous, to the problem of getting some learning under way. These solutions ranged from "infiltrate their organization with a spy," through "lock them up and let them out only when they demonstrate mastery of the subject matter," to "arrange an accident in which they all die -- *all*." Needless to say, students and professors together surmounted this stage, and learning of the subject material did begin. As noted, this learning began for most students in lecture groups and gradually became a more individual effort for the majority of the class.

Other Frustrations

The frustrations of a program, where students and faculty together design and carry out what have traditionally been activities with considerable division of labor can be enormous. Specifically, faculty are relinquishing control over areas which historically have provided considerable power. This can be demoralizing as well as frustrating, particularly when it becomes apparent that some of their most strongly held beliefs concerning effective teaching techniques turn out to be less than enthusiastically received by suddenly frank students. Students, for their part, find themselves called on to participate in redesigning a system which they had previously only criticized with no actual responsibility for change.

Frustrations for students in particular can be severe. Professors, by the time they become members of faculty, no longer require external impetus to perform. Many undergraduate students, on the other hand, have spent their lives in situations in which an external push has always been available. When the push of grades or other instructor-controlled pressures is removed, students suddenly face the reality of their own internally generated impetus. For many, this is a harsh view of themselves, and one which in some cases is unexpected. Some students reacted to this situation by demanding the organization of lectures and other classroom situations similar enough to the normal university format that their anxieties were minimized. The existence of such lectures, on the other hand, increased the anxieties of other students who found it difficult to study but who, because there was now no way to blame others for their non-achievement, were forced to recognize that such non-achievement was their own doing. Others went through a period of non-activity followed by individual or small group study. All expressed frustration during this period of readjustment to a new system (or non-system), but virtually all expressed the view that the period of frustration had been a period of personal growth or a period during which their self-understanding increased.

PLANS FOR THE FUTURE

In general, the authors are encouraged by the results of the first year of the innovative program. Plans for the 1973-74 program involve efforts to overcome deficiencies discovered the first year. Specifically, the plans call for:

1. More guidance in developing learning behaviors.
2. More practice in organizational skills.
3. Early exposure in more depth to course material.
4. Integration of course material to a greater extent.

More generally, we expect to continue to build on the good features of the first year program. Our initial hypotheses that attitude change is crucial and that better feedback, greater choice, situationally relevant learning and a sense of community provide the cornerstones for innovative learning have been confirmed. These elements will thus be included in future programs.

REFERENCES

Bachman, C.W. and P.F. Secord, *A Social Psychological View of Education*, (New York: Harcourt, Brace and World, Inc., 1968).

Boekhard, R., *Organization Development: Strategies and Models*, (Reading, Massachusetts: Addison-Wesley, 1969).

Bennis, W.G., *Organization Development: Its Nature, Origin, and Prospects*, (Reading, Massachusetts: Addison-Wesley, 1969).

Brown, G.I., *Human Teaching for Human Learning: An Introduction to Confluent Education*, (New York: The Viking Press, 1971).

Dressel, P.L. (Ed.), Mono. 7, *The New Colleges: Toward an Appraisal*, (Iowa City, Iowa: The American College Testing Program, 1971).

Dubin, R. and T.C. Taveggia, *The Teaching-Learning Paradox: A Comparative Analysis of College Teaching Methods*, (Eugene, Oregon: Center for the Advanced Study of Educational Administration, University of Oregon, 1968).

Harderoad, F.F. and J.H. Cornell (Eds.), Mono. 6, Assessment of Colleges and Universities, *The American College Testing Program*, (Iowa City, Iowa: 1971).

Lawrence, P.R. and J.W. Lorsch, *Developing Organizations: Diagnosis and Action*, (Reading, Massachusetts: Addison-Wesley, 1969).

Mann, R.D., S.M. Arnold, J.L. Binder, S. Cytrynbaum, B.M. Newman, B.C. Ringwald, J.W. Ringwald, R. Rowenwein, *The College Classroom: Conflict, Change, and Learning*, (New York: Wiley, 1970).

Miles, R.E., R.V. Rasmussen, R.J. Weber, and G.A. Walter, "Organization Simulation and Feedback: Developing Understanding in the Behavioral Sciences," (Unpublished manuscript. 1970).

Mussen, P., "Early Socialization: Learning and Identifications," in T.M. Newcomb (Ed.), *New Dimensions in Psychology III*, (New York: Holt, Rinehart, and Winston, Inc., 1967).

Runkel, P., R. Harrison and M. Runkel. *The Changing College Classroom*, (San Francisco: Jossey-Bass, 1969).

Sauer, J., "Knowledge of Results Conceptualized as subject awareness of the discrepancy between his response and a goal response." Unpublished manuscript, (Berkeley: University of California, 1968).

Sheffield, E.F. (Ed.), *Curriculum Innovation in Arts and Science*, (Higher Education Group: University of Toronto, University of Toronto Press, 1970).

Shein, E.H., *Process Consultation*, (Reading, Massachusetts: Addison-Wesley, 1969).

Schmuck, R.A. and M.B. Miles (Eds.), *Organization Development in the Schools,* (Palo Alto, California: National Press Books, 1971).

Silberman, C., *Crisis in the Classroom,* (New York: Random House, 1970).

Thelen, H.A., "Some Classroom Quiddities for People-Oriented Teachers," *J. Applied Behavioral Science,* 1, 1965, pp. 270-285.

Walton, R.E., *Interpersonal Peacemaking: Confrontations and Third Party Consultation,* (Reading, Massachusetts: Addison-Wesley, 1969).

Watson, G., "What Do We Know About Learning?", *NEA Journal,* March 1963, pp. 20-22.

FOOTNOTES

[1] Including Berkeley, Chicago, Cornell, Ohio State, and Washington.

[2] We would argue that the abilities to accomplish tasks one through three are probably most characteristic of the student of Type 4 in the Mann, et. al. study and thus the students of other types are forced either to quickly change their attitudes and behaviors or to fail.

A Critique

The Newton paper describes a comprehensive program of change implemented at a single institution during a particular time period involving a certain set of actors. It is, therefore, a case study. It represents two other contributions as well. First, it is a well-written example of some of the pre-experimental, pre-research, pre-implementation issues which confront the innovator. Second, it is an example of "action research".

Part I of the paper illustrates the diagnostic phase of problem solving. The authors and their colleagues identify a problem (the goal of "learning to learn" is not being realized), obtain data to pinpoint some of the parameters of the problem (finding that the students' attitudes seem badly awry), isolate some theory with explanatory power (defining the link between attitudes and behavior), and then (in Part II) design and implement a program of systematic and comprehensive change aimed at rectifying the attitudinal problems, among others. Ideally, the program will be monitored so that the data analysis phase and corrective mechanisms can be implemented as well. Part II also includes certain pre-quantitative, anecdotal information about the program, the kind of insight which may be invaluable to erstwhile imitators.

"Action research" is research which *intends* to create change, not just detect and measure change. The experimenter is an actor with definite goals, not a passive and neutral recorder of events. The commitment is to change of a particular type, and systematic, uncontaminated observation is subservient to the problem of inducing that change. It is useful to reflect that most educational research is of that ilk.

Therefore, the paper is purely descriptive. Control and comparison are discounted, so that generalizations are extremely limited. The authors can say, "Here's what we did and here's what happened", but extrapolations become extremely hazardous. Causal attributions are difficult to come by in this form of research due to the number of variables (controlled and uncontrolled), the "fine-tuning" of courses, teaching methods and curricula, and the lack of validated measurements.

However, as any Harvard Business School professor would hasten to point out, the case study does not seek to isolate cause-and-effect. It does provide a single, important example of how somebody else faced a similar problem. For precisely that reason, the Newton paper is a valuable contribution of this book.

It is important to note the time frame of this study (very long) and the nature of the data to be collected (demographic, testing data, success levels, attitudes, skills and so on). In addition to being a case study, it is also a "pilot" study. As such, it should be a model for later, more rigorous researchers. For Newton *et al.* vigor is preferable to rigor, at least for now.*

---

* The interested reader may wish to examine the paper by Rockart in Section IV for example of multiple and simultaneous changes.

Student Attitudes Toward Management Accounting and the Influence of the Management Accounting Course

David M. Buehlmann
Illinois State University

Introduction

The question of the formation and modification of student attitudes during college is a many faceted one that has been extensively studied by sociologists.[1] While the impact of situational variables is quite complex, Feldman and Newcomb stress high group interaction with groups that support certain attitudes as critically important to student attitude formation. Since accounting students tend to interact highly with other accounting majors and accounting faculty, it would appear that accounting education has great potential to be a supportive environment for attitude formation.

Further, the National Opinion Research Center study has demonstrated that certain attitudes, especially job related attitudes, are identifiable by college major.[2] For example, business majors tend to be money oriented and not interested in occupations that promise social service or an opportunity to be original and creative. Those differences in attitudes are accentuated by the process of attrition, as shown in Freshman to Senior studies. Thus, those that change their major during college tend to have attitudes more similar to those in the new major than in the major they left.

It would appear that attitudes are modified as a result of the collegiate experience and that the clustering of certain attitudes by the college major are apparent. Accounting educators should be curious about the nature of these attitudes. For instance, Becker found that medical students began their professional education with a desire to learn all they could to help mankind.[3] But, due to the pressures of medical school, they quickly formed groups whose primary desire was to learn enough to beat the system. Perhaps the attitudes of aspiring accounting professionals may also be a surprise.

Attitude formation in professional education is an extremely broad topic. The only purpose here is to point out the breadth of its possible impact since any study can deal only with a small portion of the problem. One possible impact is on the type of student attracted to the profession. Students are attracted to a major that appears to reward and support attitudes similar to his own. Interaction with similar majors and faculty in various situations causes pressure to subscribe to the perceived group norms. If it is true that the successful professional accountant is original and creative and has ample opportunity to provide society with valuable services, then these are the types of career goals that the better students should possess. If this is conveyed in the classroom, then we should observe attitudinal shifts in the accounting profession. These shifts would be due to a new student perspective about the profession induced by the accounting curriculum. Other impacts may be suggested in the form of unanswered questions:

What are desirable attitudes?

Should attitudes be measured toward the Code of Professional Ethics?

Should attitudes differ for work in tax, managerial or public accounting?

Are attitudes being formulated in professional curriculums in accord with attitudes in practice?

What are the most effective means to impart attitudes to accounting majors?

THE STUDY

This study is concerned with one aspect of the problem, the formation of student attitudes about management accounting and the role of the management accountant. One force that prompted this particular area of study was the comments of industrial accountants such as Warner Stoughton of Caterpillar in a speech at the April, 1972 meeting of the MBAA. He stated that students had a clearer understanding of the role of the public accountant education. He felt that equal time should be given to the management accounting option. Another force was the behavioral science literature that indicates that many of the problems with budgeting systems are caused by administration.[4] Thus, attitudes toward budget administration are important toward the adequate performance of the management accountant. Finally, this area seems particularly susceptible to attitude modification for two reasons. First, it may be conjectured that students are less aware of the potential role of a management accountant since tax work and public accounting dominate the press. Second, somewhat of a revolution is going on in text materials for management accounting as we move from the traditional routine of cost accounting to the "different costs for different purposes" approach.

This study concentrated on the one semester Managerial Accounting course and covered the academic year 1971-1972. This course has a prerequisite of six hours of principles and is usually taken by junior or senior accounting majors. The primary text is Charles Horngren's *Cost Accounting: A Managerial Emphasis* with supplemental material from Edwin Caplan's *Management Accounting and Behavioral Science*. The approach of these texts was supported vigorously by classwork.

A modified version of a questionnaire designed by David Green, Jr. and Selwyn Becker (see below) to measure attitudes about budgeting was utilized.[5] The questionnaire was administered on the first day of class to three sections of Managerial Accounting offered throughout the year (n = 95). This questionnaire was answered anonymously. Further, the instructions stressed that opinions were being solicited and that no right or wrong answers existed. Hopefully, these devices would elicit honest opinions rather than what the student perceived as a desired response. This same questionnaire was administered under similar conditions after the course was completed (n = 86).

EXHIBIT

SURVEY OF OPINION ON MANAGEMENT ACCOUNTING

Attitudes about Management Accounting and its role in the organization are diverse. This opinion survey is intended to measure the diversity of these attitudes among our students. Since this is an opinion survey, no right or wrong answers exist. This questionnaire is being given anonymously to encourage you to state your true opinions.

On the left margin appears a statement and its opposite is on the right margin. You are asked to make a check mark (✓) some place on the attitude, opinion, or preference continuum. If the respondent strongly believes that his goal is a career in Management Accounting, then his check mark should appear over the 1. If he strongly believes that his goal is a career in Financial Accounting, then the check mark should appear over the 5. Indications of 2 or 4 would indicate less strong belief for this particular item, and 3 would probably indicate ambivalence on this particular statement.

1. My goal is a career in Management Accounting

   My goal is a career in Financial Accounting

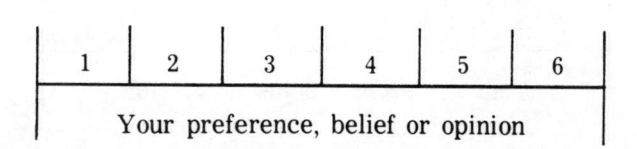

1	2	3	4	5	6

   Your preference, belief or opinion

2. Management Accounting involves a substantial amount of routine work

   Management Accounting does *not* involve a substantial amount of routine work

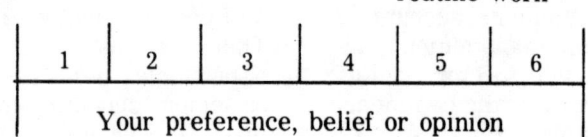

   | 1 | 2 | 3 | 4 | 5 | 6 |

   Your preference, belief or opinion

3. Management Accountants are *not* consultants or advisors to operating heads

   Management Accountants *are* consultants or advisors to operating heads

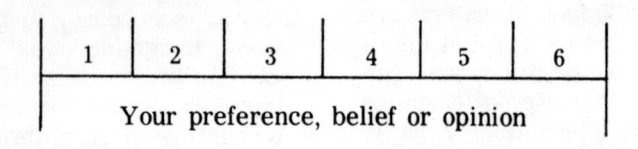

   | 1 | 2 | 3 | 4 | 5 | 6 |

   Your preference, belief or opinion

4. Budgeting is one of the general tools of management

   Budgeting is primarily an activity of the accounting department

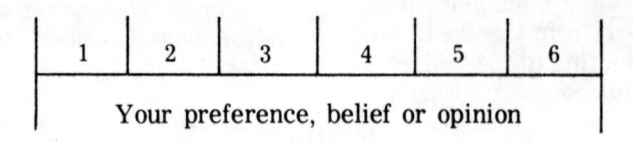

   | 1 | 2 | 3 | 4 | 5 | 6 |

   Your preference, belief or opinion

5. Achievement of good budgeting practices is expected

   Individuals who achieve good budgeting practices should be praised

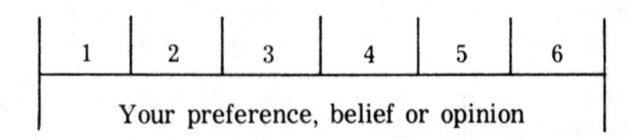

   | 1 | 2 | 3 | 4 | 5 | 6 |

   Your preference, belief or opinion

6. Reports comparing actual results to the budget serve primarily as feedback devices to operating managers

   Reports comparing actual results to the budget serve primarily as devices to evaluate operating managers' performance

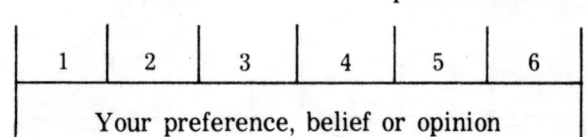

   | 1 | 2 | 3 | 4 | 5 | 6 |

   Your preference, belief or opinion

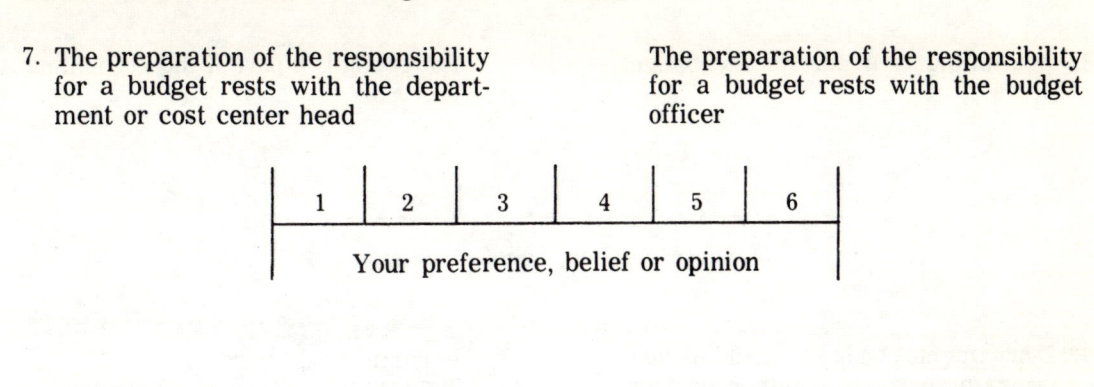

7. The preparation of the responsibility for a budget rests with the department or cost center head | The preparation of the responsibility for a budget rests with the budget officer

| 1 | 2 | 3 | 4 | 5 | 6 |

Your preference, belief or opinion

8. Budget planning and budget revising should be a year around process which involves operating people | To minimize wasted effort, operating people should not be involved with budgets except for a one month period each year

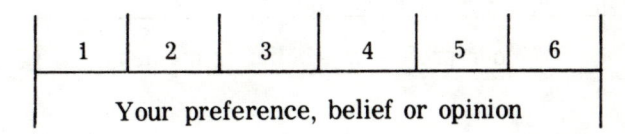

| 1 | 2 | 3 | 4 | 5 | 6 |

Your preference, belief or opinion

9. Budgets should be modified if extensive unexpected external change takes place | Budgets should stay as initially formulated so that measurements attributable to external unexpected changes can be made

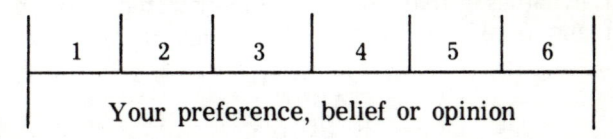

| 1 | 2 | 3 | 4 | 5 | 6 |

Your preference, belief or opinion

10. Budgets should be modified to account for unexpected internal changes | Budgets should remain unchanged throughout the period

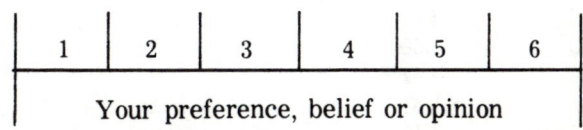

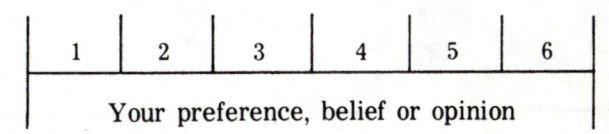

| 1 | 2 | 3 | 4 | 5 | 6 |

Your preference, belief or opinion

11. Budgets should be modified whenever performance and budget are widely divergent | Budgets should remain unchanged throughout the period

| 1 | 2 | 3 | 4 | 5 | 6 |

Your preference, belief or opinion

12. Accounting is a part of the budget process

Budgeting is a part of the accounting process

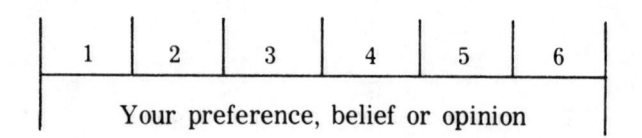

| 1 | 2 | 3 | 4 | 5 | 6 |

Your preference, belief or opinion

13. Departmental budgets should include pro rata shares of common or joint costs, such as General Corporate (home office) costs

Departmental budgets should not include any arbitrary allocation of common or joint costs

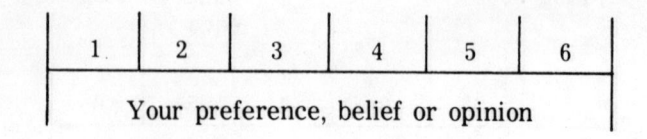

| 1 | 2 | 3 | 4 | 5 | 6 |

Your preference, belief or opinion

* The question sequence has been rearranged from the original to follow the order of discussion in the article.

RESULTS

Both the initial and final sets of questionnaire were analyzed. Using a one-tailed test, the null hypothesis that the means of the initial and final sets were equal could be rejected at a 10 percent significance level on ten of thirteen questions. The remaining questions demonstrated shifts in opinion but only at less significant levels. See Table 1 below.

TABLE 1
RESULTS

QUESTION	PRE-TEST MEAN	POST-TEST MEAN	SHIFT TO MORE FAVORABLE ATTITUDE?	LEVEL OF SIGNIFICANCE
1	3.92	3.27	Yes	1 percent
2	2.68	3.30	Yes	1 percent
3	4.04	4.47	Yes	1 percent
4	2.00	1.81	Yes	10 percent
5	2.73	3.10	Yes	10 percent
6	2.32	1.76	Yes	1 percent
7	2.39	2.41	No	NS*
8	1.61	1.36	Yes	1 percent
9	2.31	1.74	?	1 percent
10	2.04	1.96	?	NS*
11	2.53	2.87	?	5 percent
12	3.63	3.15	Yes	2 percent
13	1.91	1.94	?	NS*

*Not significant at the 10 percent level

DISCUSSION

Careers in Management Accounting (Questions No. 1, 2)

The emphasis of the course is the interesting, dynamic nature of management accounting, and on the wide variety of career possibilities that exist in management accounting.

It was not surprising that the initial sampling indicated that few students had given serious consideration to a career in management accounting. They also held the opinion that work in management accounting was routine and boring. By the final sampling, it was gratifying to note, opinions shifted toward the opposite statements with the shift demonstrating a level of significance of 1 percent.

Role of the Management Accountant (Question No. 3)

In the initial sampling, students slightly favored the notion that management accountants are consultants and advisors to operating heads by a slight margin over the opposite statement. This is surprising because accountants have a reputation for being overly concerned about their own functional area to the exclusion of the other management functions. It is possible that this result can be explained by DeCoster and Rhode's observation that current accounting graduates have significantly different personality traits than the professionals currently in practice.[6] In the final sampling, opinions strengthened in this same direction with a level of significance of 1 percent. This result is consistent with the course material which reinforces the attitude that managerial accountants should have a broad supportive role in the organization.

Human Relations (Questions No. 4, 5, 6)

Approximately one-half of the course is devoted to the planning and controlling activities of the management accountant. A continuous attempt is made in the reading and class discussion to sensitize the student to the potential dysfunctional consequences of this process on human relations. Students began the course slightly favoring the view that budgeting is a tool of management rather than primarily an activity of the accounting department. They finished the course with opinions strengthened in this direction with a 10 percent level of significance. This demonstrates the increased awareness of the potential impact of planning and control on the people of the organization.

Initially, student opinion slightly favored the proposition that the achievement of good budgeting practices is expected. This opinion shifted to favor the opposite proposition, that individuals who achieve good budgeting practices should be praised (level of significance 10 percent). That variance reports should serve as feedback devices was initially favored, but favored even more strongly on the final sampling. The emphasis appears to be upon helping the line manager achieve success rather than on the traditional view of finding fault. These attitudes are also consistent with the type of approach used in the course.

Participative Budgeting (Questions No. 7, 8)

A slight preference was stated for the preparation of budgets within cost centers and this did not change significantly. Initially, a strong preference was expressed for planning and revising budgets with the involvement of operating people on a year-around basis. This preference became even stronger. This appears contradictory since participation in the initial planning process is not as stressed as participation in the revisions. The tone of the course does emphasize the desirable affects of participative budgeting, but also stresses the dysfunctional affects of changing goals in midstream without sufficient input from operating managers. It seems as if students view the changing of goals in midstream as causing more potential disharmony than setting the original budget goals.

Budget Flexibility (Questions No. 9, 10, 11)

Student opinion strongly favors budget changes in reaction to unexpected external changes and somewhat favors such changes for unexpected internal changes. Initially students felt that budgets should be modified whenever actual performance and budget are widely divergent but in the final sampling they became neutral about such changes. It is possible that these responses demonstrate concern about holding the manager responsible for events beyond his control but also not penalizing him for good performance. This latter point is covered by Horngren in a case that describes budget cuts made in reaction to good performance. Most discussion of this case seemed to conclude that this probably would have a dysfunctional effect on the manager.

Role of the Management Accounting System (Questions No. 12, 13)

While the students initially believed that budgeting was part of the accounting process rather than the reverse, they became neutral on the question by the final sampling. It would appear that the planning and control activities of a firm are now earning a new respect from students whose predominant exposure had been financial accounting. One surprising result was a neutral opinion on the question of the allocation of common or joint costs. This neutral stand remained almost constant despite a course emphasis against arbitrary allocation of costs that are uncontrollable at lower levels.

LIMITATIONS OF THE RESEARCH

Certainly the results and observations stated here only hold for one institution, course, instructor, and set of materials. Although the results do indicate dramatic shifts in opinion, it is impossible to state which element of the education process is primarily responsible for such changes. It is also incorrect to assume that these opinions will remain constant throughout the students' professional careers. Formal education is only one influence (another major one being socio-economic) on the formation of student opinion about the profession. Job related experience and interaction with other professionals is likely to alter these opinions considerably.

The inability to conclusively demonstrate that these shifts of opinion are explained by a particular educational variable is traceable to the research design. Kerlinger, among others, warns that the simple pre-test-post-test design does not control for other factors that may have influenced the results.[7] First, the fact that a measurement procedure was applied to the group sensitized them to the issues involved in the research and, thus, may have influenced the results. Second, the study lasted a full semester, allowing for additional maturation and history to take place. Consequently, other extraneous variables (e.g., other courses) and general maturation may have influenced their final opinions even without the course in its existing form. Third, a more specific hypothesis would have allowed for specification of the treatment to be controlled for, e.g. course material.

A more complex design utilizing four randomly assigned groups would be able to overcome these limitations. One experimental group would use the experimental course materials and receive both a pre-test and post-test. The first control group would use the traditional materials and also be subject to a pre-test and post-test. The second experimental group would use the experimental materials but would only be subject to a post-test. The second control group would not use the experimental materials, not be pre-tested. Ideally, all groups would utilize the same instructor and meet at "prime" hours to control these variables. Often, the most difficult aspect of this approach is to justify the use of different materials for the first control group if the experimental materials are judged superior.

The problem of generalizability may be solved by replication at other institutions and with other instructors. Changes of opinion over time due to professional experiences are best studied in a longitudinal fashion.

A total of nine students dropped the course which represents about 9 percent of the initial group. The stated reasons were primarily academic pressures and the drops took place within the first three weeks. A decision was originally made that anonymity was important and consequently these nine questionnaires could not be removed from the initial responses. Instead it was assumed, for purposes of comparison, that these nine would have made the mean response on the final questionnaire had they stayed with the course.

CONCLUSIONS AND RECOMMENDATIONS

Illinois State University students exhibited a substantial shift in opinion about Managerial Accounting after completing the course. First, it would be interesting to know if this shift in opinion is generalizable to other schools, and other accounting courses. I suspect it is.

Second, as educators, it would be beneficial to know the degree of influence each of the variables has on attitude function. This information would help us plan our course materials, classroom technique, or even the selection process for admitting accounting majors. To be effective, we should provide those variables or combination of variables necessary for students to get "turned on" about accounting in general and Management Accounting specifically. Intuitively, I would probably agree with Gerherdt Mueller's stress on the course materials.[8] A general audience of students can be motivated very effectively with the Study Group's approach to the Introduction to Accounting. It seems reasonable that this will generate higher student interest in the course and stimulate comparatively better learning experiences. Also, it seems quite possible that this approach will attract better quality students to accounting.

Third, what attitudes should the aspiring management accountant have? Unless this is known, it will not be possible to measure the success or lack of success of the educational program. For example, I accepted the desirability of participative budgeting and that managerial accountants should be advisors to operating heads. Based upon these assumptions, the shifts of opinion demonstrated by this study were deemed desirable. Given the opposite assumptions, these shifts would have been interpreted as dysfunctional.

The classroom is not only a forum for technical material but an environment in which attitudes are formed. If positive attitudes about the expanding role of the management accountant will influence career choice and aid in success, then the formulation of these attitudes becomes a function of the Managerial Accounting course.

FOOTNOTES

[1] Feldman, Kenneth and Theodore Newcomb (Eds.) *The Impact of College on Students,* (San Francisco: Jossey-Boss, Inc., 1969).

[2] Davis, James A. *Undergraduate Career Decisions,* National Opinion Research Center, (Chicago: Aldine Publishing Company, 1965).

[3] Becker, Howard, *Boys in White,* (University of Chicago Press, 1961).

[4] Argyris, Chris, *The Impact of Budgets on People,* (New York: Controllership Foundation, Inc., 1958).

[5] Green, David Jr., and Selwyn W. Becker, "Survey of Opinion on Budgets," (Unpublished questionnaire (pretest draft) distributed at the Illinois Teachers of Accounting Conference, November, 1970).

[6] DeCoster, Don and John Rhode, "The Accountants' Stereotype: Real or Imagined, Deserved or Unwarranted," *The Accounting Review,* October, 1971.

[7] Kerlinger, Fred N. *Foundations of Behavioral Research,* (New York: Holt, Rinehart and Winston, Inc., 1964).

[8] Mueller, Gerhardt (Ed.), *A New Introduction to Accounting,* (Price Waterhouse Foundation, July, 1971).

A Critique

Aside from the case study, the pre-test/post-test design used by Professor Buehlman is the simplest sort of pre-experimental research technique. Essentially, it poses the question "How much did things change?" Unfortunately, it permits almost no causal attribution since there is little or no control over extraneous variables. Professor Buehlman is attacking an important problem, but with ineffective weapons.

First, there are problems which are built into the simple pre-test/post-test design. Most of these are discussed by the author, but they warrant reemphasis since they would seem to mitigate most of the conclusions reached. We shall pose them as rival hypotheses, indulging ourselves in our critical role for the moment. Recall that the purpose of research design is to anticipate such problems.

Explanation No. 1. The change in attitudes (or the lack of change) was due to the fact that subject's had already seen the questionnaire; i.e., the second repetition was biased by the first. This, of course, is the problem of the pre-test. As noted by the author, adding experimental and control groups would allow the researcher to isolate such an effect (See Sanders' design in this Section). Note that Professor Buehlman did try to control this feature by the use of instructions.

Alternative Explanation No. 2. The change (or lack of change) was due to the systematic elimination of certain types of students from the course. Since enrollment declined by roughly 10 percent from start to finish, the difference between pre-test and post-test could be due largely to these dropouts having attitudes dissimilar from those who remained. This is the problem of mortality, and there do not seem to be any checks or comments on these subjects. Were they systematically different in some way? Note that the researcher can obtain extra-experimental information on that point.

Alternative Explanation No. 3. The change in attitudes (or lack of change) was due, not to the management accounting course, but to (a) other courses, (b) the passage of time, (c) some significant event in the news, (d) nearness to graduation, or (e) sun spots. This is the most serious flaw with this design: aside from the management accounting course, a number of other contemporaneous events were occuring, each of which could be exercising a reinforcing or offsetting influence. Technically, this is the problem of maturation or history. Again, the problem is inherent in the design, but additional information could be gathered to provide either support for or suspicion of the change data.

The important point is that the author cannot really refute these alternative explanations. The design is simply not powerful enough.

Second, the attitude measuring instrument (the Becker & Green "Survey of Opinion on Budgets") has apparently not been tested for either validity or reliability; not is it clear that it has much relationship to "attitudes" as opposed to "opinions". While there is minimal disclosure on this point, it seems highly questionable that this instrument is appropriate to plumb any "new student perspective about the profession". For example, does an increased preference for a career in management accounting (Question No. 1) reflect the effects of this course or of some other course? Is Question No. 12 getting at attitudes or facts? Is not Question No. 13 purely a matter of taste? Not only is the link between the question and attitudes unclear, but -- for some questions -- the change in response can be interpreted either to be a "favorable" or an "unfavorable" shift.

Third, there are some minor problems with the statistical analysis. The use of the one-tailed test requires some discussion and justification. The use of multiple t-tests on questions which are not independent of one another is bothersome. And the lack of any analysis of individual differences is disturbing. Did "high change" subjects have any particular characteristics? Were "good students" more susceptible to change? The use of a Likert-type scale has implications for the type of statistical tests which may be appropriate. In any case, the pre-statistical significance of the data is almost overwhelmed by the difficulties in interpreting the results, so that the formal analysis is not very meaningful.

In short, the researcher is able to detect change. But the deficiencies of design are such that he is unable to make assertions about the nature of the change, its causes or its implications for accounting education.

The Effectiveness of Active Student Participation in Meeting the Cognitive and Affective Objectives of an Elementary Accounting Course*

Maureen H. Berry
University of Illinois

INTRODUCTION

This section defines the research problem, summarizes the research study, sets out the research hypotheses and defines the terms used.

The Research Problem

With the emergence of graduate schools of business administration calling for students from the arts and sciences,[1] and with the current demand from the public accounting profession for recruits with more varied interests and skills than the traditional business majors,[2] attention focuses on the vital point at which students can be attracted into the accounting field - the elementary accounting course.

Introductory accounting education typically emphasizes the transmission of technical skills in a highly structured learning environment. Despite the implications of findings in the area of educational psychology for improvement in ways of teaching accounting,[3] changes in student-faculty roles in the learning process, increased concern over the quality of education, and, perhaps most importantly, the fact that many beginning students bring negative impressions of accounting into the classroom with them,[4] the basic combination of lecture and blackboard problem-solving still dominates as a pedagogic technique.[5] Accounting is also taught by the case method, both computerized and noncomputerized, and business games, but rarely at the introductory level.

One of the main problems with the use of a unidirectional teaching method is that it can introduce or reinforce negative attitudes. As experiments in classroom creativity by Torrance have shown,[6] and as the experiences of other innovative educators have demonstrated,[7] students learn best when they are actively involved, both physically and mentally, in the learning experience. Although accounting educators have long been aware of the need to move towards a sharing of the responsibility for learning,[8] the basic reason for their slow response could well be due to their almost exclusive focus on cognitive learning outcomes. While some researchers in accounting education have surveyed and reported on students' emotional responses to learning situations, there is little evidence of any systematic attempt to include consideration of student attitudes in the planning and measurement of desired behavioral outcomes.[9] This in spite of the fact that reduction of negative

---

* This paper was presented at the UCLA Accounting and Information Systems Research colloquium on December 4, 1972 and benefited from comments of the participants. The helpful suggestions of Professors John Buckley, Joan Lasko and Theodore J. Mock are acknowledged, as well as the valuable contributions of Lawrence A. Tomassini.

attitudes and, hopefully, creation or enhancement of positive ones, should be of significant and particular concern to accounting educators.

Bloom and his associates have suggested several reasons for the general neglect of affective outcomes in American education.[10] One reason is that cognitive goals are much easier to define and measure than affective ones and require a narrower range of teaching methods. The widely-used and well-developed teaching techniques which involve lectures, discussions, printed materials and so forth, are most appropriate for verbal-conceptual outcomes. While such techniques produce or influence affective outcomes, they are designed to develop cognition and need to be implemented by other techniques aimed specifically at the affective area of learning. This requires an awareness of the factors which influence attitudinal response to course content as well as the development of interpersonal skills.

Another reason arises from respect for the idea that personal values are private matters which should not be subjected to classroom indoctrination. The matter of privacy can be respected by attitude surveys which assure the anonymity of the respondents. As to the "brainwashing" aspect, instructors unconciously project their personal values during the teaching process which is, in any event, an indoctrination process.

A final problem is that the evaluation of affective outcomes may well require a longitudinal study. Some of the benefits of the course, and satisfaction with the course, may not become apparent or be experienced for some time. A partial answer to this dilemma is to attempt to formulate and measure some short-run affective objectives, while recognizing that attitudinal responses in the short-run are subject to subsequent modification.

In summary, there exists, at the introductory accounting course level, a need for curriculum course design which not only encompasses the cognitive objectives of developing the individual's intellectual abilities and skills,[11] but also such affective objectives as arousing or reinforcing student interest in accounting to produce willing response to the topic as well as student satisfaction with this response.[12]

The Research Study

The purpose of the research study was to introduce an innovative pedagogic technique in an elementary accounting class and test its effectiveness in meeting the cognitive and affective objectives of the course. The technique chosen as the experimental activity, or experimental variable, was to require the students to share the responsibility for the course curriculum by assuming the instructor's role, either individually or in groups, for certain periods during each class session. While in this role, they would share with the rest of the class information about various aspects of accounting, based on personal contacts or experiences. This type of student participation is typical of graduate seminars but neglected at the undergraduate level. It was chosen because of the personal relevance to each student of the topic he brought in from his own familiar world outside the classroom. It was also thought that students would be more effective in the area of influencing attitudes because of a sense of shared values with their peers. Following the same line of reasoning, the professor was to be primarily responsible for cognitive learning because he would be more highly valued as a source of technical information than would a peer. The effectiveness of this technique was to be tested by comparing the cognitive and affective outcomes of the experimental group with those of a control group who would be taught by the conventional lecture and blackboard problem-solving method.

The learning experience for the two groups is depicted in Figure 1. The difference in curriculum design is indicated by the broken line. At the first class meeting, there was an exchange of information between the professor and the students concerning the students' needs. Affective outcomes were not discussed, but the curriculum design was somewhat modified, in terms of the professor's planned activities with cognitive learning, as a result of student feedback concerning their perceived needs.

The Research Hypotheses

After the entry attitudes of the research subjects had been surveyed and measured, the following research hypotheses were formulated:

1. H_O: Accounting proficiency achievement, as measured by scores on written examinations, would be the same for the test group as for the control group.

   H_A: Accounting proficiency achievement would not be the same for the test group as for the control group.

2. H_O: Satisfaction with accounting, as measured by attitudes towards accounting as an interesting career opportunity would be the same for the test group as the control group.

   H_A: Satisfaction with accounting as an *interesting* career opportunity would not be the same for the test group as for the control group.

3. H_O: Satisfaction with accounting, as measured by attitudes towards accounting as a *stimulating* career opportunity would be the same for the test group as for the control group.

   H_A: Satisfaction with accounting as a stimulating career opportunity would not be the same for the test group as for the control group.

4. H_O: Satisfaction with accounting, as measured by attitudes towards accounting as an *exciting* career opportunity, would be the same for the test group as for the control group.

   H_A: Satisfaction with accounting as an exciting career opportunity would not be the same for the test group as for the control group.

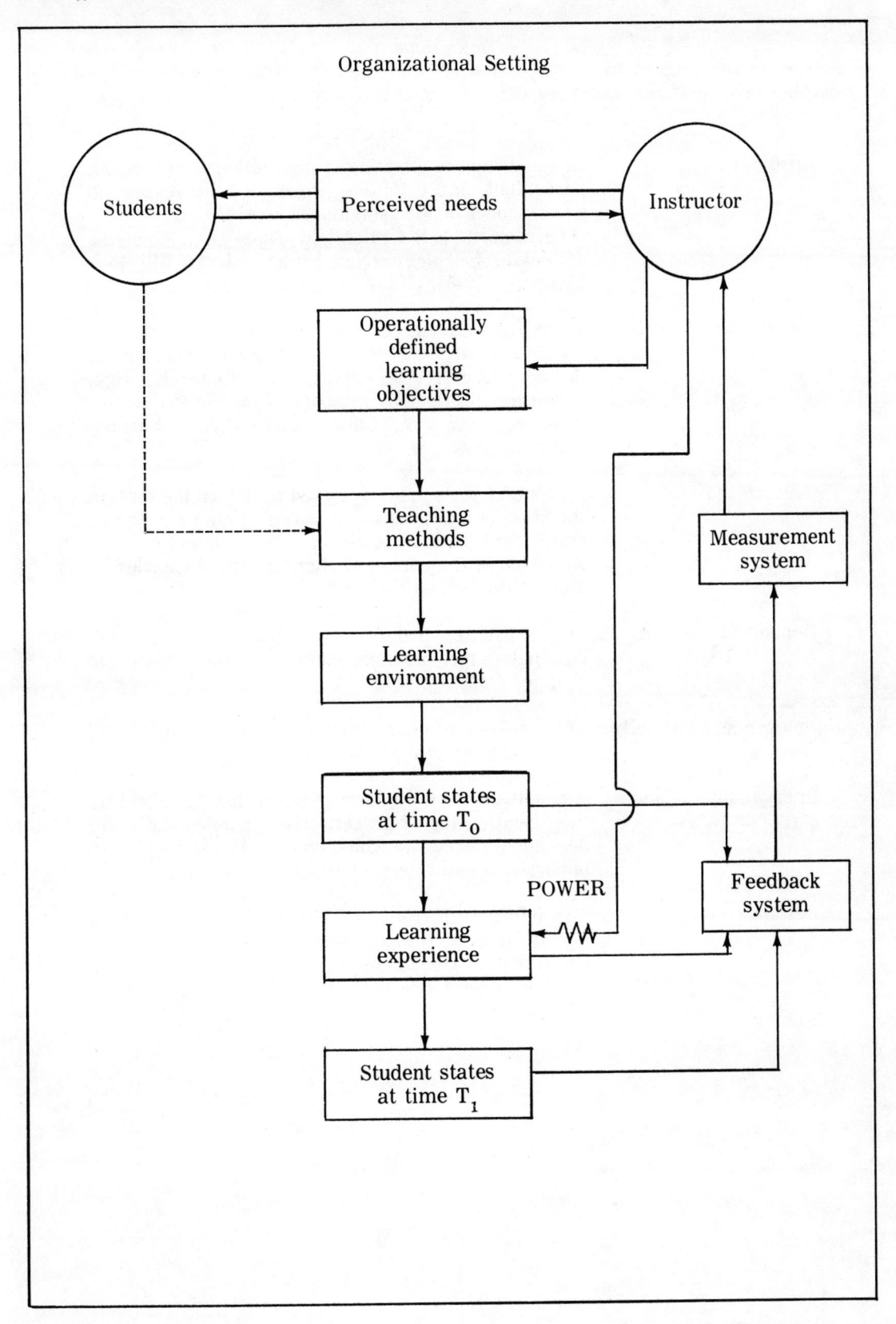

Figure 1 A learning situation

Definitions

Before proceeding with a discussion of the method used in carrying out the research study, it is necessary to define some key terms.

Attitude:
: An enduring organization of motivational, emotional, perceptual, and cognitive processes with respect to some aspect of the individual's world.
(D. Krech and R.S. Crutchfield, *Theory and Problems of Social Psychology*, (New York: McGraw-Hill Book Company, 1948), p. 152.

Concomitant variable:
: An extraneous source of variation believed to affect the dependent variable and considered irrelevant to the objectives of the experiment. (Roger E. Kirk, *Experimental Design: Procedures for the Behavioral Sciences*, (Belmont: Calif: Brooks-Cole Publishing Company, 1968), p. 457.

Content analysis:
: A group of techniques designed to determine certain specified characteristics of verbal, either written or oral, communication. (John L. Hayman, Jr., *Research in Education*, (Columbus, Ohio: Charles E. Merrill Publishing Co., 1968), p. 79.

Dependent variable:
: The attribute, property or characteristic which manipulation of the independent variable is meant to change. *(Ibid., p. 43.)*

Independent variable:
: The condition or characteristic which is manipulated in an experimental study. *(Ibid.)*

Intervening variable:
: A condition or characteristic which has an effect on the relationship between the independent and dependent variables, which can be vital in helping to understand and interpret results. *(Ibid.)*

Response set:
: The tendency to reply to attitude-scale items in a particular way, almost independent of content. (A.N. Oppenheim, *Questionnaire Design and Attitude Measurement*, (New York: Basic Books, Inc., 1966), p. 117.

METHOD

General Design

This study faced the problem, common to many educational research efforts, of potential bias resulting from the unavoidable use of intact groups. Because the investigator had no control over the selection of subjects and their assignment to the experimental and control groups, and because preliminary personal data obtained from the subjects indicated a lack of pre-experimental sampling equivalence, a non-equivalent control group design was employed.[13]

As described later, the subjects were students enrolled in two elementary accounting classes. The investigator was the instructor for both of these classes which were taught on a ten-week quarter basis. Each class met twice weekly for two-hour sessions in the same classroom and at the same time of day but on different days of the week. Consequently, the physical conditions were the same for each class, except that one class met on a Monday and Wednesday basis while the other class met on Tuesdays and Thursdays.

The assignment of the independent variable to one of the groups was made randomly. The test group was the Monday-Wednesday class. To control for a possible "Hawthorne effect", the experimental activity was designed and introduced as an integral part of the test group's course curriculum. The subjects in each group appeared to be familiar with the data collection materials and seemed comfortable with the feedback process. In an effort to minimize atypical responses, the investigator placed no stress on the importance of outcomes.

To make a preliminary estimate of possible contamination, the subjects were asked to provide certain personal information, both factual and attitudinal, at the first class meeting. Group profiles were then constructed and differences noted which indicated lack of homogeneity between the two groups. After some deliberation as to the possible impact of these intervening variables on the dependent and independent variables, it was decided not to continue the search for further contaminants, but to use pre-test scores of accounting achievement as covariates in an analysis of covariance to test the significance of the differences between means of post-test scores.

This decision inevitably delayed the introduction of the independent variable so that the preliminary accounting instruction, preceding the pre-test, would not be biased because of dissimilar learning conditions for the two groups.

Both the pre-test and the post-test of technical proficiency in accounting were written examinations consisting of short problems. These problems were designed to test the subjects' understanding of the course material, or accounting information processing ability, rather than to test recall of procedures. Thus they were intended to be appropriate for any instruction mode. All students were given identical examinations and a standardized points system was used in grading the responses. To eliminate grading bias by the investigator, who had become acquainted with the subjects on a personal basis, all the tests were graded by an independent reader. To minimize contamination through possible intergroup communication of examination content, the questions involved diversified topics and the order of presentation of the questions in the individual examination booklets was randomly varied.

Attitudinal data were elicited by two independent methods in order to generate validity checks.[14] A sentence-completion projective technique was used to obtain information about prevailing attitudes towards several aspects of accounting. Adjectives were extracted from the sentence stem responses and categorized as favorable, unfavorable, or neutral. From these data, attitude profiles were constructed. Answers to the free-response questions were also used for the selection of bipolar adjectives contained in semantic-differential questionnaires, separately administered, which explored similar concepts. The two sets of measures were compared for consistency of results.

Investigator bias in the analysis of qualitative data was controlled by employing independent coders who sorted and classified the qualitative data from the free-response sentences, using standardized coding frames and a standardized coding system.[15] Coder bias was controlled by having each coder work on the entire set of data. The coders compared results and reconciled any coding differences.

After the experiment was concluded, additional attitudinal data were obtained from questionnaires and free-response sentences for use in evaluating and interpreting the experimental results.

Subjects

The research subjects were ninety-four students enrolled in two elementary accounting classes at the University of California at Los Angeles.

From factual and attitudinal data supplied by the subjects at the first meeting of each class, group profiles were constructed as shown in Table 1.

During the first two weeks of the school quarter, two students dropped the class in the experimental group, while three dropped the class in the control group. Consequently, forty-seven subjects in each group started and completed the experiment.

The profiles of factual data showed that significant differences existed between the groups with respect to all the intervening variables initially selected for investigation. The subjects in the test group were generally younger than the subjects in the control group and contained a higher percentage of females. While each group contained about the same percentage of juniors, there was an excess of sophomores in the test group and an excess of seniors in the control group. More than forty percent of the subjects in the test group had not yet made a choice of major field of study, which is consistent with the preponderance of sophomores, whereas all the subjects in the control group had already made major field commitments and some 10 percent of them planned to major in accounting. The attitudinal data showed that the subjects in the test group were less favorably disposed towards accounting, as interpreted from their stereotypes of accountants and the accounting profession, than the subjects in the control group.

Data Gathering and Measurement Instruments

Various types of data were collected and analyzed to obtain information concerning the subjects, their technical proficiency in accounting and their attitudes towards accounting. Additional data were also obtained to help the investigator understand and interpret the experimental results and suggest any implications for further research. Because different kinds of data were collected for different purposes, different instruments and techniques were employed.

Data Collection

Both direct and indirect methods were used to gather data. Factual personal data were obtained from written answers to direct questions concerning the selected intervening variables of age, sex, year in school and major field of study. Data concerning technical proficiency were obtained from written examinations. Attitudinal data were obtained indirectly through sentence-completion methods and semantic-differential questionnaires.

The sentence-completion method is a technique which consists of asking a subject to complete a sentence fragment, or stem, which usually has been specifically devised for the particular research project. While originating at about the turn of the century as a device for measuring intellectual variables, it recently became popular for a variety of purposes, including the assessment of attitudes.[16] The assumption this method makes is that the subject will more readily provide information of research interest through an indirect approach than he would in direct questioning.[17]

The investigator conjectured that few, if any, of the subjects would already possess any academic knowledge of accounting, except, possibly, for some high-school bookkeeping. Accordingly, the subjects' attitudes towards accounting were explored indirectly by asking about their perceptions of accountants and the accounting profession.

The sentence stems, to which the subjects gave written responses, were as follows:

Pre-test only: "What I hope to get out of this course is ......"

Pre-test and post-test: "My perceptions of an accountant are ...."

"My perceptions of the accounting profession are .."

Post-test only: "The thing I like best about this class is ......"

"The thing I like least about this class is ....."

Table 1 *Group Profiles*

	Experimental Group	Control Group	Total
	N equals 49	N equals 50	N equals 99
	Percentages		

Factual Data:			
Age:			
Under 20	56	34	45
20-25	44	57	50
26-35	-	8	4
Over 35	-	1	1
	100	100	100
Sex:			
Male	76	85	81
Female	24	15	19
	100	100	100
Year in school:			
First	2	8	5
Second	64	34	50
Third	30	28	29
Fourth	4	26	14
Graduate	-	4	2
	100	100	100
Major field of study: (actual or planned)			
Economics	26	26	26
Various (1 or 2 each)	12	31	25
Undecided	42	-	21
Political Science	12	11	11
Mathematics	8	7	7
Psychology	-	7	3
Management	-	7	3
	100	100	100

Attitudinal Data:			
Attitudes towards accountants:			
Favorable	17	20	18
Neutral	9	12	10
Unfavorable	21	5	15
*Factual	30	46	38
None	23	17	20
	100	100	100
Attitudes towards the accounting profession:			
Favorable	16	33	25
Neutral	40	13	27
Unfavorable	16	10	13
*Factual	9	26	17
None	19	18	18
	100	100	100

*Provided operational definitions.

The sentence stems bearing on the experimental objectives were administered on both pre-test and post-test. The sentence stems administered only on the pre-test or post-test were designed to help the investigator with the interpretation of experimental results.

The semantic-differential questionnaire is a technique resulting from Osgood's research on the objective measurement of meaning.[18] This type of questionnaire consists of a series of seven-step scales which are bounded by polar terms. The subject is asked to check that position on the continuum between the polar terms which best indicates the direction and strength of his judgment about that particular scale. For scoring purposes, the seven positions are weighted from seven to one, a score of seven being the most favorable and a score of one being the most unfavorable. When scores are computed, the presentation of some of the scales must be reversed because the location of the favorable terms on the questionnaire is randomized to control for bias due to response set.[19]

As explained in a later section, an examination of the sentences completed by the subjects on the pre-test showed that adjectives used in expressing unfavorable attitudes towards accounting tended to concentrate, through various synonyms, on the concept that accounting is uninteresting. This particular concept became the focus of research interest. The bipolar adjectives 'interesting' and 'uninteresting', plus two other bipolar synonyms, were mingled with other scales, included as fillers, under the heading of accounting as a career. Because of the preponderance of this view of accounting as uninteresting, no attempt was made by the investigator to construct a set of scales from which group profiles of general attitudes towards accounting could be derived.

Data Measurement.

The data obtained through direct methods and the semantic-differential questionnaire were examined by statistical analysis, whereas content analysis techniques were used on the data obtained by the sentence-completion technique.

In comparing the test scores on the written examinations of accounting proficiency, analysis of covariance was used to evaluate achievement under the two different learning conditions. This technique is widely used in educational research when dealing with intact groups, in that statistical control is the only available way of dealing with potential sources of bias which cannot be eliminated by experimental control.[20] The subjects are administered a pre-test on a variable, or variables (in the case of multivariate analysis), related to the dependent variable. After the experiment, the subjects are measured on the dependent variable and the final means scores for the experimental and control groups are adjusted for pre-test differences.[21]

Careful consideration was necessary in the selection of a concomitant variable. Among the methods available for adjusting for the effects of experimental error are matching subjects with respect to intelligence, using IQ scores as pre-test measures, and-or using pretests of aptitude or achievement in some special field related to the dependent variable, a critical assumption being that the concomitant variable is unaffected by the treatment.[22] Attitudes could be ruled out as covariates, even though they might signficantly affect the outcome of the experiment, both because they could be affected by the treatment and because they could not be objectively measured at a ratio scale level. It was ultimately decided to use accounting achievement as the covariate on the assumption that, given some initial instruction in accounting under similar learning conditions, the effects of differences in intervening variables between the groups should be reflected in achievement scores on a pre-test of accounting proficiency.[23] Consequently, the independent variable was not introduced into the test group until after the pre-test had been administered.

In measuring the responses to the semantic-differential questionnaire, research interest was concentrated on the following scales:—uninteresting-interesting; boring-stimulating; and dull-exciting. Percentages were calculated, for each group, of the responses falling in each of the seven possible positions along the continuum, for all three scales. This analysis is presented, in bar-chart form, in a later section.

The content analysis methods used on

the data obtained by the sentence-completion technique were as follows—The unit of analysis was defined as the response to the sentence stem. All the responses were typed out verbatim and identified by number. Two judges, working independently, read through all responses and coded them, by identification number, using standardized coding frames. Neither judge had any knowledge of the experiment, nor any training in research methods. Both were mature men, approximately the same age, one accounting-oriented, the other history-oriented, neither previously acquainted with the other. The investigator would have preferred to use more than two judges, in case of possible bias, but was constrained by lack of resources.

The standardized frames provided for classification of the stem-responses according to direction and frequency. Classification by direction involved sorting for favorable, unfavorable, or neutral-ambivalent attitudes. Classification by frequency involved counting the number of units which fell into each category. Classifications were also provided for those responses which were nonevaluative in that the respondents either had no stereotypes of accountants or the accounting profession, which were classified as 'none', or else provided operational definitions, which were classified as 'factual'.

After the judges had completed the coding frames, they compared the two sets of frames and reconciled any coding differences. The percentages of responses from each group were then computed and tabulated.

Procedure

The test group was selected randomly and two different course outlines prepared. The course outline intended for the experimental group discussed the class participation requirement, but otherwise was the same as the course outline intended for the control group.

At the first meeting of each class, factual and attitudinal data were obtained from the subjects so that group profiles could be constructed and possible contamination, due to non-randomization of subjects, evaluated. The investigator also explored the subjects' motives for taking the course, which could affect their evaluations of the outcome, by obtaining written responses to a sentence stem on that topic.

In that the course was the first part of a two-quarter course offering, the investigator was constrained to cover certain materials in the assigned text-book which the students would be using again in the follow-on course. The subjects in the experimental group were requested to start making plans for their class participation activities, and submit them to the investigator for coordination, during the following three weeks. This delay provided time to review the preliminary data and finalize the research design.

The group profiles of factual data were reviewed during the first week of the course and the decision was made to postpone the introduction of the independent variable until after a pre-test of accounting proficiency had been administered to each group.

At the third class meeting, in the second week of the course, the subjects completed a semantic-differential questionnaire which was designed to measure three particular scales on the concept of accounting as a career opportunity. Pseudonyms chosen by the subjects protected identity and made it possible to compare scores on the pre-test and post-test for each individual.

For three weeks, each group was exposed to a lecture instruction mode, covering the basic accounting process, which included problem-solving at the blackboard by the investigator and dialogue between the investigator and the subjects.

The pre-test of accounting proficiency was administered during the fourth week of the course and from that time until the end of the quarter the learning experience for each group differed.

For the control group, the instruction mode consisted of blackboard demonstrations of accounting problem-solving, combined with lecture and dialogue which used a Socratic approach to instructor-student interaction. The same instruction mode was used with the test group for part of each class session. Otherwise the learning experience was shared. The subjects submitted their plans to the investigator who prepared a timetable designed to optimize the balance between proposed topics or activities and the established schedule for course material coverage. During the first week of the experiment, the subjects made their contributions to group learning whenever it seemed most convenient and natural in the context of on-going activities in the classroom. However, this was soon determined to be a suboptimal approach in that the subjects' interventions tended, at first, to be rambling and lengthy, leading to a lack of group involvement. Subsequently, the investigator reserved the first hour of each session for instructor-oriented learning. The class then took a ten-minute break and the sessions resumed with the subjects taking responsibility for the learning activities. An unplanned benefit of this arrangement was that it provided a means for unobtrusively measuring the success of the experiment, in terms of subject interest, by noting the degree of absenteeism in the second hours. It also satisfied the investigator's ethical problem of ensuring that the basic instruction required for the second part of the course, during the following academic quarter, would be provided. However, a significant drawback was that it established responsibility priorities rather than providing for a mutually-shared experience at all times.

Subject intervention followed a pattern of a short presentation, not necessarily from the podium, followed by discussion. The presentations were usually made on an individual basis, although sometimes joint efforts were presented. The investigator always abdicated the podium, sat in the body of the class as a constituent of the learning group, and tried to minimize intervention in order to promote free discussion. The physical facilities tended to inhibit rather than encourage group interaction. Long rows of tables, accommodating about ten subjects in each row, faced the podium and rearrangement of the furniture in order to facilitate multidirectional communication was not possible. The presentations included some topics related to personal experiences and others based on articles in the professional literature. The presentations frequently included explanatory hand-outs. A few subjects prepared solutions to unassigned accounting problems, explained them to the class, and distributed copies. The investigator provided the subjects with ditto masters and made all reproduction arrangements.

The investigator prepared a few questions during the course of each presentation in case class involvement needed some stimulating. These were generally not necessary, however, because there was always some spontaneous discussion both during and after each topic was presented.

During the last week of the quarter, at the last class meeting before the post-test a semantic-differential questionnaire, identical to the one administered on the pre-test, was administered to each group. The investigator hoped that the passage of approximately eight weeks would mitigate any contamination due to response set. The purpose of this second administration of the questionnaire was to measure any changes in scores on the three scales of primary research interest.

At the last class meeting before the post-test, the subjects completed some sentence stems concerning their perceptions of accounting. They also provided course evaluations by the same indirect method. This information later proved valuable in examining and interpreting the experimental results.

The post-test of accounting proficiency, consisting of short problems, was administered at the last class meeting. This concluded the experiment, the results of which are presented in the following section.

RESULTS

This section assesses the effectiveness of the experimental manipulation by presenting the findings of the experimental measurements.

Cognitive Objective - Accounting Proficiency

The pre-test of accounting proficiency was given during the fourth week of the quarter, with forty-seven subjects in each group. The mean score for the experimental group was 46.7 (standard deviation of 17) while the mean score for the control group was 53.5 (standard deviation of 19). The total possible score was 100. A test of the hypothesis that the pre-test scores of subjects in the two groups are equal resulted in an F ratio of 3.23, which is significant at the .90 level (one-tail.)

The post-test was given during the tenth week of the quarter, with the same forty-seven subjects in each group. The mean score for the experimental group was 58.5 (standard deviation of 15,) while the mean score for the control group was 58.8 (standard deviation of 18). The results of the analysis of covariance are presented in Table 3 below.

Table 3

Analysis of Covariance and Test of Significance of Adjusted Means of Final Scores

Source	Sum of Squares	Degrees of Freedom	Mean Squares	F Ratio
Between groups, B_{adj}	127.3	1	127.3	0.55 NS
Within groups, S_{adj}	21,052.9	91	231.4	
Total	21,180.2	92		

The computed F ratio of 0.55 is not significant. The null hypothesis of no difference in accounting proficiency achievement between the two groups could not be rejected. Matched pairs t-tests were used to analyze increases in accounting proficiency for each group. The computed t for the test group was 4.29, which is significant at 0.002 (two-tailed). The computed t for the control group was 1.93, which is significant at 0.10 (two-tailed). However, the marginal differences between pre and post-test indicate a relatively small improvement for *either* group.

Affective Objective - Arousal or Enhancement of Interest in Accounting

Attitudinal data were elicited from the subjects by a sentence-completion technique and by a semantic-differential questionnaire. Evaluation of the results of the first administration of the free-response sentences yielded several scales, involving a number of synonyms, from the subjects' perceptions of accountants and the accounting profession. These are presented in Table 4 below. The data were grouped because they were to form the basis for further measurements, involving an identical measurement instrument for each group.

Table 4

Popularity of Scales Prepared from Adjectives Used in Responses to Initial Test of Perceptions Accountants and the Accounting Profession

	% (N = 99)
Favorable Attitudes:	
Financially rewarding	30
Important	13
Interesting	13
Other (miscellaneous)	44
	100
Unfavorable Attitudes:	
Uninteresting	72
Other (miscellaneous)	28
	100

The three most popular adjectives used, involving the 'uninteresting' scale were uninteresting, boring, and dull. These adjectives were paired with polar adjectives used by the subjects as synonyms for 'interesting' and included in the semantic-differential questionnaire which was the instrument used to measure whether the experiment achieved its affective objective.

The percentages of responses, by each group, at each of the seven possible positions on three scales concerning the concept of accounting as a career opportunity is shown in figures 3.1 through 3.6 below. On all three scales, the test group scored more heavily on the negative portion of the continuum *and the post-test showed a negative shift in attitudes*. The post-test for the control group, however, showed a positive shift.

Analyses of covariance, using pre-test and post-test scores, yielded the following results:

Hypothesis	Computed F Ratio	Significance Level	Hypothesis Rejected or Not Rejected
No difference in satisfaction with accounting as an *interesting* career opportunity.	4.24	95 percent (one-tail)	Not rejected
No difference in satisfaction with accounting as a *stimulating* career opportunity.	5.49	95 percent (two-tailed)	Rejected
No difference in satisfaction with accounting as an *exciting* career opportunity	12.50	99.5 percent (two-tailed)	Rejected

DISCUSSION

From the results presented in the previous section it is clear that although the cognitive objectives were met for each group, only the control group met the affective goals of the course.

While the test group improved in accounting proficiency more than the control group, there was no significant difference between the means of the scores for the two groups on the post-test, with or without adjustment for uncontrollable differences between them. The experimental hypothesis that the groups' accounting proficiency would differ as a result of active learning involvement had to be rejected. This is consonant with other educational research which has shown little correlation between attitudes and cognitive achievement.[24]

The experimental hypotheses that active learning involvement would affect the arousal or enhancement of satisfaction with accounting was supported on two of the three scales used. However, the test group which initially had scored more negatively than the control group shifted even more negatively on the post-test, whereas the control group shifted in the other direction.

Unfortunately, the students' evaluations of the course, shed little light on these results, except with respect to the experimental variable. The aspect of student participation in the course presentation received more negative comments than positive ones, being mentioned only twelve percent of the time under the 'liked best' category, compared with twenty-two percent of the time under the 'liked least' category, by the test group. Table 5 summarizes these responses.

As an aid in further research, the following speculations are offered as to why the two groups may have differed in their affective reactions to the course.

Satisfaction of Perceived Needs

As shown in Table 6, most of the subjects had clearly defined expectations about the course. Short-run needs to learn accounting

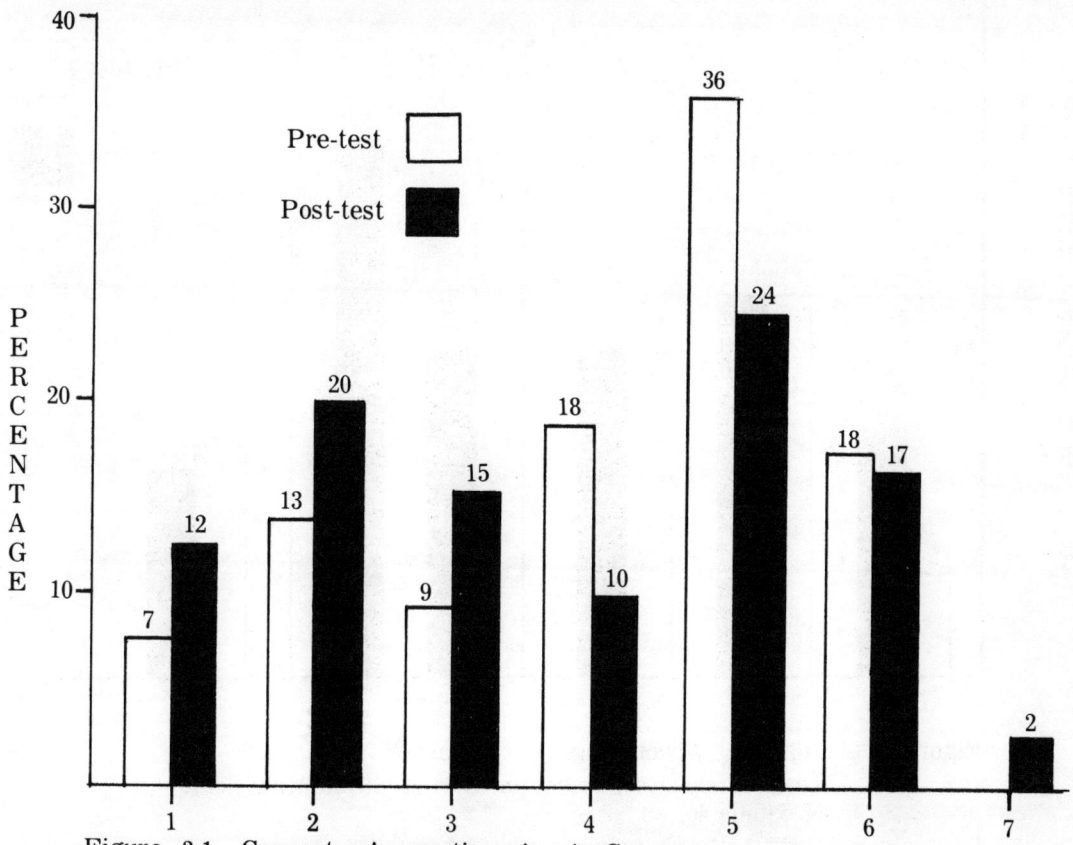

Figure 3.1. Concept: Accounting As A Career.
Test Group Responses on Uninteresting-Interesting Scale.
N equals 40.

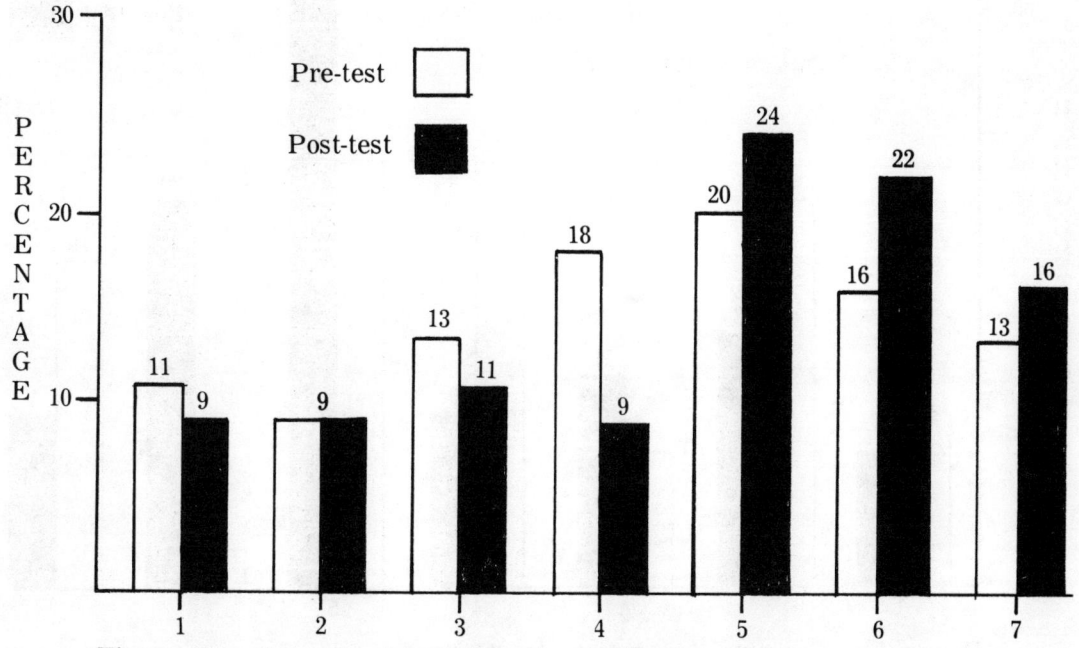

Figure 3.2. Concept: Accounting As A Career.
Control Group Responses on Uninteresting-Interesting Scale.
N equals 42.

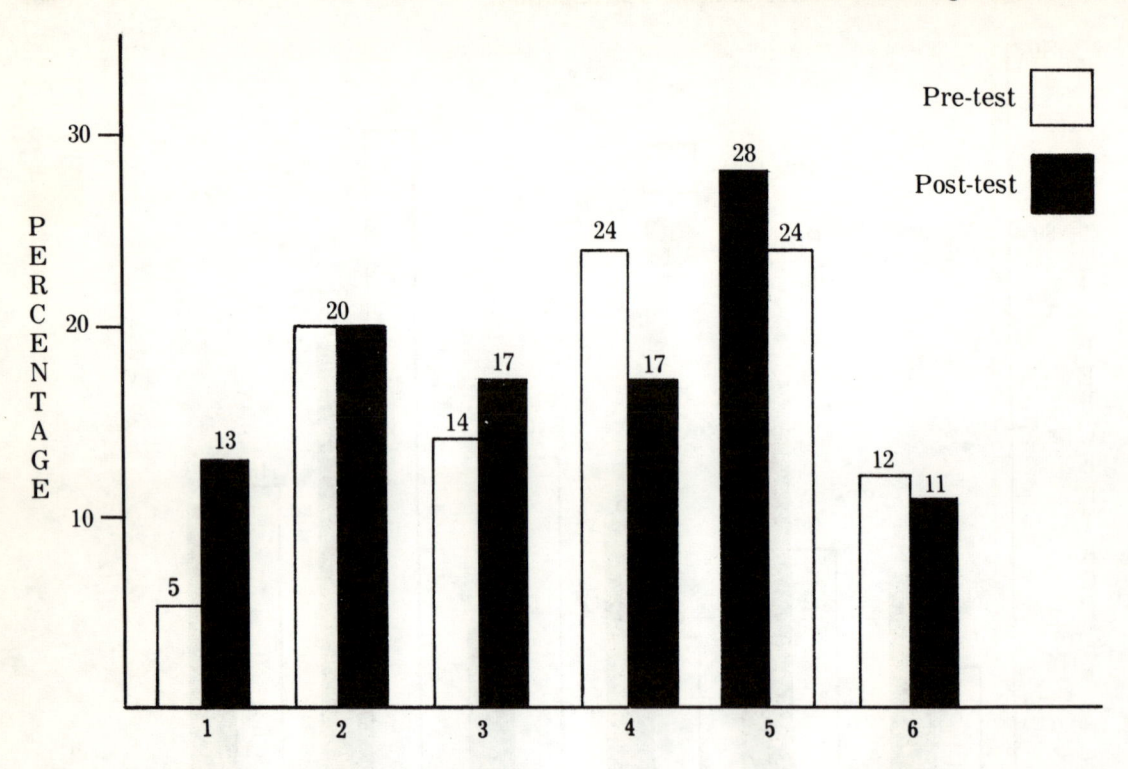

Figure 3.3. Concept: Accounting As A Career
Test Group Responses on Boring-Stimulating Scale.
N equals 40.

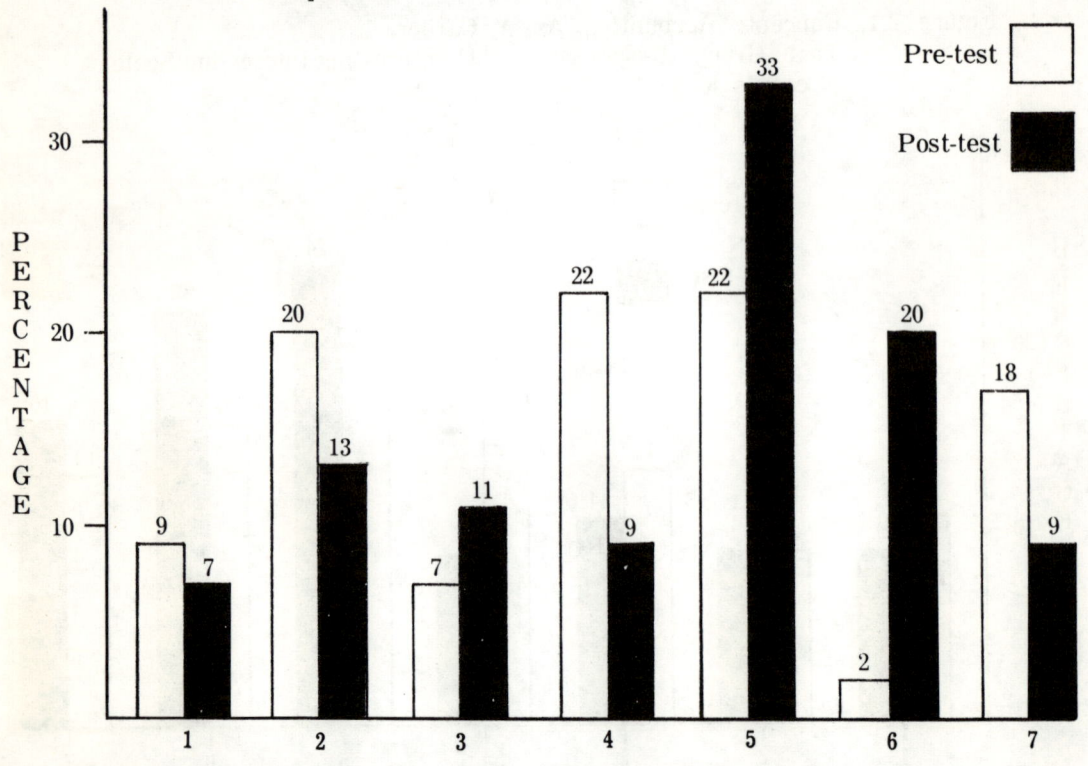

Figure 3.4. Concept: Accounting As A Career.
Control Group Responses on Boring-Stimulating Scale.
N equals 42.

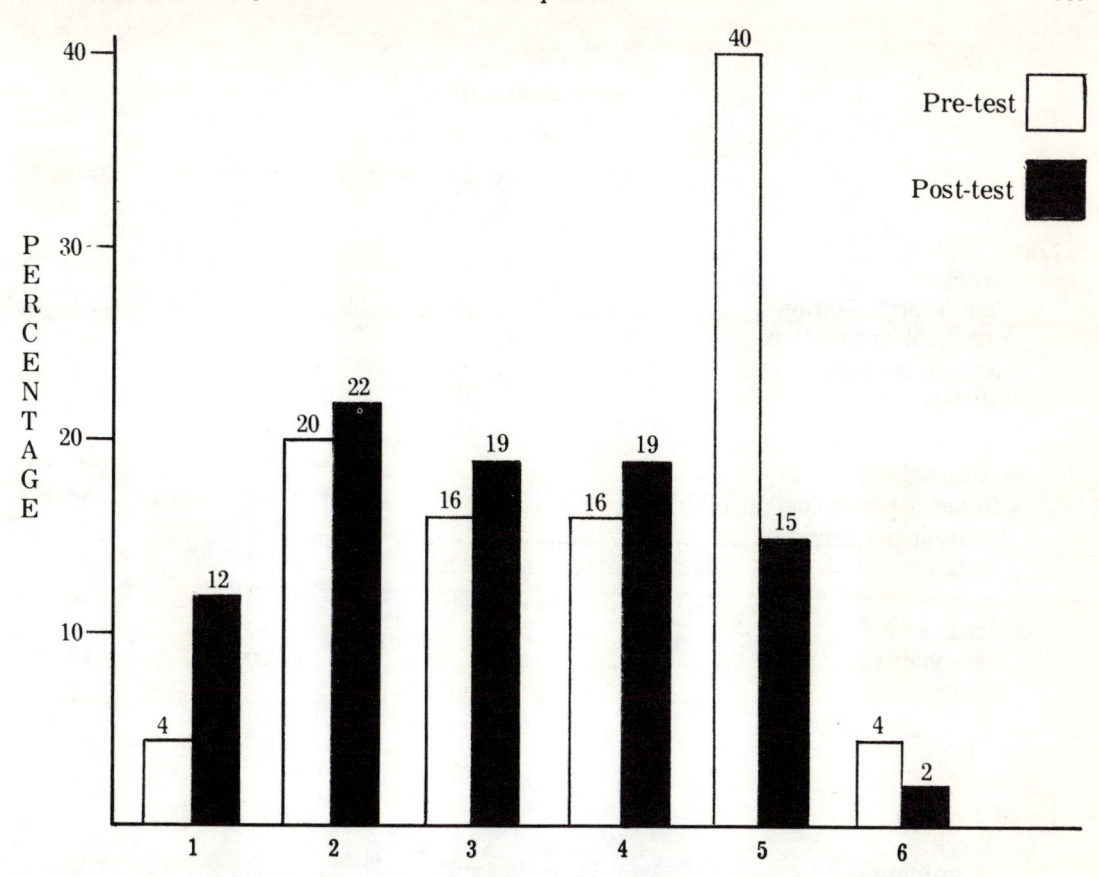

Figure 3.5. Concept: Accounting As A Career
Test Group Responses on Dull-Exciting Scale.
N equals 40.

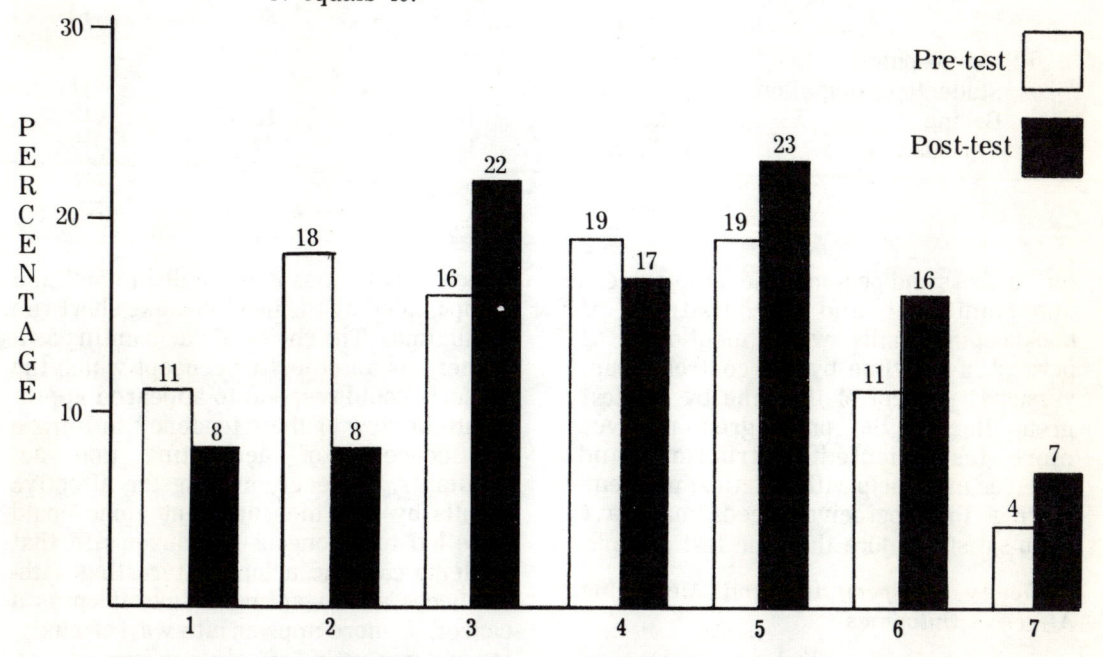

Figure 3.6. Concept: Accounting As A Career
Control Group Responses on Dull-Exciting Scale.
N equals 42.

Table 5

Course Evaluation

(%)

	Test Group N = 47	Control Group N = 47	Total N = 94
Liked Best:			
(1) Work:			
Course organization	10	7	9
Practical orientation	7	14	11
Lecture content	5	16	11
Various	19	10	15
	41	47	46
(2) Atmosphere:			
General psychological climate	17	16	17
Student participation	12	N-A	6
Various	20	17	19
	49	33	42
(3) Instructor:			
Personality	—	20	10
Various	10	—	5
	10	20	15
	100	100	100
Liked Least:			
(1) Work:			
Examinations	16	5	11
Lack of problem-solving	8	18	13
Textbook	3	20	12
Various	19	17	18
	46	60	54
(2) Atmosphere:			
Student participation	22	N-A	11
Boring	16	18	17
Various	16	22	19
	54	40	47
	100	100	100

for business and personal use, employment opportunities, and acquisition of bookkeeping skills were mentioned 62 percent of the time by the control group, versus 44 percent of the time by the test group. Because the control group received more task-oriented instruction, and received more help with practical problem-solving, their perceived needs may have been satisfied more than the test group's.

Difficulty of Specifying and Measuring Affective Outcomes

As pointed out earlier, the problem of deciding what student behavior will lend itself to inferences by the instructor about affective outcomes is difficult in itself and compounded by the need to make short-run evaluations. The choice of "accounting as a career" as an objective concept which the subjects could respond to appeared appropriate in view of their tendency to mingle the concepts of accounting and accountants. However, judging the affective results by this measurement alone could have led to erroneous conclusions in that students can find a topic interesting without necessarily wanting to take it up as a career. A more appropriate way of studying and measuring affective responses may be to take the phenomenological approach of accepting all data which appears during

Table 6
Subjects' Perceived Needs With Respect to the Course
(%)*

	Test Group N = 49	Control Group N = 50	Total N = 99
Utilitarian:			
To supplement studies in other fields	26	34	30
For business or personal use	22	34	28
To improve short-run employment opportunities	8	11	9
To acquire bookkeeping skills	14	17	15
	70	96	82
Other:			
To help decide on long-run career opportunity	16	19	17
To satisfy prerequisites	14	15	14
Miscellaneous	8	2	5
	38	36	36

*The above percentages were computed by dividing the number of times a particular category of needs was mentioned by the number of respondents. Because multiple needs were expressed, the percentages add to more than 100.

a particular experience as the subject matter of inquiry,[25] rather than selecting a few factors which may fail to give a representative or reliable account of what actually occurred. This type of approach could be tried by systematic observation of classroom behavior,[26] although this technique could, of course, only deal with the classroom aspect of the total experience and would be costly in both time and personnel resources. However, because of the potential value of classroom observation in evaluating affective outcomes, the identification of those behavioral patterns which differentiate the affective "climate", as well as the design of suitable measuring instruments, are suggested as being necessary and worthwhile areas for future research.

Need for Variety in Teaching Techniques

A teaching technique can be briefly defined as "what the teacher does to help students learn"[27] and a variety of techniques may be called for in order to achieve either single or multiple goals. Furthermore, all student groups are made up of individuals who may need different stimuli to produce looked-for responses. Consequently, individual differences should be considered in deciding upon appropriate pedagogic techniques, and feedback information should be gathered frequently as to how successfully these techniques are working. With this in mind, we could consider the approach used by Dr. Volney Faw, of Lewis and Clark College, in teaching a required introductory course in psychology, as reported by Carl Rogers.[28] Dr. Faw interviews each student before the first class meeting and places considerable emphasis on student participation in setting the learning objectives, as well as providing a variety of alternatives for obtaining course credit. Given the classroom time requirements for interpersonal activity, it might be appropriate to include a programmed text among the devices chosen to enhance the effectiveness of the instructor as a learning facilitator. Apart from the mix of media to be used with the teaching techniques, the available physical facilities must be taken into account. The lack of flexibility in the seating arrangements encountered in this study was a significant drawback in attempting to change the traditional student-instructor dichotomy.

These attempts to explain the research results can only be considered as tentative in view of the limited feedback and the disparity between the two groups in terms of maturity and interests. Future experiments with innovative pedagogies must be planned in the context of an overall strategy in which the setting of goals, the selection of teaching techniques and media, and the measurement of outcomes will be integrated for both the cognitive and affective learning areas.

Unanticipated Results

It had been expected that because of the more frequent personal contacts between students and instructor in the test group, and the less formal classroom atmosphere, a more positive student reaction to the instructor would have been evidenced by the test group as compared with the control group. This however, did not turn out to be the case. The students' course evaluations concerning the instructor were twice as favorably disposed towards the instructor by the control group as compared with the test group. This could have been due to the more dominant role played by the instructor in the control group. On the other hand, a halo effect may have colored the instructor's impressions of the experience with the test group, or again, the introduction of non-traditional methods into a traditional physical setting may have presented the test group with an ambiguous situation. In any event, the less favorable evaluation of the instructor by the test group could have implications concerning the training needs of teachers who wish to experiment with creative methods, as well as for the short-run evaluation of their teaching effectiveness.

FOOTNOTES

[1] John W. Buckley and John J. McDonough, "Three Critical Issues in Accounting Education", AIS Working Paper No. 71-8, University of California at Los Angeles, February, 1971, p. 9.

[2] John Ashworth, "People Who Become Accountants", *The Journal of Accountancy,* (November, 1968), p. 46.

[3] Norton M. Bedford, "The Laws of Learning and Accounting Instruction", *The Accounting Review,* (April, 1963), p. 406.

[4] John J. McDonough and Theodore J. Mock, "Accounting Education In A Changing World", *The California CPA Quarterly,* (September, 1970), 10. Also, Don T. DeCoster, "The CPA In The World of Psychology", *The Journal of Accountancy,* (August, 1971), 40, and L. William Seidman, "The End Of The Great Green Eyeshade", *The Journal of Accountancy,* (January, 1972), p. 51.

[5] Ronald J. Patten and Joseph W. Bachman, "Elementary Accounting Profile—1970", *The Accounting Review,* (January, 1972), 165. Also, Doyle Z. Williams, "Teaching Methods and Aids", *Accounting Instruction: Concepts and Practices,* (Cincinnati, Ohio: South-Western Publishing Co., 1968), p. 83.

[6] E. Paul Torrance, "Scientific Views of Creativity", *Daedalus,* (Summer, 1965), p. 676.

[7] The education literature is rich in this area. As examples:—Neil Postman and Charles Weingartner, *Teaching as a Subversive Activity,* (New York: Dell Publishing Co., Inc., 1969.) and Henry F. Beechhold, *The Creative Classroom,* (New York: Charles Scribner's Sons, 1971.)

[8] Charles T. Horngren, "Teaching Methods and Participation as a Major Law of Learning", *The Accounting Review,* (April, 1963), pp. 409-411, and Wiley S. Mitchell, "Relationship of Laws of Learning to Methods of Accounting Instruction", *The Accounting Review,* (April, 1963), pp. 411-414.

[9] Among the exceptions:—Ronald J. Patten and Lawrence L. Steinmetz, "What Do Your Students Think of Your Elementary Course?", *The Accounting Review,* (October, 1966), pp. 767-772, and Don Etnier, "A More Interesting Auditing Course", *The Accounting Review,* (July, 1965), pp. 648-649.

[10] Benjamin S. Bloom, J. Thomas Hastings and George F. Madaus, *Handbook on Formative and Summative Evaluation of Student Learning,* (New York: McGraw-Hill Book Company, 1971), pp. 226-227.

11 Benjamin S. Bloom (Editor), *Taxonomy of Educational Objectives: The Classification of Educational Goals, Handbook I: Cognitive Domain,* (David McKay Company, Inc., 1956.) p. 7.

12 David R. Krathwohl, et al., *Taxonomy of Educational Objectives: The Classification of Educational Goals, Handbook II: Affective Domain,* (David McKay Company, Inc., 1964), p. 49.

13 Donald T. Campbell and Julian C. Stanley, "Experimental and Quasi-Experimental Designs for Research on Teaching", *Handbook of Research on Teaching,* (Chicago, Ill: Rand McNally & Company, 1963), p. 217.

14 Eugene J. Webb, Donald T. Campbell, Richard D. Schwartz, and Lee Sechrest, *Unobtrusive Measures: Nonreactive Research in the Social Sciences,* (Chicago, Ill: Rand McNally & Company, 1966), p. 34.

15 A.N. Oppenheim, *Questionnaire Design and Attitude Measurement,* (New York: Basic Books, Inc., 1966), p. 227.

16 Philip A. Goldberg, "A Review of Sentence Completion Methods in Personality Assessment", *Handbook of Projective Techniques,* (New York: Basic Books, Inc., 1965), p. 779.

17 Amanda R. Rohde, *The Sentence Completion Method,* (New York: The Ronald Press Company, 1957), p. 3.

18 Charles E. Osgood,"The Nature and Measurement of Meaning", *Semantic Differential Technique,* (Chicago, Ill: Aldine Publishing Company, 1969), p. 3.

19 Oppenheim, *op. cit.,* p. 206.

20 B.J. Winer, *Statistical Principles In Experimental Design,* (New York: McGraw-Hill Book Company, 1962), p.581.

21 Walter R. Borg, *Educational Research,* (New York: David McKay Company, Inc., 1963), p. 304.

22 Max D. Engelhart, *Methods of Educational Research,* (Chicago, Ill: Rand McNally & Company, 1972), p. 436.

23 Fred N. Kerlinger, *Foundations of Behavioral Research,* (New York: Holt, Rinehart and Winston, Inc., 19645, pp. 347-351. (The study referred to:—R. Koenker, "Arithmetic Readiness at the Kindergarten Level", *Journal of Educational Research,* XLII (1948), pp. 218-223, involved the use of two intact groups.)

24 Krathwohl, *et al., op. cit.,* p. 7.

25 R.B. MacLeod, "Phenomenology: A Challenge To Experimental Psychology", *Behaviorism and Phenomenology,* T.W. Mann, Editor, (London: The University of Chicago Press, 1964), p. 51.

26 Donald M. Medley and Harold E. Mitzel, "Measuring Classroom Behavior by Systematic Observation", *Handbook of Research on Teaching,* N.L. Gage, Editor, (Chicago: Rand McNally & Company, 1963), p. 249.

27 Hazel Taylor Spitze, *Choosing Techniques for Teaching and Learning,* (Washington, DC: Home Economics Education Association, National Education Association, 1970), p. 1.

28 Carl R. Rogers, *Freedom to Learn,* (Columbus, Ohio: Charles E. Merrill Publishing Company, 1969), pp 36-37.

A Critique

The major premise addressed in Professor Berry's research is that "participation" by students in "the responsibility for the course curriculum by assuming the instructor's role, either individually or in groups, for certain periods during each class session," would both improve the student's proficiency and would also leave the student with a more positive attitude toward certain attributes of the area as a career.

Professor Berry's paper represents a well planned and executed experiment within the constraints set by the environment. The description of the research design, the hypotheses, the subject population, methodology, execution, evaluative process and conclusions is complete and clearly presented. The author also provides us with some of her own insights into the limitations of her research.

This attention to orderly and clear exposition is essential. If one wishes to cause readers to revise their beliefs based on an empirical research study, the reader must be able to evaluate the strengths and limitations of the design, execution and evaluation phases. In particular, the author has a responsibility to inform the reader of the limitations to both external and internal validity issues. The investigator is in the optimal position to do this; the reader is not. Professor Berry's paper should be an excellent road map for those endeavoring to study teaching innovation.

Perhaps of primary evaluative significance, we can not be sure that the treatment was in fact achieved. In order to have effective participation, the students must feel their inputs are both desired and effectively incorporated into the course structure. It would have been helpful if some means, even a questionnaire, had been used to attempt to determine whether the subjects felt effective participation had been achieved.

One insight that is relevant to this issue comes from the course evaluation. The apparent negative nature of the subject's response to the participation issue as evidenced by the larger percentage describing it as "liked least," suggests participation may not have been effectuated. The author also states that the physical conditions were not conducive to participation. But we can't really be sure if effective participation was or was not achieved since effective participation does not require that the subjects liked it, nor do we know what percentages would result under ideal conditions for the two alternative questions included in the course evaluation, and hence have no basis for comparing the percentage responses. Also, there are many means of achieving participation, only one of which was investigated in the study.

Participation is not a zero-one variable. It is not very useful to try to elect between "you have it" or "you don't" positions. More accurately, participation is a continuous variable and we would like to know in what direction and to what degree it was affected by the research approach used. In other words, it is a variable within the study and should have been measured. A naive hypothesis consistent with the findings of the Berry study is that no (significant) change in participation took place.

Let us turn now to some of the design problems in this study. As the author stressed, the assignment to groups was non-random. However, the design assumes randomness. Observation of groups by the author indicates an obvious lack of equivalence. While this does not prevent appropriate use of this experimental design, it raises issues of internal validity to the extent the groups are not comparable.

One of the more important issues is the potential interaction between the maturation effects and the selection bias represented in the groups. Maturity and attitudes of the two groups appear to differ in ways which might reinforce the failure of a new instructional method which was introduced substantially after the start of the course to achieve the expected effects. Some such problem may partially explain the attitude toward the instructor evidenced in the course evaluation.

The differences in the two groups appear to involve attributes (such as class) that would be correlated with the performance measure. (The higher pre-test score obtained by the control group is consistent with this observation). If so, the differences in the degree of shift from pre-test to post-test could reflect the effect of regression rather than any effect of the treatment variable. Indeed the group profiles reveal such dramatic differences between the experimental and the control group that we question whether any useful conclusions could be obtained from the experiment.

The author makes reference at several places to matched pairs t-tests which "were used to analyze increases in accounting proficiency for each group." It is not clear just what was done here, nor how the pairs were established, but this could also produce the regression effect. As Campbell and Stanley observe in describing the experimental design used by Berry, "if...the means of the groups are substantially different, then the process of matching not only fails to provide the intended equation but in addition insures the occurrence of unwanted regression effects." This reduces the probability of showing an experimental effect. The analysis of covariance is one means of avoiding this problem and we believe this technique was selected by the author for the major tests for precisely this reason. We are unable to determine why the matched-pairs tests were used for these additional comparisons.

The fact that the instructor for both classes was the same introduces problems in evaluating performance. The second performance given by an instructor on the same material is influenced by the first. Furthermore, since the instructor was also the experimenter, unconscious bias may have been introduced. Feedback from one class to another could have also confounded the experimental effect and it could produce the "Hawthorne" effect which the author hoped to avoid. Also, the four week hiatus before the pre-test was not common for the groups. The test group was (presumably) already planning and reacting to participation as outlined in the syllabus.

Finally we turn to some testing issues. We have already referred to the appropriate use of covariance analysis in testing the performance hypothesis. Two testing problems, however, concern us. These include the analysis of the attitude data and the use of one-tail statistical tests.

The percentage responses graphed in Figures 3.1 and 3.2 are referred to as being the results of "three combined scales." The scales are apparently combined because the reference points on the semantic-differential for each are synonyms. But, if so, the responses are not independent due to both the individual respondent and the scales themselves. It is therefore not clear what the aggregation process shows. Although we can not be sure from the data provided, the analysis of covariance given of the attitudinal data in Table 3 may be based on the same additive data. If so, the covariance analysis is not valid since the critical assumption of independence is violated.

But, further, the results of the responses to the semantic-differential questionnaire were assumed to represent more than ordinal measurement as evidenced by the use of covariance analysis. In fact such data represents at most ordinal data and nonparametric testing methods are appropriate.

Second, several statistical tests are referred to by the author as one-tail tests. Such tests are appropriate with directional hypotheses where they provide stronger (in the sense of being more likely to yield significance at a given probability level) tests. However, the hypotheses presented in the Berry study are not directional (although they could have been so stated). The Berry hypotheses refer only to differences but not to the expected direction. The hypotheses and tests should be consistent in this sense.

The individual importance of some of these issues we suspect is small. But even then one could only speculate on their combined import. We mention them in this light.

In conclusion, the group profiles reveal such dramatic differences between the experimental and the control group that we question whether any useful conclusions could be obtained from the experiment. The possible interaction of the treatment and class (selection) combined with the uncertainty whether the experimental treatment was even realized prevent any conclusions one might try to draw concerning the experiment itself from being extrapolated beyond the situation examined.

A New Introduction to Accounting Combined with a Traditional Textbook: An Empirical Research Study

Allen Sanders
Elon College

In July, 1971, the Price Waterhouse Foundation study group recommended a new approach to the first-year accounting course.[1] The Study Group provided an eight-module structure for a course directed toward all college students instead of the usual orientation toward accounting and business majors. Several reports of trials of the new approach have generally indicated favorable results in terms of student and faculty response, but actual measurements of success in terms of learning achieved have not been reported.

During the 1972-1973 academic year, handout materials were developed to adapt a traditional elementary textbook to the new approach at Elon College.[2] Following the Solomon Four-Group Research Design, two experimental sections used the materials adapting the traditional textbook to the new approach, while two control sections used the same textbook in normal cover-to-cover sequence. At the end of the two-semester course, the experimental sections achieved mean scores on the American Institute of Certified Public Accountants (AICPA) Achievement Test, Level I, that were significantly higher than the scores of the control sections.

RESEARCH DESIGN

The Solomon Four-Group Design is diagrammed as follows:[3]

$$\begin{array}{ccc} 0_1 & X & 0_2 \\ 0_3 & & 0_4 \\ & X & 0_5 \\ & & 0_6 \end{array}$$

The 0's represent observations; the X's symbolize experimental treatment. Each of the four rows in the design depicts the events that happen to a single section with passage of time from left to right. Vertical alignment of symbols--e.g., 0_1 and 0_3, indicate events that occur simultaneously.

In this study, the observations were the AICPA tests. 0_1 and 0_3 were a pre-test administered to one experimental and one control section at the beginning of the year. It was Achievement Test, Level I, Form DS (fifty-minute version), administered on September 20, 1972. The X's in the first and third row indicate that one pre-tested and one unpre-tested section were taught in an experimental manner during the entire year from the materials adapting the textbook to the Study Group approach.[4] The absence of X in the second and fourth rows indicates that one pre-tested and one unpre-tested control section were taught from the textbook alone. The right-hand column of 0's in all four rows represents a post-test administered to all four sections on May 9, 1973. The AICPA Achievement Test, Level I, Form D (two-hour version) was used for this post-test. All tests were scored by the Psychological Corporation, the testing arm of the AICPA.

ANALYSIS OF DATA

The three statistical techniques that can be used to evaluate data collected in a Solomon Four-Group Design are:[5]

1. Simple analyses of variance comparisons of the test score mean from one observation with the test score mean of another observation. This procedure simply determines whether one mean score is greater than another at a specified level

of significance.

2. Two-dimensional analysis of variance of post-test scores of all four sections. Sometimes called, analysis of variance (2 X 2 design), this technique allows the experimenter to determine whether there are significant differences in post-test score means due to main effects—in this project, experimentation and pretesting—and, to determine whether there is significant interaction between the two.

3. An analysis of covariance of post-test scores of the two pre-tested sections with pre-test scores being the covariate. Analysis of covariance is a blending of regression analysis with simple analysis of variance; it is a procedure to compare post-test score means which have been adjusted for beginning differences in level of knowledge that are indicated by the pre-test scores.

The data collected in this study were subjected to all of the above statistical procedures with a significance level of .05 selected to reject the hypothesis that one mean was greater than another. All computations were verified by computer using programs in the libraries of Call-a-Computer at Raleigh, N.C. or Triangle Universities Computing Center, Research Triangle Park, N.C.

SUBJECTS

In the academic year 1972-1973, Elon College had only four daytime sections of the first-year course in accounting. Under such circumstances, random assignment of students was impossible; the sections were allowed to form under normal registration procedures for the fall semester. All students in the four sections were aware that an experiment was taking place. Students were not allowed to switch from an experimental to a control section or vice versa at mid-year. Students who entered the elementary course after the beginning of the fall term and students who withdrew from the course were not included in the evaluation. As a result, the four sections ended the year with n = 21, n = 26, n = 27, and n = 28 students respectively.

Both experimental sections were taught by one instructor and both control sections were taught by another instructor. Each of these had about eight years experience in teaching the elementary course at Elon College. Both attempted to reduce bias by refraining from close observation of the other's courses. For example, the instructor of the control sections did not read the Student Handout Materials used in the experimental sections. They jointly supervised administration of the pre-test and post-test.

RESEARCH FINDINGS

Mean scores achieved by students in all the tests are shown in Table 1.

TABLE 1

ACTUAL MEAN SCORES ON ALL TESTS

Pre-test		Post-test	
Observation	Mean	Observation	Mean
O_1	4.07	O_2	22.19
O_3	3.00	O_4	15.71
		O_5	24.00
		O_6	10.57

Because the simple analyses of variance and the 2 X 2 analysis of variance procedures required proportional numbers in the sections, a computer program was used to draw a random sample of post-test scores of twenty students from each section. The post-test score means of the students in the samples are shown in Table 2.

TABLE 2

POST-TEST SCORE MEANS OF SAMPLES OF TWENTY STUDENTS FROM EACH SECTION

Observation	Mean
O_2	23.10
O_4	15.35
O_5	24.40
O_6	11.10

Four simple analyses of variance comparisons were made. Results are shown in Table 3.

TABLE 3

RESULTS OF ANALYSIS OF VARIANCE ON RANDOM SAMPLES OF TWENTY SCORES

Comparison	F Ratio	Significance Level
0_2 versus 0_1	47.22	$P<.001$
0_5 versus 0_3	68.24	$P<.001$
0_2 versus 0_4	7.01	$P<.010$
0_5 versus 0_6	21.76	$P<.001$

The first two comparisons in Table 3 hold little meaning for this study. 0_2 versus 0_1 is simply a comparison of post-test versus pre-test for the pre-tested experimental section. One would expect $0_2 > 0_1$ to be significant. 0_5 versus 0_3 compares post-test scores of the unpre-tested experimental section with the pre-test scores of the pre-tested control section. Accordingly, one would also expect $0_5 > 0_3$ to be significant, assuming that the course is at all effective.

The last two comparisons in Table 3 are more meaningful. 0_2 versus 0_4 is a comparison of the post-test scores of the two pre-tested sections. $0_2 > 0_4$ with an F ratio of 7.01 indicates that the mean score of the experimental section was greater than the mean score of the control section with less than one percent probability of such an occurrence by chance alone. 0_5 versus 0_6 is a comparison of post-test scores of the two unpre-tested sections. $0_5 > 0_6$ with an F ratio of 21.76 indicates that the experimental section mean was greater than the control section mean, and that the probability of such an occurrence by chance alone is less than one-tenth of one percent.

Analysis of Variance (2 X 2 Design).

Because this evaluation requires proportionality of cell frequencies, the same random samples of twenty scores from each section were used. A diagram of the organization of data for the two-dimensional analysis is as follows:

Treatment

	Control	Experimental
	Sample of twenty scores of pre-tested control section	Sample of twenty scores of pre-tested experimental section
	Sample of twenty scores of unpre-tested control section	Sample of twenty scores of unpre-tested experimental section

Differences in the column means are analyzed for significance of the experimentation effect; differences in the row means are analyzed for significance of the pre-testing effect. As mentioned earlier, this design also allows an analysis of significance of interaction between these two main effects.

Results of this procedure are shown in Table 4. The F ratio of .52 between rows indicates no significant difference in mean scores of experimental and control groups caused by pre-testing. The F ratio of 1.85 for interaction--also nonsignificant--indicates that pre-testing and experimentation are independent of each other.

The important finding in this analysis is the highly significant F ratio of 26.55 between columns. It indicates that the experimental section means were greater than control section means with a probability of less than one-tenth of one percent of such an occurrence by chance alone.

TABLE 4

2 X 2 ANALYSIS OF VARIANCE ON POST-TEST

Source Variation	df	Sums of Squares	Mean Squares	F Ratio	Significance Level
Between cols.	1	2,212.51	2,212.51	26.55	P<.001
Between rows	1	43.51	43.51	.52	N. S.
Interaction	1	154.01	154.01	1.85	N. S.
Within cells	76	6,432.96	83.46		
Totals	79	8,755.99			

Analysis of Covariance

The results of the analysis of covariance of data from the two pre-tested sections are contained in Table 5.[6]

TABLE 5

ANALYSIS OF COVARIANCE

Source of Variation	df	Adjusted Sums of Squares	Adjusted Mean Squares
Between sections	1	416.35	416.35
Within sections	52	3,494.08	67.19
Totals	53	3,910.43	

The adjusted post-test score mean for the experimental section is 21.72; for the control section, it is 16.16. The F ratio between sections is 6.20 indicating that the adjusted experimental section mean is greater than the adjusted control section mean at a significance level of P<.016. This finding is especially important because the adjustment of mean scores in the analysis of covariance compensates for section differences in pre-course knowledge of accounting.

Summary of Findings

All of the evaluation procedures indicate that experimental sections' achievement on the post-test was significantly higher than achievement of the control sections. In no case was the significance level even near the rejection rule of .05.

DISCUSSION AND CONCLUSIONS

In a joint evaluation of post-test scores in light of their individual opinions of relative ability of specific students formed during the two semesters of teaching, and recollections of their observations of attitudes of students during the post-test, the two instructors concluded that some "negative Hawthorne effect" was felt by the unpre-tested control section.[7] They are of the opinion that some portion of the difference between post-test score means of the two control sections (15.71 and 10.57) was due to the fact that some students in the unpre-tested control section felt resentment toward an unfamiliar test.

There was also some positive effect of pre-testing on one control section. Various methods are available to compute this effect.[8] In a 2 X 2 design, about all that can be determined is whether such an effect, if it exists, is positive or negative. The investigator's computations show a positive effect for the pre-tested control section. This, in addition to the "negative Hawthorne effect" appears to explain the difference in performance of the two control sections.

Reasons For Success of the Study Group Approach

Various learning theories were considered as possible explanations for the success of the new approach. Among them, B.F. Skinner's feedback and reinforcement theory was discarded.[9] All sections received about the same amount and immediacy of both, thus neither appears to have had an effect upon the experimental sections that was any different from the sections taught in the traditional manner.

The Hawthorne effect, considered earlier, does not appear to be a reason for success of the experimental sections. Although there was some evidence of increased interest during the first week or two, it soon faded. The suggestion that the students in the experimental sections worked harder over a two-semester period is not consistent with the instructor's personal observations of the students.

The real key to the success of the experimental sections appears to lie in the idea of conceptual set.[10] The new approach, by opening the first-year course with a fairly rigorous study of the uses of accounting data, appears to create a mental set that better enables the student to perceive the conventional accounting model with greater understanding of the theory which underlies it. This appears to apply especially to concepts of value and valuation methods.

Future Research

Some students from all four sections are accounting majors who will be enrolled in the intermediate course in 1973-1974. All students in that course will be taught by one instructor. Professor Charles Smith has discussed the question of how well the new approach prepares an accounting major for the intermediate course.[11] An opportunity for study of that question is an interesting by-product of this study.

CONCLUSIONS

Based upon the findings in this experiment, it is concluded that:

1. The New Introduction to Accounting, when coordinated with a traditional textbook, produces better understanding of financial and managerial accounting concepts in the first-year course than when the traditional textbook is taught in a cover-to-cover sequence.

2. Because of the measure used, The AICPA Achievement Test, Level I, this result appears to apply to accounting majors as well as to students majoring in other disciplines. However, whether a better foundation is laid for the intermediate course in accounting is a matter for additional study.

3. The reason for the success of the new approach is believed to lie in the perceptual sets successively created in the student by the ordering of the material and the emphasis placed upon the societal role of the end product of the accounting process before exposing him to the conventional accounting model.

FOOTNOTES

[1] Gerhard G. Mueller, *A New Introduction to Accounting: A Report of the Study Group Sponsored by the Price Waterhouse Foundation* (Seattle: Price Waterhouse and Co., 1971).

[2] A four-year undergraduate institution. 1972-1973 enrollment of 1873 included 282 business administration majors and 63 accounting majors.

[3] Donald T. Campbell and Julian C. Stanley, *Experimental and Quasi-Experimental Designs for Research* (Chicago: Rand McNally, 1963).

[4] The textbook used for all four sections was Albert Slavin, Isaac N. Reynolds, and John T. Miller, *Basic Accounting for Financial and Managerial Control,* 2nd. ed. (New York: Holt, Rinehart and Winston, 1972).

[5] For explanation of these procedures and simple examples, see John T. Roscoe, *Fundamental Research Statistics for the Behavioral Sciences* (New York: Holt, Rinehart and Winston, 1969).

[6] For this evaluation, a computer program that does not require proportionality was used. All scores in the sections are included in the analysis.

[7] F.J. Roethlisberger and W.J. Dickson, *Management and the Worker* (Cambridge: Harvard Univ. Press, 1939).

[8] See either Louis B. Barnes, "Organizational Change and Experimental Methods;" in *Methods of Organizational Research*, ed. Victor H. Vroom (Pittsburgh: Univ. of Pittsburgh Press, 1967) or Bernard Ostle, *Statistics in Research,* 2nd. ed. (Ames, Iowa: The Iowa Univ. Press, 1963).

[9] B.F. Skinner, *Science and Human Behavior* (New York: The Macmillan Co., 1953).

[10] David Krech, Richard S. Crutchfield, and Norman Livson, *Elements of Psychology,* 2nd ed. (New York: Alfred A. Knopf, Inc., 1969).

[11] Charles H. Smith, "A New Introduction to Accounting: Some Explanations," *The Accounting Review, p. 48 (1973).*

A Critique

Professor Sanders provides an excellent research example of the strengths and the inherent limitations of experimental approaches to teaching effectiveness. Of all the papers in this section, his is the only one to approach a "true" experimental design in the formal sense. In keeping with the experimental emphasis, his variables are well-defined: he is concerned solely with the effect of alternative course structures on the learning of accounting skills. Since one of the alternative structures is that one recommended by the Price Waterhouse Study Group, the study is of intrinsic interest to most accounting educators.

Strengths

The Solomon Four-Group Design makes full use of the available data and controls for certain threats to internal and external validity, such as pre-testing effects and differential experience for the experimental groups. It is an appealing design, both for its simplicity and its rigor. Professor Sanders uses it well, with certain inevitable exceptions to be noted.

The numerical observations are based on a widely used and validated instrument, the AICPA achievement tests. Furthermore, different forms are used from pre to post test, thereby helping to offset the pre-test effect, if it exists.

The author attempts to tie his findings into a theoretical framework, although the brevity of the paper makes this difficult to achieve. There is a great deal of criticism of "dust bowl empiricism" in educational research and it is always pleasing to find data fitted into an overriding concept. However, it is difficult for the reader to make the link between the notion of "conceptual set" and the fact that the experimental group did better on the average. The interested reader is referred to the citations given by Professor Sanders or to his thesis (of which this paper is a highly condensed version).

Some Deficiencies

As the author (and most other educational researchers) would be quick to point out, it is difficult and often impossible to meet all of the theoretical niceties of experimental research when doing such research. Certainly, it would be unfortunate if such niceties precluded ever doing the research.

For example, one of the deficiencies in the experiment is the non-random selection of intact groups for the experimental and control groups in this experiment. This is a clear violation of the requirement for complete randomization if the design is to be completely experimental. Similarly, instructors were probably not randomly assigned to sections. Two confounding effects (rival explanations) are possible due to this fact.

First, the highly significant difference between the control and experimental group (the Price Waterhouse Study Group sections doing better) could be explained by the teaching skills of the two instructors rather than by the different course structures. The instructor effect is entangled with the structure effect. Second, if any one or more of the four sections had a differential educational experience during the academic year, this effect is buried somewhere in the results.

As noted by the author (in correspondence), these features were institutional necessities and beyond his control. However, it would be possible to do some post-experimental analysis to test for the likelihood of such effects. For example, is there any objective evidence (e.g., formal course evaluations) to indicate differential teaching abilities between the two instructors? What did the students think? Did the four sections have a totally common curriculum? How did they differ? Was the composition of the sections similar in terms of social, economic, age profiles? (The study by Berry illustrates the use of profiles to investigate such potential confounders).

Another problem concerns the long time span (one academic year). Given that the students had close contact with one another and were well-informed about the character of the experiment and the different course structures, it is impossible to associate the higher performance for the experimental sections entirely with the different structure. Professor Sanders discusses the likelihood of Hawthorne effects associated with pre-testing, but does not discuss such effects caused by the knowledge that the subject was in a "traditional" control group, or in a "modern" experimental group. Again, some assessment of student attitudes—both before and after—would have provided some insights into this possibility.

It would have been helpful to gain some intermediate feedback about relative performances. Was the differential performance created at any particular time phase or was it gradual throughout the year?

The statistical analyses used (primarily analysis of variance techniques) warrant some testing of the underlying assumptions, especially since there is a significant question about the independence of the error terms which is important to ANOV.

Finally, it is commendable to advocate future research building on these results. It also seems premature. Replication of Professor Sanders' work would seem highly desirable, preferably at another institution and with some attention to the imperfections mentioned above. Simultaneously, more linkages between the underlying theory and the observed outcomes should be carried forth.